Statistics for Social Science and Public Policy

Advisors:
S. E. Fienberg   D. Lievesley   J. Rolph

Springer
New York
Berlin
Heidelberg
Barcelona
Hong Kong
London
Milan
Paris
Singapore
Tokyo

Statistics for Social Science and Public Policy

Joseph L. Gastwirth

Editor

Statistical Science in the Courtroom

With 30 Illustrations

Springer

Joseph L. Gastwirth
Department of Statistics
315 Funger Hall
George Washington University
Washington DC 20052

Advisors

Stephen E. Fienberg
Department of Statistics
Carnegie Mellon University
Pittsburgh, PA 15213
USA

Denise Lievesley
Institute for Statistics
Room H.113
UNESCO
7 Place de Fontenoy
75352 Paris 07 SP
France

John Rolph
Department of Information and
  Operations Management
Graduate School of Business
University of Southern California
Los Angeles, CA 90089
USA

Library of Congress Cataloging-in-Publication Data
Statistical science in the courtroom / editor, Joseph L. Gastwirth.
     p. cm. — (Statistics for social science and public policy)
     Includes bibiliographical references.
     ISBN 0-387-98997-8 (hardcover : alk. paper)
     1. Evidence, Expert.   2. Forensic statistics.   I. Gastwirth, Joseph L.   II. Series.
     K5485.S73 2000
     614′.1—dc21   00-024955

Printed on acid-free paper.

Production managed by Jenny Wolkowicki; manufacturing supervised by Jacqui Ashri.
Typeset by The Bartlett Press, Inc., Marietta, GA.
Printed and bound by Hamilton Printing Co., Rensselaer, NY.
Printed in the United States of America.

9 8 7 6 5 4 3 2 1

ISBN 0-387-98997-8   SPIN 10751205

Springer-Verlag New York Berlin Heidelberg
A member of BertelsmannSpringer Science+Business Media GmbH

Preface

The last twenty-five years has seen an increasing use of scientific evidence, and, in particular, statistical evidence, by the legal system. The trial of O.J. Simpson highlighted the potential importance of DNA evidence, while problems with the care of blood samples by the police and crime laboratories involved, introduced the public to these issues in a rather sensational way. In 1977 the U.S. Supreme Court decided that without formal statistical analysis, comparison of the proportion of minorities in the population eligible for jury service and the proportion actually called was no longer appropriate. Replacing a rule of thumb allowing a 10 to 15% difference between the two proportions, the Court, in *Castenada v. Partida*, adopted formal hypothesis testing as the standard analytic method. It left the required level of significance imprecise by stating that the statistic giving the normal approximation for the probability of observing a difference between the observed number of jurors and their expected number should be at least two to three standard deviations in order that the data support a *prima facie* case. While two standard deviations correspond to a significance level or probability of .05, three correspond to a level of only .0026.

After 1977 the use of statistical analysis in discrimination cases became commonplace, and more sophisticated methods, such as regression and combination of tests applied to appropriately stratified data, were accepted by the courts. Today, statisticians are routinely hired by parties in cases concerning possible discrimination, antitrust violations, goods that infringe on patents, environmental hazards, and harm caused by products such as drugs. Most of the books on statistics in law describe the methods used to analyze data rather than on how involvement in the area of legal statistics affects statisticians and their research programs. The authors of the articles in this book were asked to write about cases in which they were experts or consultants or about areas of the law that rely on quantitative research or how their interest in the use of statistical evidence in legal cases has influenced their research. They were also encouraged to give their views on whether the courts give appropriate weights to statistical testimony. Some authors focused on just one of these topics, while others tried to comment on several of them.

As noted previously, discrimination, product liability, and DNA evidence are areas that rely heavily on statistical studies and analyses. Statistical issues and problems faced by experts involved in discrimination cases are discussed by Drs. Pollard, Rosenblum, Mann, and the editor, Dr. Gastwirth. Several experts, Drs. Balding, Chaseling, Geisser, and Weir, who have testified on the subject in many cases, survey DNA evidence. In addition to discussing important technical issues some describe their experiences with the legal system. Professors Mellen and Stockmarr discuss the importance of the likelihood ratio in interpreting a DNA match. Product liability and toxic tort cases rely on various types of medical evidence involving quantitative toxicology and epidemiology. Professors Loue and Wagner provide a survey of these areas of the law.

Statistical analysis is also used in estimating monetary damages and in determining drug sentences. Professors Rubin and Zeger were opposing experts in the Minnesota tobacco case and present their views. Professors Aitken and Izenman discuss statistical issues arising in drug sentences, and the book closes with a fairly detailed examination of the data in the *Shonubi* drug sentencing case.

The role of probabilistic ideas and the need for careful statistical thinking in properly interpreting evidence are discussed by Dr. Aitken. The article introduces the reader to several fallacies that are all too common in forensic calculations of "match probabilities." Although the likelihood ratio is considered by statisticians as the best way to summarize evidence when the model underlying the data is known, the article reports the results of a survey of individuals involved with the judicial process, which indicate that many were confused by the concept. The last section of the article summarizes the research of Dr. Aitken and his colleagues on determining the appropriate sample size to reliably estimate the proportion of a large consignment of goods that contain an illegal substance.

Professor Izenman discusses several types of cases that rely on evidence based on a sample of the relevant population. Cases concerning trafficking in pornography over the Internet rely on samples of files from floppy or hard disks to determine the proportion of these that contain illicit material. The article notes the importance of designing a sampling plan that accords with the circumstances of the available evidence in the particular case. Uses of samples to assess damages in Medicaid fraud and copyright infringement are described. In the United States, the federal government has established guidelines for sentencing drug offenders that rely on estimates of the amount of illegal drugs involved. As the available data may not be a true random sample, issues concerning the methodology underlying an estimate based on fragmentary data have arisen. In drug trafficking cases, sentences increase sharply at specific drug amounts, so that sampling error and other sources of uncertainty can become critical in determining the amount of drugs ascribed to the defendant.

The calculation of the probability that a suspect's DNA matches the evidence at the crime scene depends on several important assumptions. Since the relative frequencies of the alleles at the loci used in forensic testing vary among racial and ethnic groups, which group's frequencies should be used? The importance of assessing the effect of this and other assumptions is summarized by Professor Balding. The article introduces the reader to the Bayesian approach, which focuses on the probability of interest, namely the probability that the accused is the culprit given the evidence. A careful examination of the likelihood ratio in the important situation where the culprit and the defendant have the same DNA profile answers the question as to which population to use. It is the population of alternative possible culprits. The article ends with a discussion of how probability-based reasoning has fared in U.K. courts as well as some common fallacies in the presentation of statistical evidence.

Professor Weir has testified in numerous trials involving DNA evidence and its interpretation. Readers familiar with the O. J. Simpson case will recognize him as the prosecution's expert. He describes his long involvement with statistical problems stemming from the use of DNA profiles. In particular, the effects of population structure, the validity of the assumption of independence between the alleles at the loci used in the calculation, and complications arising from mixed stains, e.g., when there are two victims and one defendant, are described. Professor Weir discusses how his work in the forensic arena raised interesting problems for his research and convinced him of the importance of educating the press and the public about statistical concepts.

Professor Geisser has been a testifying or consulting expert for defendants in many cases, including the O. J. Simpson case. His article reviews several statistical issues that arose in the interpretation of DNA evidence using a variable number of tandem repeats (VNTR) to classify an allele. He raises important questions concerning the assumption of independence and the sampling techniques used to determine the allele frequencies. Professor Geisser also describes the litigation process, emphasizing that the adversary process is not a fair scientific inquiry. Readers concerned with keeping the scientific traditions of encouraging independent replication of results and of peer review by an impartial referee may find the last section of the article discouraging but interesting. It is very important that scientists, judges, and the public become aware of the threat to independent research as well as the ethical issues concerning the refereeing process that are raised by Professor Geisser.

Professor Chaseling describes her experience as an expert witness interpreting DNA evidence in the Australian court system. In addition to the difficulties the adversarial system imposes on one's testimony, the importance of obtaining a thorough knowledge of the background of the case from the lawyer is emphasized. Moreover, the testimony needs to be presented in a way that jurors can comprehend. Professor Chaseling shows how jurors' knowledge of betting on a well-known horse race can be used to explain the meaning of a low probability. The article concludes by presenting some suggestions for improving the legal system so that the real issues are identified and the evidence presented at trial focuses on them.

In light of the recent Supreme Court decisions in *Daubert, Joiner, and Kumho Tire* that focused on evidential relevance, reliability, and how reliability is determined, Dr. Mellen's article on the likelihood approach to DNA evidence is a timely addition to the statistical forensics literature. In the context of DNA evidence in criminal trials, Dr. Mellen not only presents the connection between evidential relevance and likelihood ratios used as weights of evidence, but also proposes the use of estimated probabilities of observing misleading DNA evidence as a measure of evidential reliability. The article includes a review of the genetic background underlying the types of DNA evidence that have been used in actual cases.

Professor Stockmarr describes several interesting problems that arose during his work with the forensic genetics department at the University of Copenhagen. As other authors have noted, the likelihood ratio is the fundamental statistical concept, and he uses it in all the analyses presented. In the cases he discusses, the available evidence created special situations. In the first example, two different samples were found at the crime scene, and there were two suspects. Since the case against each suspect had to be made separately, one could not assume that the other suspect was also guilty, i.e., that their DNA was part of the sample. The implications for both the calculations and the presentation of the results are noted. DNA analysis is also used to determine paternity in admitting children of refugees or legal immigrants into a country. The potential effect of mutation on the analysis used in a case in Denmark is described.

Dr. Rosenblum traces the increasing level of sophistication required by courts in equal employment cases, integrating this development with three recent cases, *Daubert, Joiner, and Kuhmo Tire Co.*, which established new criteria for the admissibility of expert evidence in U.S. federal courts. These and a number of other major cases concerning the requisite level of statistical refinement are discussed. Recent lower court decisions illustrating a trial judge's "gatekeeper" function are also described. Potential experts should be aware of the importance of the discovery process, especially those aspects dealing with the timely presentation of their opinion and its underlying assumptions, methodology, and results to the opposing party and the court. Otherwise, the proposed testimony may be excluded. On balance, the author regards these developments favorably, since they help to refine the process in which analytical proof and statistics are used in employment law cases.

Professor Pollard provides a detailed study of the juror selection process he carried out as an expert for the Connecticut Public Defender's Office. Although both sides agreed that minorities, especially Hispanics, were underrepresented, the issue for the court was whether the state was responsible for it. His study helped focus the case on the fact that a far greater proportion of jury summonses to Hispanics could not be delivered than was the case for summonses sent to Whites. It should be mentioned that the opposing expert was invited to comment on Professor Pollard's article, but he declined. An interesting aspect of Professor Pollard's participation in the case was that he accepted a much lower payment for his services, primarily for his court appearances, in return for having the data made available for teaching purposes.

Dr. Mann gives us the perspective of a statistician who earns a living from statistical consulting. The first part of the article tells the reader what statisticians may expect when they become involved in legal consulting. The importance of the discovery process, especially deposition, is emphasized. Several interesting statistical problems are described, in particular, appropriate methodology for the allocation of damages to a class and for determining minority availability (their share of the qualified and available labor pool for a job). He discusses some ethical issues faced by statistical experts and presents his resolution of an actual ethical dilemma. Since the problem occurs often, it deserves attention. It might also be noted that it is not easy simply to "quit" a case if the lawyer asks you to do something that you feel is unethical or improper *very near* the trial date. If one has prepared an analysis that supports the claims of individuals harmed by discriminatory employment practices or defective products and withdraws for ethical reasons, the lawyer may not be permitted by the court to obtain an alternative expert. Is it right to leave the plaintiffs without an expert?

Professor Loue describes the role of epidemiological studies as evidence in legal cases. The article carefully distinguishes the purposes of law and science and describes the consequent different requirements needed for causal determination in the two areas. After describing measures of risk and the various types of studies used to estimate them, the article discusses their use in actual cases. A brief description of the legal process in civil cases is presented, including the role of interrogatories in discovery and various motions both sides may submit to the judge. The reader will note that courts and commentators do not agree on a specific threshold or minimal value of relative risk to use in assessing liability in toxic exposure cases. Scientists may be somewhat uncomfortable with this; however, courts do not view the scientific evidence as determinative. Judges and juries are free to take into account other factors, such as the prior health status of the plaintiff, in deciding a particular case.

Professor Wagner discusses the need to improve the legal process's review of agency regulatory decisions. Since some courts have required a more definitive quantitative analysis than the available scientific knowledge allows, the Environmental Protection Agency has tended to avoid mentioning the inherent statistical uncertainties with its risk estimates. After illustrating the types of problems arising in the area, Professor Wagner provides useful suggestions for improving the setting of environmental standards and subsequent judicial review. Government agencies that clearly explain the rationale underlying the rules they promulgate would receive deference from the courts as to technical aspects, such as the model assumed, as long as the reasoning and justification for those decisions are laid out. In their review, courts would ensure that the agencies explained their decisions and followed scientifically accepted practices.

The estimation of monetary damages due to plaintiffs who prevail in a toxic tort case is quite important. We are fortunate in having the experts on both sides of the Minnesota tobacco case present their views of how the problem should be formulated. Professor Zeger and coauthors describe the process they used to estimate the expenditures the state made that were attributable to smoking. Since the question arose only after smoking was scientifically linked to harmful health, a cohort study of individuals could not be conducted. Thus, existing data sets, originally collected for other purposes and medical billing records, were combined to yield an estimate.

Professor Rubin describes an approach based on comparing the actual expenditures with what would have occurred in a counterfactual world, one in which the tobacco companies had acted in accordance with the laws they allegedly violated. This approach underlies the way damages are assessed in equal pay cases where the difference in salary between a female employee and a higher paid but similarly situated male is typically awarded women who prevail. Because the court would not allow the industry to take credit for any reduction in expenditures that the state would have made on behalf of smokers who would have lived longer and received other state money in the counterfactual world, the approach had to be suitably modified. The article also discusses the important issue of apportioning damages when the harm was jointly caused by two agents.

Professor Kadane reviews several areas where statistical methodology has played an important role and describes how legal issues framed new problems for his research. His early work with Professors Lehoczky and David Kairys on the need to use multiple sources to compile a list of eligible jurors is still relevant today (see Professor Pollard's article). Decision-theoretic issues that arose in examining strategies lawyers should use in deciding which potential jurors should be challenged were analyzed in his research with the late Professor DeGroot. Professor Kadane is an expert in Bayesian methods, which typically utilize the statistical analyst's prior background knowledge. In legal applications one also needs to convince juries or a judge or regulatory administrator that the analysis presented is sound. Thus, one should consider how these individuals might look at the data. This led Professor Kadane to develop methods that incorporate the prior views of a group of individuals. He calls such methods multiparty Bayesianism. While some of the mathematical details in the articles that he and his coauthors have published in the statistical literature are complex, his article in this book conveys to the reader the motivating problems and potential applications.

Everyone who has purchased a large household appliance is familiar with warranties. Professor Singpurwalla, who has served as an expert in cases concerning the reliability of products, discusses the need for contracts to consider the probabilistic ideas inherent in assessing the reliability of products. After summarizing an actual case, he proceeds to formulate the problem as a probabilistic model and calculates the expected losses to both parties (buyer and seller). The loss to the seller depends on the probability of observing a predetermined number of failures of the product in the time period specified by the contract and how much the buyer will be reimbursed. The corresponding loss to business buyers depends on how much profit from the end product they expect to make minus the reimbursement they will receive from the seller should too many items fail. In the tradition of the literature on economics of contract law, the article has a mathematical focus; however, the general reader can appreciate the need for this type of analysis and the issues the author raises for future research. The article shows how Professor Singpurwalla's involvement in warranty cases led him to consider three concepts of probability.

Two major quantitative social studies have influenced the legal and policy debate over the death sentence. A major issue in the arguments over capital punishment is whether it deters murder and other very serious crimes. Professor Cottrol reviews the studies and their effect in legal decisions, emphasizing the difficulty of determining causality from observational data. Statistical methodology played an important role in the two major studies, and major advances in econometric and statistical methods in the intervening years have enabled researchers to incorporate more potential variables into the analysis. Professor Cottrol reminds the reader that the study supporting the deterrent effect also showed that increasing the probability of arrest or conviction had an even greater effect. Yet this finding received much less attention than the first. He concludes that jurists have not given careful scrutiny to studies in the area but should be open to doing so if the deterrence issue remains a main justification for the death penalty.

The *Shonubi* case concerns sentencing drug offenders, where the standard of proof is less than the "beyond a reasonable doubt" criterion used at trial. The case is interesting, since the trial judge and the appellate court disagreed on the utility of the statistical evidence. Professor Izenman introduces the case and two articles discussing the statistical issues in the case. His introduction includes the relevant data sets.

Finally, the reader should know that in two instances where a statistical expert was interested in writing about a case, the lawyers involved discouraged them. In one instance, the lawyer did not want the expert to write anything on the topic, since it might limit his testimony. In the second, the lawyers felt that articles on the topic might encourage more suits. The editor believes that discussion of these issues would bring them to the attention of the scientific community. This also raises a concern about the comprehensiveness of the published studies concerned with occupational health and environmental hazards. If lawyers advise firms not to publish findings indicating a potential increased risk of a product or chemical to which the public or its workers are exposed to, then meta-analyses of the published results will underestimate the risk of harm to the public. As the editor and Professor Wagner have written elsewhere, firms should have an incentive to provide as much information as possible to regulatory bodies and the public at large.

George Washington University   Joseph L. Gastwirth
March 2000

Acknowledgments

This book would not have come to fruition without the enthusiastic assistance and support of many individuals. First of all, I wish to thank the authors, who took time from their busy schedules to write. A number of them, David Balding, Alan Izenman, Beverly Mellen, Weiwen Miao, and Mark Rosenblum, served as reviewers for several articles and provided numerous helpful comments and suggestions. Several other scholars, Shari Seidman Diamond, Michael D. Green, and Arnold Reitze, reviewed some articles and offered most helpful advice to the authors and editor. I am most grateful for the support of John Kimmel and the staff at Springer as well as the editors of the series. Special thanks go to Jenny Wolkowicki, the Production editor for her excellent handling of the final stages of the editing and production process. My Ph.D. students Gang Zheng, Binbing Yu, and Jinyu Yuan willingly assisted me in many of the organizational and computer related tasks. The secretarial staff of the department of statistics, especially Bickie Pham and Stephanie Mohr, were most cooperative. The book was completed while I was on sabbatical leave as visiting scientist at the Division of Cancer Epidemiology and Genetics of the National Cancer Institute. It is a pleasure to thank Dr. Mitchell Gail, chief of the biostatistics branch, and Dr. Joseph Fraumeni Jr., the division director, for providing such a stimulating and encouraging research environment that allowed me to pursue new interests and complete this project.

Contents

Contributors

Colin G.G. Aitken is a Reader in Statistics at The University of Edinburgh. He has been involved in the use of statistical evidence in forensic cases since he was a graduate student and is the author of "Statistics and the Evaluation of Evidence for Forensic Scientists" as well as numerous papers in the area. His research focuses on the Bayesian approach to the interpretation of evidence and design of studies. A major force in the creation of the series of Conferences on Forensic Statistics, he has served on the program committee for all four conferences held to date and is on the program committee for the fifth. He has been consulted by police, lawyers and forensic scientists for advice on general policy as well as on issues arising in specific cases.

Mailing address: Department of Mathematics and Statistics, The University of Edinburgh, James Clerk Maxwell Building, King's Buildings, Mayfield Road, Edinburgh EH9 3JZ, Scotland.
Email: cgga@maths.ed.ac.uk

David J. Balding is Professor of Applied Statistics at the University of Reading and holds the degrees of B. Math, (Newcastle, Australia, 1984) and D. Phil, (Oxford, UK, 1989). He has taught and researched at Oxford and Queen Mary & Westfield, London. He has investigated statistical and population genetics issues in the interpretation of DNA evidence, and has advised defense lawyers and given expert witness testimony in numerous UK criminal cases.

Mailing address: Department of Applied Statistics, University of Reading, Harry Pitt Building, Whiteknights Road, P.O. Box 240, Reading RG6 6FN, England.
Email: d.j.balding@reading.ac.uk

Janet Chaseling teaches in the Faculty of Environmental Sciences at Griffith University. She began her career as a Biometrician and is an Accredited Statistician, a status awarded by the Australian Statistical Society. Over the past six years she has served as an expert witness for the prosecution in over twenty trials involving DNA evidence. In addition, she has worked with the National Institute of Forensic Science and other forensic laboratories to develop a national DNA database of consistent loci for use in these cases. Dr Chaseling's expert witness work has stimulated her to think about how statistical concepts can be communicated to judges and jurors.

Mailing address: Applied Statistics, Faculty of Environmental Sciences, Griffith University, Nathan Campus, Queensland 4111, Australia.
Email: j.chaseling@mailbox.gu.edu.au

Robert J. Cottrol is the Harold Paul Green Research Professor of Law and Professor of History and Sociology at George Washington University. He received the B.A. and Ph.D. in American Studies from Yale University and the J.D. from Georgetown University. He has written extensively in the fields of U.S. legal and social history having published three books. His articles and essays have appeared in the *American Journal of Legal History*, the *Yale Law Journal*, the *Georgetown Law Journal*, the *Law and Society Review*, the *Cardozo Law Review*, the *University of Colorado Law Review*, the *Tulane Law Review*, and *Slavery and Abolition*, among other journals. Professor Cottrol has testified before Congress on criminal justice issues.

Mailing address: George Washington Law School, 2000 H Street, N.W., Washington, D.C. 20052.
Email: bcottrol@main.nlc.gwu.edu

Boris Freidlin is a mathematical statistician at the Biometric Research Branch of the National Cancer Institute, in Bethesda, Maryland. He received his Ph.D. in Statistics from George Washington University. His research has focused on statistical methodology useful in the analysis of data arising in clinical studies as well as in legal applications.

Mailing address: Biometric Research Branch, Division of Cancer Treatment and Diagnosis, National Cancer Institute, 6130 Executive Blvd. EPN 739, Bethesda, MD 20892-7434.
Email: freidlinb@ctep.nci.nih.gov

Joseph L. Gastwirth is Professor of Statistics and Economics at George Washington University. He is a Fellow of the American Statistical Association and the Institute of Mathematical Statistics. He has served several terms as an Associate Editor of the *Journal of the American Statistical Association*. In 1985 he received a Guggenheim Fellowship to continue his research in the area of statistical problems arising in the legal setting. He is the author of "Statistical Reasoning in Law and Public Policy," published in 1988 as well as articles concerning the use of statistical evidence in cases concerning discrimination, environmental protection, product liability, pyramid fraud and unfair tax assessment. He has testified for both plaintiffs and defendants in equal employment cases, and for the government in consumer and environmental protection cases as well as the use of sampling.

Mailing address: Department of Statistics, 315 Funger Hall, George Washington University, Washington D.C., 20052
Email: jlgast@research.circ.gwu.edu

Seymour Geisser is Professor and Director of the School of Statistics, University of Minnesota. Previously he was Chief of a Biometry section at the National Institutes of Health and chairman of the Department of Statistics at the State University of New York at Buffalo. He has published in the following areas: prediction, multivariate analysis, Bayesian analysis, growth curves, classification, discriminant analysis, perturbation analysis, interim analysis, sampling curtailment, diagnostics, sample reuse, discordancy testing, influential observations, repeated measurements, profile analysis, biostatistical applications, model selec-

tion, screening tests, control procedures and DNA forensics. He is a Fellow of the American Statistical Association and the Institute of Mathematical Statistics as well as a member of the International Statistical Institute. He has edited several volumes of statistical papers and is the author of the book "Predictive Inference."
Mailing address: School of Statistics, University of Minnesota, 313 Ford Hall, 224 Church Street SE, Minneapolis, MN 55455.
Email: geisser@stat.umn.edu

Alan J. Izenman is Senior Research Professor of Statistics in the Department of Statistics, Fox School of Business and Management, Temple University, Philadelphia. He received his Ph.D. in Statistics from the University of California, Berkeley, in 1972. He has held faculty positions at Tel-Aviv University and at Colorado State University, and visiting positions at the University of Chicago, the University of Minnesota, Stanford University, and the University of Edinburgh. During 1992–94, he was Director of the Statistics and Probability Program at the National Science Foundation. He is a Fellow of the American Statistical Association and has been an associate editor of the *Journal of the American Statistical Association*. His research interests are primarily in multivariate analysis, time series analysis, nonparametric curve estimation, and the application of statistical methods to law and public policy. He has been a consultant to numerous companies, government agencies, city police departments, and law firms. He has testified on statistical issues in state courts, where he has appeared for either the plaintiffs or the defendants depending upon the case. He has also testified on statistical issues in state legislative council hearings.
Mailing address: Department of Statistics, Temple University, Philadelphia, PA 19122.
Email: alan@surfer.sbm.temple.edu

Joseph B. Kadane is Leonard J. Savage University Professor of Statistics and Social Sciences at Carnegie Mellon University, where he has taught since 1971, and served as Department Head in Statistics from 1972 to 1981. He is a Fellow of the American Statistical Association and the Institute of Mathematical Statistics. He was Applications and Coordinating Editor of the *Journal of the American Statistical Association* from 1983 to 1985. He is coeditor of the book "Statistics and the Law," published in 1986, and co-author of "A Probabilistic Analysis of the Sacco and Vanzetti Evidence" published in 1996. He has testified as an expert on whether draw poker machines require skill to play, and on the census undercount. His other testimony has concerned discrimination by age, race, and sex in employment, housing, jury venire selection, and policing, often, although not always, for plaintiffs. Additionally, he has worked on sampling issues in large corporate disputes, for the defense.
Mailing address: Department of Statistics, Carnegie Mellon University, Pittsburgh, PA 15213.
Email: kadane@stat.cmu.edu

Sana Loue holds a J.D. from the University of San Diego School of Law (1980), an M.P.H. from San Diego State University (1989), and a Ph.D. in epidemiology from the School of Public Health at the University of California, Los Angeles (1993). She practiced immigration and HIV-related law for fourteen years prior to joining the School of Medicine at Case Western Reserve University. Her current areas of research include behavioral interventions to reduce HIV transmission, immigrant health and intimate partner violence. Dr. Loue is the author of "Forensic Epidemiology: A Comprehensive Guide for Legal and Epidemiology Professionals" (1999). She has served as a consultant to attorneys, primarily plaintiffs and epidemiologists, in cases involving tobacco and work-related exposures.

Mailing address: Department of Epidemiology and Biostatistics, Case Western Reserve University, Metro Health Center, 2500 Metrohealth Drive, Cleveland, OH 44109-1998.

Email: sxl54@po.cwru.edu

Charles R. Mann is President of Charles R. Mann Associates Inc., a Washington, D.C. based consulting firm specializing in providing statistical, economic, data processing and other technical services to the legal and human resource professions since 1977. He received his Ph.D. in Statistics from the University of Missouri and has been a member of the Statistics faculty of The George Washington University. Dr. Mann is an elected Fellow of the American Statistical Association and has served as Chair of its Committee on Professional Ethics. He has been providing expert witness services since 1971. Dr. Mann provides consulting services and litigation support with a concentration on equal opportunity and affirmative action matters on behalf of both defendants and plaintiffs. His clients include corporations, federal agencies, local governments and individuals. Major cases in which he has provided testimony include: *Bazemore v. Friday*, 478 U.S. 385 (1986), *Sledge v. J.P. Stevens Inc. & Co.*, 585 F.2d 625 (4th Cir. 1978), *Price Waterhouse v. Hopkins*, 490 U.S. 228 (1989), *Chewning v. Seamans*, C.A. No. 76-0334 (D.D.C.), and *Roberts v. Texaco, Inc.*, C.A. No. 94-2015. (S.D.N.Y.).

Mailing address: Charles R. Mann Associates, Inc., 1101 Seventeenth St., N.W., Washington, D.C. 20036-4704.

Email: crmann@attglobal.net

Beverly Mellen is Assistant Professor in the Section on Biostatistics in the Department of Public Health Sciences at Wake Forest University School of Medicine. She received an M.S. degree in Human Genetics in 1987 from the Medical College of Virginia and a Ph.D. degree in Biostatistics in 1997 from Johns Hopkins University School of Hygiene and Public Health. Her areas of research include statistical theory and methods for evaluating human DNA data as identification evidence, as well as topics in epidemiologic and genetic statistics.

Mailing address: Department of Public Health Sciences, Wake Forest University School of Medicine, Medical Center Boulevard, Winston-Salem NC 27157-1063.

Email: bmellen@wfubmc.edu

Weiwen Miao is Assistant Professor of Mathematics at Macalester College. She received her Ph.D. from Tufts University, specializing in probability and statistics. Prior to joining the faculty at Macalester she taught at Mount Holyoke and Colby College. Her research interests include theoretical issues arising in maximum likelihood estimation, statistical education and forensic uses of statistics.

Mailing address: Mathematics and Computer Science Department, Macalester College, Saint Paul, MN 55105.
Email: miao@macalester.edu

Leonard S. Miller, Ph.D., is an economist and Professor, University of California, Berkeley. His research is on the evaluation of programs to achieve efficient social service systems. His prior tobacco research (with Bartlett, Rice and Max) produced the first national estimates of smoking-attributable expenditures (SAEs) based on data from the National Medical Expenditure Survey, 1987. State estimates of these SAEs and of Medicaid SAEs (with Zhang) were the basis for determining individual State shares from the Master Settlement Agreement between the States and the tobacco industry. He worked for more than two years on the State of Minnesota-Blue Cross/Blue Shield claims estimates, the article reported in this volume.

Mailing address: Department of Biostatistics, University of California, Berkeley, CA 94720.
Email: lsmiller@uclink4.berkeley.edu

David Pollard teaches statistics and probability at Yale University, where he has spent most of his career since receiving his Ph.D. in mathematical statistics from the Australian National University in 1976. He is a fellow of both the American Statistical Association and the Institute of Mathematical Statistics, and an elected member of the International Statistical Institute. His work for the Public Defender in the *King*, *Rodriguez*, and *Gibbs* cases has been his only excursion into the application of statistics to the law.

Mailing address: Department of Statistics, Yale University, 24 Hillhouse, New Haven, CT 06520.
Email: david.pollard@yale.edu

Marc Rosenblum, an economist and a lawyer, has been with the Equal Employment Opportunity Commission since 1979. He has a Ph.D. from the University of Minnesota (1972) and a JD from the Georgetown University Law Center (1989). He previously taught at John Jay College (City University of New York), and has been on the adjunct law faculty at Georgetown since 1992, teaching employment discrimination law. He also served as a Judicial Fellow during 1992–93 at the Administrative Office of the U.S. Courts. Dr. Rosenblum is the author of six law and several economics journal articles, as well as several chapters in various treatises.

Mailing address: Chief Economist, EEOC, 1801 L Street N.W., Washington, DC 20507.
Email: marc.rosenblum@eeoc.gov

Donald B. Rubin is Professor in the Department of Statistics, Harvard University, which he chaired for three consecutive terms from 1985–1994 and will chair again starting in 2000. He has over 250 publications (including several books) on a variety of topics, including computational methods, causal inference in experiments and observational studies, techniques for handling nonresponse and other issues in survey sampling, and applications in many areas of the social, economic, and biomedical sciences. Professor Rubin is a Fellow of the American Statistical Association, the Institute of Mathematical Statistics, the International Statistical Institute, the Woodrow Wilson Society, Phi Beta Kappa, the John Simon Guggenheim Society, the New York Academy of Sciences, American Association for the Advancement of Science, and the American Academy of Arts and Sciences. He is also the recipient of two of the most prestigious awards for statisticians: The Samuel S. Wilks Medal of the American Statistical Association and the Parzen Prize for Statistical Innovation.

Mailing address: Department of Statistics, Harvard University, Cambridge, MA 02138.
Email: rubin@hustat.harvard.edu

Jonathan M. Samet, M.D., M.S. is Professor and Chairman of the Department of Epidemiology of the Johns Hopkins University School of Hygiene and Public Health. He is Director of the Institute for Global Tobacco Control and Co-Director of the Risk Sciences and Public Policy Institute. His research has addressed the effects of inhaled pollutants in the general environment and in the workplace. He has written widely on the health effects of active and passive smoking and served as Consultant Editor and Senior Editor for Reports of the Surgeon General on Smoking and Health. He has served on the Science Advisory Board for the U.S. Environmental Protection Agency and was Chairman of the Biological Effects of Ionizing Radiation Committee VI of the National Research Council. He is presently Chairman of the National Research Council's Committee on Research Priorities for Airborne Particulate Matter. He was elected to the Institute of Medicine of the National Academy of Sciences in 1997.

Mailing address: Department of Epidemiology, W6041 Johns Hopkins School of Public Health, 615 North Wolfe St., Baltimore, MD 21205.
Email: jsamet@jhsph.edu

Nozer D. Singpurwalla is Professor of Operations Research and of Statistics at George Washington University, Washington, D.C. His interests are in the statistical and probabilistic aspects of reliability, warranties, and quality control. He is a Fellow of the American Statistical Association, the Institute of Mathematical Statistics, and the American Association for the Advancedment of Science. He has served as an expert witness on several cases involving issues of product quality and system reliability. He has also been involved with cases pertaining to the use of reliability and survival analysis concepts on cases of age discrimination, taxation, and patent infringement. He has represented plaintiffs and defendants both from government and industry.

Mailing address: Department of Operations Research, George Washington University, 707 22nd Street, N.W., Washington, D.C. 20052.
Email: nozer@research.circ.gwu.edu

Anders Stockmarr received his Master's and Ph.D. degrees from the Institute of Mathematical Statistics at the University of Copenhagen. For two and a half years he worked at the Department of Forensic Genetics, which provides independent expertise to courts in Denmark. He assisted forensic scientists in preparing DNA-based testimony requested by the prosecution in several cases. His work on the database search problem has appeared in *Biometrics*. Currently, Dr. Stockmarr is with the Department of Plant Biology and Biogeochemistry of Risoe National Laboratory, Denmark, and an associated researcher of the Institute of Public Health, Department of Biostatistics of the University of Copenhagen.

Mailing address: Risoe National Laboratory, Plant Biology and Biogeochemistry Department, Building 301, Frederiksborgvej 399, P.O. Box 49, DK 4000 Roskilde, Denmark.

Email: anders.stockmarr@risoe.dk

Wendy Wagner is Professor at Case Western University School of Law and Weatherhead School of Management in Cleveland, Ohio. After receiving a master's degree in environmental studies from the Yale School of Forestry and Environmental Studies and a law degree from Yale Law School, Professor Wagner clerked for Judge Albert Engel of the U.S. Court of Appeals for the 6th Circuit. Then she worked as an honors attorney with the Environmental Enforcement section of the Environment and Natural Resources Division of the U.S. Department of Justice in Washington D.C. and served as the Pollution Control Coordinator for one year in the Office of General Counsel, U.S. Department of Agriculture. Dr. Wagner currently teaches courses in torts, environmental law, advanced environmental law, and seminars in law and science and in complex problem solving. Her research focuses on the law-science interface in environmental law, and her articles include: "The Science Charade in Toxic Risk Regulation," *95 Columbia L. Rev.* 1613 (1995); "Choosing Ignorance in the Manufacture of Toxic Products," *82 Cornell L. Rev.* 773 (1997); and "Congress, Science, and Environmental Policy," 1999 *U. of Illinois L. Rev.* 181.

Mailing address: CWRU School of Law, Case Western Reserve University, 11075 East Boulevard, Cleveland, OH 44106-7148

Email: wagner9@attglobal.net

Bruce S. Weir received an undergraduate education in Mathematics from New Zealand, and then received a Ph.D. in Statistics from NC State University in 1968. After a short stay back in New Zealand he returned to NC State as a faculty member, and is now William Neal Reynolds Professor of Statistics and Genetics. He works on developing statistical methodology for genetic data, and has been involved with DNA forensic data for the past 10 years. This involvement has included testifying for the prosecution, in support of DNA profile evidence, in nearly 30 trials. He has published over 120 scientific papers. His text, "Genetic Data Analysis" is now in its second edition, and his book, "Interpreting DNA Evidence" with Ian Evett was published in 1998. He has been elected an honorary fellow of the Royal Society of New Zealand, and is a fellow of the American Association for the Advancement of Science and the American Statistical Association.

Mailing address: Department of Statistics, North Carolina State University, Raleigh, NC 27695-8203.

Email: weir@stat.ncsu.edu

Timothy Wyant, Ph.D., is a statistical consultant with Decipher, Inc. His litigation work has included testimony in employment discrimination and asbestos cases, and in the Dalkon Shield bankruptcy. Dr. Wyant is a specialist in statistical methods for large, complex data systems. He was an expert witness for the States of Minnesota, Maryland, and Wisconsin in their suits against the tobacco industry. *Mailing address*: DECIPHER, 17644 Raven Rocks Rd., Bluemont, VA 20135. *Email*: tw@deciph.com

Scott L. Zeger, Ph.D., is Professor and Chair of Biostatistics at Johns Hopkins University School of Hygiene and Public Health in Baltimore, Maryland. He has served as expert witness to the States of Minnesota, Maryland, and Wisconsin in their civil suits against the tobacco industry. Dr. Zeger is a Fellow of the American Statistical Association, Co-Editor of the Oxford Press journal Biostatistics, and International Biometrics Society ENAR Past-President for 1997. Dr. Zeger's research focuses on the design and analysis of data from public health and biomedical studies and his specialty is on drawing inferences from correlated data. He has made substantive contributions to studies of smoking and health and environmental health.
Mailing address: Department of Biostatistics, The Johns Hopkins University, 615 N. Wolfe St., Room 3132, Baltimore, MD 21205-2103.
Email: szeger@jhsph.edu

Interpretation of Evidence, and Sample Size Determination

C.G.G. Aitken

Abstract

Two aspects of the role of probabilistic ideas in the legal process are discussed. The first is the evaluation and interpretation of evidence, where a clear understanding of conditional probability is required. Various errors in interpretation are examined. The second aspect is the sampling of a large consignment of material to determine the proportion that contains illegal substances. A Bayesian approach is used, and inferences are presented in probabilistic terms, with due account taken of prior beliefs and the outcome of the sampling process.

Keywords: Bayesian methods, evaluation of evidence, interpretation of evidence, sampling.

1 How I Became Involved in Forensic Statistics

In the mid-1970s a forensic odontologist, Dr. Gordon McDonald, came to the Department of Statistics at the University of Glasgow seeking advice on the analysis of some data on bite marks that he had collected at the Glasgow Dental Hospital. He was interested in assessing their evidential worth. He examined bite marks at the scenes of crimes and compared them with the bite mark provided by a suspect. From his own experience he was able to make a subjective judgment concerning the worth of the evidence. However, he wanted an objective judgment. Therefore, he had collected data from two hundred patients at the hospital and wanted to use these data to determine a probability distribution for the characteristics that he had measured on these data. The data were categorical concerning the position and rotation of teeth with reference to the natural arch of the jaw.

I was doing a Ph.D. at the time under the supervision of Professor John Aitchison. The subject was probability estimation for categorical data. Professor Aitchison referred Dr. McDonald to me, an act of great confidence in a raw Ph.D. student. I did some work for Dr. McDonald that was eventually published in *Applied Statistics* (Aitken and McDonald, 1979). However, I do not believe that the methodology described in the paper has ever been used in courts. This is a fate that has befallen other attempts to introduce statistical advances into the courtroom.

In 1977 I moved to a lectureship at Strathclyde University, one of only two universities in Europe at the time to have a forensic science unit. My appetite for forensic problems had been whetted by my discussions with Dr. McDonald, and I approached the forensic science unit. This was partly because there was a risk that I was about to be called as an expert witness to explain my methodology in a case involving bite marks, and I wanted advice as to how to present my evidence. It was also partly to see whether they had any interesting problems. I was not called as an expert witness but they did have interesting problems.

The first problem concerned hair identification. A forensic scientist and a statistician in Canada had published some work concerning the analysis of a set of pairwise comparisons of hairs that they had done to assess the value of such evidence for identification purposes. James Robertson, one of the lecturers in the Strathclyde unit and now Director of Forensic Services for the Australian Federal Police, was not happy with the interpretation. The problem was that the Canadian researchers were using discriminating power (see below) as a measure of the value of evidence in an individual case. However, discriminating power provides only a measure of the general value of an evidential type. It does not help in an individual case. This is now well known but was not so well appreciated then.

Consider the selection of two individuals at random from some population. The probability that they are found to match with respect to some characteristic (e.g., blood phenotype) is known as the probability of nondiscrimination or the probability of a match. The complementary probability is known as the probability of discrimination or discriminating power, DP, say. A low value for DP implies that a match by chance between samples of materials from two different sources in the system being studied is likely. A high value of DP implies that a match is unlikely and could be forensically significant. However, DP provides a general result. It does not measure the importance of a match in a particular case. This is done by the likelihood ratio, which is described below.

As an example, consider Table 1, which gives the phenotypic frequencies in the ABO system (Grunbaum et al., 1980).

The probability of a match by chance of two individuals selected at random from this population is $0.441^2 + 0.417^2 + 0.104^2 + 0.039^2$, which equals 0.381. The discriminating power is then given by

$$DP = 1 - (0.441^2 + 0.417^2 + 0.104^2 + 0.039^2) = 0.619.$$

This says nothing about the evidential value in a particular case. Suppose a crime is committed. A bloodstain is found at the scene and is determined to have come from the perpetrator. The stain is of group AB. A suspect is detained on evidence other than blood grouping. His blood group is found to be AB. If the suspect was not at the crime scene, then the perpetrator is a person other than the

Table 1. Phenotypic frequencies in the ABO system from Grunbaum et al. (1980)

Phenotype (j)	O	A	B	AB
Frequency (p_j)	0.441	0.417	0.104	0.039

suspect. The probability that a person would be of group AB by chance alone, and thus match the blood group of the suspect, is 0.039. This, and not the discriminating power, provides a measure of the value of the evidence in this particular case.

Discriminating power provides only a general measure of evidential value. High values for DP have been obtained by experimental means using pairwise comparisons in situations where frequency probabilities are not available and for which a classification system has not been devised. Examples are in the areas of paint fragments (Tippett et al., 1968), head hairs (Gaudette and Keeping, 1974) and footwear (Groom and Lawton, 1987). A discussion of the problems associated with the work on head hairs is provided by Aitken and Robertson (1987).

Since then I have been involved in various aspects of evidence evaluation and interpretation. My work has emphasized in particular the use of the likelihood ratio for evaluation, and this statistic is discussed briefly in Section 2. Various applications of the likelihood ratio to evidence evaluation have been brought together in Aitken (1995). Section 3 discusses interpretation and several possible errors of interpretation. Section 4 determines the evidential value, as measured by the likelihood ratio of the outcome of a sampling procedure from a consignment of discrete units that may contain illegal material. Section 5 discusses technical issues of sample size determination in sampling from such a consignment. Section 6 provides a brief conclusion.

2   The Evaluation of Evidence

Consider evidence E, which is thought relevant to a comparison of two issues, H_1 and H_2, respectively the case for the prosecution and the case for the defense. Then the odds form of Bayes's theorem shows how the relative beliefs in favor of H_1 and H_2 are altered by E:

$$\frac{\Pr(H_1 \mid E)}{\Pr(H_2 \mid E)} = \frac{\Pr(E \mid H_1)}{\Pr(E \mid H_2)} \times \frac{\Pr(H_1)}{\Pr(H_2)}. \tag{1}$$

The prior odds in favor of H_1 are converted into posterior odds in favor of H_1 by the likelihood ratio $\Pr(E \mid H_1)/\Pr(E \mid H_2)$. The likelihood ratio has been defined as the value (V) of the evidence (Aitken, 1995).

A likelihood ratio greater than 1 lends support to H_1; a likelihood ratio less than 1 lends support to H_2. If logarithms are taken, then the relationship between log posterior odds, log likelihood ratio, and log prior odds is additive. The logarithm of the likelihood ratio has been called the weight of evidence (Good, 1985). These ideas are not new. Taroni et al. (1998) discuss their use in the famous criminal case of Dreyfus at the beginning of the century. Good (1985) refers to work in the Second World War involving weights of evidence. The use of a verbal categorical scale has been suggested by Evett (1987), with an upper category for V from $10^{5/2}$ upwards. Such a scale is not practical with the very large values provided, for example, by DNA profiles. An alternative suggestion using logarithms, based on medical examples of risk and which has an upper category of 10^{10} upwards, has been made by Aitken and Taroni (1998).

The odds form of Bayes's theorem provides a strong intuitive argument for the use of the likelihood ratio (V) as a measure of the value of the evidence, and Good (1989) has provided a mathematical argument to justify its use.

3   The Interpretation of Evidence

Once the evidence has been evaluated by the scientist it has to be interpreted in order that the court may fully understand its value. It has been shown in Section 2 that the way to evaluate evidence is to use a likelihood ratio. It is thus relatively straightforward to detect errors in interpretation. If the interpretation is not based on an evaluation that itself is based on a likelihood ratio, then the interpretation will be wrong.

A colleague of mine, Dr. Franco Taroni, and I conducted a survey of forensic scientists and lawyers in Scotland to investigate their understanding of several different interpretations of DNA evidence. Some of the interpretations were correct, while others were wrong, and we were concerned to see whether the participants in the survey could detect which was which.

First, the notation introduced in Section 2 has to be defined in this context.

- H_1:   the prosecution hypothesis. This could be that the defendant is guilty (the ultimate issue) or that he was present at the scene of the crime (an intermediate issue);
- H_2:   the defense hypothesis. This could be that the defendant is innocent (the ultimate issue) or that he was not present at the scene of the crime (an intermediate issue);
- E: the evidence that is being assessed. This would come in two parts, evidence E_1 found at the scene of the crime and evidence E_2 associated with a suspect. It is similarities in E_1 and E_2 that lead to the suspect being considered as such.

These three items are related using (1).

The scientist is concerned with the likelihood ratio,

$$V = \frac{\Pr(E \mid H_1)}{\Pr(E \mid H_2)}. \tag{2}$$

At its simplest, the numerator of V is taken to be 1. The concern here is with the interpretation of the value that is obtained for V in a particular case, not with the evaluation itself. For interpretation, it is not necessary to be too concerned with the derivation of V. For evaluation, it is of concern whether the numerator is 1 or not. In the case where the numerator of V is 1, then V is just the reciprocal of the probability $\Pr(E \mid H_2)$. Note, though, that there are several reasons why the numerator may not be 1. These include the existence of more than one criminal or the existence of a mixed sample in DNA profiling. There are various erroneous ways in which the value of the evidence has been interpreted, and these are familiar to students of what may be called forensic statistics; the terminology for the most part is that of Koehler (1993).

- Prosecutor's fallacy;
- Defense fallacy;
- Source probability error;
- Ultimate issue error;
- Probability of a match in two pieces of evidence;
- Probability (another match) error;
- Numerical conversion error.

Various examples of interpretation, some correct and some wrong, were distributed among lawyers, forensic scientists, and students of forensic medicine and of forensic science, within Scotland, by Dr. Taroni and myself. People to whom the examples were sent were asked to comment on the correctness or otherwise of the experts' summaries. A full report is available from me; full summaries are published in Taroni and Aitken (1998a, 1998b). A brief summary with an emphasis on evidence interpretation and evaluation is given here. Note that the source probability error and the ultimate issue error are variations on the prosecutor's fallacy.

3.1   Prosecutor's Fallacy

This fallacy is sometimes difficult to detect. Mathematically it equates $\Pr(E \mid H_2)$ with $\Pr(H_2 \mid E)$. The former probability is reported by the scientist, where H_2 is a conjecture that the accused was not present at the crime scene or that the accused was not the source of semen (in a rape), for example. Suppose this probability is very small. This is then interpreted by the prosecutor to mean that $\Pr(H_2 \mid E)$ is very small; in other words, there is a very low probability that the accused was not present at the crime scene or that he was not the source of the semen. Alternatively, the scientist himself gives an opinion that the accused was present at the crime scene or was the source of the semen.

An example of this is to be found in *Ross v. Indiana* (1996), where the expert reported that "after conducting DNA testing on the vaginal swab samples taken from Anderson (the victim) and blood samples from Ross (the suspect), the DNA expert opined that Ross was the source of the seminal fluid." This associates a high probability with $\Pr(H_1 \mid E)$ and a corresponding low probability to $\Pr(H_2 \mid E)$, where H_1 is the hypothesis that Ross was the source of the seminal fluid and H_2 is the hypothesis that Ross was not the source of the seminal fluid. Comments from participants in the survey included one that the lack of background information available to the expert made it impossible to reach a conclusion on the issue. This emphasizes the problem of interpretation with the prosecutor's fallacy: In order to determine $\Pr(H_2 \mid E)$ from $\Pr(E \mid H_2)$ it is necessary to know $\Pr(H_2)$, the prior belief in H_2, and $\Pr(E \mid H_1)$, the probability of evidence under H_1; see equation (1).

3.2 Defense Fallacy

As the name suggests, this is an argument proposed by the defense. Consider a frequency of q for some genetic characteristic C, known to be possessed by the criminal. A suspect is identified who has C. There is a population of size N to which the criminal belongs. Thus there are Nq individuals with C. The suspect is only one of Nq individuals. Therefore, he has a probability of $(Nq - 1)/Nq$ of innocence. *The evidence is therefore not relevant.*

This argument assumes that all Nq people with the characteristic were equally likely to have left the evidence. This is not particularly reasonable when there is other evidence that may place the suspect near the scene of the crime. In the absence of any such evidence (which seems to be the situation in some reported cases involving DNA profiling), the probability argument is correct. However, it is fallacious to argue that the evidence is not relevant. Before the genetic evidence was put forward the accused was one of N individuals. After the genetic evidence was put forward he is one of Nq individuals. In many cases, the reduction could be from one in many millions to one in a few. Evidence such as this is highly relevant.

3.3 Source Probability Error

In *U.S. v. Jakobetz* (1992) the frequency of the trait in the population was reported to be 1 in 300 million. The FBI concluded that there was one chance in 300 million that the DNA from the semen sample could have come from someone in the Caucasian population other than the defendant. The FBI conclusion is a statement about the value of $\Pr(H_2 \mid E)$. The report of the frequency of the trait is a statement about the value of $\Pr(E \mid H_2)$. This is similar to the prosecutor's fallacy. In the prosecutor's fallacy, the expert gives an *opinion* about the source of the evidence. With the source probability error, the expert gives a *probability* for the source of the evidence.

3.4 Ultimate Issue Error

This error extends the hypothesis that the suspect is the source of the evidence to the hypothesis that the suspect is guilty of the crime in question (Koehler, 1993). Consider a case in which $\Pr(E \mid \text{suspect not present at crime scene})$ equals 1 in 5 million. The ultimate issue error would interpret this as a probability of 1 in 5 million that the suspect was innocent. Again, this is similar to the prosecutor's fallacy but uses a probability rather than an opinion. It is also similar to the source probability error but is now, as the name suggests, an error related to the ultimate issue of guilt rather than an intermediate issue about the source of the evidence.

3.5 Probability of a Match in Two Pieces of Evidence

In *State of Arizona v. Robert Wayne Johnson* (1995), the frequency of the concordant genetic characteristic in the population was reported to be 1 in 312 million. The expert calculated the possibility of a random match—*two* unrelated individuals having the same DNA pattern across five alleles—to be one in 312 million.

This interpretation is wrong (assuming that the quoted frequency is correct). The probability of a match of two unrelated pieces of evidence is not of interest. Consider the value V of evidence E as defined above, where now E is written as (E_1, E_2), where E_1 is the evidence of a DNA profile from a stain found at the crime scene and E_2 is the evidence of the DNA profile of the suspect. Also, H_1 is the hypothesis that the suspect was present at the crime scene, and H_2 is the hypothesis that the suspect was not present at the crime scene. Then

$$V = \frac{\Pr(E_1, E_2 \mid H_1)}{\Pr(E_1, E_2 \mid H_2)}$$
$$= \frac{\Pr(E_1 \mid E_2, H_1)\Pr(E_2 \mid H_1)}{\Pr(E_1 \mid E_2, H_2)\Pr(E_2 \mid H_2)}.$$

Now, note that $\Pr(E_2 \mid H_1) = \Pr(E_2 \mid H_2)$, since the evidence of the DNA profile of the suspect is independent of whether he was at the crime scene or not. It has the same probability whether or not the suspect was present at the crime scene. Also, if the suspect was not present at the crime scene, then $\Pr(E_1 \mid E_2, H_2) = \Pr(E_1 \mid H_2)$, since the evidence at the crime scene is independent of the evidence from the suspect under these circumstances. Thus,

$$V = \frac{\Pr(E_1 \mid E_2, H_1)}{\Pr(E_1 \mid H_2)}.$$

In the simplest case, if the suspect was at the crime scene, there is certain to be a match between his evidence E_2 and that of E_1 found at the scene, and $\Pr(E_1 \mid E_2, H_1)$ equals 1. Then,

$$V = \frac{1}{\Pr(E_1 \mid H_2)}.$$

This is just the reciprocal of the frequency of the characteristic in the population. A more general approach, taking account of factors such as the possible relatedness between a suspect and the criminal is given in Balding and Donnelly (1995).

In the case of *Arizona v. Johnson* (1995), $V=312$ million. This is the reciprocal of the probability that *one* individual selected at random from the population has the DNA profile found at the crime scene. However, the expert quoted above believed that 1/312 million was the probability of *two* unrelated individuals having the same DNA pattern. This is not so. The probability that two unrelated individuals selected at random have the same characteristics is $\{\Pr(E_1 \mid H_2)\}^2$, and this is not relevant to the evaluation of evidence.

3.6 Probability (Another Match) Error

Consider the case of *Arizona v. Johnson* (1995) again. Let the number of innocent members of the relevant population be N and let q be the relative frequency of the genetic characteristic C in the relevant population. The probability that an individual member of the population has C is taken to be q, independent of all other members of the population. Notice that $1/q$ can be larger than N. This is possible because q is estimated from some large superpopulation (e.g., Caucasians in USA.), whereas N is defined by the circumstances of the particular case under investigation. The probability that no innocent member of the relevant population has C is then $(1 - q)^N$, and the probability that at least one innocent member of the population has C is $1 - (1 - q)^N$. This is the probability that an innocent member of the population matches the crime evidence. An alternative interpretation is that it is the probability of finding a match other than that between the evidence of the crime scene and the suspect.

Consider *Arizona v. Johnson* (1995), with $q = 1/312$ million. Suppose N equals 1 million. Then $1 - (1 - q)^N = 0.0032$. This probability has been used as a method of evaluating evidence, but it is very difficult to interpret. It is not a likelihood ratio so does not fit into Bayes's theorem. It is an error to equate $1/312$ million to the probability that at least one other person has the profile. This error is known as the probability (another match) error (Evett, 1995).

3.7 Numerical Conversion Error

In the case of *Ross v. State* (1992), the frequency q of the concordant genetic characteristic C was 1 in 209,100,000. The expert was asked, "how many people (n) would we have to look at before we saw another person like this?" The answer given was 209,100,000 ($1/q$). This is not so, and the error is known as the numerical conversion error (Koehler, 1993). It equates n with $1/q$. However, it is possible to determine n if and only if the probability P of at least one other match is specified. For example, if P equals 0.5, then n can be obtained from the equation

$$1 - (1 - q)^n = 0.5,$$

where $q = 1/209,100,000$. The solution of the equation gives a value of 145 million for n. For P equal to 0.9, n equals 482 million, and to obtain n equal to 209,100,000, then P is 0.632 (Taroni and Aitken, 1998a).

Note that in Section 3.6 it is q and N that are fixed, and it is the probability of another match that is then determined. In this section it is q and P that are fixed, and n is then determined.

3.8 Likelihood Ratio

The likelihood ratio (2) was used to summarize the evidence in *R. v. Montella* (1992). The frequency of the concordant genetic characteristic in the population was 8.06×10^{-5}, or 1 in 12,400. The evidence was summarized by saying that the likelihood of obtaining such results (a match between a DNA profile from the semen stain found at the crime scene and a DNA profile from the accused) was at least 12,400 times greater if the semen stain originated from the accused than from another individual.

This is the best way to summarize the evidence. There are two conditioning events, one that the semen stain originated from the accused, the other that it originated from some other person. For the first event, the probability of the evidence is taken to be 1; if the semen stain came from the accused, then the probability of a match is certain. For the second event, the probability of the evidence is taken to be 1/12,400; if the semen stain did not come from the accused, the probability of a match is 1/12,400. The ratio of these two probabilities is 12,400. This is then reported as above or in a similar way: The evidence is 12,400 times more likely if the accused were the donor of the semen than if he were not.

Unfortunately, the use of the likelihood ratio caused the greatest confusion among those surveyed, and many participants confessed to not understanding what the summary meant.

More education is needed to explain how to interpret probabilities. These responses came from people involved in the judicial process and thinking a lot about it. However, others are involved in juries. It was difficult for those participating in our survey to obtain the correct answer. How much more difficult will it be for others? Help may be given if the presentation of evidence is standardized. One suggestion as to how this may be done is to use a logarithmic scale of evidence as proposed by Aitken and Taroni (1998).

4 Sampling

4.1 Introduction

Another area of forensic science in which statistics has a role to play is that of sampling a large consignment of material to determine the proportion that contains illegal substances.

Consider a large consignment (of size N) of discrete units, such as pills or computer disks. It is thought that some, or all, of these units may contain illegal material. Some or all of the consignment of pills may contain illegal drugs, some or all of the consignment of disks may contain some disks that contain illegal material, such as pornographic images. It is neither feasible nor desirable to inspect all the units in the consignment. A sample is necessary. The question than arises, "How big a sample should be taken?"

If a sample is inspected from the consignment, uncertainty remains as to the contents of the units in the rest of the consignment that have not been inspected. The question as phrased in the previous paragraph can be extended to, "How big a sample should be taken in order to make some claim about the consignment as a whole?" Even then, one needs to know the claim that one is trying to make. It will not be possible to make most claims with certainty, since the whole consignment has not been inspected.

The most sensible assertion to try to make is that the proportion θ of the consignment that contains illegal material is greater than some value, θ_0 say. The value of θ_0 needs to be specified in advance in order to determine the sample size. If one wants to be certain that all of the consignment contains illegal material then the whole consignment has to be inspected.

Let m be the number of units examined. The proportion examined is m/N. If all m of the sample are found to contain illegal material, then it can be said with certainty that at least m/N of the consignment contains illegal material. However, this will usually not be a very efficient way of proceeding. Consider a consignment of 10,000 computer disks. To be certain that at least 50% (5,000) contain pornographic images, say, it would be necessary to inspect at least 5,000 disks. If one is prepared to tolerate a little uncertainty, then the number of disks it is necessary to inspect may be reduced considerably.

The uncertainty one is prepared to tolerate can form part of the sampling criterion. The criterion can then be stated as, "It is desired to choose a sample size m such that it can be said with probability p that at least a proportion θ_0 of the entire consignment contains illegal material."

The consignment size N will be taken to be sufficiently large relative to m such that sampling may be considered to be with replacement. The sample size will then be independent of the consignment size.

The sample size is to be determined according to a criterion such that with probability p at least a proportion θ_0 of the consignment contains illegal material. In what follows it will be assumed that each unit among those inspected is found to contain illegal material. The discussion about the value of the evidence follows from Section 2.

Let the true proportion of the consignment that contains illegal material be θ. The sample size criterion enables a probability p to be attached to the event $\theta > \theta_0$, given that m units have been examined and all found to contain illegal material. The evidence E is the result of the inspection. The two issues H_1 and H_2 being compared are $\theta > \theta_0$ (H_1) and $\theta < \theta_0$ (H_2). The posterior odds in favor of H_1 (see Section 2) are

$$\frac{\Pr(\theta > \theta_0 \mid E)}{\Pr(\theta < \theta_0 \mid E)} = \frac{p}{1-p}.$$

This is a statement about an issue. As such it should not be the responsibility of the scientist. The scientist should be concerned with the value V of the evidence. In this context

$$V = \frac{\Pr(E \mid \theta > \theta_0)}{\Pr(E \mid \theta < \theta_0)}.$$

Let the prior probability density function $f(\theta)$ for θ be a beta distribution, a very common distribution when the parameter space is defined on [0,1]. For a given θ and m, the probability of E is θ^m, since if an individual unit contains illegal material with probability θ and each unit is independent of the others, then the probability that all m units contain illegal material is θ^m. Thus,

$$V = \frac{\int_{\theta_0}^1 \theta^m f(\theta)d\theta}{\int_0^{\theta_0} \theta^m f(\theta)d\theta}.$$

For the so-called uniform beta distribution in which $f(\theta) = 1$ $(0 < \theta < 1)$ and for $\theta_0 = 0.5$,

$$V = \frac{\int_{0.5}^1 \theta^m d\theta}{\int_0^{0.5} \theta^m d\theta}$$

$$= \frac{1 - \left(\frac{1}{2}\right)^{m+1}}{\left(\frac{1}{2}\right)^{m+1}}$$

$$= 2^{m+1} - 1.$$

Notice that $V = 1$ when $m = 0$. When no sampling has been done, the evidence is neutral.

It is easy, mathematically, to determine how V varies as the specifications of θ under H_1 and H_2 vary. For example, again for the uniform beta distribution, and with $H_1 : \theta > \theta_1$, $H_2 : \theta < \theta_2$, $(\theta_2 < \theta_1)$, then

$$V = \frac{(1 - \theta_1^{m+1})}{\theta_2^{m+1}}$$

when all units inspected contain illegal material. For situations in which the beta distribution is not uniform (and thus prior beliefs place more weight on certain ranges of proportions than others) or some of the units inspected do not contain illegal material, then V is a ratio of incomplete beta functions. Analytic solutions are not possible, though numerical ones are, given access to a suitable statistical package. Further details of the general beta distribution are given in Section 5.

4.2 Relationship to Legislation

Various questions arise from the analyses in Section 4.1. How should the value of θ_0 be chosen? Should H_1 and H_2 be complementary or should it be that H_1 is $\theta > \theta_1$ and that H_2 is $\theta < \theta_2$ (where $\theta_1 > \theta_2$)? How should the value of p be chosen? These may be questions that legislators should be considering. Values of $\theta_1 = 0.5$ and $p = 0.95$ used in Section 5 were specified to me in discussions with forensic scientists.

The idea that statistics may be used as an aid to the formulation of legislation is not new. Bisgaard (1991) suggested that statisticians should take a "more proactive role by helping legislators, lawyers, and other legal experts in designing laws that are concise, and to the widest possible extent unambiguous."

In the sampling issues discussed here, the measure of interest is the *proportion* of a large consignment that contains illegal material. Legislation already exists in the USA for the consideration of a *quantity* of illegal material, namely the amount of drugs handled, to be taken into account at sentencing. The quantities are compared with so-called base offense levels. Legislation has been framed in sentencing guidelines (U.S. Sentencing Commission, 1995) so that the quantity of drugs is one of the factors used in determining the length of the sentence handed down. For example, the estimation of the quantity of drugs involved was a key issue in the Shonubi case, discussed elsewhere in this volume. The quantity relevant for sentencing includes not only the amount under the current charge but also the amounts "that were part of the same course or common scheme or plan as the offense of the conviction" (U.S. Sentencing Commission, 1995). Some attention has been paid to the probabilistic aspect of this quantity estimation (Aitken et al., 1997; Bring and Aitken, 1996, 1997).

Is it possible to determine equivalent criteria for the proportion of a consignment that contains illegal material? For example, if it can be shown with probability p that a proportion θ, at least as great as θ_0, of a consignment of computer disks contains pornographic material, then can it be stipulated that a certain length of sentence, say in the interval k to l months, be handed down, where k and l are specified in suitable guidelines? Thus, it may arise that the prosecution wish to use $H_1 : \theta > \theta_1$, whereas the defense may wish to use $H_2 : \theta < \theta_2$, where $\theta_1 > \theta_2$, and different sentencing lengths apply.

The base offense levels are restrictive and leave judges little room in which to maneuver in sentencing, though the sentence can be adjusted by consideration of other circumstances. Similar guidelines for sampling offense levels may also be thought restrictive. The base offense levels as currently published (U.S. Sentencing Commission, 1995) have no explicit probabilistic component. In practice, a quantity of drugs relevant for sentencing purposes has only to be determined on the *balance of probabilities*. More explicit probabilistic criteria may aid the judges in their decisions.

Two points have to be borne in mind in determining such criteria. First, for the quantity of drugs, the amount is determined not only by the amount associated with the defendant at the time of his arrest. Judges are allowed also to consider noncharged criminal activity that is "part of the same course or common scheme or plan as the offense of the conviction" (U.S. Sentencing Commission, 1995) in computing a defendant's sentence. Second, in most federal courts, for sentencing purposes the quantity of drugs handled is an issue of fact that must be established by a preponderance of the evidence, or balance of probabilities. In many state courts, the quantity is an essential element of the possession charge and as such must be proved beyond reasonable doubt. For the consideration of proportions, should similar noncharged criminal activity be included in the sentencing decision? This line of thought is not pursued further here. However, some comments on the burden of proof may be relevant.

From a probabilistic perspective, there seems to be good agreement among judges that the preponderance standard is just above 50%. However, there is disagreement concerning the interpretation of "beyond reasonable doubt," with values ranging from 76% to 95% (*U.S. v. Fatico*, 1978). The value of 76%, if believed, would imply that the judges who supported that figure were prepared to tolerate an error rate such that 1 in 4 people found guilty were, in fact, innocent. This does not seem correct. It suggests rather that judges do not really understand the meaning of probability.

In 1991, the preponderance standard was incorporated as an amendment to the sentencing guidelines. This standard is used to establish disputed facts at sentencing and allows judges to consider even noncharged criminal activity in computing a defendant's sentence (Greenwald, 1994; Izenman, 1999). Consider the Shonubi case again. There was evidence that the defendant had made eight trips. The court considered them all at the time of sentencing, by multiplying the amount, t_0 say, determined from the charged criminal activity by eight to give a value t_1 say, where $t_1 = 8t_0$. However, t_1 is an estimate of the total amount T smuggled by Shonubi. This total amount is a random variable whose distribution may be estimated (Bring and Aitken, 1997). The preponderance of the evidence is generally taken to be equivalent to a probability of 0.5. Shonubi could then be sentenced for smuggling a total amount t that would be the largest amount for which it could be said that $\Pr(T > t) > 0.5$.

In order to find someone guilty "beyond reasonable doubt," values for the probability of guilt, $\Pr(G)$, have been reported from 0.9 upwards (Gastwirth, 1992), though values as low as 0.6 have been suggested (Taroni and Aitken, 1998a). In *Bater v. Bater* (1951), Lord Denning said, "In criminal cases the charge must be proved beyond reasonable doubt, but there may be degrees of proof within that standard. As Best, C.J. and many other great judges have said, 'in proportion as the crime is enormous so ought the proof be clear' " (Eggleston, 1983). The reference to Best, C.J. is to *Despard's Case* (1803), a trial for high treason. In *R. v. Sarah Hobson* (1823), Holroyd, J. said, "The greater the crime, the stronger is the proof required for the purpose of conviction." Research carried out by Simon and Mahan (1971) supports this suggestion. Simon and Mahon administered a questionnaire to judges, jurors, and students of sociology in which they asked the respondents to assign a probability to the phrase "beyond reasonable doubt" for various crimes. The answers ranged from a mean of 0.93 provided by the students for a charge of murder to a mean of 0.74 provided by the jurors for a charge of petty larceny. Thus it is that there is no clear specification for "beyond reasonable doubt." This is understandable. However, there is another factor to be considered earlier in the legal process than determining the level of proof and that is the choice of prior values.

Should legislators be concerned with prior specifications? The sample size determinations and the value for V specified above depend on a prior distribution. Is it fair for the forensic scientist to have to shoulder the responsibility for choosing the parameters for the prior distribution? Are the legislators prepared to do this?

If not, then there is scope for discussion at trials as to what the correct prior distribution is. This is not a good way forward. Can one discuss priors after the data have been collected?! Can guidelines be provided for scientists to enable them to make a judgment about priors that can then be justified in court?

5 Technical Aspects of Sample Size Determination

5.1 Introduction

The criterion that with probability p at least a proportion θ of the consignment contains illegal material is a probability statement about a proportion. As such it suggests a Bayesian approach for the solution of the problem. Solutions based on a frequentist approach have been suggested (Tzidony and Ravreby, 1992, Frank et al., 1991, Colón et al., 1993). Suppose m units are examined and x ($\leq m$) are found to contain illegal material. The observed proportion is x/m, which may be used as an estimate for θ. A frequentist approach determines a value for θ_0 as the lower confidence bound for θ. This considers the probability of the observed proportion given a value for θ. The analysis is considered as a hypothesis test. The null hypothesis is that $\theta > \theta_0$; the alternative is that $\theta < \theta_0$. In the case where $x = m$, the null hypothesis is rejected in favor of the alternative, for size p, if $\theta_0^m \leq p$.

Consider as an example the case where $x = m = 5$ and $\theta_0 = 0.7$. Then $\theta_0^5 = 0.17$. The frequentist argument is then that there is 83% *confidence* that θ, the true proportion of drugs in the consignment, is greater than 0.7.

However, such a probability is the transpose of what is required. This is recognized by the use of the word *confidence* rather than *probability*. What is required is a probability distribution for θ given the observed proportion in the sample. Thus arises the usual conflict between the Bayesian and frequentist approaches to statistical analyses. The conflict is resolved in a limiting case, as explained below, when both approaches give the same answer. The Bayesian approach provides greater flexibility but at the expense of requiring prior beliefs to be stated explicitly.

The Bayesian analysis for large consignments is given here. A detailed comparison of this analysis with the frequentist approach and similar analyses for small consignments are given in Aitken (1999).

5.2 A Bayesian Method for the Estimation of θ

In order to make probability statements about θ, it is necessary to have a probability distribution for θ to represent the variability in θ. The most suitable distribution in this context for θ is the beta distribution (Bernardo and Smith, 1994). Its use in another forensic context, that of sampling glass fragments, is described in Curran et al. (1998). A special case has been discussed in Section 4.1.

The general beta distribution for θ, parametrized by $(\alpha, \beta; \alpha > 0, \beta > 0)$ and denoted by $\mathrm{Be}(\alpha, \beta)$, has a probability density function

$$f(\theta \mid \alpha, \beta) = \theta^{\alpha-1}(1-\theta)^{\beta-1}/B(\alpha, \beta), \qquad 0 < \theta < 1, \tag{3}$$

where

$$B(\alpha, \beta) = \frac{\Gamma(\alpha)\Gamma(\beta)}{\Gamma(\alpha + \beta)}$$

and

$$\Gamma(z) = \int_0^\infty t^{z-1}e^{-t}dt$$

is the gamma function. Integer and half-integer values of the gamma function are found from the recursive relation $\Gamma(x + 1) = x\,\Gamma(x)$ and the values $\Gamma(1) = 1$ and $\Gamma(\frac{1}{2}) = \sqrt{\pi} \simeq 1.7725$.

The beta distribution is a conjugate prior distribution for the binomial distribution. Suppose m units are examined and x are found to contain illegal material. The distribution of X (the number of illegal units in m units inspected) given that θ is binomial, is

$$\Pr(X = x \mid m, \theta) = \binom{m}{x}\theta^x(1-\theta)^{m-x},$$

which is the same functional form for θ as in (3). Thus

$$f(\theta \mid x, m) \propto \Pr(X = x \mid m, \theta)\,f(\theta).$$

Then the probability density function that combines this information with the prior distribution is given by

$$f(\theta \mid x, m, \alpha, \beta) = \frac{\theta^{x+\alpha-1}(1-\theta)^{m-x+\beta-1}}{B(x+\alpha, m-x+\beta)}, \qquad 0 < \theta < 1,$$

denoted $\mathrm{Be}(x + \alpha, m - x + \beta)$. In the particular case where $x = m$, the density function is given by

$$f(\theta \mid m, m, \alpha, \beta) = \frac{\theta^{m+\alpha-1}(1-\theta)^{\beta-1}}{B(m+\alpha, \beta)}, \qquad 0 < \theta < 1.$$

Assumptions made in this model include independence and homogeneity of material. In the example of pills these assumptions have the following interpretation. All pills are similar in appearance, weight, and texture. The whole consignment is uniform in nature. There are not different bottles that may contain different types of pill. The process by which the consignment is put together is assumed to ensure that each pill is equally likely to contain drugs, independently of other pills. Queries may be made of these assumptions. Different assumptions may lead to a different model. However, the principle remains the same. There is a probabilistic model for the distribution of illegal units. From this model, probabilistic statements may be made about the proportion of the consignment that contains drugs.

The conflict between the Bayesian and frequentist formulations of the sampling problem is resolved, as mentioned earlier, in a limiting case. Let $\alpha \to 0$ and let $\beta = 1$. This gives rise to an improper prior distribution. Assume that $x = m$. The posterior distribution is then

$$f(\theta \mid m, m, \alpha, \beta) \to \frac{\theta^{m-1}}{B(m, 1)} = m\theta^{m-1}.$$

Thus,

$$\Pr(\theta < \theta_0 \mid m, m, \alpha, \beta) \to \int_0^{\theta_0} m\theta^{m-1} d\theta = \theta_0^m,$$

the same expression as used in the frequentist case of Section 5.1 but with a clear interpretation, since it is now a probability statement about θ (rather than a statement of confidence).

For $m = x = 5$ and $\theta_0 = 0.7$,

$$\Pr(\theta < 0.7 \mid 5, 5, \alpha, \beta) \to 0.7^5 = 0.17,$$

the same numerical value as before, but with a much more coherent interpretation. The probability that $\theta > 0.7$ is 0.83. Note that this is independent of the size of the consignment.

A commonly used prior distribution is one in which $\alpha = \beta = 1$, the uniform beta distribution of Section 4.1. Then

$$f(\theta \mid 1, 1) = 1, \quad 0 < \theta < 1.$$

This is often used to represent maximum uncertainty about θ. Another representation of uncertainty is the case where $\alpha = \beta = \frac{1}{2}$, where greater belief is placed at the ends of the range than in the middle. Thus, one's prior belief is that either all (or nearly all) units or no (or nearly none of the) units contain illegal material. Then

$$f(\theta \mid 0.5, 0.5) = \pi^{-1}\theta^{-\frac{1}{2}}(1 - \theta)^{-\frac{1}{2}}.$$

In practice, as well as the specification of the prior distribution, a criterion has to be specified in order that the sample size may be determined. Consider the criterion that the scientist wishes there to be a 95% probability that 50% or more of the consignment contains illegal material when all units sampled contain illegal material. (This was a criterion given to me by forensic scientists in Scotland whose question about sample sizes provided the motivation for this work. The question was, "How many units should be inspected to satisfy this criterion?") The criterion may be written mathematically as

$$\Pr(\theta > 0.5 \mid m, m, \alpha, \beta) = 0.95,$$

or

$$\frac{1}{B(m + \alpha, \beta)} \int_{0.5}^{1} \theta^{m+\alpha-1}(1 - \theta)^{\beta-1} d\theta = 0.95. \tag{4}$$

The solution for general p and θ_0 is obtained by finding the value of m which solves the equation

$$\frac{1}{B(m + \alpha, \beta)} \int_{\theta_0}^{1} \theta^{m+\alpha-1}(1 - \theta)^{\beta-1} d\theta = p. \tag{5}$$

Such integrals are easy to evaluate using standard statistical packages (e.g., SPLUS, Venables and Ripley, 1997) given values for m, α, and β. Specified values for θ_0 and p and given values for α and β are substituted in (5). The choice of values for α and β is the subject of the questions asked at the end of Section 4.2. The number m of units to sample is then selected by solving (5) through trial and error.

Example. Consider the following pairs of values for α and β: (1,1), (0.5, 0.5), and (0.065, 0.935) (the last pair suggested by Professor T. Leonard, personal communication). For the first two pairs there is a prior probability of 0.5 that $\theta > 0.5$; for the third pair there is a prior probability of 0.05 that $\theta > 0.5$. This third choice was made because 0.05 is the complement of 0.95. Table 2 shows the results of inserting various values of m, α, and β into the left-hand side of (4).

Thus for large consignments (sufficiently large that the sampling of five units may be considered as sampling with replacement), the scientist need examine only 4 units, in the first instance to satisfy the criterion that there be a 95% probability that 50% or more of the consignment contains illegal material. If all are found to contain illegal material, then the criterion is satisfied. This can be compared with a frequentist approach using a normal approximation to the binomial distribution that gives a value of 12 for the sample size (Cochran, 1977). These sample sizes are surprisingly small. However, on reflection, there is not very much information gained about the exact value of θ. It has been determined only that there is probability of 0.95 that $\theta > 0.5$. This is a wide interval (from 0.5 to 1) within which the true proportion may lie.

Table 2. The probability that the proportion of illegal material in a large consignment is greater than 50% for various sample sizes m and prior parameters α and β. All m units inspected contain illegal material. (*Reprinted, with permission, from the Journal of Forensic Sciences, July 1999, copyright American Society for Testing and Materials, 100 Barr Harbor Drive, West Conshohocken, PA, 19428.*)

α	β	m			
		2	3	4	5
1	1		0.94	0.97	
0.5	0.5	0.92	0.97	0.985	0.993
0.065	0.935		0.90	0.95	0.97

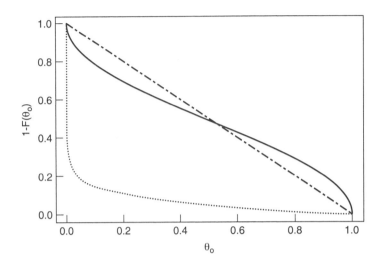

Figure 1. The prior probability that the proportion of units in a consignment that contain drugs is greater than θ, for various choices of α and β: $\alpha = \beta = 1(- \cdot --)$, $\alpha = \beta = 0.5(- - -)$, $\alpha = 0.065$, $\beta = 0.935(\cdots)$. (*Reprinted, with permission, from the Journal of Forensic Sciences, July 1999, copyright American Society for Testing and Materials, 100 Barr Harbor Drive, West Conshohocken, PA, 19428.*)

Figures 1 and 2 illustrate how varying prior beliefs have little influence on the conclusions once some data have been observed. Figure 1 shows the prior probability that $\theta > \theta_0$ for $0 < \theta_0 < 1$, for the values of (α, β) given in Table 2, decreasing from a value of 1 when $\theta_0 = 0$ to a value of 0 when $\theta_0 = 1$. There are considerable differences in the curves. Figure 2 shows the corresponding posterior probabilities for $\theta > \theta_0$ given that four units have been observed and all have been found to contain drugs, with the values for $\theta_0 = 0.5$ emphasized. There is very little difference in these curves. There may be concerns that it is very difficult for a scientist to formalize his prior beliefs. However, if α and β are small, large differences in the probabilities associated with the prior beliefs will not lead to large differences in the conclusions.

The methodology can be extended to allow for units that do not contain illegal material. For example, if one of the original four units inspected is found not to contain illegal material, then three more should be inspected. If they all contain illegal material, then it can be shown that the probability that $\theta > 0.5$, given that six out of seven contain illegal material, is 0.96.

The dependency of the sample size on the values of p and θ_0 is illustrated in Table 3. The prior parameters α and β are set equal to 1. Consider $p = 0.90$, 0.95, and 0.99 and consider values of $\theta_0 = 0.5$, 0.6, 0.7, 0.8, 0.9, 0.95, 0.99. The sample size m required to have a probability of p that θ is greater than the

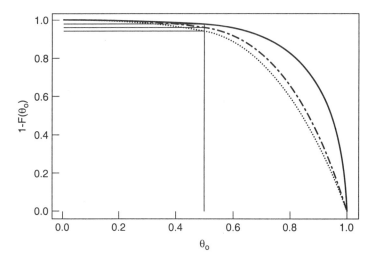

Figure 2. The posterior probability that the proportion of units in a consignment that contain drugs is greater than θ, after inspection of $m = 4$ units has shown them all to contain drugs, for various choices of $\alpha = \beta$: $\alpha = \beta = 1(- \cdot -\cdot)$, $\alpha = \beta = 0.5(- - -)$, $\alpha = 0.065$, $\beta = 0.935(\cdots)$. The solid lines show the probabilities that $\theta > 0.5$ for the various choices of $\alpha = \beta$ (from Table 2, with $m = 4$, the probabilities are 0.97, 0.985, and 0.95, respectively, for $(\alpha, \beta) = (1, 1), (0.5, 0.5)$, and $(0.065, 0.935)$). (*Reprinted, with permission, from the Journal of Forensic Sciences, July 1999, copyright American Society for Testing and Materials, 100 Barr Harbor Drive, West Conshohocken, PA, 19428.*)

specified value is then given by the value of m that satisfies the equation

$$\Pr(\theta > \theta_0 \mid m, m, 1, 1) = 1 - \theta_0^{m+1} = p,$$

a special case of (5). The value of m is thus given by the smallest integer greater than

$$[\log(1 - p)/\log(\theta_0)] - 1.$$

Note that the sample size has to be small with respect to the size of the consignment. For the last row in particular to be useful, the size of the consignment from which the sample is to be taken will have to be on the order of several tens of thousands.

There may be situations in which different choices of α and β may be wanted. It may be that the scientist has some substantial prior beliefs about the proportion of the consignment that may contain illegal material. These have to be beliefs that he is willing to testify to in court; for example, they may arise from previous experiences of similar consignments. In such cases, use can be made of various properties of the beta distribution to assist the scientist in choosing values for α and β. For example, consideration of the mean and variance may be used (Aitken, 1999). Alternatively, if it was felt that β could be set equal to 1 (so that the probability density function

Table 3. The sample size required to be $100p\%$ certain that the proportion of units in the consignment that contain illegal material is greater than θ_0, when all the units inspected are found to contain illegal material. The prior parameters $\alpha = \beta = 1$. (*Reprinted, with permission, from the Journal of Forensic Sciences, July 1999, copyright American Society for Testing and Materials, 100 Barr Harbor Drive, West Conshohocken, PA, 19428.*)

θ_0	p		
	0.90	0.95	0.99
0.5	3	4	6
0.6	4	5	9
0.7	6	8	12
0.8	10	13	20
0.9	21	28	43
0.95	44	58	89
0.99	229	298	458

was monotonic increasing with respect to θ) and that there was a prior belief about a lower bound for the proportion, say that

$$\Pr(\text{Proportion} > \theta \mid \alpha, \beta = 1) = p,$$

then

$$\alpha = \frac{\log(1 - p)}{\log(\theta)}.$$

For example, if the scientist had a prior probability of 0.95 ($p = 0.95$) that the proportion was greater than 90% ($\theta = 0.90$), then α could be taken equal to 30. Notice from (5) that if α is large, then large samples (large values of m) have to be inspected to have an effect on θ_0. This is no more than a statement of the effect that results from large samples are needed to alter strong prior beliefs. The solution of (5) for $\beta = 1$ and general α gives

$$m = \frac{\log(1 - p)}{\log(\theta)} - \alpha.$$

This expression could give negative values for m in certain situations. If one's prior beliefs are large, then the criterion specified by p and θ_0 may be satisfied without sampling.

6   Conclusion

The Bayesian approach in general and the likelihood ratio in particular provide a sound basis for the evaluation and interpretation of evidence. Overt use of the Bayesian approach in the courtroom has met with resistance among lawyers and the courts ("Evidence of Bayes's theorem or any similar statistical method of analysis plunged the jury into inappropriate and unnecessary realms of theory and complexity deflecting them from their proper tasks. It is not appropriate for use in jury trials"; *R. v. Adams* (1996)). The likelihood ratio is found to be a confusing method for summarizing evidence. It is easy to suggest that better education of lawyers in the principles of conditional probabilities is necessary. It is not so easy to implement the suggestion.

The Bayesian approach depends on a clear specification of prior beliefs. This is a good thing. Are lawyers unhappy with the consequences of their prior beliefs being exposed so explicitly? The Bayesian approach and the use of likelihood ratios require consideration of conditional probabilities. These are not easy concepts but are crucial to most facets of everyday life. People are happy to agree that a monkey has two arms and two legs and also that something with two arms and two legs need not necessarily be a monkey. However, the legal analogy causes problems. People are happy to agree that a rapist will have a DNA profile that matches that of semen found on the victim but are not so happy to agree that someone whose DNA profile matches that of semen found on the victim need not necessarily be the rapist.

All that is needed for the likelihood ratio to be accepted as the best method of evaluating evidence is the recognition that in the evaluation of evidence two probabilities are necessary: the probability of the evidence if the prosecution's case is true and the probability of the evidence if the defense case is true. This may seem obvious stated in print. However, often, as in the prosecutor's fallacy, a small probability for the evidence if the defense case is true is deemed sufficient to decide that the prosecution's case is true.

A fear of numbers on the part of lawyers and jurors has to be overcome. Perhaps the verbal scale based on logarithms will help (Aitken and Taroni, 1998) in that it will allow evidential value to be considered in a way similar to that in which other phenomena, such as the strength of earthquakes, are considered.

Acknowledgments

Thanks are due to various people and institutions who have helped my understanding of this subject. These include John Aitchison, Derek Bain, Ian Evett, Joe Gastwirth, Alan Izenman, Tom Leonard, Dennis Lindley, Gordon McDonald, James Robertson, Franco Taroni, Peter Tillers, the International Forensic Statistics Conference, and the Fourth Framework Programme of the European Union, Training and Mobility of Researchers Project numbers ERB4001GT953876 and ERB4001GT963536.

7 Cases Cited

Bater v. Bater (1951) p. 35.
Despard's Case (1803) 28 St. Tr. 345.
R. v. Adams (1996) 2 Cr. App. R. Part 3, p. 467.
R. v. Montella (1992) 1 NZLR High Court, 63–68.

R. v. Sarah Hobson (1823) 1 Lewin 261; 168 E.R. 1033.
Ross v. Indiana (1996) Indiana Court of Appeal, 13 May 1996.
Ross v. State (1992) B14-9–00659, Tex. App. 13 Feb. 1992.
State of Arizona v. Robert Wayne Johnson (1995) 905 P. 2d 1002: 192 Ariz Adv. Rep. 19.
U.S. v. Fatico (1978) 458 F. Supp. 388, E.D., N.Y.
U.S. v. Jakobetz (1992) 955 F. 2d 786 (2nd Cir.).

REFERENCES

[1] Aitken, C.G.G. (1995) *Statistics and the Evaluation of Evidence for Forensic Scientists.* Chichester: John Wiley and Sons Ltd.

[2] Aitken, C.G.G. (1999) Sampling—how big a sample? *Journal of Forensic Sciences*, 44, 750–760.

[3] Aitken, C.G.G., Bring, J., Leonard, T., and Papasouliotis, O. (1997) Estimation of quantities of drugs handled and the burden of proof. *Journal of the Royal Statistical Society, Series A*, 160, 333–350.

[4] Aitken, C.G.G. and MacDonald, D.G., (1979) An application of discrete kernel methods to forensic odontology. *Applied Statistics*, 28, 55–61.

[5] Aitken, C.G.G. and Robertson, J. (1987) A contribution to the discussion of probabilities and human hair comparisons. *Journal of Forensic Sciences*, 32, 684–689.

[6] Aitken, C.G.G and Taroni, F. (1998) A verbal scale for the interpretation of evidence. Letter to the Editor. *Science and Justice*, 38, 279–281.

[7] Balding, D.J. and Donnelly, P. (1995) Inferring identity from DNA profile evidence. Proceedings of the National Academy of Sciences of the USA, 92, 11741–11745.

[8] Bernardo, J.M. and Smith, A.F.M. (1994) *Bayesian Theory.* Chichester: John Wiley and Sons Ltd.

[9] Bisgaard, S. (1991) Design of standards and regulations. *Journal of the Royal Statistical Society, Series A*, 154, 93–96.

[10] Bring, J. and Aitken, C.G.G. (1996) *United States v. Shonubi* and the use of statistics in court. *Expert Evidence*, 4, 134–142.

[11] Bring, J. and Aitken, C.G.G. (1997) Burden of proof and estimation of drug quantities under The Federal Sentencing Guidelines. *Cardozo Law Review* 18, 1987–1999.

[12] Cochran, W.G. (1977) *Sampling Techniques*, 3rd edition. Chichester: John Wiley and Sons Ltd.

[13] Colón, M., Rodriguez, G., and Diaz, R.O. (1993) Representative sampling of "street" drug exhibits. *Journal of Forensic Sciences*, 38, 641–648.

[14] Curran, J.M., Triggs, C.M., and Buckleton, J. (1998) Sampling in forensic comparison problems. *Science and Justice*, 38, 101–107.

[15] Eggleston, R. (1983) *Evidence, Proof and Probability* (2nd edition). Weidenfeld and Nicolson, London.

[16] Evett, I.W. (1987) Bayesian inference and forensic science: problems and perspectives. *The Statistician*, 36, 99–105.

[17] Evett, I.W. (1995) Avoiding the transposed conditional. *Science and Justice*, 35, 127–131.

[18] Frank, R.S., Hinkley, S.W., and Hoffman, C.G. (1991) Representative sampling of drug seizures in multiple containers. *Journal of Forensic Sciences*, 36, 350–357.

[19] Gastwirth, J.L. (1992) Statistical reasoning in the legal setting. *American Statistician*, 46, 55–69.

[20] Gaudette, B.D. and Keeping, E.S. (1974) An attempt at determining probabilities in human scalp hair comparison. *Journal of Forensic Sciences*, 19, 599–606.

[21] Good, I.J. (1985) Weight of evidence: a brief survey. *Bayesian Statistics 2* (Bernardo, J.M., DeGroot, M.H., Lindley, D.V., Smith, A.F.M. (eds.)) Elsevier Science Publishers B.V. (North-Holland), pp. 249-270.

[22] Good, I.J. (1989) Weight of evidence and a compelling meta principle. C139 in *Journal of Statistical Computation and Simulation* 31, 54–58.

[23] Greenwald, L. (1994) Relevant conduct and the impact of the preponderance standard of proof under the Federal Sentencing Guidelines: a denial of due process. *Vermont Law Review*, 18, 529–563.

[24] Groom, P.S. and Lawton, M.E. (1987) Are they a pair? *Journal of the Forensic Science Society*, 27, 189–192.

[25] Grunbaum, B.W., Selvin, S., Myrhe, B.A. and Pace, N. (1980) Distribution of gene frequencies and discrimination probabilities for 22 human blood genetic systems in four racial groups. *Journal of Forensic Sciences*, 25, 428–444.

[26] Izenman, A.J. (1999) Statistical and legal aspects of the forensic study of illicit drugs. Submitted for publication.

[27] Koehler, J.J. (1993) Error and exaggeration in the presentation of DNA evidence at trial. *Jurimetrics*, 34, 21–39.

[28] Simon, R.J. and Mahon, L. (1971) Quantifying burdens of proof. *Law and Society Review*, 5, 319–330.

[29] Taroni, F. and Aitken, C.G.G. (1998a) Probabilistic reasoning in the law, part 1: assessment of probabilities and explanation of the value of DNA evidence. *Science and Justice*, 38, 165–177.

[30] Taroni, F. and Aitken, C.G.G. (1998b) Probabilistic reasoning in the law, part 2: assessment of probabilities and explanation of the value of trace evidence other than DNA. *Science and Justice*, 38, 179–188.

[31] Taroni, F., Champod, C., and Margot, P. (1998) Forerunners of Bayesianism in early forensic science. *Jurimetrics*, 38, 183–200.

[32] Tippett, C.F., Emerson, V.J., Fereday, M.J., Lawton, F., and Lampert, S.M. (1968) The evidential value of the comparison of paint flakes from sources other than vehicles. *Journal of the Forensic Science Society*, 8, 61–65.

[33] Tzidony, D. and Ravreby, M. (1992) A statistical approach to drug sampling: a case study. *Journal of Forensic Sciences*, 37, 1541–1549.

[34] U.S. Sentencing Commission (1995) *U.S. Federal Sentencing Guidelines Manual*, ch. 2, part D (http://www.ussc.gov/guide/ch2ptd.htm). Washington DC: U.S. Sentencing Commission.

[35] Venables, W.M. and Ripley, B.D. (1997) *Modern Applied Statistics with S-Plus* (2nd edition). Springer-Verlag, New York.

Statistical Issues in the Application of the Federal Sentencing Guidelines in Drug, Pornography, and Fraud Cases

Alan Julian Izenman

Abstract

The United States Sentencing Guidelines adopted by Congress for use within the federal justice system require that sentencing in criminal cases depends primarily on the calculation of certain quantitative amounts related to the crime. Previously, no such need existed. Examples of the types of cases that fall under this description include cases involving illicit drug trafficking, trafficking in pornography via the Internet ("cyberporn"), large-scale unauthorized duplication for sale and distribution of computer software programs, motion pictures, live and recorded musical performances, and video games ("piracy" or "counterfeiting," depending upon how much the packaging is intended to deceive), Medicare, Medicaid, and Food Stamp fraud ("welfare fraud"), and securities fraud. In such cases, the total weight of the drugs seized, the amount of monetary loss caused to the victim, or the market value of all items seized acts as a proxy for the severity of the crime. Often, however, the quantities that need to be determined are, for one reason or another, difficult to obtain. Therefore, in practice a statistical sampling and inference approach to estimating the appropriate quantity is used. In this article we discuss the statistical issues involved in these types of cases, including possible choices of sampling plans, and how federal courts recognize and deal with the presence of selection bias due to unscientific sampling. We also provide some case studies that illustrate how these issues become relevant to federal sentencing.

Key words and phrases: Capture–recapture, copyright infringement, counterfeiting, cyberporn, Food Stamp fraud, illicit drug trafficking, Medicare/Medicaid fraud, sampling, software piracy, statistics and the law.

1 Introduction

One rarely sees an actual sentencing hearing on television. While scenes of dramatic courtroom testimony abound, the foreperson entering the sentence as "death" is perhaps the only hint that there is another step in the process. In fact, in most criminal cases, sentencing is divorced from the trial itself. In a secondary phase of a federal criminal proceeding following conviction, the defendant's sentence is determined by the judge. In some strictly limited instances (such as a "continuing criminal enterprise"), federal sentences are statutorily mandated, and the elements constituting a mandatory sentence must be determined by the jury. Furthermore, trial and sentencing proceedings in the federal system have very different standards of proof. Whereas the defendant has the right to demand that guilt be proven beyond a reasonable doubt at trial (*in re Winship* 1970), the standard of proof for disputed facts at sentencing is preponderance of the evidence (*McMillan v. State of Pennsylvania* 1986). Because the Federal Rules of Evidence (FRE) do not apply at a sentencing hearing, the use of hearsay is allowed as well as other kinds of evidence that are inadmissible at trial.

It is important to note that sentencing in federal courts may use a different standard of proof than that used in non-federal (state or local) courts. The difference depends upon what are considered to be the essential elements of the crime in question. For example, state legislatures were given the authority in *Patterson v. New York* (1977) to define the "elements" of a crime and to design statutes to control what has to be proved beyond a reasonable doubt. Thus, in illicit drug cases, most state courts consider the total quantity Q of drugs seized from the defendant to be an essential element of the offense. As a result, state prosecutors must prove beyond a reasonable doubt that the amount Q was actually found in the defendant's possession. In all but a few of the federal circuits, however, the amount Q is not considered to be an essential element of the offense as defined under 21 U.S.C. §841 and hence for sentencing purposes has only to be proved by a preponderance of the evidence. For more detailed discussion of these issues, see Aitken, Bring, Leonard, and Papasouliotis 1997 and Izenman 1999. In this article we shall be dealing only with issues of federal sentencing where disputed facts (such as the value of Q) must be established by the preponderance standard.

Current federal sentencing practices owe their origin to the dramatic change brought about in 1984 when Congress passed the Comprehensive Crime Control Act, which included the Sentencing Reform Act. As part of the latter Act, the United States Sentencing Commission was created as an independent, permanent agency within the judiciary charged with establishing sentencing guidelines to determine appropriate types and lengths of sentences for every category of federal offense and every type of defendant. The primary focus of the Sentencing Commission was to

> provide certainty and fairness in meeting the purposes of sentencing, avoiding unwarranted sentencing disparities among defendants with similar records who have been found guilty of similar criminal conduct while maintaining sufficient flexibility to permit individualized sentences when warranted by mitigating or aggravating factors not taken into account in the establishment of general sentencing practices (28 U.S.C. §991(b)(1)(B)(1985)).

In order to tie sentencing to past actual practice, a statistical study of tens of thousands of convictions and presentence reports was commissioned, and in November 1987, based in part upon the results of this study, the United States Sentencing Guidelines (*U.S.S.G.* or "Federal Sentencing Guidelines") became law.

All federal crimes are governed by the Federal Sentencing Guidelines, and federal judges are now required to follow these guidelines. Sentencing decisions have to be documented in great detail and can be subject to rigorous appellate review. In 1991, the preponderance standard was incorporated as an amendment to the Federal Sentencing Guidelines.

Federal crimes that have a statistical element in the determination of the defendant's sentence will be discussed in this article. Such crimes include illicit drug trafficking; trafficking in pornography via the Internet ("cyberporn"); large-scale unauthorized duplication for sale and distribution of computer software programs, motion pictures, live and recorded musical performances, and video games; and welfare fraud involving the Medicare, Medicaid, and Food Stamp programs. Unauthorized duplication is called "piracy" if the copy is accurate, but the packaging does not resemble that of the original, and is called "counterfeiting" if both the underlying work and packaging are accurately reproduced, including all labels, art, logos, and trademarks, specifically with intent to deceive. Securities fraud and insider trading are treated essentially as a sophisticated fraud for sentencing purposes (*U.S.S.G.* §2F1.2(b), Application Note 1), and so will not be discussed here.

The financial incentives created by cyberporn, piracy, and counterfeiting are enormous and growing rapidly. For example, sexually explicit material available on the Internet can be accessed easily and inexpensively, and includes text and pictures that range from "the modestly titillating to the hardest core" (*Reno v. ACLU* 1997). In 1996, revenues from the adult cyberporn market exceeded $50 million (Weber 1997, quoted in *United States v. Black* 1997). An even bigger market is that derived from software piracy, which has been documented at great length in recent years; see, for example, *United States v. LaMacchia* (1994). Computer software programs can be considered as literary works and hence are copyrightable if original (17 *U.S.C.* §102(a)(1)). Unauthorized duplication and distribution of software programs are prohibited by U.S. copyright law; see Saunders (1994). A survey and statistical analyst testifying in *Vault Corporation v. Quaid Software Limited* (1988) estimated that revenue losses due to software piracy were $1.3 billion during 1981–84 and $800 million in both 1985 and 1986. In 1992, testimony to the Subcommittee on Intellectual Property and Judicial Administration of the House Committee on the Judiciary stated that software manufacturers and the video game industry were losing $2.4 billion and $1 billion, respectively, in United States revenues annually as a result of piracy, while worldwide losses were estimated at $10–$12 billion annually (Saunders 1994). In 1996, software piracy accounted for an estimated $2 billion in the United States and over $11 billion worldwide (*Congressional Record*, November 13, 1997, p. S12691).

This article is organized as follows. In Section 2, the origins of the work in this article are described. In Section 3, we explain the main ideas behind the application of the Federal Sentencing Guidelines. In Section 4, we discuss the various sampling issues that are relevant to the application of those guidelines. In that section, we describe the legal status of sampling in the context of federal sentencing, possible choices of sampling plans, and how federal courts recognize and deal with the presence of selection bias due to unscientific sampling. Section 5 provides an overview of the issues raised in this article.

2 Origins and Questions

My initial involvement in this general area was through Sam Hedayat, who at that time was doing statistical consulting with the Illinois State Police Department on statistical methods for estimating the total weight Q of the illicit drugs seized from a defendant. Drugs such as cocaine or heroin may be packaged in thousands of plastic baggies, some of which may contain inert powder rather than the "real thing." Interest centered upon whether Q could be determined statistically from the contents of a small sample of those baggies. In Hedayat, Izenman, and Zhang 1996 we introduced the idea of sequentially estimating Q in a procedure designed specifically for use in plea-bargaining situations. This was followed by an extensive study (Izenman 1999) of the legal and statistical issues in using various sampling plans for estimating Q. The Hedayat et al. paper was presented at the 3rd International Conference on Forensic Statistics, held in Edinburgh, Scotland. An EPSRC Visiting Fellowship at the University of Edinburgh then enabled me to carry out joint research with Colin Aitken and Tom Leonard, who were also working in the general area of illicit drug quantity estimation. This research led to a Bayesian treatment of the measurement error problem in estimating Q (Izenman, Papasouliotis, Leonard, and Aitken 1998).

Whilst at the University of Edinburgh, I joined Colin Aitken in a consulting session with Mr. John Dunn, a Procurator Fiscal with the Crown Office, Edinburgh. Procurators Fiscal are the local representatives of the Lord Advocate and are responsible within their district in Scotland for the investigation of crime and the prosecution of offenders. Mr. Dunn's specific enquiry was concerned with the prosecution of child pornography cases, where huge numbers of such images are distributed throughout the Internet. In a Scottish case recently completed, over seven thousand images of child pornography that had been downloaded from the Internet had been found on the defendant's personal computer. After carefully reviewing and identifying all seven thousand images, the police officers needed to be given substantial desk leave for rest and recuperation!

The question posed by Mr. Dunn was whether one could view only a small number of these computer images rather than study every single one of them for purposes of prosecution. In Britain, sentencing does not depend upon any specific quantitative amount connected with the seriousness of the crime as is now required in federal cases in the United States. For example, in drug cases, sentencing in Britain depends only on whether it can be proved that the defendant possessed illicit drugs for personal use or for purposes of trafficking. Intent, therefore, is the primary determinant of sentence length, although quantity helps to establish whether personal use or trafficking is the more likely possibility in a given case.

We might expect, therefore, that similar arguments as were used in dealing with problems of sampling in drug cases should exist for dealing also with pornographic images.

This consultation led naturally to questions about how the U.S. federal justice system deals with such crimes. The transmission of child pornography over the Internet is treated in the U.S. as a federal crime because the crime crosses state lines. In prosecuting those who traffic in child pornography over the Internet, U.S. federal courts allow the use of scientific sampling and statistical inference procedures for dealing with the often gigantic and potentially heterogeneous volume of such material seized by the police.

3 Federal Sentencing Guidelines

Before the sentencing guidelines became law, judges had the exclusive, and often unlimited, authority to decide for themselves which factors were relevant to sentencing and what the sentence would be. With the advent of the guidelines, "offender-specific" factors (such as age, educational background, mental and emotional condition, physical condition, employment record, family ties) were generally dropped in favor of "offense-specific" factors (Herman 1992).

Sentencing in federal cases now boils down to essentially two factors. The first factor, which reflects the severity of the crime, is expressed in terms of a "base offense level," or BOL, numbered from 1 to 43. In general, the more serious the crime, the higher the BOL, and the longer the sentence. The severity of the crime, and hence the BOL, is often determined by a quantitative finding that depends upon the type of crime committed. In drug cases, the BOL is determined primarily from a "Drug Quantity Table" (*U.S.S.G.* §2D1.1(c)) by the total amount (by weight) of the illicit drugs seized from the defendant. The sentencing guidelines also specify (at *U.S.S.G.* §1B1.3(a)(2)) that drug weight be calculated from all activities "that were part of the same course of conduct or common scheme or plan as the offense of conviction," without time constraints, whether or not charged in the indictment.

Departures from a defendant's BOL can be made either upwards or downwards depending upon the circumstances of the crime and any "relevant conduct" to arrive at the "adjusted offense level" for that crime. For crimes such as trafficking in cyberporn, software piracy, and fraud cases, the primary adjustment of the BOL is an increase in level based upon the quantitative finding for the crime. A conviction of trafficking in material involving the sexual exploitation of a minor, for example, results in a BOL of 15, which is then increased by the retail value of all the pornographic items found in the defendant's possession (*U.S.S.G.* §2G2.2(b)(2)). In a software piracy or fraud case, the BOL of 6 is increased by the amount of monetary loss caused to the victim (*U.S.S.G.* §2B5.3). In cases of welfare fraud involving diversion of government program benefits, the definition of "loss" is the value of the benefits diverted from intended recipients or users (*U.S.S.G.* §2F1.1(b), Application Note 7(d)). In general, a "Fraud and Deceit Table" (*U.S.S.G.* §2F1.1(b)(1)), which is a graduated scale of progressively increasing offense levels, is used to govern the increase in the BOL for such crimes. The table uses "loss" as a generic term for the financial value of the crime, which, depending upon context, can refer to wholesale or retail value. Thus, if the loss exceeds $2,000, there is an increase of one level to the BOL; if the loss exceeds $5,000, the BOL is increased by two levels; if the loss exceeds $10,000, the BOL is increased by three levels; and so on up to an increase of 18 levels to the BOL if the loss exceeds $80 million. Additional adjustments to the BOL include the importance of the defendant's role in the crime, whether a dangerous weapon was involved, whether obstruction of justice took place, and the defendant's willingness to accept responsibility for the crime.

The second factor used to determine the sentence is the defendant's previous criminal history, which is listed as ordered categories ranging from I (no prior criminal history) to VI.

These two numbers, the adjusted offense level and the defendant's prior history, are then referred to a 43-row, six-column, two-way "Sentencing Table" (*U.S.S.G.* §5A) to determine the appropriate Guideline Sentencing Range, expressed in terms of months in prison (United States Sentencing Commission 1995). The sentencing judge has to pick a sentence within the range specified. These ranges are quite narrow, with six months being typical. The Supreme Court in *Witte v. United States* (1995) held that there is no "bright-line distinction" between the concept of relevant conduct (used to adjust the BOL) for row determination and the criminal history factor for column determination in the Sentencing Table. The two concepts were deemed to be overlapping and each could be broadly interpreted.

4 Statistical Issues in Sentencing

In many cases, the exact quantitative amounts cannot easily be measured, either because of the difficulty in obtaining the information, or because of the tremendous volume of information to be collected, or some combination of the two reasons. The guidelines are reasonably flexible on this issue and allow sampling to be used to extrapolate for sentencing purposes. In particular, the guidelines state (*U.S.S.G.* §2F1.1(b), Application Note 8) that

> The loss need not be determined with precision. The court need only make a reasonable estimate of the loss given the available information. This estimate, for example, may be based on the approximate number of victims and an estimate of the average loss to each victim, or on more general factors such as the nature and duration of the fraud and the revenue generated by similar operations. The offender's gain from committing the fraud is an alternative estimate that ordinarily will underestimate the loss.

In *United States v. Scalia* (1993), a case involving marijuana possession, where 15 plants were randomly selected for testing from the 112 plants seized, the court noted that "statistically based drug-quantity extrapolations predicted on random test samples" were acceptable, "drug-quantity estimates need not be statistically or scientifically precise," and while case law permits extrapolation in general, the government has to be able to demonstrate "an adequate basis in fact for the extrapolation and that the quantity [had to be] determined in a manner consistent with the accepted standards of [reasonable] reliability."

One of the main problems with a statistical approach to extrapolation involves the sampling plan to be used to produce the sample data for inference. In many instances, sampling is carried out informally, haphazardly, and unscientifically. Sampling is then followed by statistical inference procedures to provide estimates of the quantitative information required for sentencing based upon the sample data. Typically, because of the way that the sentencing guidelines have been formulated, estimates of unknown quantities have meant point estimates only. Recently, however, this attitude seems to be changing as expert statistical witnesses draw the court's attention to the idea of sampling variation of the point estimate.

In this section we discuss issues that arise from the need to provide quantitative amounts related to the criminal activity. For the most part, this means sampling the seized evidence and extrapolating from sample results to the entire evidence using methods of statistical inference. Aspects of sampling and inference where legal controversies have arisen include questions relating to the extent of homogeneity of the population to be sampled, situations where the population of items to be sampled turns out to be highly structured with many hierarchical levels or categories, situations in which sampling is not feasible but statistical inference is still required, and situations in which selection bias is prevalent due to unscientific sampling procedures. As we shall see, the relevance of these issues usually depends upon the type of crime in question.

4.1 Illicit Drug Trafficking

The practice of sampling to determine the total quantity of illicit drugs seized has been well-documented (Izenman 1999). If all the drugs seized are found in a number of containers, such as plastic baggies, then a sampling plan can be devised in a straightforward way. The primary issue that a court has to consider in such drug cases is whether or not sampling has been carried out in a scientific manner that would permit a valid extrapolation from the total weight of drugs in the sample to the entire quantity of drugs seized. Sampling plans used by forensic chemists can differ from jurisdiction to jurisdiction, usually depending upon how the drugs were found (in a single container, or in multiple containers possibly grouped within batches), what form the drugs take (pills, tablets, capsules; rocks or bricks of crack cocaine; loose cocaine or heroin powder; LSD on blotter paper), and which courts (federal or state) allow which types of plans. When a forensic chemist does not follow the specific sampling rule (usually, simple random sampling for a single container or some form of stratified sampling or multistage sampling for multiple containers) laid down by the relevant jurisdiction, the appeals court will typically reduce the BOL and hence the sentence decided by the trial judge.

In some circumstances, a sampling plan for estimating total drug quantity cannot be implemented. When the amount of illicit drugs seized forms only a portion of the entire quantity of drugs associated with the defendant, the sentencing phase tends to dwell upon how to treat the missing data and whether the court will affirm imputation of those values. Examples include scenarios in which (1) the defendant is successful in destroying evidence prior to arrest; (2) it may be physically impossible to seize all contraband; (3) the quantity found in the possession of the defendant at the time of the arrest may constitute the latest part of a "continuing criminal enterprise." In such situations, the sentencing judge is required (*U.S.S.G.* §2D1.1, Application Note 12) to "approximate" the amount of drugs involved "where there is no drug seizure or the amount seized does not reflect the scale of the offense." Extrapolation can then be described as "filling in the gaps" by extending the seized evidence obtained in one time period to the entire duration of the illegal activity, or from a few seized packages to many packages not available at all. In *United States v. Walton* (1990), Judge Kennedy wrote that

> If the exact amount [of drugs] cannot be determined, an estimate will suffice, but here also a preponderance of the evidence must support the estimate. Thus, when choosing between a number of plausible estimates of drug quantity . . . a court must err on the side of caution.

Methods suggested by the guidelines for imputing such unknown drug quantities include "the price generally obtained for the controlled substance, financial or other records, similar transactions in controlled substances by the defendant, and the size or capability of any laboratory involved."

There are many instances of judges accepting missing data imputation for sentencing purposes. In *United States v. Hilton* (1990), for example, the U.S. Coast Guard was in the process of intercepting a sailboat in mid-ocean on suspicion of carrying contraband when a fire broke out on the sailboat following a sudden explosion. After the fire was extinguished, one of the boarding party observed approximately twenty-two plastic-wrapped packages floating in the ocean each of similar size and appearance. Only one of the packages (with a gross weight of 14 lbs or approximately 5 kg) was retrieved, which turned out to contain marijuana. The court, in affirming the fifteen-year prison sentence for trafficking in more than 50 kg of marijuana, agreed with the sentencing judge that it was reasonable to believe that the remaining twenty-one packages each contained at least ten pounds of marijuana, even though they were never seized, nor were their contents analyzed.

In *United States v. Sklar* (1990), twelve similar mail packages were received by the defendant over a short period of time, but only the last was intercepted. This package was examined, weighed (11.3 oz), and found to contain 2.65 oz (75 grams) of cocaine. The first eleven packages were "never produced in court, inspected by government agents, or chemically treated." Postal records gave the gross weights of the missing eleven packages (in time order) as 3 oz, 10 oz, 5 oz, 1.9 oz, 7 oz, 8.3 oz, 7 oz, 9 oz, 8 oz, 5.8 oz, and 5 oz. The court concluded that the mailings were part of a common scheme: The packages mailed to the defendant from a "fictitious entity at a series of fictitious addresses were of the same ilk as the package actually intercepted." The sentencing judge assumed that each of these eleven packages contained *at least one-third as much cocaine as the last package*, thereby obtaining an estimated total drug weight of at least (11 × 25 grams) + 75 grams = 350 grams for all twelve packages. The defendant's BOL was then set at level 22 (for 300–400 grams of cocaine). The judge's estimate was conservative and designed to "safely insulate [it] from clear-error attack." The court, while affirming the sentencing decision, cautioned that special care should be taken in extrapolating in such situations because of the obvious impact upon the length of a sentence. The extent of such caution can be seen by noting that a larger estimate than 350 grams might also have been acceptable in this case. We know that the total gross weight of all twelve packages was 81.3 oz (or 2305 grams) and that cocaine formed 23.5% of the total weight of the last package. So, if we apply that same percentage to all packages (a not unreasonable assumption), the total amount of cocaine in all twelve packages could have been estimated instead at 2305 grams × 0.235 = 541.64 grams, resulting in a BOL of 26. To compare our alternative estimate with the judge's estimate of at least 25 grams of cocaine in each of the eleven missing packages, we note that our estimate is based upon an average weight of 42.4 grams for each of those packages. Actually, an average weight of at least 38.7 grams for the eleven missing packages would have still yielded a BOL of 26.

In *United States v. Whiting* (1994), the issue was to estimate the amount of cocaine handled by an ongoing illicit drug conspiracy over a period of three years when the evidence consisted not of seized packages of drugs but of (1) general comments by various defendants estimating average volume of drug business; (2) corroborating comments by cooperating co-defendants that particular quantities of cocaine were handled at particular times; (3) controlled buys by government undercover operatives; and (4) evidence indicating the size and scope of the organization itself. Based upon such testimony, the court affirmed the district court's conservative estimate of cocaine distribution of two kilograms per week over the three years.

An anomaly in this regard was provided by *United States v. Shonubi* (1997), in which a similar scenario as above led to quite a different result. In this case, the defendant was found to have swallowed 103 balloons of heroin (with a total weight of 427.4 grams) when arrested at JFK International Airport. The defendant's passport and employment record indicated seven previous overseas trips to Nigeria from the United States whose purposes were not satisfactorily explained; there was also strong evidence that the other trips were also smuggling trips. A sequence of three sentencing decisions was made by the sentencing judge, Jack B. Weinstein, of the Eastern District of New York, following an appeal. The main question was how to estimate Q, the total amount smuggled from all eight trips. Several statistical imputation procedures were considered by the judge. The first estimate was simple: 8×427.4 grams $= 3419.2$ grams, leading to a sentencing range of 151–188 months and a prison term of 151 months. The court agreed with Weinstein that the defendant's travel was part of the same course of conduct as the latest trip, but was not satisfied with the determination of Q. The second estimate was much more complicated, with extensive evidentiary hearings and reports by experts, but boiled down to the same sentence as before. Ultimately, the appeals court reversed and ordered that Shonubi's sentence be derived solely from the evidence on the night of his arrest. Their decision was based upon a requirement that "specific evidence" of Shonubi's drug activities had to be presented in order to prove the "relevant-conduct quantity" of drugs for which the defendant was responsible under the sentencing guidelines. In resentencing Shonubi to a sentencing range of 97–121 months with a prison term of 97 months, Weinstein was highly critical of the appellate court opinion, arguing that it was based upon "a radical interpretation of the Federal Rules of Evidence, the Sentencing Guidelines, and the Supreme Court precedents." The problem of estimating Q in the *Shonubi* case is discussed in more detail by Izenman (2000) and Gastwirth, Freidlin, and Miao (2000). See also Aitken, Bring, Leonard, and Papasouliotis 1997.

4.2   Trafficking in Cyberporn

Whilst investigating a case involving trafficking in computer pornography, FBI agents typically seize a defendant's personal computer containing a large number of computer files and floppy disks that are suspected of being pornographic. This type of crime is fairly new, with the first federal criminal prosecution for distributing child pornography through a computer bulletin board system occurring in 1995. In *United States v. Thomas* (1996), a computer bulletin board system operated by the defendants was found to contain approximately 14,000 files of graphical depictions of pornographic images; in *United States v. Drew* (1997), over 3,000 computer files were found containing pictures of preteen girls posing nude or engaging in sex acts; in *United States v. Sassani* (1998), 382 floppy disks were discovered containing a total of 6,731 files, of which 120 were identified as being graphic images of minors engaged in sexually explicit conduct, and 16,226 files on the computer hard disk, of which 56 were identified as similar types of pornographic images; and in *United States v. Hall* (1998), 403 files on the defendant's floppy and hard disks were found to contain video images of child pornography. In *United States v. Coenen* (1998), the defendant admitted that "for a relatively short period of time, he had 1,000 or more images of child pornography on his computer hard drive." Zanghi (1995) reports an investigation of an employee of Lawrence Livermore Laboratories, a nuclear weapons laboratory in California, who stored 91,000 photographs of nude women, adults having sex, and child pornography on laboratory computers and was allowing people outside the laboratory access to the pornographic images via the Internet.

These examples give some idea of the scope of cyberporn cases and the difficulty of laboriously searching through and viewing the many thousands of computer files to identify those that can be classified as pornographic. In order to arrive at an adjusted BOL for the crime, the sentencing judge has to be provided with the number of pornographic images found on the defendant's computer, from which their total market value may be calculated. This is similar to the problem of determining how many of the seized pills or tablets actually contain illicit drugs. Federal courts have accepted the general idea of sampling of suspected pornographic images. In *United States v. Black* (1997), for example, a Board-certified pediatrician testified that she examined forty of the numerous printed photographs found in the defendant's residence (many apparently derived from downloading computer images from the Internet) and stated that twenty of those images were of prepubescent children.

Sampling plans should always take into account the circumstances in which the evidence is discovered. Pornographic images downloaded from the Internet are usually found in different computer files located in various directories or subdirectories of a hard disk on a personal computer, and with directory names that may be coded for security reasons and known only to the defendant. These images may then be listed by different coded categories that reveal the type of pornography stored there. A defendant may use an alternative storage medium such as floppy disks (diskettes) or Zip disks on which the images are downloaded and stored in different containers according to subject matter. The sampling plan should, therefore, be carefully formulated in such a way that takes into account the stratified and possibly hierarchical nature of the target population. For example, in *United States v. Ownby* (1997), 1,612 images, over 62% of which were pornographic, were found on 76 floppy disks located in differently labeled boxes organized by their content.

4.3 Copyright Infringement and Software Piracy

A closely related sampling problem concerns cases involving software piracy. Defendants in such cases are charged with the unauthorized possession and distribution of a large quantity of counterfeit software programs to be sold privately at a deeply discounted price. In presenting the case, the contents of these disks have to be compared with the original software. In the absence of direct evidence of copying, which is generally not available, courts have examined circumstantial evidence to show that the defendant had access to the copyrighted work and that the accused work is *substantially similar* to the copyrightable work; see, for example, *Computer Associates International, Inc. v. Altai, Inc.* (1992). Note that copyright law protects against copying, not just against similarity (*Gates Rubber Co. v. Bando American, Inc.* 1992). Because no hard and fast rule or percentage has been given for determining the meaning of "substantial similarity," the extent that one work can be substantially similar to another is the subject of much copyright litigation, with survey evidence often being used to gather information on similarity (Kegan 1985).

In cases where complex computer programs need to be compared for piracy, courts often rely on expert testimony (using FRE 702), possibly from a special master or court-appointed expert (using FRE 706), to determine the degree of similarity. The courts have recognized that an exact duplicate is a copy of the original that satisfies the substantial similarity test. Substantial similarity can be shown through a direct comparison of lines of source code. In *SAS Institute, Inc. v. S&H Computer Systems, Inc.* (1985), for example, the court held that there was substantial similarity even though only 44 lines out of the total of 186,000 lines of *S&H*'s code had been shown to have been copied directly by the defendants from *SAS* source code. The expert for *SAS* testified that these 44 specific instances of copying were not the result of an exhaustive comparative study of the two programs, "but were limited by the limited time and resources available in view of the sheer magnitude of the task" (see Gastwirth 1988, pp. 667–8). In *United States v. Manzer* (1995), one of the few cases in which a specific percentage was given, it was held that more than 70% similarity of seized computer programs to copyrighted software for unauthorized decryption of premium channel satellite broadcasts was sufficient evidence for the court to affirm copyright infringement of software.

Carrying out an investigation comparing software programs can be a daunting task for an investigator faced with thousands of computer disks to examine. Again, this identification problem is similar to the illicit drugs and computer pornography identification problems. One can argue that floppy disks are like pills containing a controlled substance, and so, under the preponderance standard of proof, not every disk need be tested. In principle, one should be able to sample and test only a small number of the entire collection of seized disks. The primary issue here, as in the drugs and pornography cases, is the *homogeneity* issue. One has to be confident that the computer files or floppy disks are sufficiently homogeneous (at least visually) to start the sampling process. If there is reason to believe, possibly from just a visual inspection, that the disks are multiple copies of a single software program, then the homogeneity question has been resolved and simple random sampling can proceed. If, however, the disks were found in several boxes, or at several different locations, or if there was any indication that more than one type of unauthorized software program might be found on the seized disks, then a more elaborate sampling plan would be required. Compounding the sampling issue further is the recognition that some of the seized disks may not contain counterfeited software.

In civil courts, parties can bring copyright infringement lawsuits. Because the standard of proof in civil cases is also the preponderance standard, the use of sampling in such suits is relevant to federal criminal sentencing for cases involving copyright infringements. In *Microsoft Corporation v. Grey Computer* (1995), a federal district court civil case, for example, the defendants were found liable for copyright and trademark infringement by selling or distributing counterfeit copies of Microsoft's software products. Simultaneous raids at seven Houston-area locations resulted in seizures of 35,000 copies of MS-DOS and Windows, with a street value of approximately $2 million, and further evidence existed that approximately 45,000 more copies had already been sold. It is instructive to see what happened in the *Microsoft* case. The court was of the opinion that examining all of the seized units would "place an unreasonably high burden on Microsoft to show that each and every unit of software [that the] Defendants ever shipped was counterfeit." The court went on to say that "Microsoft has met its burden by showing that Defendants had access to and copied Microsoft's copyrighted work and that is all it is required to do." Furthermore,

> [t]he Court is satisfied that [Microsoft's expert] conducted a thorough examination of the software units. The Court is also satisfied that the counterfeit units that [the expert] did examine were substantially similar to the approximately 45,000 units [the Defendant] had already distributed. [Microsoft's attorney] stated that he examined the outside of the boxes containing the counterfeit software which had an "Allstates Air Cargo" label affixed to them. He then opened the boxes and found that they contained counterfeit versions of Microsoft's MS-DOS 6, MS-DOS 6.2, and Windows 3.1. He examined every unit therein to determine if they were identical. After determining that the units in a particular box appeared identical, he removed one unit and compared them with a sample unit and determined that the sample unit appeared identical. Only after [the attorney] examined each box did he forward one unit of each software product to [the expert].

Microsoft's attorney correctly recognized that three different types of units were present in the seized materials and that the sampling method had to reflect that fact. Therefore, he adopted a stratified sampling approach: Each box became a stratum, and a single unit in each box was (randomly?) selected and (visually?) compared with a unit of legitimate Microsoft software. In this way, the expert examined the packaging and software and accompanying manuals of about 1,000 of the seized units and declared them to be counterfeit software.

The opinion hints, but does not state explicitly, that the software units with differently labeled operating systems were packed in different boxes. If that were indeed the case, the sampling procedure could be resolved straightforwardly as follows. First, divide the boxes into three groups, one for each of the three operating systems; second, from each group, randomly select a subset of the boxes; and then from the selected boxes randomly select some of the software units. We also note that for the above case, no attention appears to have been paid to the fact that the units were seized from seven different locations, which might have added another layer to the sampling plan.

If the three types of operating system units had been mixed together ("comingled") in the same boxes, then a more complicated sampling plan would have been needed. We can think of this sampling problem as follows. Suppose there are J different types of units in a closed population, such as a box, where J may be known or unknown, and suppose the jth type consists of N_j items, $j = 1, 2, \ldots, J$, where the values of the $\{N_j\}$ are unknown and need to be estimated. Set $N = \sum_{j=1}^{J} N_j$. For the type of courtroom situations of this article, N will be very large. There are therefore two parameters, J and N, for this problem, both of which may be known or unknown. The simplest situation is where $J \geq 1$ and N are both known, and we wish to estimate the values of $\{N_j\}$. Let p_j be the probability that a unit in the population is of jth type, $j = 1, 2, \ldots, J$, where $\sum_{j=1}^{J} p_j = 1$. We can take a simple random sample (without replacement) of n items from the box and find the number n_j of units of the jth type in the sample. The joint distribution of $(n_1, n_2, \ldots, n_J)$ is therefore multinomial with parameters N and $(p_1, p_2, \ldots, p_J)$. The maximum likelihood estimator (MLE) of p_j is given by the relative frequency $\hat{p}_j = n_j/n$, and the MLE of N_j is given by $\hat{N}_j = N\hat{p}_j, j = 1, 2, \ldots, J$. Variances and covariances of these estimators can be found, for example, in Johnson and Kotz 1969, Chapter 11.

A more interesting problem occurs when either J or N is unknown. If N is unknown and $J = 1$, then the literature gives estimates for N using capture–recapture methods. The basic idea behind capture–recapture is as follows. Take an initial simple random sample of size n_1 from the population, mark all the units in that initial sample, and replace all sample units into the population. Then, take an independent, second, simple random sample of size n_2 from the same population and identify the number, say m, in the second sample that were previously marked from the initial sample. Equating the proportion of marked units in the second sample m/n_2 to the population proportion n_1/N of marked units leads to the so-called Petersen estimator $\hat{N} = n_1 n_2/m$, which when suitably rounded to an integer yields the MLE of N. See, for example, Seber 1982, Pollock 1991, and Thompson 1992, Chapter 21. When N is unknown and $J = 3$, Otis (1980) obtained the MLEs of N, N_1, N_2, and N_3, together with their asymptotic variances and covariances. The general problem of estimating N and the $\{N_j\}$ when J is known is open. If J is unknown, this is called the "number of species problem" (Bunge and Fitzpatrick 1993; Haas and Stokes 1998), and estimation of J is more complicated.

The above discussion of sampling in cases involving software piracy also applies to the counterfeiting of copyrighted motion pictures, audio cassettes, and video games. The counterfeited videotapes, cassettes, and cartridges should be considered to be just like floppy disks containing pirated software, but where the level of deception is much higher, with packaging (including trademarks and photos) designed to convince the purchaser of the legitimacy of the items. The numbers of such counterfeited items are typically in the thousands (*United States v. Larracuente* (1992), where 2,652 counterfeit videotapes of movies were seized; *Columbia Pictures Industries, Inc. v. Landa* (1997), where 4,000 videocassettes containing 216 different movies were seized from five video stores and a residence) or even millions (*United States v. Hernandez* (1991), where 2,613,600 usable counterfeit inlay cards—the paper that wraps up the cassette inside the plastic case, containing the trademark and the photo of the group performing on the tape—were seized). With such large numbers, sampling would help provide information as to the identity of these counterfeited items and determine their market value without anyone having to listen to or view every tape.

4.4   Waste, Fraud, and Abuse of Welfare Programs

The existence of federal–state welfare programs, such as Medicare, Medicaid, Food Stamp, and Aid to Families with Dependent Children, has necessitated some sort of control by the federal government of the possibilities of "waste, fraud, and abuse." Accordingly, quality control systems have been set up by the federal government to monitor payments made to welfare recipients. Auditing is carried out "post-payment" to discover improper billing practices or where welfare assistance was obtained through fraudulent means. The amount of overbilling has to be assessed for sentencing purposes and to recoup any excess compensation paid.

The courts quickly recognized that auditing every one of a huge number of claims, where legitimate as well as illegitimate claims should be expected, is impossible. For example, in *State of Georgia Department of Human Services v. Califano* (1977), the court noted that an "[a]udit on an individual claim-by-claim basis of the many thousands of claims submitted each month by each state [under Medicaid] would be a practical impossibility as well as unnecessary." Even though Congress has neither authorized nor expressly disallowed the use of random sampling for auditing publicly-funded reimbursements of medical services where the number of claims is large, "sample audits" are more the rule today than the exception (Heiner, Wagner, and Fried 1984). For example, the court in *Illinois Physicians Union v. Miller* (1982) held that "[the Illinois Department of Public Aid] processes an enormous number of claims and must adopt realistic and practical auditing procedures." The *Illinois* court then went on to say that "[i]n view of the enormous logistical problems of Medicaid enforcement, statistical sampling is the only feasible method available." In *Mile High Therapy Centers, Inc. v. Bowen* (1988) the court noted that sampling was one way of maintaining the integrity of the Medicare payment system. Indeed, testimony by the U.S. Department of Health and Human Services in *Mile High* stated that some form of sampling (in Medicare/Medicaid audits) had been used since at least 1972, and that sample audits for post-payment reviews were carried out using instructions published by the Health Care Financing Administration (1986).

The sampling issue was placed into a broader public policy perspective by the court in *Ratanasen v. State of California Department of Health Services* (1993) when, after approving the general use of sampling and extrapolation as part of the audit process in connection with Medicare and other similar programs, it opined that

> To deny public agencies the use of statistical and mathematical audit methods would be to deny them an effective means of detecting abuses in the use of public funds. Public officials are responsible for overseeing the expenditure of our increasingly scarce public resources and we must give them appropriate tools to carry out that charge.

Sampling is thus used routinely to investigate the extent of suspected welfare overpayments and to determine whether claims were made that involved non-covered services that the provider knew or should have known were not covered. In *United States v. Freshour* (1995), for example, a medical equipment business located in Tennessee had 240 Medicaid patients, and a random sample of approximately 23% of them were used to audit for mail fraud and money laundering relating to Medicaid fraud.

One of the really interesting points to be made about the use of audit sampling of health care providers is that a study of such cases reveals the wide range of sampling percentages that are acceptable to the courts. Although a specific sampling percentage is not mandated by case law, the federal courts have approved sampling percentages in such cases that have ranged from a tiny 0.4% of the total number of payment authorizations to clients in *Michigan* to "a substantial portion [27%] of the physician's records" in *Illinois*. Other small sampling percentages, such as 3.4% in *Ratanasen* and 5.4% in *Chaves County Home Health Services, Inc. v. Sullivan* (1991), have also been approved by federal courts. In Heiner et al. 1984, a worked example was given whereby 400 patient files from a large metropolitan hospital were randomly selected for a sample audit from a total of 14,433 patient files, a sampling percentage of only 2.8%. From Table 1, it can be seen that even with very small sampling percentages the smallest approved sample size was 100; however, it is not clear from these published cases whether there exists a minimum number for auditing purposes. We can also point to a case in which a random sample of total cases was not approved, namely that of *Daytona Beach General Hospital, Inc. v. Weinberger* (1977), where the court held that a recoupment claim based upon a sampling percentage of less than 10% was a denial of due process.

Generally, health care providers are given the opportunity to challenge the statistical validity of the sample audit. In *Michigan Department of Education v. United States Department of Education* (1989), for example, the court noted that "[w]hen, as here, the state is given every opportunity to challenge each disallowance as well as the audit technique itself, it appears that the state has been treated as fairly as is practicable under the circumstances." This is important, since the full amount of the provider's overpayment liability for the time period in question is extrapolated from the percentage of sample claims that are denied. In *Michigan*, the government audited a random, stratified sample of 259 (out of 66,368) cases using five strata defined by specified levels of expenditures. Thirteen of those cases were declared to be unallowable expenditures, but of the nine disputed by the state, only one was ultimately reversed.

Georgia has been used as a landmark case that supports the use of sampling and extrapolation in auditing health care providers. The Department of Health, Education, and Welfare (HEW) had refused to reimburse Georgia for $3.5 million the state had paid to doctors who provided services to Georgia Medicaid recipients for three years in the 1970s. An audit was carried out, in which claims paid during a five-quarter period were sampled. The audit revealed that the state had paid some claims in excess of ceilings imposed by federal statutes. As a result, HEW's

Social Rehabilitation Services regional commissioner disallowed $2.86 million in matching federal funds (later reduced to $1.45 million) and made a demand for a refund of that money. Georgia appealed, claiming that the administrator's decision was arbitrary and capricious, because "the amount of overpayment was determined by use of a statistical sample, rather than by an individual, claim-by-claim review." In finding for defendant HEW, the district court concluded that

> The use of statistical samples was not improper. Projection of the nature of a large population through review of a relatively small number of its components has been recognized as a valid audit technique and approved by federal courts in cases arising under Title IV of the Social Security Act. Moreover, mathematical and statistical methods are well recognized as reliable and acceptable evidence in determining adjudicative facts. However, to find that statistics may be admitted as evidence of a proposition is not to say that the statistical model will always be conclusive. The weight which must be given to such statistical evidence is necessarily one which must be considered by the fact finder in light of the practical difficulties in obtaining a claim-by-claim review. In the instant case, a statistical sampling was the only feasible method of audit available to HEW.

A list of cases in which sampling and extrapolation were at issue in the determination of the amount of overpayment by health care providers is given in Table 1. The *Illinois* and *Daytona Beach* cases are discussed by Gastwirth (1988, p. 493). Most of these cases cite the *Georgia* case as precedent in approving random auditing. Detailed discussion and analysis of the many statistical issues involved in estimating overpayment error rates in federal welfare programs may be found in Fairley and Izenman 1989 and Fairley, Izenman, and Bagchi 1990.

4.5 Welfare Fraud and Selection Bias

Selection bias in sampling refers to the bias that occurs when the sampling mechanism does not select items randomly from the target population, when it randomly selects items but in a way that is not independent of the variable(s) of interest, or when the mechanism behaves in ways not originally intended; see Wei and Cowan 1988. Samples that are not randomly collected are referred to as convenience or judgment samples (Hahn and Meeker 1993) depending upon how they are selected. Such nonprobability samples invalidate the probabilistic basis for statistical inference and can lead to seriously biased results.

Federal and state courts, however, have accepted nonprobability sampling in surveys of large numbers of individuals. Examples include Lanham Act cases (surveys of consumer perception used in determining trademark infringement and claims of false advertising) and employment discrimination cases. An Advisory Committee's Note to FRE 703, which deals with opinion testimony by experts, points out that for determining the admissibility of survey evidence the court's attention should be directed to "the validity of the techniques employed" rather

Table 1. Federal Cases That Used Sampling to Audit for Welfare Fraud and Medical Reimbursement.

Case (Year)	Program	Cir./D.C.	N	n(%)	Sampling
United States v. Freshour (1995)	Medicaid	6th	n.a.	240 (23%)	Approved
Ratanasen v. State of California DHS (1993)	Medi-Cal	9th	8,761	300 (3.4%)	Approved
Yorktown Medical Lab., Inc. v. Perales (1991)	Medicaid	2d	n.a.	100	Approved
Chaves County Home Health Serv., Inc. v. Sullivan (1991)	Medicare	D.C.	13,000	700 (5.4%)	Approved
Michigan DOE v. United States DOE (1989)	voc. rehab.	6th	66,368	259 (0.4%)	Approved
Illinois Physicians Union v. Miller (1982)	Medicaid	7th	1,302	353 (27%)	Approved
State of Georgia DHR v. Califano (1977)	Medicaid	N.D. Ga	n.a.	n.a.	Approved
Daytona Beach General Hospital, Inc. v. Weinberger (1977)	Medicare	M.D. Fla	3,500	(< 10%)	Not Approved
Mount Sinai Hospital v. Weinberger (1975)	Medicare	5th	n.a.	710	

Note: Cir./D.C. = Federal Circuit Court of Appeals/Federal District Court; N = total number of patient files available for audit; n = number of patient files included in sample audit; n.a. = not available (published opinion did not include this information); Sampling = position of the court on the application of audit sampling of patients' records.

than to "fruitless" enquiries as to whether surveys violate the hearsay rule. Rule 703 has been interpreted (Diamond 1994, p. 227) to mean that survey evidence would be admissible if the survey were "conducted in accordance with generally accepted survey principles" and if the survey results were applied in "a statistically correct way." See Gastwirth 1996.

Nonprobability sampling has also been used in cases that try to document fraud, and especially welfare fraud. Sample surveys are often carried out to investigate the seriousness of the fraud perpetrated on insurance providers and particular welfare programs. In fraud cases, just as in trademark infringement cases, the collection of survey data usually does not permit the luxury of randomization. Sentencing in a fraud case depends upon a determination of the total amount of financial loss incurred. Such a total is usually a combination of several different types of losses, some of which may be proved at trial or based upon testimony of witnesses and records obtained post-trial. At issue in many of these cases is an unknown loss figure that must be computed based upon losses not proved at trial. In this section, we will describe some welfare fraud cases in which the court of appeals recognized the presence of selection bias in the estimation of unknown losses from a nonprobability sample survey.

Selection bias from nonrandom sampling was an issue in *United States v. Caba* (1996), where it was established at trial that the defendant had devised a scheme by which he received food stamps for prohibited purposes, including selling the food stamps to small retailers and self-employed truck drivers at a 4% premium. The evidence established that the defendant had laundered approximately $11.7 million in proceeds from such unauthorized food stamp transactions. The court noted that the true loss incurred by the government as a result of the defendant's activities was almost impossible to calculate with any degree of precision. Indeed, the total amount of actual proven loss (as determined beyond a reasonable doubt at trial) was only $65,650, which was unsatisfying to the court "because common sense indicates that the loss to the Government must be much greater." To estimate the unknown losses in this case, the court used an innovative and "not inappropriate" approach. It decided to rely solely upon a recent government report entitled "The Extent of Trafficking in the Food Stamp Program" (Macaluso 1995). Possibilities of both overestimation (investigators chose "highly-suspicious stores and moderately-suspicious stores to monitor for the study rather than purely a random sample") and underestimation ("some violating stores only traffic with people they know, not strangers, and thus investigators cannot catch this type of trafficking") of fraud in the program were noted in the report and by the court. The court resolved this issue by giving the defendant the greatest benefit of the doubt. Using the lowest reported trafficking percentage, 4.2%, led to an estimated loss to the Government of $491,400 (= $11.7 million × 4.2%). The resulting sentencing level for the defendant was a BOL of 6 for unlawful acquisition of food stamps, plus 9 for the amount of loss over $350,000. With additional adjustments, the total offense level was determined to be 19, with a sentencing range of 30–37 months in prison. This was much reduced from the total offense level of 34 argued by the government, which would have given a sentencing range of 151–188 months in prison.

In *United States v. Skodnek* (1996), a psychiatrist was convicted of engaging in various schemes to defraud insurance providers and the Medicare program by requesting payment for professional services he did not actually provide. The defendant had charged insurance providers for longer sessions than were held, for sessions included within periods of time when he was on vacation or out of the state, and for treatment of individuals whom he had never seen as patients. It was proven at trial that the defendant's misconduct during the nineteen-month period from August 31, 1992, until March 31, 1994, resulted in a documented loss of $157,460 to the victim insurance carriers. At sentencing, however, the government claimed that the actual loss amount was $1,218,454.50 and that the defendant's BOL of 6 (for crimes involving fraud) should be increased by 11, representing a loss amount in excess of $800,000. The loss projections were derived from a number of factors, including the testimony of additional witnesses not present at trial and extrapolations from known losses.

The court accepted the known losses (which had either been proved beyond a reasonable doubt at trial or were based upon detailed interviews with actual witnesses and records obtained post-trial) totalling $358,682. The court, however, was unconvinced by the government's estimate of total losses, which were extrapolated assuming *the same rate of fraudulent billing as for the known losses* over the six-year period, January 1989 through December 1994. The government argued that this assumption was based upon an investigation of the defendant's entire billing records and the fact that no person interviewed could verify the accuracy of the billings made out in his or her name. The defendant counterargued that although some of the individuals interviewed disputed the government's assumption, they were not included in the random sample of individuals used in the investigation. The court rejected the government's extrapolated amount, saying that the sentencing decision could not be based upon a quantity that was so unreliable. In its opinion, the court referred to an affidavit of a professor of statistics and Kaye and Freedman 1994 for guidance on possible interviewer bias in sample surveys. The court concluded that

> [t]he data on which the government relies is skewed.... [T]he government did not begin with a random sample [of individuals interviewed]. Instead it was a convenience sample, garnered by a unit whose purpose is to investigate fraud. It was conducted not by dispassionate interviewers, but by fraud and abuse investigators, including some from the FBI, the Office of Inspector General, and the Medicare Abuse Unit. Clearly, the interviewers were searching out "horror" stories, the stuff of which criminal prosecutions can be made or sentencing increased. Indeed, there were instances in which reports apparently inconsistent with the overall conclusions were ignored.

The *Skodnek* court rejected the government's invitation "to extrapolate from known losses in ways not supported by statistical theory, to cover a period outside that covered by the superseding indictment, based on flawed assumptions inadequately grounded in the trial evidence or sentencing data." Furthermore, the court noted that "the extrapolation was not done according to the usual statistical [protocols which] represent standards for determining whether and under what circumstances it is reasonable to extrapolate from a known universe to an unknown one." Even under the preponderance standard, the court declined to believe this assumption because it would mean that the defendant "almost never honestly billed a single patient, never forgot to bill for time he had actually spent with them (and thus underestimated his work), and that his illegal activities never ebbed and flowed over the whole period."

The court was highly critical of the way the case had been presented, saying that the government could have conducted surveys of the defendant's records for the entire six-year period for which losses were extrapolated to verify that billing fraud was constant over the longer time period, but that it chose not to do so. The defendant's BOL of 6 was increased by a loss amount of only 9 levels (representing a loss of more than $350,000). In essence, then, the court decided to ignore any possible fraud by the defendant during that part of the six-year period not covered by the known losses. The court's rejection of the poor statistical work by the government in this case had a significant effect on the defendant's sentence. In the end, the total offense level of 25 (based upon a loss estimate of just over $1.2 million) and suggested sentence of 80 months in prison that was requested by the government was reduced on appeal to a level of 23 and a sentence of 46 months in prison.

5   Discussion

We have shown in this article that sampling and statistical inference often have an important role to play in the determination of sentences handed down by judges in federal criminal cases.

For crimes in which an (often large) finite number of similar physical items (packages of drugs, computer files and disks containing pornographic material, computer disks containing pirated software, etc.) are seized as evidence of the severity of the crime, a sampling plan can and should be designed and implemented. For most of these types of crimes, statistical procedures yield appropriate total quantitative amounts that may be used as a basis for sentencing. Whether that amount is the total weight of illicit drugs or the market value of all items seized, the sampling and inference principles are similar, and if they are carried out according to approved statistical practice, the results should be accepted by the federal courts.

In the event that the government samples from a large number of seized items and then extrapolates its findings from the sample data to all items seized, it is a common defense strategy to claim that such extrapolations are not precise enough for sentencing purposes. Defendants argue that every item in the population should have been examined to determine the total quantitative amount necessary to establish the correct offense level for the crime. As we have seen, the response to this argument should depend upon the court's perception of how the sampling and extrapolation were carried out. If sampling is carried out by the government using properly randomized procedures, whether simple or sophisticated as appropriate to the case, and if extrapolations follow the principles of statistical inference, then the defendant should not prevail. On the other hand, if the government does not explain its sampling and inference methodologies sufficiently, the courts should be receptive to the defendant's position by giving less credence to any statistical conclusions derived from a poorly conceived sampling plan. With this in mind, the courts should encourage prosecutors to detail their sampling and inference procedures in cases in which a sampling plan is necessitated by a large-scale seizure of items. For example, in *United States v. Scalia* (1993), a videotape of the randomization procedure that selected 15 marijuana plants from 112 plants seized was received into evidence.

In cases investigating fraud, the legal and statistical issues of survey sampling practice need to be addressed, since they are different from the issues of randomized sampling of large finite populations, The government, in fraud cases, often has to rely on interviewing a large number of individuals to document the extent of the fraud. In such cases, survey sampling, which is routinely used in the courts to demonstrate trademark infringement or employment discrimination, has been used to estimate the total loss amount that would be necessary for making a sentencing decision. Because of the inherent difficulty in obtaining a probability sample from these populations, courts have often accepted evidence from nonprobability sampling. In trademark infringement cases, for example, mall survey results have been accepted if a substantial number of the individuals surveyed showed confusion over similar-looking products.

In some fraud cases, however, populations may be such that one can carry out a probability sampling of the individual victims. If that is possible, the courts tend to be very critical of prosecutors who make no effort to obtain (possibly more balanced) evidence from a random (rather than a judgment) sample of those individuals. Random sampling of the population would enable any perception of selection bias to be reduced or eliminated. Courts have also been critical of prosecutors in fraud cases making possibly unwarranted statistical assumptions in extrapolating from one audit period to another without investigating the validity of those assumptions.

As a concluding remark, we note that Congress has recently passed a number of laws that order the Sentencing Commission *to provide substantially increased penalties* for persons convicted of the types of crimes discussed in this article. Amendments to the sentencing guidelines have been ordered for drug trafficking (Comprehensive Methamphetamine Control Act of 1998, which amends the Controlled Substances Act, 21 U.S.C. §801 *et seq.*), pornography (Protection of Children and Sexual Predator Punishment Act of 1998, which amends 18

U.S.C. §2251 *et seq.* to take account of child pornography on the Internet), fraud (Telemarketing Fraud Prevention Act of 1998, and a proposed extention of the Criminal Fraud Statute, 18 U.S.C. §1343, to deal with telemarketing fraud over the Internet), and copyright and trademark infringement, especially software piracy (No Electronic Theft (NET) Act of 1998, which closes a loophole in the Copyright Act). However, due to lengthy political wrangling, the Sentencing Commission has not yet been in a position to make any of these recommended amendments to the sentencing guidelines.

Acknowledgments

The author thanks Joseph Gastwirth for the invitation and editorial suggestions that improved the presentation of this material, Colin Aitken and John Dunn for providing me with a motivation to investigate this research topic, Betty-Ann Soiefer Izenman for advice and guidance on the many legal issues that arose during the writing of this article, Richard Heiberger for his LaTeX expertise, and two anonymous reviewers. The research was partially supported by a United Kingdom EPSRC Visiting Research Fellowship held at the University of Edinburgh during Fall 1997.

6   Cases Cited

Chaves County Home Health Service, Inc. v. Sullivan (1991), 931 F.2d 914 (D.C. Cir.).

Columbia Pictures Industries, Inc. v. Landa (1997), 974 F.Supp. 1 (D.D.C.).

Computer Associates International, Inc. v. Altai, Inc. (1992), 982 F.2d 693 (2d Cir.).

Daytona Beach General Hospital, Inc. v. Weinberger (1977), 435 F.Supp. 891 (M.D. Fla.).

Gates Rubber Co. v. Bando American, Inc. (1992). 798 F.Supp. 1499 (D. Col.).

Illinois Physicians Union v. Miller (1982), 675 F.2d 151 (7th Cir.).

in re Winship (1970), 397 U.S. 358, 90 S.Ct. 1068, 25 L.Ed.2d 368.

McMillan v. State of Pennsylvania (1986), 477 U.S. 79, 106 S.Ct. 2411, 91 L.Ed.2d 67.

Michigan Department of Education v. United States Department of Education (1989), 875 F.2d 1196 (6th Cir.).

Microsoft Corporation v. Grey Computer, et al. (1995), 910 F.Supp. 1077 (S.D. Md.).

Mile High Therapy Centers, Inc. v. Bowen (1988), 735 F.Supp. 984 (D.Colo.).

Patterson v. New York (1977), 432 U.S. 197, 97 S.Ct. 2319, 53 L.Ed.2d 281.

Ratanasen v. State of California, Department of Health Services (1993), 11 F.3d 1467 (9th Cir.).

Reno v. ACLU (1997), 521 U.S. 844, 117 S.Ct. 2329, 138 L.Ed.2d 874.

SAS Institute, Inc. v. S&H Computer Systems, Inc. (1985), 605 F.Supp. 816 (M.D. Tenn.).

State of Georgia v. Califano (1977), 446 F.Supp. 404 (N.D. Georgia).

United States v. Black (1997), 116 F.3d 198 (7th. Cir.).

United States v. Caba (1996), 911 F.Supp. 630 (E.D.N.Y.).

United States v. Coenen (1998), 135 F.3d 938 (5th Cir.).

United States v. Drew (1997), 131 F.3d 1269 (8th Cir.).

United States v. Freshour (1995), 64 F.3d 664 (E.D. Tenn.).

United States v. Hall (1998), 142 F.3d 988 (7th Cir.).

United States v. Hernandez (1991), 952 F.2d 1110 (9th Cir.), *cert. denied* 506 U.S. 920, 113 S.Ct.334, 121 L.Ed.2d 252.

United States v. Hilton (1990), 894 F.2d 485 (1st Cir.).

United States v. LaMacchia (1994), 871 F.Supp. 535 (D. Mass.).

United States v. Larracuente (1992), 952 F.2d 672 (2d Cir.).

United States v. Manzer (1995), 69 F.3d 222 (8th Cir.).

United States v. Ownby (1997), 131 F.3d 138 (4th Cir.), unpublished opinion (available on LEXIS at 1997 U.S. App. LEXIS 33592).

United States v. Sassani (1998), 139 F.3d 895 (4th Cir.), unpublished opinion (available on LEXIS at 1998 U.S. App. LEXIS 3731).

United States v. Scalia (1993), 993 F.2d 984 (1st Cir.).

United States v. Shonubi (1997), 962 F.Supp. 370 (E.D.N.Y.). See also 103 F.3d 1085 (2d Cir. 1997), 895 F.Supp. 460 (E.D.N.Y. 1995), 998 F.2d 84 (2d Cir. 1993), 802 F.Supp. 859 (E.D.N.Y. 1992).

United States v. Sklar (1990), 920 F.2d 107 (1st Cir.).

United States v. Skodnek (1996), 933 F.Supp. 1108 (D. Mass.).

United States v. Thomas (1996), 74 F.3d 701 (6th Cir.), *rehearing and suggestion for rehearing denied, cert. denied* 117 S.Ct. 74, 136 L.Ed.2d 33.

United States v. Walton (1990), 908 F.2d 1289 (6th Cir.), *cert. denied* 111 S.Ct. 273, 112 L.Ed.2d 229 (1990).

United States v. Whiting (1994), 28 F.3d 1296 (1st Cir.).

Vault Corporation v. Quaid Software Limited (1988), 847 F.2d 255 (5th Cir.).

Witte v. United States (1995), 515 U.S. 389, 115 S.Ct. 2199, 132 L.Ed.2d 351.

Yorktown Medical Laboratory, Inc. v. Perales (1991), 948 F.2d 84 (2d Cir.).

REFERENCES

[1] Aitken, C.G.G., Bring, J., Leonard, T., and Papasouliotis, O. (1997), Estimation of quantities of drugs handled and the burden of proof, *Journal of the Royal Statistical Society*, 160, 333–350.

[2] Bunge, J. and Fitzpatrick, M. (1993), Estimating the number of species: a review, *Journal of the American Statistical Association*, 88, 364–373.

[3] Diamond, S.S. (1994), Reference guide on survey research, in *Reference Manual on Scientific Evidence*, Federal Judicial Center, Washington, D.C.: U.S. Government Printing Office, pp. 221–271.

[4] Fairley, W.B. and Izenman, A.J. (1989), Welfare quality control programs: how much is misspent by the welfare system?, *Chance: New Directions for Statistics and Computers*, 2, 10–17.

[5] Fairley, W.B., Izenman, A.J., and Bagchi, P. (1990), Inference for welfare quality control programs, *Journal of the American Statistical Association*, 85, 874–890.

[6] Gastwirth, J.L. (1988), *Statistical Reasoning in Law and Public Policy: (Vol. 1) Statistical Concepts and Issues of Fairness; (Vol. 2) Tort Law, Evidence, and Health*. San Diego, CA: Academic Press.

[7] Gastwirth, J.L. (1996), Review of Diamond (1994), *Jurimetrics Journal*, 36, 181–191.

[8] Gastwirth, J.L., Freidlin, B., and Miao, W. (2000), The *Shonubi* case as an example of the legal system's failure to appreciate statistical evidence, this volume.

[9] Haas, P.J. and Stokes, L. (1998), Estimating the number of classes in a finite population, *Journal of the American Statistical Association*, 93, 1475–1487.

[10] Hahn, G.J. and Meeker, W.Q. (1993), Assumptions for statistical inference, *The American Statistician*, 47, 1–11.

[11] Health Care Financing Administration (1986), HCFA Ruling 86–1: Use of statistical sampling to project overpayments to Medicare providers and suppliers.

[12] Hedayat, S., Izenman, A.J., and Zhang, W.G. (1996), Random sampling for the forensic study of controlled substances (with discussion), *ASA Proceedings of the Section on Physical and Engineering Sciences*, 12–23.

[13] Heiner, K.W., Wagner, N.L., and Fried, A.C. (1984), Successfully using statistics to determine damages in fiscal audits, *Jurimetrics Journal*, 24, 273–281.

[14] Herman, S.N. (1992), The tail that wagged the dog: bifurcated fact-finding under the Federal Sentencing Guidelines and the limits of due process, *Southern California Law Review*, 66, 289–356.

[15] Izenman, A.J. (1999), Legal and statistical aspects of the forensic study of illicit drugs. Submitted for publication.

[16] Izenman, A.J. (2000), Assessing the statistical evidence in the *Shonubi* case, this volume.

[17] Izenman, A.J., Papasouliotis, O., Leonard, T., and Aitken, C.G.C. (1998), Bayesian predictive evaluation of measurement error with application to the assessment of illicit drug quantity, unpublished manuscript.

[18] Johnson, N.L. and Kotz, S. (1969), *Discrete Distributions*. New York: John Wiley.

[19] Kaye, D.H. and Freedman, D.A. (1994), Reference guide on statistics, in *Reference Manual on Scientific Evidence*, Federal Judicial Center, Washington, D.C.: U.S. Government Printing Office, pp. 331–414.

[20] Kegan, D.L. (1985), Survey evidence in copyright litigation, *Journal of the Copyright Society of the U.S.A.*, 32, 283–314.

[21] Macaluso, T.F. (1995), *The Extent of Trafficking in the Food Stamp Program*, Washington, D.C.: United States Department of Agriculture, Food, and Consumer Service, Office of Analysis and Evaluation.

[22] Otis, D.L. (1980), An extension of the change-in-ratio method, *Biometrics*, 36, 141–147.

[23] Pollock, K.H. (1991), Modeling capture, recapture, and removal statistics for estimation of demographic parameters for fish and wildlife populations: past, present, and future, *Journal of the American Statistical Association*, 86, 225–236.

[24] Saunders, M.J. (1994), Criminal copyright infringements and the Copyright Felony Act, *Denver University Law Review*, 71, 671–691.

[25] Seber, G.A.F. (1982), Capture–recapture methods, in: *Encyclopedia of Statistical Sciences* (eds. S. Kotz and N.L. Johnson), 1, 367–374, New York: John Wiley.

[26] Thompson, S.K. (1992) *Sampling*, New York: John Wiley.

[27] United States Sentencing Commission (1995), *Federal Sentencing Guidelines Manual*. St. Paul, MN: West Publishing Company.

[28] Weber, T.E. (1997), For those who scoff at Internet commerce, here's a hot market, *Wall Street Journal*, May 20, 1997, p. A1.

[29] Wei, L.J. and Cowan, C.D. (1988), Selection bias, in *Encyclopedia of Statistical Sciences* (eds. S. Kotz and N.L. Johnson), 8, 332–334, New York: John Wiley.

[30] Zanghi, J.S. (1995), Community standards in cyberspace, *Dayton Law Review*, 21, 95–118.

Interpreting DNA Evidence:
Can Probability Theory Help?

David J. Balding

Abstract

The interpretation of DNA evidence has been the subject of substantial controversy, both in the courtroom and in the scientific and legal literatures. The debate revolves around a number of topics, including population genetics issues, the role of possible laboratory errors, the effect of database "trawls" on evidential weight, and criteria for establishing the "uniqueness" of a profile. In large measure, the confusion surrounding the controversy can be attributed to the concepts of classical statistical inference, with which most scientists are familiar, but which are inappropriate in this setting. I argue for an affirmative answer to the question in the title, showing how many of the areas of controversy are readily resolved by insights obtained from probability-based reasoning focused on the relevant question, which is typically, Is the defendant the source of the crime scene DNA? The argument developed here is inspired by my experiences of advising courts, lawyers, and defendants in many UK criminal cases, in addition to researching relevant statistics and population genetics issues.

Keywords: identification, DNA profiles, weight-of-evidence, population genetics, relatedness, databases, uniqueness.

1 A Forensic Identification Problem

When the defendant in a criminal legal case shares with the true culprit a rare characteristic, such as a DNA profile, how incriminating is this evidence? How convinced should a juror be, based on this information, that the defendant is the perpetrator of the crime?

I encountered this forensic identification problem early in 1990, not long after obtaining my Ph.D. in mathematics, and at the start of a career teaching and researching in probability and statistics. It seemed like a routine statistical inference problem—a decision must be made among competing hypotheses on the basis of data. At that time I had some familiarity with statistical theory, through undergraduate courses, through having worked for most of a year as a research assistant in medical statistics before my Ph.D., and through having spent a year teaching mathematical statistics after it. This ought to be adequate preparation, I assumed, for tackling a seemingly straightforward statistical inference problem. And it would make an interesting, but not too challenging, problem to help establish my statistical career.

Years later, I had not only more respect for the subtleties underlying this important problem, but also less respect for the classical statistical methods that I had been taught. I had come to see that the paradigm underlying classical statistics, in which one considers the outcomes that might be obtained from imagined repetitions of an "experiment," is not relevant to the forensic identification setting. Courts are concerned with particular instances—did this man commit this crime? I came to see that inappropriate ideas from classical statistics had caused much confusion about the interpretation of DNA profile evidence.

But I also came to appreciate that appropriate statistical ideas were available, and could be enormously helpful to courts. The key principle turned out to be astonishingly simple: Focus on the relevant question. Many misleading statistical approaches turned out to be providing valid answers to the wrong questions.

In criminal legal cases, the relevant question is usually whether or not the defendant is guilty. In cases involving DNA identification evidence, "is guilty" is often effectively equivalent to "is the source of the crime scene DNA" and, for convenience, I will treat these as equivalent, although this is not necessarily the case in practice. The statistician's role should be to assist a rational juror to evaluate his/her probability that the defendant is guilty. This "direct probability" approach can be viewed as an instance of the Bayesian paradigm for statistical inference, about which I knew very little in 1990. Of course, probability theory provides no automatic procedure that resolves all difficulties by turning a mathematical "handle." But the direct probability approach is firmly grounded in logic, leads to important insights, and forms a framework for resolving the areas of confusion and controversy that caused so much difficulty for courts during the early 1990s.

2 The Population Genetics Debate

DNA profiles were still new in 1990, in routine use for not much more than a year, but the euphoria surrounding their introduction was beginning to be replaced by signs of a reaction. Was the science reliable? Were the statistics reported in court valid? These questions rose to prominence with the landmark paper of Lander (1989), strongly critical of some aspects of the handling and interpretation of DNA profile evidence in the US case *People v. Castro* (1989).

One particular issue that was developing into a controversy in 1990, a controversy which broke out fully after the publication of Lewontin and Hartl (1991), was that of the role of population subdivision. It was common for DNA evidence to be accompanied by an estimate of the relative frequency of the matching profile: It seemed intuitively clear then, as now, that the rarer the profile, the stronger the evidence for identity of defendant with culprit. DNA profiles are typically so rare that direct estimates of their relative frequencies, based on sample frequencies of entire profiles, were impractical because most samples have no instances of the profile(s) arising in an actual case. Instead, indirect estimates were obtained via the so-called "product rule," based on an assumption of independence of profile components.

The validity of the independence assumption underpinning the product rule was open to challenge. A closely related, and perhaps more fundamental, question was, "in which population?" Profile relative frequencies can vary from one population to another, with differences between two populations tending to be larger if the populations are isolated from each other, and if one or both of the populations is small. A defendant may be convicted on the basis of a frequency estimate pertaining to the wrong population: Perhaps the defendant belongs to a small, isolated religious or social group in which the profile, though rare in the general population, is relatively common. Alternatively, perhaps not the defendant but the true culprit came from such a population, and is it not the population of the culprit that matters, not that of the defendant?

The debate on these questions was fuelled by Krane et al. (1992), who reported that even within the ethnic group usually identified as "Caucasian," often regarded as practically homogeneous, substantial differences in profile frequencies could arise. Specifically, the profile relative frequency could be understated by an order of magnitude if estimated from a mixed Caucasian database when an Italian or a Finnish population was relevant. The methodology of Krane et al. was criticized (see Sawyer et al., 1996, references therein, and Balding and Nichols, 1997), but the existence of the phenomenon could not be denied. Despite a large literature on population genetic issues in forensic DNA profiling (for a bibliography, see Weir, 1995), Krane et al. seemed to be alone at that time in presenting data that focused directly on the relevant issue—comparing frequencies from a general Caucasian sample, similar to typical forensic databases, with sample frequencies pertaining to a specific subpopulation, from which both a defendant and many alternative possible culprits may be drawn.

The "in which population?" debate used up much ink in academic journals (see, e.g., Roeder, 1994, and references therein), and generated more heat than light. Nor could it generate much light, since the debate was based on a misconception, engendered by attempts to shoehorn the forensic identification problem into the classical hypothesis-testing framework.

3 The Classical Framework

The jury in a criminal case must reason from the evidence presented to it, to a decision between the hypotheses

G: the defendant is guilty;
I: the defendant is not guilty.

Within the classical framework, it was generally accepted that the legal maxim "innocent until proven guilty" implied that I should be the null hypothesis. A critical region could then be identified, consisting of all (measured) DNA profiles that match the crime scene profile, where "match" means "differs in each component by less than the accepted measurement-error tolerance." Therefore, the strength of the DNA profile evidence could be measured by the significance level α, which is the probability, under I, that the defendant's profile matches the crime scene profile.

Unfortunately, hypothesis I does not determine a statistical model under which α can be calculated. The usual approach to overcoming this problem, adopted by the report[1] NRC2, replaces I with a more precise hypothesis:

I': the defendant has been chosen randomly from a population of innocent individuals.

With I' as the null hypothesis, α is simply the *profile frequency*, the relative frequency in the population of profiles that match the crime profile.

The "in which population?" question is clearly central to this formalization of the forensic identification problem. Just as clear is that, posed in this way, the question is unanswerable. The null hypothesis is patently false: Nobody was chosen randomly in any population, and so a debate about the precise definition of the population has something in common with a debate about the precise number of wings on the tooth fairy.

Even if it were accepted that the "in which population?" question has no logically compelling answer, it might be hoped that there is an answer that satisfies some notion of fairness or reasonableness. But if the population is defined broadly, this tends to be unfavorable to the defendant. If narrowly, how narrowly? The smallest population containing the defendant consists of one person and has a 100% relative frequency for the defendant's DNA profile.[2]

The fact that it created unnecessary confusion over the "in which population?" question is not the only weakness of the classical hypothesis testing paradigm, as applied to forensic identification. Other difficulties that the classical approach could not adequately deal with include:

- How can the significance level in assessing the DNA evidence be incorporated with the other evidence? What if the defendant produces an apparently watertight alibi? What if additional incriminating evidence is found?

---

[1] In 1996, the National Research Council of the USA issued its report *The evaluation of forensic DNA evidence* (NRC2), which attempted to settle the controversies and confusions surrounding the use of DNA evidence in courts. Some of the controversies existed because of a 1992 report by the same body that was criticized by commentators from all sides of the debate. NRC2 adopted the classical framework for most of its statistical deliberations, and some of its conclusions are flawed; see Balding (1997).

[2] My first attempts at addressing the problem (Nichols and Balding, 1991) were framed within the classical setting, and tried to overcome the problem by choosing as null the hypothesis that the defendant is not directly related to the culprit, but is drawn from the same subpopulation, partly isolated from the population for which sample frequencies are available. See Balding and Donnelly (1995) for later developments.

- What if the defendant has a brother not excluded by the other evidence from being a possible culprit?
- How should the possibility of laboratory or handling error be taken into account?
- What if the defendant was identified only after a number of other possible culprits were investigated and found not to match?

Perhaps the most important weakness is the first: the problem of incorporating the DNA evidence with the other evidence. Hypothesis tests are designed to make accept/reject decisions on the basis of the scientific evidence only, irrespective of the other evidence. Legal decision-makers must synthesise all the evidence, much of it unscientific and difficult to quantify, in order to arrive at a verdict.

These weaknesses have been overlooked by many courts and legal commentators, at great cost in terms of confusion and unnecessary disputes. Fortunately, a superior framework for the statistical interpretation of DNA evidence has gained currency, and now predominates in the UK and elsewhere.

4   A Direct Probability Framework

The principal unknown of interest to the jury is whether or not hypothesis G is true. A rational juror is therefore concerned with evaluating $P(G|E)$, the probability of G based on the evidence E presented to the court. It is helpful to partition E into the DNA evidence, E_d, and the other evidence, E_o. By Bayes's theorem[3], we can write

$$
\begin{aligned}
P(G|E) &= P(G|E_d, E_o) \\
&= \frac{P(E_d \cap G|E_o)}{P(E_d \cap G|E_o) + P(E_d \cap I|E_o)} \\
&= \frac{P(E_d|G, E_o)P(G|E_o)}{P(E_d|G, E_o)P(G|E_o) + P(E_d|I, E_o)P(I|E_o)}.
\end{aligned} \tag{1}
$$

Hypothesis I' is irrelevant: There is no need to invoke a fictitious "random man." Although this concept can be helpful in presenting probabilities to a lay audience, it has no role in the rational assessment of evidential weight.

While valid, (1) is not useful in practice because $P(E_d|I, E_o)$ is not straightforward to evaluate. We can proceed by partitioning I into subhypotheses of the form "x is the culprit" for various individuals x. Writing C and s for the names of

---

[3]The standard version of Bayes's theorem given two possibilities G and I, and some evidence (or data) E, is

$$
P(G|E) = \frac{P(E|G)P(G)}{P(E|G)P(G) + P(E|I)P(I)}.
$$

Equation (1) is slightly more complicated because $E = \{E_d, E_o\}$ and (1) analyzes the effect of E_d, while E_o is assumed to have already been accounted for.

the culprit and of the defendant (or suspect), and assuming that E_d is independent of E_o, given C, we can write

$$P(C=s|E) = \frac{P(E_d|C=s)P(C=s|E_o)}{P(E_d|C=s)P(C=s|E_o) + \sum_{x \neq s} P(E_d|C=x)P(C=x|E_o)}, \quad (2)$$

where the summation is over all the alternative possible culprits.[4]

It is sometimes helpful to rewrite (2) in terms of $R_s(x)$, the likelihood ratio (LR), defined by[5]

$$R_s(x) = \frac{P(E_d|C=x)}{P(E_d|C=s)}, \quad (3)$$

and the "other evidence" ratio, $w_s(x)$, defined by

$$w_s(x) = \frac{P(C=x|E_o)}{P(C=s|E_o)}. \quad (4)$$

If the DNA profile of x is known, then either it also matches the crime scene profile, so that $R_s(x) = 1$, or it does not, and $R_s(x) = 0$ (assuming that, e.g., gross error or fraud can be ruled out). Typically, the DNA profile of an alternative culprit x is unknown, and $0 < R_s(x) \ll 1$.

The $w_s(x)$ measure the weight of the non-DNA evidence against x *relative to* its weight against s. If the case against s rests primarily on DNA evidence, there may be many x for whom $w_s(x) \approx 1$. For most sexual or violent crimes, $w_s(x) \approx 0$ for women, children, and invalids. When the defense presents evidence in favor of s, such as a convincing alibi or nonidentification by a victim, a juror may reasonably assign $w_s(x) \gg 1$ for many x.

Equation (2) can now be rewritten in terms of a sum of LRs, weighted by the $w_s(x)$:

$$P(C=s|E) = \frac{1}{1 + \sum_{x \neq s} R_s(x)w_s(x)}. \quad (5)$$

Each term in the summation measures the plausibility, in the light of all the evidence, of the hypothesis that x is the true culprit. The overall case against s is compelling only if this summation is small, i.e., if the total weight of evidence against all the alternative culprits is small. Some of the confusion about DNA evidence has arisen because the hypothesis of guilt is inappropriately compared with

---

[4]Equation (2) applies when there is only one contributor to the crime sample and only the crime and defendant profiles are reported to the court. Modifications are required for other scenarios, such as when the DNA profiles of other individuals have been observed and found not to match and when the crime sample has more than one source.

[5]Many authors prefer to work with the inverse of (3). The present definition has the advantage that the LR simplifies in standard settings to a (conditional) match probability, given below at (9).

a *particular* alternative, such as that a "random" person is the culprit, rather than the cumulative weight over *all* alternatives.

Similarly, there is not just one LR, but many. In principle, there can be a distinct LR for every alternative culprit. In practice, groups of alternative culprits will have a common LR, and it may suffice to report to the court only a few important values. These might include LRs corresponding to a brother of s, another close relative such as a cousin, and a person apparently unrelated to s, but with a similar ethnic background.

A DNA expert may be able to advise jurors on appropriate values for the LRs, but it will not usually be appropriate for them to assign explicit values to the $w_s(x)$. Nevertheless, it may be reasonable for an expert to guide jurors by illustrative calculations that might involve, for example, a group of individuals for whom jurors assess that $w_s(x) \approx 1$, and another group for whom the total value of $w_s(x)$ over all x in the group is negligibly small. Useful approximations to (5) may then be available.

5   Consequences of the Probability Analysis

5.1   Non-DNA Evidence

Consider the two cases of assault outlined in the box below. The overall cases against the two defendants differ dramatically: In the first case the evidence against s seems overwhelming; in the second, a jury would have to make careful judgments about the validity of the alibi, the possibility of traveling such a distance, and the strength of the DNA evidence. Reporting only the profile frequency allows the jury no framework for comparing the DNA evidence with the non-DNA evidence and hence sensibly distinguishing such cases.

Two Assault Cases

Case 1
- victim recognizes alleged assailant and reports his name, s, to the police;
- s is found to have injuries consistent with the victim's allegation and cannot give a convincing alibi for his whereabouts at the time of the alleged offense;
- s is profiled and found to match the crime profile.

Case 2
- victim does not see assailant and can give no useful information about him;
- the crime profile is compared with DNA profiles from many other individuals until a matching individual s is found.
- s lives in another part of the country, has a good alibi for the time of the crime and no additional evidence can be found linking him to the alleged offense.

In the direct probability approach, the difference between these two cases is encapsulated in different values for the other evidence ratio $w_s(x)$. On the basis of a plausible allegation by the victim in Case 1, a juror is likely to set $w_s(x) < 1$ for any x about whom no special information is available. Lacking such an allegation, and presented with strong alibi evidence, a juror in Case 2 may set $w_s(x) \gg 1$ for many x. It is not usually necessary for a juror to assign precise values to the $w_s(x)$: It suffices to distinguish the moderately small and extremely large values that may be appropriate in these two examples.

5.2   Many Possible Culprits

Because DNA evidence is typically very strong, cases are coming to courts in which there is very little non-DNA evidence. In such cases, there may be large numbers of individuals who, if not for the DNA evidence, would be just as likely as s to be the culprit, i.e., for whom $w_s(x) \approx 1$.

As an illustration, suppose that there are N individuals other than s who could have committed the crime, and that the non-DNA evidence does not distinguish among them, so that $w_s(x) \equiv 1$. Suppose also that the profile of s is observed to match the crime profile, whereas the profiles of the other possible culprits are unknown, and that the LR is constant over x, i.e., $R_s(x) \equiv r$. In this scenario, (5) simplifies to

$$P(C{=}s|E) = \frac{1}{1 + \sum_{x \neq s} r} = \frac{1}{1 + Nr}. \tag{6}$$

Even a very small LR (or a very small profile frequency) may not suffice to imply a high probability of guilt—it is not enough that r is small, the product Nr must be small. A juror told only that the profile frequency is 1 in 1 million may incorrectly conclude that this amounts to overwhelming proof of guilt. This error can be extremely detrimental to defendants when large values for N might be appropriate (see box on page 59).

5.3   Relatives

Because DNA profiles are inherited, closely related individuals are more likely to share a DNA profile than are unrelated individuals. Many commentators, including NRC2, take the view that unless there is specific evidence to cast suspicion on them, close relatives of s need not be considered in assessing the DNA evidence.

The direct probability analysis shows this view to be mistaken. Consider a case in which there is DNA profile evidence against s, but the DNA profiles of the other possible culprits—a brother of s named b and 100 unrelated men—are

---

The weight of evidence fallacy: examples

Many commentators, presumably reasoning within the classical framework, seem to take the view that a small profile frequency alone establishes guilt. Some examples of statements which seem to be based on this fallacy are:

- "There is absolutely no need to come in with figures like 'one in a billion', 'one in ten thousand' is just as good" (P. Reilly, quoted in Anderson, 1992).
- "The range may span one or two orders of magnitude, but such a range will have little practical impact on LRs as large as several million" (Roeder, 1994).
- "population frequencies ... 10^{-5} or 10^{-7}. The distinction is irrelevant for courtroom use" (Lander & Budowle, 1994).
- "If the calculated profile probability is very small, ... even a large relative error will not change the conclusion" (NRC2, 1996).

These statements are misleading because in the presence of many possible culprits, or strong exculpatory evidence, small profile frequencies may be consistent with acquittal and differences of one or two orders of magnitude may be crucial.

---

not available.[6] Suppose that the non-DNA evidence does not distinguish among these 102 individuals, so that $w_s(x) \equiv 1$, and that the LRs are, for the brother, $R_s(b) = 10^{-2}$, and for all other possible culprits $R_s(x) = 10^{-6}$.

Under these assumptions, (5) gives

$$P(C=s|E) = \frac{1}{1 + 10^{-2} + 100 \times 10^{-6}} \approx 99\%. \qquad (7)$$

The probability that s is innocent in this scenario would thus be about 1%. A juror may or may not choose to convict on the basis of such a calculation. The pertinent point is that ignoring b would be very misleading: We would then have

$$P(C=s|E) = \frac{1}{1 + 100 \times 10^{-6}} \approx 99.99\%,$$

so that the probability of innocence would be calculated as 0.01%, understating the correct value by two orders of magnitude. It is easy to think of similar situations, involving additional unexcluded brothers or other close relatives, in which the probability of innocence is substantial, even after apparently strong DNA evidence has been taken into account. As a rough guide, the probability that s is innocent is

---

[6]It may be helpful to profile brothers in such cases, if possible. The brother may, however, be missing, or refuse to co-operate with investigators. It may not even be known whether or not the defendant has any brothers.

at least the match probability for brothers times the number of brothers for whom the non-DNA evidence has much the same weight as it does for s.

In practice, the calculation of $P(C=s|E)$ is more complex than in this example, but the example illustrates that unexcluded close relatives may cause reasonable doubt about guilt *even when there is no direct evidence to cast suspicion on the relatives.*

5.4 Population Genetics

We now return to the issue that caused so much controversy in the DNA profiling debate: the role of population genetic effects. The direct probability approach illuminates a path to resolving the problem. The key point is that it is the LR that is directly relevant, not the profile relative frequency α. The latter is useful only as an approximation that is adequate under some circumstances.

For the moment, let us ignore the possibility of error, and assume that the DNA evidence E_d consists of the information that the culprit C and the defendant s have the same DNA profile D. To indicate this, we will now use the notation $\mathcal{G}_C = \mathcal{G}_s = D$ instead of E_d. Substituting into (3), the LR becomes

$$R_s(x) = \frac{P(\mathcal{G}_C = \mathcal{G}_s = D | C = x)}{P(\mathcal{G}_C = \mathcal{G}_s = D | C = s)}. \tag{8}$$

When $C = s$ (and ignoring error), $\mathcal{G}_C = \mathcal{G}_s = D$ is equivalent to just $\mathcal{G}_s = D$. Assuming also that the fact that an individual committed the crime does not of itself alter the probability that they have a particular profile, (8) can be simplified further to

$$R_s(x) = \frac{P(\mathcal{G}_x = \mathcal{G}_s = D)}{P(\mathcal{G}_s = D)} = P(\mathcal{G}_x = D | \mathcal{G}_s = D). \tag{9}$$

Thus, $R_s(x)$ is the conditional probability, called the "match probability," that x has the profile *given* that s has it. It is thus the alternative possible culprit x who defines the appropriate population for obtaining estimates of genetic frequencies. Crucially, however, population genetic effects arise, and can be dealt with, via the conditioning in (9): The possibility of shared ancestry between x and s (perhaps many generations in the past) implies that the match probability is typically larger than the profile frequency α.

The important distinction between the LR and α is that the former takes account of *both* the observed profiles that form the match, whereas α involves only one profile. Some authors, including the authors of NRC2, misleadingly refer to α as a "match probability," which is inappropriate, since the concept of "match" involves two profiles, rather than just one. To emphasize the distinction, Weir (1994) employs the term "conditional genotype frequency."

The direct probability approach highlights the genetic correlations that must be modeled in order to evaluate (9). This in itself represents an important advance, but the remaining task of formulating appropriate population genetics models, defining the relevant correlations, and estimating their values is substantial, and a discussion of it is beyond the scope of this chapter. See, for example, Weir (1994), Balding, Greenhalgh and Nichols (1996), Foreman, Smith and Evett (1997), and Balding (1999a).

5.5 Laboratory and Handling Errors

If crime and defendant profiles originate from the same individual, the observation E_d of matching profiles is not surprising. Nonmatching profiles could nevertheless have arisen through an error in the laboratory or at the crime scene, such as an incorrect sample label or laboratory record, a contaminated sample, or a software error in a computer-driven laboratory procedure.[7] The common practice of neglecting the fact that a false exclusion could have occurred favors the defendant, although the effect is typically small (e.g., ϵ_1 does not appear in the approximate LR calculated in the box below).

Profiling Errors: A Simplified Illustration

Calculation of likelihood ratios taking error probabilities into account can be difficult. Nevertheless, it is important for courts to obtain some understanding both of the possible errors and of their effects on evidential weight. The following simplified illustration may be helpful.

Suppose that the possible culprits have profile D independently and with probability p. Suppose further that profiling errors are independent and that the probability that an individual having true profile D will be correctly profiled is $1 - \epsilon_1$, while the probability that a non-D individual will be incorrectly recorded as having profile D is ϵ_2. Finally, we assume that each of p, ϵ_1, and ϵ_2 is sufficiently small that the product of any two is negligible compared with any one of them.

If $C = s$, the probability of both crime and defendant profiles being recorded as D is

$$P(\mathcal{G}_C=\mathcal{G}_s=D|C=s) = (1-\epsilon_1)^2 p + \epsilon_2^2(1-p) \approx p.$$

The corresponding probability when $C = x$ is

$$P(\mathcal{G}_C=\mathcal{G}_s=D|C=x) = ((1-\epsilon_1)p + \epsilon_2(1-p))^2 \approx (p + \epsilon_2)^2.$$

Therefore, $R_s(x) \approx (p+\epsilon_2)^2/p$, which always exceeds the value p that would apply if errors were assumed impossible (e.g., exceeds by a factor of four if ϵ_2 has about the same magnitude as p). The value of ϵ_1 is irrelevant, to a first approximation.

---

[7]We do not consider here measurement errors—small variations in results due to variable laboratory conditions. These are dealt with by adopting an appropriate match criterion.

On the other hand, ignoring the possibility of a false inclusion error is always detrimental to s, sometimes substantially so. Under the hypothesis that $C = x$, for some $s \neq x$, the evidence E_d could have arisen in at least two ways:

(a) x happens to have a DNA profile that matches that of s and no error occurred;
(b) the DNA profile of x is distinct from that of s, and the observation E_d of matching profiles is due to an error in one or both recorded profiles.

Forensic scientists are highly trained and generally take great care to avoid errors, so (b) is typically unlikely. However, (a) may also be very unlikely, and hence ignoring (b) may have the effect of greatly overstating the strength of the evidence against the defendant (see box on page 61).

Error probabilities are difficult to assess. Even if error rates from external, blind trials are available, there will usually be specific details of the case at hand that differ from the circumstances under which the trials were conducted, and that make it more or less likely that an error has occurred. In the criminal legal setting, it is ultimately jurors who must assess the error probabilities, but an expert can be helpful in pointing out some broad conclusions of the probability analysis, such as:

1. In order to achieve a satisfactory conviction based primarily on DNA evidence, the prosecution needs to persuade the jury that the relevant error probabilities are small.
2. If the probability of error (b) is much greater than the probability of matching profiles (a), then the latter probability is effectively irrelevant to evidential weight. Extremely small match probabilities can therefore be misleading unless the relevant error probabilities are also extremely small.
3. What matters are not the probabilities of *any* profiling or handling errors, but only the probabilities of errors that could have led to the observed DNA profile match.

5.6 Database Searches

In many countries, databases of the DNA profiles of named individuals have been established for criminal intelligence purposes (distinct from anonymous databases used for statistical purposes only). The question thus arises as to the appropriate method for assessing the DNA profile evidence when s was identified following a search through a database. In many jurisdictions, the number of individuals involved in such a search, and even the fact that there was a search, is not reported to the court.[8] It is therefore crucial to know whether or not omitting this information tends to favor the prosecution.

---

[8]The reason for not reporting details of a search is that intelligence databases often consist of the DNA profiles of previous offenders. Admitting that such a search has been conducted is thus tantamount to admitting that the defendant is a previous offender, which is not permitted in Anglo-American courts.

Within the classical statistics framework, the strength of evidence is assessed, broadly speaking, according to how probable such evidence would be in conceptual repetitions of an "experiment" that leads to the identification of innocent defendants. Such repetitions are fundamental to classical inference, but can be problematic due to the choice of what constitutes the "experiment." Often, as in the present setting, there is no actual repetition, and so the choice of protocol for the imaginary repetitions amounts to a subjective choice by the scientist or statistician.

In the database search setting it is difficult to see what "experiment" should be assumed for the purposes of classical statistical analysis. For the standard forensic identification problem discussed above, NRC2 chose to assume that innocent defendants are chosen by a process, which we have labeled hypothesis I', of random selection in a population of innocent defendants, leading to a significance level α that equals the profile frequency. We have argued that I' is inappropriate in any case, but it is even less tenable in the database search context because it does not account for the individuals in the database who were inspected and found not to match. Instead, a natural analogue of I' for database searches is

I_d: The database contains the DNA profiles of N individuals chosen independently and at random from a population of innocent individuals.

Like I', hypothesis I_d is patently false: The individuals whose profiles are in a DNA profile database were not chosen by any "random" process. However, classical statistics requires some such assumption, and NRC2 seems to have adopted this choice (which it attempted to justify using a misleading coin-tossing analogy).

If, as is usually the case, $N\alpha \ll 1$, then the significance level associated with hypothesis I_d, given that the defendant's DNA profile is the only one in the database to match the crime profile, is approximately $N\alpha$. NRC2 recommended that this value be reported to courts as a measure of the strength of DNA evidence when it results from a database search.

Since $N > 1$, this analysis implies that DNA evidence following a database search is weaker, usually much weaker, than in the standard setting. This conclusion seems intuitively attractive to many scientists who are familiar with the dangers inherent in "hypothesis trawling." Omitting to tell a jury that the defendant was identified on the basis of a database search can, from this perspective, be seriously detrimental to the defendant, since the evidence is much weaker in this setting. Moreover, a similar analysis applies in many related scenarios involving a, possibly ad hoc, search of the DNA profiles of possible culprits. Some sort of search is likely to be common in actual crime investigations, but for practical and/or legal reasons, it may not be possible to report the details of the search to a jury. The NRC2 approach to assessing evidential strength thus seems to undermine seriously the forensic use of DNA profiles.

Fortunately, the conclusions drawn in the classical framework, and the recommendation of NRC2, are misguided. The fact that a match seems less surprising when it results from a search is not directly relevant to the weight of evidence against s. Focusing instead on the relevant question, the direct probability analysis shows that DNA evidence is usually slightly stronger in the database search setting, so that omitting information about the search tends to favor s, although usually the effect is small. The typical forensic situation differs from the "hypothesis trawls" familiar to scientists because we know in advance that a culprit having the profile exists. To guide intuition, consider a database which records the DNA profiles of everyone who could possibly have committed the crime (perhaps even everyone on earth). If the profile of s were the only one in this database to match the crime profile, then the evidence against him would clearly be overwhelming. Yet the reasoning underpinning NRC2 would imply that the evidence is relatively weak because the database is large.[9]

Although the DNA evidence may be slightly stronger in the context of a database search, the overall case against s may tend to be weaker because there may often be little or no incriminating non-DNA evidence; see Balding and Donnelly (1996), and Donnelly and Friedman (1999).

6 Probability-Based Reasoning in the Courtroom

6.1 Bayes's Theorem in Court

In my own casework, I usually avoid trying to teach lawyers or jurors how to perform calculations using Bayes's theorem. Instead, I try to use informal language to convey insights that I have obtained via a more formal analysis, on the role of relatives or laboratory error, for example, or on cumulating over alternative hypotheses rather than considering them separately.

In some cases, however, the arguments for an explicit introduction of Bayes's theorem into the courtroom are very strong. In the UK case *R. v. Adams* (1996), the prosecution presented strongly incriminating DNA evidence, whereas the defense could produce non-DNA evidence that might also be characterized as strong—perhaps the most important component was a statement by the victim that the defendant did not resemble the man who had attacked her. The defense team was concerned that jurors may well be overwhelmed by the impressive numbers cited in support of the DNA evidence, and not give appropriate weight to the less easily quantified nonscientific evidence. They therefore engaged an expert witness statistician to, in effect, tutor jurors in how to perform their own Bayes's theorem calculations, based on their own assessments of the various items of evidence.

After two convictions, separated by a successful appeal, Adams's legal process terminated with an unsuccessful appeal. In the course of both appeals, the Court expressed disapproval of the introduction into the courtroom of a mathematical formalism, Bayes's theorem, to guide jurors in quantifying the non-DNA evidence and combining it with the DNA evidence.

---

[9]The report acknowledged this counterexample, and admitted that its approach did not apply in this setting. However, it did not explain how evidence gets weaker as N increases, yet becomes overwhelmingly strong when N is very large.

Many observers will sympathize with the Court's position, although the judgment was marred by a misunderstanding of the sequential application of Bayes's theorem to several items of evidence. Yet it must be regarded as unfortunate that explicitly logical reasoning should be ruled inadmissible in English courts. However, the ruling has little impact in practice because instances of Bayes's theorem being explicitly introduced in a criminal trial are so rare.

Although ruling out explicit introduction of formalized probability reasoning, the method of presenting DNA evidence advocated by the Court of Appeal is, fortunately for justice, rooted in the logic of Bayes's theorem. In its approach, an expert statistician can advise the court on the expected number X of individuals (in, e.g., England) who share the defendant's DNA profile. Jurors would then be invited to consider whether or not the non-DNA evidence suffices to persuade them that the defendant, and not one of these possibly X other individuals, is the culprit. Thus, the Court in effect advocates starting with an equal probability of guilt for all members of some appropriate population and updating these equal probabilities in the light of the DNA evidence, with the other evidence being assessed last.

There are a number of difficulties in practice with the Court's approach (Lambert and Evett, 1998), but it has clear merits. For the two assault cases outlined on page 57, for example, suppose that in each case the crime occurred in London and an expert testified that he/she expected only one other individual in England to share the defendant's profile. A juror may, in the light of the other evidence, think it plausible that the (possible) other individual is the true culprit in Case 2, whereas this possibility may well seem highly implausible to a juror in Case 1.

6.2 Two Common Fallacies

The prosecutor's fallacy is an error of logic that can arise in reasoning about DNA profile evidence, and may be regarded as a generalization of the error in elementary logic of confusing "A implies B" with "B implies A." The fallacy consists in confusing $P(A|B)$ with $P(B|A)$. It is a special case of what statisticians may prefer to call "the error of the transposed conditional."

The probability of DNA evidence given that s is innocent is often taken to be very small. It does not, however, immediately follow that the probability that s is innocent, given the DNA evidence, is also very small. Transcripts of actual court cases very often record statements that indicate that the profile frequency is being confused with the probability that the defendant is innocent (see box on page 66). This error can amount to a substantial overstatement of evidential strength. The fallacy was one of the grounds for a successful appeal in the case of *Deen* and subsequent UK cases. For further examples, and discussion, of the prosecutor's fallacy in the DNA evidence setting, see Koehler (1993), Balding and Donnelly (1994), Robertson and Vignaux (1995), and Evett (1995).

Another error of logic that can arise in connection with DNA evidence usually favors the defendant and is consequently dubbed the "defendant's fallacy." Suppose that a crime occurs in a nation of 100 million people and a profile frequency is

---

The Prosecutor's Fallacy: Examples

In each of the quotations below, an expert witness has made a "transposed conditional" error.

- "We end up with a probability of the semen having originated from someone other than Andrew Deen of 1 in 700,000" (*R. v. Deen*, UK, 1994).
- "I can estimate the chances of this semen having come from a man other than the provider of the blood sample . . . less than 1 in 27 million" (*R. v. Adams*, UK, 1997).
- ". . . the chance that anyone else but the appellant left the hairs at the scene of the crime is 6 billion to 1" (*People v. Axell*, 1991).

These statements concern the probability that the defendant is not the source of the crime profile, whereas the appropriate statement refers to the probability of the DNA evidence *if* the defendant is not the source of the crime profile.

---

reported as 1 in 1 million. The fallacy consists of arguing that since the expected number of people in the nation with a matching profile is 100, the probability that the defendant is the culprit is only 1 in 100.

This conclusion would be valid if jurors were given no other information about the crime, but this does not arise in practice. Even if there is little or no directly incriminating evidence beyond the DNA profile match, there is always background information presented in evidence, such as the location and nature of the alleged offense, that will make some individuals more plausible suspects than others.

A closely related fallacy consists in arguing that since it is expected that many people in the nation share the profile, the DNA evidence is almost worthless.

6.3 Uniqueness

Because DNA evidence involves scientific issues beyond the knowledge of the general public, courts contemplating DNA evidence often make use of an expert witness to help with the assessment of such evidence. Any individual, including the expert witness, can make their own assessment of the probability that the defendant is guilty, based on the DNA evidence and any background information that they feel appropriate. A juror's reasoning is, however, constrained by legal rules. For example, although it may be reasonable to believe that the fact that a person is on trial makes it more likely that they are guilty, a juror is prohibited from reasoning in this way. (Among other reasons, this prohibition is intended to avoid double-counting of evidence.) It follows that it is not appropriate for the expert witness to report to the court their own assessment of the probability that the defendant is guilty.

A closely related issue is whether or not it might be appropriate for an expert witness to assert that, provided that no laboratory or handling error has occurred, and that the defendant has no identical twin, his/her DNA profile is almost certainly unique in some relevant population. Such an approach shifts attention away from the directly relevant question, but has the advantage that very small match probabilities, which may overwhelm or confuse jurors, can be avoided.

Asserting uniqueness is fraught with difficulties, not least of which is the effect of the non-DNA evidence in a case. Suppose that a defendant's profile matches the crime scene profile, and is thought to be unique. If, later, overwhelming new evidence comes to light that appears to establish that s is innocent, then the new evidence also makes it more likely that the defendant's profile is not unique. More generally, any evidence in favor of the innocence of s is evidence against uniqueness.

Focusing on uniqueness, rather than the directly relevant issue, guilt, makes less efficient use of the evidence. Under the assumption that there is no evidence in favor of s, Balding (1999b) estimates that at least ten short tandem repeat (STR) loci will be needed to routinely establish uniqueness, whereas six loci usually suffice for satisfactory convictions in current practice. Additional loci imply additional possibilities for error, and it seems likely that the substantial development effort required to validate the additional STR profiling tests, as well as the recurrent cost of the extra profiling runs, would not justify the gains obtainable by reporting "uniqueness" in court. In any case, the assumption of no evidence in favor of s is required, which will often not be appropriate, and there seems no generally valid approximation.

7 Conclusion

The direct probability approach to reasoning about DNA evidence embodies rules for coherent reasoning in the presence of uncertainty. Although there are compelling arguments for adhering to these rules (see, for example, Bernardo and Smith, 1994) there is also a substantial literature pointing to the conclusion that typical jurors may not do so (see, for example, Kerr 1993). The value of a logical framework for helping experts, lawyers, and commentators understand issues affecting the weight of DNA evidence seems self-evident. Just as evident is the fact that there remains a substantial challenge in the task of incorporating the insights obtained from the logical analyses into presentations in court that are soundly based, yet also accessible to jurors.

I have illustrated some of the insights that can be obtained from the direct probability approach to assessing evidential weight; others have been omitted, such as in cases involving mixed stains and paternity (for evaluating LRs in these and other settings, see Evett and Weir, 1998). I started off in 1990 having no experience or familiarity with direct probability reasoning: The spur in this direction has been the practical necessity of advising lawyers and jurors about the issues arising in actual cases. The direct probability approach to reasoning about DNA evidence is relatively easy to convey to nonspecialists, reflecting both (1) that the rules of probability encapsulate elementary rules of logical reasoning and (2) that the approach focuses on the relevant questions.

Having the direct probability framework available has been invaluable to me in consulting with lawyers and giving expert witness testimony. It gives reliable guidance on how to approach new issues arising in cases with unusual features, which is especially helpful in clarifying my thoughts when caught "on the spot" in the courtroom. Lessons I have learned from my study of forensic identification have also had an impact on my other scientific work. Although classical methods work well in many applications, I have become aware of the potential danger of being led astray by not focusing on the directly relevant issue.

Acknowledgments

This chapter was written while the author was visiting the Isaac Newton Institute for Mathematical Sciences, Cambridge, UK.

8   Cases Cited

People v. Axell (1991) 235 Cal App 3d, 836, 844.
People v. Castro (1989) 545 N.Y.S.2d 985.
R. v. Adams (Dennis John) (1996) 2 Cr App R 467; 61 JCL 170.
R. v. Adams (Gary Andrew) (1997) 1 Cr App R 369.
R. v. Deen (1994) *The Times*, January 10.

REFERENCES

[1] Anderson, C. (1992), FBI attaches strings to its DNA database, *Nature*, **357**, 618.

[2] Balding, D.J. (1997), Errors and misunderstandings in the second NRC report, *Jurimetrics Journal*, **37**, 469–476.

[3] Balding, D.J. (1999a), Forensic applications of microsatellite markers, Ch. 15, pp 198–210, in *Microsatellites: evolution and applications*, D. Goldstein and C. Schlotterer eds., Oxford UP, 1999.

[4] Balding, D.J. (1999b), When can a DNA profile be regarded as unique?, *Science & Justice*, Vol 39 pp 257–260.

[5] Balding, D.J. and Donnelly, P. (1994), The prosecutor's fallacy and DNA evidence, *Criminal Law Review*, October 1994, 711–721.

[6] Balding, D.J. and Donnelly, P. (1995), Inferring identity from DNA profile evidence, *Proceedings of the National Academy of Sciences of the USA*, **92**, 11741–11745.

[7] Balding, D.J. and Donnelly, P. (1996), Evaluating DNA profile evidence when the suspect is identified through a database search, *Journal of Forensic Sciences*, **41**, 603–607.

[8] Balding, D.J., Greenhalgh, M., and Nichols, R.A. (1996), Population genetics of STR loci in Caucasians, *International Journal of Legal Medicine*, **108**, 300–305.

[9] Balding, D.J. and Nichols, R.A. (1997), Significant genetic correlations among Caucasians at forensic DNA loci, *Heredity*, **78**, 583–589.

[10] Bernardo, J.M. and Smith, A.F.M. (1994) "Bayesian Theory," Chichester: Wiley.

[11] Donnelly, P. and Friedman, R. (1999), DNA database searches and the legal consumption of scientific evidence, Vol 97 pp 931–984 *Michigan Law Review*.

[12] Evett, I.W. (1995), Avoiding the transposed conditional, *Science & Justice*, **35**, 127–131.

[13] Evett, I.W. and Weir, B.S. (1998), *Interpreting DNA evidence: statistical genetics for forensic scientists*, Sinauer, Sunderland MA.

[14] Foreman, L.A., Smith, A.F.M., and Evett, I.W. (1997), Bayesian analysis of DNA profiling data in forensic identification applications, *Journal of the Royal Statistical Society*, **A 160**, 429–459.

[15] Kerr, N. (1993), Stochastic models of juror decision making, Chap. 5 of *Inside the Juror: The Psychology of Juror Decision Making*, R. Hastie Ed., Cambridge Series on Judgement and Decision Making.

[16] Koehler, J.J. (1993), Error and exaggeration in the presentation of DNA evidence at trial, *Jurimetrics Journal*, **34**, 21–39.

[17] Krane, D.E., Allen, R.W., Sawyer, S.A., Petrov, D.A., and Hartl, D.L. (1992), Genetic-differences at 4 DNA typing loci in Finnish, Italian, and mixed Caucasian populations, *Proceedings of the National Academy of Sciences of the USA*, **89**, 10583–10587.

[18] Lambert, J.A. and Evett, I.W. (1998), The impact of recent judgements on the presentation of DNA evidence, *Science & Justice*, **38**, 266–270.

[19] Lander, E.S. (1989), DNA fingerprinting on trial, *Nature*, **339**, 501–505.

[20] Lander, E.S. and Budowle, B. (1994), DNA-fingerprinting dispute laid to rest, *Nature*, **371**, 735–738 .

[21] Lewontin, R.C. and Hartl, D.L. (1991), Population genetics in forensic DNA typing, *Science*, **254**, 1745–1750.

[22] National Research Council (1996), *The evaluation of forensic DNA evidence* (NRC2), Washington DC: National Academy Press.

[23] Nichols, R.A. and Balding, D.J. (1991), Effects of population structure on DNA fingerprint analysis in forensic science, *Heredity*, **66**, 297–302.

[24] Robertson B., and Vignaux, G.A. (1995), *Interpreting Evidence*, Wiley.

[25] Roeder, K. (1994), DNA fingerprinting: a review of the controversy, *Statistical Science*, **9**, 222–278.

[26] Sawyer, S., Podleski, A., Krane, D., and Hartl, D. (1996), DNA-fingerprinting loci do show population differences—comments on Budowle et al., *American Journal of Human Genetics*, **59**, 272–274.

[27] Weir, B.S. (1994), The effects of inbreeding on forensic calculations, *Annual Review of Genetics*, **28**, 597–621.

[28] Weir, B.S. (1995), A bibliography for the use of DNA in human identification, *Genetica*, **96**, 179–213.

Statistics, Litigation, and Conduct Unbecoming

Seymour Geisser

Abstract

This paper discusses the statistical analysis involved in DNA cases in court and the difficulties and impediments placed in the way of defense experts.
Key words: DNA profiles, Hardy–Weinberg equilibrium, linkage equilibrium, restricted frequent length polymorphisms, variable number of tandem repeats.

1   Introduction

My experience in litigation involving statistical issues encompasses a large variety of cases. They range from gender, disability, and domestic partner discrimination to mail fraud, drug side effects, workmen's compensation, commercial disputes, hockey injuries, scientific misconduct, and tobacco reimbursements. These account for about one-eighth of the cases. A further one-sixth relate to paternity suits. The rest involve criminal cases that include homicide (a not insignificant number of these are death penalty cases), rape, and armed robbery.

In paternity and criminal cases the major statistical issues involve problems of genetic forensic identification. In most of the paternity cases, red cell and human leukocyte antigens were used. Recently, it has not been uncommon for several DNA probes to have been added to this forensic identification battery. DNA is the active substance of genes carrying the hereditary code for all organisms.

In the criminal cases, where I have almost always been called by a public defender's office, forensic identification has included anywhere from two to six DNA probes. Up until rather recently, these have been mainly restricted fragment length polymorphisms (RFLP) where a sample of DNA is cut with an enzyme into fragments whose lengths depend on the location of the cuts recognized by the enzyme. One form of RFLP that is probed are variable numbers of tandem repeats (VNTR), which are sequences of nucleotides of four types represented by the letters A, C, G, and T. Currently, polymer chain reaction (PCR) and short tandem repeats (STR) probes also have come to be used, but I shall restrict my attention to VNTR.

Giving expert testimony in a legal setting whether under a *subpoena duces tecum*, a Kelly–Frye judicial hearing, or testimony during a trial is an experience quite unlike teaching a class or giving a talk to colleagues. It resembles, but only slightly, a doctoral dissertation defense, in which, however, the interrogators are knowledgeable, friendly, helpful, unrestricted by legal custom and regulation concerning testimony, and the examination of the candidate is relatively short with a final result announced rather quickly. In comparison, in a criminal case, and these constitute the majority of cases in which I have been used as an expert, the prosecutor is none of the above. He is often hostile, not very knowledgeable about statistical issues, determined to either trip you up, make you appear foolish, or highlight any apparently contradictory statement made in all the years you have ever made statements on almost any topic. Having access through prosecutorial networks and other means, the prosecutor's office has scrutinized all previous testimony, statements, papers, and books in which you have ever ventured an opinion, expert or otherwise, for the slightest inaccuracy, potential contradiction, or apparent inconsistency. The intent of this exercise is to come up with something, whether or not it has relevance to the current case, in order to portray you as a congenital liar or complete ignoramus. If this is not successful, the next line of attack is that you are obviously in it only for the money, so your testimony is obviously bent. This line of attack is rather strange, because the prosecution invariably has much deeper pockets than a public defender and spends considerably more on its experts than the defense can possibly afford. Even someone as affluent as O. J. Simpson, who succeeded in his case, could or would not pay all expert witnesses' bills, while the prosecution did remunerate its experts.

An appreciable portion of the cases in which I have testified are death penalty cases. Here there appears to be much more tension between the defense attorneys and prosecutors, and of course, this is reflected in the treatment of experts on the stand.

In what follows, I shall discuss mainly the statistical issues I have encountered in criminal cases and the difficulties in working with public defenders induced by prosecutors, the FBI, commercial forensic laboratories, and the adversarial nature of the judicial process, which is somewhat orthogonal to the presentation of statistical evidence.

2   Use of VNTR Loci for Identification

DNA typing or profiling (or, less accurately, DNA fingerprinting) was introduced in England by Jeffreys et al. (1985 a, b) using VNTR loci for forensic identification. By 1987 two commercial laboratories in the USA, Cellmark and Lifecodes, were using single locus probes for DNA profiling for forensic identification. It has been suggested that these two laboratories engaged in a race to the courthouse to gain some competitive advantage by establishing the admissibility of its particular version of the DNA test (Neufeld and Coleman 1990). Shortly thereafter, the FBI entered this race, and by offering free training and other assistance to public criminal laboratories induced many of these units to use the FBI methods in an attempt to create an FBI standard as a national one. With each ensuing year more and more of state, county, and city forensic laboratories joined in this forensic frenzy. Many of these laboratories use FBI criteria for matching two profiles and also for calculating the relative frequency of a profile in particular so-called racial populations. Others may deviate slightly from them. While the technology could often clear an innocent person, there were often problematic methods, necessarily statistical, that led to disputes as to the calculation for the relative frequency of genetic profile of VNTR loci in a designated population when a match of two profiles was asserted.

A simplified explanation of the genetic setup is that at each VNTR locus on a chromosome, an individual's identity is exhibited by two alleles, one inherited from each parent. Each allele is then represented as a discrete number of hypervariable tandem repeats. Without going into the molecular-biological issues or into laboratory procedure for their measurement, it suffices to say that the electrophoretic procedure and subsequent laboratory techniques used induce some measurement error requiring statistical methods for their analysis.

In the past, depending on circumstances, anywhere from one to eight of these loci, with two alleles at a locus, are probed and presented as evidence in court cases. They are usually used in criminal cases to aid in the identity of those who may have left one or more of a variety of tissues or body fluids such as blood, semen, hair, and saliva at a crime scene. Because at these highly polymorphic VNTR loci there may be 30–100 alleles or more, they have much greater discriminatory power for individual identity than many of the genetic markers, such as red cell and human leukocyte antigens, that had been used in the past for such a purpose. While this is a major advantage, there is one drawback, as previously noted. These VNTR loci are subject to measurement error using the RFLP method. Because of the measurement error a procedure is required for determining a match or the similarity of crime scene material with a sample taken from a suspect or victim depending on circumstances. Forensic laboratories have established their own criteria for determining a match. Once they have decided that two profiles match, or are similar at each band, they then attempt to estimate the relative frequency of the entire profile of loci that they have probed. The asserted match of these bands and a minuscule relative frequency of the entire profile of bands are presented as evidence of a crime committed by a alleged perpetrator.

3   The Matching Criterion

Aside from an initial visual inspection, the FBI, using computerized methods, will generally assert that the two bands match if their difference is no larger than 5% of their average size (Budowle et al. 1991). This was called a ±2.5% match window by the FBI, but it clearly is a ±5% interval (Fung 1996). A study of repeated measurements on pairs of bands from the same individuals on the same electrophoretic gel yields an estimate of the standard deviation of the difference to be 0.74% of the band size, while on different gels it is 1.35%. This results in a tolerance interval for a match made on the same gel of about 6.7 standard deviations. Based on normally distributed measurement error, a false exclusion (negative) rate (falsely asserting that bands from the same individual are from

different individuals), based on, say, four loci, is of order 10^{-10} (Geisser 1996).
Thus in the long run, virtually no "guilty" person will evade the DNA net, though
some innocent ones will be entangled.

Information on standard deviation studies was shielded from defense experts until a court-ordered discovery yielded these results (*Minnesota vs. Johnson*, Fourth Judicial District Court, 1991). False inclusion (positive) rates (falsely asserting that the bands are from the same individual when they are not) are not possible to obtain theoretically in a sensible manner. They can be estimated empirically from a direct count comparison of the entire profiles of all possible pairs in a database consisting of different unrelated individuals. The relative frequency of different individuals in the database asserted to be the same is found to be between 10^{-4} and 10^{-5} for a four-locus profile profile (see Table 4 in Geisser 1998). Thus it would appear that the false exclusion rate is many orders of magnitude less than the false inclusion rate. This not only denies but reverses the adage that it is preferable to acquit many who are guilty rather than to convict one who is innocent.

Among the commercial forensics laboratories, Cellmark is the one most frequently used by the prosecution for DNA profiling. Cellmark uses a system of resolution limits on the autoradiograph to define the match interval. A match is declared if the two bands are within one resolution limit, but sometimes two resolution limits are used. There are limited data from Cellmark that indicate that a resolution limit will vary from 1.1 to 5.15% of the band size—the larger the band size, the larger the precentage. Calculation shows that the single resolution limit results in a tolerance between the two bands to be matched that will vary between 2 and 6 standard deviations. Thus no overall false exclusion rate is easily obtained, except that it is known to be larger than the rate for the FBI. As regards the false inclusion rate, there is some evidence from proficiency tests that it is large, relative to the false exclusion rate. The only time external proficiency tests were performed was in 1988 by the California Association of Crime Laboratory Directors, Report #6, and these were not blind. The results at that time were two false inclusions out of 100. No external blind proficiency tests have been performed since then. This is further evidence that the rate of false inclusions is substantially larger than that of false exclusions.

Both the FBI and Cellmark have consistently claimed that their procedures are conservative, i.e., that they favor the defendant. The evidence from their match criteria, in regard to false exclusion and inclusion rates, which are never reported in court by the laboratories, would indicate that for these characteristics the opposite is true.

4   Estimating the Relative Frequency of the Profile

Once a match has been asserted, the forensic laboratory presents as estimate of the relative frequency of the matching profile in several racial populations. These estimates are obtained by certain databases available to the laboratory. They depend on the following assumptions: (a) random samples of unrelated individuals from designated homogeneous populations; (b) statistical independence of the pair of alleles within each locus—termed Hardy–Weinberg equilibrium in genetic parlance; (c) mutual statistical independence among the several loci used—termed linkage or gametic phase equilibrium.

When these assumptions are met, they may provide good estimates of the population characteristics of the profile, given that the procedure for obtaining these estimates is consistent with the original matching window.

The statistical validity of assumptions (a)–(c) and the consistency of the relative frequency estimates with the match criterion will be discussed in greater detail in a later section.

5 Enter—Statistical Expert Witnesses

With this methodology, as with any new scientific evidence, most state courts may schedule a preliminary hearing (often called a Frye or Kelly–Frye hearing) so that a judge may rule on the admissibility of this particular kind of evidence. At first, at these hearings, the expert witnesses were laboratory forensicists, molecular biologists, and population geneticists. But is was soon noticed by defense attorneys that except for the laboratory procedures and the genetic principles involved, much of this evidence was statistical in nature. Some sought help from statisticians regarding the sampling of populations, the estimates obtained, and other issues. I was first brought in by the Hennepin County Minnesota Public Defenders office in early 1989 to help them understand the statistical calculations offered as evidence by the forensic laboratories.

There were generally two steps in the giving of expert testimony on DNA evidence. The first was the Kelly–Frye hearing before a judge who would hear the novel scientific issues and testimony by experts as to whether this DNA evidence was generally accepted by the scientific community. The judge would then rule on whether this novel procedure was admissible. If the ruling was positive, the evidence would then be used in the upcoming jury trial. In some cases the defense did not request this type of hearing and went directly to a jury trial. In many other instances the defense, concerned about the validity of the DNA evidence, engaged experts who strongly questioned the reliability of the evidence in Kelly–Frye hearings.

One of the first aspects of the Kelly–Frye hearing was to qualify the experts who were brought to testify. Statistical defense experts were usually closely questioned as to whether they had formal training in the genetics of DNA and whether or not they have had ever worked in a DNA laboratory by the prosecutors, who hoped for a quick disqualification if the answers were negative. Oddly enough, other kinds of experts were permitted to testify about statistical issues without being subjected to extensive questions on their statistical background. Of course, anybody can do statistics.

These Kelly–Frye hearings were conducted by judges who ruled in their state districts as to the admissibility of the novel DNA evidence. Appeals from either side would often be settled by the highest state court. However, as either a new laboratory or new methods such as PCR came into the picture, these would frequently occasion further Kelly–Frye hearings for a ruling on admissibility of their "novel" DNA evidence. Since 1993 there has been a different standard in federal cases. The United States Supreme Court in Daubert vs. Merrell Dow held that the Federal Rules of Evidence (especially rule 702), not Kelly-Frye, provide the standard of admitting expert scientific evidence in federal court. This is known as the "Daubert" standard, which suggested several criteria judges could use in assessing the reliability of scientific evidence. One of which was the "Frye" standard of general acceptance by the scientific community. However, it gave the court greater latitude in ruling on the legal admissibility of DNA evidence.

6   Flawed Sampling

For RFLP–VNTR profiling the FBI and Cellmark have established statistical procedures that I and others have criticized as flawed in affidavits, depositions, hearings, and court testimony. It is to be noted that both laboratories have consistently claimed in case after case that their methods favor the suspect. We have already disposed of this claim for the initial match criterion as either being false or without support.

Expert "statistical" testimony engaged by prosecutors and forensic laboratories has been mainly from population geneticists and biomathematicians. They have supported the statistical estimates submitted by the laboratories. Remembering that the relative frequency estimates depend on assumptions (a)–(c) of Section 4, we shall investigate their validity. We first examine (a) random sampling from a homogeneous racial population. Cellmark is probably the worst offender in this regard. Their entire African-American, or Black, database was obtained from donors to a Detroit blood bank except for a relatively small number of Cellmark paternity cases. The Detroit group were all rare blood donors and self-described as Black. The head of the blood bank, who had sent the samples to Cellmark, stated when asked whether the sampling was random and the individuals unrelated that he was not familiar with random sampling nor did he have knowledge concerning familial relationships among the donors nor had he any interest in creating a population genetics database.[1]

The Caucasian database was obtained from the Blood Bank of Delaware, whose director was told that the specimens would be used only for research. He was upset that Cellmark was using these specimens as a part of their marketing

---

[1]Letter from A. W. Shafer, executive director, Southeastern Michigan Chapter and Regional Blood Services, American Red Cross, to D. Wymore, Colorado chief deputy public defender. March 19, 1990.

strategy. He also questioned (as of course anyone would) how Cellmark could claim these specimens to be a cross section of the U.S. Caucasian population.[2] The Hispanic database was obtained from two blood banks in California and one in Miami. The California database consisted of individuals who probably were of Mexican heritage, and the one in Miami probably consisted primarily of those of Cuban heritage.

Less egregious were the FBI racial databases, obtained mostly from medical institutions that were larger in size and somewhat more dispersed. Caucasian specimens were obtained from Texas, California, Florida, and from FBI recruits. Black data were obtained from those three states as well. while Hispanic data was secured from Florida and Texas. It was also claimed that the individuals in the databases were unrelated. However, in a cleansing of their databases, it was discovered that using the FBI match criterion there were twenty-five apparent matches. A number were tracked down to duplicated submissions; other "matches" were deleted based solely on the match criterion (Sullivan 1992). In order words, they used the criterion to justify the criterion.

It became obvious that the initial attempt to justify the sample databases of both laboratories as random or even haphazard was hopeless. After a while expediency dictated that they assign some novel pseudo-technical term to their sampling procedures. These were now denoted as "convenience" sampling by prosecution experts, which rendered them devoid of any precise meaning for estimation.

7 Flawed Independence Assumption

The multiplication of each of the allele relative frequency estimates for the profile estimates requires mutual independence of alleles within and between loci for each of the populations sampled. Even if all of the assumptions were correct, it is clear that this product estimator is biased and has a sampling distribution so skewed that most of the time it will underestimate the population profile relative frequency (Balding 1995, Geisser 1996), once again belying claims of favoring the suspect.

An analysis using χ^2 tests from quantile contingency tables proposed by Geisser and Johnson (1992) demonstrated that most of the loci used by the FBI are not in Hardy–Weinberg equilibrium (Geisser and Johnson 1993). A test for pairwise independence of the loci was developed in Geisser and Johnson (1995), and several pairs can be shown not to be independent (unpublished).

With regard to Cellmark's RFLP–VNTR probes, four our of five loci were found not to be in Hardy–Weinberg equilibrium for all three racial databases. Some of the results for the Black databases appear in Geisser and Johnson (1995). There is some difficulty in testing linkage equilibrium on all the pairs of Cellmark's

---

[2]Letter from R. L. Traver, executive vice-president, Blood Bank of Delaware, to A. Sincox, assistant public defender, Cook County, Illinois. October 19, 1992

data because of the paucity of observations that were measured on all of the loci. See Table five of Geisser 1996. Tests for mutual dependence on the five loci are virtually precluded because of the very small number of individuals who are measured on all 5 probes, e.g., 2 for Blacks, 75 for Caucasians, and 59 Hispanics. However, tests on many of the pairs indicate pairwise dependence. In many court cases judicial protective orders prohibited publication of tests of independence on Cellmark data by defense experts (*Michigan vs. Chandler*, Washtenaw County, 1992). However, prosecution experts were permitted by Cellmark to publish their results on the data (Weir 1992). Prevention of publication of analysis of data by defense experts is a reprehensible tactic used by both laboratories. A publication carries significantly more weight in a Kelly–Frye or "Daubert" hearing than a submitted report which the judge probably will not understand. Thus it becomes a tactic promoted by forensic laboratories and aided and abetted by prosecutors.

A survey of various independence tests for RFLP–VNTR data is given by Mueller (1999).

8   Biased and Inconsistent Estimation Procedures

Estimation of the relative frequency of a pair of alleles in a locus from a homogeneous population using the product rule requires independence. Simply put, it means that if a_1 has probability p_1 of occurring and a_2 has probability p_2 of occurring, and they are different alleles, then the probability of the pairs is $2p_1p_2 = q$. Estimates of p_1 and p_2 are obtained from the data base, assuming that it is a random sample of unrelated individuals from a homogeneous population said to be in Hardy–Weinberg equilibrium. Multiplication of the q's for the various loci in that population results in the probability of the profile (assuming that the profile is made of distinctive alleles at each locus).

The FBI carries out estimation of the p_i's for a locus by arranging the alleles in the database in bins according to their size. At the start they used 31 different bins, but due to the size of the databases, they were soon reduced to a minimum of 13 and a maximum of 26, depending on the locus. They estimate the relative frequency of an allele a_i as the fraction of the total of the alleles that lie in the same bin as a_i, with a slight modification if a_i is too close to a bin boundary. Thus $\hat{p}_i = f_i/(2N)$, where f_i is the number of database alleles in the bin and $2N$ the total number of alleles in the database. Then for two distinct alleles at a locus their estimate is $\hat{q} = 2\hat{p}_1\hat{p}_2$, and for several loci in linkage equilibrium the entire estimated relative frequency of the profile is the product of the $\hat{q}$'s of the individual loci. As mentioned, their estimator is biased in the direction of underestimating the true value even when the mutual independence assumption holds. This is one kind of bias, but there is a much larger one. Fung (1996), in criticizing the FBI's assertion that their binning procedure favored the defendant, showed that this was not the case, as generally more than half the bins had a percentage width relative to its midpoint in excess of 10%, i.e., ±5% as their match criterion dictated for the original 31 bins. Geisser (1998) also showed that this was true even for the reduced number of bins that came into current use.

However, there is even a much more serious bias. The appropriate or fair percentage should be ±9.1%, or 18.2%, because the alleles are on a different gel than the ones in the database. Recall that the standard deviation of the difference between the suspect and a database gel is 1.82 larger than the initial comparison made on the same gel. In order to make a fair and consistent assessment of the procedure for the initial match and the match of the suspect allele with the database alleles one should use the same type of floating bin procedure. However, since the suspect allele and alleles from the database are on different gels, the match window should now be increased to ±9.1% instead of ±5% as the initial match comparison that is made on the same gel. A comparison was made between the FBI fixed bin cum product rule approach and one that uses the ±9.1% floating bin using the FBI's Caucasian base. Geisser (1998) considered the number of direct pairwise matches and compared it to the use of the FBI procedure in the database. It became apparent that the FBI underestimation of the relative frequency was a factor between 10^2 and 10^5 for four loci. This factor will increase with increasing loci. It had generally been assumed that a six-locus match between unrelated individuals was impossible to find. In fact, a six-locus match was found in the Caucasian database. Certainly, this demonstrates that the FBI's claim of favoring the defendant has no basis in fact. Indeed, the opposite is true.

9   Scientific and Legal Conduct

For those who are asked to become expert witnesses in criminal cases, it may be instructive to relate my experiences in several cases in which I served as an expert witness. Early on it became apparent that there was great difficulty in obtaining the databases from the forensic laboratories. It should be noted that prosecution experts had access to the databases and published analyses based on them. While the defense attorneys, at my insistence, would request the databases, they were initially not overly disappointed by a refusal on the grounds the data were proprietary. Their hope was that the judge would then throw out the evidence. It must be remembered that the job of the prosecutor is to attempt to secure the admissibility of any "evidence" that can potentially incriminate the defendant. The defense attorney, on the other hand, will attempt to have the court dismiss any evidence that may be harmful to the defendant's case. When the defense attorneys fail to have evidence from the databases dismissed, they will then work hard to get court orders to obtain them. Finally, in a specific case, when a judge ordered this to happen, the form in which databases were surrendered by the FBI was unusable for a proper analysis by the defense. However, the material was supplied, in the form requested, to one of the prosecution experts. Hearing my complaint, this expert generously sent me an appropriate diskette, to the chagrin of the FBI.

Since there is great stress on the "science" of this technology in Kelly–Frye-type hearings, an unpublished expert's report carries far less weight than a peer-reviewed article in a scientific journal. When I first submitted a coauthored paper on a method for testing Hardy–Weinberg equilibrium, interesting things happened. I had been engaged by the Hennepin County Minnesota Public Defender to examine data and offer expert testimony at a DNA admissibility hearing (*Minnesota vs. Alt*, Olmstead County, 1992). Seven days before my scheduled court date, a faxed letter was sent to me by the prosecutor in the Alt case. The fax was sent to me at 4:19 p.m. The letter asked that I produce copies of any forensic DNA articles (along with correspondence and peer review comments) I had authored and submitted to a scientific journal.

The paper that had been under submission was entitled, "Testing Hardy–Weinberg Equilibrium on Allelic Data from VNTR Loci." This short coauthored paper presented statistical methods for assessing the validity of certain procedures used by forensic laboratories engaged in DNA profiling.It avoided some of the problems associated with other statistical tests that had been used. The manuscript was submitted to the *American Journal of Human Genetics* on November 19, 1991. As of January 15, 1992, I had not received any peer review comments from the journal editor, nor had the manuscript been circulated to other scientists or to any lawyers.

At approximately 4:34 p.m., just fifteen minutes after receiving the demand from the prosecutor. I received a fax from the editor of the *American Journal of Human Genetics* with a review of the paper. See Anderson (1992a).

Originally, there were two referees for the paper, and then a third was employed because the original two disagreed. All these were anonymous and confidential according to editorial policy. Reviewer A delivered an unusually virulent attack on the paper composed mainly of a series of trivial comments and accusations of ignorance. In addition, several substantive comments made by the reviewer were mathematically incorrect. (He claimed that the degrees of freedom we gave for the suggested quantile χ^2 test were wrong and according to him should have been much larger than what we derived.) In particular, he made a series of in-nuendoes about a critical result in the paper. He initially insinuated that it had been previously published by others. Then he stated that it was wrong. Finally, even if it were correct, he declared it to be a student exercise. This inconsistent line of reasoning was essentially refuted by reviewer B, who affirmed the correctness of the critical result. Reviewer C, who first thought the degrees of freedom to be in error in a different direction, later conceded it to be correct. Reviewer B accepted our results, but intimated that he knew "the author's stated position on the FBI." This raised my suspicion as to the identity of the referees because there was nothing in the paper that expressed a position regarding the FBI.

By their reviews (ye shall know them), it became abundantly clear who these "anonymous reviewers" were. Clearly, A and B had worked closely with the FBI and their databases. Later, in court, with great reluctance and pleading confidentiality, reviewer A was compelled by a judge in Seattle to admit his identity as a reviewer. My suspicion concerning reviewer B's identity was confirmed by an admission of the editor's assistant. Both reviewers A and B had special arrangements with the FBI for DNA research and appear in court as proponents of the FBI's methods. As a consequence, the ethical course would have been for them to recuse themselves from reviewing our paper or at least to relinquish anonymity with an accompanying disclaimer and a declaration of interest.

In particular, I regard A's review as a singularly blatant attempt, cloaked under the guise of anonymous peer review, to discredit me in court, knowing that I would be compelled to produce all reviewers' comments. Clearly, the FBI must have learned of this paper, probably from reviewer A or B or both, and forwarded this knowledge to the prosecutor, who pretended lack of such knowledge but unfortunately was just a little too quick with his request. It was also disclosed that reviewer A et al. in a National Institute of Justice grant application (*Washington vs. Copeland*, King County, January 1992), which was funded, stated in the proposal that the expected product of the grant was to generate publications and make presentations at national meetings that will lend credibility to the FBI's statistical methods. As evidenced by his handling of my manuscript, reviewer A behaved as if his funding from the Justice Department requires not only that he endorse the methods used by the FBI but that he denounce manuscripts that could potentially question FBI methods. The face that A did not recuse himself but attempted anonymity was, in my view, unethical and contrary to the proper function of peer review. The paper was published later that year (Geisser and Johnson 1992). Cases of FBI meddling, pressure, and prosecutorial interference in the refereeing process are related in greater detail in a report of the AAAS Newsletter, and there aptly summarized, for the most part, by Barry Scheck (1992).

At any rate, a bit later, I was somewhat perplexed when B sent me a paper by A to referee for the journal *Genetics*. But I declined, as I regarded it as a conflict of interest.

After these events were learned by the editor, he wrote that if he had known of the situation, neither A nor B would have been engaged as reviewers. He also suggested that I and my coauthor prepare a paper analyzing all the FBI databases according to our methods, which we welcomed. I told him, however, that I strongly doubted that the FBI would give us permission to make an independent analysis for publication. They had continually balked at providing the data in a utilizable form that allowed testing of the critical assumptions that they make. When they finally acceded to court orders to do so, they arranged to have the data sealed under a protective order. The editor suggested that I prepare an analysis anyway. I asked him whether such a protective order could be legally contravened. An opinion was solicited by the editor from his lawyer as to his potential liability as well as ours (the authors) if such data were used without the generator's permission. The opinion by his lawyer clearly indicated no liability for the editor, but uncertain liability of the authors of such a publication. In light of this fact, the editor instructed me to seek permission from the FBI to make such an analysis of their databases. With some reluctance, because of my past experience with the FBI and prosecutors working closely with them, I finally requested permission of Bruce Budowle, an employee of the FBI, who generated the data and who devised the FBI procedures using fixed bins and the product rule. Dr. Budowle had already testified in Minnesota vs. Alt that the Hennepin County prosecutor had given him the paper and the reviewers' comments prior to my receipt of the fax letter from the editor. Under questioning he also revealed that he had balked at a request by the counsel for the *American Journal of Genetics* to allow publication of an analysis of the FBI database by me.

A response came about a month later from James Kearney, then head of the section on forensic science research. After first expressing concern regarding the use of FBI databases by me, he also questioned my intent. He then criticized me for not seeking such permission earlier (as if it would have been granted). He went on to indicate that the FBI had already provided the data to A and B as well as to Bernard Devlin and Neil Risch. Finally, he wrote, "We are willing to approve your use of FBI population data with certain provisions. You must be sensitive to the fact that previous commitments have been made with other researchers, and the particular study you are doing must not conflict with these projects. The FBI data may be used only in a joint collaboration with Dr. Budowle." He further wrote, "The use of the data is restricted to this one paper. All parties (i.e., the authors) must agree to the entire contents of a final manuscript prior to submission to a journal. Any changes whatsoever in the manuscript must be agreed upon by all collaborating parties." It is also interesting to note that Kearney sat on panels that awarded a National Institute of Justice grant to A.

Obviously, an independent study under such provisions would be totally compromised, if not impossible. It completely violates the 1992 National Academy of Sciences report on DNA technology in *Forensic Science*, page 91, which states, "It scientific evidence is not yet ready for scientific scrutiny and public re-evaluation by others, it is not yet ready for court." By the way, A and B, as well as other prosecution experts, Devlin and Risch, had all published articles based on the FBI databases without Budowle as a coauthor.

In late August of 1992, I received a letter from John Hicks, then director of the laboratory division of the FBI, saying that Kearney's letter had been misunderstood and that FBI approval was not necessary for my use of the data, since it was in the public domain. Of course, one might ask why a protective order (Washington vs. Copeland, King County, July 1991), was put on the data. The answer is, of course, to conceal, if possible, and probably to intimidate. For further details on this incident see Anderson 1992 a, b. An analysis of the FBI databases was published the following year (Geisser and Johnson 1993).

As an interesting and current aftermath, a major scandal involving the FBI laboratory was reported by the Associated Press on August 7, 1998. The Assistant Attorney General of the United States, Stephen Colgate, wrote as part of his report that "consistent and often spirited FBI opposition [is made] to any conclusion that its employees have engaged in misconduct or performed poorly." He also indicated that had John Hicks and James Kearney not retired, he would have also proposed disciplining them regarding their negligence.

Another interesting side-note was a review paper by Kathryn Roeder (1994), who discussed our quantile contingency tests. She dismissed them because of some simulations in a paper by Devlin and Risch (1993), using sextiles. That paper claimed that simulation indicated that coalescence (a blurring on the autoradiograph such that presumably close but different bands are erroneously judged to be the same) would tend to make the quantile χ^2 test overly sensitive to finding dependence. It was now raised from insensitive, by reviewer A, to overly sensitive, a remarkable test indeed. The latter would have some modest force only if a large number of quantiles had been used. But most of the tests that indicated dependence used only two or three quantiles, where coalescence plays a negligible part if any at all. We had responded to the Devlin and Risch criticism, in Geisser and Johnson (1993), but this was not cited.

I wrote to the editor to indicate that Roeder had again gotten the degrees of freedom wrong for the test (the third person to do so), and I inquired whether I could respond to her criticism. The editor of *Statistical Science* denied me that opportunity but agreed to bring to her attention the correct degrees of freedom. In a later issue, she acknowledged her error regarding the degrees of freedom. It turned out that Bernard Devlin has been an expert witness for the FBI and Lifecodes (a forensic laboratory that had been active early on in DNA cases). He and I have had strong disagreements about the statistical analysis of DNA data in the various court cases in which we both have appeared on opposite sides. Further, I later learned that Devlin is Roeder's husband. I also thought that since the editor was a member of the same statistics department as Roeder, he should have allowed me to respond for the sake of dispelling the appearance of showing favoritism, but perhaps that was pushing the envelope on my part.

Other defense-expert witnesses have been harassed and pressured by prosecutors. For example, a California prosecutor, threatened Lawrence Mueller, a defense expert population geneticist, with jail because Mueller had not yet changed this out-of-state license for a California driver's license. Two distinguished population geneticists, Daniel Hartl and Richard Lewontin, who testified in a case for the defense, were "lobbied" by a federal prosecutor, who had obtained galleys of their paper prior to publication in *Science*, not to publish. This was described by Hartl as an attempt at intimidation, while the prosecutor benignly called it an "amiable chat." To avoid this type of pressure, Hartl ceased testifying. Simon Ford, a British citizen who is a defense expert, alleges that he was sufficiently intimidated by the same California prosecutor, who threatened to see to it that his immigration status would be revoked so that he no longer could testify. Much of this and more is described by Roberts (1992).

These incidents, while extremely disturbing and actually having untoward consequences in the pursuit of justice, are still not quite as flagrantly unethical and deceitful as what was perpetrated by the Washington County of Oregon prosecutor in the Libby Affair.

Randall Libby is a molecular biologist and court-appointed expert witness who testified for the defense in a murder case, *Oregon vs. Cunningham*, Washington County, 1994. The prosecutor, irritated with Libby's affidavit, initiated grand jury proceedings alleging perjury on the part of Libby. He obtained an indictment against Libby in May, 1995. That a prosecutor can "get an indictment against a proverbial ham sandwich" is borne out to a great extent by the prosecutor's deputy, who testified in *Oregon vs. Cunningham* under oath that grand juries in Washington County are accusatorial and inquisitorial. As soon as the indictment was obtained, the prosecutor faxed copies of it around the country in hopes of discrediting Libby. After considerable travail, Libby was acquitted in a trial in 1996. Discovering what the prosecutor had done, he demanded that he advise all those individuals to whom he had sent copies of the indictment that Libby was now acquitted of the charges for which the state had prosecuted him. The prosecutor refused, and Libby brought a civil rights claim against him. This was finally settled out of court, resulting in the Oregon Department of Justice sending letters to all of the prosecutor's correspondents that Libby had been acquitted.

What is to be learned from these incidents? Clearly, testifying for the defense in high-profile murder cases can subject one to abuse, harassment, intimidation, witch hunts, accusations of criminal conduct, indictment, and a criminal trail. Winning high-profile cases is a boon for a politically active prosecutor, and some will go to any length to achieve this objective. The defense expert witness can refrain from getting involved or get angry and testify despite potential consequences. If one does so, it is advisable to make certain that you have the backing of excellent attorneys and a good deal of available funds, as justice can be very expensive.

10   Remarks

At the request of the editor and publisher, the identity of journal reviewers, editors, and prosecutors has been withheld.

11   Cases Cited

Minnesota vs. Johnson, Fourth Judicial Court, 1991.
Michigan vs. Chandler, Washtenaw County, 1992.
Minnesota vs. Alt, Olmsted County, July 1991, January 1992.
Oregon vs. Cunningham, Washington County, 1994.
Washington vs. Copeland, King County, July 1991, January 1992.

REFERENCES

[1] Anderson, C. (1992a). Conflict concerns disrupt panels, clouds testimony. *Nature* 355 753–754.

[2] Anderson, C. (1992b). FBI attaches strings to its database. *Nature* 357.

[3] Balding, D.J. (1995). Estimating products in forensic identification using DNA profiles. *Journal of the American Statistical Association*, 90 839–844.

[4] Budowle B., Giusti, A.M., Wayne, J.S. Baechtel, F.S., Fourney, R.M., Adams, D.E., Presley, L.A., Deadman H.A., and Monson, K.L. (1991). Fixed bin analysis for statistical evaluation of continuous distributions of allelic data from VNTR loci for use in forensic comparisons. *American Journal of Human Genetics* 48 841–855.

[5] Delvin, B. and Risch, N. (1993). Physical properties of VNTR data and their impact on a test of allelic independence. *American Journal of Human Genetics* 53 324–328.

[6] Fung, W.K. (1996). 10% or 5% match window in DNA profiling, *Forensic Science International* 111–118.

[7] Geisser, S. (1996). Some statistical issues in forensic DNA profiling, *Modeling and Prediction*, eds. J.C. Lee et al., Springer, 3–18.

[8] Geisser, S. (1998). The statistics of DNA forensics. *Utilitas Matematica*, 63. 125–140.

[9] Geisser, S. and Johnson, W. (1992). Testing Hardy–Weinberg equilibrium on allelic data from VNTR loci. *American Journal of Human Genetics* 51 1084–1088.

[10] Geisser, S. and Johnson, W. (1993). Testing independence of fragment lengths within VNTR loci. *American Journal of Human Genetics* 53 1103–1106.

[11] Geisser, S. and Johnson, W. (1995). Testing independence when the form of the bivariate distribution is unspecified. *Statistics in Medicine*. 14 1621–1639.

[12] Jeffreys, A.J., Wilson, V. and Thein, S.L. (1985a). Hypervariable "minisatellite" regions in human DNA. *Nature* 314 76–79.

[13] Mueller, L.D. (1999). The DNA typing controversy and NRC II. *Statistics in Genetics*, IMA Vol. 114 eds. M.E. Halloran et al, Springer, 1–23.

[14] Neufeld, P. and Coleman, N. (1990). When Science Takes the Witness Stand, 262 *Scientific American* 46.

[15] Roberts, L. (1992). Science in court: A culture clash. *Science* 257 732–736.

[16] Roeder, K. (1994). DNA fingerprinting: A review of the controversy. *Statistical Science* 9 222–278.

[17] Scheck, B. (1992). Newsletter of AAAS, Frankel, M.S. ed., V, 2, 7–8.

[18] Sullivan, P. (1992). DNA Fingerprint matches. *Science* 256 1743–1744.

[19] Weir, B.S. (1992). Independence of VNTR alleles defined as floating bins. *American Journal of Human Genetics* 51 992–997.

The Consequences of Defending DNA Statistics

B.S. Weir

Abstract

I describe my involvement with the forensic uses of DNA evidence. This involvement has centered on the statistical aspects of assigning weight to matching DNA profiles, with particular attention to issues of independence, population structure, mixtures, and uniqueness. Many pitfalls in interpreting DNA evidence can be avoided if a coherent approach based on the use of likelihood ratios is used. These ratios are of the probabilities of evidence given alternative propositions, and should not be confused with probabilities of the propositions given the evidence.

Keywords: DNA profiles, likelihood ratios, uniqueness, independence, population structure.

1 Introduction

My experience with statistical science in the courtroom began in late 1989 when I received a call from the FBI scientist responsible for developing DNA technology for forensic identification in the US. He was concerned by the claims of a population geneticist that DNA evidence is unreliable because there is too much variation between human races—maybe even bigger differences in the frequencies of DNA types between races than between humans and other primates. This claim turned out not to be true, and forensic DNA profiles are now known to follow the same evolutionary relationships as do other genetic systems. I then attended some meetings of the FBI's Technical Working Group on DNA Methods and began to hear of the statistical challenges to this new identification tool.

By the end of 1990 I had been called to serve as an expert witness in a murder trial, where the same population geneticist had given evidence suggesting a lack of independence between components of a DNA profile. He had based his argument on the misapplication of an earlier paper of mine (Weir, 1979). I was asked to explain to the jury why the statistical reasoning used by the prosecution gave strong weight to the DNA evidence. I had the distinct impression at that time that the jury was absorbing what I said and believing my conclusions. I still remember the plane ride home, during which I checked my calculations yet again to make sure that I had not misled that jury. The defendant was convicted, as has been the situation in virtually every DNA case.

From 1990 to mid-1997 I testified for the prosecution in twenty-seven criminal trials and for the plaintiff in one civil trial, the most notable being the two trials involving football star O. J. Simpson. I ended my testifying days after a case in

Colorado when the defense objected that my use of Fisher's exact test was hearsay and that the prosecution needed to call Mr. Fisher to the stand. It was clear that the public defender was not at all interested in hypothesis testing and was simply interrupting my testimony. I was wasting my time.

The most satisfying aspect of my court work was the knowledge that I was helping with the introduction of a technology that has a huge potential benefit in many areas requiring individual identification. The negative aspects have been the public disagreement with statisticians whose work I respect, and my present failure to convince some US forensic scientists to adopt a coherent approach to interpreting DNA evidence. In this chapter I will describe some of the statistical issues that have arisen, and that have affected my research. Many of the issues have been summarized in a recent text (Evett and Weir, 1998).

2   Independence

Individuals receive genetic information from each parent, and it will be convenient here to describe this information as the material, or pairs of alleles, that an individual receives at a series of loci. There has been a recent move in the US to standardize forensic DNA typing on a set of 13 core loci, so that a DNA profile will consist of 26 alleles. Each locus may have from two to ten or more alleles in the population. A locus with m allelic types has $m(m + 1)/2$ possible allelic pairs, or genotypes. The number of possible genotypes at the 13 loci far exceeds the number of people living on earth.

When the DNA profile from a crime sample matches that from a known person, either a suspected perpetrator of the crime or a victim of the crime, that person is not excluded as a possible source of the sample. A preliminary indication of the strength of this DNA evidence is provided by an estimate of the probability of finding the matching profile in a "random" member of the population. Although this does not lead to the best description of the evidentiary strength of the DNA match, it will be useful here to pursue the idea of estimating the probability. Unless very few loci have been typed, it is virtually certain that the profile will not be seen in any sample from the population, so there is a problem in estimating the probability of the profile from that sample. One solution would be to add the profile seen in the known person and/or in the crime sample so that the probability could be estimated as one or two divided by the sample size increased by one or two. The problem is that this "counting method" would give the same answer regardless of how many loci were typed for the profile, whereas it would seem that the strength of the match should be greater as more loci were used.

The simplest remedy is to assume the constituent alleles are independent and estimate the profile probability as the product of the many separate sample allele frequencies. It is not unusual for an allele to have an observed relative frequency of about 0.1, so that the product can be an extremely small number. Numbers like 1 in 7.87 trillion are reported (OIC, 1998). Because the "product rule" rests so heavily on allelic independence, there were immediate challenges to this assumption, and most of my early involvement centered on responding to these challenges. Assumptions of independence have often been made with little justification in forensic science: downstrokes in a signature in the Howland will case of 1868 (Meier and Zabell, 1980), and physical attributes described by an eyewitness of two robbers in the Collins case of 1968 (Finkelstein, 1978). The conviction of Mr. Collins was reversed by the California Supreme Court, in part because of the probability calculations.

The independence of the two alleles an individual receives at one locus is an assumption that pervades population genetics, in applications ranging from evolutionary studies to the locating of human disease genes. Independence would be expected if individuals mated at random within infinite populations and there were no evolutionary forces such as mutation or selection. Such conditions do not hold for real populations, but statistical methods were in place (e.g., Weir, 1990) to test for departures from Hardy–Weinberg equilibrium, as this independence is known. These methods had been devised for loci with relatively small numbers of alleles, and the forensic scientists in 1990 were using loci with 20 to 30 alleles. We explored several strategies (Weir, 1992a, 1992b, 1993e; Evett et al., 1996; Hamilton et al., 1996; Maiste and Weir, 1995; McIntyre and Weir, 1997; Zaykin et al., 1995) and found little evidence for departures from Hardy–Weinberg. This work has some implications for population genetics (e.g., Weir, 1996b), and had immediate implications for the acceptance of DNA profile evidence. The longer-term forensic implications, however, may be slight. There has been a move towards an acknowledgment of some departures from independence, and adoption of a formulation that accommodates these departures (e.g., NRC, 1996). The work on testing for independence has shown that the level of dependence in many different populations is likely to be low.

There is also the statistical issue of power. The probability of detecting small departures from independence is low in samples of realistic size: A sample of over 100,000 is needed for 90% probability of detecting the levels of departure from the Hardy–Weinberg likely value for a two-allele locus in human populations. The problem is worse for tests with multiple loci. We explored exact tests for multiple loci (Zaykin et al., 1995) but realize (J.S. Buckleton, personal communication) that such tests are of limited use when every multilocus genotype occurs once or not at all in a sample. Alternatives to assuming independence between loci have not yet been developed. As for within-locus dependencies, however, the magnitude of between-locus dependencies must be low. It is straightforward, for example, to conduct empirical studies that show the numbers of matches at n loci between all pairs of profiles in a forensic database declines with n at the rate expected under independence assumptions. These demonstrations can be used to great effect in the courtroom.

3   Population Structure

Human populations are not homogeneous. Geography and culture both raise barriers to random mating and therefore contribute to allelic dependencies. An early concern was that a crime may have been committed by someone belonging to a subpopulation for which allelic frequencies were not available. What relevance would population-wide frequencies have? The answer lay in population genetic theory, which was brought into prominence by Nichols and Balding (1991) and Balding and Nichols (1994). My late colleague C.C. Cockerham pointed me to the role of his methodology in formulating the probability of an unknown person having a specific genotype when it is known that another person in the (sub)population has that genotype. This was developed in Weir 1994c, 1996b and Evett and Weir 1998. Briefly, the theory allows for variation of allele frequencies among subpopulations and uses population-wide frequencies in expressions that apply in expectation to all subpopulations. Although this is a population-genetic argument, use is made of a fundamental concept in evidence interpretation—the need to consider alternative explanations for the evidence. The explanation that a particular biological sample did not originate from the defendant in a trial leads naturally to the need for conditional DNA profile probabilities.

The concept is embedded in the conclusion (Evett and Weir, 1998) that what is needed to interpret DNA evidence is the probability, under alternative scenarios, of finding a particular profile when it has already been seen at least once. This, in turn, rests on the need to compare the probabilities of the DNA evidence under alternative hypotheses. The prosecution hypothesis H_p may be

$$H_p : \text{the suspect left the crime sample,}$$

and the defense hypothesis H_d may be

$$H_d : \text{some other person left the crime sample.}$$

The evidence E is that the profiles G_S and G_C of the suspect and the crime sample are both of type G, and then the ratio of probabilities (the likelihood ratio) is (Evett and Weir, 1998)

$$\text{LR} = \frac{\Pr(E|H_p)}{\Pr(E|H_d)}$$
$$= \frac{1}{\Pr(G_C = G|G_S = G, H_d)}.$$

It is the conditional probability that can incorporate the effects of population structure or other dependencies between individuals, such as that imposed by family relationships. The need to assume independence of allele frequencies in the whole population (but not in the subpopulation) is removed with this formulation.

One of my great disappointments has been the failure of the US forensic bureaucracy to embrace current forensic science literature and join other countries in adopting the use of likelihood ratios. There has been concern that this approach would be too complex to explain in court, although my experience would suggest otherwise. The problem may lie in the lack of sufficient statistical training within forensic science training programs.

4 Mixtures

In many crimes there are samples containing biological material from more than one person. For example, a person who cut himself while stabbing other people may have both his own blood and the victims' blood on his glove, which could then be transferred to his car as he drove away from the crime scene. This was the explanation put forward by the prosecution in the Simpson case to account for several of the blood stains found in Simpson's car and on a glove found at Simpson's house (Weir, 1995c). At the time of the trial, the US forensic community felt constrained by a single sentence in a report of the National Research Council (NRC, 1992):

> If a suspect's pattern is found within the mixed pattern, the appropriate frequency to assign such a "match" is the sum of the frequencies of all genotypes that are contained within (i.e., that are a subset of) the mixed pattern.

If a locus has only two alleles, A and B, in the population, there are three genotypes AA, AB, and BB. If a DNA profile AB is known to be from a sample that had two contributors, then these people could have been of types AA, AB or AA, BB or AB, AB or AB, BB. Two people who were both of type AA or both of type BB do not have the AB profile between them, so there are some pairs of people who would be excluded as contributors. In other words, the evidence is not certain under the hypothesis of two contributors. The NRC procedure, however, would add the frequencies of all genotypes AA, AB, and BB so that the assigned frequency would be 100% and the DNA evidence from the sample would have no probative value. The Simpson defense wished to use this argument, and objected to prosecution plans not to present any statistical weight for mixed stains. The court agreed that statistics should be presented, and I was called to testify to the method that took into account the number of contributors. Even though the method had been published by Evett et al. (1991), it had not been adopted by the US forensic community, in part because of the NRC report (NRC, 1992).

I was able to convince the court that Evett's method was appropriate. This success was largely nullified when the defense found that I had made an error during some late-night computing during the period of my testimony. Subsequently, we were able to derive simple algebraic expressions to handle mixtures (Weir et al., 1997, Evett and Weir, 1998) and even to allow for the effects of population structure (Curran et al., 1999).

Because the Simpson case did not lead to an Appellate Court decision, my testimony there could not lead to any case law, although my colleagues and I have subsequently testified on mixtures using our published approach. US forensic agencies generally continue either to follow the 1992 NRC report, or not to give any statistical calculations at all for mixtures.

5 Uniqueness

Attaching probabilities to the event that two DNA profiles match when they are from different people becomes increasingly difficult as the profiles become based on more and more loci. It appears to be increasingly unlikely that two people, even if as closely related as sibs (identical twins excepted), could have equal profiles, and DNA profiles can be expected to lead to claims of identity in the same way as do fingerprints. Statistician Stigler (1995) considered that this universal acceptance of fingerprints as proof of identity had three sources: the ability to demonstrate the similarity of fingerprints in court, the successful use of fingerprints in high-profile cases, and the lack of any situation of different people being shown to have the same fingerprints. I have previously stated (Weir, 1995c) that I share Stigler's view (Stigler, 1995) that DNA profiles will come to have the same acceptance. Numbers will not be attached in most cases for DNA evidence, just as they are not attached to fingerprints.

In an attempt to hasten this declaration of identity, the 1996 NRC report suggested that uniqueness might be claimed when the probability of the profile not existing in a population (other than for the known person) was small. If the profile probability is P, the probability that N people do not have the profile was assumed by the NRC report to be the binomial expression $(1 - P)^N$. This led the FBI to announce a policy of declaring identity when P is estimated to be less than 1 in 260 billion, for then the probability of no one in the US population of 260 million having the profile is 99.9%. In a report written for the Office of the Independent Counsel, the FBI stated:

> Based on the results of these seven genetic loci, specimen K39 (CLIN-TON) is the source of the DNA obtained from specimen Q3243-1, to a reasonable degree of scientific certainty.

This argument ignores the effects of relatives, and the effects of evolutionary relatedness that provided the formulations for population structure mentioned above (Weir, 1999). Once again, sound statistical reasoning has not been applied.

6 Bayesian Statistics

The use of likelihood ratios leads to a full Bayesian approach to the interpretation of DNA evidence, by means of the equation

Posterior odds on guilt = Likelihood ratio × Prior odds on guilt.

Although this approach is used routinely in paternity case calculations, it has not been used very often in a forensic context, mainly because of the difficulty of assigning prior probabilities.

Bayesian analyses are being used increasingly in this field, however, just as they are in many areas of statistics. My interest in forensic uses of DNA has led to an examination of departures from Hardy–Weinberg (Shoemaker et al., 1998) in work that complements that of other authors (e.g., Lindley, 1988).

7 Educational Issues

This review has covered some of the scientific issues that I have been led to consider as a result of being asked to defend DNA statistics. At least as much of my energy has been devoted to educational efforts. This has included expository writing (Weir 1992d, 1993a–d, 1994a–b, 1995a–c, 1996a,c–d, 1998a–c; Weir and Hill, 1994) and joint authorship of a textbook (Evett and Weir, 1998). I have able to direct Ph.D. studies on the statistical issues (Li, 1997; Maiste, 1993; McIntyre, 1995; Shoemaker, 1998). A very enjoyable experience has been the presentation of short courses to forensic scientists, and this has led to the use of the Internet for distance learning (http://www.stat.ncsu.edu, click on "statistical genetics").

Not all of my educational efforts have been successful. Like many other statisticians (e.g., Berry, 1992) I have tried to explain the transposed conditional to members of the news media. They persist in writing statements like this from *Science* on November 21, 1997:

> Even in O.J. Simpson's trial, prosecutors could say only that the odds were billions to one that the blood found at the scene was not O.J.'s.

Reporters brush aside any suggestions that they have a responsibility to report accurately. Not only did my own local newspaper fail to include the issue in a story they wrote after sending a reporter from Raleigh, North Carolina, to Seattle, Washington, to interview me and listening to an explanation of the dangers of transposing the conditional (*News and Observer*, Raleigh NC, February 17, 1997), but also they edited my subsequent "Letter to the Editor" in a way that obscured the issue (*News and Observer*, Raleigh NC, February 24, 1997). Finally, the newspaper did publish the following crucial statement:

> When numbers are presented in court they are based on an estimated probability of finding a matching DNA profile in a random member of the population. They are not the probabilities of guilt or innocence.

(*News and Observer*, Raleigh NC, March 1, 1997.)

8 Conclusion

My involvement as a statistician in the issues surrounding the forensic use of DNA has been largely positive. It has introduced me to a fascinating area of research, it has taken me into the warm and dedicated forensic science community, and it has opened up new teaching opportunities. It has brought some prominence, although this has not always been complimentary. There have been frustrations with media distortions, with disingenuous arguments by some of my scientific colleagues in court who have challenged DNA statistics, and with the reluctance to accept sound statistics by others. In short, it has been a rich experience.

REFERENCES

[1] Balding, D.J. and R.A. Nichols. 1994. DNA profile match probability calculation: how to allow for population stratification, relatedness, database selection and single bands. *Forensic Science International* 64:125–140.

[2] Berry, D.A. 1992. Statistical issues in DNA identification, Billings (ed.) *DNA On Trial*, Cold Spring Harbor Laboratory Press.

[3] Buckleton, J.S., I.W. Evett, and B.S. Weir. 1998. Setting bounds for the likelihood ratio when multiple hypotheses are postulated. *Science and Justice* 38:23–26.

[4] Curran, J.M., C.M. Triggs, J.S. Buckleton, and B.S. Weir. 1999. Interpreting DNA mixtures in structured populations. *Journal of Forensic Sciences* 44: 44:987–995

[5] Evett, I.W., C. Buffery, G. Willott, and D. Stoney. 1991. A guide to interpreting single locus profiles of DNA mixtures in forensic cases. *Journal of the Forensic Science Society* 31:41–47.

[6] Evett, I.W., P.D. Gill, J.K. Scranage, and B.S. Weir. 1996. Establishing the robustness of STR statistics for forensic applications. *American Journal of Human Genetics* 58:398–407.

[7] Evett, I.W., J.A. Lambert, J.S. Buckleton, and B.S. Weir. 1996. Statistical analysis of a large file of data from STR profiles of British Caucasians to support forensic casework. *International Journal of legal Medicine* 109:173–177.

[8] Evett, I.W. and B.S. Weir. 1992. Flawed reasoning in court. *Chance* 4:19–21.

[9] Evett, I.W. and B.S. Weir. 1998. *Interpreting DNA Evidence*. Sinauer, Sunderland, MA.

[10] Federal Bureau of Investigation. 1998. Report of Examination. FBI File No. 29D-OIC-LR-35063, 08/17/98.

[11] Finkelstein, M.O. 1978. *Quantitative Methods in Law: Studies in the Application of Mathematical Probability and Statistics to Legal Problems*. The Free Press, New York.

[12] Hamilton, J.F., L. Starling, S.J. Cordiner, D.L. Monahan, J.S. Buckleton, G.K. Chambers, and B.S. Weir. 1996. New Zealand population data at five VNTR loci: validation as databases for forensic identity testing. *Science and Justice* 36:109–117.

[13] Li, Y-J. 1996. *Characterizing the Structure of Genetic Populations.* Ph.D. thesis, Department of Statistics, North Carolina State University, Raleigh NC.

[14] Lindley, D.V. 1988. Statistical inference concerning Hardy–Weinberg equilibrium. *Bayesian Statistics* 3:307–326.

[15] Maiste, P.J. 1993. *Comparison of Statistical Tests for Independence at Genetic Loci with Many Alleles.* Ph.D. thesis, Department of Statistics, North Carolina State University, Raleigh NC.

[16] Maiste, P.J. and B.S. Weir. 1995. A comparison of tests for independence in the FBI RFLP databases. *Genetica* 96:125–138.

[17] McIntyre, L.M. 1996. *DNA fingerprinting and Hardy–Weinberg Equilibrium: A Continuous Analysis of VNTR Data.* Ph.D. thesis, Department of Statistics, North Carolina State University, Raleigh NC.

[18] McIntyre, L.M. and B.S. Weir. 1997. Hardy–Weinberg testing for continuous data. *Genetics* 147:1965–1975.

[19] Meier, P. and S. Zabell. 1980. Benjamin Peirce and the Howland will. *Journal of the American Statistical Association* 75:497–506.

[20] National Research Council. 1992. *DNA Technology in Forensic Science.* National Academy Press, Washington, DC.

[21] National Research Council. 1996. *The Evaluation of Forensic DNA Evidence.* National Academy Press, Washington, DC.

[22] Nichols, R.A. and D.J. Balding. 1991. Effects of population structure on DNA fingerprint analysis in forensic science. *Heredity* 66:297–302.

[23] Office of the Independent Counsel. 1998. Report to Congress. Narrative Section B.1 Physical Evidence.

[24] Shoemaker, J. 1998. *A Bayesian Characterization of Genetic Disequilibria.* Ph.D. thesis, Department of Statistics, North Carolina State University, Raleigh NC.

[25] Shoemaker, J., I.S. Painter, and B.S. Weir. 1998. A Bayesian characterization of Hardy–Weinberg disequilibrium. *Genetics* 149:2079–2088.

[26] Stigler, S.M. 1995. Galton and identification by fingerprints. *Genetics* 140:857–860.

[27] Weir, B.S. 1979. Inferences about linkage disequilibrium. *Biometrics* 25:235–254.

[28] Weir, B.S. 1990. *Genetic Data Analysis.* Sinauer, Sunderland, MA.

[29] Weir, B.S. 1992a. Independence of VNTR alleles defined as fixed bins. *Genetics* 130:873–887.

[30] Weir, B.S. 1992b. Independence of VNTR alleles defined as floating bins. *American Journal of Human Genetics* 51:992–997.

[31] Weir, B.S. 1992c. Discussion of "Statistical inference in crime investigations using DNA profiling" by D.A. Berry et al. *Applied Statistics* 41:528–529.

[32] Weir, B.S. 1992d. Population genetics in the forensic DNA debate. *Proceedings of the National Academy of Sciences, USA* 89:11654–11659.

[33] Weir, B.S. 1993a. Forensic population genetics and the National Research Council (NRC). *American Journal of Human Genetics* 52:437–440.

[34] Weir, B.S. 1993b. DNA fingerprinting report. *Science* 260:473.

[35] Weir, B.S. 1993c. The Status of DNA fingerprinting. *The World & I.* November, 1993, 214–219.

[36] Weir, B.S. 1993d. Review of "DNA on Trial: Genetic Identification and Criminal Justice" edited by P.J. Billings. *American Journal of Human Genetics* 53:1158–1160.

[37] Weir, B.S. 1993e. Tests for independence of VNTR alleles defined as quantile bins. *American Journal of Human Genetics* 53:1107–1113.

[38] Weir, B.S. 1994a. DNA profiling on trial. *Nature* 369:351.

[39] Weir, B.S. 1994b. Discussion of "DNA fingerprinting: A review of the controversy" by K. Roeder, *Statistical Science* 9:222–278.

[40] Weir, B.S. 1994c. The effects of inbreeding on forensic calculations. *Annual Reviews of Genetics* 28:597–621.

[41] Weir, B.S. 1995a. Discussion of "Inference in forensic identification" by D.J. Balding and P. Donnelly, *Journal of The Royal Statistical Society* 158:21–53.

[42] Weir, B.S. (editor) 1995b. *Human Identification: The Use of DNA markers.* Kluwer, Dordrecht.

[43] Weir, B.S. 1995c. DNA statistics in the Simpson matter. *Nature Genetics* 11:365–368.

[44] Weir, B.S. 1996a. Statistics in court. Stats 16:15–17.

[45] Weir, B.S. 1996b. *Genetic Data Analysis II.* Sinauer, Sunderland, MA.

[46] Weir, B.S. 1996c. Presenting DNA statistics in court. *Proceedings of the Sixth International Symposium on Human Identification* 128–136.

[47] Weir, B.S. 1996d. Invited editorial: The second National Research Council report on forensic DNA evidence. *American Journal of Human Genetics* 59:497–500.

[48] Weir, B.S. 1998a. Statistical methods employed in evaluation of single-locus probe results in criminal identity cases. pp. 83–96 in P.J. Lincoln and J. Thomson (eds.) *Methods in Molecular Biology* 98: Forensic DNA Profiling Protocols. Humana Press, Totowa, NJ.

[49] Weir, B.S. 1998b. The coancestry coefficient in forensic science. *Proceedings of the 8th International Symposium on Human Identification*, 87–91.

[50] Weir, B.S. 1998c. Quantifying the genetic structure of populations with application to paternity calculations, pp. 31–44 in M.E. Halloran and S. Geisser (eds.) *Statistics in Genetics* Volume 112 of IMA Volumes in Mathematics and its Applications. Springer-Verlag, New York.

[51] Weir, B.S. 1999. Are DNA profiles unique? *Proceedings of the 9th International Symposium on Human Identification* pp. 114–117.

[52] Weir, B.S. and J.S. Buckleton. 1996. Statistical issues in DNA profiling. *Advances in Forensic Haemogenetics.* 6:457–464.

[53] Weir, B.S. and I.W. Evett. 1992. Whose DNA? *American Journal of Human Genetics* 50:869.

[54] Weir, B.S. and I.W. Evett. 1993. Reply to Lewontin. *American Journal of Human Genetics* 52:206.

[55] Weir, B.S. and B.S. Gaut. 1993. Matching and binning DNA fragments in forensic science. *Jurimetrics Journal* 34:9–19.

[56] Weir, B.S. and W.G. Hill. 1994. Population genetics of DNA profiles. *Journal of Forensic Science* 33:219–226.

[57] Weir, B.S., C.M. Triggs, L. Starling, L.I. Stowell, K.A.J. Walsh, and J.S. Buckleton. 1997. Interpreting DNA mixtures. *Journal of Forensic Sciences* 42:213–222.

[58] Zaykin, D., L.A. Zhivotovsky, and B.S. Weir. 1995. Exact tests for association between alleles at arbitrary numbers of loci. *Genetica* 96:169–178.

DNA Statistics Under Trial in the Australian Adversarial System

Janet Chaseling

Abstract

The adversarial legal system as practised in Australian criminal courts presents considerable difficulties for the statistical expert witness who appears for the prosecution (Crown). In particular, while full disclosure of all evidence is required of prosecution witnesses, the legal "right to silence" of the accused is enforced such that the defense and their witnesses have no similar requirement. The prosecution witnesses may find themselves in court completely unaware of what challenges to their evidence, or self, will be forthcoming. This chapter provides a review of the common situations that can be expected by an expert statistical witness appearing for the prosecution in an Australian criminal case involving the interpretation of DNA evidence. The information has been gained from experiences over a six-year period in the various state and territory legal systems. Eight separate legal jurisdictions are in operation throughout the Australian States and Territories, and some of the difficulties that arise because of differences within the systems are raised and explored. The critical need to communicate effectively to judge and jury is demonstrated through examples of specific difficulties that have been encountered. A number of the strategies that have been found to work successfully in explaining to judge and jury traditionally feared "statistical" issues are presented in full.

Key Words: forensic DNA profiles, multiplication rule, statistical models, genetical models, statistical communication, statistical education.

1 Introduction

The opinions expressed in this chapter come from the author's experience as a statistical expert witness in the interpretation of DNA profile evidence for criminal identification. Examples of misunderstandings and typical challenges come from cases encountered throughout Australia over the past six years. Also included are the visual aids and analogies that have been used successfully in assisting counsel, judge, and jury to understand and make effective use of the statistical aspects of DNA evidence.

It is widely acknowledged that the *adversarial legal system* leads to an environment in which an expert witness will undoubtedly be placed in a threatening situation in which the process of presenting carefully reasoned evidence in an objective way is extremely difficult and stressful. Even the practice of court transcription, in which every word uttered is recorded verbatim, can be daunting—in what other situation would a scientist have unprepared responses recorded without a chance of clarification? The expert witness cannot help but feel that they are "on their own." Fienberg (1997) describes the "seduction that occurs when a statistician becomes an expert witness" and states that "Learning the game and how to play it well often appear in conflict with the tenets of the profession."

Clearly, there is a *game* to be played, but is it appropriate in the search for justice for this game to include the expert witness whose task should be to assist the court?

Roberts (1998) provides a summary of the use of DNA profiling for criminal investigations in Australia since the mid 1980s. He reports a number of cases in which sound inferential argument based on appropriate assumptions was vital in the defense of the DNA evidence. Experiences in Australian criminal cases since 1993 strongly support the beliefs expressed by Fienberg and others (see, for example, Meier, 1986; Gastwirth, 1988a and 1988b) of the difficulties faced by a statistical expert witness under the adversarial system. While these difficulties are similar in any specialized area, there is certainly an added set of problems placed on the statistical expert by virtue of the attitude of society in general to anything perceived as "mathematical."

Evidence can be seen in court transcripts that in some cases, experts use their opportunity in the witness box as a forum to raise academic argument. Scientific debate is necessary, but the forum for it is not a criminal court of law with a judge and jury as arbiters; such debate should occur in an environment where expert can discuss with expert, without mediation through a barrister who may have little understanding of the issues. Points of agreement and disagreement should be reached with a minimum of misunderstanding and confusion, and communicated to the court objectively. A judge and jury have the right to evaluate the evidence without the diversion that may be caused by the presentation skills of the expert.

In the process of a trial by jury, the role of the expert witness is to provide the best possible description and/or explanation of issues that relate to the crime and that involve their particular area of expertise. Each expert provides one component of the overall "jigsaw"; the jury's decision-making process involves assessment of the totality of interrelated evidence.

2   Giving Expert Evidence in the Australian Adversarial System

2.1 The Adversarial System

The implications of the adversarial legal system on the expert witness in general are well documented—see, for example, Selinger 1986, Meier 1986, Robertson and Vignaux 1995, and Angell 1996. Regardless of personal beliefs, experts who give evidence under the adversarial system are perceived as representing one particular side of the argument; rarely will they be seen as objective. Despite this, many experts clearly see their role as unbiased regardless of which side has enlisted their help, and regard themselves as acting for the court to provide the best information they can to assist the jury in its deliberations. This impartiality needs to be reinforced whenever possible during time in the witness box. Credibility as an objective witness will be enhanced by a display of total frankness during cross-examination. Unfortunately, the opposing expert may not have the same personal beliefs and may well see their role as one of raising confusion with the aim of "muddying the water" and thus having evidence excluded because it is confusing. This potential situation of differing "ethics" is supported by Fienberg (1997) when he says:

> we must recognize that some of our colleagues are fully aware that they have been hired as experts precisely because their testimony is expected to help win the case and that they exploit this situation by securing high fees for their services . . . [this] becomes a problem if and when the high fees buy "testimony."

The expert whose opinion does not support the barrister's case will not be used.

Additional problems may arise through poor communication between barrister and expert. Details associated with the case are provided to the expert by the relevant barrister, and it is possible for experts on opposing sides to be given different information, or to have received information with different emphasis. Sharing of the information between opposing experts can only benefit the quest for truth. For example, in the case of *R v Humphrey* (1999) a murder had taken place in a shantytown, or camp of "humpies," on the banks of the River Murray in South Australia. These dwellings were occupied by people from mixed racial backgrounds including Caucasians and full and partial Aboriginals. DNA matching that of the victim had been found on the clothes of the accused, and an estimate of the probability of occurrence of this observed DNA profile was required. Experts for the prosecution had presented statistical estimates based on a general database for South Australia. The opposing expert challenged the appropriateness of the general database, saying that the correct database would be one taken from the population of people who inhabit the banks of the River Murray where the crime occurred. Under cross-examination, it was pointed out to the defense expert that many of the people inhabiting the area, including the defendant, were itinerants who live for short periods in a variety of areas including the city of Adelaide and numerous townships throughout South Australia. This was new information to the expert, and he conceded that it altered his opinion; he now felt that the population he had proposed would not be appropriate.

Experts need to be aware of the relevance of their expertise to the specific case. This awareness depends on a clear understanding of the "real" question being asked of them. There appear to be no formal procedures in Australian criminal courts for the instruction of an expert witness by the barrister. In the absence of a formalized mechanism, the statistical expert must insist on adequate briefing through pretrial conferences. It is advisable to have a "practice run" through the approach to be taken during the presentation of evidence in chief, and to "role play" potential challenges. The expert witness must prepare and provide to the court a written statement in which the question answered in formulating the opinion should be clearly documented. Parts of the evidence seen as important by the expert may not be elicited by their barrister and thus not formally presented to the court. Provided that the comprehensive written statement is "tendered" in court as an exhibit, the jury will have access to all of the expert's opinion. Potential challenges should be anticipated and written answers prepared and kept readily available in notes during cross-examination. Despite careful preparation, when questioned by someone whose sole aim is to find errors in one's work or credibility, it can be difficult to retain composure, think clearly, and maintain a flow of responses that are carefully reasoned. For example, in the case of *R v Jarrett* (1994), the same question was asked of the expert twenty-three times throughout a two hour session, in the hope that the response would be transposed, resulting in commitment of one of the famous "fallacies" (for example, see Aitken, 2000). Fortunately, the expert had the answer written down, and on every occasion was able to respond by reading from the prepared notes and saying: "As I responded last time in answer to that question . . . ."

The process of court transcription results in a record that can be used against the expert, not only in the current trial but also at any time in the future. This is a challenge that few scientists will experience and with which even fewer will feel comfortable. It is a situation that would usually be avoided. For example, many university lecturers are reluctant to have lectures taped by students for the very reason that should they later correct or expand on some point, they cannot be sure that the original recording will be effectively amended and placed in the appropriate context. Unlike a court transcript, most permanent records become available only after extensive preparation and redrafting; consider for example, the preparation and formal scripting that goes into a television documentary.

The good expert witness will be a competent communicator who clearly "informs" all parties involved, and ensures that the decision-makers, the members of the jury, engage with the expert's evidence. Judge and jury should be approached as though they were a class of students none of whom has knowledge of the specialist's technical area (Justice Olsson, personal communication). This "class" needs to be convinced that the expert has the required expertise and has applied it in the correct way; results must be presented as simply as possible using a minimum of technical jargon and symbols. Visual aids can be an invaluable way of conveying technical information, provided that they are totally objective and balanced. The use of visual aids is at the discretion of individual judges, and while some actively encourage their use, others refuse, often citing a concern that they may distract the jury from consideration of the full oral evidence on which their decision must be made. An expert witness wishing to use visual aids must discuss them in detail with their barrister, who will in turn raise the specific proposals with the judge prior to the trial. The judge will need to know what aids are proposed, their content, and the purpose of their use.

An expert witness will be subject to extreme scrutiny, especially in their early court experiences. If the area of expertise is not apparent in formal qualifications, there will be a need to justify the relevance of experience; failure to recognize this and prepare appropriately may lead to embarrassment and subsequent loss of credibility. A witness's past will inevitably be raised. For example, undergraduate grades from more than twenty-five years ago were cited in *R v Jarrett* (1994) as evidence of lack of credentials as a statistical expert. Everything the expert witness has ever uttered in a court or published professionally will be sought out and used against that expert—the witness will be *"an expert on trial."*

2.2 Admissibility of Evidence—The Voir Dire or Pretrial

One of the parties may challenge the admissibility of some component of the evidence. In Australia, this will mean the holding of a *voir dire* in which no jury is present and the judge listens to argument from both parties (prosecution and defense) as to why and why not the evidence at issue should be placed before the jury. The judge then makes a judgment as to whether or not the disputed evidence will be admitted in the trial by jury. Either side may call expert witnesses during this process. The voir dire enables the judge to perform a "filtering" process to ensure that evidence that may turn out to be inadmissable does not go before the jury resulting in a possible mistrial. Although the voir dire usually occurs before the start of the trial, it may occur at any point during the trial.

A judge may exclude evidence for a variety of reasons, but the key areas attacked during a voir dire are the expertise of the witness, the reliability of the evidence, and the factual frame of reference in which the evidence is based. Giving evidence in the absence of a jury is not the same as giving evidence before a jury; "the game" played by the barrister during cross-examination will be very different. With no jury present, the opposing barrister makes a more concerted effort to discredit the witness and their evidence—no holds are barred! Time under cross-examination will almost always be much longer during the voir dire; it is not unusual for a day and a half in the voir dire to become less than an hour in front of the jury. An inexperienced expert witness faced with their first voir dire will find it difficult to obtain advice on what to expect.

Although negatives far outweigh positives, there are some advantages for the expert in giving evidence in a voir dire. Without the jury, there will usually be more opportunity to interact with the judge, who will often question the expert in order to clarify the evidence. For example, in a case in which confidence intervals were used for an estimate of a probability, the judge led the questioning during a two-hour period, requesting examples that "did not involve coins." If the barrister has not elicited a component of evidence that the expert feels is important, there is more chance in a voir dire of being able to include the relevant points by direct appeal to the judge.

2.3 The Adversarial System in Australia

Australia has a system of state and federal governments, which results in separate legal administrations within each of its six states and two territories. All criminal courts use an adversarial system, which is, in general, similar to that used in the UK and USA. There is increasing concern and published recognition that this system is less than adequate for the presentation of expert evidence. In a recent article, the director of the National Institute for Forensic Science in Australia (Ross, 1998), stated:

> We have a system which is cumbersome and out of date. A system which to the outsider may appear to be a game of smoke screens and mirrors and to be vigorously protected by vested interest. A thorough review of the presentation of expert evidence within the adversarial system in Australia is long overdue.

The real impediment to obtaining the best expert opinion of the facts in an Australian criminal trial lies with the principle of "the accused's right to silence." This "right" while primarily designed to prevent self-incrimination by the accused, results in a system in which full disclosure is required by one side, the prosecution, but not by the other side, the defense. In a recent article, "To How Much Silence Ought an Accused be Entitled," Justice Olsson (1999) states:

> The right to silence at trial creates problems for judicial management . . .
> (it) allows an "ambush defense."

The prosecution must provide full, written details of all proposed evidence, in a timely manner to enable due consideration of the material by the defense and associated experts. On the other hand, prior to the formal presentation at the trial, the defense need provide none of its proposed argument and in some Australian courts does not even need to divulge the areas in which experts will be called. If proposed defense experts are named, pretrial discussion between experts from opposing sides is discouraged and may be opposed by counsel on either side.

In Australian criminal courts, the defense expert is used to identify some area of doubt that will provide an angle for the defense barrister to use to discredit either the evidence of the experts or the experts themselves. The prosecution expert may have no awareness of what particular challenges are to be made before they arise during cross-examination. Although there will be some opportunity during a period of reexamination by their own barrister for the expert to defend and explain decisions reached and to correct misinterpretations rising during the cross-examination, effective countering of an opposition challenge needs to occur at the time the challenge is raised. To achieve this, the expert must seek opportunities during the cross-examination process, a task that will be made very difficult by a skilled and experienced opposing barrister. A prosecution expert is placed in the unenviable situation of facing an effective ambush with information obtained from scrutiny of the evidence they are required to provide. There is no opportunity (let alone requirement) for a similar scrutiny of the evidence presented by the defense expert, who may not have provided any form of written statement. At best, it may be possible to raise issues under cross-examination of the defense expert, but any such debate must take place through a third party, the barrister, who is unlikely to have the knowledge to ensure meaningful debate. Nothing can be more frustrating than to sit as an advisor during cross-examination, having prepared carefully worded written questions, only to have the witness respond in a totally unexpected way, leaving the barrister speechless. The opposing expert may well be able to rebuff the witness's response, but the adversarial system leaves as the only options for such input the passing of notes or a call for adjournment to allow further discussions between expert and barrister.

Despite provisions within the various criminal legislations throughout Australia for a judge to enlist the assistance of a court expert, no record could be found in Australian courts of this happening in the case of statistical evidence associated with the interpretation of DNA evidence.

In general, the expert witness in an Australian criminal trial has no opportunities for informed discussion with the opposing expert in order to explore differing processes used and assumptions made in reaching the opinions expressed. However, in a recent trial in the Northern Territory, after much debate, the expert witnesses on opposing sides were given permission by their respective barristers to have pretrial discussions with the expectation of coming to agreement and presenting a single opinion for the court. The process was lengthy, but after compromises on both sides, agreement was reached, and a single statement signed by both experts was submitted to the court. Unfortunately, this story does not end successfully with a case that can be quoted and used as a precedent, as the very next day the supposed victim withdrew the complaint and no case was heard!

The plethora of criminal courts throughout Australia also results in a number of perhaps seemingly trivial differences that are rarely, if ever, discussed. Each court system has slightly different protocols, which can cause problems for the uninformed expert witness who appears sporadically before the different systems. For example, will the expert witness sit or stand? Will they be allowed to refer to notes in the witness box? Will a formal subpoena be issued? Will the expert be allowed in court during the evidence given by other experts on the same side and/or on the opposing side? The different court systems also vary with respect to the availability of presentation facilities for visual aids, the number of people on the jury, and whether or not precedents from other states will be accepted. In 1998, visual aid facilities in supreme courts in Australia ranged from modern technology (Queensland), through an easel and sheet of cardboard (Western Australia), to refusal of anything (Australian Capital Territory, federal).

The current adversarial system also places extreme demands on expert witnesses with respect to timing, resources, and associated inconvenience. Under a system where the defense will in general have revealed little if anything of the components of the prosecution evidence that it will attack or of the evidence that it will present, in the words of Justice Olsson (1999):

[the court] will be at the mercy of the defense lawyer and/or the accused, rather than having control over the progress of the case. Credible trial dates and the reduction of adjournments will remain a court administrator's dream.

Clearly, there is a component of the "game" that works against optimal use of experts' time. Australia is a large country, and it is not unusual for an expert to be required to make flights of over six hours in order to give evidence. It is equally not unusual for that expert to be told on arrival that they are no longer required, or to find that their testimony will not be required for a number of days.

3   The Statistical Expert Witness

3.1   Problems Facing the Statistical Expert

Just as the use of statistics arises in almost every area of research, the statistical expert witness may be found in a variety of legal situations. Considerable literature is available describing these various roles together with the difficulties and potential risks facing someone who takes on the role of statistical expert; see, for example, Fienberg 1997, Gastwirth 1988a and 1988b, Meier 1986, and Weinstein 1988. One of the safeguards offered to the statistical expert by authors such as Fienberg (1997) is to abide by the professional codes or guidelines issued by the various statistical associations such as the American Statistical Association, the International Statistical Institute, the Royal Statistical Society, and, most recently, the Statistical Society of Australia. However, these codes invariably omit two aspects that are crucial in the legal setting, namely, that the approach used should be the simplest possible to achieve valid conclusions and that the statistical processes should be communicated clearly without recourse to complex theory.

Before a statistician begins to give evidence, they must accept that the first problem to be overcome relates to the disease within society known as *mathphobia*. This is a disease, which is currently in plague proportions in much of the Western world, where there is a general fear in the community of anything mathematical. The statistical expert would do well to follow the "KISS" (keep it simple, statistician) principle.

By definition, the jury consists of "ordinary people" selected from the community. It is no secret that over the years, statistical education in primary and secondary schooling in Australia and other countries has been less than inspiring, and has led to a perception by society in general that statistics is difficult, confusing, and even magical. Walking past a jury to the witness box the statistical expert often hears murmurs from the jurors such as: "I hated maths at school" or "I could never understand stats and maths" (words not recorded in transcript, unfortunately). Many people mistrust statistics. The linking of statistics with mathematics has in many ways been unfortunate in that it has tended to hide the nonmathematical aspects of statistics, that is, the way of thinking. It is easy to see the difficulty faced by the general public when even mathematical colleagues argue that: "statistics is just mathematics" and when judges make statements such as "It should be pointed out that statistics are nothing more than the application of symbolic logic" (*R v Mitchell*, 1997). The critical aspect of statistics needed in the interpretation of evidence in court is the *inferential process*. While complex mathematics will undoubtedly provide the underpinning for the implementation of this process, it is the understanding of the process itself that is vital if a jury is to make valid assessment of the evidence. No matter how theoretically sound an argument may be, if it is not understood, then it is of little value to the court; a lack of understanding by a judge may lead to the statistical evidence being disallowed on the grounds that it will be too confusing for the jury. This occurred in the cases of *R v Mitchell* (1997) and *R v Love, Smith and Wanganeen* (1998).

Many statisticians are unaware of the real gap in knowledge between themselves and the general public. Others may acknowledge the problem but be unable to bridge that gap. The use of basic statistical terms such as *estimate, statistic, parameter, probability, odds, likelihood ratio, random, power, sample*, and *population*, without effective definitions will cause immediate glazing of the eyes in most juries. Statisticians often believe that it is easier to understand something if it is expressed in symbolic form—this is not necessarily true for many nonmathematical people. Few examples are given in the legal literature of ways for improving communication of specialized content. However, the teaching literature abounds with suggestions that are eminently relevant for the statistical expert witness (see, for example, the *Journal of Statistical Education, Teaching Statistics*, and the proceedings from the *International Conference On Teaching Statistics—ICOTS*). One particular strategy that has worked effectively in Australia is the use of analogies to assist in the clarification of complex issues.

Statistical evidence will fall on deaf ears and have little value unless judge and jury have a basic understanding of the concept, process, and use of statistical inference. The statistical expert must ensure that this understanding is there **before** beginning. Box 1 contains the visual aid that has been used successfully in Australian courts to introduce the general concept of the *inferential process*. Where possible, the aid is presented as an overhead and also as a handout to the jury; the expert explains the various components using examples as necessary. During the explanation it is pointed out that if all the information were available (measurements were available for all the population), there would be no need for statisticians—usually a point that evokes some laughter and wishful thinking!

Judge and jury may feel uncomfortable in the presence of variability and the consequential answer that includes uncertainty rather than an exact number. Even when the concept of uncertainty has been embraced and the importance of sample size accepted, there may be genuine confusion about the meaning of a stated degree of certainty. The visual aid in Box 2 has been used with great success in explaining the concept of a *confidence interval* and the need for an interval estimate rather than a point estimate, to incorporate sample size.

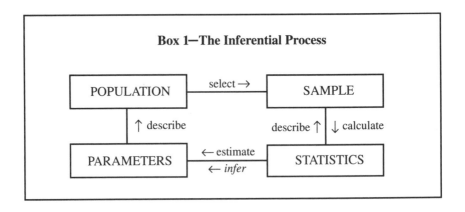

Box 1—The Inferential Process

POPULATION — select → SAMPLE

↑ describe   describe ↑ | ↓ calculate

PARAMETERS ← estimate / ← *infer* — STATISTICS

A similar approach is reported in Gastwirth (1988a), in the US discrimination case of Capacci (1983), where it was argued that as long as females formed **at least** 2% of the qualified pool of workers, then the data were significant. The plaintiffs presented several plausible comparative labor pools showing that females formed **at least** 15% of each of them and 19% of the applicants after the charge was filed were women. In this case, the use of a range of estimates was accepted by the appeals court.

An additional problem is the overreaction by a judge to the presence of uncertainty and the consequent rejection of all the statistical evidence because it is "unreliable." This occurred in the case of *R v Love, Smith and Wanganeen* (1998), when in an attempt to address the problem of the appropriate population, confidence interval results were presented from a number of different databases representing different geographical areas and different racial groups. Although the results varied for the different racial groups, the greatest probability of occurrence in any was 1 in 230 million. The judge determined that because there was variation between the racial groups, no figure should be used at all, and instructed the jury that they could consider the DNA evidence of a profile match, but that they were not to attach to it any measure of probability.

Interestingly, in the case described in Section 2.1, of *R v Humphrey* (1999), in the same court before a different judge, confidence intervals for the true proportion were again presented for a number of different databases. For each racial group, the upper limits representing the greatest probability of occurrence were similar, and all intervals overlapped considerably. The opposing expert challenged the confidence intervals on the grounds that they were different, as they had varying **lower** limits. During the opposing expert's evidence in chief, the judge pointed out the substantial degree of overlap between the various limits. He then expounded on the importance to the accused of the **upper** limit, compared with the lower limit of the interval, explaining to the expert and jury that while the upper limit gives an estimate of the most conservative value, the one most favorable to the accused, the lower limit is an expression of the least conservative value.

Box 2 — The Need for Confidence Intervals

The accuracy and reliability of estimates of population values based on samples of data depend on the size of the sample. If sample size is not incorporated into the estimate, the numerical value may be misleading. Statistical theory provides a way of building in the sample size effect through the use of interval estimates instead of the simple but possible misleading, point estimates. Interval estimates have a known degree of reliability, which relates directly to the sample size. This effect is illustrated below with a simple example.

How many women in Australia use Hormone Replacement Therapy?

Survey Results: one sixth or approximately 17%

But, how large was the sample size used?

6 women	and 1 uses HRT	proportion $= 1/6 = 0.17$	(17%)
60 women	and 10 use HRT	proportion $= 1/6 = 0.17$	(17%)
600 women	and 100 use HRT	proportion $= 1/6 = 0.17$	(17%)

In all cases, the point estimate of the proportion of women who use HRT is the same, 17%.

Which survey gives you more confidence? One based on 6 people or one based on 600?

Using statistical theory and the knowledge from the samples, confidence intervals can be constructed which allow a statement of a range of values which it is believed will include the true population value. These intervals can be calculated for different degrees of confidence; typical values are 95% and 99%. The interval given with 99% confidence will necessarily cover a wider range than the one given for 95% confidence.

The 95% confidence intervals for the HRT example are:

6	0% to 64%	0.00 to 0.64
60	7% to 27%	0.07 to 0.27
600	14% to 20%	0.14 to 0.20

These results are now illustrated in graphical form:

| 0 | 0.1 | 0.2 | 0.3 | 0.4 | 0.5 | 0.6 | 0.7 | 0.8 | 0.9 | 1 |

More women result in a smaller range for the 95% confidence interval

Inferences based on a sample of only six women will have little meaning. To be 95% sure that the interval given will cover the true proportion, an interval of 0 to 0.64 must be given—not much better than saying somewhere between none and 100% of women use HRT!

However, if a sample of 600 women is available, a reasonably tight range can be stated, within which there is a good deal of confidence (95%) that the true population value will lie—namely, between 14% and 20% of women use HRT.

Note that the change from six to 60 is much greater than the change from 60 to 600—as the sample size increases, it reaches a stage where additional observations do not contribute appreciably to further information.

The value of large sample sizes is evident.

The need to include confidence intervals instead of just point estimates to reflect sample size is evident.

3.2   The Importance of the Question

Experience in Australian courts supports the opinion of many of the authors cited throughout that the most crucial problem with which the statistical expert witness must contend is maintaining an active awareness of the real question(s) to be addressed. Definition of the problem is of primary concern in any consulting statistician's task; however, in the activities of the adversarial system it can easily be lost or become confused. Statistical experts must limit their opinion to the specific question that they have been asked to address; they must be able to distinguish between this question and the "ultimate question." Under the heading "Where Expertise Ends and the Jury Begins," Selinger (1986) provides a sound warning to any expert witness, but in particular to the statistician, with an example in which there was "failure to separate out a scientific procedure from legal evaluation." Unless the statistician has been engaged by the court specifically to provide expert advice on interpreting the evidence in total—see, for example, the case of *People v Collins* as reported by Fairley and Mosteller (1974)—he or she must not provide comment beyond answering the specific question for which their expertise has been sought. This will in most cases relate to the statistical inference involved.

While it might be tempting for statisticians to feel that their expertise in problem solving through application of basic probability would be useful for the jury in its deliberations, this must be avoided. As Allen (1998) points out:

> There is no reason to believe that statisticians are any better than members of any other profession, or lay witnesses for that matter, at identifying data that are critical to resolving a question of historical fact . . . .

The decision-making process practiced by jurors is extremely complex and has been the focus of considerable research by experts in a variety of areas. Hastie (1993) provides a comprehensive summary and description of four models that are based on probability theory, "cognitive" algebra, stochastic processes, and information processing, respectively. Study of these models has arisen from the belief that their application would improve the performance of a juror, by providing a uniform, formalized structure to the decision-making process. Hastie (1993) reports that:

> Although alternative formulations of probability theory have been proposed and a variety of interpretations of the term "probability" have been advanced, one approach, now called Bayesian probability theory, has been dominant for centuries.

But he continues that of all the possible models:

> The Bayesian approach . . . runs into the greatest difficulties. [It] predicts stringent limits on behavior because of its strong requirements for numerically precise internal consistency among a static system of beliefs . . . there is substantial empirical evidence that human behaviour does not exactly conform to probability theory principles.

The suggestion that all people carry out a decision-making process in a common, formalized way appears unwarranted. It cannot be assumed that jurors consider evidence in a one-dimensional framework, taking individual components of evidence one by one, and reaching a single verdict based solely on their progressive interpretation of these individual pieces of evidence. Judgments made by a juror about individual items of evidence are not necessarily "coherent" in any formal sense, and it cannot be assumed that at any given point in deliberation, a juror has a clearly defined, numerical probability of guilt in mind. The statistical expert must realize the importance of other components of human decision making behavior. Allen (1998) reports on research in which:

> Jurors construct stories as they hear evidence and the stories are subject to revision or modifications as they acquire additional information. When they make a decision, jurors consider whether the story (or alternative stories) they have constructed forms a permissible verdict ... Models of formal logic may certainly play a role in construction and evaluation of stories, but in a much different fashion than would more traditional evidence. It seems very doubtful that formal symbols interact with knowledge stored in memories as words, physical objects or even demeanor of witnesses might.

Hastie and Pennington (1995) also discuss the use made in the jury decision-making process of the "story" model. A juror's decision as to whether or not to acquit does not rest solely on their assessment of the evidence; a juror has the right to take into account other issues such as the circumstances and the potential costs of different decisions. A jury can do what a judge cannot, namely, apply the prerogative of mercy. The circumstances may be such that a jury may choose to acquit even though they believe the suspect to be technically guilty (Judge Olsson, personal communication). Indeed, the study of Kalven and Zeisel (1966) indicates that jurors acquitted "sympathetic" defendants that judges would have found guilty.

The process of clearly defining the question involves identification of the *variable* that has been measured and a statement of the *parameter* of interest. For example, the question may appear to relate to a *mean* when really it is a *median* that is of interest. Failure to identify the real parameter may lead to a classic case of the *Type III* error, in which a perfect, theoretically sound statistical analysis is obtained to the wrong question!

3.3   Communicating the Results and Defending Opinion

Having identified the question and carried out appropriate statistical analysis, the expert must decide how to present the results. For example, the statistical expert should not need to include mathematical formulae in the evidentiary statement; all mathematical formulae can be expressed in written language, and the challenge is to do this in an informative way. Concerns for communication are expressed by the barrister Graham Cooke (1999) when he says:

It is not good enough for mathematicians and logicians to produce symbolic formulae; they must come down and find a way to put their logical concepts into ordinary language . . . .

At the very basic level is the problem of how to express a probability. Should it be as a decimal number, a proportion, a percentage, or as '1 in . . . ' ? All these methods have their associated problems of potential misunderstandings, which are enhanced by the general public's fear of extreme numbers. Regardless of which mode of expression is adopted, the statistician cannot be sure that a judge will understand the meaning of a probability. For example, in the case of *R v Abbott* (1996) the expert witness quoted as the most conservative estimate of the probability of occurrence of an observed DNA profile, approximately one in 23 billion. After a brief guffaw, the judge said to the expert:

> "That's more than the population of the world, it's meaningless. Are you saying you have found something that can't occur in the number of people in the world?"

The analogy given in Box 3 was used by the expert to redress the judge's misunderstanding; relating this to the DNA profile probability follows with little difficulty, and the exercise is usually accompanied by some amusement.

Opposing counsel may try to present the statistical expert as a "technical whiz," someone who cannot communicate and who can only understand complex mathematical procedures. Appeal will be made to the belief that all statistical calculation must be complex and no one else but a statistician can understand it. There may be a request for further calculation to be performed in the witness box to demonstrate that the analysis is straightforward. Such a request should be resisted at all times, regardless of how confident and free of stress the statistician feels. In the case of *R v Jarrett* (1994) the barrister handed the statistical expert a calculator

---

Box 3 — The Extreme Probability

A Famous Australian Horserace—The 'Melbourne Cup'

On the first Tuesday of November, almost all of Australia comes to a standstill for a famous horse race known as the 'Melbourne Cup'. Some incredible amounts of money are gambled on this race through formal betting and the traditional 'sweep' held in offices, family groups and at social gatherings. Most Australians will be aware of the race and many will have some interest in it, to the extent of knowing that there will be a 'favorite' and that other horses will be at 'long odds'. A total of 24 horses is allowed to run in the race. In most years some horses will be 'long shots' and run at 100 to 1 or more.

Experience has shown that most people have no difficulty with the concept that a horse has a stated chance of winning of one in a hundred even though there are only 24 horses in the race. They also accept that the horse might actually win! In this context people clearly relate the 'chance' to a 'probability'.

with six significant figures and requested that he be shown how a figure of 1 in 12 million had been obtained.

The statistician will need to untangle *theory* and *assumptions* and present each in the context of the case at issue. This may mean resorting to simple analogies and the need to forgo the beauty of mathematical complexity. It is not sufficient simply to state the assumptions; the implications of their violations within the context of the case in question must be conveyed to the jury of lay people. Some statistical experts show a definite reluctance to focus on the specific case, preferring to relate general theory and its associated assumptions without addressing them in the context of the real issue facing the court. In the case of *R v Jarrett* (1994) the defense expert witness was arguing that the probability quoted was incorrect because of various general theoretical considerations. After giving much criticism of the prosecution expert's figures the defense expert had still not provided any alternative figures or any real indication of the implications of his arguments on the estimated probability of the profile at issue. The judge finally asked him:

> "And if all these possible problems were taken into account what, in your opinion, would be the rarity of the profile? Would it be rare or not?"

Without any hesitation, the expert responded: Oh, it would still be extremely rare.

3.4   Statistical and Underlying Process Models

The concept of a statistical model as it relates to the process of statistical inference may need to be explained and contrasted with the underlying theoretical process model (physical, biological, or social). The statistical model is used to make inference from sample to population: Something is believed of the population, do the observed sample data support this belief? Inevitably, it will be necessary to make clear that most theoretical process models represent simplifications of the real world that rely on assumptions that may or may not be true, and that may or may not have significant impact on any particular situation. Should evidence be given that draws solely on the underlying theory of the process involved, without appropriate statistical testing of data relevant to the particular case, it is imperative that all assumptions required in the theoretical process model be clearly stated and their implications to the case at issue be evaluated. Both expert and barrister must ensure that the jury is fully versed with the differences between the two types of models, is aware that they both involve assumptions, has understood the implications of all assumptions on the current case, and is aware that the proposed underlying process model represents a current theoretical belief that may change over time. The assessment that a particular theoretical process model fits well will have been based on a statistical model measuring goodness of fit. Box 4 provides an analogy that has been used successfully to illustrate the difference between the *statistical model* and the *underlying process model*.

Box 4 — Statistical Model versus
Underlying Process Model

Throughout Australia, people participate in weekly-televised 'lotteries'. These vary slightly from state to state, but in general involve some type of a rotating machine into which 45 balls are released. The balls are then agitated for a period of time before six are drawn one by one from the group to represent the winning numbers. Each ball has a different number, and sets of numbers may occur on balls with different colours. Participants will have selected a number of 'games' in each of which they have nominated six numbers as those they believe will be drawn. Anyone who has all six of the numbers drawn by the machine in the same game will share in the first prize.

The machine has been designed by engineers to ensure that numbers will be selected by the mechanism at random. This will have involved consideration of the various underlying physical processes such as Newton's laws of motion and the conservation of energy. In the design process the various components, including the mechanism for motion, the shape of the container, the way in which the balls are introduced into the machine, the process of agitation and the method used to select each successive ball, will have been evaluated to ensure that all come together to produce a random selection of six balls. If balls are of different colours, underlying processes of chemistry and physics will be needed to ensure that balls of different colour are the same with respect to weight, coefficient of friction, etc.

The government runs stringent checks on these 'gaming' machines to ensure that selection of numbers does occur at random and that the public are not being 'cheated'. In doing this, the government does not appeal to the theory of the underlying processes. Rather, it takes a sample of observations giving the number of times each ball has been selected over various time periods, and applies statistical tests of the null hypothesis that random selection is occurring. It is true that each of the underlying processes could be reviewed and used for validation, but the real question relates to the final outcomes and whether or not the net result of all the inter-related and possibly unknown processes, is a random selection of numbers.

Assuming that the outcome of the machine is truly random by testing an observed sample of results against what should have occurred (random selection), is analogous to assessing the independence between DNA alleles by testing an observed sample (the database) against what should be seen (independence between alleles).

In the gaming machine, there is no need to justify each of the underlying physical processes and theory, some of which may be unknown or not strictly correct, others of which may have assumptions which cannot be confirmed. Similarly, in assessing the independence of alleles or genotypes, there is no need to draw on underlying genetical theory which may be incomplete or not strictly correct, and which may have assumptions which cannot be confirmed.

3.5   Limitations

All expert witnesses must acknowledge the limits of their knowledge. The expert statistician must recognize that they will *not* necessarily have the knowledge to define some components needed to determine which statistical procedures are relevant; they will need to accept direction from their barrister or from the court. Some of the required knowledge will come from other evidence and may not be available to the specific expert. Wherever necessary, clear statements should be included in the written statement of the assumptions made and the limitations placed on the expert's opinion by lack of knowledge.

Finally, the statistical expert will need to be aware that within the legal system there appears to be a belief that anything to do with misinterpretation of scientific evidence tends to be branded as a statistical problem. In particular, the errors referred to as the *prosecutor's* and the *defender's* fallacies, in which valid statements are incorrectly reversed, have no more basis in statistics than they do with, for example, English grammar. For a detailed discussion on these "fallacies" refer to the chapter by Aitken in this book (Aitken, 2000). Certainly, the statistician must avoid making such fallacious statements, but the statistical community should not take upon itself the role of the sole arbiter of such errors.

4   The Statistician and DNA Evidence

4.1   Jargon and Understanding

The first problem a statistician will face when being briefed is the specific jargon used by DNA biologists for statistical aspects. For example, DNA biologists tend to use the word "database" for "sample" or in some cases "population database," which can be even more confusing. In general, when they refer to "frequency" they mean "relative frequency" or "probability." The more general use of "frequency" is replaced with "count." While the statistician will quickly adapt to these slight differences in terminology, under the pressure of cross-examination it may be difficult to retain the meaning familiar to the court. Once an expert displays inconsistent use of apparently simple words such as "sample" and "frequency," understanding by judge and jury is quickly lost.

Another area causing confusion and frustration to the statistician is the apparent belief that forensic DNA data are in some way different from similar data found in other disciplines, and that statistical methods that have been widely and successfully used in other areas have no role in the analysis of forensic data. Even the techniques used by population geneticists in the study of animal populations are not willingly adopted into the forensic context.

4.2   The DNA Evidence

Presenting DNA evidence can be seen to involve two distinct stages:

(a) Do the relevant DNA profiles match?
(b) If so, how likely is the observation of such a match if the accused is not in fact the person who left the crime scene sample?

Opinion from an expert statistician is usually sought for part (b), since determining the accuracy of the stated components in a DNA profile is usually beyond the expertise of a statistician. Implied within part (b) is the possibility that there is "someone else" who could have committed the crime; there is some *population of possible perpetrators*. Definition of this population must be based on other evidence associated with the crime and, except in rare cases, will be undefined to the statistical expert. This is the first stage at which the question asked of the statistician becomes unclear; without knowing the exact population to which inference must be made, can the statistician contribute anything of value? The answer to this question is the province of the jury. As stated by Justice Bleby in his *Reasons for Ruling* in the voir dire of *R v Humphrey* (1999)—refer to Section 2.1 for details of this case):

> For the Court to determine before the trial begins what is the appropriate description of the population from which the sample might have come is to make a judgement on evidence which it has not heard, and which judgement may or may not turn out to be correct when the evidence unfolds before the jury ... It is not for the trial judge to make a factual determination as to the population group which the data base would represent ... to do so is to usurp the function of the jury.

4.3   The Variables in DNA Evidence

As an initial stage in identifying the real question, it is necessary to have a clear definition of the *variables* that have been measured. A typical DNA profile presented to a statistician in Australia in 1999 will consist of a series of paired numbers for each DNA sample at issue in the case. In general there will be at least one sample from the crime scene and one or more from the accused; each sample will have one DNA profile record. Each pair in a record will refer to a different *locus* (part of the DNA). The components of each pair represent the values of the two *alleles* (separate pieces received, one from mother, one from father) that the particular individual whose DNA profile has been measured has at each of these loci. The values will appear as two numbers separated by a nonnumeric character such as a comma or a slash.

Currently, in Australia each locus used in forensic DNA can be defined as a place on the DNA strand where a certain known pattern repeats a variable number of times. Each possible number of times the pattern could be repeated is regarded as one possible allele for that locus. For example, for a particular locus, one individual might have eight repeats of the specified pattern from one parent and ten repeats from the other parent, giving a recording of 8, 10; another individual might have eight repeats from both parents, giving a recording of 8, 8. An example of a typical

Table 1. Typical DNA Profile in Australian Forensic DNA in 1999.

DNA locus	D3S1358	vWA	FGA	D8S1179	D21S11
observation	14,15	15,15	20,21	13,13	30,31.2
DNA locus	D18S51	D5S818	D13S317	D7S870	
observation	14,15	11,12	8,11	8,9	

DNA profile is given in Table 1.

The initial impression is that the variables concerned are *allelic values* at each of a number of loci, and the profile represents a multivariate observation with the number of variables given by twice the number of loci. However, once a number of such profiles are provided it becomes clear that in every case, the smallest of the two allelic values is presented as the first number in the pair. Further enquiry will reveal that the variable actually measured by the forensic biologist is the *genotype*, a combination of two alleles. In normal forensic casework there is no way in which the alleles from the respective parents can be identified. Thus, at each locus, the separate values of two alleles are given; however, once the observation is considered across a number of loci, any consideration of individual alleles as coming from a particular parent is impossible. The multilocus profile represents a multivariate observation with the number of variables equal to the number of loci; each variable is the single *genotype value* as distinct from two *allelic values*. In the profile in Table 1 there are nine variables, each the genotype of one of the loci. Despite this, statistical components in DNA evidence have almost always involved calculations involving the probabilities of the alleles. This anomaly is discussed further below.

Part (b) of the DNA evidence question relates to the weight that is to be placed on the DNA match. This will require some measure of the *probability* of occurrence of the multilocus profile observed at the scene of the crime in some population of interest; that is, the *parameter* will be some measure of probability. The real question may, of course, be that of the values of the relative probability of the observed DNA profile (the evidence) under different scenarios. In this case, the most informative answer will be a likelihood ratio. Two of the typical scenarios that will be encountered are "the crime scene sample was left by the accused" and "the crime scene sample was left by someone other than the accused." The sample to be used for estimation will be the one or more *databases* usually provided by the forensic scientist. An initial assumption that the statistician must make is that the data in the database are correct, and that any description provided as to the demographics of the individuals in the database is correct. The statistician must be told and/or deduce the composition of the database with respect to racial groups, and have some idea of how the data were collected. The potential debates that inevitably arise with the appropriateness of the database have been illustrated above. A clear statement must be provided by the statistician of the assumptions made in using a particular database(s). Ultimately, however, the decision of the relevance of the database(s) requires a definition of the *population of possible perpetrators*, something that can be made only by the jury.

4.4 Estimating the Match Probability of a DNA Profile: The Product Rule and Independence

Much controversy has occurred concerning the methods used to estimate the probability of a multilocus DNA profile. At the centre of this controversy is the debate as to whether the problem is one of a statistical model or a genetic model. Recall that the real measurements taken are *genotypes*, but traditionally *alleles* have been the measurement unit used to estimate the probability, and the most furious debate has been over the use of the "product rule" in estimating a genotype probability from observed allele relative frequencies. Can the probability of the composite event (genotype occurrence) be estimated by the product of the simple events (allele occurrences) that make up the composite? Are the simple events independent? Using statistical notation: Is $\Pr(AB) = \Pr(A)\Pr(B)$?

In the DNA profile, each locus can be considered separately; for example, the FGA locus in Table 1 has a genotype of 20, 21. What is the probability of observing an FGA genotype of 20, 21? The simplest way to answer this question is to count the number of times the genotype has been observed in the database and use the ratio of this to the database size as the estimate. This is known as the 'counting' method, and the assumptions required to accept the resulting estimate as meaningful are that the database be a true random and representative sample of the relevant population, and that it be of adequate size (see Box 2 for discussion of this point). If instead of a single genotype, each individual's measurement is regarded as two simple events, for example, a 20 allele from one parent and a 21 allele from the second parent, then the sample size is effectively doubled. The question now becomes, Can the probability of the genotype be estimated from the product of the probabilities associated with the occurrence of each allele? These allelic probabilities will need to be estimated from the available data, and are not determined by knowledge of the parental genotypes. If the contribution of the allele from each parent is *independent* and the probabilities of observing each allele are known, then the probability of the genotype can be estimated as the product of these two known probabilities. A multiplier of two will be needed for cases such as this example, to accommodate the possibility of each allele, the 20 and the 21, coming from either of the two parents. A similar argument leads to estimates for a genotype consisting of two of the same allele—the probability of the genotype will be the square of the probability associated with the single allele.

The validity of this product rule as a means of estimation depends on whether or not the occurrence of one allele is independent of the occurrence of the other allele, that the dependence between them is zero. The statement of independence forms a null hypothesis that is subjected to statistical testing. However, the nature of the scientific method that underpins all statistical hypothesis testing states that a hypothesis can only be disproved; it can never be proven true (Popper, 1959).

Thus no statistical test can ever prove that two variables are independent, and the statistician must resort to consideration of the power of the tests to detect various degrees of dependence. Whether the power is adequate depends on how much dependence can be tolerated before its presence will substantially change the weight of the evidence. What is a meaningful degree of dependence for the court's purpose?

An alternative approach is to call on the underlying genetic theory regardless of the observed data, and invoke the Hardy–Weinberg principle, which states that under a number of assumptions, an individual receives the two alleles from the parents independently. The formal definition of this genetical theorem, together with the related assumptions, can be found in most basic genetics textbooks. If the Hardy–Weinberg law holds, then the two alleles forming the genotype will be independent, and it will be valid to use the multiplication of the allele frequencies.

Both approaches (statistical and genetical) require assumptions about the individuals on whom measurements of a genotype have been made. Statistical assumptions will usually include that the sample of individuals were selected at random from the population, something that may be contentious for the typical forensic database. The genetically imposed Hardy–Weinberg theory requires numerous assumptions, including random mating and zero migration, most of which are unlikely to be valid in a population representing possible perpetrators.

The population geneticist will argue that no human population will be in Hardy–Weinberg equilibrium and therefore the alleles must be dependent, thus violating the use of the multiplication rule.

The statistician will argue that the issue is not whether or not Hardy–Weinberg equilibrium exists, but whether or not in the population of interest, the two alleles forming a genotype are independent, for whatever reason. The reason for two alleles associating independently may be complex, involving many known and unknown genetic processes and potential interactions.

To the statistician, the question is one of statistical independence, a simple reflection of the theory of independent events in probability theory. The geneticist sees the question as one of genetic independence and attempts to justify such a condition through current genetic theory. Who, if either, is right?

It is crucial to return to the real question. The court requires the probability of occurrence of an observed profile in a specific population. In an ideal situation, the population would be known and it would be possible to measure the profiles of all individuals in that population and thus find the true relative frequency of the profile of interest. Since it is not possible to measure the profiles of all individuals in the population, the process of statistical inference is used to provide an estimate based on a sample of individuals whose profiles can be measured. The final sections of the analogy given in Box 4 provide further explanation of this point.

Independence at a single locus has really become a nonissue, since as in most cases there should be no need to turn to allelic relative frequencies to provide the estimated probability. The variable measured is clearly the genotype, and with forensic databases now containing thousands of individuals and loci in use with a maximum of 100 genotypes, the observed relative frequency from the database, together with its standard error, provides a valid and appropriate estimate of the true probability of the genotype.

Multilocus profiles, almost by definition, will be seen only once in any population. Thus, no database can be expected to contain the observed profile for which an estimate of probability of occurrence is required. If independence *between* the genotypes at different loci can be established, then the overall probability can be estimated using multiplication of the estimated probabilities for the individual loci. Once again, there has been a tendency to resort to underlying genetical theory in opposing this multiplication process; statements such as: "the loci are on the same chromosome, therefore, they must be dependent," are commonly seen in defense experts' transcripts. The fact that physical proximity does not necessarily equate to dependence between values can be extremely difficult to communicate. Box 5 provides an analogy that illustrates the difference between physical dependence and dependence of values; these two dependencies are sometimes referred to by forensic scientists as "genetic dependence" and "statistical dependence," respectively.

It should be noted that the challenge raised in connection with dependence or otherwise between loci that might be physically close within a chromosome, relates to *alleles* and not to *genotypes*, the true variables whose independence is at issue. The debate over the relationships between dependence of alleles and possible necessary dependence of corresponding genotypes is beyond the scope of this chapter.

5 Discussion

There are many more typical areas of challenge that a statistical expert may face when providing evidence relating to the interpretation of DNA profile evidence. The loci used for forensic identification are hypervariable, and are known to have a range of possible alleles. As more and more loci are measured routinely, one would expect that the need for statistical inference will decline. In the case of *R v Harrison* (1998), twenty-one loci were measured and found to match, and it is difficult to see how an estimated probability of occurrence can provide "value added" evidence.

The statistician who embarks on the role of expert witness for DNA evidence is strongly advised to heed the advice given in Chapter 9 of Evett and Weir 1998, and to be constantly aware that:

> In spite of the elegant mathematical arguments . . . we stress that the final
> statistical values depend wholly on the initial assumptions. The validity
> of these assumptions in any given case (is) a matter for expert opinion,
> so that we claim "objective science" can exist only within the framework
> of the subjective judgement.

Box 5 — Statistical Dependence versus Genetical Dependence

Dependent Geographically versus Dependent Numerically

Suppose a car manufacturer makes car bodies in three colours, red, white and silver, and car interiors (upholstery, carpets, etc) in two colours, beige and red. Suppose also, that there is no plan as to how car bodies are matched with car interiors; any car body may be matched with any interior. That is, the chance of the interior being beige is the same whether the car body is white, red or silver. Once the car is completed and sold, the two components, body and interior, will stay together over time and a multiplicity of owners, assuming of course that no owner decides to change one or other of the colours (a mutation). If at some point in time a sample of cars is selected to investigate a proposed dependency between body colour and interior colour, based on the belief that these two features are held together by the single car unit, the hypothesis of independence should be accepted—body and interior were initially assigned to each other at random.

Suppose now that the car firm makes a decision that its red car bodies are to be matched with red interiors, whereas the silver cars are to have beige interiors. Clearly, once the cars are completed, there will be dependency between body colour and interior colour and this dependency will be maintained throughout time.

Without the knowledge of what actually happened at the time of car manufacture, the only way of assessing whether or not car body colour and interior colour are dependent would be to take a random sample of cars, measure the colours of their body and interior, and apply an objective statistical test. The numbers of each combination of body and interior colours which would be expected if there was no dependence would be compared with the numbers of each combination actually seen in the sample.

The car with its different characteristics (body and interior colour) remains together as a physical unit; however, this does not necessarily mean that the colours of body and interior are dependent. Dependence between body and interior colours will depend on how the cars were manufactured. The car can form an analogy to a chromosome with its different characteristics (loci). Although these loci remain together physically during inheritance, whether or not their values (alleles) are dependent will depend on the initial circumstances. Since these circumstances are unknown, the fact of two loci being physically close together should not be equated to the values of their alleles being related to each other.

The way forward for the expert statistical witness in criminal trials in Australia is not clear. If expert evidence is to be used effectively as a tool in the pursuit of justice in criminal cases, there needs to be some mechanism for the academic arguments to be resolved in pretrial conference; there must be full disclosure by both parties, as is currently required in civil courts in Australia. In the words of Justice Olsen (1999):

> The prohibition on defense disclosure does not serve the goal of efficiency in the administration of justice.

In late 1998, the Federal Court of Australia released a *Practice Direction: Guidelines for Expert Witnesses in proceedings of the Federal Court of Australia*, a copy of which is to be provided "to any expert witness [counsel] propose to retain for the purpose of giving a report and giving evidence in a proceeding." This document states clearly that the paramount duty of an expert witness: "is to the Court and not to the person retaining the expert." A written report is required of all expert witnesses, and details are given of the information that must be included in such a report. Reports are to be exchanged, and the expert must convey any change of opinion resulting from the viewing of an exchanged report or for any other reason, in writing to the court. Provision is made for experts' conferences, which would occur "at the direction of the Court", and at which: "it would be improper conduct for an expert to be given or to accept instructions not to reach agreement."

In the trial of *R v Humphrey* (1999; refer to Section 2.1 for details of this case) following a substantial voir dire and subsequent ruling admitting all components of the DNA evidence, the barristers on both sides were able to agree on the statistical issues, and a single document of *Statement of Fact* was read to the jury during the trial by the court associate; neither expert witness was called. These are small steps, but it is hoped that they will "catalyse a review of entrenched cultural attitudes [and allow a criminal justice system in which] the real issues in contention are identified and focussed on; and that formal evidence and debate is limited to those issues." (Olsson, 1999).

Without change, it is likely that the pressures and apparent injustices imposed by the adversarial system as applied in Australia will exclude those experts who could provide valuable information to a jury's deliberation. One may well ask, "Why does anyone do it?"

Acknowledgments

My thanks go firstly to Joe Gastwirth for the invitation to contribute this material and for his encouragement and patience, through times when it seemed a hopeless task. His advice, guidance, and editorial suggestions have been greatly appreciated.

I would like to acknowledge the assistance of The Honourable Justice Olsson (South Australian Supreme Court) in preparing this chapter. He gave willingly of his time and expertise, and offered much encouragement. Thanks also to the biologists in the state forensic laboratories, particularly in Darwin, Adelaide, Perth, and Brisbane, who made valuable comments and suggestions on early drafts of this work, and who have assisted me at various points in my experiences as an expert statistical witness. Their patience in persevering with explanations until I understood enough of the science of DNA to talk sensibly, and their advice to me on court protocols and "acting" in the witness box in the different Australian jurisdictions, are greatly appreciated. Wendy Abraham (QC) has been a continuing source of legal information and encouragement, having provided my initial training as an expert witness. Robert Curnow, David Balding, and two anonymous referees also provided valuable suggestions and editorial comments, and I thank them for this advice.

Some of the material in this chapter was developed while the author was on secondment to the Australian National Institute of Forensic Science.

6   Cases Cited

Capacci v Katz and Besthoff Inc. (1983) 711 F.2d 647 (5th Cir. 1983).
People v Collins, reported in Fairley and Mosteller (1974).
R v Abbott (1996) Supreme Court of Queensland, Brisbane, Australia.
R v Humphrey (1999) SASC 67, Supreme Court of South Australia, Adelaide, Australia.
R v Harrison (1998) Supreme Court of the Northern Territory, Darwin, Australia.
R v Hobby and Zaggit (1997) Supreme Court of Western Australia, Perth, Australia.
R v Jarrett (1994) 62 SASR 443, Supreme Court of South Australia, Adelaide, Australia.
R v Love, Smith and Wanganeen (1998) Supreme Court of South Australia, Adelaide, Australia.
R v Mitchell (1997) ACTR 48, Federal Supreme Court, Australian Capital Territory, Canberra, Australia.
R v Staats (1997) Supreme Court of the Northern Territory, Darwin, Australia.
R v White (1998) Supreme Court of Queensland, Brisbane, Australia.
R v Williams (1997) Supreme Court of Western Australia, Perth, Australia.

REFERENCES

[1] Aitken, C.G.G. (2000) Evidence interpretation and sample size determination. In *Statistical Science in the Courtroom*. Editor: J.L. Gastwirth. Springer-Verlag, New York.

[2] Allen, C.R. (1998) *Adams* and the Person in the Locked room. *International Commentary on Evidence*, August, 12 pages.

[3] Angell, M. (1996) *Science on Trial*. Norton, New York.

[4] Cooke, G. (1999) The DNA Database. Letter to the Editor—*Criminal Law Review* pp. 175–176.

[5] Evett, I.W. and Weir, B.S. (1998) *Interpreting DNA Evidence*. Sinauer Associates, Inc., Massachusetts.

[6] Fairley, W.B. and Mosteller, F. (1974) A conversation about Collins. *University of Chicago Law Review*, **41**: 541–613.

[7] Federal Court of Australia (1998) *Practice Direction: Guidelines for Expert Witnesses in Proceedings in the Federal Court of Australia*, Law Council of Australia, Canberra.

[8] Fienberg, S.E. (1997) Ethics and the expert witness: statistics on trial. *Journal of the Royal Statistical Society: A*, **160:** Part 2, 321–331.

[9] Gastwirth, J.L. (1988a) *Statistical Reasoning in Law and Public Policy*, vol. 1, *Statistical Concepts and issues of Fairness*. Academic Press: San Diego.

[10] Gastwirth, J.L. (1988b) *Statistical Reasoning in Law and Public Policy*, vol. 2, *Tort Law, Evidence and Health*. Academic Press: San Diego.

[11] Hastie, R. (1993) Introduction, in *Inside the Juror: The psychology of juror decision making*. Ed. Reid Hastie, Cambridge University Press.

[12] Hastie, R. and Pennington, N. (1995) Cognitive Approaches to Judgement and Decision Making. *The Psychology of Learning and Motivation* **32**.

[13] Kalven J. and Zeisel H. (1966) *The American Jury*. Little and Brown, Boston MA.

[14] Meier, P. (1986) Damned liars and expert witnesses. *Journal of American Statistical Association*, **81**, 269–276.

[15] Olsson, L.J. (1999) To how much silence ought an accused be entitled? *Journal of Judicial Administration*, **8**, 131–134.

[16] Roberts H. (1998) Interpretation of DNA evidence in courts of law. *Australian Journal of Forensic Science*, **30**, 29–40.

[17] Ross, A.M. (1998) Controversy corner: the quest for truth. *Australian Journal of Forensic Sciences*. **30**:41–44.

[18] Schum, D.A. and Martin, A.W. (1993) Formal and empirical research on cascaded inference in jurisprudence. in: *Inside the Juror: The psychology of juror decision making*. Ed. Reid Hastie, Cambridge University Press.

[19] Selinger, B. (1986) Expert evidence and the ultimate question. *Criminal Law Journal* **10:** 247–254.

[20] Weinstein, J.B. (1988) Litigation and statistics. *Statistical Science*, **3**, 286–297.

A Likelihood Approach to DNA Evidence[1]

Beverly G. Mellen

Abstract

Evidence based on human deoxyribonucleic acid (DNA) is now widely admitted in court in both civil and criminal cases. The overall objective of presenting DNA and other evidence in court is to help the trier of fact to understand past events. Critical to this objective are the legal concepts of relevance and reliability, or trustworthiness. In this article, logical connections are put forward between evidential relevance and reliability on the one hand, and statistical concepts and associated statistical tools available for assessing and presenting DNA evidence on the other. Among the tools discussed are likelihood ratios and probabilities of weak evidence and strong misleading evidence. For the purpose of introducing some of the molecular tools used to classify DNA types in court, RFLP and PCR-based methods are described.

Key words and phrases. Daubert, deoxyribonucleic acid, evidentiary reliability, likelihood ratio, polymerase chain reaction, probabilities of weak and misleading evidence, profile likelihood function, relevance, restriction fragment length polymorphism, scientific evidence.

1 Introduction

Evidence based on deoxyribonucleic acid (DNA) is now widely admitted in court in both civil and criminal trials. As with longtime evidentiary staples such as fingerprints and blood-typing, DNA evidence can link a defendant to a crime scene. DNA evidence can have extraordinary power either to implicate, as when a "match" is observed between DNA from a defendant and a crime scene, or to exclude, as when there is not a match. This power derives from the high degree of stability of DNA in an individual, combined with the high level of variation among individuals. But the introduction of this powerful source of evidence into court has brought considerable controversy. As described in other articles in this volume, including "The Consequences of Defending DNA Statistics," by Weir, and "Interpreting DNA Evidence: Can Probability Theory Help?" by Balding, statistics has played a central role.

In the present article, the role of statistics in DNA evidence is presented with the following aims:

---

[1] Work on this article was performed while the author was at Vanderbilt University School of Medicine.

1. To describe statistical tools specifically designed to

    (a) objectively measure the strength of evidence embodied in a particular set of observations (Section 3.1), and to
    (b) measure and control probabilities that weak evidence or strong misleading evidence will be generated in evidence-gathering procedures (Section 3.2)

    (Mellen and Royall 1997; Royall 1998).
2. To argue that these statistical tools are appropriate for presenting and assessing DNA evidence in legal cases (Sections 2 and 4).

These items draw on statistical thinking, or reasoning, which is a major theme in this article. But precisely what is statistical reasoning?

Mallows explored the nature of the statistical reasoning process in a recent Fisher Memorial Lecture (1998). In his paper, Mallows stressed early steps in the process: deciding what the relevant population is, what the relevant data are, and how these relate to the purpose of a statistical study. He also described the overall process, stating:

> Statistical thinking concerns the relation of quantitative data to a real-world problem, often in the presence of variability and uncertainty. It attempts to make precise and explicit what the data has to say about the problem of interest (Mallows 1998).

All of these elements of statistical reasoning come into play in the context of DNA evidence. What is described in the present article is one approach to making precise and explicit what DNA evidence has to say.

Before describing in some depth the needed statistical tools (probability models, likelihood ratios, and probabilities of misleading evidence), the next section introduces two U.S. court requirements of scientific evidence: relevance and reliability. These are discussed later in the article in connection with the statistical tools. In the context of DNA data, the theory of likelihood ratios addresses issues of relevance, whereas probabilities of misleading evidence address aspects of reliability.

2 Scientific Evidence: Relevance and Reliability

In a legal case, the objective of presenting and assessing evidence is to describe clues that enable the trier of fact, either judge or jury, to understand the past. It is important to understand the past only when it relates to consequential facts. Thus, "clues" are offered in court only when they constitute relevant evidence, where *relevance* is defined in Rule 401 of the Federal Rules of Evidence as "having any tendency to make the existence of any fact that is of consequence to the determination of the action more probable or less probable than it would be without the evidence." The trier of fact may "weigh" the evidence, and thereby reach a closer understanding of the past in order to make a judgment.

Scientific evidence most often finds its way into the courtroom in the form of expert testimony. As laid out in Rule 702 of the Federal Rules of Evidence, expert witnesses may be allowed to testify as follows:

If scientific, technical, or other specialized knowledge will assist the trier of fact to understand the evidence or to determine a fact in issue, a witness qualified as an expert by knowledge, skill, experience, training, or education, may testify thereto in the form of an opinion or otherwise.

Thus, for an expert's scientific knowledge to be admissible as evidence, it too must assist the trier of fact.

In a 1993 U.S. Supreme Court decision, *Daubert v. Merrell Dow Pharmaceuticals*, the Court told us that scientific knowledge will assist the trier of fact only if it is also *reliable*, or trustworthy:

In short, the requirement that an expert's testimony pertain to "scientific knowledge" establishes a standard of... evidentiary reliability—that is, trustworthiness.

In a case involving scientific evidence, evidentiary reliability will be based upon scientific validity.

Thus, scientific knowledge that is presented as expert testimony must have a valid scientific basis. This may be established through elaboration of the process by which the conclusions were reached.

In a more recent U.S. Supreme Court decision, *Kumho Tire Co., Ltd. v. Carmichael* (1999), the Court revisited issues of evidentiary reliability, specifically "whether, or how, *Daubert* applies to expert testimony that might be characterized as based not upon 'scientific' knowledge, but rather upon 'technical' or 'other specialized' knowledge." After noting that "[the language of Rule 702] makes no relevant distinction between 'scientific' knowledge and 'technical' or 'other specialized' knowledge," and "there is no clear line that divides the one from the others," the Court concluded:

Daubert's general principles apply to the expert matters described in Rule 702. The Rule, in respect to all such matters, "establishes a standard of evidentiary reliability." 509 U.S., at 590.
And where such testimony's factual basis, data, principles, methods, or their application are called sufficiently into question ... the trial judge must determine whether the testimony has "a reliable basis in the knowledge and experience of [the relevant] discipline." 509 U.S., at 592.
... the law grants a district court the same broad latitude when it decides *how* to determine reliability as it enjoys in respect to its ultimate reliability determination.

Thus, all expert testimony covered by rule 702 must have a reliable basis. The determination of reliability and the basis for this determination are the responsibility of the trial judge.

3 Likelihood Paradigm

3.1 Statistical Evidence and Likelihood Ratios

The aim of this section is to introduce methods that can be used to measure the strength of statistical evidence. What is meant by *statistical evidence* are observations interpreted under a *probability model*. The model consists of a collection of probability distributions, and the observations are conceptualized as having been generated from one of the distributions (Royall 1998).

The basic rule for interpreting statistical evidence in this framework is what Hacking (1965) named the *law of likelihood*. It states:

> If hypothesis A implies that the probability a random variable X takes the value x is $P(X = x|A)$, while hypothesis B implies that the probability is $P(X = x|B)$, then the observation x is evidence supporting A over B if $P(X = x|A) > P(X = x|B)$, and the *likelihood ratio*, $P(X = x|A)/P(X = x|B)$, measures the strength of this evidence (Royall 1998).

This law tells us how to evaluate whether an observation x is evidence favoring one hypothesis over another. It also provides us with a measure of the strength of that statistical evidence via the likelihood ratio. The larger the ratio, the stronger the evidence in favor of hypothesis A over hypothesis B; the smaller the ratio, the stronger the evidence in favor of hypothesis B over hypothesis A. (For a more complete discussion of the law of likelihood, see Edwards 1972 and Royall 1997.)

A second, related, meaning for the likelihood ratio is provided in the following argument. If we can suppose that $P(A)/P(B)$ is the probability ratio or prior odds for hypothesis A relative to hypothesis B before X is observed, then after the observation $X = x$, this probability ratio becomes the posterior probability ratio or odds, $P(A|X = x)/P(B|X = x)$, according to the equation

$$\frac{P(A|X = x)}{P(B|X = x)} = \frac{P(X = x|A)}{P(X = x|B)} \times \frac{P(A)}{P(B)}. \tag{1}$$

That is, the likelihood ratio is the factor by which the prior odds $P(A)/P(B)$ is multiplied to obtain the posterior odds given the observation x. More generally, this factor is the *Bayes factor* of Bayesian statistics.

To illustrate the use of likelihood ratios, consider the following example. Suppose a population of individuals is known to have N members, and associated with each member there is a constant that is equal to either 1 or 0, indicating the presence or absence of a particular trait. Let $1, 2, \ldots, N$ denote the members of the population, and let $x_1, x_2, \ldots, x_N$ denote the corresponding constants for the trait.

Now suppose that what is of interest is the total number in the population having the trait, that is, the value of the sum $T = \sum_{i=1}^{N} x_i$. But suppose the observation of only a subset of the total N is possible, through selection of a simple random sample. (A simple random sample of size n is one that is generated using any one of a number of sampling schemes that assigns the same probability of selection to all possible subsets of size n from the population.) The observed traits (i.e., x values) from the sample tell us something about the population total, $T = \sum_{i=1}^{N} x_i$.

Let S denote a (random) sample of size n selected using such a sampling procedure, and let the sum $\sum_{i \in S} x_i$ denote the total number having the trait in the sample, called the sample total. Then the probability distribution for this sample total is the hypergeometric distribution,

$$P\left(\sum_{i \in S} x_i = t\right) = \frac{\dbinom{T}{t} \dbinom{N-T}{n-t}}{\dbinom{N}{n}}, \tag{2}$$

where t can take integer values that satisfy $\max\{n - (N - T), 0\} \leq t \leq \min\{T, n\}$.

Equation (2) is a function of the population total T when N, n, and the sample total are held constant. This function, denoted by $L(T)$ in equation (3) below, is called the *likelihood function*, and can be used to derive likelihood ratios that measure the evidence in an observed sample total favoring one value of the population total, say T_A, over another, say T_B. Since it is likelihood ratios like $L(T_A)/L(T_B)$ and not the likelihood function itself that have meaning, the likelihood function is usually defined only to within an arbitrary constant. In this case, it is

$$L(T) = \begin{cases} \dbinom{T}{t} \dbinom{N-T}{n-t} & \text{if } T \in \{t, t+1, \ldots, t + (N - n)\}, \\ 0 & \text{otherwise.} \end{cases} \tag{3}$$

(Note that the likelihood function equals zero at impossible values for T, including those values ruled out by the observed sample total t, e.g., $T = t - 1$.) If T_A and T_B are possible values for the population total based on both the observed sample total t and the known values of N and n, then equation (3) leads to the general form for the likelihood ratio

$$\frac{L(T_A)}{L(T_B)} = \frac{\dbinom{T_A}{t} \dbinom{N - T_A}{n - t}}{\dbinom{T_B}{t} \dbinom{N - T_B}{n - t}}. \tag{4}$$

For illustration, suppose a sample total $t = 1$ is observed in a sample of $n = 90$ members from a population of size $N = 100$. Based on this sample, possible values for the population total are $1, 2, \ldots$, and 11. Applying the law of likelihood, we find that the evidence supports a population total of $T = 1$ over each of the other possible totals, and there is support in favor of $T = 2$ over each value $T > 2$, since the likelihood decreases with increasing values of $T > 1$. The law of likelihood also tells us that a measure of the strength of the evidence in favor of the total $T = 1$ over $T = 2$ is the likelihood ratio

$$\frac{L(1)}{L(2)} = \frac{\binom{1}{1}\binom{100-1}{90-1}}{\binom{2}{1}\binom{100-2}{90-1}} = 4.95. \tag{5}$$

A question that arises is, "How strong is the evidence when the likelihood ratio is 4.95?" Based on benchmarks from a set of canonical experiments, likelihood ratios can be calibrated as follows. Suppose either of two urns—one containing only white balls (A), and another containing equal numbers of white and black balls (B)—is selected for drawing balls with replacement. Then the likelihood ratios $2, 4, 8, \ldots$ measure the strength of evidence in favor of urn A over B after observing only white balls from $1, 2, 3, \ldots$ consecutive draws (Royall 1997, pp. 11–12). Therefore, the likelihood ratio 4.95 represents evidence that is stronger than that of only two white balls, but is not as strong as that of three white balls, as drawn in the canonical experiments. Using these benchmarks, most would consider this weak evidence.

A related interpretation of the likelihood ratio 4.95 is as the factor by which prior odds are multiplied to obtain posterior odds, given the observed data. In this framework, suppose the prior odds $P(T = 1) : P(T = 2)$ are $1 : 99$, for example. Then these odds, increased by a factor of 4.95, yield posterior odds equaling $1 : 20$. If the prior odds were exactly $1 : 4.95$, then the posterior odds would be even ($1 : 1$). In summary, the observation of only 1 person with the trait in the sample is still only weak evidence in favor of a population total $T = 1$ over $T = 2$—specifically, it is evidence only strong enough to convert odds of $1 : 4.95$ to even odds—when the number of unobserved persons in a population of size $N = 100$ is $N - n = 10$.

3.2 Probabilities of Weak Evidence and Strong Misleading Evidence

The aim of this section is to introduce methods that can be used to measure and control probabilities that weak evidence or strong misleading evidence will be generated in evidence-gathering procedures. In the context of the previous example, how might an observed sample that represents weak evidence with a likelihood ratio of only 4.95 be avoided? How might strong evidence in favor of a false hypothesis be avoided?

As before, suppose we have a population of size $N = 100$ and we are interested in the total number in the population with a particular trait. If we set out to observe a simple random sample of size n, then what is the probability we will observe only

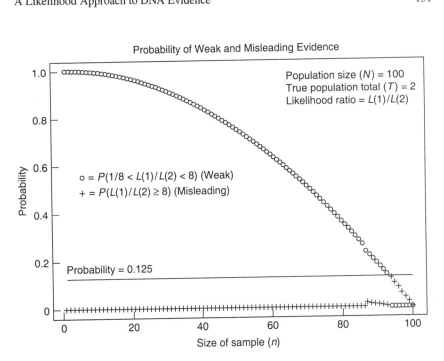

Figure 1. Probability of observing weak evidence, $P(1/k < L(1)/L(2) < k)$, and probability of observing strong evidence favoring the false hypothesis (population total $(T) = 1$), $P(L(1)/L(2) \geq k)$, in hypergeometric example, where population size $(N) = 100$ and $k = 8$. These two probabilities, represented by circles and plus signs, respectively, are functions of sample size, n.

weak evidence? What is the probability we will observe strong evidence favoring a false hypothesis over the truth?

These probabilities depend on not only the size of the sample but also (1) the true population total, (2) the particular false hypothesis, and (3) the likelihood ratio threshold that is used to delineate strong evidence. Suppose we are planning to assess a sample total as evidence with respect to whether the trait is unique within the population, i.e. $T = 1$, versus $T = 2$. Furthermore, suppose $T = 2$ is the truth. Then if we use as the likelihood ratio threshold for strong evidence the value 8 (i.e., three white balls in the canonical experiment), then the probability of observing *weak evidence* in favor of $T = 1$ over $T = 2$, or vice versa, can be denoted by $P(\frac{1}{8} < L(1)/L(2) < 8)$. The probability of observing *strong evidence* favoring the false hypothesis $T = 1$ over $T = 2$ can be denoted by $P(L(1)/L(2) \geq 8)$.

These two probabilities, calculated using the distribution function (2), are illustrated in Figure 1. As might be expected, the probability of observing weak evidence (i.e., the failure to observe strong evidence in either direction) is close to 1 for small samples. As sample size increases, this probability decreases, reaching zero for large samples. This decrease is accounted for by corresponding increases in the probabilities of observing strong evidence—predominantly, in the probability of observing strong evidence in favor of the true hypothesis. The probability of observing strong evidence in the opposite direction, i.e., observing strong misleading evidence in favor of $T = 1$ over $T = 2$, remains quite small, as desired, regardless of sample size. However, for large sample sizes, this probability is positive, and it reaches its maximum value when the sample size is $n = 94$.

Probability theory tells us that the probability of strong misleading evidence defined in this manner is always bounded by a value less than 1. Specifically, for any given distinct statistical hypotheses A and B, if B is true, then

$$P(P(X|A)/P(X|B) \geq k) \leq 1/k, \tag{6}$$

where k is any given positive constant greater than 1 (Royall 1997, p. 7). Thus, for a likelihood ratio threshold $k = 8$, we can say that in our example the probability is at least as small as $\frac{1}{8} = 0.125$ that the sampling procedure will result in a likelihood ratio $L(1)/L(2)$ as great as 8 when $T = 2$, regardless of sample size (see Figure 1). Note that in this case, the bound is not attained, and the maximum probability is equal to 0.117.

The probabilities of weak evidence and strong misleading evidence can be used to plan sample sizes and thereby control the frequency of these undesirable outcomes. In our example, we know that if evidence is gathered about the true population total by observing a sample, then the probability that strong misleading evidence will result is no greater than 0.125 (when strong evidence is defined by a likelihood ratio ≥ 8). However, in the case of $T = 2$, the probability that weak evidence will be observed with respect to $T = 1$ versus $T = 2$ falls below 0.5, for example, only if the sample size n is greater than 70. The probability of weak evidence is less than 0.125 only if the sample size is greater than 93 (see Figure 1). After considering such probabilities and our tolerance for observing weak evidence, we might decide that a sample of $n = 71$ is sufficient for gathering evidence about the true population total, or that a larger sample is needed.

In summary, the avoidance in evidence-gathering procedures of generating observations that represent weak evidence or strong misleading evidence is desirable. Probabilities of weak evidence and strong misleading evidence are measures of the propensity of evidence-gathering procedures for generating these undesirable outcomes. Natural limits on the probability of observing strong misleading evidence together with the relation between sample size and the probability of weak evidence allow for control over the frequency with which weak and misleading evidence is generated.

The overall aim of the next three sections is to make the argument that these statistical tools based on likelihoods are appropriate for presenting and assessing DNA evidence in legal cases. For example, the idea of using likelihood ratios as measures of evidential strength, and controlling undesirable outcomes by measuring and controlling probabilities of observing strong misleading evidence, is extended to the context of DNA evidence. The first of these sections provides some genetic background on DNA evidence.

4 DNA Evidence as Statistical Evidence

4.1 Human DNA

DNA evidence admitted for the purpose of human identification provides information about DNA molecules derived from individuals. DNA molecules are found in nearly all cells. These molecules are usually duplicated during cell division, and as a result, nearly all cells within a person contain a complete copy of the person's DNA.

Within cells, DNA molecules are paired. One molecule in each pair derives from DNA belonging to the person's mother, and the other derives from DNA of the father. This pairing is important for interpreting DNA samples. Two distinct components, called alleles, are typically observed from testing the DNA of one person at a single location (locus) among the DNA molecules. One allele is observed if the maternally and paternally derived versions are indistinguishable. Testing at multiple DNA locations (loci) in an individual results in what is called a multilocus genotype. It is composed of the maternally and paternally derived alleles for each locus tested. For example, an individual i's genotype at three loci (a, b, c) can be denoted by $(\{a_{i1}, a_{i2}\}, \{b_{i1}, b_{i2}\}, \{c_{i1}, c_{i2}\})$. A second person, j, has an identical or "matching" three-locus genotype if $\{a_{i1}, a_{i2}\} = \{a_{j1}, a_{j2}\}$, $\{b_{i1}, b_{i2}\} = \{b_{j1}, b_{j2}\}$, and $\{c_{i1}, c_{i2}\} = \{c_{j1}, c_{j2}\}$.

Before discussing how DNA testing yields multilocus genotypes, some background on the structure of DNA molecules is needed. Each DNA molecule is composed of (1) two long strands twisted to form a double helix, and (2) components called bases (denoted by A, T, G, and C) bound along each strand, yielding what are called base sequences. Bonding between pairs of bases on the separate strands holds the double helix together. Since a stable helix requires that bases of the types A and T be paired with one another and the bases G and C be paired with one another, the strands of a DNA molecule usually have sequences that are complementary (e.g., $GAATTC\ldots$ and $CTTAAG\ldots$). These complementary sequences constitute the overall DNA molecule sequence. [Further information on DNA and fundamentals of molecular genetics can be found at http://www.ornl.gov/hgmis/publicat/primer/intro.html (Human Genome Program 1992).]

Most human DNA sequences at a given locus tend to be similar, even between unrelated people. However, with the vast amount of genetic material in each person, many DNA loci exhibit considerable between-person variation. It is this variation between individuals, and the constancy of DNA within individuals, that are critical to the success of human identification through DNA evidence. Loci that tend to have a high level of between-person variation are selected for testing.

For multilocus genotype testing there are currently two general procedures used in the courtroom. The first procedure, called restriction fragment length polymorphism (RFLP) analysis, was introduced in the late 1980s. In RFLP analysis, DNA molecules are first separated from cells and other materials in the sample. The DNA is then exposed to restriction enzymes, which cut DNA molecules into smaller pieces, or fragments. Each restriction enzyme consistently cuts the DNA at all copies of an enzyme-specific short sequence, so that the resultant mixture of fragments is always the same within a person but might vary between people due to DNA sequence variation. The DNA fragments from the sample are placed in a small well at the end of a thin rectangular gel plate. When an electrical field is applied to the gel using a procedure called electrophoresis, the DNA fragments spread in a lane across the gel, ordered by fragment length, with the smallest fragments farthest from the well. Without disrupting this length-ordering, the DNA is transferred and affixed to a nylon membrane, and the strands are chemically separated within the double helix. The strands are then exposed to copies of a radioactively-labeled, single-stranded DNA molecule called a probe. The probe has a base sequence that is complementary to a strand from a unique locus, called the target locus, within the original molecules. The probe binds to strands that contain some or all of this target-locus complementary sequence. After excess probe is removed, a technique called autoradiography is used to record the locations of strands to which the probe has bound.

In RFLP analysis, a pattern of dark bands appears on the autoradiograph where a substantial amount of probe has bound. If the sample contains DNA from one person, then each band is part of either the maternally or paternally derived allele, or both. To classify the resultant single-locus genotype (e.g., $\{b_{i1}, b_{i2}\}$, where b_{i1} and b_{i2} are alleles at locus b in individual i), the band locations are compared with those from known alleles. (Because some small DNA fragments are undetectable due to migration off of the gel during electrophoresis, care must be taken not to misinterpret results with only one allele.) Multiple loci—typically 4 to 6 for purposes of human identification—are tested by repeating this procedure using different restriction enzyme and probe combinations.

The name RFLP, or "restriction fragment length polymorphism," refers to the between-person variation in DNA sequences that leads to fragments of differing lengths when the DNA is cut by restriction enzymes. The term RFLP is usually reserved for DNA sequence variants that result from between-person differences in the pattern of DNA sites cut by the restriction enzyme within the locus. In human identification applications, the term RFLP is used more generally. Loci that tend to be selected for the RFLP procedure are "variable number tandem repeat" (VNTR) loci, which means that the restriction fragments are composed of tandemly repeated sequences of DNA. The number of repeats determines the fragment length, and the greater the variation in repeat number, the greater the variation among genotypes at the locus. The use of VNTR loci with a very high level of variation has been instrumental in the success of these analyses for human identification.

The second general procedure for testing genetic loci, often referred to as polymerase chain reaction (PCR), was introduced in the courtroom in the mid-1990s. PCR is a method for the repeated replication of relatively short targeted DNA segments—typically < 350 base pairs in length. The replication step of PCR is useful when samples are small, old, or otherwise partially degraded due to conditions adverse to the stability of DNA molecules. DNA is isolated from the sample, and is then used as a template to make new copies. This DNA "amplification" is accomplished by first mixing the DNA from the original sample with (1) short pieces of single-stranded DNA called primers, which are complementary to the DNA sequences flanking the target locus (one requirement of PCR is that the flanking DNA must have a known sequence for making the primers); (2) DNA polymerase, the enzyme that is primarily responsible for DNA replication in living organisms; and (3) other chemicals needed for DNA replication. The mixture is then heated so that the DNA strands in the double helix separate, and the primers of single-stranded DNA bind to the exposed complementary flanking strands. DNA polymerase acts to produce copies of the target locus by extending the flanking primer strands across the intervening single-stranded target sequence. This procedure may be repeated to produce a sufficient amount of DNA to complete genotype testing (description below). Typically, two or more loci are amplified simultaneously using what is called multiplex PCR. One drawback of the replication process of PCR is that additional precautions must be used to prevent the introduction of contaminants, especially other human DNA, into samples. If other DNA is introduced, then alleles from this DNA might undergo amplification and appear in the results along with alleles from the original sample.

Loci that tend to be used with PCR in human identification belong to a subset of VNTR loci, called "short tandem repeat" (STR) loci. For human identification purposes, "short" typically means repeats of 4 or 5 base pairs. The amount of between-person variation for STRs is generally not as great as it is for RFLPs. However, STR loci are quite plentiful in humans, and the lower level of variation can be offset by genotype testing at a greater number of loci (the addition of loci also has the benefit of diminishing the importance of a full sibling and others who, for example, might be accused of a crime and have a greater chance of sharing the same multilocus genotype with a true perpetrator due to relatedness through mothers and fathers). Though fewer than 13 loci might be used in routine cases, the FBI has designated a standard set of 13 STR loci, called the loci of the "Combined DNA Index System" (CODIS). (CODIS is part of an ongoing effort in the U.S. to create a large database of genotypes from individuals convicted of a felony sex offense or other violent crime, and from crime scene samples such as semen stains and blood.)

Following the replication step of PCR, genotype testing is based on the analysis of STR fragments using gel electrophoresis, as in RFLP analysis. However, allele-specific probes and fluorescent detection systems are used, which make PCR-based methods less expensive and less time-consuming than the previous methods. Furthermore, since alleles are more directly identified in PCR-based STR methods, the procedures required for declaring a match between two multilocus genotypes and for estimating the probability of specific alleles is more straightforward than in RFLP analysis. New developments in genotype testing continue, which will impact procedures for human identification using DNA evidence. In 1998, the National Commission on the Future of DNA Evidence was formed in part to make recommendations on such developments (for further information, see http://www.ojp.usdoj.gov/nij/dna/welcome.html).

4.2 Likelihood Ratios, Weighing DNA Evidence, and Relevance

DNA identification evidence in the form of multilocus genotypes (described above) is commonly evaluated as statistical evidence in court. The aim in this and the next section is to provide reasoning behind the presentation and assessment of these DNA observations using statistical tools: probability models, likelihood ratios, and probabilities of misleading evidence. The connection between these statistical tools and the legal concepts of relevance and reliability is discussed as well.

Likelihood ratios provide an objective means for weighing DNA evidence. Accordingly, they may assist a judge or jury in understanding a consequential fact in a case. Such a fact that might be at issue is whether the DNA that is presented in court as evidence from a crime scene is derived from the same person as that presented as DNA from the defendant. Suppose the DNA from the crime scene and that from the defendant are found to match, as determined using either RFLP or PCR procedures at several loci, each with a high level of between-person variation. There are various hypothetical situations in which one person is the common source of these two DNA samples as presented, including the following:

1. The defendant leaves some of his or her DNA at the crime scene, and both the crime scene and defendant's sample are handled and tested properly.
2. Someone other than the defendant who has access to a sample of the defendant's blood leaves some of it at the crime scene, and both the crime scene and defendant's sample are handled and tested properly.
3. The same situation as 1, except that the samples are mishandled, and the defendant's blood is mistakenly tested as both the crime scene and defendant's sample (important aspects of this unusual type of situation are discussed elsewhere in this volume by Balding, in "Interpreting DNA Evidence: Can Probability Theory Help?").

(In the event that there is reason to believe that two or more individuals contributed DNA to a sample, methods for interpreting "mixed samples" must be used; see Weir et al. 1997.)

The likelihood ratios described in this section are relevant for comparing any of the three situations above with the one in which DNA left at the crime scene is from someone who is distinct from the defendant but whose multilocus genotype is the same as the defendant's. In order to keep track of these two types of situations, some notation is needed. Let the label s denote the unknown *source* of the crime scene DNA, and let d denote the *defendant*. Thus, $s = d$ denotes the situation in which the two are the same person. Let $s \neq d$ denote the situation in which they are *not* the same person, but the source s is instead another possible suspect, either known or unknown, in the same crime.

A simplified version of this notation is used below to write an expression for the likelihood function. The likelihood in this case is a function of δ, which is defined as

$$
\delta = \begin{cases} 1 & \text{if the defendant is the source of the crime scene DNA } (s = d), \\ 0 & \text{if another possible suspect is the source } (s \neq d). \end{cases}
$$

Thus, the values of δ correspond with two hypotheses—namely, the DNA is from one person, or it is from two different people.

In order for the DNA observations to be evaluated as statistical evidence, they must be conceptualized as having been randomly generated according to a probability distribution. (For a discussion of how to handle non-DNA evidence and distinct alternative suspects within this framework, see Mellen 1997, and Mellen and Royall 1997.) Let the notation Z_i represent the random multilocus genotype from person i. Then under the hypothesis $\delta = 1$, Z_s and Z_d are the *same* random variable, and therefore must be modeled using the same probability distribution. In contrast, under $\delta = 0$, these two random variables are distinct. Consequently, they might or might not share the same probability distribution, and the joint distribution between the two must also be specified (in this volume, see Weir, "The Consequences of Defending DNA Statistics" for a discussion of possible dependencies between these two genotypes).

Now suppose a match is observed between the DNA from the source and defendant: $Z_s = Z_d = z$, where z denotes the particular genotype that is observed, for example a six-locus genotype (loci a–f), represented by ($\{a_{i1}, a_{i2}\}, \{b_{i1}, b_{i2}\},$ $\ldots, \{f_{i1}, f_{i2}\}$). In the absence of information about the rarity of z, the observation of a match has little evidential value. To evaluate the match, another piece of evidence is critical: a collection of genotypes observed at the same loci as in the source and defendant, but from a *reference sample*, that is, in individuals who serve as references. Let n denote the number of individuals in this reference sample, and let the vector $\mathbf{Z}_n$ denote the corresponding random genotypes with observations $\mathbf{z} = (z_1, z_2, \ldots, z_n)$. Then the probability distribution for the observed genotypes can be denoted by

$$
\begin{aligned}
& P(Z_s = z, Z_d = z, \mathbf{Z}_n = \mathbf{z}) \\
&= P(Z_s = z, Z_d = z | \mathbf{Z}_n = \mathbf{z}) P(\mathbf{Z}_n = \mathbf{z}) \\
&= \begin{cases} P(Z_d = z) P(\mathbf{Z}_n = \mathbf{z}) & \text{if } \delta = 1, \\ P(Z_s = z | Z_d = z) P(Z_d = z) P(\mathbf{Z}_n = \mathbf{z}) & \text{if } \delta = 0, \end{cases}
\end{aligned}
\tag{7}
$$

assuming independence between the matching and reference genotypes.

The likelihood function for all of the DNA data is given in equation (8) below. In this expression, the reference sample size n and the genotypes z and $\mathbf{z}$ are implied constants. That is, the likelihood function is defined using both the reference sample size, n, and the observed matching genotype, z. The parameter of interest, δ, and the DNA probabilities (see equation (7)) are unknown variables. To further simplify the appearance of the likelihood function, let θ_d and $\theta_{s|d}$ denote the probabilities

$P(Z_d = z)$ and $P(Z_s = z|Z_d = z)$, respectively, and let a vector parameter θ contain the elements $\theta_d, \theta_{s|d}$, and $P(\mathbf{Z}_n = \mathbf{z})$. Then the likelihood function can be written as

$$L(\delta, \theta) = \begin{cases} \theta_d L_R(\theta) & \text{if } \delta = 1, \\ \theta_{s|d}\theta_d L_R(\theta) & \text{if } \delta = 0, \end{cases} \tag{8}$$

where $L_R(\theta)$ is the likelihood function for the observed reference sample.

The likelihood function in (8) is used to derive likelihood ratios that measure the strength of the DNA evidence in favor of the defendant being the source of the crime scene DNA ($\delta = 1$) versus another possible suspect being the source ($\delta = 0$). The general form for this ratio is thus

$$\frac{L(1, \theta)}{L(0, \theta)} = \frac{1}{\theta_{s|d}}, \tag{9}$$

assuming that θ_d and $L_R(\theta)$ do not depend on δ. If under $\delta = 0$ the probability $\theta_{s|d} = P(Z_s = z|Z_d = z)$ is close to 1, as is generally the case when the genotype z is expected to be common among possible suspects in the crime excluding the defendant, then the strength of the DNA evidence that implicates the defendant is not great. On the other hand, if the probability $\theta_{s|d}$ is small, as is generally the case when the genotype z is expected to be rare among other possible suspects, then the strength of this implicating evidence is great.

When the likelihood ratio assumes a value other than 1, the DNA evidence is *relevant* in the legal sense of relevance. A likelihood ratio greater than or less than 1 "speaks to" the issue of whether the source of the crime scene DNA is in fact the defendant. Only if the likelihood ratio equals 1 is the evidence entirely irrelevant. Thus, the likelihood ratio is a direct indicator of the relevance of the DNA evidence with respect to these two hypotheses.

Though equation (9) provides the formula for the likelihood ratio that weighs the DNA evidence, the value of the probability $\theta_{s|d} = P(Z_s = z|Z_d = z)$ is not known. The likelihood ratio cannot be calculated directly. For this reason, $\theta_{s|d}$ is called a *nuisance parameter* (Mellen 1997; Mellen and Royall 1997). Various techniques have been proposed for "eliminating" nuisance parameters in statistics. However, only those in a small subset are widely applicable. The most direct general approach is to eliminate a nuisance parameter by replacing it with an estimate in the likelihood function. Problems with this approach are discussed by Mellen and Royall (1997) in the context of DNA identification evidence. Another general approach is that of constructing a likelihood ratio based on the *profile likelihood function*. In the DNA evidence context this amounts to separately estimating the vector parameter θ under $\delta = 1$ and $\delta = 0$ (see equation (8)), and using these estimates, say $\hat{\theta}_1$ and $\hat{\theta}_0$, to calculate the so-called *profile likelihood ratio*,

$$\frac{L_p(1)}{L_p(0)} = \frac{L(1, \hat{\theta}_1)}{L(0, \hat{\theta}_0)} \tag{10}$$

(Mellen and Royall 1997). A final general approach is that of constructing a Bayes factor by assuming particular prior probability distributions for the nuisance parameters under each hypothesis (for example, see Foreman, Smith, and Evett 1997). These latter two approaches are expected to produce similar results under many prior probability distributions. However, no formal comparison of the two under various models has yet appeared in the literature.

4.3   Probability of Observing Strong Misleading Evidence as Measure of Reliability of DNA Evidence

Probabilities of strong misleading evidence can assist the trier of fact in understanding a DNA evidence-gathering procedure by providing a measure of the propensity of that procedure for generating misleading observations. These probabilities are distinct from weights of evidence provided by likelihood ratios. When weak or strong evidence is generated, we know when it is weak, and when it is strong. However, when strong evidence is generated, we do not know, with certainty, whether it is misleading. A probability of strong misleading evidence might indicate that the evidence-gathering procedure is trustworthy, that is, it is worthy of confidence, if in fact the procedure is expected to produce strong misleading evidence with extremely low probability. Alternatively, a probability of strong misleading evidence might indicate that the procedure is untrustworthy if it is expected to commonly produce strong misleading evidence. In the legal context, probabilities of observing strong misleading evidence can thus speak to issues of reliability.

How are probabilities of strong misleading evidence calculated in the context of DNA identification evidence? One of the problems introduced along with the nuisance parameter (see previous section) is the inapplicability of the general bound on probabilities of strong misleading evidence (equation (6)). This is not to say that in the presence of nuisance parameters these probabilities tend to be large, but rather, the nuisance parameter introduces another element into the probability distribution, and thus, the study of these probabilities is more complex than it is without this parameter.

This increased complexity also becomes apparent in the consideration of the DNA evidence-gathering procedures. The evidence is composed of observed genotypes from (1) the crime scene, (2) the defendant, and (3) individuals in the reference sample. Which procedure(s) for gathering evidence should be evaluated with respect to their propensity for generating strong misleading evidence?

Recall that the main purpose of presenting these probabilities is to assist the trier of fact *in a particular case*. Therefore, it might be appropriate to evaluate one of the procedures for gathering evidence while conditioning on a different component of the evidence. The particular choice of probability might vary from one set of circumstances to the next, but a natural choice is to condition on the evidence directly related to the crime—that is, the crime scene DNA evidence. Then a probability of interest, calculated under the hypothesis that the defendant is not the source of the crime scene DNA ($\delta = 0$), is $P(L_p(1)/L_p(0) \geq k | Z_s = z)$, where $L_p(1)/L_p(0)$ indicates the use of the profile likelihood ratio for weighing the evidence.

In this case, the probability of misleading evidence must be no greater than the probability $P(Z_d = z | Z_s = z)$: Under $\delta = 0$ ($s \neq d$),

$$P(L_p(1)/L_p(0) \geq k | Z_s = z)$$
$$= P(L_p(1)/L_p(0) \geq k, Z_d = z | Z_s = z)$$
$$= P(L_p(1)/L_p(0) \geq k | Z_s = z, Z_d = z) P(Z_d = z | Z_s = z)$$
$$\leq P(Z_d = z | Z_s = z) \tag{11}$$

(Mellen and Royall 1997). (Note that as in the case with the likelihood ratio, this probability must be estimated.) As might be expected, if the genotype z tends to be rare among individuals in the same genetic subset of the population as the defendant, then the probability of observing genotypes in the defendant and the reference sample that constitute strong misleading evidence is not great. If on the other hand the genotype z tends to be quite common in this subpopulation, then the probability might be larger. These tools provide the means to measure the expected frequency of observing strong misleading evidence in a particular case.

5   Cases Cited

Daubert v. Merrell Dow Pharmaceuticals, Inc., 509 U.S. 579 (1993).
Kumho Tire Co., Ltd. v. Carmichael, 526 U.S. 137 (1999).

REFERENCES

[1] Balding, D.J. (1999) Interpreting DNA evidence: can probability theory help? (this volume).

[2] Balding, D.J., Donnelly, P., and Nichols, R.A. (1994) Some causes for concern about DNA profiles (comment on paper by Roeder, K.). *Statistical Science*, 9, 248–251.

[3] Edwards, A.W.F. (1972) *Likelihood*. Cambridge: Cambridge University Press.

[4] Foreman, L.A., Smith, A.F.M., and Evett, I.W. (1997) Bayesian analysis of DNA profiling data in forensic identification applications (with discussion). *Journal of the Royal Statistical Society*, Ser. A, 160, 429–469.

[5] Hacking, I. (1965) *Logic of Statistical Inference*. Cambridge: Cambridge University Press.

[6] Human Genome Program (1992) *Primer on Molecular Genetics*. Washington, D.C.: U.S. Department of Energy.

[7] Mallows, C. (1998) The zeroth problem. *The American Statistician*, 52, 1–9.

[8] Mellen, B.G. (1997) Statistical reasoning about DNA evidence in human identification problems. Ph.D. dissertation, Johns Hopkins University, Baltimore.

[9] Mellen, B.G., and Royall, R.M. (1997) Measuring the strength of deoxyribonucleic acid evidence, and probabilities of strong implicating evidence. *Journal of the Royal Statistical Society*, Ser. A, 160, 305–320.

[10] Royall, R.M. (1997) *Statistical Evidence: A Likelihood Paradigm*. London: Chapman and Hall.

[11] Royall, R.M. (2000) The likelihood paradigm for statistical evidence (to appear).

[12] Weir, B.S. (1999) The consequences of defending DNA statistics (this volume).

[13] Weir, B.S., Triggs, C.M., Starling, L., Stowell, L.I., Walsh, K.A.J., and Buckleton, J. (1997) Interpreting DNA mixtures. *Journal of Forensic Sciences*, 42, 213–222.

The Choice of Hypotheses in the Evaluation of DNA Profile Evidence

Anders Stockmarr

Abstract

The use of statistics in the evaluation of forensic DNA evidence has been standard for some time, but the area is still in a state where principles for a systematic evaluation have been only partly established. A major problem is the translation from court issues like the possible guilt of a person and linking persons to crime scenes or objects, to the corresponding statistical issues of data evaluation, expressed in the choice of suitable statistical hypotheses. This is not necessarily automatic, and problems that arise are illustrated with three case studies.

Keywords: DNA fingerprint, evidence evaluation, likelihood ratio, paternity

1 Introduction: Judicial and Statistical Hypotheses

The power of the DNA profiling technique became apparent to me during a case in Denmark in 1993, where a mentally retarded person was charged with attempted sexual assault on a seven-year old girl. At the crime scene (an exterior staircase) a number of hairs were found containing sheath cells, which allowed DNA profiling to be carried out. A preliminary enzyme analysis showed that the hairs could not have come from the suspect, of which the court was informed. But shortly thereafter, the suspect confessed, and the DNA evidence was disregarded as being from a third, irrelevant, source. The actual DNA profile was kept in the case file at the Department of Forensic Genetics, and about half a year later the department became aware of a case from 1989 (the Malene-case 2, conviction date January 16, 1990), concerning abduction and sexual abuse of a small girl. The DNA profile from the 1993 case matched the one from 1989 perfectly, but when this was communicated to the court, the suspect had already been convicted on the basis of his confession, on August 5, 1993. The result was a retrial of the 1993 case, where the prosecution had to plead that the convicted suspect should be acquitted of the crime, which he was on February 7, 1995. A new trial was then held, where the 1989 perpetrator was charged with and subsequently convicted of the 1993 crime (*Ugeskrift for Retsvæsen (1996)*). The original confession was simply false and a result of the man's retardedness combined with the desire to "solve" the case. Here, an obvious case of miscarriage of justice was prevented, solely from the DNA profile evidence in the case, and the massive media coverage of the case introduced the technique to the public.

DNA profile evidence in crime cases has had a reputation of a sort of "absolute evidence," which could not be wrong and had a certainty of 100%. We know that this is not so, but nevertheless, it may be an extremely powerful tool when one has to link a person to a crime scene or to a certain object. DNA profile evidence can be ranked together with evidence from eyewitnesses and fingerprints. When it comes to evaluation of the evidence, it may be questioned how reliable a certain eyewitness is, and an expert has to compare two sets of fingerprints. This usually results in a statement from the fingerprint expert that the two sets of fingerprints are (or are not) identical, which the court has to rely on, and an assessment of a certain level of credibility of an eyewitness. In both cases, an uncertainty, which may be infinitesimal or may be substantial, remains. This uncertainty will have to be incorporated into the minds of the decision-makers, who have to decide on a verdict in a case where the evidence is presented. These decision-makers will often be a jury, and let us therefore refer to them as "the jury."

Unlike these two forms of evidence, DNA profile evidence may be treated as measurements where the laws of probability and population genetics allow us to quantify parts of this uncertainty, in the sense that we can calculate probabilities of observing the DNA evidence $\mathcal{E}$ in question from "a randomly chosen person in a given population" (or a more specific alternative), or at least a good approximation thereof. These probabilities have to be related to the decision problem of the jury to be of any use. This problem (we shall not consider it as a decision problem in the strict statistical sense, since the penalty for making a wrong decision is hard to quantify) consists in deciding which one of two competing scenarios describes the sequence of events that led to the observation of the DNA evidence $\mathcal{E}$-scenarios that are more or less specified versions of the following two:

> *The prosecution's scenario:* "The suspect is guilty of the crime."
>
> *The defense's scenario:* "The suspect is not guilty of the crime."

From these scenarios, the statistician derives hypotheses that model the DNA profile data of which the evidence consists, in terms of the suspect and the "true perpetrator," representing the real donor of the DNA evidence who may or may not be identical to the suspect. These MAY be direct translations of the prosecution's and the defense's scenarios, for example,

> H_p : *"The suspect and the true perpetrator are one and the same person"*

and

> H_d : *"The profiles of the suspect and the true perpetrator are obtained from different, unrelated individuals"*

with H_p and H_d signifying the hypotheses put forth under the prosecution's and the defense's scenario, respectively.

An important difference between the seemingly identical approaches is that the hypothesis describing the data under the defense's scenario has to specify how the profiles of the suspect and the true perpetrator relate to one another. The usual way of doing this is to assume that the suspect and the true perpetrator are "unrelated," so that their DNA profiles may be thought of as the result of independent stochastic variables.

Remark 1.1. In practice, the DNA profiles of "unrelated" individuals are not necessarily independent, and adjustments need to be made. But as this has no direct connection to the scope of this paper and will only blur the arguments, these are omitted for the sake of clarity. Unless otherwise stated, DNA profiles are throughout the article considered as stochastic variables, drawn from a population of stochastically independent, identically distributed "profiles," which for each locus are in Hardy-Weinberg equilibrium, making the two alleles at the locus stochastically independent as well. The reader is referred to Balding and Nichols 1994 and Evett and Weir 1998.

Denote a person X's DNA profile by $[X]$, and assume that the DNA evidence is $\mathcal{E} = \{[D] = A, [S] = A\}$, where D is short for the true perpetrator (Donor) and S denotes the suspected perpetrator (Suspect), so that the two, perhaps identical, persons share a common profile A. There is a broad consensus in the forensic community (Berry 1991 and Roeder 1994) that the weight one should assign to such evidence, as a measure of the extent to which it affects our belief in whether H_p or H_d is true, is given by the point value of a likelihood ratio related to the two hypotheses:

$$\text{LR}_A(H_p, H_d) = \frac{P_p(\mathcal{E})}{P_d(\mathcal{E})} = \frac{P_p([D] = A, [S] = A)}{P_d([D] = A, [S] = A)} = \frac{P_p([D] = A)}{P_d([D] = A)P_d([S] = A)},$$
(1)

where P_p, respectively P_d, signifies the probability distribution of the evidence if H_p, respectively H_d, is true. This way, one can state from (1) that one is LR_A times more likely to observe the evidence if H_p is correct than if H_d is correct. In contrast to usual statistical significance testing, where one accepts a hypothesis unless the data speak against it through a test statistic, the method of using the point value of the likelihood ratio as a direct measure for H_p versus H_d is more suitable when one has to make a decision whether the null hypothesis is to be considered as true "beyond reasonable doubt," subject to the condition that any other description of the data be contained in the alternative hypothesis. The approach is termed *likelihood testing* by Dempster (1997). An approach based on similar considerations can be found in Edwards 1972 ("the method of support," pp. 31–35).

Assuming that under H_d, D and S belongs to the same population, so that in particular, $P_p([D] = A) = P_d([D] = A) = P_d([S] = A)$, we let q be the probability of observing the common profile A of the suspect and the donor. If q

is known, it holds that

$$\text{LR}_A(H_p, H_d) = \frac{P_p([D] = A)}{P_d([D] = A)P_d([S] = A)} = \frac{q}{q^2} = \frac{1}{q}. \tag{2}$$

However, the parameter q and thus the probabilities $P_p(\mathcal{E})$ and $P_d(\mathcal{E})$ are usually not known, and they must be estimated in order to obtain an estimate for LR_A in (1). For this, a reference database containing already measured DNA profiles is used, and modeled simultaneously with the matching DNA profiles. Suppose that the matching profile A consists of the allele types B and C with $B \neq C$, and that the reference database consists of n alleles, of which x_b are of type B and x_c are of type C. The probabilities $P_p([D] = A)$, $P_d([D] = A)$, and $P_d([S] = A)$ in (1) are then all equal to $2p_b p_c$ with p_b, p_c the theoretical probabilities that an allele is of type B, respectively C. The probability of an allele being something other than B or C is $1 - p_b - p_c$, and for this estimation we may group the alleles in the database as being of type B, type C, or type "anything other than B or C." We can thus model the database counts by a multinomial distribution of dimension 3, and assuming that neither donor nor suspect has donated alleles to the reference database, so that independence applies, the likelihood function under H_p is then

$$L_p(p_b, p_c) = \text{constant} \times 2p_b p_c \cdot p_b^{x_b} p_c^{x_c}(1 - p_b - p_c)^{n - x_b - x_c}$$
$$= \text{constant} \times p_b^{x_b+1} p_c^{x_c+1}(1 - p_b - p_c)^{n - x_b - x_c}, \tag{3}$$

while the likelihood function under H_d is

$$L_d(p_b, p_c) = \text{constant} \times 2p_b p_c \cdot 2p_b p_c \cdot p_b^{x_b} p_c^{x_c}(1 - p_b - p_c)^{n - x_b - x_c}$$
$$= \text{constant} \times p_b^{x_b+2} p_c^{x_c+2}(1 - p_b - p_c)^{n - x_b - x_c}. \tag{4}$$

The functions (3) and (4) are maximized for (p_b, p_c), attaining the values

$$(\hat{p}_b, \hat{p}_c) = \left(\frac{x_b + 1}{n + 2}, \frac{x_c + 1}{n + 2}\right)$$

in (3) and

$$\left(\hat{\hat{p}}_b, \hat{\hat{p}}_c\right) = \left(\frac{x_b + 2}{n + 4}, \frac{x_c + 2}{n + 4}\right)$$

in (4). From this, the maximum likelihood estimates $2\hat{p}_b \hat{p}_c$ for $P_p([D] = A)$ and $2\hat{\hat{p}}_b \hat{\hat{p}}_c$ for $P_d([D] = A)$ and $P_d([S] = A)$ follow. Similarly, if B and C were equal, the estimate of the common allele probability would be

$$\hat{p}_b = \frac{x_b + 2}{n + 2}, \qquad \hat{\hat{p}}_b = \frac{x_b + 4}{n + 4}.$$

This estimation differs from H_p to H_d, since under H_d the alleles are observed twice and not once, and therefore the estimate of the corresponding probability parameter is higher. When rare alleles are involved, this estimation may differ from H_p to H_d by up to a factor of 2 per (rare) allele. If only common alleles are involved, the difference is immaterial. We shall revisit the issue later in the example on evidence separation, but for the moment abstain from discussing it.

The above is how the weight of the evidence is usually presented (although often with an estimator for q based on the reference database only, corresponding to (2)); this estimation procedure is discussed by Mellen and Royall (1997), who also consider alternative likelihood-based approaches. The weight that is assessed to the evidence is therefore the ratio of the approximated probabilities of observing the DNA profile evidence under the hypotheses H_p and H_d.

The expert witness has to stick to the interpretation of the likelihood ratio, since conducting a formal test of H_p versus H_d will cause him to interfere with the jury's decision-making by assessing the level of significance. The jury has to base its decision upon the estimated value of the likelihood ratio, its interpretation, and perhaps a comment from the expert witness about whether this value of the likelihood ratio is large or not. But the expert witness still has a major impact on the testing, because it is he or she that specifies the hypotheses H_p and H_d and therefore chooses how to interpret statistically the options that the jury has to consider for the DNA evidence. This has to be done with great care. Though the consequences may be inferior, the wrong questions may be asked, which in some cases may point towards wrong persons as donors. Problems that may arise are illustrated in three examples in the following section.

2   Examples

Example 2.1 (Evidence Separation).   In a 1997 case, a crime occurred and two suspects were arrested. Two items with traces of DNA were found at the crime scene; we shall refer to these DNA samples as sample 1 and sample 2. The samples contained a DNA profile at 5 different loci, but for sample 2 the profile was only partial, since no results were found for two of the loci, while two other loci resulted in three alleles and the last locus only in two alleles. Readers unfamiliar with the genetic terms should consult, for example, Weir 2000. Although much of the DNA profile was missing, it was clear from the loci where three alleles appeared that the sample could not have originated from a single person. Sample 1 showed a DNA profile of what appeared to be DNA from one person only. Under the circumstances it was believed that the person who donated DNA to sample 1 was also a donor to sample 2. At least 2 persons had therefore donated DNA to the evidence samples, and the calculations that follow assume that the number was exactly 2. We shall refer to these two as donor 1 and donor 2, so that donor 1 donated the DNA to sample 1 and the (partially observed) sample 2, while donor 2 donated DNA to the partially observed sample 2 only. The measurements matched the suspects' DNA profiles in the sense that the DNA profile of suspect 1 matched sample 1, and the DNA profiles of suspects 1 and 2 together contained all the alleles in sample 2. The system where two alleles were observed on item 2 is known as D1S80, and

Table 1. Types from suspects and evidence samples in D1S80.

suspect 1:	suspect 2:	sample 1:	sample 2:
20,24	14,36	20,24	14,20

in this system the observations were as shown in Table 1. We shall consider only this system.

Based on this evidence, we set up the hypothesis

H_{12} : *Suspect* 1 *is identical to donor* 1, *and suspect* 2 *is identical to donor* 2.

One alternative hypothesis is that the DNA traces did not come from the suspects:

H_{UU} : *Suspect* 1, *suspect* 2, *donor* 1, *and donor* 2 *are four unrelated persons.*

We can then compute the estimated likelihood ratio of the hypothesis H_{12} versus the hypothesis H_{UU}, but the number obtained is not of any use, since this number tells us that "it is LR times more likely for these data to be obtained if suspect 1 and 2 are the donors, rather than if it is two unknown persons." The LR tells us nothing about the strength of the evidence against each of the two individuals. To obtain separate evidence for or against the individuals, we must set up hypotheses that list the possible explanations for these data, where, for example, suspect 1 is thought to be donor 1, and those where suspect 1 is thought not to be donor 1. This can be accomplished in terms of the hypotheses

H_{1U} : *Suspect* 1 *is identical to donor* 1; *suspect* 2 *and donor* 2 *are unrelated,*

H_{2U} : *Suspect* 2 *is identical to donor* 2; *suspect* 1 *and donor* 1 *are unrelated,*

together with H_{12} and H_{UU}, since the possible donor combinations that link suspect 2 to sample 2 correspond to H_{12} and H_{2U}, whereas H_{1U} and H_{UU} reflect those that do not. The hypotheses to be compared in assessing the strength of the evidence against suspect 2 are therefore

$$H_{12} \cup H_{2U} \qquad \text{versus} \qquad H_{1U} \cup H_{UU},$$

where $\cup$ denotes set union, since $H_{12} \cup H_{2U}$ contains the two possible explanations that we will consider with suspect 2 donor to sample 2—either together with suspect 1 or together with an unknown, unrelated person. A similar interpretation holds for the alternative hypothesis, $H_{1U} \cup H_{UU}$.

Since every fixed relation between the donors and the suspects increases the probability of this evidence, the likelihood ratio that compares the two composite hypotheses above is exactly the same as the likelihood ratio for comparing H_{12} versus H_{1U}. The resulting message that the maximum likelihood method sends us is therefore to calculate the strength of the evidence against one suspect as if the other suspect were a donor.

This is highly problematic, since the result has to be communicated to the jury and rests on assumptions about which they must make decisions. Therefore, it is preferable to present the likelihood ratio for H_{12} versus H_{1U} and the likelihood ratio for H_{2U} versus H_{UU}. This allows for statements like "if suspect 1 is a donor, the strength of the evidence against suspect 2 is $< this\ number >$, and if suspect 1 is not a donor, the strength of the evidence is $< that\ number >$." This way the expert witness leaves the problem of whether suspect 1 is a donor or not to the jury, as it should be. If these two numbers are close to each other, the evidence against suspect 2 is separated from the full evidence. Otherwise, the jury must consider the context of the two numbers.

Returning to Table 1, we would like to state this evidence in a way that allows probabilistic considerations. The problem is how to describe sample 2, the partial sample. What have we actually seen? We have seen some, maybe all, of the combined D1S80 profile for the persons donor 1 and donor 2. We can therefore state the DNA evidence as

$$\mathcal{E} = \{[S1] = \{20, 24\}, [S2] = \{14, 36\},$$
$$[D1] = \{20, 24\}, \{14, 20\} \subset [D1, D2]\}.$$

The calculations are further complicated by the fact that the allele 14 has not been observed before in the relevant population and thus has a database allele count of 0, which makes it impossible to base estimation solely on the reference database. Of course, the allele does exist, since it has just been observed. The way we will deal with this is to follow the estimation procedure described in Section 2 for the simple comparison hypotheses H_p and H_d, and simply include the allele observations confirmed by the data in the material used to estimate the probability parameters by the corresponding frequencies (and file confirmed observations to the reference database for future use). The price one has to pay is that the probability estimators differ with the various hypotheses. For example, under H_{UU} one has observed allele 14 twice and not just once. The interpretation of this is that if the hypothesis H_{UU} is correct, then allele 14 may not be that rare after all. This technique is applied to all of the estimations made in this example; the value of the estimators are shown in Table 2. Based on these estimates, the profile probability estimates under the various hypotheses can be calculated using standard methods. For example, if I denotes the set of all possible D1S80 allele types, the probability of the evidence $\mathcal{E}$ subject to H_{1U} being true is

$$P_{1u}(\mathcal{E}) = P_{1u}([S1] = \{20, 24\}, [S2] = \{14, 36\}, [D1] = \{20, 24\}, \{14, 20\} \subset [D1, D2])$$
$$= P_{1u}([D1] = \{20, 24\}, [S2] = \{14, 36\}, \{14\} \subset [D2])$$
$$= 2p_{20}p_{24} \times 2p_{14}p_{36} \times \left(p_{14}^2 + \sum_{i \in I \setminus \{14\}} 2p_{14}p_i\right)$$
$$= 4p_{14}p_{20}p_{24}p_{36}(p_{14}^2 + 2p_{14}(1 - p_{14}))$$
$$= 4p_{14}p_{20}p_{24}p_{36}(2p_{14} - p_{14}^2),$$

where we have used that $S1$ and $D1$ are identical, and where "\" denotes set difference. Results are shown in Table 3, which result in the estimated likelihood ratios as shown in Table 4. One could say that this was overdoing it; the evidence

Table 2. Probability estimation formulas based on confirmed allele observations, relative to the various hypothesis. The number of alleles in the database, n, was 2968. Hypotheses marked with an asterisk disregard person 1 and sample 1.

Hypo-thesis:	Confirmed observations	$\hat{p}_{14}$	$\hat{p}_{20}$	$\hat{p}_{24}$	$\hat{p}_{36}$
H_{12}	4	$\dfrac{x_{14}+1}{n+4}$	$\dfrac{x_{20}+1}{n+4}$	$\dfrac{x_{24}+1}{n+4}$	$\dfrac{x_{36}+1}{n+4}$
H_{1U}	5	$\dfrac{x_{14}+2}{n+5}$	$\dfrac{x_{20}+1}{n+5}$	$\dfrac{x_{24}+1}{n+5}$	$\dfrac{x_{36}+1}{n+5}$
H_{2U}	6	$\dfrac{x_{14}+1}{n+6}$	$\dfrac{x_{20}+2}{n+6}$	$\dfrac{x_{24}+2}{n+6}$	$\dfrac{x_{36}+1}{n+6}$
H_{UU}	7	$\dfrac{x_{14}+2}{n+7}$	$\dfrac{x_{20}+2}{n+7}$	$\dfrac{x_{24}+2}{n+7}$	$\dfrac{x_{36}+1}{n+7}$
H_{2U}^{*}	3	$\dfrac{x_{14}+1}{n+3}$	$\dfrac{x_{20}+1}{n+3}$	$\dfrac{x_{24}+0}{n+3}$	$\dfrac{x_{36}+1}{n+3}$
H_{UU}^{*}	4	$\dfrac{x_{14}+2}{n+4}$	$\dfrac{x_{20}+1}{n+4}$	$\dfrac{x_{24}+0}{n+4}$	$\dfrac{x_{36}+1}{n+4}$
alleles in database		$x_{14}=0$	$x_{20}=140$	$x_{24}=1075$	$x_{36}=23$

Table 3. Profile probabilities under various hypotheses. Hypotheses marked with an asterisk disregard person 1 and sample 1.

Hypothesis:	Profile Probability Formula	Probability Estimate
H_{12}	$4p_{20}p_{24}p_{14}p_{36}$	$1.87 \cdot 10^{-7}$
H_{1U}	$4p_{20}p_{24}p_{14}p_{36}(2p_{14} - p_{14}^2)$	$5.01 \cdot 10^{-10}$
H_{2U}	$8p_{20}^2 p_{24}^2 p_{14}p_{36}$	$6.49 \cdot 10^{-9}$
H_{UU}	$8p_{20}^2 p_{24}^2 p_{14}p_{36}(2p_{14} - p_{14}^2)$	$1.74 \cdot 10^{-11}$
H_{2U}^{*}	$2p_{14}p_{36}(2p_{20} - p_{20}^2)$	$5.04 \cdot 10^{-7}$
H_{UU}^{*}	$24p_{14}^2 p_{20}p_{36}(1 - p_{14} - p_{20})$ $+4p_{14}^2 p_{20}p_{36}(2(p_{14} + p_{20})^2 - p_{14}p_{20})$	$3.97 \cdot 10^{-9}$

against suspect 1 could be found on item 1, and the evidence against suspect 2 could be found on item 2. Indeed, this is true for suspect 1, since the profile of the alternative donor can be found on item 1, and item 2 does not contribute any new evidence. This is not so for suspect 2, however, since disregarding item 1 means

Table 4. Likelihood ratios.

Likelihood ratio	Estimated value
$LR_{H_{12},H_{2U}}$	28.8
$LR_{H_{1U},H_{UU}}$	28.8
$LR_{H_{12},H_{1U}}$	372.3
$LR_{H_{2U},H_{UU}}$	372.8
$LR_{H_{2U}^*,H_{UU}^*}$	127.03

that you lose information on which of the allele bands on item 2 that belongs to the same donor. Disregarding the evidence from sample 1 and suspect 1 would leave us with the evidence

$$\mathcal{E} = \{[S2] = \{14, 36\}, \{14, 20\} \subset [D1, D2]\}.$$

When we take item 1 into consideration, we know under the hypotheses H_{2U} and H_{UU} that one of the two donors has D1S80 types 20 and 24. By disregarding this information, calculations as shown in Tables 2–4 (formula (5) in example 2.2 can be used to derive this) show that the weight of the evidence, the estimate of $LR_{H_{2U}^*,H_{UU}^*}$, is reduced to 127 : 1, a reduction of nearly two-thirds.

An attempt to operate with the likelihood ratio (2) and solve the problem that allele 14 has not been observed prior to this case by operating with a "minimum frequency" of one over the size of the database will in this case dispose of the need to distinguish between $LR_{12,1U}$ and $LR_{2U,UU}$, since their theoretical expressions will be identical. But it will give results that are significantly different from those of Table 4. For example, $LR_{12,1U}$ will attain the value 1484.25 compared to 372.3, as is seen by dividing the two profile probability formulas from Table 3 corresponding to the hypotheses H_{12} and H_{1U} and afterwards inserting $1/2968$ for p_{14}. When several loci are considered, the difference will increase exponentially.

Example 2.2 (Mixed Samples).   In 1996, a man was killed with a knife during a quarrel with a group of youngsters. The group fled from the scene, and subsequently a small group of young men were arrested. During a search, a folding knife was recovered with a tiny amount of blood in the shaft. The small amount of blood allowed only a single DNA system (D1S80) to be typed, and the resultant evidence $\mathcal{E}$ consisted of 6 different D1S80 types:

$$\mathcal{E} = \{18, 24, 28, 31, 33, 36\}.$$

The probability parameters in the population of possible perpetrators of these types were estimated by the frequencies in a database consisting of 2968 alleles as 0.2487, 0.3622, 0.0657, 0.0738, 0.0044, and 0.0077, respectively. The victim's D1S80 types were $\{24, 33\}$, so he could have donated DNA to this knife. The owner of the knife was taken into custody, but it turned out that neither he nor the rest of the group could have donated DNA to the sample. The investigators therefore faced a mixed sample with 6 bands, of which they could only hope to account for 2, which may have originated from the victim.

In order to link the knife to the victim, a likelihood ratio to weigh the evidence should be formulated and estimated. From the 6 bands on the knife it was obvious that at least 3 persons had donated DNA to the sample, but it was not obvious that the number was exactly 3. In an attempt to clarify the impact of a higher number of donors, the hypotheses for the prosecution and the defense were formulated in terms of the number of unknown donors:

H_p : *The donors to $\mathcal{E}$ are the victim and $n - 1$ unknown, unrelated persons.*

and

H_d : *The donors to $\mathcal{E}$ are n unknown, unrelated persons.*

The probability of obtaining the evidence $\mathcal{E}$ from n individuals may be derived from the mixed sample formula: For any set of k alleles $\mathcal{E}_k = \{A_1, \ldots, A_k\}$ with corresponding probabilities $p_1, \ldots p_k$, the probability that a set of n unrelated persons together has this profile may be calculated as

$$P^{(n)}(\mathcal{E}_k) = \sum_{\substack{\Delta \subset \{1,\ldots,k\} \\ \Delta \neq \emptyset}} (-1)^{k-|\Delta|} \left(\sum_{i \in \Delta} p_i \right)^{2n}, \tag{5}$$

where the first sum extends over all nonempty subsets Δ of $\{1, \ldots, k\}$, and $|\Delta|$ signifies the number of elements in Δ. Another way of writing formula (5) is

$$P^{(n)}(\mathcal{E}_k) = \left(\sum_{i=1}^{k} p_i \right)^{2n} - \left(\sum_{i=2}^{k} p_i \right)^{2n}$$
$$- \left(p_1 + \sum_{i=3}^{k} p_i \right)^{2n} - \left(p_1 + p_2 + \sum_{i=4}^{k} p_i \right)^{2n} - \cdots$$
$$+ \left(\sum_{i=3}^{k} p_i \right)^{2n} + \left(p_1 + \sum_{i=4}^{k} p_i \right)^{2n} + \cdots,$$

thus raising the sum of the p_i's to the power $2n$, subtracting the sums where one index is missing (raised to the same power), adding the sums where two indices are missing, and so on. The proof of the formula can be found in Weir et al. 1997. A later, but less tedious, proof is in Fukshansky and Bär 1998.

Working conditionally on the profile of the victim (the term corresponding to the victim's profile cancels in the (simplified) likelihood ratio 2, which was the approach used in this case) it is immediate from (5) that we can calculate the probabilities of the evidence as

$$P_p(\mathcal{E}) = P^{(n-1)}(\mathcal{E} \setminus \{24, 33\}) + P^{(n-1)}(\mathcal{E} \setminus \{24\})$$
$$+ P^{(n-1)}(\mathcal{E} \setminus \{33\}) + P^{(n-1)}(\mathcal{E}),$$

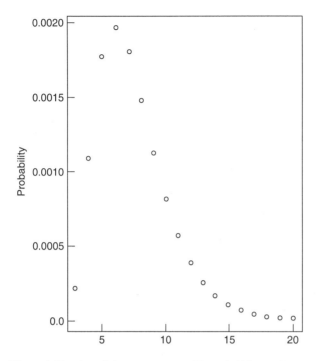

Figure 1. Number of donors versus profile probability, under H_p.

$$P_d(\mathcal{E}) = P^{(n)}(\mathcal{E}).$$

where "\" denotes set difference. The result as a function of the number of donors n is shown in Figures 1 and 2.

Note that the numbers of donors to which the highest event probability for the observations is assigned are 6 and 7 for the two hypotheses, respectively. If the number of donors is 3, the event probability is very small compared with the event probability in the case of 6 or 7 donors, under both hypotheses. The likelihood ratio, derived from this, follows in Figure 3.

There are several things to notice from these figures. First, the estimated likelihood ratio does not change much as long as the number of donors is within a reasonable range. The likelihood ratio that results from 3 donors is estimated as 20.92 in favor of the victim being a donor, and this fits relatively well with the cases where the profile probability is highest, within a difference of 10–20%. What does not fit is the profile probabilities though, which differ by a factor of 10. The reason for this is the combination of some very common alleles, 18 and 24, with a high number of rare alleles, a combination that invites the belief that more than three persons have donated DNA. As we have seen, this does not change the weight of the evidence drastically, but this is only after we have gone through the effort of investigating it. If we had kept the number of donors fixed at 3, a well-

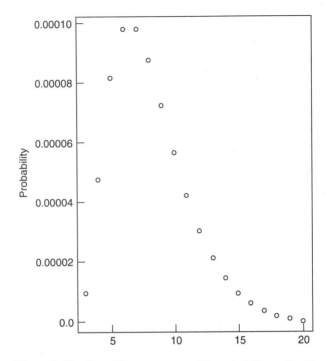

Figure 2. Number of donors versus profile probability, under H_d.

prepared defense lawyer could use the profile probability calculations to question the validity of the evidence, since it was calculated under "unlikely circumstances." Also worth noting is that if we did not impose the restriction that we are describing the experiment "n people donate DNA to a sample" subject to two different sets of circumstances (hypotheses), but allowed the number of donors to be incorporated in the hypotheses, the evidence could be as low as 2.2 : 1, if a rushed forensic scientist and a careful defense lawyer selected the hypotheses.

The suspect (the owner of the knife) was eventually convicted on the basis of the DNA evidence and other evidence, the appeal as described in *Ugeskrift for Retsvæsen (1998)*.

Example 2.3 (Paternity Cases and Mutations). In a 1997 case, a paternity analysis was carried out on a male who was granted refugee asylum, and a child, in order to investigate whether the male (AF, the alleged father) was the true father of the child. If so, the child would be granted asylum as well. An analysis over 12 loci showed 10 matches and two inconsistencies. If the male, the alleged father, actually is the true father of the child, the inconsistencies may arise from mutations, and so the analysis did not rule out the male as the father. A likelihood ratio ("Paternity Index"; see for example Weir 1996) for the hypotheses

$$H_{AF} : \text{ The true father of the child is the alleged father}$$

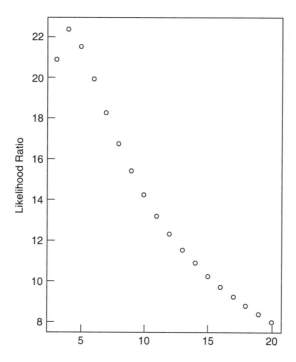

Figure 3. Number of donors versus likelihood ratio, H_p versus H_d.

versus

H_U : *The true father of the child is a person not related to the alleged father*

was constructed in order to quantify the weight of the DNA evidence. The U subscript indicates that the true father under this hypothesis is considered as an unknown "random man"—a man picked at random from a background population. In the following, all likelihood ratios are simplified by letting probability parameters cancel as in (2), and thus using the same estimate under the two competing hypotheses, since this is what is assumed in the calculations presented.

Suppose that at a certain locus, AF has alleles A and B, and that the child (CH) has alleles A and C with $B \neq C$ (we restrict ourselves to heterozygotes for simplicity). If we again denote the DNA profile of an individual X by $[X]$, then the probability of observing these profiles subject to the hypothesis H_{AF} being correct is

$$P_{AF}([AF] = \{A, B\}, [CH] = \{A, C\})$$
$$= P_{AF}([AF] = \{A, B\}, CH \text{ inherits } A \text{ from } AF, [CH] = \{A, C\})$$
$$= 2p_A p_B \cdot \frac{1}{2} \cdot p_C$$
$$= p_A p_B p_C,$$

assuming that no mutations occur and that the alleles of the mother may be thought of as statistically independent of alleles of AF. If H_U is true, the profiles of AF and CH are statistically independent, so the probability of observing the profiles is $4p_A^2 p_B p_C$, which yields the (simplified) likelihood ratio

$$\text{LR}_{H_{AF}, H_U} = \frac{1}{4p_A}.$$

Now, for a locus where there is no overlap between $[AF] = \{A, B\}$ and $[CH] = \{C, D\}$, things are not so obvious. Subject to H_{AF} being true, such an observation can occur only through a mutation of one of the alleged father's alleles. Denote the probability of an allele mutating to an other allele by μ. This probability does not depend on the alleles involved, which may be a problematic assumption; we shall not discuss the issue though, the assumption is necessary to reach commonly used LR formulas. The probability of observing the profiles may be calculated as follows, assuming that any mutated allele is distributed according to the allele probabilities:

$$P_{AF}([AF] = \{A, B\}, [CH] = \{C, D\})$$
$$= P_{AF}([AF] = \{A, B\}, inherited\ allele\ mutates\ to\ C, [CH] = \{C, D\})$$
$$+ P_{AF}([AF] = \{A, B\}, inherited\ allele\ mutates\ to\ D, [CH] = \{C, D\})$$
$$= 2p_A p_B ((\mu p_C) \cdot p_D + (\mu p_D) \cdot p_C)$$
$$= 4p_A p_B p_C p_D \mu .$$

The probability of observing the profiles subject to H_U being true is here $4p_A p_B p_C p_D$, which in this case gives us the likelihood ratio

$$\text{LR}_{AF,U} = \mu .$$

Now, supposing that H_{AF} is true, the factor in the likelihood ratio from a locus where a mutation has occurred will be outweighed by a sufficient number of other loci where AF and CH share alleles. In the case from which this example is taken, this was true, since the estimated overall likelihood ratio attained a value of 34300 favoring paternity (both mutation rates set to 0.001), and the resolution seems obvious.

Not so. A necessary condition for this number to be appropriate is that the alternative explanation that is considered reasonable is included in the alternative hypothesis; if AF is not the father, then what is he? In this case, seeing the two inconsistencies, one might get the idea that the actual father was the brother of AF; in other words, that AF is CH's uncle. This makes the observations much more likely, since the probability that an uncle and his nephew will share an allele by descent is 0.5 at each locus. This is an option that is sometimes built into software packages, for example Kinship (see Brenner 1997) for calculating paternity indexes, and seeing that the data fit this option, one may be tempted to calculate an index. Formulas for profile probabilities may be found in Evett and Weir 1998, but we shall not consider the analytic expression for this likelihood ratio, since it is a tedious expression and irrelevant for the argument; it is found easily through standard pedigree analysis. Using the nephew–uncle relationship as the alternative hypothesis, the conclusion is suddenly reversed; now an estimated likelihood ratio of 980:1 favors AF as CH's uncle rather than CH's father, and the resolution seems obvious.

Not so. There lies a problem in how the alternative hypothesis is selected, since in this case the idea that AF's brother should be CH's father is triggered by the two inconsistencies. Even if the inconsistencies are true inconsistencies and not mutations, the true father could be a person with a weaker degree of relationship to AF than his brother. If we instead impose a second-order relative to AF as the father under the alternative hypothesis (for example, AF and CH are really cousins), the evidence favors this option with a value of 16.5:1 rather than AF being the true father; if the alternative father is chosen to be a third order relative, the "conclusion" is reversed again, since the estimated likelihood ratio attains a value 2.73:1 in favor of AF being the true father.

For this number of loci tested (12), further calculations of averages show that the problem is greatest when 2 loci are inconsistent. If 3 loci are inconsistent, the likelihood ratio would favor even distant relatives, and usually it will not favor AF's paternity at all; if only 1 locus is inconsistent, AF's brother may be favored, but usually not with a high coefficient, and AF may even be favored over any type of relatives. When alleles are not shared, the likelihood ratio for AF versus the uncle alternative can be shown to equal 2μ. When alleles are shared, the likelihood ratio for the uncle alternative attains a value between 1 and 2 for each locus, so once a common mutation with a mutation rate of say 0.01 occurs, no fewer than 6 loci are needed to outweigh it. For the case considered here, the existence of two inconsistencies means that no matter what the allele probabilities are, the likelihood ratio value will favor AF being CH's uncle with a factor of no less than 244:1. If a laboratory handles a number of cases each year of which, say, 2000 includes a child and the actual father, the probability of one of these having a double mutation can be calculated to be about 12%, assuming as in this case that the mutation rate is 0.001. Many of these pitfalls will be dealt with by a reasonable jury, but others will not, and comments like, "It is his brother, the index is 3:1" have been heard. With a higher mutation rate, double mutations will be common. In the case discussed here, both the likelihood ratio with a random, unrelated person as alternative and the likelihood ratio with the brother as alternative were communicated. The ruling in the case is presently unknown by the author.

It is important to distinguish between DNA profiling analysis for criminal cases and paternity cases. In the latter, the burden of proof is not obvious, and the estimate of the point value of a likelihood ratio is no longer obviously the best way of evaluating the evidence. In an asylum case like the above, the child could be granted asylum unless the likelihood ratio (in the absence of other evidence) shows that AF is not the father of CH "beyond reasonable doubt." Another scenario may be that the alleged father is filing a case in order to obtain custody of the child. Third, it may be that a third party is filing a case against AF in order to make him pay for the child's expenses. In the first case, the hypothesis of interest to test is the alternative, and AF's interest is H_{AF}; In the second, the hypothesis of interest to test is the H_{AF}, which is also the interest of AF; and in the third case, the hypothesis of interest to test is H_{AF}, but AF's interest is the alternative.

3   Conclusion

DNA evidence may provide strong and crucial evidence in the courtroom, provided that hypotheses are chosen with care by the expert, so that he or she maintains neutrality toward the sides in a trial. In many nonstandard cases, pitfalls occur, which can give rise to serious misinterpretations. The proper way for the expert to counter these is to indicate the hypotheses that have to be evaluated. Things that must be considered are which side bears the burden of proof, which interests the sides have, and whether the statistical alternatives describe the possible real alternatives reasonably. These issues are not always routine, and directions are essential for circumstances that are nonstandard. The examples have shown that pitfalls occur in all of the possible types of analyses, both as a result of poor measurements, unavailable background information, misinterpretations of likelihood ratios, rare events, and failure to do thorough analyses that could reveal a need for modifications. A common denominator for these pitfalls is that they can be avoided by an expert who describes the observations carefully. The task of describing the observations carefully is for use in the courtroom just as important as the formulation of the results. This level of care exceeds the level that statisticians involved with other applications of probability need. In the courtroom one has to be right every time, and hypotheses have to be formulated so that they do not lead to error rates that over time will prove essentially positive. In other areas, measurements and their analysis and description will lead to a degree of belief in certain details about the data-generating mechanism, but seldom to actual conclusive evidence in precisely how the mechanism works. This near conclusive evidence for use in the courtroom can often be obtained thanks to the diversity of human DNA; as long as experts prevent misuse, DNA analysis in the court is an invaluable tool.

Acknowledgments

I am grateful to one anonymous referee for careful and thorough refereeing. Part of this work was done at the Department of Forensic Genetics, University of Copenhagen.

REFERENCES

[1] Balding, D.J. and Nichols, R.A. (1994): DNA profile match probability calculation: How to allow for population stratification, relatedness, database selection and single bands. *Forensic Science International* **64**; 125–140.

[2] Berry, D.A. (1991): Inferences Using DNA Profiling in Forensic Identification and Paternity Cases. *Statistical Science* **6,2**; 175–205.

[3] Brenner, C.H. (1997): Symbolic Kinship Program. *Genetics* **145**; 535–542.

[4] Dempster, A.P. (1997): The direct use of likelihood for significance testing. *Statistics and Computing* **7**; 247–252.

[5] Edwards, A.W.F. (1972): *Likelihood.* Cambridge University Press.

[6] Evett, I.W. and Weir, B.S. (1998): *Interpreting DNA Evidence.* Sinaur Assc., Sunderland, Massachusetts.

[7] Fukshansky, N. and W. Bär, (1998): Interpreting Forensic DNA Evidence on the Basis of Hypothesis Testing. *International Journal of Legal Medicine* **111**; 62–66.

[8] Mellen, B.G. and Royall, R.M. (1997): Measuring the Strength of Deoxyribonucleic Acid Evidence, and Probabilities of Strong Implicating Evidence. *Journal of the Royal Statistical Society* **A 160,2**; 305–320.

[9] Roeder, K. (1994): DNA Fingerprinting: A Review of the Controversy. *Statistical Science* **9,2**; 222–278.

[10] Ugeskrift for Retsvæsen A (1996): 1996.470H (in Danish). Gad, Copenhagen.

[11] Ugeskrift for Retsvæsen A (1998): 1998.1503H (in Danish). Gad, Copenhagen.

[12] Weir, B.S. (1996): *Genetic Data Analysis II.* Sinaur Assc., Sunderland, Massachusetts.

[13] Weir, B.S. (2000): The Consequences of Defending DNA Statistics. This volume.

[14] Weir, B.S., Triggs, C.M., Starlling, L., Stowell, L.I., Walsh, K.A.J., and Buckleton, J.S. (1997): Interpreting DNA mixtures. *Journal of Forensic Science* **42**; 113–122.

On the Evolution of Analytical Proof, Statistics, and the Use of Experts in EEO Litigation[1]

Marc Rosenblum

1 Introduction and Overview

Approximately twenty-five years ago, in my first case as an expert in federal equal employment opportunity (EEO) litigation, *Rios v. Steamfitters Local 638* (1975), a comparison of the difference in racial and ethnic proportions between the union's membership and the area civilian labor force (CLF) was regarded as an acceptable analytic approach. The district court accepted my estimates that the differences were statistically significant and ordered the union to admit more black and Hispanic members.

Under today's evidentiary standards, the idea that the simple difference in racial proportions between one organization's workforce profile and the overall labor force can, without additional information, be validly compared to provide prima facie proof of discrimination is no longer regarded as probative. More likely, many trial judges would regard such an opinion as not just methodologically deficient but inadmissible. The economist or statistician holding that opinion would possibly not even be allowed to testify.

This chapter illustrates the substantial evolution of statistical evidence in employment discrimination cases that has taken place over the past quarter century. It considers the way in which analytical proof and expert opinion in EEO law has evolved, some of the factors responsible for those changes, and some thoughts on how further change may develop.

The changes in substantive interpretation of Title VII law in the evaluation of statistical evidence (and the experts offering it) during the 1970s and on into the 1980s illustrate the problem faced by the courts. It should be remembered that during that time period, courts were both fact-finders and interpreters of the law, rather than, as now, simply the latter. Fact-finding is now a jury responsibility.[2]

This meant that courts were required to evaluate analytical proof and statistical evidence without, in most instances, the training and understanding (and in some instances the inclination) needed to competently do so.[3] The result was an

---

[1] This chapter was written by the author in his private capacity. No support or endorsement by any agency of the United States is intended or should be inferred.

[2] The right to jury trials was added to Title VII as part of the 1991 Civil Rights Act, Pub.L. 102–166 (1991).

[3] As explained elsewhere in this chapter, trial judges, as "gatekeepers," are required to scrutinize proposed expert reports and opinions, permitting juries to hear only what is scientifically sound and thus able to assist the fact-finding process.

inconsistent body of decision law, where courts assigned different weight to and reached opposite conclusions from similar statistical evidence, further exacerbating the problem. Several commentators, including Dorseano (1975), Gastwirth and Haber (1976), and Rosenblum (1977, 1978), advocated clearer analytic standards to interpret Title VII statistics, but to no avail.

Changes through that time period and beyond were evolutionary and incremental. Without coherent guidance from the Supreme Court (similar, for example, to the Court's repeated refinement to the law covering Title VII and ADEA proof burdens), and burdened by the Court's repeated ambiguity with respect to clearcut standards regarding statistical proof (like *Johnson v. Transportation Agency)* (1987), progress was relatively gradual.

The reader must, for example, look to *Wards Cove Packing Co. v. Atonio* (1989) for even a glimmer of clarity in this regard. Overshadowed by the *Wards Cove's* ruling on disparate impact proof burdens that was reversed two years later by Congress is that case's restatement of the law on statistical workforce comparison that remains intact—a decade later—as the Court's last (and clearest) statement in this area.

Meanwhile, over the past half decade the legal standard to evaluate statistical evidence—and all other expert testimony—has become more precise. At the same time, litigants have also adjusted to procedural rule changes that require greater pretrial disclosure of experts' reports and reasoning.

A trilogy of Supreme Court cases interpreting the evidence Rules, primarily Rule 702 governing the admissibility of expert testimony—*Daubert* (1993), *Joiner* (1996), and *Kumho Tire Co.* (1999)—require the district judge to determine whether a proposed expert's testimony will assist the jury in its role as trier of fact, and exclude it if it will not. To the extent that pattern and practice or disparate impact EEO cases usually depend on expert testimony, litigants must now ensure that their analytical proof is not only helpful, but also relevant, as that term is formally understood in evidence law.[4]

This leads to a conclusion not immediately obvious to the casual reader: The effects on EEO litigation brought about by the procedural and evidentiary changes alluded to here are far more important than has generally been acknowledged to date, especially in comparison with the effects that followed passage of the 1991 Civil Rights Act. With respect to the development and introduction of analytical proof and statistics, present admissibility requirements may constitute even more of a shift from prior practices than the legislative influence on substantive law of the 1991 amendments, and the cases that followed.

These developments have clearly complemented each other. That is, to be admissible as reliable scientific knowledge, the expert opinion must first represent a valid methodology that "fits" and applies to the facts at issue.[5] At the same time,

---

[4]Fed.R.Evid. 401.
[5]*Daubert,* 509 U.S. at 591 (1993).

the judiciary was moving to eliminate, or at least reduce, procedural problems such as pretrial discovery abuse by lawyers in civil litigation, including employment discrimination.

The 1993 procedural rules changes now require that the identity of proposed testifying experts and their qualifications must be made known to the opposing party in a timely manner, followed similarly by the expert's report and opinion, including assumptions, methods, and data.[6] Previous discovery process abuses left some litigants ill-informed regarding an opponent's expert analyses, particularly during the limited time available to develop a rebuttal response.

While the remedy for "hiding the ball" expert tactics is the exclusion of the withheld evidence,[7] courts have not always applied such sanctions to effectively deter abuse. To an increasing extent, however, courts, as in *Darby* (1995), are excluding or limiting the testimony of experts whose existence (as well as their identity) is not disclosed in a timely manner.

Thus, reduction of both discovery abuse and the temptation to use "hired-gun" expert opinion appears to be having a positive effect on the analytical process in EEO litigation. The emerging legal focus on statistical comparisons, in terms of determining their admissibility as well as their evidentiary weight prior to trial, is especially salutary. Methodologically slipshod analyses that previously were admitted into the decision-making process are now increasingly subjected to gatekeeper evaluation and exclusion. As a result, the use of analytical proof and statistics in EEO litigation remains a viable—and valuable—scientific enterprise.

2   Evolution of the Analytical Process

Four distinct factors have led to the evolution under review here, steadily but inevitably changing the character of analytical proof and statistics in EEO law over the past quarter century. They are identified and then discussed in turn as (1) the nature of the statistical comparisons from which judges and juries could infer the presence or absence of employment discrimination, (2) the delineation and definition of geographic labor markets, (3) the appropriate level of occupational specificity that reflects the at-issue comparison pool, and (4) the inclusion of additional variables that are relevant to evaluating a firm's employment practices.

To understand this process, the reader should also keep two things in mind: first, that changes in any one of these four areas inevitably affected others. The unifying theme of greater rather than less refinement applies in all instances. Second, the structure of our judicial system—where decisions from federal district courts in all fifty states initially go to twelve appellate courts, and in turn are subject to

---

[6]Fed.R.Civ.P. 26(a)(2).

[7]Fed.R.Civ.P. 37(b). See, also, *Sierra Club* (1996) as an example of a case where the court of appeals upheld the exclusion of an expert for failure to reveal, as required by Rule 26, other cases in which he had testified during the preceding four years.

possible Supreme Court review—permits and tolerates a wide range of inconsistency regarding the facts that lead to legal conclusions. Thus, over a time frame now measured in decades, a clearer picture emerges than may be apparent at any specific point in time.

2.1 The Statistics

The first round of changes entailed steady increases in understanding by experts of how their methods and techniques were interpreted judicially. A period of low-threshold statistical proof ignored analytical questions that later arose, but compared with the subjective "eyeball" responses that preceded them represented an initial step forward for employment discrimination cases.

The use of statistical comparisons in school desegregation and jury selection cases like *Sims* (1967) and *Jefferson County* (1966) during the 1960s set the paradigm for measuring the racial effect of an employer's practices that would not be apparent from a review of particular decisions. As one of the early holdings under this approach, *Ochoa* (1971), noted, "gross statistical disparity amounts to a prima facie showing of discrimination, thus shifting to the opposing party the burden of going forward."

Demographic statistics measured differentials in black employment relative to other area workers, with the results at first expressed primarily in percentage terms. Comparative statistics, on the other hand, measure the results of particular practices, like use of tests and other selection devices to disproportionately screen out minority applicants.

Reflecting the entrenched pre–Civil Rights Act exclusion of blacks from most nonmenial jobs throughout the South, differences in the early cases, assessed under either type of comparison, were usually so large and apparent as to obviate the need for expert analysis. Following the amendment of Title VII in 1972,[8] discrimination was increasingly seen as being against groups or classes of persons rather than just individuals. Litigation covering industry-wide discrimination in trucking, paper manufacturing, and construction unions, illustrated by *Local 36* (1969), *Local 86* (1970), *Local 189* (1969), *Hayes* (1972), and *Rowe* (1972), set the legal precedents and evidentiary comparisons. Employer defenses focused on the absence of qualified blacks or random variation in employment patterns, often without success.

This is primarily why, at first, descriptive statistics satisfied the evidentiary burden. Where exclusionary policies had limited black employment in nonmenial positions, the early-case disparities were obvious enough so that simple percentage comparisons sufficed to lead to an inference of intentional discrimination. *Griggs v. Duke Power Co.* (1971), defining disparate impact theory, did not itself involve statistical inference, but its emphasis on the racial effects of facially neutral policies,

---

[8]Equal Employment Opportunity Act of 1972, P.L. 92–261 (1972).

primarily preemployment tests, quickly implicated industrial psychologists' test validation methodology into the discrimination law arena.[9]

Once significance testing became established, several issues faced legal practitioners and their experts, particularly whether there was a difference between the level required under disparate treatment and disparate impact theory.[10] In practice, the appropriate level of significance that satisfied case-by-case proof burdens depended on the degree of analytical refinement contained in the litigants' statistical evidence.

This relationship between analytical refinement and the level of statistical significance at which courts comfortably accept the results is now intuitively obvious, but few decisions articulated it clearly before decisions like *Segar* (1984) and *Palmer* (1987). As explained below in Section 3.3, district judges now must consciously decide that question as part of their "gatekeeper" responsibilities before admitting or excluding expert opinions, presumably supported by statistical inference.

Initially, however, the total or near complete exclusion of blacks did not require statistical proof, even though pattern and practice treatment of classes was involved. *Teamsters v. United States* (1977) exemplifies that line of cases. As will be explained below in Section 3.1, no case decided by Supreme Court had more influence on the application of statistical evidence, and no case was, from an analytical perspective, more wrongly decided than *Teamsters*.

The *Teamsters* court indicated that statistical evidence could support the claim of intentional discrimination where it was shown that a "longstanding and gross" disparity existed.[11] The Court was able to avoid defining what level of disparity is gross enough in terms of significance because of the "inexorable zero" fact pattern, although few cases then or later faced inexorable zero fact patterns that permitted such a resolution.[12]

---

[9]Testing cases and their methodology have historically remained a separate element of Title VII law, although little test-validity litigation occurs today. The 1969 EEOC testing guidelines, 29 C.F.R. Part 1607.5(c), 35 Fed. Reg. 12333 (1970), measuring validity through statistical significance at the .05 level, thus served as a precedent for later application of inferential measures to demographic and comparative statistical applications covering all aspects of discrimination. While the decision in *United States v. Georgia Power Co.* (1973) cautiously characterized the .05 level as "a desirable goal and not a prerequisite," it then went on to say that "Conversely, the pure common sense of this guideline cannot be ignored."

[10]Disparate treatment theory requires proof, statistical or otherwise, of an intent by the employer to discriminate by treating women or minorities differently from males or nonminorities. Disparate impact refers to the unintended but measurable disadvantaging effects of facially neutral employment practice on women or minorities.

[11]431 U.S. at 340, n.20.

[12]Where the workforce was totally gender-segregated, as in *Babrocky v. Jewel Food Co.* (1985), even descriptive statistics sufficed to demonstrate the "inexorable zero" and intentional discrimination. Conversely, it is possible to construct an example, like *Falcon* (1980), in which even zero is not statistically significant, because of low Hispanic availability, the

Arguably, the major reason that courts resorted to criteria like "gross," "substantial," "marked," or "compelling" to assess statistical imbalances was an awareness that the underlying comparisons were imprecise and unrefined. Put another way, there were reservations that a statistical significance level might not always have a "practical" significance of similar magnitude, e.g., .05 could not necessarily always be trusted to provide the underpinning for a legally sound decision.

Because of two related opinions issued the same term as *Teamsters, Castenada v. Partida*, and *Hazelwood School District v. United States*, the lower courts further disagreed on the alternative methods to determine significance, as well as the standard for determining significance. Given the strong scientific consensus around the .05 probability level as the usual and customary cutoff point, many courts, like *Contreras* (1981), *Trevino* (1981), *Martin* (1985), *Hilton* (1980), *White* (1979), and *Segar* (1984), adopted that measure.[13] Others, however, following Castenada and Hazelwood, used the Z score test-statistic to determine significance.

Not surprisingly, not all commentators agreed on a significance standard. Some, like Braun (1980), favored the .05 level primarily to promote consistent decision-making. Others, like Kaye (1983) or Smith and Abram (1981), regarded the benefit of a bright line rule on significance levels as outweighing their concerns that statistical significance may not be a proper judicial tool in the first place, or one with more limited applications than courts were accepting.

Meier, Sacks, and Zabell (1986) agreed on a .05 level, for example, but only on a two-tailed basis. Shoben (1983) favored differential significance levels, .001 for disparate treatment and .05 for disparate impact, because the legal consequences of an intentional discrimination finding (in 1983, when her article was published) were more severe than the consequences of disparate impact.

The "greater than two to three standard deviation" language in *Hazelwood*, a weakly articulated description of significance, triggered further disagreement over the use of statistics in Title VII cases. Defendant employers and their experts then argued that "greater than two to three" must mean four or more standard deviations, a probability level in the .001 range and much more difficult to reach. Such an interpretation of *Hazelwood's* "gross disparities" language[14] was generally rejected by the appellate courts in favor of an increased emphasis on proper comparison pools and refinements, such as the decisions in *Kilgo* (1986), *Cook* (1985), and *Palmer* (1987), but the continued absence of regulatory guidance on this question makes an unambiguous consensus more difficult to achieve.

---

small number of decisions, and the low number of Hispanics expected to be hired in a race-neutral setting.

[13] For the contrary view that "There is no arbitrary cutoff point for statistical significance," see *Eubanks v. Pickens Bond Construction Co.* (1980).

[14] "[w]here gross statistical disparities can be shown, they alone in a proper case constitute prima facie proof of a pattern or practice of discrimination." 433 U.S. at 307-08.

2.2   Geographic Labor Market Issues

The definition of an appropriate labor market for comparing workforce profiles on the basis of race was for many years a basic Title VII conundrum. This dilemma stemmed from two diverse factors, largely unrelated to each other. First, the earliest, precedent-setting, cases paid little attention to the geographic areas within which defendant employers operated, because either proof of intentional discrimination was developed directly rather than through the use of statistics, or the statistical disparities were so stark as to focus attention on the racial rather than the geographic component of the comparison.

Second, there were limitations inherent in the principal data source relied on for benchmarking external availability, the decennial census. Data from the 1970 and 1980 censuses on persons' socioeconomic characteristics, particularly occupation, was not even available below the metropolitan area level for Hispanics and Asians in much of the country, and not available for blacks in counties where their presence fell short of minimum enumeration levels.[15] Tests to estimate availability had to be developed by experts, who applied labor market principles and statistical methods to the legal issues raised by litigants.

Even where such information was published, the census reports enumerated persons by residence location, rather than where they were employed. This left unresolved questions of availability for blacks or other minorities when firms were located across geographic boundaries from where the job-seekers lived, and sustained numerous expert disputes that the courts then resolved, sometimes arbitrarily.[16]

Thus, the geographic boundary for demographic comparisons was primarily framed in terms of persons living in the city or metropolitan area in which an employer operated. Plaintiffs claimed, and many courts accepted, the idea that simple statistical discrepancies between an employer's workforce and the area's racial profile suggested discrimination.

Before long, employers and their experts offered analyses to rebut the premise that differences unexplained by such simple comparisons in employment were racially motivated. For example, it was held in *North Hills-Passavant Hospital* (1979) that an employer was not liable for a drop in minority employment when it moved from an inner-city to a suburban location, where the decline in black workers was due to reduced availability in the new area and race-neutral transportation and commuting problems.

---

[15]Despite these problems, most commentators, like the *Virginia Law Review* note, focused on legal rather than labor market questions and asserted that relevant labor markets are defined by standard metropolitan statistical areas (SMSAs).

[16]This writer in 1977 and 1978, and others, pointed out that arbitrary application of geographic labor market proxies could, and often did, have inconsistent and outcome-determinative effects on litigation.

By the mid-1970s the evolution of analytical refinement with respect to labor market geography had begun. This took several forms, primarily by weighting procedures across geographic boundaries in cases like *Markey* (1981) or *Clark* (1982) or in some instances like *Mister v. Illinois Gulf Central RR Co.* (1987), determining whether employer recruitment had included gerrymandering techniques to eliminate potential minority candidates.[17]

Hazelwood School District was the Supreme Court's first attempt to resolve geographic labor market questions, having largely ignored the issue in *Teamsters*.[18] The decision raised more questions than it answered, but at least clearly illustrated how the choice of geographic comparisons could directly determine the analytical result. *Hazelwood* concerned whether the city of St. Louis is part of the labor market for teacher hiring in a nearby suburban school district, and whether an active affirmative hiring effort by the St. Louis schools diverted black applicants who would otherwise have been available to teach in Hazelwood.

After identifying the problem, the Supreme Court remanded the case to the lower courts for resolution of this question. Because a settlement was reached before trial, the issue was left unresolved. Thus, litigants and their experts continued to define geographic labor markets using model estimates to reconcile differences between employee residence locations and employer job sites, hypothesizing the number and proportion of persons available in different locations. Not surprisingly, the results emphasized a range of fact-specific outcomes, and presented little clear precedent for other courts to rely on.[19]

The matter was only fully resolved when the 1990 decennial Census EEO File was revised to provide empirical data on availability for all places of work, as well as places of residence. Given this new data, experts no longer need to make labor supply estimates by race, occupation, and residence.

The information is now sorted in a manner that matches EEO-1 employer annual reports by geography, that is, by worksite location as well as other EEO-related characteristics. This development may, in part, be responsible for the decline in

---

[17] Judge Easterbrook rejected defendant expert's model because it measured weighted availability by primarily white hiree residence locations, thereby leapfrogging over and undercounting concentrations of potential black applicants, and ignoring relevant commuting distances for railroad jobs.

[18] The statistical comparison broadly outlined in *Teamsters* compared the employer's workforce to "the population in the community from which the employees are hired." 431 U.S. at 339-40 n.20 (1977).

[19] In one case, *County of Fairfax* (1979), plaintiffs failed to persuade a trial court that the Washington, D.C., SMSA represented the labor market for employment in Fairfax County, Virginia, a suburb of Washington, because black availability was substantially lower there than in the overall area. Plaintiffs eventually did establish liability, but only after the court of appeals found that defendants' weighted zip-coded availability estimates by race were also flawed. In another case, *Chicago Miniature Lamp Co.* (1991), the court of appeals reversed a trial court verdict for plaintiffs, whose expert demographer limited the geographic labor market to Chicago itself, while omitting nearby suburbs closer to the employer's facility than some locations within the city's boundaries that were included.

disputes over labor market definition in recent litigation, although the decline in class-based hiring cases that would rely on this information to develop evidence of significant disparities by race is probably of greater importance.

2.3 Occupational Comparisons

Disagreement over the proper level of occupational specificity for comparison purposes has historically been more pronounced than any other aspect of EEO analysis, even beyond the geographic labor market issue. The Supreme Court has not been especially helpful in this regard.

None of the Court's Title VII decisions have addressed the occupation issue squarely, or acknowledged that occupation was a measurable if not entirely accurate proxy for individuals' qualifications by race or sex. While *Teamsters* assumed that, absent discrimination, each employer's workforce would match the race and sex distribution of the area population and labor force, such an unexamined assumption could be made only in cases where the total exclusion or segregation of blacks made more precise comparisons unnecessary.[20]

Once more refined comparisons started being necessary in subsequent cases, the real question evolved into how much of the differential between groups was the result of discriminatory practices and how much the result of benign labor market factors. Because qualifications, measured through census occupational data could be interpreted differently by experts and the courts, substantial variation in parity estimates occurred. The related question of demonstrating that some stated qualifications were artificially set to exclude minorities or women further enmeshed this issue with proof burden questions, allowing the lack of judicial clarity or consensus to persist through *Hazelwood* and, to some lesser degree, even beyond *Wards Cove*.

While *Hazelwood* reiterated the *Teamsters* view that in some cases generalized comparisons were appropriate,[21] the Court clearly recognized that qualifications had to be taken into account. Beyond that, the decision was vague and provided little concrete guidance to the courts below, litigants, or experts asked to make such comparisons on behalf of parties in Title VII actions.[22]

Wards Cove marked progress in the area of occupational comparison, by expressly specifying that disparate impact requires a measured disparity between "the racial composition of qualified persons in the labor market and the persons

---

[20] See, *Teamsters*, 431 U.S. at 339-40 n.20 (1977), stating that "absent explanation, it is ordinarily to be expected that nondiscriminatory hiring practices will in time result in a work force more or less representative of the racial and ethnic composition of the population in the community from which the employees are hired."

[21] See, *Hazelwood*, 433 U.S. at 308 n.13 (1977).

[22] *Id.* "When special qualifications are required to fill particular jobs, comparison to the general population (rather than to the smaller group of individuals who possess the necessary qualifications) may have little probative value."

holding the at-issue jobs."[23] This approach requires comparison to some particular segment of the labor force, either occupation-specific or limited to related jobs requiring similar skills. It eliminated the population or overall labor force comparisons that had plagued EEO analysis since *Teamsters*.

Where possible disagreement remains among experts calculating availability for hiring comparison purposes is in the extent to which undifferentiated census occupational data is an accurate supply estimator, rather than adding further refinement based on education and wage levels. While there has been a distinct decline in the number of hiring cases litigated in recent years, the decisions covering this issue suggest increased judicial reliance on additional factors in evaluating statistical comparisons whenever such information can be factored into the analysis.[24]

3   Evolution of the Legal Precedents

EEO law does not operate in a vacuum, but represents litigation under specific federal statutes, particularly Title VII, the Equal Pay Act, and the Age Discrimination in Employment Act (ADEA). It is also influenced by developments affecting all civil litigation, particularly the body of rules governing civil procedure and evidence in federal courts.[25]

Changes in these arenas, particularly in recent years, have also had substantial effects on the way challenged employment practices are analyzed and litigated. This section considers the three distinct areas of law that interact to shape the full range of legal precedents governing the analytical process, statistics, and the use of expert testimony in EEO cases: substantive employment discrimination law (primarily Title VII decisions), procedural rule changes, and significant changes in evidence law (both as to Supreme Court decisions and their interpretation of the evidence rules).[26]

---

[23] *Wards Cove*, 490 U.S. at 650 (1989).

[24] See, for example, *EEOC v. Consolidated Service Systems* (1993), affirming a district court decision that plaintiffs' statistical analysis should have controlled for and excluded persons uninterested in defendant's low-wage jobs.

[25] This is, of course, a two-way street. Some of those changes resulted from issues raised first in EEO settings and then applied elsewhere in civil litigation.

[26] A fourth area, noted here but not discussed in detail, is the line of cases applying analytical refinement to race-conscious contracting preferences. While some readers might consider this as unrelated to the increased refinement of analysis and statistical proof in employment discrimination cases, I do not. In particular, see Justice O'Connor's opinion in *City of Richmond v. J.A. Croson Co.* (1989), clearly emphasizing that plan defenders must put into evidence a refined factual predicate, differing from the analysis of employment cases only by reference to at-issue contractors in the relevant area rather than occupations. See also *Adarand Constructors v. Pena* (1996). The importance of these two cases as corroborating the Court's recognition that EEO statistics have matured cannot be underestimated.

3.1 Title VII Case Law

Aside from *Griggs* (which distinguished the disparate impact theory of employment discrimination from disparate treatment), there have only been five Supreme Court decisions that materially affected the way in which the lower courts, regulators, scholars and litigants look at the analytical process and statistics in EEO cases: *Teamsters, Hazelwood, Beazer* (1979), *Bazemore* (1986), and *Wards Cove*, discussed in turn below. Inferences and clues can be decoded from several other decisions, but the basic quantum of legal doctrine is amazingly limited, given the number of EEO cases litigated over the past three decades and their importance to the nation's social and economic framework. These decisions are looked at with an eye toward the changes that each engendered in the way that experts framed and developed their opinions.

3.1.1 *Teamsters v. United States*

Like *Griggs* before it, *Teamsters* was decided under both disparate treatment and disparate impact theories. The motivation to discriminate can be inferred from the same statistical disparities that also demonstrate the effects of race-neutral practices. But *Teamsters* differed in one key respect. Whereas the impact in *Griggs* stemmed from the effects of an educational requirement (without regard for occupation), the at-issue over-the-road truck driver jobs in *Teamsters* could have been compared to a proxy pool more closely related to interest in and affinity for truck driving than the general population data relied on by Justice Stewart.

Stewart, who wrote the majority opinions in both *Teamsters* and *Hazelwood*, reiterated in the latter more clearly what he was trying to achieve in both cases: While there was a need for more accurate statistics, areawide population comparison was also probative where disparities were wide. Unfortunately, his doubly incorrect translation of those aims into practice created analytical chaos that lasted until *Wards Cove* was decided a decade later, and then some.

The first assumption was that the areawide general population was highly probative of the racial proportion that would be employed, absent discrimination, because "the job skill there involved—the ability to drive a truck–is one that many persons possess or can fairly readily acquire."[27] The second assumption was that "When special qualifications are required to fill particular jobs, comparisons to the general population (rather than to the smaller group of individuals who possess the necessary qualifications) may have little probative value."[28]

While such language did not affect the *Teamsters* case directly—blacks had been virtually excluded from over-the-road driver positions however they were measured and compared—the premise that such inaccurate comparisons could

---

[27] See, *Hazelwood*, 433 U.S. at 308, n.13 (1977), quoting *Teamsters*, 431 U.S. at 337, n.17 (1977).
[28] *Id.*

serve to statistically suggest discrimination in less clear-cut circumstances ignores the range of particular labor market criteria related to differences between all jobs.

The second assumption is, in one sense, correct: General population comparisons have little probative value, but because they overinclusively include persons with no interest in jobs above or below those for which they are qualified, those who have no interest in any job, and those who are too young, old, infirm, or institutionalized and not even enumerated as part of the workforce, rather than as suggested in Justice Stewart's opinion.

The technical infirmity of Justice Stewart's argument is not salvaged by the caveat in *Teamsters* that "... evidence showing that the figures for the general population might not accurately reflect the pool of qualified job applicants would also be relevant."[29] Footnote 20 suggests that Stewart may have had two possible purposes in mind that, in effect, overrode the need for statistical precision.

First, it would be defendant's rebuttal burden, rather than plaintiff's prima facie burden, to define the occupational pool narrowly rather than broadly. Second, barely a decade after the effective date of Title VII, when both the lingering effects of pre-Act discrimination and ongoing societal differences by race were still evident, statistics overstating black availability would to some degree offset and counterbalance the residual differences presumably attributable to discrimination that could otherwise not be taken into account.

An alternative assumption, however, superseding that of Justice Stewart, could easily have been that all jobs, from the highest to lowest, attract a definable pool of persons in any area who can be estimated on various dimensions, including race or ethnicity. Expert analysis on a case-by-case basis could develop such estimates.

In turn, some courts might then have accorded statistical evidence greater probative value, rather than discounting it as inaccurate and unreliable, as many of them did.[30] By defining the terms of the legal balance in a manner that thwarted the need for more clearly defined analytical parameters, Justice Stewart's effect on EEO enforcement was, ultimately, detrimental.

3.1.2 *Hazelwood School District v. United States*

This case represents the Supreme Court's first real foray into the thicket of EEO analysis. Had it been followed in short order by decisions clarifying the issues of geographic labor markets, workforce, and demographic benchmark comparisons and the role of statistical significance in establishing the prima facie case, Hazelwood would be regarded as a solid first step. Because the Court chose not to revisit these issues soon, however, *Hazelwood*'s value is undercut by the unresolved issues it left strewn in its wake.

---

[29]*Teamsters*, 431 U.S. at 340, n.20 (1977).

[30]As a *Virginia Law Review* note (1973) observed, "The uneven reliability of statistics used to establish the plaintiff's prima facie case ... may give rise to judicial uncertainty."

Turning first to statistical significance, the two-to-three standard deviation approach is still among the range of methodologies considered appropriate by some courts despite its inferiority to the exact probabilities. The binomial normal approximation approach had been used by the Court earlier that year to decide a grand jury exclusion case, *Castenada v. Partida* (1977), and then applied in *Hazelwood*.

The number of employees expected was substituted for the number of jurors in the formula. Where the difference between the number expected and the number employed exceeded two-to-three standard deviations, "then the hypothesis that teachers were hired without regard to race would be suspect."[31]

In one sense, this represented some improvement over the prior approach, e.g., whether the disparity was large enough for a trial judge to subjectively link the challenged employment practice to race. Until *Hazelwood*, there was little assurance that a decision to accept or reject statistical disparities was analytically sound, because the point at which differences were significant was not ascertained.

On the other hand, the "two-to-three" language unleashed an interpretive quandary that has not fully been resolved to this day. Accepting the widely held scientific protocol that rejects null hypotheses at the .05 level, 1.96 or, rounded, two standard deviations is a two-tailed cutoff point, and would appear to be the test-statistic equivalent. Defendants and some judges, ignoring or unmindful of the non-linear character of the normal distribution, argued that at least three, or more than three standard deviation differences were necessary for significance.[32]

With respect to geographic labor market definition, the Court at least clarified the point that some external comparison was necessary in recruitment and hiring cases, although not in cases involving promotion or other internal questions. While data on actual applicants is preferable when it is available or not otherwise compromised,[33] the absence of such information in the record led to reliance on a comparison between the proportion of black teachers hired subsequent to 1972 and the proportion available.

---

[31] *Hazelwood*, 433 U.S. at 308-09, n.14 (1977).

[32] That would, of course, set the equivalent probability to less than the .01 level, rather than the .05 otherwise generally regarded as sufficient to demonstrate significance. The Fourth Circuit in particular was a hotbed of statistical illiteracy during that time. See, for example, *EEOC v. American National Bank*, (1981) which held that while courts should not reject a difference beyond three standard deviations to establish significance, they should be cautious about accepting deviations in the one to three range. See, also, *EEOC v. Federal Reserve Bank of Richmond*, (1983) a decision interpreting *Castenada-Hazelwood* as requiring a disparity of more than two to three standard deviations.

[33] Most courts have held that applicant flow comparisons are more probative than workforce statistics, except where minority or female applicants are deterred by employer-raised barriers. See, for example, *EEOC v. Rath Packing Co.* (1986) and *EEOC v. Joe's Stone Crab, Inc.* (1997), a case where borderline statistical probabilities were combined with evidence that delegation of hiring responsibilities to gender-stereotyping subordinates resulted in female underemployment.

The Court then remanded the case for resolution of an atypical complicating factor involving possible alternative labor market definitions: did St. Louis's effort to hire large numbers of black teachers influence the labor market in nearby suburban Hazelwood? Depending on how that question was answered, the difference would or would not be statistically significant.

Subsequent cases thus reflected arguments and expert calculations that structured the labor market to increase or decrease availability. As explained above, the lack of worksite-based availability data prior to the 1990 Census EEO File left this issue unresolved until that time. While external labor markets can vary for jobs where the employer recruits beyond the local area, this issue in general should now diminish as a point of contention in EEO law.

The *Hazelwood Court* looked to its *Teamsters* decision to repeat that, absent discrimination, the employer's workforce should in the long run mirror the area's proportion of minorities or women.[34] At the same time, the decision clearly specified that qualifications are to be taken into account. "When special qualifications are required to fill particular jobs, comparisons to the general population (rather than to the smaller group of individuals who possess the necessary qualifications may have little probative value."

The lower courts then fractured on which jobs required skills not possessed by the general population, and the broader questions of qualifications and the ability to statistically measure productivity and performance differences across various workforce segments. Not until *Wards Cove* was decided in 1989 did the Court specify that the comparison should be between the proportion of minority workers seeking the at-issue jobs and their proportion in the area workforce. Unadjusted population data finally appears to have dropped out of the employment equation.[35]

3.1.3 *New York City Transit Authority v. Beazer*

Among all the cases discussed in this section, *Beazer* is unquestionably the one least familiar to readers not intimately familiar with the development of EEO law. It marked the first decision in which the Court rejected a party's disparate impact statistical proof as methodologically deficient, based on problems that the Court assumed an active role in identifying. To some, it marked a step back from the policy interpretation plaintiffs had given *Griggs*, namely that the measured effects of employer practices (rather than motivation or intent) determined discrimination.

Subsequent to *Griggs*, relatively broad statistical comparisons were used to prove discrimination covering a range of employment practices, such as educational requirements, height–weight limits, and disqualification on the basis of

---

[34]This long-term equilibrium notion may not always apply in the short run, a distinction largely ignored by litigants, their experts, and the courts.

[35]One recent exception to insistence on comparison to the at-issue workforce occurred in *McNamara v. City of Chicago* (1998) when the appeals court considered a community's racial population proportion relevant to promotion targets for affirmative relief purposes, where past unlawful practices had reduced prior entry-level firefighter hiring.

arrests or garnishments, among others.[36] Practices determined to have disparate impact constitute prima facie proof of discrimination, which an employer can defeat either by showing that the challenged practice has "a manifest relationship to the employment in question"[37] or, initially, by rebutting the statistics as "insufficient or inaccurate."

As mentioned earlier, the magnitude of disparity necessary to demonstrate a prima facie case rarely arose in the early cases, given the substantial differences by race between black plaintiffs and comparison pools. In *Griggs* itself, for example, a high school completion requirement for coal-shoveling jobs at a utility was held to impact North Carolina blacks who, measured by the 1960 Census, had a 12% rate compared with 34% for Whites.[38]

Prior to *Hazelwood*, the Court treated the racial composition of a population as a sufficient proxy for the racial composition of the at-issue workforce to assume equivalence. It further glossed over the imprecision of the comparisons it did recognize, given limits in the statistical data.[39] As mentioned above, *Hazelwood* represented the first step toward statistical refinement, with respect to both geographic and occupational requirements.

Beazer went one quantum step further, holding that plaintiffs statistics fell short of demonstrating the disparate effect of the employer's policy barring employment of persons using methadone, a medical substitute for heroin. Plaintiffs relied on a series of imprecise comparisons, which the Court rejected as irrelevant and insufficient to establish a prima facie case: statistics on the proportion of employees suspected of any narcotics use, not just methadone; no record of terminations under the enforcement policy; and, most critically, comparison of minority (black and Hispanic) methadone program participants in publically funded programs with the workforce-age population of the New York metropolitan area.[40]

Calling this grab bag of demographic statistics "virtually irrelevant,"[41] the Court then held that the population data overinclusively contained persons unavailable for work of any kind, let alone for the transit authority. The real

---

[36]In particular, see Blumrosen (1972), emphasizing descriptive statistical differences rather than inference.

[37]*Griggs*, 401 U.S. at 431-32 (1971).

[38]*Id.*, 401 U.S. at 430 n.6.

[39]In *Griggs* the Court recognized no need to compare the educational attainment of blacks in Duke Power Company's labor market area rather than all of North Carolina. Similarly, in *Dothard v. Rawlinson*, nationwide height and weight data were used to demonstrate the exclusionary effect by gender of specified limits that eliminated most women. The Court assumed that such characteristics were distributed uniformly by state and were sufficiently accurate to be applicable in Alabama. See 433 U.S. at 329-30, n.12 (1977).

[40]The Court regarded the omission of private methadone clinic data critical, given the much higher proportion of nonminority participants in such programs. To establish a prima facie case, plaintiffs would have had to show that even combining private and public programs, blacks and Hispanics would have been excluded at a significantly greater rate than others. 440 U.S. at 586, n.30 (1979).

[41]440 U.S. at 586 (1979).

doctrinal importance of *Beazer* for interpreting disparate impact theory goes beyond rejecting plaintiffs' incorrect assumption that any statistics would suffice.

It is, rather, articulation of the Court's belief that, absent an intent to discriminate, neutral-rule challenges must clearly specify and demonstrate the claimed harm before an employer's defense is required. The case thus suggests that the justices were growing uneasy with the way that *Teamsters* had generated a string of population-related comparisons for jobs where identifiable skills were required, and was suggesting that attacks on the effects of discrimination were not incompatible with a clearer focus on who had been harmed, and by how much.

3.1.4 *Bazemore v. Friday*

Bazemore represents an interesting element in the development of EEO statistical proof in several respects. First, it considers the evidentiary weight of multivariate models in the proof process, holding that a regression cannot be given no weight and excluded simply because it does not include every possible independent variable.

Second, it recognizes that analytical proof is not limited to hiring cases or difference in proportion comparisons between minority and nonminority employee pools. Like most Title VII cases using regression evidence, *Bazemore* concerned pay differences. In this instance, salary by race.

The key aspect of *Bazemore* is the Court's adoption of scientific logic as a rationale for its legal ruling, and the extent to which sound methodology and legal proof burdens coincide in the decision. Reversing an appellate court that had ruled to the contrary, the Supreme Court held that a theoretical critique of a party's regression is no substitute for empirically addressing the claimed fault. So long as the regression includes the major explanatory factors, it is sufficiently refined to be admissible and have evidentiary value.[42]

Neither mere conjecture on the part of defendant's expert, nor defendant's legal argument that a statistically significant negative wage coefficient is attributable to unmeasured nondiscriminatory factors rather than to race, satisfies defendant's burdens—analytical or legal. To defeat the inference created by plaintiff's significant statistics, defendant must introduce evidence to support its contention that some missing factor explains the disparities, rather than simply hypothesize about that possibility.

In statistical terms, defendant could rebut plaintiff's prima facie case by reducing the salary coefficient difference to zero. This could occur if some relevant criterion, omitted from plaintiff's regression, was added by the defendant to its model so that enough of the salary variance initially attributed to race is now explained by that new factor, say productivity or performance.

In legal terms, this is wholly consistent with recognized Title VII proof burdens. Plaintiff's statistics, if sufficiently persuasive to the trier of fact, can shift

---

[42]But see *Coward v. ADT Security Systems, Inc.* (1998), where the plaintiff's regression analysis was rejected as invalid under *Bazemore* for omitting a major factor.

the production burden to defendant. In turn, to satisfy that burden, defendant's evidence must rebut the initial showing. As the Court said in *Teamsters*, "evidence showing that the figures for the general population might not accurately reflect the pool of qualified applicants would also be relevant."[43]

The opinion seemed to suggest an understanding of several things: first, the ability to control for several independent variables at once gave a properly specified regression additional weight over other EEO statistics, especially because the data referred to the actual employer, and not an external referent pool. This is analogous to the judicial preference for applicant flow data rather than snapshot comparisons between an employer's workforce and an external referent, so long as the flow data is untainted.[44]

Second, the Court's treatment of multivariate regression analysis is in that respect consistent with its evolving broader interpretation of other statistical evidence. That is, there must be some minimum level of refinement; otherwise, statistical comparison is inappropriate. Beyond that, the level of refinement becomes a matter of the weight to which this evidence is entitled in the decision-making process.

The real distinction is the presence of two elements of refinement that must be satisfied here. The refinement is both methodological, as to the scientific procedure used to properly specify the model, and substantive, concerning how well the actual data fits the model as specified.[45]

3.1.5 *Wards Cove Packing Co. v. Atonio*

Wards Cove created much ado when it was decided in 1989, primarily by articulating what was widely construed as a lessening of the employer's disparate impact rebuttal burden. Following two years of contentious debate in Congress and a pres-

---

[43]431 U.S. at 340, n.20 (1977).

[44]Plaintiffs in some cases successfully argued that regressions can also be tainted, if independent variables reflect unlawful employer decisions. See, for example, *James v. Stockham Valves & Fittings Co.* (1977), where the model specified by defendant's expert economist relied on skill as an independent variable to explain wages by race, attributing skill differences to rank as a means of explaining wage differences. But because the employer defined rank as having higher skill, and defined skill in terms of the higher rank of being incumbent in those upper-level jobs from which blacks were totally excluded, the court rejected the regression as invalid and the defense argument as circular.

[45]Commentators have expressed concerns over the problems of interpreting multivariate analysis in the legal process for the past quarter century, going back to Finkelstein (1973, 1980). Review articles summarizing the literature on this issue that may be of interest to the reader include Dempster (1988), and Ananda and Gilmartin (1992). Other specific articles, like the 1975 *Harvard Law Review* Note and Fisher (1980), have also contributed to the broader understanding of these issues. Technical problems with regression analysis will be recognized by readers familiar with this approach, such as the inclusion of tainted variables, the exclusion of necessary variables, measurement error, specification error and multicollinearity, among others.

idential veto of the 1990 version, the 1991 Civil Rights Act[46] restored the status quo ante burden scheme, where it rests today.

Largely unnoticed at the time and ignored in the legislative process, the decision specified that in hiring cases disparate impact is demonstrated by comparing "the racial composition of qualified persons in the labor market and the persons holding the at-issue jobs."[47] Holding that plaintiffs statistical evidence was insufficient to establish a prima facie case, the Court expressly rejected the claim that incumbent cannery laborers were qualified and part of the comparison pool for craft and similar positions.

The decision goes on to say that if the imbalance "is due to a dearth of qualified nonwhite applicants," then there is no disparate impact.[48] The emphasis on qualification, properly understood, invalidates the simple, unadjusted demographic approach, general population or the undifferentiated civilian labor force, as simultaneously under- and overinclusive of the particular segment within the labor force whose skill, training, and education (or in some instances, lack of it) identifies such persons as legitimate job candidates.

While this language attempted to draw lower courts' attention to the variables involved in labor market comparisons, the opinion ignored the seasonal nature and remote island location of the fish cannery. *Wards Cove* could have spoken more clearly to hiring versus promotion differences and the range of labor supply decisions facing employers, but did not. As the Court put it, correctly but with little real guidance, "isolating the cannery workers as the potential 'labor force' for unskilled noncannery positions is at once both too broad and too narrow in its focus."[49]

Delineation of availability comparison pools on a case-by-case basis is thus a matter of expert analysis and opinion, particularly where further analytical stratification within occupation is required on the basis of income, education, or other factors that must be taken into account.[50] In addressing the burden of proof issue, Congress showed no inclination to review or reject the labor market refinements the Court had articulated.

But by restating the employer's rebuttal burden as "a reasoned review of the employer's justification for his use of the challenged practice,"[51] or justifiable practice standard, the Court abandoned the long-held "business necessity" criterion set forth in *Griggs*. What *Wards Cove* said, in effect, was that plaintiffs prima facie case required a determination that the challenged practice was both statistically

---

[46]Pub. L. 102-166 (1991).

[47]*Wards Cove*, 490 U.S. at 650-51 (1989).

[48]*Id.*, 490 U.S. at 650 (1989).

[49]*Id.*

[50]See, for example, *Grauer v. Federal Express Corp.* (1994), where the court rejected plaintiff's assertion, offered without either a statistical showing or an expert opinion, that a certain job-skill requirement (knowledge of accounting) had disparate impact on women.

[51]*Wards Cove*, 490 U.S. at 659 (1989).

significant and unjustified. Previously, the justification aspect was part of the employer's rebuttal burden, after the prima facie case had been established. Congress then disagreed.

Wards Cove also reiterated the Court's earlier decision in *Watson v. Ft. Worth Bank & Trust* (1988) that disparate impact plaintiffs must identify specific practices that result in significant disparities. The plurality in *Watson* had held that, standing alone, even a statistically significant imbalance cannot establish a prima facie case.[52]

This provision was also modified by the 1991 Title VII amendments, so that if the disparate effects of particular practices cannot be analytically isolated, plaintiffs may still demonstrate the overall disparate impact of an employer's human resource system. Furthermore, the overall effects approach (rather than the identifiable practices theory) is in no way inconsistent with the refined availability requirement set forth in *Wards Cove*.

3.2 Procedural Rule Changes Affecting EEO Testimony

In 1993 the procedural rules governing discovery were amended to require more substantial disclosure of the material and experts that a party to civil litigation intends to use in the proof process.[53] The underlying reasoning for these changes is to help streamline the litigation process at a time when growing federal court caseloads have far outstripped the judicial resources needed to resolve them in a timely manner. By requiring more complete disclosure between litigating parties, the aim was to eliminate unfair surprise and conserve scarce resources—both judicial and those of the parties.[54]

The rules changes require, among other things, voluntary disclosure (without waiting for specific requests) of all relevant data and documents that are relevant to the party's claim. In practice, this requires defendant employers to reveal to plaintiffs the type and amount of data that can be used to evaluate the challenged employment practices, in more detail than under the previous rules. These initial disclosures must also be augmented or updated if and when new information becomes available.

These changes are intended to provide plaintiffs with sufficient information so that statistical analysis of class-based data is as complete and accurate as possible.

---

[52]The identifiable practices standard was one of the judicial responses to the overinclusive evidentiary criteria (like undifferentiated civilian labor force comparisons and across-the-board class certification of broad Title VII plaintiff classes dissimilar in many respects other than race) that became widespread following the development of disparate impact theory in *Griggs*. Where more precise analyses result in significant disparities, the absence of an identifiable practice should not arbitrarily be dismissed.

[53]See Fed.R.Civ.P. 26(a)(1),(2) (1998).

[54]This reasoning was articulated unambiguously in *Sylla-Sawdon v. Uniroyal Goodrich Tire Co.* (1995).

Presumptions of significant disparities can thus be confirmed or shown to be incorrect, and litigation decisions shaped accordingly.[55] Previously, some litigation strategies included delay or total withholding of statistical data to which plaintiffs were entitled, untimely disclosure of opposing experts' identity and opinions, and insufficient disclosure by such experts in their reports or depositions of the bases on which their opinions were reached.

Under the revised rules EEO litigants may still engage nontestifying experts to evaluate their own and the opponents' statistical evidence without disclosure, but testifying experts must, within thirty days of being retained, provide a written report containing their opinion, along with the basis and reasoning underlying that opinion. The expert must also provide a detailed statement of qualifications, disclose the compensation rate covering her services, a list of all publications produced over the past ten years and, most importantly, a list of all cases within the past four years in which the expert testified or was deposed.

The supplemental disclosure requirement is intended to cover instances where the original response is in some material way incorrect or incomplete.[56] The criterion by which judges will determine whether an expert's report is sufficiently complete is whether surprise and unnecessary depositions can be avoided, as well as reducing costs.

Sanctions against parties who violate Rule 26 include exclusion of the expert testimony in part or in its entirety.[57] The threat of such exclusion promotes compliance, although in practice courts are reluctant to invoke that provision. Exclusion primarily occurs where the opposing party would be substantially prejudiced by admission of the questioned opinion, or there is evidence of bad faith noncompliance with the rule.[58]

One final aspect of the Rule 26 revisions deserves mention in the context of statistical evidence and experts in EEO litigation. Courts now hold that material prepared by lawyers but disclosed to experts (so the experts will better understand the legal framework in which their opinion will be used) can now be discovered by the opposing party. Previously, the "work product" doctrine, first enunciated by

---

[55]Litigants who refuse to introduce statistical evidence through experts but instead assume that courts should regard claimed disparities as proof of discrimination can, in that regard, be seen as frivolously wasting scarce judicial time. In particular, see *Frazier v. Consolidated Rail Corp.* (1988), where the court of appeals rejected plaintiffs claim that the trial judge erred in refusing to evaluate the statistics or take judicial notice of the Z scores (incorrectly) calculated by counsel. See also *Wilkins v. University of Houston* (1981), which held that, absent a contrary expert opinion from plaintiffs, there was no basis for the trial judge to reject defendant expert's interpretation of the R-square of a regression analysis.

[56]Fed.R.Civ.P. 26(e)(1), (2) (1998).

[57]Fed.R.Civ.P. 37(c)(1) (1998).

[58]See, for example, *In re Paoli RR Yard PCB Litigation* (1994), where the court of appeals reversed the district court's exclusion decision because it determined that the prejudice was "extremely minimal."

the Supreme Court in *Hickman v. Taylor* (1947), shielded from discovery written materials containing the attorney's legal thinking and strategy.

Several courts and commentators have interpreted the 1993 rule amendments to hold that when a lawyer gives work product to an expert who then uses that information in forming an opinion that will be introduced into evidence at trial, the information is no longer privileged and must be disclosed. This disclosure provision does not apply to nontestifying experts, since the work product will not in any way be translated into evidence. In effect, an internal conflict between disclosure and work product protection (within Rule 26) has been resolved in favor of disclosure where the material could influence the expert's opinion, and in favor of protection when it will not.

This disclosure provision carries an additional benefit that becomes clearer in light of the evidence law changes covered elsewhere in this section. Even though some experts may be marginally qualified under the criteria described below, their opinions may not be of genuine assistance to the fact-finder (as required for admissibility). The weakness of their opinions can more clearly be probed by evaluating the source material they relied upon as to its scientific validity. This further permits courts to determine how much of the opinion represents the expert's own work, or as the court in *Karn v. Rand* (1996) explained, how much represents the "facts chosen and presented by an attorney advocating a particular position."

3.3   Changing Evidence Law

As covered above, the role of statistical analysis and expert testimony in EEO litigation has evolved slowly over the past twenty-five years, reflecting changes in the experts' solutions to EEO problems and in substantive legal doctrine. In general, the courts have not enthusiastically embraced these developments, but pragmatically recognized that class-based discrimination claims are most effectively evaluated using quantitative proof.

In contrast to the incremental changes in EEO analysis, there have been major changes in evidence law over the past half decade covering all federal court litigation, including EEO law. A series of Supreme Court decisions has reinterpreted Evidence Rule 702, covering expert testimony, with a resultant increase in pretrial judicial scrutiny of proposed experts and their opinions. Rather than, as in the past, almost automatically admitting into evidence almost any opinion labeled "expert," trial judges must initially act as "gatekeepers" and determine that the proposed opinion is not scientifically baseless, and that it will assist the trier of fact (the jury) before permitting the expert to testify.

Since passage of the 1991 Civil Rights Act, the Title VII trier of fact is the jury.[59] Previously, by statute, the trial judge wore both hats; Title VII plaintiffs did

---

[59] ADEA and Equal Pay Act plaintiffs have always had the right to a jury trial, so the role bifurcation between judge and jury did not apply.

not have the right to a jury trial. Thus, the trial judge often found it easier (as the legal decision-maker) to admit questionable expert testimony, often over objection, and then (as the fact-finder) give the opinion no weight, rather than risk an appeal on the admissibility issue. Now, the preliminary ruling on admissibility that the court must reach is critical: If the judge determines that the proposed expert's testimony and opinion will not be of aid the fact-finder, the opinion is excluded and does not reach the jury.

This shift in evidence law began in 1993, when the Supreme Court finally addressed and resolved a long-standing disagreement between the various appeals courts concerning the correct criteria for admitting expert testimony. That decision, *Daubert v. Merrell-Dow Pharmaceuticals, Inc.*, is discussed below. Like other landmark decisions, *Daubert* generated additional questions as to how it should be interpreted that took the Court several years to reach and address. *General Electric Co. v. Joiner* and *Kumho Tire Co. v. Carmichael* then followed. Taken together, the Supreme Court's expert trilogy has clarified the expert admissibility sequence, the criteria and bases for exclusion, and the level of appellate review of contested admissibility decisions.[60]

As several decisions discussed below show, application of the revised admissibility paradigm to EEO law resulted in the exclusion of proposed expert testimony, and the concomitant inability of litigants relying on those opinions to establish a statistical inference of discrimination. The effect of these changes on the role of analytical proof in employment discrimination cases follows.

3.3.1 *Daubert v. Merrell-Dow Pharmaceuticals, Inc.*

Prior to *Daubert*, the admissibility of scientific evidence in federal trials was evaluated on a "general acceptance" standard, known widely as the *Frye* test, after an appellate decision articulated three-quarters of a century ago. The criterion was that a theory or methodology must be generally accepted by the scientific community covering that area of expertise before it could be admitted. The Federal Rules of Evidence, promulgated in 1975, established a different standard, based solely on the scientific validity of the opinion without regard for what Faigman (1997)

---

[60]In addition, proposed changes would codify the *Daubert* interpretation of admissibility. The Committee on Rules of Practice and Procedure of the Judicial Conference of the United States issued for public comment in August 1998 proposed amendments to Evidence Rule 702, expressly extending the trial court's gatekeeper responsibility set forth in *Daubert* and extended in *Kumho Tire* to all expert testimony, be it scientific, technical, or based on other specialized knowledge. The expanded rule requires a showing of reliable methodology, facts, and data, and specifies that the expert must reliably apply those principles and methods to the facts of the case, e.g., the proper "fit." Following public hearings and comment, the proposed changes then go to the Judicial Conference, the federal courts' governing body. If approved by the Judicial Conference, the proposed changes are submitted to the Supreme Court for its approval. If approved, and then unless legislatively overruled by Congress, the amended rule takes effect.

characterized as the "protracted waiting period that valid scientific evidence and techniques must endure before gaining legal acceptance."

Daubert holds that the Rules of Evidence superseded Frye, deemphasizing general acceptance from the sine qua non of admissibility to only one of a flexible series of criteria that judges, fulfilling their "gatekeeper" role, could look to.[61] The decision did not intend for the "checklist" to be exclusive or dispositive, as not all factors apply to every type of expert testimony.

Under *Daubert*, a proposed opinion must be grounded in some scientific knowledge and method, not just speculation or conjecture on the expert's part.[62] The opinion's credibility is established by being scientifically valid. This translates loosely as the expert having "good grounds" for the opinion, and that the opinion clearly represents a "fit" between theory and its application to the at-issue fact pattern in the case.

Courts have identified other reliability indicia. These include Judge Kozinski's benchmark in the remand appeal in *Daubert* (1995) (1) whether the opinion was expressly developed for litigation, rather than growing out of research conducted in a more objective forum; (2) Judge Posner's measure in *Braun v. Ciba-Geigy Corp.* (1996) of whether the expert's litigation opinion is as intellectually rigorous as the expert's other professional work;[63] and (3) the perspective expressed in *Claar v. Burlington Northern R.R.* (1994) whether the opinion considers all relevant factors, or whether it ignores those variables that could undercut or invalidate the expert's conclusion.

Some courts, dubious of the professional witness or "hired gun," require the party whose expert testimony was not based on research conducted independently of the litigation to come forward with other, objective and verifiable, evidence that the expert testimony is scientifically valid before admitting it. This could include peer-reviewed studies affirming the expert's methodology, or the like.

The post-*Daubert* trial judge is responsible for screening proposed opinions and, as the court held in *Bammerlin v. Navistar International Transportation* (1994), must be confident that the expert "knows whereof he speaks" as a precondition for admissibility. Various additional indicia, beyond those cited above, have been relied on in making such determinations.

---

[61] The other *Daubert* criteria are whether the expert's methodology can be tested, replicated, and objectively evaluated (as opposed to a subjective and conclusory opinion whose reliability cannot be assessed); whether the methodology has been subjected to peer review and publication; and whether the expert's conclusion, based on applying a methodology or theory to the at-issue facts, takes into account known or potential rates of error that might affect the expert's opinion.

[62] *Daubert*, 509 U.S. at 589-90 (1993).

[63] Unfortunately, this criterion may not be as effective in the case of professional experts who do not conduct any research independent of litigation.

These include, as the court suggested in *Summers v. Missouri Pacific Railroad* (1995), the judicial evaluation of the proposed expert's opinion in previous cases.[64] Similarly, as in *U.S. v. Artero* (1997), judges are wary regarding the extent to which the proposed expert is seen as advocating a party's position rather than offering an objective opinion.[65] Finally, as held in *Lust v. Merrell-Dow Pharmaceuticals, Inc.* (1996), an expert may be excluded where the opinion is regarded by the court as "influenced by a litigation-driven financial incentive."

3.3.2 *General Electric Co. v. Joiner*

Joiner resolved a particular legal issue that had arisen: the standard for appellate review of trial court decisions to admit or exclude expert testimony. More important, however, is how *Joiner* relates to the admissibility issue generally, and as applied to EEO law specifically. The decision clearly reaffirmed and strengthened the trial court's gatekeeper responsibility in several respects.

The case arose when an appeals court, applying its own interpretation of how the matter should be resolved, reversed a district court ruling to exclude a proposed expert's opinion. Normally, the appellate court would apply an "abuse of discretion" standard, and overrule the trial judge only if the admissibility decision was legally erroneous, giving the lower court the benefit of the doubt in most instances.

Believing that the plaintiff's expert should have been excluded, defendant General Electric Company sought Supreme Court review. It argued that by reinstating the excluded expert and sending the case back for trial, the appeals court had erred in two respects. First, the panel had held that appellate courts should take a "hard look" at district court rulings to exclude expert testimony that are outcome determinative, e.g., eliminate the entire evidentiary basis of that party's case, as opposed to exclusions that deprive the party of some, but not all, of their proof.

Second, General Electric contended that the reasoning articulated by the court of appeals as to why it reversed the district court was also wrong. The appellate judges had interpreted Evidence Rule 702 to say that the district court's gatekeeper evaluation is limited to the expert's principles and methodology, but not the expert's conclusion in terms of the actual case.

---

[64]*Summers* cited two previous appellate decisions upholding exclusion of the same expert's opinion as of no assistance to the fact-finder, one of which expressly characterized the individual's testimony as "[The party's] testimony dressed up and sanctified as the opinion of an expert."

[65]In *Artero* a demographer's study that failed to correct for salient explanatory variables was excluded. The opinion noted that the proposed expert's well-credentialed academic resume does not protect the court against "tendentious advocacy research." Similarly, a court of appeals in *Tokio Marine & Fire Insurance Co.* (1992) found no error in the exclusion of a proposed engineering expert who referred to himself in testimony "as a member of the team that was preparing this case."

The district judge had indicated a belief that there was "too great" an analytical gap between Joiner's expert's conclusions and the underlying data, in effect moving from the expert's theory to an evaluation of the results. That methodology–conclusions dichotomy was one of the post-*Daubert* interpretations of that point, thus requiring Supreme Court resolution.

The Supreme Court reaffirmed and extended the principles enunciated in *Daubert*. First, the appellate courts were directed to apply an "abuse of discretion" standard, rejecting the "stringent review" approach used by the Eleventh Circuit. The fact that an expert exclusion might prove outcome-determinative to a party's evidentiary case does not permit the heightened review advocated by the court of appeals.

Second, and again, more importantly, the gatekeeping trial judge is not limited to evaluating the expert's methodology, and can determine whether the expert's conclusions validly follow application of theory to the at-issue facts. This permits the district judge to assess whether the expert's opinion is, in the first instance, inadmissible, rather than admissible but subject to later challenge only as to the weight of the opinion.

3.3.3 *Kumho Tire Co. v. Carmichael*

One other area where the lower federal courts had split over interpreting *Daubert* concerned the earlier decision's scope. That is, did the *Daubert* admissibility analysis apply to all expert testimony, irrespective of the nature of the expertise, or as some judges believed, only to "hard science" expertise and not qualifications derived from higher education, training, experience, or other criteria.

Under the latter interpretation, *Daubert* was inapplicable to technical or otherwise specialized expertise in those circuits where that distinction had been adopted. The question arose in several instances regarding engineering experts, including *Kumho Tire* itself.

Where *Daubert* does not apply, trial judge gatekeepers rely entirely on the evidence rules to evaluate proposed expert testimony, rather than the combination of the rules and *Daubert*. Where *Daubert* does apply, irrespective of the nature of the experts' claimed qualifications, the likelihood that marginal or questionable experts would be excluded increases. To some extent, especially after *Joiner*, the distinction had become one more of form than substance, since the rules increasingly were being interpreted in light of the Court's teachings, and vice versa. Cases on the margin, like this one, prompted the Court to revisit the matter once more.

Kumho Tire arose from an appellate decision reflecting that narrow area where a proposed expert's opinion lacked any scientific methdological foundation whatsoever, whereas the at-issue question clearly had to be addressed through more rigorous analysis. Reversing a district court decision to exclude a mechanical engineer's opinion concerning the cause of a tire failure, the Eleventh Circuit held that the expert's opinion was admissible based on his twenty-some years of experience evaluating tires, despite the engineer's lack of expertise in the underlying theories of chemistry and physics affecting tire performance.

Like the Eleventh Circuit in *Kumho Tire*, almost half of the other courts of appeal had interpreted *Daubert* similarly. These included the Second Circuit in *Iacobelli v. County of Monroe* (1994), the Fourth Circuit in *Freeman v. Case* (1998), the Sixth Circuit in *U.S. v. Jones* (1997), the Ninth Circuit in *McKendall v. Crown Control Corp.* (1997), and the Tenth Circuit in *Compton v. Subaru of America, Inc.* (1996). This view emphasized the difficulty in applying the admissibility checklist factors, namely, testability, error, peer review, and publication, to all varieties of expert opinion, and assumed that if certain experts could not be evaluated on all the criteria, then Rule 702 alone covered the admissibility determination rather than the rule and *Daubert*.

The alternative view was that *Daubert* applied to all expert testimony, including the social as well as natural sciences. This position was exemplified by the en banc decision of the Fifth Circuit in *Moore v. Ashland Chemical Corp.* (1998) along with the Third Circuit in *Paoli Railroad Yard* (1994), the Seventh Circuit in *Tyus v. Urban Search Management* (1996), the Eighth Circuit in *Peitzmeier v. Hennessy Industries* (1996), as well as the Fifth Circuit's own earlier decision in *Watkins v. Telsmith, Inc.* (1997). The Moore court focused on the broad flexibility of *Daubert*'s principles, recognizing that the methodology appropriate to a medical research lab is not applicable to assessing the reliability of evidence drawn from clinical medicine, and reversing the exclusion of a treating physician who was qualified to offer a medical opinion concerning the cause of plaintiff's illness.

In a March 1999 decision by Justice Breyer, this alternative view prevailed. *Kumho Tire* repeated that *Daubert* is to be read comprehensively, and emphasized that the checklist is not exhaustive, is to be interpreted flexibly, and should not create a barrier to the admissibility of otherwise reliable and probative evidence simply because an expert is unable to meet the four basic criteria.

Conversely, *Daubert* and *Kumho Tire*, read in tandem, make clear that every scientific community has some methodological underpinning that can be applied to evaluate opinions concerning that particular field. The principles and methodology may differ, but the fundamental emphasis on scientific process unifies this search and distinguishes an expert opinion from mere conjecture and speculation, which abound in the marketplace.

Where no scientific methodology is implicated, all the more reason exists to either exclude the opinion or require its proponent to explain with unambiguous specificity why it qualifies for admission. Otherwise, as Capra (1998) noted, wily litigants would seek some perverse advantage by labeling their experts as nonscientists to avoid *Daubert*'s admissibility review.

This danger supports the proposed Rule 702 amendment, which clearly forecloses any distinction between scientists and other experts as to their admissibility burden. As *Watkins* (1997) reiterated, nonscientists' expert opinions should be scrutinized as closely as scientists', if not more so.

The question raised by *Kumho Tire's* fact pattern, e.g., should the court of appeals have deferred to the gatekeeper's decision to exclude the proposed expert, was thus answered affirmatively as follows: The proposed expert failed to meet any of the *Daubert* criteria, not just one or two of them. Ultimately, it was the expert's heavy reliance on his own subjective judgment, lack of appropriate scientific methodology of any kind, and his inability to articulate how his opinion was derived, that distinguish this case from ones where deference would have been warranted. As Justice Breyer noted in his opinion, the abuse of discretion appellate review standard covering admissibility determinations "applies as much to the trial court's decisions about how to determine reliability as to its ultimate conclusion."[66]

Finally, the expert's opinion cannot be reconciled with *Joiner's ipse dixit* criterion, and also required rejection on that basis. This principle denies admissibility to opinions based on nothing but the expert's *ipse dixit*, or assertion that something is so because the expert says that it is.

3.3.4 A Summary of the Changes in Evidence Law

Litigants have quickly incorporated these developments affecting the use of expert testimony into contemporary trial practice. Expert challenges, as a specific form of litigation strategy, are becoming even more widespread.

In particular, where a party's evidentiary proof relies on an expert opinion, a decision to exclude that evidence is often fatal to that party's case; particularly after the Supreme Court in *Joiner* rejected the rationale of the court of appeals that the potentially outcome-determinative consequence of expert exclusion justified heightened rather than deferential review of the trial court's ruling to exclude. Similarly, albeit with lesser impact on the overall litigation, the more open and extensive discovery of opposing expert reports permitted by the 1993 procedural rule changes also contributes to greater scrutiny of experts' opinions prior to trial.

Clearly, the expert challenge phase of litigation has developed a life unto itself. And as noted, some cases do not survive these issues. Challenges may arise where an expert is deemed by the opposing party to lack the appropriate knowledge, skill, experience, training, or education to formulate the proffered opinion. In particular, degrees and expertise in unrelated areas do not qualify an expert on a specific issue.

In that context, even following the expert trilogy, some issues are still in dispute. For example, does the district court's gatekeeper responsibility extend to the distinction between a minimally or marginally qualified expert and one clearly better equipped to assist the trier of fact?

Where the evidence rules are interpreted to favor admissibility, the answer appears to be no. The court of appeals in *Kannankeril v. Terminex* (1997) treated as error a trial judge's ruling to exclude the proposed expert as not the most appropriate witness on the issue at hand.

---

[66]526 U.S. at 152 (1999).

But where judicial concern is focused on proposed experts who have general knowledge about an overall field but lack expertise regarding a particular subfield or the specific problems raised by a case, the balance shifts. Several courts, like those in *Whiting* (1995) and *Sutera* (1997), thus justified their decisions to exclude as justified under the "fit" criterion articulated in *Daubert*.

Daubert was initially interpreted simply to extend and expand expert admissibility criteria beyond *Frye*. Increasingly, and in particular subsequent to *Joiner* and *Kumho Tire*, the issue has broadened to the interplay and balance between liberal admissibility standards and the Evidence Rules' emphasis on reliability and relevance.

The proposed Evidence Rule 702 amendment further suggests that proposed experts will be subject to more, rather than less, scrutiny by gatekeeping trial judges. It may also mean that if the two policy objectives conflict, then reliability and relevance will prevail over liberal admissibility.

4   On the Evolution of EEO Law

Has there been a tangible shift in the use of analytical proof, statistics, and related expert testimony in EEO cases over the past decade as a result of the issues covered above? Such a broad question is complicated by the clear decline in the number of employment discrimination cases involving class claims and statistical evidence litigated, although in some instances the more rigorous proof standards may have dissuaded litigants from proceeding to trial with evidence that previously would have been put before a trier of fact.

The best, albeit admittedly rough, indicator supporting an affirmative response to this question stems from the number of reported cases where district and appellate judges have referred to the statistical evidence upon which they have passed legal judgment, and the outcomes of those decisions. Based on a close reading of all reported and many unreported cases over the past decade, clearly more litigation has been lost by parties whose analytical proof, statistical evidence, and expert testimony have been deemed deficient in comparison to the number of cases where the winning party prevailed despite defective evidentiary proof.

Several such cases are described briefly below, to illustrate instances where the lawyers or their experts failed to prepare their evidence in a manner that would satisfy the evolving standards considered above. In one instance, *Thomas v. National Football League Players Association* (1997), the court of appeals affirmed a trial court ruling that plaintiff failed to establish a prima facie case because, in comparing applicants for promotion by race, the expert labor economist failed to consider and control for the minimum occupational qualifications needed for promotion. The court was critical of both the expert and plaintiff's counsel, who chose not to request the data necessary for such an analysis from the defendant during discovery, thereby ensuring that the expert's opinion was methodologically flawed.

With respect to the *Daubert/Kumho Tire* line of expert admissibility cases (as they now will be called), two prime examples relating to EEO law are cited. First, in an age termination case, *Sheehan v. Daily Racing Form*, (1997) plaintiff's statistical expert incorrectly assumed that all employees were fungible and equally likely to be terminated.

He thus used Fisher's exact test to infer an age effect rather than a multivariate technique or stratification. The expert also omitted, without comment, other potentially explanatory variables, as well as not including several employees who should have been part of the analytical pool. Chief Judge Posner of the Seventh Circuit, who typifies the rigorous expert admissibility standard line of judicial thinking, affirmed the trial court's exclusion of the proposed expert as scientifically unsound (given the faulty methodological approach to the termination pattern).

The second case, *Allard v. Indiana Bell Telephone* (1998), also covered an age reduction-in-force analysis, but involved the inadmissibility of four plaintiff experts, including two labor economists and an industrial psychologist. All were rejected on the grounds of their proposed testimony being neither reliable nor of assistance to the jury. Additionally, the record included evidence that one of the experts did not write the report attributed to and signed by him, that the opinions offered by the other three experts were the same as those offered by them and rejected by the court in a companion case, and the fact that similar coordinated opinions by the two labor economists had also been rejected by a trial judge and court of appeals elsewhere.

The court rejected as inadmissible the approach of one of the economists, whose analysis was regarded as methodologically flawed because he did not have the information necessary to control for the factors other than age that affected termination decisions, and assumed that all differences were the result of discrimination. The court was particularly critical of that economist and plaintiff's counsel for framing their theory of the case and the analysis in such a way that ignored the range of reasons causing disparity in termination rates, and treating any gross disparity as proof of discrimination. Summary judgment was granted to the defendant.

This entire volume, not just this entire chapter, could be filled with similar illustrations. The reader should regard this as the tip of the iceberg rather than a series of isolated incidents. Given the refinements in EEO law, statistical proofs as applied to equal employment cases, and the law covering expert admissibility, the predilection of some litigants to advance cases of limited analytical refinement may become at least somewhat deterred by the increasing probability of judicial rejection.

5   Summary and Conclusions

The use of analytical proof in EEO cases has slowly but steadily matured, especially considering the imprecise and overinclusive precedents set in the early cases twenty-five years ago. Today, statistical evidence is not accepted automatically or uncritically as proof of discrimination. To the degree that courts sometimes drew inferences from statistics that were poor proxies for what they were measuring, especially during the 1970s and 1980s, that is no longer the case.

Courts are increasingly critical of statistical proof, rejecting inferences not based on refined assumptions and data. In particular, the statistics must be refined to address the at-issue employment practice. These refinements specifically distinguish between legitimate and illegitimate factors, focus on relevant occupational and geographic labor market comparisons, and use correct statistical assumptions and techniques.

The most critical case in the evolution of EEO statistical proof is not *Teamsters* or *Hazelwood*, but *Wards Cove*. As a result of that decision, courts now understand that the qualification requirement applies to the entire occupational spectrum, and is not limited to positions requiring formal qualifications (like the schoolteachers addressed by the Court in *Hazelwood*).

The *Wards Cove* plaintiffs had prevailed in the courts below by showing that a high proportion of minority workers held laborer positions while nonminority workers held craft and other nonlaborer jobs. The Supreme Court rejected such comparisons as "nonsensical." While the burden-shifting language in *Wards Cove* was overruled by the 1991 Civil Rights Act, the refined statistical comparison holding remained undisturbed.

In terms of expert opinion prepared to support EEO litigants, the evidence trilogy of Supreme Court cases between 1993 and 1999 requires that the expert's report and testimony meet reliable levels of scientific knowledge and method, ruling out subjective belief or unsupported speculation. *Daubert* and *Kumho Tire* emphasize that the trial judge is the gatekeeper with respect to admissibility issues, and must ascertain that any proposed expert testimony rests on a reliable methodological foundation, is relevant to the case, and will assist the jury in its fact-finding responsibility.

The two lines of legal analysis, substantive regarding EEO and procedural concerning expert admissibility, are clearly consistent, supportive, and interacting. That is why their force is likely to become more effective in coming years, to the benefit of those who regard statistical science as an appropriate means of helping to resolve legal disputes.

6   Cases Cited

Adarand Constructors v. Pena, 515 U.S. 200 (1996).
Allard v. Indiana Bell Telephone Co., 1 F.Supp.2d 898 (S.D. Ind. 1998).
Babrocky v. Jewel Food Co., 773 F.2d 857 (7th Cir. 1985).
Bammerlin v. Navistar Int'l. Transp. Co., 30 F.3d 898, 901 (7th Cir. 1994).
Bazemore v. Friday, 478 U.S. 385 (1986).

Braun v. Ciba-Geigy Corp., 78 F.3d 316 (7th Cir. 1996), *cert.* denied, 519 U.S. 819 (1996).

Carmichael v. Samyang Tire, Inc., 131 F.3d 1433 (11th Cir. 1997), reversed, *sub nom, Kumho Tire Co. v. Carmichael*, 526 U.S., 137 (1999).

Castenada v. Partida, 430 U.S. 482 (1977).

Claar v Burlington Northern R.R., 29 F.3d 499 (9th Cir. 1994).

City of Richmond v. J.A. Croson Co., 488 U.S. 469 (1989).

Clark v. Chrysler Corp., 673 F.2d 921 (7th Cir. 1982), cert. denied, 459 U.S. 873 (1982).

Compton v. Subaru of America, Inc., 82 F.3d 1513 (10th Cir. 1996), *cert. denied*, 519 U.S. 1042 (1996).

Contreras v. City of Los Angeles, 656 F.2d 1267 (9th Cir. 1981).

Cook v. Boorstin, 763 F.2d 1462 (D.C. Cir. 1985).

Coward v. ADT Security Systems, Inc., 140 F.3d 271 (D.C. Cir. 1998).

Darby v. Godfather's Pizza, Inc., 45 F.3d 1212, 1214 (8th Cir. 1995).

Daubert v. Merrell-Dow Pharmaceuticals, Inc., 509 U.S. 579 (1993).

Daubert v. Merrell-Dow Pharmaceuticals, Inc., 43 F.3d 1311 (9th Cir. 1995), *cert. denied*, 516 U.S. 869 (1996).

Dothard v. Rawlinson, 433 U.S. 321 (1977).

EEOC v. American National Bank, 652 F.2d 1176, 1193 (4th Cir. 1981).

EEOC v. Consolidated Service Systems, 989 F.2d 233 (7th Cir. 1993).

EEOC v. Chicago Miniature Lamp Co., 947 F.2d 292 (7th Cir. 1991).

EEOC v. Federal Reserve Bank of Richmond, 698 F.2d 633 (4th Cir. 1983).

EEOC v. Joe's Stone Crab, Inc., 969 F.Supp. 727 (S.D. Fl. 1997).

EEOC v. North Hills-Passavant Hospital, 466 F.Supp. 783 (W.D. Pa. 1979).

EEOC v. Rath Packing Co., 787 F.2d 318 (8th Cir. 1986), cert. denied, 479 U.S. 910 (1986).

Eubanks v. Pickens Bond Construction Co., 635 F.2d 1341 (8th Cir. 1980).

Falcon v. General Telephone of the Southwest, 626 F.2d 369 (5th Cir. 1980), *vacated and remanded on other grounds*, 450 U.S. 1036 (1981).

Frazier v. Consolidated Rail Corp., 851 F.2d 1447 (D.C. Cir. 1988), *affirming Cox v. Conrail*, 47 F.E.P. Cases 685, 711 (D.D.C. 1987).

Freeman v. Case, 118 F.3d 1011 (4th Cir. 1998).

Frye v. United States, 293 F. 1013 (D.C. Cir. 1923).

General Electric Co. v. Joiner, 522 U.S. 136 (1996).

Grauer v. Federal Express Corp., 894 F.Supp. 330, 333 (W.D. Tenn. 1994), *aff'd.*, 73 F.3d 361 (6th Cir. 1996).

Griggs v. Duke Power Co., 401 U.S. 424 (1971).

Hazelwood School Dist. v. United States, 433 U.S. 299 (1977).

Hickman v. Taylor, 329 U.S. 495 (1947).

Hilton v. Wyman-Gordon Co., 624 F.2d 379 (1st Cir. 1980).

Iacobelli v. County of Monroe, 32 F.3d 19 (2d Cir 1994).

In re Paoli RR Yard PCB Litigation, 35 F.3d 717, 792-93 (3d Cir. 1994), *cert. denied, sub nom, General Electric Co. v. Ingram*, 513 U.S. 1190 (1995).

James v. Stockham Valves & Fittings Co., 559 F.2d 310, 332 (1977), cert. denied, 434 U.S. 1034 (1978).

Johnson v. Transportation Agency, 480 U.S. 616, 652 (1987) (O'Connor, J concurring).

Kannankeril v. Terminex Int'l., Inc., 128 F.3d 802 (3d Cir. 1997).

Karn v. Rand, 168 F.R.D. 633, 639 (N.D. Ind. 1996).

Kilgo v. Bowman Transportation Co., 789 F.2d 859 (11th Cir. 1986).

Kumho Tire Co. v. Carmichael, 526 U.S., 137 (1999).

Lust v. Merrell-Dow Pharmaceuticals, Inc., 89 F.3d 594 (9th Cir. 1996).

Markey v. Tenneco, Inc., 635 F.2d 497 (5th Cir. 1981).

Martin v. Citibank, 762 F.2d 212 (2d Cir. 1985).

McKendall v. Crown Control Corp., 122 F.3d 803 (9th Cir. 1997).

McNamara v. City of Chicago, 138 F.3d 1219 (7th Cir. 1998), *cert. denied*, 525 U.S., 981 (1998).

Mister v. Illinois Gulf Central RR Co., 832 F.2d 1427 (7th Cir. 1987), *cert. denied*, 485 U.S. 1035 (1988).

Moore v. Ashland Chemical Corp., 151 F.3d 269 (5th Cir. 1998).

New York City Transit Authority v. Beazer, 440 U.S. 568 (1979).

Ochoa v. Monsanto Co., 335 F.Supp. 53, 58 (S.D. Tex. 1971).

Palmer v. Shultz, 815 F.2d 84 (D.C. Cir. 1987).

Peitzmeier v. Hennessy, Ind. Inc., 97 F3d 293 (8th Cir. 1996), *cert. denied*, 520 U.S. 1196 (1997).

Rios v. Steamfitters Local 638, 400 F.Supp. 993 (S.D. N.Y. 1975), *on remand from* 501 F.2d 622 (2d Cir. 1974).

Rowe v. General Motors Corp., 457 F.2d 348 (5th Cir (1972).

Segar v. Smith, 738 F.2d 1249, 1278 (D.C. Cir. 1984), cert. denied, 471 U.S. 1115 (1985).

Sheehan v. Daily Racing Form, Inc., 104 F.3d 940 (7th Cir. 1997), *cert. denied*, 521 U.S. 1104 (1997).

Sierra Club v. Cedar Point Oil Co., 73 F.3d 546, 571 (5th Cir. 1996).

Sims v. Georgia, 389 U.S. 804 (1967) (jury).

Summers v. Mo. Pacific RR System, 897 F.Supp. 535 (D. Okla. 1995).

Sutera v. Perrier Group of America, Inc., 1997 WL 659076 (D. Mass. 1997).

Sylla-Sawdon v. Uniroyal Goodrich Tire Co., 47 F.3d 277, 284 (8th Cir. 1995), *cert. denied*, 516 U.S. 822 (1995).

Teamsters v. United States, 431 U.S. 324 (1977).

Thomas v. National Football League Players Ass'n., 131 F.3d 198 (D.C. Cir. 1997).

Tokio Marine & Fire Ins. Co., Ltd. v. Grove Mfg. Co., 958 F.2d 1169 (1st Cir. 1992).

Trevino v. Holly Sugar Corp., 811 F.2d 896, 902 n.11 (5th Cir. 1981).

Tyus v. Urban Search Management, 102 F.3d 256 (7th Cir. 1996).

United States v. Artero, 121 F.3d 1256 (9th Cir. 1997).

United States v. County of Fairfax, 19 F.E.P. Cases 753 (E.D. Va. 1979), *vacated and remanded*, 629 F.2d 932 (4th Cir. 1980).

United States v. Georgia Power Co., 474 F.2d 906, 915 (5th Cir. 1973).

United States v. Hayes Int'l. Corp., 456 F.2d 112, 120 (5th Cir. 1972).

United States v. Ironworkers, Local 86, 443 F.2d 544 (9th Cir. 1970), *cert. denied*, 404 U.S. 984 (1971).

United States v. Jefferson Co. Bd. of Ed., 372 F.2d 836 (5th Cir. 1966), *cert. denied*, 389 U.S. 840 (1967).

United States v. Jones, 107 F.3d 1147 (6th Cir. 1997), *cert. denied*, 521 U.S. 1127 (1997).

United States v. Local 36, Sheet Metal Workers, 416 F.2d 123 (8th Cir. 1969).

United States v. Local 189, Paperworkers, 416 F.2d 980 (5th Cir. 1969), *cert. denied*, 397 U.S. 919 (1970).

Wards Cove Packing Co. v. Atonio, 490 U.S. 642 (1989).

Watkins v. Telsmith, Inc., 121 F.3d 984 (5th Cir. 1997).

Watson v. Ft. Worth Bank & Trust, 487 U.S. 977 (1988).

White v. City of San Diego, 605 F.2d 455 (9th Cir. 1979).

Whiting v. Boston Edison Co., 891 F.Supp. 12 (D. Mass. 1995).

Wilkins v. Univ. of Houston, 654 F.2d 388, 408 (5th Cir. 1981).

REFERENCES

[1] Ananda, S. and Gilmartin, K. (1992) Inclusion of Potentially Tainted Variables in Regression Analyses for Employment Discrimination Cases, *Industrial Relations Law Journal* 13, 121–152.

[2] Blumrosen, A. (1972) Strangers in Paradise: *Griggs v. Duke Power Co.*, and the Concept of Employment Discrimination, Michigan Law Review 71, 59–110.

[3] Braun, L. (1980) Statistics and the Law: Hypothesis Testing and Its Application to Title VII Cases, *Hastings Law Journal* 32, 59–89.

[4] Capra, D.J. (1998) The *Daubert* Puzzle, *Georgia Law Review* 32, 699–782.

[5] Dempster, A.P. (1988) Employment Discrimination and Statistical Science. *Statistical Science* 3, 146–161.

[6] Dorseano, W.V. (1975) Statistical Evidence in Employment Discrimination Litigation: Selection of the Available Population, Problems and Proposals, *Southwestern Law Journal* 29, 859–875.

[7] Faigman, D.L., Kaye, D.H., Saks, M.J., and Sanders, J. (1997) *Modern Scientific Evidence: The Law and Science of Expert Testimony. St. Paul: West.*

[8] Finkelstein, M.O. (1973) Regression Models in Administrative Proceedings, *Harvard Law Review* 86, 1442–1475.

[9] Finkelstein, M.O. (1980) The Judicial Reception of Multiple Regression Studies in Race and Sex Discrimination Cases, *Columbia Law Review* 80, 737–754.

[10] Fisher, F.M. (1980) Multiple Regression in Legal Proceedings, *Columbia Law Review* 80, 702–736.

[11] Gastwirth, J.L. and Haber, S.E. (1976) Defining the Labor Market for Equal Employment Standards, *Monthly Labor Review* 99 (3) 32–36.

[12] Kaye, D.H. (1983) Statistical Significance and the Burden of Persuasion, *Law & Contemporary Problems* 46, 13–23.

[13] Meier, P., Sacks, J., and Zabell, S.L. (1986) What Happened in *Hazelwood*? in *Statistics and the Law* DeGroot, M., Fienberg, S. and Kadane, J., editors, 1–40. New York: John Wiley & Sons.

[14] Message From the President of the United States Returning Without My Approval S.2104, The Civil Rights Act of 1990, S. Doc. No. 35, 101st Cong., 2d Sess. (1990).

[15] Note (1973) Employment Discrimination: Statistics and Preferences Under Title VII, *Virginia Law Review* 59, 463–491.

[16] Note (1975) Beyond the Prima Facie Case in Employment Discrimination Law: Statistical Proof and Rebuttal, *Harvard Law Review* 89, 387–422.

[17] Rosenblum, M. (1977) The Use of Labor Statistics and Analysis in Title VII Cases: *Rios, Chicago* and Beyond, *Industrial Relations Law Journal* 1, 685–710.

[18] Rosenblum, M. (1978) The External Measures of Labor Supply: Recent Issues and Trends, *Connecticut Law Review* 10, 892–919.

[19] Shoben, E.W. (1983) The Use of Statistics to Prove Intentional Employment Discrimination *Law & Contemporary Problems* 46, 221–245.

[20] Smith, A.B. and Abram, T.G. (1981) Quantitative Analysis and Proof of Employment Discrimination, *U. Illinois Law Review* 1981, 33–74.

A Connecticut Jury Array Challenge

David Pollard

Abstract

This article describes a detailed statistical study of the system used for summoning jurors to serve in the State of Connecticut's Superior Courts. The study was made at the request of the Connecticut Public Defender's Office, to provide a factual basis for a series of (ultimately unsuccessful) jury array challenges in capital felony cases, culminating with *State v. Gibbs* (1997). Application of geocoding and Hispanic surname matching to several hundred thousand individual juror records provided a detailed picture of how Hispanics were being lost to the jury system.

Key words and phrases: statistical analysis of juror records; geocoding to census tracts; Hispanic surname matching; undeliverable juror summonses.

1 Introduction

The Sixth and Fourteenth Amendments to the United States Constitution promise defendants in criminal trials "an impartial jury of the State and district wherein the crime shall have been committed" and the "due process" and "equal protection of the laws."

Citing these Constitutional rights, and analogous rights promised in the Connecticut State Constitution, attorneys from the Connecticut Public Defender's Office recently mounted a series of challenges to the composition of the pool from which juries for the state's superior courts were being chosen. Specifically, they claimed underrepresentation of Hispanics, which they asserted to be a violation of the requirement that juries be summoned from a fair cross section of the community.

In order to establish a prima facie case, the public defender had to satisfy the three "prongs" of the test spelled out by the Supreme Court in *Duren v. Missouri* (1979):

> (1) that the group alleged to be excluded is a "distinctive" group in the community; (2) that the group's representation in the source from which juries are selected is not fair and reasonable in relation to the number of such persons in the community; and (3) that this underrepresentation results from systematic exclusion of the group in the jury-selection process.

The Court had further explained (p. 366) that it understood "systematic" to mean "inherent in the particular jury-selection process utilized."

For a fair cross section claim it was *not* required that underrepresentation be the result of deliberate discrimination, as emphasized by the Connecticut Supreme Court in its most recent pronouncement on jury array challenges, *State v. Castonguay* (1984), citing the *Duren* decision:

> ... in a fair cross section claim, the defendant need not prove intent. "[S]ystematic disproportion itself demonstrates an infringement of the defendant's interest in a jury chosen from a fair community cross section. The only remaining question is whether there is adequate justification for this infringement."

To gather evidence to satisfy the second prong of the *Duren* test, before I became involved with the challenge, the public defender had arranged for potential jurors arriving at the main Hartford courthouse to fill out a questionnaire, indicating both race and ethnicity (Hispanic or not).

My work for the public defender began only after the first round of questionnaires had been filled out and collected. For my February 1996 testimony in *State v. King*, I was asked to make routine calculations, comparing the responses from the questionnaires with the proportions of Blacks and Hispanics in the total population of the judicial district, as counted by the 1990 Census. The request was in accord with the direction (in the context of an equal protection challenge to grand jury selection) of the Supreme Court in *Castaneda v. Partida* (1977), that

> ... the degree of underrepresentation must be proved, by comparing the proportion of the group in the total population to the proportion called to serve as grand jurors, over a significant period of time.

It seemed strange to me that the workings of the system should be judged by means of a comparison of questionnaire proportions with proportions in the total population. Clearly, the system had not been designed to mirror the total population. For example, persons under 18 years of age were not eligible for jury service; others were disqualified for various reasons, such as inability to understand English or lack of citizenship; and others, such as those over 70 years of age, could choose not to serve.

The challenge in *King* was denied, having failed the second prong of *Duren*, partially on the grounds that many of the questionnaires had not been completely filled out—many who answered the race question did not answer the ethnicity question, possibly because "... many survey respondents tend to use the terms 'race' and 'ethnic origin' interchangeably, and they do not clearly distinguish between the two concepts" (Gerber and de la Puente 1996, pp. 3–4). The challenge was successful in one respect, however, because it paved the way for the public defender to gain access (at my suggestion) to records maintained by *Judicial Information Systems* (JIS), the part of the Office of the Chief Court Administrator in the Connecticut Judicial Branch responsible for the process of summoning jurors.

In my opinion, it would have been futile to pursue a challenge using only data collected at the courthouses, without further information about the effects of disqualifications and other mechanisms by which persons were eliminated from the pool of potential jurors. For example, only with JIS data could I investigate suggestions made by the state during the *King* hearing that the shortfall of Hispanics among the questionnaire respondents could be explained through the action of citizenship and language disqualifications of Hispanics. I undertook the task of discussing with JIS which data might be relevant to further study of the jury system.

The public defender also obtained a court order requiring collection of an improved questionnaire from more courthouses, but the focus of the challenge had shifted to the data from JIS. I agreed to continue the routine tabulation and calculation for the questionnaire results, but my main goal became the analysis of the JIS data. My arrangement with the attorneys from the public defender's office was that I would extract from the JIS data an accurate picture of how the summonsing procedure had actually been operating for several years. I did not see myself as an advocate for the defense. I saw it as the public defender's job to argue about whether the state was, or was not, responsible for what was happening.

The analysis of the JIS data formed the basis for my subsequent testimony in *State v. Rodriguez*, in January 1997. That trial ended abruptly, in April 1997, with the challenge still unresolved. With the agreement of both the state and the public defender, the challenge (and the record from *Rodriguez*) was carried over to *State v. Gibbs*. The February 1998 challenge for *Gibbs* was also denied, for reasons that I discuss in Section 9: In short, Judge Spada accepted that "Hispanics are less likely to receive summonses and more likely to be subject to disqualification," but he regarded these facts as reflecting "legitimate differences between Hispanic and non-Hispanic participation—based on factors external to the system," and concluded that they do "not prove significant underrepresentation."

In my opinion, the challenge was not a wasted effort. During the period from *King* to *Rodriguez*, the arguments before the courts shifted from interpretation of isolated summary percentages (as in *State v. Castonguay*) to consideration of the actual workings of the Connecticut jury system. The disagreements shifted away from disputes about what was happening to questions of why it was happening and judgements of whether the State should be required to remedy the problems.

Outline of the Article

2   Construction of the Jury Pool

It took a surprising amount of effort to determine the procedure by which jurors are actually summoned in Connecticut. The task was made difficult by a confusion of terms in the documents from which I had to work. For example, the important distinction between a summons returned to JIS as undeliverable and a summons sent to a person who subsequently did not show up at the court ("no-shows") was often blurred. In addition, for many months during the *Rodriguez* trial, JIS was unable to correctly explain how it combined the source lists (voter lists plus list of licensed motor vehicle operators, for the period covered by the JIS data) from which it chose potential jurors. I expended a lot of statistical effort shooting down successive JIS explanations, which did not jibe with their own summary reports.

Here is an outline of the procedure followed by JIS, as best as I could reconstruct it. JIS used the procedure to build a separate master list of potential jurors for each of the twelve judicial districts in Connecticut. (As one reviewer has noted, the master list could be thought of as the statistical frame from which potential jurors were sampled.) Almost all evidence in the *Rodriguez* and *Gibbs* cases focused on the largest judicial district, Hartford–New Britain (HNB).

(i) Jury Administration estimated the court requirements for the coming court year. The total requirement was allocated among the towns in the district, with each town's quota being proportional to its total population according to the 1990 census.

(ii) In essence, for each town, JIS combined a sample from each source list, with duplicates discarded. The procedure is much harder to carry out than it sounds (Munsterman 1996, Element 2), because of the extreme technical difficulties involved in identifying matches based on partial information. For example, names might be abbreviated, addresses might have changed, middle initials might be present for only one list, and so on. The precise procedure for combining source lists in the correct proportions was based on the method described by Kairys, Kadane, and Lehoczky (1997, page 819).

Clearly, JIS did not understand the logic behind the procedure. The statute clearly stated that a sample from the voter list for each town should have been compared against the DMV list, and that duplicates should have been discarded from the *voter* sample. Initially, JIS claimed to be following a different procedure, equivalent to the discarding of duplicates from the DMV list before a sample was drawn from that list. The jury administrator asserted that the deviation from the statute would be of no consequence. Actually, as I explained at great length during *Rodriguez* testimony, it would have caused an oversampling from the set of persons who appeared on both the voter and DMV lists. The issue was finally resolved, during the time period between the end of the *Rodriguez* trial and the start of *Gibbs* testimony, by a detailed examination of computer code and the retrieval of intermediate output from the most recent construction of the master list. The output proved to be consistent with the statute.

(iii) From the combined samples (from the voter and DMV lists) for each town, JIS took a simple random sample of size equal to the town quota, then added it to the master list for the judicial district. Juror IDs were applied to the master list in random order.

(iv) As jurors were needed, names were drawn from the master list in order of juror ID, and summonses were mailed, about two months before the date (the "summons date") at which the juror was required to serve at the court. *It is important to any understanding of problems with undeliverable summonses that one be aware of the delay—in some cases more than two years—between the time at which a name and address were added to a source list and the time when the summons was actually mailed.*

(v) In response to the summons, some potential jurors claimed disqualifications (such as lack of citizenship or inability to speak and understand the English language), and some postponed service to a later date. Summonses that were undeliverable according to the postal service were returned to JIS, whereupon the master file was updated to show a "disqualification code" 13. Some persons did not respond at all to the summons.

(vi) For jurors not disqualified and not listed as code 13, further information about jury service was mailed out, about two weeks before the summons date. Undeliverable mailings at this step were marked as code 17.

(vii) Prior to the summons date, some jurors had their service canceled, because of changes in the courts' needs. (Those jurors are still listed with code OK, in my scheme explained in the next section.)

(viii) At the courthouse, a small proportion of jurors were excused, for reasons such as extreme hardship or health-related problems. Some small proportion also postponed service to a later date, and there were also persons who turned up on the wrong day for their service.

(ix) Jurors who did not turn up for service were sent further mailings. After one year from the summons date, if the matter of nonappearance was not resolved satisfactorily, such jurors were declared delinquent. (The no-shows, with code NS in my scheme.)

(x) Jurors who were qualified, and whose service was not canceled, remained at the courthouse for at most one day, and were required to serve on at most one trial jury.

From this abbreviated account, it should be apparent that there were several ways in which persons might not have ended up in a jury pool.

(a) They might not have been on either of the source lists. Any group whose proportions on the source lists did not mirror the proportions in the "community" (however that may be defined) would have lost some representation at step (ii).

One reviewer has suggested that "If the community is defined to control legitimate nondiscriminatory reasons ... the disparity might be eliminated at step (i) and not be an issue at step (ii)." Another reviewer suggested that "the community ... presumably would be all members of the group of the appropriate age range for jury service." As I argue in Section 7, the definition of the first reviewer's concept of the community is not as straightforward as it might seem. I agree that comparisons would be simpler if all parties could agree on a precise definition of the community, or of the "eligible population," but I see conceptual difficulties in the concept. The issue became moot when the Defense for *Rodriguez* chose to focus its claim on the steps in the selection process subsequent to construction of the master list, forgoing claims related to composition of the source lists.

(b) A name on the combined source list might not have been selected into the master list. However, this fact alone should *not* have caused underrepresentation if the sampling in step (iii) were carried out correctly.

(c) A person who was assigned a juror ID on the master list might not have been sent a summons, because the courts' needs were overestimated. Again, this fact alone should *not* have caused underrepresentation if assignment of juror IDs were correctly randomized.

(d) Persons sent summonses could claim disqualifications, or be missed because of undeliverability problems, in steps (iv) and (vi). Some jurors became delinquent. Disqualification, undeliverability, and delinquency had a very large combined effect on the jury pool, an effect captured in the records that JIS kept for all summonses drawn from the master list.

(e) At step (viii), disqualifications for hardship or health might fall unevenly on different groups in the population. In particular, exemptions for hardship might have been expected to be driven in part by poverty, which is often associated with minority status.

(f) The effects of challenges following voir dire might have had further effects on underrepresentation, but they were not reflected in the JIS data.

Vast amounts of court time—not just for the cases with which I was involved—would have been saved if a clear and accurate description of the JIS procedure had been written out in the early 1990s, when the system was first adopted.

3   The JIS Data

The data that I received from JIS—in several installments, from August 1996 until February 1997—were the key to understanding how the procedure for summoning jurors was actually working. They contained the answer to the question of exactly how Hispanics were disappearing from the system.

The data included records for each person sent a summons for the court years 1992–93 through 1995–96, together with about half the summonses for the 1996–97 court year. Among other information, each record showed the name and address of the person summoned, together with various "disqualification" codes indicating whether the person was qualified to serve or was disqualified for some reason. I put the word disqualification in quotes, because not all of the codes correspond to statutory disqualifications. To avoid tedious repetition, all subsequent quoting of the word will be omitted, but the reader should remember the caveat. JIS used the codes as a matter of administrative convenience. I extended their scheme to get a unique descriptive code for each person to whom a summons was sent.

The data were originally contained in extracts from multiple JIS summary files, with records sorted according to the date at which the person's jury service was resolved—for no-shows that involved at least a year's time lapse. For my analysis it was important to rearrange by date of original summons, for otherwise various important time effects and peculiarities of particular court years would have been disguised. For example, time trends in undeliverable rates would have been hidden.

Table 1 gives the breakdown of summonses by disqualification code for each of the court years. The column heading HNB9293 means court year 1992–93 for the HNB judicicial district, and so on. To conserve on space in tabulations, and to concentrate attention on the more significant types of disqualification, I eventually consolidated the counts for eleven of the codes into two broad categories: **xjd** to mean "out of the judicial district" (or, more precisely, not a current resident of the judicial district), and **rest** as a residual category. The column headed DBPcode shows the result of the consolidation. In subsequent tabulations for this article, the counts or estimates for codes 02, 15, and 16 will be combined into the single xjd category, and for codes 03, 05, 07, 10, 11, 14, 18, and 99 into the single rest category.

Some records contained a blank disqualification code. I had to deduce what had happened by means of other information in the record. I created the code **NS** to denote a *no-show*: a person who failed to serve, or failed to be disqualified in some way, within one year of the date of summons to serve. Such a person might have deliberately ignored the summons or follow-up communications from JIS, or might not have received the summons in the first place. I created the code **OK** to denote those persons confirmed for jury service: Either the person turned up at court, and was not disqualified there, or the person's service was canceled, because of changes in the courts' needs. The OK code group corresponds to the jurors that I decided to treat as the *jury pool*. Finally, for some of the 9596 and many of the 9697 records, I created the code **??** to indicate that the disqualification status of the person was not yet determined. My experience with earlier batches of data suggested that most of the ?? would have eventually turned into either NS or OK.

For confidentiality reasons, JIS completely omitted, or edited out identifying information from, records for code 04 or code 09. My statistical techniques could not be applied to the edited records, so I omitted them from most analysis. (Rough checks, based on counts by town and month for those code 04 and 09 records that I did receive, reassured me that my overall conclusions were scarcely affected by the omission.)

Table 1. HNB summonses, by court year and disqualification code: JIS codes at far left; DBP abbreviated codes at far right; breakdown for each court year in columns headed HNB9293 through HNB9697.

code	description	HNB9293	HNB9394	HNB9495	HNB9596	HNB9697	DBPcode
01	not US citizen	2113	1598	1988	1922	979	01
02	not CT resident	3100	2688	3339	3314	1325	xjd
03	under 18	1	0	0	1	2	rest
04	found by judge to be "impaired"	—	—	—	—	—	—
05	convicted felon	333	230	278	291	110	rest
06	can not speak/understand English	1787	1320	1788	1981	934	06
07	member of general assembly while in session	1	0	4	0	3	rest
08	older than 70, chooses not to serve	9751	7483	9832	10159	5117	08
09	physical/mental disability	—	—	—	—	—	—
10	elected state official	17	11	13	16	4	rest
11	served in last 2 years	1066	2004	2831	3042	1998	rest
12	extreme hardship	3758	3013	5603	5102	1208	12
13	summons undeliverable	10523	9072	12297	11154	4629	13
14	deceased	1090	861	1109	1326	497	rest
15	moved out of judicial district	1282	957	1244	1151	492	xjd
16	moved out of state	413	69	290	401	201	xjd
17	other [followup material] undeliverable	912	932	1469	1661	698	17
18	received summons for this court year	233	123	165	149	35	rest
99	juror excused by court	2586	1573	1585	1093	286	rest
??	status not yet determined (DBP)	0	0	0	4483	20754	??
NS	noshow (DBP)	4145	2938	3678	1865	0	NS
OK	"yield" (DBP)	45873	32951	39096	38867	12764	OK
	TOTAL	88984	67823	86609	87978	52036	

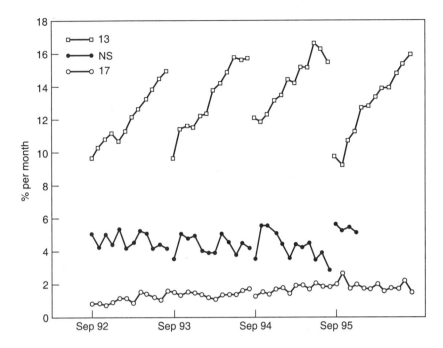

Figure 1. Percentage disqualifications by month of summons date for all HNB summonses: two types of undeliverable (codes 13 and 17), and no shows (NS). Series broken at the end of each court year.

In theory, persons under 18 were screened out of the DMV lists at a preliminary stage of the JIS selection procedure, and they should not even have been on the voter lists, but a few code 03 slipped through.

Patterns Across Time

Figure 1 shows the percentages of all HNB summonses for each month that were lost from the pool by means of undeliverability or no-shows. I have broken the plots at the end of each court year, so that each segment refers to disqualifications from a different master list. The incomplete data from 1996–97 are omitted.

The code 13 undeliverable rate increased fairly steadily through each court year, an increase that was consistent with the observations of Munsterman (1996, page 50). Addresses would go "stale," making it harder for the postal service to deliver a summons to the addressee. The code 17 undeliverable rate seldom got above 2%. I would have expected the code 17 rates to change relatively less during a court year, because they reflected only a two-month delay between receipt of initial summonses and mailing of the follow-up. I do not know why the rate slowly crept up over the four years. The no-show rate seemed to stay fairly constant, at around 5% of all summonses sent out. The rates for all other disqualification

Table 2. HNB judicial district disqualifications, percentages within towns and town group-ings: summonses sent to the two main cities (Hartford and New Britain), to all 27 other towns in HNB combined (otherHNB), and to addresses outside HNB (nonHNB).

[HNB9293]	01	06	08	12	13	17	NS	OK	xjd	rest	total
HARTFORD	4	5	8	2	27	3	12	35		5	100
NEW BRITAIN	5	5	15	3	15	1	6	44		5	100
nonHNB									97	2	100
otherHNB	2	1	12	5	9	1	3	60	1	7	100
Total	2	2	11	4	12	1	5	52	5	6	100

[HNB9394]	01	06	08	12	13	17	NS	OK	xjd	rest	total
HARTFORD	3	5	8	2	31	3	10	33		4	100
NEW BRITAIN	4	5	15	3	17	2	6	42		7	100
nonHNB									98	2	100
otherHNB	2	1	12	5	10	1	3	57		8	100
Total	2	2	11	4	13	1	4	49	5	7	100

[HNB9495]	01	06	08	12	13	17	NS	OK	xjd	rest	total
HARTFORD	3	5	7	3	36	4	10	27		4	100
NEW BRITAIN	4	6	17	5	16	2	5	37		7	100
nonHNB									98	2	100
otherHNB	2	1	13	8	10	1	3	53		8	100
Total	2	2	11	6	14	2	4	45	6	7	100

[HNB9596]	01	06	08	12	13	17	??	NS	OK	xjd	rest	total
HARTFORD	3	5	8	2	28	5	8	5	31		4	100
NEW BRITAIN	4	6	17	5	15	2	6	2	37		6	100
nonHNB										98	2	100
otherHNB	2	1	13	7	10	1	5	2	51	1	8	100
Total	2	2	12	6	13	2	5	2	44	6	7	100

categories (except for OK, which was forced to decrease through the court year because of the increase in code 13 undeliverables) were fairly stable within each court year; they are not shown in the figure.

Patterns Across Towns

The proportions of disqualifications were not uniform across the 29 towns in the judicial district. (I use the term town as a synonym for city, for the sake of a uniform terminology.) The two largest towns—the cities of Hartford and New Britain—stand out from the general pattern, as shown in the four tabulations grouped as Table 2.

Each tabulation corresponds to a different court year of summons. The four rows give the percentage breakdown by disqualification category for summonses sent to persons in Hartford town, New Britain town, towns outside the judicial dis-trict (nonHNB), or one of the other 27 towns that make up the district (otherHNB).

The bottom rows (total) give the breakdown for all summonses to courthouses in the district.

For all four years, Hartford town had a very low yield of qualified jurors—at most 35% of mailed summonses fell into the OK category—and a very high rate of undeliverable summonses. The Hartford no-show rate ran at about three times the "other HNB" group. New Britain was slightly less extreme, but still rather different from the "other HNB" group. It was also striking that the undeliverability rates were consistently higher for Hartford (and, to a lesser extent, New Britain) than for the other towns in the district: Roughly 30% of the summonses sent to an address in the city of Hartford were returned by the postal service as undeliverable (disqualification code 13). The story for the incomplete 1996–97 court year appeared to be similar.

According to the 1990 Census, Hartford and New Britain accounted for a large fraction of the minority population of the whole district: Hartford contained almost 60% of the Hispanic over-18 population, and almost 62% of the black over-18 population; New Britain contained more than 16% of the Hispanic over-18 population, and more than 6% of the black over-18 population.

Thus the JIS data showed unequivocally that the two towns in the HNB judicial district that together accounted for a large proportion of the over-18 minority population had much the highest rates of undeliverable summonses and no-shows.

I strongly suspected, based on the JIS data broken down by town, that undeliverable summonses (and perhaps no-shows) would be a major part of the explanation of the low Hispanic proportions on the questionnaires. It appeared that language and citizenship disqualifications were less significant than might have been predicted, and that significantly lower code 08 disqualifications (requests for excusal from persons over 70 years of age) might have a mitigating effect on the undeliverability problem in Hartford.

Of course, there was also the possibility that the undeliverables were more concentrated in some parts of the towns than others, and hence that it was some subpopulation of the towns that was being affected. To follow through on this possibility, I had to carry the analysis down to smaller regions within towns.

4   Estimation via Geocoding and Hispanic Surname Matching

The JIS records contained no explicit information about race or ethnicity of the persons to whom summonses were sent. To learn more about the effects of the various disqualifications (including undeliverable and no-shows) on the minority population, I had to draw inferences based on the information that was contained in the JIS records.

I used two distinct methods of statistical inference. The first method was based on *geocoding*, that is, the matching of addresses in the summons records to small subregions of the judicial district. For a number of technical reasons, I chose to use the regions called *census tracts*. (For example, the town of Hartford is divided into 49 disjoint census tracts.) I was then able to estimate the numbers of disqualifications for each minority group, using the census data for each tract.

In essence, my method was to multiply the number N_α of summonses, geocoded to each tract α by the fraction h_α of the over-18 population of that tract counted as Hispanic by the 1990 census, then calculate the sum $\sum_\alpha h_\alpha N_\alpha$ over all tracts in a particular region to estimate the total number of summonses sent to Hispanics in the region. Repeating the exercise separately for each type of disqualification, I then estimated the total numbers of Hispanics *who were on the master list and who were disqualified or eliminated for various reasons*. Actually, my eventual implementation of the method was slightly more complicated. For instance, as only persons over 70 years of age should have been eligible to claim code 08 disqualifications, I applied the estimation method to the over-70 populations (according to the 1990 Census) of the tracts. I developed similar refinements for code 01 and code 06 disqualifications.

My second method used data collected by the Bureau of the Census, in the form of a "Spanish surname list" (SSL), to draw inferences about Hispanic origin based on a person's surname. (Compare with the identification of Mexican-Americans with "persons of Spanish language or Spanish surname" at footnote 5 of *Castaneda*.) From the SSL I estimated the proportion of Hispanics among each surname in the census sample. I applied that proportion to each surname from the JIS records, then added over all records with a given disqualification code to get an estimate of the number of Hispanics with that code. For example, the SSL rated the surname "Garcia" as heavily Hispanic, with 94.5% of Garcia's being Hispanic; so each Garcia in the JIS records contributed 0.945 Hispanics toward the totals. The SSL rated "Smith" as a rare Hispanic surname, even though about 1% of the Census Bureau sample was named Smith. Accordingly, I let each Smith contribute zero Hispanics towards the totals.

Initially, I was skeptical that surname matching could provide any sort of reliable estimate. For example, women who change their surnames after marriage create some difficulties for any method of identification based on surnames. A Hispanic Ms. Garcia who married a Mr. Smith would not be counted as Hispanic; a non-Hispanic Ms. Smith who married a Mr. Garcia would be miscounted as Hispanic. However, sampling experiments that I carried out with the HNB questionnaire data (see Section 8) suggested that the systematic error was not large, presumably because of a cancellation effect between the two types of error.

The geocoding method suffers from the disadvantage that it must work with estimates of minority populations derived from the 1990 census. I would expect the estimates of total counts to increase over time if up-to-date minority proportions could be used. Estimates of total counts via geocoding would also suffer from the undercounts of minority populations that are known to have occurred with the 1990 census. The percentage breakdown across disqualifications would be less affected, unless the undercount concentrated on minorities who were prone to a particular type of disqualification.

Table 3. Percentage breakdown of estimated disqualifications for Hispanics (by geocoding in the rows labeled Hgeo, and by surname matching in the rows labeled SSL) and non-Hispanics (by surname matching, in the rows labeled nonH). Estimates for the incomplete year 1996–97 omitted.

HNB9293	01	06	08	12	13	17	NS	OK	rest	xjd	total
Hgeo	3	14	3	3	29	3	12	27	5		100
SSL	3	13	2	2	29	3	12	32	3	2	100
nonH	2	1	12	4	11	1	4	53	6	6	100
HNB9394	01	06	08	12	13	17	NS	OK	rest	xjd	total
Hgeo	3	13	3	3	33	3	10	26	5		100
SSL	3	11	2	2	32	4	10	31	3	2	100
nonH	2	1	12	5	12	1	4	50	7	6	100
HNB9495	01	06	08	12	13	17	NS	OK	rest	xjd	total
Hgeo	3	13	3	4	37	4	10	22	5		100
SSL	2	11	2	3	36	5	10	26	3	2	100
nonH	2	1	12	7	13	1	4	47	7	6	100

HNB9596	01	06	08	12	13	17	??	NS	OK	rest	xjd	total
Hgeo	3	15	3	4	29	5	8	5	24	5		100
SSL	2	13	2	3	31	5	7	4	28	3	2	100
nonH	2	1	12	6	11	2	5	2	45	7	6	100

In contrast, the SSL estimates (based on surname matching) turned out to increase over time, tracking the increasing proportion of Hispanics in the HNB population.

The estimates of the *total numbers* obtained by geocoding and surname matching did diverge over time, but the two methods were remarkably consistent regarding the *relative proportions*: As shown by Table 3, for both Hispanics and non-Hispanics, both methods were in close agreement for every court year for the proportions of summonses in each of the main categories of disqualifications.

For 1996, my best estimate for the fraction Hispanic on the master list was something in the range of 7.0%–7.5%, a figure reasonably consistent with the 1996 Census Bureau estimates of 7.77% Hispanic for the over-20 population of Hartford County.

My analysis boiled down to a set of estimates for the numbers of Hispanics and non-Hispanics in each disqualification category. Table 3 gives the estimates expressed only as percentages of the estimated totals. Complete tabulations for various estimated counts are to be found at my web site: http://www.stat.yale.edu/~pollard.

Notice the consistency between the two breakdowns for Hispanics, by geocoding (Hgeo) and by surname matching (SSL). Estimated standard errors (not shown) reassured me that the agreement was real. I inferred with some confidence that about 30% of the Hispanics who made it to the master list were being lost because of undeliverable summonses. By contrast, only about 12% of non-Hispanics (nonH) who made it to the master list were lost in the same way. At best, about 30% of the Hispanics on the master list survived the effects of undeliverable summonses and other disqualifications to reach the OK category—the yield. By contrast, the yield for non-Hispanics was usually close to 50%.

The estimated yields (% OK) of Hispanics versus non-Hispanics were roughly consistent with the 4.2%–4.7% Hispanic response to the questionnaires: If about 7% of summonses were sent to Hispanics, and only 30% of them were OK, whereas 50% of the remaining (93%) non-Hispanics were OK, the proportion of Hispanics in the combined yield would be about

$$(*) \qquad\qquad 4.3\% = \frac{30\% \times 7\%}{(30\% \times 7\%) + (50\% \times 93\%)}.$$

The final proportion depends on both yields and on the proportion of Hispanics on the master list, a slightly subtle point that I found difficult to explain to the court.

I also presented my estimates to the court in the form of thematic maps, showing the proportion of undeliverable summonses in each of the Hartford City tracts juxtaposed with a map showing the 1990 proportions of Hispanics in the over-18 populations of those tracts (as in Figure 2). These maps seemed more effective in convincing the court of the undeliverable problem with Hispanics than my carefully compiled estimates, despite the shortcomings of graphical presentations that I pointed out. For example, several of the areas that attract the eye, such as the large tract in the northeast corner, represent only small contributions to the overall counts. (The tract in the northwest corner with the high undeliverable rate contains the mail room for the University of Hartford—apparently students can be hard to reach by mail.)

The thematic maps for each of the other court years showed a similar tendency for undeliverable summonses in Hartford to correspond roughly with the Hispanic areas of the city. The effect was consistent over time. The suggestion from the maps was that the undeliverable problem was particularly bad in the traditionally Hispanic areas of the city.

The message from the cross-tabulations could also have been conveyed graphically, in a bar graph (as in Figure 3), which, with hindsight, I might perhaps have included in my testimony. The plot summarizes the estimated disqualifications for each of the court years, separately for Hispanics and non-Hispanics. I have made the vertical depth of each bar proportional to the estimated totals (for Hispanic or non-Hispanic, summed over all disqualifications). The stripes on each bar corresponds to the 100% breakdown of the total into disqualification categories. (Thus the area of each of the stripes is proportional to the estimated count for the corresponding category.) To the right of the vertical line, the bars contrast the consistent disparity between the yields (the percentages in the OK category) for Hispanics and non-Hispanics. To the left of the vertical line, the most striking difference is seen in the dark segments, corresponding to code 13 undeliverables.

One reviewer has remarked that the bars for 1996–97 seem uninformative, with so much incomplete data, and only a part of a court year. It is indeed simpler to

% undeliverable   % Hispanic

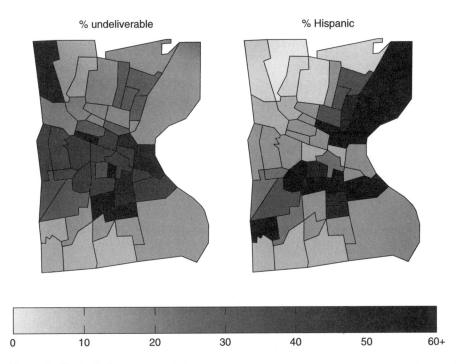

0   10   20   30   40   50   60+

Figure 2. Hartford city tracts. On left: estimated percentage undeliverable (code 13) for court year 1993–94 for each tract. On right: percentage Hispanic of over-18 population within each tract, according to 1990 census.

concentrate on the data for the first four years. One can, however, see the beginnings of the pattern from previous years, with higher undeliverability rates for Hispanics. It seemed reasonable to expect that the patterns from earlier years might prove to have been repeated when the full data for 1996–97 became available.

The pairs of bars for each court year look similar; the disparity between disqualification rates and yields for Hispanics and non-Hispanics was consistent over four (and probably five) court years. The corresponding barplots for estimates based on geocoding would paint an almost identical picture. The two methods tell the same story.

There are a few other interesting features in the plot. The no-show rates (checkered pattern, labeled NS) for Hispanics are indeed slighly higher than for the rest of the population. The citizenship disqualifications (fifth bar from the left end, shaded grey, labeled 01) accounted for a quite small proportion of the Hispanics—with hindsight, an expected outcome, given that most Hispanics in the Hartford area are Puerto Ricans, and American citizens. The language disqualification (code 06) did account for a larger proportion of Hispanics than non-Hispanics, but the difference was dwarfed by the disparity in undeliverables. The over-70 disqualification (code 08) was taken by a much larger proportion of non-Hispanics than Hispanics—again, not unexpected, given the marked skewing of the His-

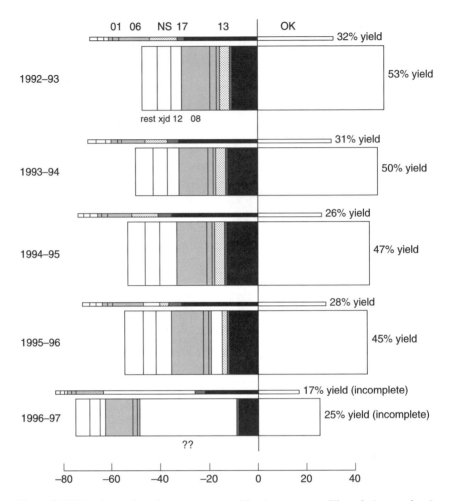

Figure 3. HNB estimates based on surname matching by court year: Hispanic (narrow bars) versus non-Hispanic (wide bars). Yield (percentage OK among Hispanics/non-Hispanics for each year) to the right of vertical axis; contributions from other disqualifications to the left of the axis.

panic population toward younger ages—with the effect of slightly narrowing the disparity in yields.

Readers who wish to study the estimates might do better to work from the cross-tabulations, such as Table 3, with reassurance from estimated standard errors and accompanying estimates for total counts, rather than trying to extract too much numerical detail from Figure 3.

In order to have confidence in my analysis, it was very important for me to have two relatively independent methods—the geocoding based on the addresses, and the surname matching based on the juror names—to arrive at estimates for the proportions of Hispanics, and the proportions of non-Hispanics, disqualified in various ways. I was able to reassure myself about possible systematic errors by comparing surname estimates for all records with surname and geocode estimates based on just those records to which I could assign a unique census tract.

In summary: The story told by the estimates was consistent over time and consistent between the two methods. Hispanics did suffer from a much higher undeliverability rate than non-Hispanics. The problem was largely driven by what was happening in the city of Hartford.

The bulk of my two years of work for the *Rodriguez* and *Gibbs* cases was devoted to developing, refining, and cross-checking my geocoding method. The effort to push the matching of summonses with tracts to a rate over 90% for some towns involved much tedious investigation of problem cases. The labor did help to move the argument about Hispanic underrepresentation away from sterile comparisons of isolated summary figures to more fruitful areas of disagreement, but it was an effort that I would not like to have to repeat.

The state and its expert, Dr. Michelson, eventually accepted most of my estimates, and agreed (Michelson 1997*b*, page 19) that undeliverable summonses were a problem:

> Everyone involved in this topic has concluded that a disproportionate number of summonses sent to Hispanics failed to be delivered, and every analysis I have seen concludes that non-delivery or non-response are the primary reasons why Hispanics fail to appear among qualified jurors.

Perhaps Dr. Michelson had in mind documents such as a memorandum ("Minority Representation," dated 6/27/94) written by Richard Gayer, the state's jury administrator, which was eventually entered as an exhibit in both the *Rodriguez* and *Gibbs* trials:

> Disqualifications. We need to look at the disqualifications individually and consider the impact on minorities versus entire demographics. The following numbers are for the court year 92–93:
>
> ⋮
>
> M.   Summons Undeliverable   11.88%   −High Impact
>
> ⋮

It appears that 49% of all disqualifications have high impact. Of that 49% more than half are related to undeliverable addressing points back to DMV and VTR files.

However, state officials did not initially acknowledge the existence of the problem:

> Q. Mr. Gayer, have you ever, over the last four years or five years as jury administrator, had any indications that there is an undeliverable problem amongst Hispanic voters?

A. No.

Q. Have you ever had any indications that there's an undeliverable problem in the Hartford/New Britain Judicial District?

A. No.

Rodriguez transcript, page 66 (17 January 1997)

5 Interpretation of My Estimates

My analysis was based mostly on the JIS data. I estimated (race and) ethnicity for the subset of names on the master list for which a summons was actually mailed. Given that summonses were effectively drawn from the master list in random order (see Section 2), for each court year, the percentages in Table 3 may be regarded as estimates of conditional probabilities: the probability that a summons was undeliverable, given that it was sent to a Hispanic or to a non-Hispanic. That is, effectively I was estimating, for each type of disqualification,

$P\{DISQ \mid$ person is Hispanic on master list$\}$,

$P\{DISQ \mid$ person is non-Hispanic on master list$\}$.

The geocoding and surname matching were in close agreement, at least for the most important categories, such as DISQ = 13 or DISQ = OK. The two methods were in less agreement regarding the estimates of conditional probabilities such as

$P\{$person is Hispanic $\mid$ person is on master list$\}$,

$P\{$person is Hispanic $\mid$ person is on combined source list$\}$.

By expressing my estimates in the form of percentages of totals (with the estimated counts relegated to separate exhibits), I separated out the question of representation or underrepresentation on the source lists from the question of what happened subsequent to the construction of the master list.

The state's expert argued that the estimates could be better interpreted via a different set of conditional probabilities. For example, one could ask for estimates of the probability that a summons resulted in an 'OK' classification, given that the summons was not undeliverable and that it was sent to a Hispanic. Or one could contemplate differences between Hispanics and non-Hispanics for the estimates of various other conditional probabilities. It is a straightforward matter to calculate any such conditional probability, or an estimate thereof, from my (estimated) probabilities for each event, conditional on selection into the master list.

6 The State's Rebuttal

As the challenge developed, the defense increasingly focused its claim on the differential effect of undeliverable summonses on the Hispanics who had reached the master list, with specific reference to the combined effect of disqualifications, undeliverability of summonses, and no-shows. The state countered that the system was not responsible for the "behavior of individuals," arguing that it was characteristics—such as a propensity to greater mobility, a greater likelihood of being a noncitizen or not speaking English, and even a reduced inclination to vote or take out Connecticut driver's licenses—that accounted for the smaller yield of Hispanics. Apparently, these effects were supposed to justify the higher rate of undeliverable summonses for Hispanics.

Some of the State's initial counterarguments became less relevant after the defense narrowed its claim to refer to the steps in the jury selection process between construction of the master list (as described in Section 3) and the point at which JIS was able to assign its disqualification codes. For example, possession (or the lack) of a Connecticut driver's license played no further role in the selection process once a person was included in the master list. Moreover, the citizenship qualification had only a minor effect on the Hispanics in the HNB judicial district, most of whom were of Puerto Rican origin, and hence almost certainly US citizens. Also, it seemed to me that fragmentary evidence regarding mobility of the general Hispanic population was less relevant to the population of Hispanics chosen from the source lists—the mere fact that a person was listed among the voters or licensed drivers argued against the transitory behavior imputed to the broader population of all Hispanics in the city of Hartford, or in the whole judicial district.

With the master list as the starting point of the analysis, the question of representation on the source lists became irrelevant.

To bolster his assertions about Hispanic behavior, the state's expert, Dr. Michelson, relied heavily on regression analysis at the town level. He argued repeatedly that one could eliminate Hispanic effects (that is, produce nonsignificant coefficients for the predictors that counted the number or proportion of Hispanics in a town) by adding other predictors to a regression. For example, he argued that linguistic isolation, the vacancy rate for housing in a town, and even lack of access to a car, each to some extent accounted for the undeliverability problem.

I objected strongly to Dr. Michelson's use of regression. He was content, in most cases, to justify a fit by pointing to the (suspiciously) large R^2, or adjusted R^2, values and by noting very small p-values. He presented no other evidence (such as the standard graphical diagnostics for regression fitting) that the implicitly assumed models were appropriate at the town level.

The defense singled out the following example of Dr. Michelson's methods for detailed criticism. On the basis of a regression, he estimated (Michelson 1997b, pages 1 and 9 of Appendix A) that "92.7 percent of adult non-Hispanics obtain a drivers licence, but −61.9 percent of Hispanics will. Hispanics are less likely to obtain drivers licenses than non-Hispanics."

He reached this conclusion by regressing the number of licensed drivers (dmv94 = counts of motor vehicle licences per town, derived from data supplied to JIS by the Department of Motor Vehicles for the construction of the 1994–95 master list) on the 1990 Census counts for both Hispanics and non-Hispanics over 18 years of age in each town.

Table 4. Coefficients from the regression of numbers of drivers on numbers of Hispanics and non-Hispanics over 18 years of age for each of the 29 towns in the HNB judicial district.

	Value	Std. Error	tvalue	$Pr(> |t|)$
(Intercept)	916.4836	291.7129	3.1417	0.0042
nonhisp18	0.9271	0.0135	68.4264	0.0000
hisp18	−0.6193	0.0475	−13.0347	0.0000
Multiple R-Squared: 0.9965

Dr. Michelson deemed the fitted regression "almost uninterpretable," but nevertheless, he seemed content to overlook the problem in other parts of his report (Michelson 1997*b*, page 11):

> It is easy to ask if the higher the percent Hispanic in a town, the lower the number of voters or drivers, holding the town's adult population constant. I have done so in Appendixes A and C, and the answer is "yes" to both questions. In its simplest form, one might say the higher the percent Hispanic, the lower the percent of adults who are Connecticut license holders. If one interprets this as the estimation of behavioral parameters (roughly, I accept this interpretation), one would say that the propensity of Hispanic adults to register to vote, or to obtain a Connecticut drivers license, is lower than those propensities among non-Hispanics.

I claim that the high R^2 and small *p*-values for the regression are largely due to one of the standard pitfalls of regression analysis, a phenomenon that is particularly dangerous when predictors vary over a wide range. To understand my claim, first note that for the purposes of model fitting it is equivalent to regress on total over-18 population (pop18) and over-18 Hispanic population (see Table 5).

The regression phenomenon is easiest to explain when the least-squares procedure is broken conceptually into two steps (compare with Section 12C of Mosteller and Tukey 1977):

(i) Regress both dmv94 and hisp18 on pop18.
(ii) Regress the dmv94 residuals from step (i) on the hisp18 residuals from step (i).

Table 5. Coefficients from the regression of numbers of drivers on numbers of Hispanics over 18 and all persons over 18 for each of the 29 towns in the HNB judicial district. Compare with Table 4.

	Value	Std. Error	tvalue	$Pr(> |t|)$
(Intercept)	916.4836	291.7129	3.1417	0.0042
pop18	0.9271	0.0135	68.4264	0.0000
hisp18	−1.5464	0.0581	−26.6330	0.0000
Multiple R-Squared: 0.9965

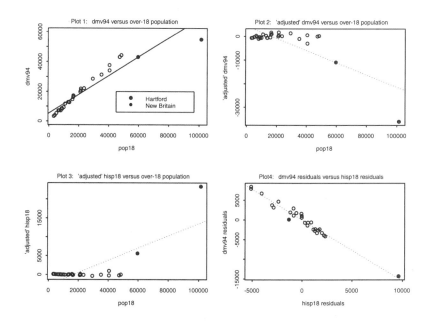

Figure 4. A two-step explanation of regression of 1994 driver counts on over-18 population counts and over-18 Hispanic counts.

The residuals from step (ii) are the same as the residuals from the regression of dmv94 on both pop18 and hisp18 simultaneously. All details of the two-predictor fit can be recovered using simple algebra from the results of steps (i) and (ii).

Figure 4 represents a small variation on the two-step procedure. Plot 1 shows the relationship between dmv94 and pop18, with the regression line superimposed. For the 27 smallest towns, notice that the points in the plot almost lie along a straight line; for most of those towns, the numbers of drivers are close to the over-18 population count. For the larger, urban, areas the story is different. The city of Hartford contributes a point of high (0.95) influence, which pulls the least-squares line away from the linear fit for the 27 smallest towns. The line passes close to the point for New Britain, which has low (0.15) influence.

For Plot 2, dmv94 is adjusted by subtraction of $1121.7 + 0.89 \times \text{pop18}$, the prediction based on the smallest 27 towns alone. Such an adjustment has no effect on the residuals from the regression of dmv94 on pop18. The new regression line (shown dotted) is easily calculated from the regression line from Plot 1. Of course, the line again comes close to the point contributed by New Britain.

Plot 3 shows hisp18, similarly adjusted for pop18 (by subtraction of the predicted values based on regression for the 27 smallest towns alone), plotted against pop18, with the regression line for all 29 towns superimposed. Notice that the line again passes close to the point for New Britain, due to the high influence of the point for Hartford.

As Plot 4 shows, the final fit is largely controlled by Hartford. In effect, hisp18, when adjusted for the over-18 population of the 27 smallest towns, acts as a dummy variable for Hartford. New Britain makes only a small contribution to the fit because its residuals from the regression lines in Plots 2 and 3 are both close to zero. Algebraically speaking, the 27 smaller towns are acting like a single point for the determination of the two-predictor regression. The whole regression procedure behaves much like an exercise in fitting a model with three parameters to three points, an operation almost guaranteed to produce a high R^2. Most of the explanatory power comes from pop18; the regression of dmv94 on pop18 alone has an R^2 of 0.9. Interpretation of the regression coefficients for such a fit makes little sense.

Another way to see that the adjusted hisp18 is acting as a dummy variable for Hartford would be to plot "adjusted dmv94$-C\times$ adjusted hisp18" against pop18, where the constant C is chosen to force the Hartford difference to zero. It would then become clear that almost all predictive power of hisp18 comes from the Hartford value.

The same phenomenon occurs when the hisp18 variable is replaced by another predictor with the same sort of behavior across the 29 HNB towns: a roughly linear association with pop18 for the 27 smaller towns, and a least-squares line pulled close to New Britain by the highly influential Hartford point. Figure 5 includes two of several possible choices: the number (noplumb) of housing units in each town without complete plumbing facilities, and the number (unemployed) of unemployed persons over the age of 16 in each town. The dotted line superimposed on each panel shows the least-squares fit based on all 29 towns.

Both the regression of dmv94 on pop18 and unemployed, and the regression of dmv94 on pop18 and noplumb, mimic the behavior of the regression on pop18 and hisp18. What do these fits imply about a quantitative (or causal) relationship between propensity to obtain a Connecticut driver's license and unemployment

Table 6. Coefficients from the regressions of numbers of drivers on numbers of all persons over 18 years of age and either numbers of housing units without plumbing or numbers of unemployed persons over 16, for each of the 29 towns in the HNB judicial district.

	Value	Std. Error	tvalue	$Pr(>|t|)$
(Intercept)	609.4928	418.4323	1.4566	0.1572
pop18	1.1821	0.0313	37.7942	0.0000
unemployed	−9.3858	0.4994	−18.7945	0.0000
Multiple R-Squared: 0.9933				
	Value	Std. Error	tvalue	$Pr(>|t|)$
(Intercept)	1641.2347	467.6011	3.5099	0.0017
pop18	0.8942	0.0215	41.6592	0.0000
noplumb	−47.2950	3.0755	−15.3778	0.0000
Multiple R-Squared: 0.9903				

or lack of plumbing? Not much, I would assert, without convincing answers to several troubling questions.

(i) Does it even make sense to assume that the rate at which persons without plumbing (or unemployed persons) obtain licenses is roughly the same within each of the 29 towns? Is the underlying model even plausible? Remember that the interpretation of p-values assumes existence of some underlying linear relationship between dmv94 and the predictor variables, with departures from linearity behaving like independent normal errors with constant variance.

(ii) What are the effects of working with grouped data? It is well known that aggregation can produce higher correlations.

(iii) Is it possible, even in theory, to disentangle the effects of the many variables whose values for Hartford tend to be very different from the values for the other towns? Will town-level data suffice?

(iv) Should we not worry about the large differences between Hartford and most of the other towns? It is particularly dangerous to work with raw counts when the

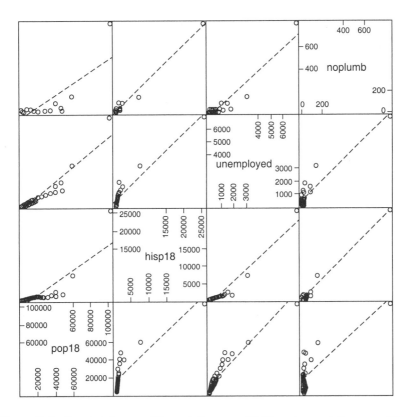

Figure 5. Scatter plots for over-18 population, over-18 Hispanic population, over-16 unemployed, and numbers of housing units without complete plumbing, for the 29 towns in the HNB judicial district.

values spread over a large range—compare with the discussion in Chapter 6 of Mosteller and Tukey (1977). Should we not worry about points with high influence?

Similar questions arise in the interpretation of many of Dr. Michelson's regressions, such as those with the counts of Hispanic over-18 population by town as one of the predictors.

7   What Population Is, or Should Be, Represented?

The word *underrepresentation* implies a comparison between two figures, a comparison between representation in some target population and representation in something like the pool from which jurors are selected.

In the landmark case *Castaneda v. Partida* (1977), the Supreme Court took the target as the total population of the county, despite the dissenting opinion of Chief Justice Burger that "*eligible* population statistics, not gross population figures, provide the relevant starting point." (This important case is well discussed, in some statistical detail, by Gastwirth 1988, Chapter 4.)

The choice of total population has been seen by some courts as a matter of practicality. For example, the Supreme Court of California in *People v. Harris* (1984, page 54) explained:

> Comparing the makeup of the actual jury pool with that of the entire population of persons presumptively eligible for jury service would be preferable to comparing with total population because if the cognizable class has a lower percentage of jury eligibles than the general population, a showing that that class' representation in the jury pool is less than the group's percentage of the general population does not necessarily show that the group is underrepresented. "Nevertheless, because it may be difficult to obtain full and accurate figures for jury eligibles and to require such data may place an insuperable burden on a litigant, this preference must accede to tolerance." (*Foster v. Sparks* (5th Cir. 1975) 506 F.2d 805, 833, Appen., An Analysis of Jury Selection Decisions by Hon. Walter P. Gewin, U.S. Circuit Judge.)

Some courts have preferred the over-18 or "voter-eligible" population, which is just as easily obtained from census figures as the total population, as a better first cut at the eligible population.

To me the key question seems to be, Is it actually possible to determine, or even to define, the eligible population?

Dr. Michelson (1997*a*, Section 3) calculated a proxy for the eligible population for each HNB town from 1990 Census data:

total over-18 − number over-18 noncitizens

− number over-18 not institutionalized

$$- \tfrac{1}{2}(\text{number over-18 who do not speak English well}).$$

The factor of $\tfrac{1}{2}$ was an attempt to eliminate the overlap between noncitizens and those who do not speak English well. He then determined the percentage of Hispanics in the eligible population by "multiplying the number eligible in each town by the percent Hispanic in that town, summing over towns, and dividing by the total number of eligible," a calculation that incorporates quite a number of simplifying assumptions.

I feel that the concept of an eligible population is not so easily captured. Consider, for example, the treatment of language ability. Table P28 of Census Summary Tape File 3A, from which the counts were taken, allows self-identified categories "speak only English," and speak English "very well," "well," or "not at all." It is not clear where one should put the dividing line for the purposes of calculating an eligible population. [When faced with a similar difficulty while estimating Hispanics, by geocoding, among the code 06 language disqualifications, I chose the proportion that would be most favorable to the state's explanation.] In Connecticut it is rather easy to be granted a language disqualification. I would also hazard an opinion that jury service is not a universally popular activity. Should the eligible population exclude only those who would certainly be justified in claiming a language disqualification, or all those who could get away with it? It makes a difference.

Similarly problematic is the question of how to handle the over-70 population. Persons over the age of 70 are granted disqualification if they claim it, but they are not excluded if they do not claim a disqualification. Should all persons over 70, or only some proportion of them, be included in the eligible population?

Other categories, such as hardship, would require equally arbitrary choices. Should we count as ineligible anyone with income below a certain level?

On top of these questions of how to handle disqualifications that are subject to some interpretation or personal choice, there sits the sheer technical problem of how to account for all the possible overlaps. Are Hispanics over 70 who speak English well more likely to opt for a disqualification than non-Hispanics over 70 who are living close to the poverty level, for example? Moreover, all this complicated exercise would be carried out using data that might be almost ten years old.

I doubt that the effort could produce a figure that is likely to be accepted by both sides to any future jury array challenge.

8 What Use Were the Questionnaires?

Interpretation of the questionnaires was complicated by many factors. There were irregularities in the collection process (some courts opted out; some courts forwarded questionnaires from periods during which there were supposed to be no cases; and there were disagreements over the numbers of questionnaires collected) and disagreement over the population that was being sampled—not all persons listed as OK actually filled out questionnaires, because of cancellations of service.

The state's expert argued convincingly that some of those persons canceled would have been no-shows if they had actually been pressed to appear. He argued that the estimated fraction of Hispanics among the OK's should actually be larger than the fraction of Hispanics filling out the questionnaires. There were also differences between courthouses, which I did manage to sort out eventually, but with little effect on the overall conclusions.

In the end I made only limited use of the questionnaires. The answers to the Hispanic question provided a sample on which to test the method of surname matching using the SSL. I was encouraged to see that SSL estimates agreed very well with the tabulated counts. Monte Carlo methods gave me a good feel for the level of bias in the SSL method, and backed up theoretical estimates of sampling variability.

The questionnaires also provided a cross-check on the estimated yields, for Hispanics and non-Hispanics, from the JIS data, as shown by the calculation ($*$) from Section 4, for the proportion of Hispanics in the combined yield.

9 Judge Spada's Decision in State v. Gibbs

The JIS data had shown that the main legal issue was whether the relatively high undeliverable rate for Hispanics could be justified. The state's main explanation was that Hispanics were highly mobile.

Judge Spada settled the question of the appropriate target population by direct reference to the analysis of the master list:

> The Connecticut cases utilizing total population as the relevant measure, however, are inapplicable to the unique facts here. Unlike typical challenges to the jury selection system, the challenge here is not based on lack of representation in the initial pool of potential jurors. Rather, the defendant's challenge is based on factors which deter Hispanics from appearing as jurors *after* the summonses are sent to a randomly selected group of persons from the master list. The defendant argues that the English-language requirement, undeliverables and no-shows disproportionately affect Hispanics. That is, after summonses are mailed based on the master list, the fact of disqualification for lack of English comprehension, the inability to deliver summonses because of stale addresses, and the failure of Hispanics to report for jury duty are the grounds for arguing unconstitutional jury selection. Because the defendant's claim defines the particular population to be examined; *United States v. Rioux, supra*, 930 F.Sup. 1558; the population of Hispanics on the master list is the appropriate pool to which to compare the number of Hispanics on the jury arrays.
>
> [pages 35–36]

(The page numbers refer to the judge's written decision.)

He determined that the appropriate comparison was between an assumed 7% Hispanic on the master list and an apparent 4.2% Hispanic on the questionnaire responses, despite the fact that the two figures were disputed.

> In order to assess underrepresentation, the proper method of comparison of the percentage of Hispanics on the master list with the population of appearing jurors must first be determined. The results are then evaluated to determine whether the underrepresentation is constitutionally significant.
>
> [pages 40–41]

That is, he was faced with an *absolute disparity* of 2.8% = 7% − 4.2%, and a *relative disparity* of 40% = 2.8/7. The absolute disparity could also be expressed as a *substantial impact*: for a 100 person venire, 2.8% corresponds to 2.8 persons.

He rejected the use of absolute disparity because of the size of the Hispanic population: less than 8% of the master list. He rejected the use of relative disparity because of fears that it tends to magnify disparities for small groups. (Compare with the discussion in Kairys et. al. 1977.) However, citing Connecticut and federal case law, he concluded that the observed discrepancy between Hispanic representation on the master list and the Hispanic representation among the questionnaires was insufficient to satisfy the second prong of the *Duren* test, on the basis of the substantial impact calculation.

I am puzzled by the rejection of absolute disparity but acceptance of the mathematically equivalent concept of substantial impact.

The judge also commented briefly on the so-called SDT method (Gastwirth 1988, Chapter 4). The test calculates the probability of observing 4.2% or fewer Hispanics in a sample (of the size given by the questionnaires) from a population with 7% Hispanic. Both experts had pointed out the inappropriateness of SDT in the context of this case: It makes little sense to test a hypothesis that everyone has already rejected. The judge understood why the hypothesis test made little sense.

> This result is not probative of the significance of underrepresentation, however, because the prospective jurors who appear are not selected randomly; rather, disqualifications and other factors intervene to exclude some of the persons on the master list.
>
> [page 48]

He also spoke to the appeals court:

> The SDT calculation, nevertheless, is the calculation applied by the courts to evaluate equal protection claims . . . Given the acceptance of SDT, this court will not attempt to fashion a new calculation of underrepresentation despite its reservations about the efficacy of SDT. It is unnecessary to do so because the defendant has failed to meet the third prong of the Castaneda test, see infra. Thus, even though per arguendo defendant can meet the

second prong using SDT, the defendant cannot establish a prima facie case.

[page 53]

I am also puzzled that the judge should understand the consistency check (∗), as described in Section 4, as a proposal for a new test:

> Because the defendant's expert believes that none of the four tests is measuring the correct thing, Pollard put forth a test calculating the yield of Hispanic appearing jurors. . . . The evidence, put forth by the defendant, has shown that Hispanics are less likely to receive summonses and more likely to be subject to disqualification. The fact that fewer Hispanics receive summonses, make it through the disqualification screen, and report for jury duty does not support a finding of significant underrepresentation. The factors which lead the Hispanics to report for jury duty in fewer numbers are not controlled by or influenced by the system and cannot support a finding of substantial underrepresentation. As discussed infra, the undeliverable problem, no-show problem and requirement of English ability are either non-systematic factors or legitimate qualifications. Although this determination blurs the line between underrepresentation and systematic exclusion, "the unfair representation and systematic exclusion prongs of the *Duren* tests are intertwined inextricably." *United States v. Rioux*, supra, 930 F. Supp. at 1568. Thus, the "comparative analysis of yield" calculation advocated by the defendant merely serves to highlight the legitimate differences between Hispanic and non-Hispanic participation—based on factors external to the system—and does not prove significant underrepresentation. The court therefore declines to adopt the defendant's method of measuring underrepresentation.

[page 49]

The bottom line: The judge decided that the undeliverability problem was not caused by state actions, and therefore it did not constitute underepresentation.

10   What Statistical Analysis Is Appropriate?

Very early in the course of my involvement with the challenge I made several decisions that guided my analysis. I decided that the traditional arguments over measures of disparity, whereby the challenge would be reduced to assertions about how to compare two summary numbers, were a dead end and pointless if the effect of "disqualifications" were not taken into account. Recognizing that courts have been wary of statistical arguments ("we must enter the statistical morass that has developed in this area," *Castonguay*, p. 426), I also decided that my testimony should rely only on easily described and justified assumptions. The more assumptions one feeds into a model, the more one deduces from data—but also the more the conclusions rest on judgments about which experts can honestly disagree. I do not regard a more detailed model based on shakier assumptions as necessarily better than a simple model. Given the large amount of JIS data available, I feel that the techniques I used were quite adequate and appropriate for the task of settling disagreements about how the jury system had actually been working.

I felt it most important for the court to get a clear picture of what the JIS data actually showed, with imprecise anecdotal explanations (such as those regarding the effects of citizenship or language ability) put to rest by the evidence from the actual summons records.

As support for my approach to the analysis, I would point out that the state did eventually accept most of my estimates drawn from the JIS data, thereby elevating the argument to differences in interpretation of a bigger picture, rather than disagreements over the relative merits of different ways of expressing a percentage.

11   Conclusions, and Lessons Learned

After over two years of work, and far too many hours spent giving testimony in court, I drew some lessons from my experience with the jury array challenges

I feel sympathy for judges who must decide statistical issues without the benefit of statistical training. Technical points and disagreements that would have been disposed of rapidly in one of our departmental seminars consumed vast amounts of court time. I felt the problem most keenly when I was attempting to criticize the state expert's use of regression. I suspect the exchanges came across to the court as just some esoteric matter of style. At times I would have appreciated the presence of a statistical referee. Of course, if there were court appointed experts to assist the judge, I suppose the choice of the expert would become another point over which parties could disagree.

I learned some lessons about tactics. When asked to provide the state with some idea of where my study was headed, I naively rushed to put together draft copies of my report, describing work in progress. Of course, minor discrepancies between drafts and final versions later provided ample ammunition for the state's cross-examinations. With hindsight, it would have been better to keep the half-baked ideas to myself, and not be so obliging about generating premature drafts.

On the purely technical level, I encountered problems that are surely worthy of more attention from a wider audience of professional statisticians. For example: How can, or should, one merge multiple source lists when there is uncertainty in the identification of duplicate names? See the conference proceedings edited by Alvey and Jamerson (1997) for some idea of what has already been achieved in this area.

Finally, I believe that arguments presented in the form of (estimates of) conditional probabilities could provide a systematic way for the courts to disentangle the combined effects of incomplete source lists, disqualifications, and the other obstacles facing would-be jurors, and for courts to judge which differences in conditional probabilities reflect benign or acceptable mechanisms (such as citizenship disqualifications) and which do not. Without some attempt at quantification, it is difficult to counter plausible explanations that too easily fit with comfortable prejudices and expectations. Sometimes the data can contradict what everyone has thought to be true.

Acknowledgments

I am grateful to Michael Courtney, both for his legal advice and for his unswerving insistence that the job of an expert witness is to tell the truth. I also thank the reviewers of the first version of this article for their helpful criticisms and suggestions.

12   Cases cited

Duren v. Missouri, 439 U.S. 357, 357 (1979).
State v. Castonguay, 194 Conn. 416 at 421, (1984).
State v. King, CR92-0137614 (Hartford Judicial District, 1996).
Castaneda v. Partida, 430 U.S. 482 (1977).
State v. Rodriguez, CR94-456268 (Hartford Judicial District 1997).
State v. Gibbs, CR93-00899ST (Hartford Judicial District 1997).
People v. Harris, 36 Cal.3d 36 (1984).

REFERENCES

[1] Alvey, W. and Jamerson, B., eds (1997), *Record Linkage Techniques*. Proceedings of an International Workshop and Exposition, Arlington, VA, March 20–21. Published by Ernst and Young, LLP, Washington, DC.

[2] Gastwirth, J.L. (1988), *Statistical reasoning in law and public policy*, Academic Press. In two volumes: 1. Statistical concepts and issues of fairness; 2. Tort law, evidence and health.

[3] Gerber, E. and de la Puente, Manuel (1996), The development and cognitive testing of race and ethnic origin questions for the year 2000 decennial census, Technical report, US Bureau of the Census. (Paper presented at the Bureau of the Census 1996 Annual Research Conference, March 17–19, Arlington, Virginia. Published in the proceedings of the Annual Research Conference.)

[4] Kairys, D., Kadane, J.B., and Lehoczky, J.P. (1977), Jury representativeness: a mandate for multiple source lists, *California Law Review* **65**, 776–827.

[5] Michelson, S. (1997a), An empirical analysis of the Connecticut Juror Selection System, Dated 2 April 1997 and 2 January 1998. Entered as a full exhibit in *State v. Gibbs*.

[6] Michelson, S. (1997*b*), Review of David Pollard's "Connecticut Juror Selection," Dated 15 May 1997 and 12 January 1998. Entered as a full exhibit in *State v. Gibbs*.

[7] Mosteller, F. and Tukey, J.W. (1977), *Data Analysis and Regression: A Second Course in Statistics*, Addison–Wesley.

[8] Munsterman, G.T. (1996), *Jury System Management*, Court Management Library Series, National Center for State Courts, Williamsburg, Virginia.

Issues Arising in the Use of Statistical Evidence in Discrimination Cases

Joseph L. Gastwirth

Abstract

As the use of statistical data and methodology in legal proceedings, especially those concerning alleged discrimination, has increased substantially during the last twenty-five years, more statisticians are becoming involved as expert witnesses and consultants. Potential experts should be aware of difficulties and pitfalls arising from the adversarial nature of legal proceedings. In particular, an expert needs to be involved early in the proceedings, especially in the discovery phase, in order that information on variables relevant to a planned analysis may be obtained. Otherwise, recent cases suggest that the statistician's testimony may not even be admitted as evidence. Some methodological developments that grew out of the application of statistical techniques to data used in equal employment cases are described.

Keywords: assessing explanations, discrimination law, expert witness, measures of teacher–pupil segregation, omitted variables, statistical evidence

1 Introduction

Statistical evidence was used to support a claim of discrimination against Chinese applicants for permits to operate laundries in *Yick Wo v. Hopkins* (1886) and in early cases concerning discrimination against blacks in jury selection in the 1930s and '40s (Gastwirth, 1988, pp. 154–156). While those cases involved alleged violations of the U.S. Constitution, the statistical disparities were so substantial that formal methods of inference were not needed. After the passage of the equal pay and civil rights laws in the 1960s some minority individuals became jurors or were hired in jobs they had previously been excluded from. Issues such as whether minorities were limited to a maximum number of jurors or were treated the same as similar whites when they applied for a job or promotion arose. More formal statistical methods were needed and accepted by the courts. In *Castenada v. Partida* (1977) and *Hazelwood School District v. U.S.* (1977) the Supreme Court accepted hypothesis testing, deeming a difference of two to three standard deviations between the actual and expected numbers of jurors or hires evidence supporting a *prima facie* case.

Although early cases concerning possible discrimination by government entities in jury selection or school segregation dealt with constitutional violations, most cases today concern violations of civil rights statutes. These are civil cases using the "preponderance of the evidence" standard of proof rather than the "beyond a reasonable doubt" standard used in criminal cases. In most discrimination cases, experts for the defendant, e.g., employer or government, have much easier access to the relevant information and databases, since the defendants possess the data and plaintiffs must obtain it during discovery. Both experts are working with observational data, however, rather than data from a randomized study or experiment. Thus, the analyses developed should account for other variables that influence the outcome of interest, e.g., education and prior experience in a hiring case, in addition to membership in a protected group.

In Section 2 we discuss some general issues concerning the way one obtains relevant data. Reasons why an expert should be involved in the discovery process, as well as problems arising in pretrial proceedings such as depositions, are presented. Section 3 describes several statistical problems arising from the author's involvement in cases. The final section summarizes the main points.

2 Problems Faced by Statistical Experts in Obtaining Relevant Data

Some time after a claim is filed in court, there is a period of time designated for discovery, i.e., each side can acquire information from the other. In equal employment cases, the plaintiff's lawyers generally ask for the criteria used by the defendant in its hiring and promotion decisions. This usually involves copies of computerized personnel files of all applicants for the jobs at issue in a hiring case, or eligible employees in a promotion case, for several years before and after the charge. Then the plaintiff's statistical expert will compare similarly qualified minority and majority individuals to determine whether their success rates were equal. At the same time the defendant's expert will analyze the data and may even put together a more comprehensive database by combining the existing personnel records with further information, e.g., annual evaluations, from the employer's personnel records.

Federal Rule of Civil Procedure 26(a) (1) (B) requires the parties to describe all documents and data compilations relevant to the disputed facts alleged with particularity in the litigation. Thus, the employer's personnel files are available for analysis. The plaintiff's expert often relies primarily on the computerized records and will likely have more difficulty developing a more comprehensive database. Even when both sides utilize the same computerized data, it is much easier for the defendant's expert to obtain information concerning a possible unusual or "outlying" observation than the plaintiff's, who must then specifically request that information. This increases the difficulty judges and juries have in understanding statistical evidence, since different results may be presented. Even slightly different estimated regressions relating the effect of productivity variables and membership in the protected group to salary can confuse jurors and judges, who may not feel comfortable with quantitative techniques. Unfortunately, courts have not adopted a protocol along the lines suggested by a committee of the New York Bar Association (reprinted in Appendix F of Fienberg, 1989) that would require the exchange of the databases prior to trial. The 1993 change in Rule 26 (a)(2)(B) of the Federal Rules of Civil Procedure requiring experts to submit reports summarizing their findings and expected testimony prior to the trial should enable the trial judge to resolve issues of database discrepancies before trial. This process of exchanging the data and analyses should assist the parties in creating a settlement and avoiding a trial.

Nesson (1991) notes that courts do not systematically penalize defendants who hide or destroy evidence or simply fail to preserve business records. While some states have created a new tort of discovery abuse to allow plaintiffs to obtain damages for their loss of the chance of proving their case in chief, recently California did not allow such a suit to proceed. Examples of the difficulties plaintiffs face when data, especially for the critical six-month to one-year period prior to the event responsible for the complaint, e.g., an adverse employment action, are missing are given in Gastwirth (1991).

The process of deposing or questioning potential witnesses about their likely testimony during the discovery process is intended to expedite the trial proceedings, since the parties may agree on some facts and also can prepare for an effective and efficient presentation and cross-examination of witnesses. Statistical experts may face a problem if they are deposed at an early stage of discovery about the results of their analysis, since *subsequently* the opposing party may produce additional data or corrections to the data that affect the statistical inference. Errors in the database and information missing at the time of the original charge can reasonably be assumed to have occurred randomly. It is highly questionable that additional data provided by a party *after* they have seen the preliminary findings of the opposing expert resulted from an unbiased search.

In *Daubert v. Merrell Dow Pharmaceuticals, Inc.* (1995) Judge Kozinski expressed similar doubts about expert testimony in the following passage:

> One very significant fact to be considered is whether the experts are proposing to testify about matters growing naturally and directly out of research they have conducted independent of the litigation, or whether they have developed their opinions expressly for purposes of testifying. That an expert testifies for money does not necessarily cast doubt on the reliability of his testimony, as few experts appear in court merely as an eleemosynary gesture. But in determining whether proposed expert testimony amounts to good science, we may not ignore the fact that a scientist's normal workplace is the lab or the field, not the courtroom or the lawyer's office.

Statistical experts for both parties face the possibility that the lawyers will not inform them of all the available data. For instance, if in addition to completed application forms there was a log kept of applications received, the lawyer is not obligated to inform the expert of the existence of this other data. Hence, each expert may be asked to analyze the database the lawyer using them believes will yield the most favorable results. Even if the two data sets are basically consistent with each other, explaining why some counts disagree can be awkward. Under such circumstances it is best to admit that one was unaware of the other database and would need time to learn how the data was collected before attempting to apply formal statistical procedures. In our example, the log might contain multiple applications from the same individual, while only one completed application per person was kept on file.

While the defendant's expert in an equal employment case usually will have an easier time in learning about how a data set provided them was assembled, they may also have difficulty obtaining data that might assist them. Most firms do not consider trials as a search for the "truth" but a cost of doing business. Indeed, in the part of a case I worked on that concerned fairness in promotions, after visiting the plant and looking at a few records I thought that minority employees might have had a higher rate of absenteeism and asked for that information. I was told that it would not be provided. Even if the idea turned out to be correct they would not submit the data and analysis because the firm was also involved in product liability cases. If a substantial fraction of employees had a high level of absenteeism, it might be used to question the quality of the product. Since the potential monetary loss in those cases far exceeded the potential award in the discrimination case, it was not cost-effective for the firm to provide that data.

Potential statistical experts should be aware of the importance of being involved with the discovery process to ensure that relevant available data is obtained. In particular, courts expect that similarly situated minority and majority employees will be compared. In *Thomas v. NFL Players Ass'n.* (1997) the court stated that to establish a *prima facie* case a plaintiff's analysis must include the minimum objective qualifications. Plaintiff's expert submitted a simple comparison of the termination rates of black and white employees that did not consider job held or seniority. The appellate court upheld the trial court's refusal to admit that evidence and observed that the plaintiffs' expert could not have incorporated relevant qualifications because the lawyer had *never requested* them in discovery. We will return to the issue of which job-related factors should be included in the statistical analyses of plaintiffs and defendants in Section 3c. Kaye and Freedman (2000) discuss this topic, citing relevant cases.

3 Statistical Research Problems Arising in Discrimination Law

Since a substantial literature (Conway and Roberts, 1983; Levin and Robbins, 1983; Dempster, 1988; Gray, 1993, 1997; and Monette, 1997) has been devoted to the issue of the effect of errors in variables on the regressions submitted in equal employment cases, other problems will be emphasized. Several problems are similar to ones arising in biostatistics, e.g., combination methods and assessing the potential effect of omitted variables on inferences drawn from observational data, while others relate to economics. In legal applications it is important that the statistical analysis fit the process being analyzed, i.e., accord with both subject matter and general knowledge, since fact finders, especially juries, try to integrate the evidence into a story (Pennington and Hastie, 1990).

3.1   Defining the Minority Share of the Qualified Labor Force

When fair hiring is the issue, the standard statistical approach is to compare the success rate of minority applicants with that of majority applicants. The data would be organized in a 2 × 2 table and Fisher's exact test would be used to test whether the hiring rates were equal. The odds ratio or the simple ratio of the two hiring rates measures the differential effect. In cases initiated a few years after the Civil Rights Act was passed in 1964, it turned out that there were few black applicants before the suit was filed because those who did apply were turned down or were restricted to low-paying jobs. Courts then asked what percentage of hires should have been black so they could assess whether the very few or no black hires was a plausible outcome of a fair recruitment and hiring process. Usually, the precomplaint data were so clear that courts simply used the minority proportion of the population in the area as a benchmark, e.g., *Jones v. Tri-County Elec. Coop.* (1975), discussed in Gastwirth (1988, 168–170).

Once firms began to hire blacks and women for more desirable jobs it was necessary to develop models to estimate minority availability, i.e., their share of the qualified labor pool available to an employer. For jobs not requiring special skill, census data on the composition of the labor force, individuals aged 16 years or older who are either employed or looking for work in the area, was used. At that time, the data were published primarily for large metropolitan areas, while an employer typically is located in a city or smaller place. Since people prefer to work near their homes, i.e., to minimize commuting time and cost, Gastwirth and Haber (1976) developed a model that gave greater weight to nearby areas than to outlying ones in determining the probability $P(B)$ that an applicant is black.

Specifically, consider a firm where workers come from K distinct residential areas $A_1, \ldots, A_k$ ordered by increasing distance (or commuting time) to the plant. For each residential area, let L_i be the area's total labor force and let b_i be the fraction of minority members (say blacks) in the area's labor force. Then the fraction of the entire labor market that blacks form is $\sum b_i L_i / \sum L_i$. Let p_i be the probability that a resident of the ith area applies to the firm so that $P(B)$ is given by

$$P(B) = \frac{\sum_{i=1}^{k} L_i p_i b_i}{\sum_{i=1}^{k} L_i p_i} = \sum_{i=1}^{k} q_i b_i, \tag{1}$$

where

$$q_i = (L_i p_i) \Big/ \sum_{i=1}^{k} L_i p_i.$$

The denominator of the first term above is the expected number of all applicants to the plant from all areas, and the numerator is the expected number of black applicants. Notice that q_i is the fraction of a firm's labor pool residing in the ith area, and $\sum q_i = 1$.

While we know that the p_i's should decrease as the commuting time increases, they are difficult to estimate directly. For the larger metropolitan areas, commuting data is available and can be used to estimate the p_i's. If the fairness of recruitment were not an issue, the q_i's could be estimated from applicant data. Starting with the 1990 census, information is available by place of work at the city and county level. Unless the defendant is the dominant employer in the area, so that the census data would reflect its hiring practices, this data file should provide reasonable estimates of minority availability.

Some defendants used the residence of current employees or recent hires to estimate the q_i terms in (1). Courts realized that this yields an underestimate of minority availability, since if minorities were not hired fairly, they would be underrepresented among the hires. In *Markey v. Tenneco* (1985) the court upheld the calculation based on applicant weights after it previously rejected the use of the residence of new hires. Using applicant data, minority availability was 42.8%, while it was only 33% using new hire data. In that case, the data for the L_i was restricted to individuals in the appropriate occupation.

In determining availability for new hires, most of which are made at the entry level, use of all individuals in the relevant occupational labor force in the area includes workers currently earning more than the job pays. Gastwirth (1981) suggested that excluding workers earning 10 to 15% more than the entry-level salary, to allow some job changes for convenience, would be an appropriate refinement. When using a wage cut-off one should use the salaries paid by the employer for the year the census data was collected. The same approach can be applied to analyze the fairness of hiring more experienced workers by eliminating much lower paid individuals from the census data, as most of them will not have had the requisite experience. The 1990 EEO Special File permits this type of analysis.

For some positions, e.g., taxi drivers and other jobs where tips are a large portion of earnings and typically are underreported, official data on income and earnings may not be sufficiently accurate to be relied on. An alternative method is to eliminate people *employed* in professional and other highly skilled occupations in the area who would not be potential applicants.

3.2 A Problem Arising in Classifying Schools as Racially Identifiable

The Supreme Court's *Brown v. Board of Education* (1954) decision that racial segregation in public schools is unconstitutional is widely regarded as one of the most important in the twentieth century. In the 1980s several jurisdictions that were under court orders to desegregate their educational facilities claimed that they had complied with the original orders and requested to be relieved of further court supervision. In determining whether a school system is "unitary" rather than segregated, courts examine several criteria, e.g., student assignments and physical facilities. One difficult aspect of these cases is distinguishing demographic patterns resulting from private decision-making, such as white families with school children moving to the suburbs, from demographic patterns arising from past school segregation. In *Freeman v. Pitts* (1992) three justices noted that two of the factors, resource allocation and teacher assignment, considered in examining whether a system is unitary are primarily under the control of the city or county and not affected by residential patterns.

Most segregation measures (White, 1986) focused on measuring the segregation of students. Gastwirth and Nayak (1994) proposed to measure pupil–teacher segregation by a statistic analogous to the relative risk or selection ratio, i.e., the ratio γ of the probability that a black student has a black teacher to the probability a white student has a black teacher. In a unitary system the value of γ should be near its expected value 1.0. Assuming random placement of students and teachers, they derived the large sample theory for γ so that one can carry out the standard tests and derive confidence limits for it.

To formally define γ we assume that the number of schools in the system is k, and that the system employs n_i teachers with m_i students at school $i, i = 1, \ldots, k$. Among the $m = \sum m_i$ students, b are black (minority) and w are white (majority). The number of black (white) students attending the ith school is b_i (w_i). Thus, $b_i + w_i = m_i, \sum b_i = b, \sum w_i = w$, and $b + w = m$. Of the $n = \sum n_i$ teachers, x are black and y are white. The number of black (white) teachers assigned to the ith school is x_i (y_i). Hence, $x_i + y_i = n_i, \sum x_i = x$ and $\sum y_i = y$. Then,

$$\gamma = \left[\sum_{1}^{k} \left(\frac{b_i}{b} \right) \left(\frac{x_i}{n_i} \right) \right] \bigg/ \left[\sum_{1}^{k} \left(\frac{w_i}{w} \right) \left(\frac{x_i}{n_i} \right) \right]. \tag{2}$$

Under random placement, the numerator of (2), the probability that a black student has a black teacher and the denominator is the probability a white student has a black teacher.

To illustrate the use of the measure we analyzed data from *Brown II* (1989), which was initiated by the same woman who as a child was the plaintiff in the original case. When the Topeka School Board requested a judicial determination that the system was now unitary, Ms. Brown and other black parents objected, since they believed that the schools were still racially identifiable. The value of γ on the data for elementary schools yielded a value of 1.53 with a standard error of .093. Thus, the observed γ exceeds its expected value, 1.0, by $.53/.093 = 5.7$ standard deviation units, a highly significant (p-value $< 10^{-6}$) result. This analysis supports the majority opinion's conclusion, which was reconfirmed in *Brown III* (1992), that Topeka's schools were not unitary with respect to faculty/staff assignment, not withstanding over thirty years of court supervision.

Another problem in *Brown II* and similar cases is that only schoolwide data were available. Especially for elementary schools, where pupils have one main teacher, the actual proportions of black and white students who had a black teacher could be calculated and compared. The calculation of γ on schoolwide data using (2) assumes that the probability each pupil has of being assigned a teacher of each race is that race's proportion of all teachers in the school. Thus, when race is a factor in teacher assignments the calculated value of γ from schoolwide date is likely to be an underestimate of what its value would be if data for each class were available.

While the measure was developed for assessing whether teacher–pupil assignments are influenced by racial considerations it can also be used to assess whether minority store managers are predominantly assigned to stores located in ethnic areas. Similar measures can be developed to assess whether blacks applying for loans for homes in mainly black residential areas have a higher probability of receiving a mortgage than similarly situated blacks applying for loans for houses in predominantly white areas.

3.3 The Adequacy of Statistical Analysis and Assessing "Explanations" of Highly Significant Disparities

In employment discrimination cases concerning disparate treatment (Paetzold and Wilborn, 1994; Rosenblum, 2000) after a plaintiff has demonstrated a statistically significant and meaningful disparity in hiring or promotion rates or in the pay of *similarly situated* minority and majority individuals, the employer must provide a justification or explanation. In *Texas Dep't. of Comm. Affairs v. Burdine* (1981) the Supreme Court stated that the defendant's reasons should "frame the factual issue with sufficient clarity so that the plaintiff will have a full and fair opportunity to demonstrate pretext." The Court noted that the reason offered does not need to be the true one but must be a legitimate one. If the defendant submits a satisfactory justification, then the plaintiff needs to prove pretext, i.e., the proffered reason was not the actual one and that the employer acted with discriminatory intent. In *St. Mary's Honor Center vs. Hicks* (1993) the Court held that the fact-finder *may* but *need not* find for the plaintiff if it does not believe the employer's reason (italics added). The plaintiff needs to convince the fact-finder that discrimination was a substantial factor in the decision.

Statistical methods can be quite useful in clarifying whether the defendant's reasons are able to explain the disparity. Sometimes the defendant asserts that plaintiff's analysis is faulty because some job-related variables were not included. Courts do not always require the critic to demonstrate that the omitted factors were sufficiently job-related to reduce the disparity to a statistically insignificant or legally minimal one, e.g., by including them in their own analysis. Since no data set is perfect, it is important for statisticians to continue developing statistical methods that quantify the potential effect of omitted or mismeasured variables (Finkelstein and Levin, 1990 pp. 409–418; Fuller, 1987; Rosenbaum, 1995) so that basically sound analyses are given their proper evidentiary weight.

Before discussing specific methods we should mention that the U.S. Supreme Court in *Bazemore v. Friday* (1986) stated that plaintiffs presenting a regression analysis need not incorporate *all* measurable variables but should account for the major ones. Otherwise, the analysis may be disregarded. In *Coward v. ADT Security Systems Inc.* (1998) a multiple regression of salaries that incorporated only race and seniority was deemed inadmissible. The trial judge excluded it because it did not include education or prior work experience as predictors, while the appellate opinion found the omission of job title or other variable representing the type of work performed rendered the regression unreliable.

In an interesting concurring opinion, Judge Sentelle observed that there are a variety of ways to select a set of independent variables that will group together employees who are more or less similarly situated. His opinion suggests that the majority might have been overly restrictive by requiring a regression equation to include job title or type of work performed, since other characteristics could also reflect their qualifications. Indeed, if minority employees with the appropriate educational background and experience for professional positions are placed in lower-level jobs, it would appear that education would be a more suitable predictor to measure discrimination than job title, since that variable would reflect the discriminatory practice at issue.

I believe a sensible approach to deciding which variables need to be included in order for a statistical analysis to be admissible into evidence was given in *Boykin v. Georgia Pacific Co.* (1983). When the plaintiff's analysis was criticized for not including other factors when it considered *all* the information on the application form, the court decided that it was adequate. As the defendant controls what information is used in employment decisions and what data is preserved in its files, it is reasonable to assume that information on the important factors for on-the-job success are systematically obtained for all applicants or eligible employees and kept in their personnel records. This is why plaintiffs should consider all the job-related factors for which the employer has gathered data. If they do, then the employers should not be able to use information that was not obtained for all job candidates to rebut an inference derived from a statistical analysis using their complete files, since this would not give plaintiffs a "full and fair opportunity" to show pretext.

As plaintiffs are required to compare similarly qualified applicants or employees, an employer's explanation of a statistical disparity should also be comparative. The approach adopted in *Barnes v. Gen Corp Inc.* (1990) of examining the defendant's comparisons of the qualifications of the individual plaintiffs to younger employees in similar jobs is preferable to the one in *Graffam v. Scott Paper Co.* (1994). That decision allowed the defendant to indicate weaknesses, e.g., did not volunteer for overtime, of the plaintiffs who were laid off without showing whether retained employees met those criteria. When courts do not require the defendant to show that those employees retained did not have the alleged deficiencies of the plaintiffs they allow defendants to avoid submitting the comparative evidence plaintiffs need to offer.

After plaintiffs have established a *prima facie* case of hiring or promotion discrimination based on comparing the success rates of similarly qualified minority and majority applicants, suppose the defendant asserts that another factor such as possessing a higher degree or special education would "explain" the disparity. Courts should follow Judge Posner's skepticism expressed in *Allen v. Seidman* (1989) when the defendant has not submitted an analysis, e.g., a logistic regression incorporating that factor. The following slight generalization (Gastwirth, 1988) of Cornfield's lemma (Greenhouse, 1982) clarifies the required degree of association of the omitted variable (OV) to job success and how much its prevalence in the two groups must differ in order for the factor U to "explain" an observed relative risk $R_0 = p_2/p_1$, where p_1 and p_2 are the majority and minority success rates and f_1 and f_2 the prevalence of U in the two groups:

(a) The relative risk R_u associated with factor U must exceed R_0, and
(b) the prevalence ratio $\theta = f_2/f_1$ *must be at least*

$$R_0 + \frac{R_0 - 1}{R_u - 1} \frac{1}{f_1}, \tag{3a}$$

or equivalently that

$$f_2 \geq R_0 f_1 + \frac{(R_0 - 1)}{(R_u - 1)}. \tag{3b}$$

To account for sampling error we can replace R_0 by the lower end of a confidence interval (Koopman, 1984). If we have information about the strength R_u of the OV and its prevalence in both groups f_1 and f_2, we can adjust the estimated relative risk (Breslow and Day 1980, p.96).

This and similar results have been extensively used by Rosenbaum (1995) to analyze the sensitivity of inferences in biostatistics to omitted variables. We use its analogue (Gastwirth, 1992) for the binomial model to examine potential omitted variables raised in Judge Manion's dissent in *EEOC v. O&G Spring Wire Forms* (1995). As in Section 3.1, the minority share of the qualified and available labor pool is denoted by π. Let s be the fraction of actual hires. For a job-related factor U omitted from the calculation of π to explain a disparity between s and π, it must increase a person's probability of being hired by R_0, where

$$R_0 = [\pi(1 - \pi)]/[s/(1 - s)]. \tag{4}$$

Moreover, θ, the ratio of the prevalence f_2 of U in the majority to its prevalence f_1 in the minority group needs to satisfy (3a) or (3b). To allow for sampling error for a statistical test at the .05 level one replaces s by u, the upper end of a 97.5% one-sided (or 95% two-sided) confidence interval for π based on s.

Plaintiff's expert developed several potential labor pools using several potentially relevant occupational categories and a weighted labor market as in Section 3.1. Since the job involved operating a kick and punch press, the closest occupational category in the census data is punch and stamp press operators. For this category $\pi = .225$. As no blacks were among 85 hires, the data is highly significant (p-value $< 10^{-6}$). The upper end of a confidence interval for π is $u = .0425$.

The trial court found for the plaintiffs, and the appellate majority affirmed the decision, noting that even if several criticisms of the plaintiff's labor market were correct they would not reduce π to a value sufficiently low (.06) to make the disparity insignificant. My calculation indicates that the court used the two-tailed .01 level rather than the .05 one. Substituting u for s in (4) indicates that R must be at least 6.54.

Judge Manion noted two potential flaws. First, the firm preferred experienced and skilled workers. Secondly, the firm did not require workers to know English, and indeed, both Polish and Spanish were spoken at the plant. He opined that English-only speakers might feel uncomfortable and might not apply. As the occupational data reported in the census is based on those employed and the unemployed with experience in the specific occupation, the first factor appears to have been included in the determination of π. While it is conceivable that applicants with a Polish or Hispanic background were more qualified than blacks, none of the opinions indicate that the defendant submitted such an analysis.

To examine the language factor, let U denote desire to work in a non–English-speaking workplace. We assume that the prevalence f_1 of U in Polish and Hispanic workers is 1.0, although some of them might prefer a diverse environment, while in blacks and other groups it would be f_2. Unfortunately, the labor market availability was given only for blacks, so we do not know what fraction of the labor pool non-Polish and non-Hispanic whites formed. To be most favorable to Judge Manion let us assume that the only potential employees were black, Polish, and Hispanic and assume that $(R_0 - 1)/(R_u - 1)$ is negligible. Then (3b) implies that if at least 15.3% of the black members of the available labor force were willing to work where English was not the common language, this factor could *not* reduce the disparity to insignificance.

The above analysis raises serious doubts that the factors mentioned could fully explain the strong statistical evidence. It also shows the wisdom of Judge Posner's observation in *Allen* (1989) that it is easy to take "potshots" at a statistical analysis, and a critic should demonstrate that the flaw is sufficient to affect the ultimate inference. This can be accomplished by submitting an analysis incorporating the omitted factor that shows that any difference between the minority and majority groups is not statistically significant. Alternatively, the critic can provide evidence of the strength of the relationship between U and the job and of a substantial difference between the prevalence of the factor in the two groups that satisfies Cornfield's conditions. It should be emphasized that the analysis we presented assesses the reasonableness of the explanation submitted to the court in the *O & G Spring Wire Forms* case, not whether the statistical disparity is explicable by other means.

3.4 The Importance of Time and Context in the Analysis of Data

Courts prefer analyses that closely follow the selection process actually used. In a fair hiring case *Harper v. Godfrey* (1993), a supervisor described that he selected

17 permanent employees from 87 substitutes by writing down a list of workers his supervisors recommended, placing them in order as he went. His list consisted of 35 from the 87, of which 17 were ultimately hired. Of the 87 workers, 25 were black, and 8 blacks were among the 35 on the list. Plaintiff's expert considered the actual hires, 1 black out of 17, as a sample from the 35 and found a statistically significant result using Fisher's exact test and the Wilcoxon test (applied to the rankings, which were not given in the opinion). The expert did not analyze the results for the first stage (selecting 8 blacks out of 25 when 35 substitutes were chosen from the 87). Fisher's exact test yields a two-sided p-value of .3464, which presumably was presented by the defendant. If this two-stage process had been followed, how should a judge combine these two results? This problem is similar to one described in Gastwirth and Greenhouse (1995) and Sprent (1998). Statisticians need criteria from the legal system to choose the most appropriate of several reasonable procedures.

An interesting aspect of the *Harper* data is that if one analyzes the data according to the process described by Judge Randa, i.e., the ordering was done from all 87 substitutes, then one can ask whether blacks received their fair share of the top 17 ranks? Fisher's test yields a statistically significant p-value of .0331, and the estimated odds ratio was .12, indicating that a black substitute worker had only one-eighth the odds of being hired as a white one. While it is not clear that this analysis would have had an effect on the final decision, since the judge raised the question, it might have.

As processes unfold in time, one needs to examine data in a way that is consistent with the major events. In a discrimination case the employer's practices and/or applicant flow may change in response to one or more of the following: the time a charge is filed with the EEOC, when the EEOC gives the complainant a right-to-sue letter, when the individual files a formal suit, and when it becomes clear that a trial will be held. Freidlin and Gastwirth (1998) modified change-point procedures based on the CuSum chart to aid courts in their determination of when, if any, discrimination might have occurred and also when it ended, which would limit a defendant's liability.

3.5 Some Other Topics

Statisticians have developed a wide variety of methods for handling unusual observations (Barnett and Lewis, 1994; Sprent, 1998). However, the routine discarding of them may not be appropriate in a legal case. For example, if someone's file contains an error, such as a miscoding of their level of education that led to their not being considered eligible for a promotion, and the few similar errors were random, then that individual would not have suffered discrimination. An honest error is not discrimination; see *Riordan v. Kempiners* (1987). While the firm's database should be corrected for future use, changing the data could lead to an underestimate of the effect of education in the promotion process *at the time* of the complaint.

Sometimes outliers in a data set reflect the basic issue. In an equal pay case, *Craik v. Minnesota State Univ. Board* (1984), the plaintiffs included administrators who held academic rank in their regression analysis comparing male and female faculty members. The university's expert asserted that they should have been deleted as "outliers" but did not reanalyze the data to show that this would have reduced the coefficient of sex to insignificance. More importantly, as the rate at which women advanced to positions such as departmental chair was less than the corresponding rate for men, the fact that the administrators were mostly male reflected the employment practices being scrutinized.

Although methods (Cochran, 1954; Mantel and Haenszel, 1959) for combining data in several 2×2 tables have been used in biostatistics for many years and related procedures such as Fisher's summary chi-square and Lancaster's mid-p modification of it for discrete data are available, they were not immediately accepted in discrimination cases. In *Hogan v. Pierce* (D.D.C. 1981), Judge Robinson's opinion accepted the test and notes its exact p-value. The case concerned the fairness of promotions to Grade 14 in the computer division of a governmental unit, and the data is discussed in Gastwirth (1988), Agresti (1996), and Strawderman and Wells (1998).

Before using a combination method one should know the issue of concern to ensure that the data sets refer to jobs of similar skill or the same time period. For instance, in a case concerning whether black college graduates had the same hiring opportunities as whites, it is reasonable to combine data analyses for entry-level managerial, sales, and computer-related jobs. One should not, however, include analyses for positions that do not require a college degree, since excess minority hires in these lower-paying jobs could mask underhiring in the positions relevant to the case. The need to analyze hiring data using the binomial model stimulated Louv and Littel (1986) to carefully examine the summary chi-square procedure in that context, and Gastwirth and Greenhouse (1987) obtained the analogue of the MH and ML estimators of a common odds ratio for such data.

This article has focused on problems that arose from the author's involvement in the area, but some other topics should be mentioned. Most age discrimination cases involve termination data, and there is a need to modify existing techniques to account for the fact that all employees under 40 are not covered by the law and should be considered as one age category. Thus, a logistic regression simply using age as a predictor along with other relevant covariates might yield a distorted estimate of the effect of age relevant for the case. The issue may be further complicated when several layoffs occur over a period of time. Finkelstein and Levin (1994) proposed a modification of Cox's proportional hazards model. Although Paetzold and Willborn (1998) raised some questions about the appropriateness of the method, the problem is an important one, and more research, including goodness of fit tests, should be carried out.

Disparate impact cases concern whether a job requirement excludes a disproportionate fraction of a minority group. Typically, one applicant's passing a test does not affect the chance of any other applicant, so the data are unconditional. Recent research (Berger and Boos, 1994) on exact and approximate tests for the 2×2 table and their extension (Freidlin and Gastwirth, 1999) to the stratified setting may lead to more powerful tests (Goldstein, 1985).

4 Summary

Statistical reasoning has been useful in resolving claims of discrimination. However, courts may not always give statistical evidence the weight it deserves. If the legal system insists on the preservation of data relevant to employment decisions for several years, then an adequate database concerning the fairness of the practices that led to the charge would be available to both parties for analysis.

It is very important for statistical experts to be involved in the discovery process, so that data on all the factors used by the employer is requested. Testifying experts should be aware that the lawyer hiring them may not provide them with all the data and may have hired a consulting expert first so they see only the "favorable" data, leaving them open to being cross-examined as to why they failed to analyze the other database. An indication that this may be happening is the request to do a particular type of analysis shortly before trial. Careful judicial oversight of the discovery process can limit the potential for manipulation of the database or misleading the opposing party about the nature of the statistical analysis. Courts should consider revising the procedural rules so that the parties must exchange the underlying data as well as the statistical analysis they intend to offer at trial prior to the trial.

Courts expect statistical analyses to compare similarly situated individuals of the minority and majority groups. Thus, experts should consider all the available information on the major factors related to successful job performance. Statistical methodology for examining alleged omissions or the flaws in an analysis have the potential for playing a more important role, especially at the pretext stage of disparate treatment cases, as they enable the fact finder to evaluate the likely effect of the "flaw" on the final inference.

The use of statistical evidence in discrimination cases has renewed interest in assessing the potential effect of omitted variables and measurement error on statistical inferences, combination methods, and the study of the properties of statistical methods on unbalanced data sets (Gastwirth and Wang 1987). In has also created new demands for census data on minority groups, which may be useful in other areas of public policy.

Acknowledgments

It is a pleasure to thank Joseph Cecil, Bruce Levin, Weiwen Miao, Frank Ponti, and Marc Rosenblum for reviewing the article and offering many helpful suggestions.

5   Cases Cited

Allen v. Seidman, 881 F.2d 375 (7th Cir. 1989).

Barnes v. Gen Corp, Inc., 896 F.2d 1457 (6th Cir., 1990).

Bazemore v. Friday, 478 U.S. 385 (1986).

Boykin v. Georgia Pacific Co., 706 F.2d 1384 (1983).

Brown v. Board of Education, 347 U.S. 483 (1954).

Brown II, 892 F.2d 851 (10th Cir. 1989).

Brown III, 978 F, 2d 585 (10th Cir. 1992).

Castenada v. Partida, 430 U.S. 482 (1977).

Coward v. ADT Security Systems Inc., 140 F.3d 271 (DC Cir. 1998).

Craik v. Minnesota State Univ. Board, 731 F.2d 465 (8th Cir. 1984).

Daubert v. Merrell Dow Pharmaceuticals, Inc., 43 F.3d 1311 (9th Cir. 1995).

EEOC v. O & G Spring Wire Forms, 38 F.3d 872 (7th Cir. 1995).

Freeman v. Pitts, 503 U.S. 467 (1992).

Graffam v. Scott Paper Co. 870 F.Supp. 389 (D.C. Me. 1994).

Harper v. Godfrey, 839 F.Supp. 583 (E.D. Wi. 1993).

Hazelwood School District v. U.S., 433 U.S. 299 (1977).

Hogan v. Pierce, 31 FEP Case 115 (D.D.C. 1981).

Jones v. Tri-County Elec. Coop., 515 F.2d 13 (5th Cir. 1975).

Markey v. Tenneco, 707 F.2d 172 (5th Cir. 1985).

Riordan v. Kempiners, 831 F.2d 690 (7th Cir. 1987).

St. Mary's Honor Center vs. Hicks, 509 U.S. 502 (1993).

Texas Dep't. of Comm. Affairs v. Burdine, 450 U.S. 258 (1981).

Thomas v. NFL Players Ass'n., 131 F.3d 198 (DC Cir. 1997).

Yick Wo v. Hopkins 118 U.S. 356 (1886).

REFERENCES

[1] Agresti, A. (1990), *Categorical Data Analysis*. New York: Wiley.

[2] Agresti, A. (1996), *An Introduction to Categorical Data Analysis*. New York: Wiley.

[3] Barnett, V. and Lewis, T. (1994), *Outliers in Statistical Data*, 3rd ed. Chichester: John Wiley.

[4] Berger, R.L. and Boos, D.D. (1994), *P* values maximized over a confidence set for a nuisance parameter. *Journal of the American Statistical Association*, 89, 1012–1016.

[5] Breslow, N.E. and Day, N.E. (1980), *Statistical Methods in Cancer Research*, vol. I, *The Analysis of Case-Control Studies*. Lyon: International Agency for Research on Cancer.

[6] Conway, D.A. and Roberts, H.V. (1983), Reverse regression, fairness and employment discrimination. *Journal of Business and Economics Statistics*, 1, 75–85.

[7] Dempster, A.P. (1988), Employment discrimination and statistical science. *Statistical Science*, 3, 146–161.

[8] Fienberg, S.E. (ed.) (1989), *The Evolving Role of Statistical Assessments in the Courts.* New York: Springer.

[9] Finkelstein, M.O. and Levin, B. (1990), *Statistics for Lawyers.* New York: Springer.

[10] Finkelstein, M.O. and Levin, B. (1994), Proportional hazards models for age discrimination cases. *Jurimetrics*, 34, 153–164.

[11] Fleiss, J. (1981), *Statistical Methods for Rates and Proportions* (2nd ed.), New York: John Wiley.

[12] Freidlin, B. and Gastwirth, J.L. (1998), The application of change point tests to data occurring in fair hiring cases: in *Asymptotic Methods in Probability and Statistics (ICAMPS '97)* Szyszkowicz B., editor, Amsterdam: Elsevier Science, 551–562.

[13] Freidlin, B. and Gastwirth, J.L. (1999), Unconditional versions of several tests commonly used in the analysis of contingency tables. *Biometrics*, 55, 264–267.

[14] Gastwirth, J.L. (1981), Estimating the demographic mix of the available labor force. *Monthly Labor Review*, 104, 50–57.

[15] Gastwirth, J.L. and Wang, J.L. (1987) Nonparametric tests in small unbalanced samples: Application in employment discrimination cases. *The Canadian Journal of Statistics*, 15, 339–348.

[16] Gastwirth, J.L. (1988), *Statistical Reasoning in Law and Public Policy.* Orlando: Academic Press.

[17] Gastwirth, J.L. (1991), Comment on Nesson. *Cardozo Law Review*, 13, 817–829.

[18] Gastwirth, J.L. (1992), Methods for assessing the sensitivity of statistical comparisons used in Title VII cases to omitted variables. *Jurimetrics*, 33, 19–34.

[19] Gastwirth, J.L. and Greenhouse, S.W. (1987), Estimating a common relative risk: application in equal employment. *Journal of the American Statistical Association*, 82, 38–45.

[20] Gastwirth, J.L. and Greenhouse, S.W. (1995), Biostatistical concepts and methods in the legal setting. *Statistics in Medicine*, 14, 1641–1653.

[21] Gastwirth, J.L. and Haber, S.E. (1976), Defining the labor market for equal employment standards. *Monthly Labor Review*, 99, 32–36.

[22] Gastwirth, J.L. and Nayak, T.K. (1994), Statistical measures of racially identified school systems. *Jurimetrics*, 34, 173–192.

[23] Goldstein, R. (1985), Two types of statistical errors in employment discrimination cases. *Jurimetrics*, 26, 32–47.

[24] Gray, M.W. (1993), Can statistics tell us what we do not want to hear?: the case of complex salary structures. *Statistical Science*, 8, 144–158.

[25] Gray, M.W. (1997), Pay equity: the role and limitations of statistical analysis. *Canadian Journal of Statistics*, 25, 281–292.

[26] Greenhouse, S.W. (1982), Jerome Cornfield's contributions to epidemiology. *Biometrics*, 38, 33–38.

[27] Kaye, D.H. and Freeman, D.A. (2000), Reference guide on statistics, in *Reference Manual on Scientific Evidence*. Washington, DC: Federal Judicial Center.

[28] Levin, B. and Robbins, H. (1983), A note on the under-adjustment phenomenon. *Statistics and Probability Letters*, 1, 137–139.

[29] Louv, W.C., and Littell, R.C. (1986), Combining one-sided binomial tests. *Journal of the American Statistical Association*, 81, 550–554.

[30] Monette, G. (1997), Is there a role for statisticians in pay equity? *Canadian Journal of Statistics*, 25, 293–319.

[31] Nesson, C.R. (1991), Incentives to spoliate evidence in civil litigation: the need for vigorous judicial actions. *Cardozo Law Review*, 13, 793–807.

[32] Paetzold, R.L. and Willborn, S.L. (1994), *The Statistics of Discrimination*. Colorado Springs: Shepard's/McGraw Hill.

[33] Paetzold, R.L. and Willborn, S.L. (1998), *Supplement to The Statistics of Discrimination*. Colorado Springs: Shepard's/McGraw Hill.

[34] Pennington, N. and Hastie, R. (1991), A cognitive theory of juror decision making: the story model. *Cardozo Law Review*, 13, 519–557.

[35] Rosenbaum, P.R. (1995), *Observational Studies*. New York: Springer.

[36] Rosenblum, M. (2000), On the evolution of analytic proof, statistics, and the use of experts in EEO litigation. (this volume).

[37] Sprent, P. (1998), *Data Driven Statistical Methods*. London: Chapman Hall.

[38] Strawderman, R.L. and Wells, M.T. (1998), Approximately exact inference for the common odds ratio in several 2×2 tables. *Journal of the American Statistical Association*, 93, 1294–1307.

[39] White, M.J. (1986), Segregation and diversity measures in population distribution. *Population Index*, 52, 198–221.

Statistical Consulting in the Legal Environment

Charles R. Mann

Abstract

This paper discusses characteristics of the legal environment as an arena in which a statistician might work. It is intended to help those who would like to know what they may be getting into before they agree to accept such an assignment.

Key words: court; courtroom; eighty percent rule; expert witness; four-fifths rule; forensic statistics; law; legal statistics; litigation; statistics; statistics profession; underutilization analysis; utilization analysis.

1 Introduction

One of the major lures of the statistical profession is the opportunity to explore and work in a variety of fields of application. Statisticians' consulting tends to cluster in certain academic environments with some few specialties absorbing them in greatest number. Biostatistics, agriculture, economics, engineering, and the social sciences are among the major such areas. The consulting statistician choosing a field in which to work may be influenced by a variety of factors including technical strengths and interests, personal preferences with respect to subject matter, the consulting environment, and the availability of work. The purpose of this paper is to identify and describe the characteristics of the legal environment to assist statisticians in deciding whether they consider it attractive.[1] By its nature, the material presented contains personal opinions and examples from the author's experience. It is hoped that they will be provocative as well as informative.

2 The Legal Arena

Perhaps the most important distinction of forensic statistics is that the work of the statistician is ultimately evaluated by nonstatisticians who may lack even a rudimentary knowledge of statistics except for that which they have obtained in the courtroom. So, after years of study and preparation, the statistician must be prepared to be judged not by his peers, but by members of the field of application in which work is being performed or even by laypersons serving as jurors. While some statisticians have argued that this should be changed to allow statisticians to

---

[1] More detailed and technical discussions of statistical aspects of litigation may be found, for example, in Fienberg (1989), Finkelstein and Levin (1990), and Gastwirth (1988).

define the rules, this appears to be an unlikely possibility. As a practical matter it is virtually unthinkable that either the courts or the populace would permit such an event. It must be kept in mind that if statistics were to take over the rule of law, then statisticians would be required to make judgments on nonstatistical matters. Why would the field of statistics, one among many scientific disciplines used within the legal system, be chosen for that unique role? Our legal system has evolved over centuries, is respected as among the best ever devised, and is not about to undergo such a change.

The heart of our legal system is the advocacy principle. In our courts of law, plaintiff and defendant are each represented by advocates who are expected to do their utmost to represent their clients' interests in the best light possible, subject to the condition that they not mislead the court, be it judge or jury. This is in strong contrast to the general scientific system, which calls for each researcher to seek truth about the (natural) laws that govern our existence. Of course, in both cases the ultimate goal is supposed to be the truth.

Working under this system adds additional burdens not usually associated with consulting in other fields. Not surprisingly, an adversarial relationship may develop between the statistician and opposing counsel. More surprisingly, an adversarial relationship may develop between the statistician and the opposing statistician. Most surprisingly, however, is that a form of adversarial relationship may develop between the consultant and the retaining attorneys (those by whom he has been hired). Although the interests of all parties are interrelated, they are not identical. For another discussion of the relationship between statistics and the law, see Meier 1986.

The attorneys seek to present their client's case. The statistician might like to present what he considers to be the best explanation and interpretation of the data, but is generally allowed to provide only that which counsel considers to be supportive of the client's cause. Under Federal Rule of Civil Procedure 26(a)(2)(B) the courtroom expert statistician is required[2] to have provided a signed written report containing "a complete statement of all opinions to be expressed and the basis and reasons therefore; the data or other information considered by the witness in forming the opinions; any exhibits to be used as a summary of or support for the opinions; the qualifications of the witness, including a list of all publications authored by the witness within the preceding ten years; the compensation to be paid for the study and testimony; and a listing of any other cases in which the witness has testified as an expert at trial or by deposition within the preceding four years." (It is worth noting that a statistician who insists on providing a report identifying all observations and conclusions, both supporting and opposing his client's interests, should expect to be replaced. There is ample opportunity through deposition and courtroom testimony for opposing counsel to elicit opinions favorable to

---

[2]Individual federal district courts may waive or modify this requirement.

their positions.) It is the statistician's responsibility to convincingly explain their methodology, logic, and conclusions to the court or jury, as opposed to simply proclaiming them as though they are too complex to be grasped by a layperson. It is also the statistician's responsibility to criticize the opposing expert's analysis and to explain the superiority of their own.

The interpersonal difficulties that arise appear to be due, at least in part, to a strong sense of caution that attorneys appear to bring to the table. Consultants, in turn, react in a variety of ways including an "I'll show them" attitude or a haughty "ivory tower" response. It is not surprising that neither of these succeeds very well.

To begin with, the rules by which any expert, including the statistician, must play are established and administered by legal experts and not by statisticians or scientists. A description of the overall process may be of help here.

Briefly, litigation begins with one party (the complainant or plaintiff) accusing another party (the defendant) of an illegal act and seeking redress. Both parties initially enter into a process known as "discovery" that involves requests for information (interrogatories) and requests for production of documents from each side. This may be an iterative process, but ultimately discovery is closed after a date set by the court. Plaintiffs may then argue their case in writing, possibly seeking a preliminary judgment or the establishment of a class of plaintiffs for whom the handling of the complaint as a single unit is efficient in terms of the time and efforts of the courts and the parties. Often the decision with respect to class certification makes use of statistical results. In any case, the plaintiffs initially identify their complaint, and the defendants respond to it by identifying flaws in the presentation or by proposing alternative explanations to those that would hold their clients responsible. It has often been my experience that whichever of the attorneys has spoken last is the one I tend to believe—at the moment. To the extent that the plaintiff's case is bolstered by statistical analysis of any form, it becomes incumbent upon the statistician working for the defense both to identify shortcomings of the original presentation and to develop alternative analyses supporting the client's position. Generally speaking, if for any reason they cannot or will not do both, they will be replaced.

It should be immediately clear as to how this process may lead to animosity between the opposing attorneys and statisticians. Ad hominem attacks are common, and unsupported assertions with regard to motivation are often made. The statistician is frequently an academic or former academic and as such is used to the respect accorded by students to a faculty member. He or she is not used to having to defend his positions, even (perhaps particularly) when they are not in his own field, and he often resents being asked to do so. Attorneys are well aware of this attitude and seek to exploit it by provoking the statistician into taking an overstated or otherwise embarrassing position. Consider the following quotation from a plaintiff's statistician's declaration (a report that is not produced under the pressures of immediacy or cross-examination). He had performed nine one-sample tests of proportions, corresponding to each of nine aggregations of broadly similar jobs,[3] each comparing the proportion of African-Americans to a known proportion that he believed identified the corresponding expectation. No additional explanatory factors such as education, specific occupation, or interest were taken into account in any way.

> The fact that there are significant differences in seven of the nine EEO-1 Categories indicates these inferences cannot be attributed to chance and *can only be attributed to [Defendant's] systematic discriminatory employment practices* [emphasis added].

The causality conclusion is not merely overstated. It is completely without basis, since no attempt was made to eliminate any explanatory variable beyond EEO-1 category and geographic recruitment area. Consider the following from Kendall and Stuart 1961, p. 279: *"[S]tatistical relationship, of whatever kind, cannot logically imply causation."*

The effect of such hyperbole is a strong reaction from both opposing counsel and opposing statistician. The reputation of the plaintiff's expert is certain to be attacked.

The forum for the initial examination of the statistician's efforts and opinions is the "deposition." Here the testifying expert is questioned by opposing counsel concerning any reports produced, analyses done, or relevant opinions held. It should be noted that although the attorney for whom the statistician is working "defends" the deposition, that attorney is representing the client and not the expert. As a rule, experts appear without counsel and have the added burden of looking after their own interests.

The purpose of the deposition is to allow the opposing counsel to learn whatever it can about the statistician's conclusions, methodology, beliefs, technical experience, consulting experience, testifying experience, oral abilities, style, and temperament. Depositions are taken under oath, and individuals working in this field may find excerpts of decades-old depositions being read back to them in connection with a current matter.[4] While the same is true of old papers or speeches, there is usually an opportunity to edit them prior to publication. Deposition testimony is, of course, spontaneous and cannot be easily retracted, although the deponent is allowed to attach corrections and supplemental statements on an errata sheet.

Another problem is that counsel may request the statistician not to prepare a written report initially. A defense counsel may want to have his consultant wait until

---

[3]The nine aggregations were the EEO-1 categories as defined by the U.S. Equal Employment Opportunity Commission: Officials and Managers, Professionals, Technicians, Sales Workers, Office and Clerical, Craft Workers, Operatives, Laborers, and Service Workers.

[4]Reports may also be provided in a sworn format. Affidavits and declarations may state, among other things, that they are being presented subject to the penalties of perjury.

plaintiff's report is received and then address only the issues raised in that report. On the other hand, plaintiff's counsel may prefer to delay providing a report so that defense counsel's consultant has minimal time to prepare a response. Attorneys are not always successful in protecting, as privileged, the work of the consultant. The importance of this is that if the statistician prepares a report in violation of counsel's instructions, this work may be revealed during the discovery process and may do harm to the client's position.

3   The Role of the Statistician

Statisticians may argue that as professionals they are obligated to provide an unbiased report, one that they could submit regardless of who retained them. This is not only inappropriate under our legal system, it may not even be desirable. The advocacy system, as will be discussed below, has evolved other means for attorneys to take responsibility for handling this problem. The statistician must respect the concept that representation of the client's interests is in the hands of the attorney.

It is rare, however, that statistical methodology itself is attacked by an attorney. That is not their field of expertise, and they are aware that their limited knowledge may make them appear unprepared or even foolish to the court or the jury. Instead, the attorney generally focuses on the statistician's underlying assumptions. Even the most basic of modeling assumptions can give rise to a string of questions that make the opposing statistician's results appear questionable at least. For example, when an eminent statistician was goaded into averring that he knew the workings of a federal personnel system because he paid his federal taxes each year, the court ignored whatever else he had to say. The rest of his presentation was not considered credible.

Ultimately, assuming that the case is not settled out of court, there will be a trial. Various legal television dramas notwithstanding, efforts are usually made to avoid surprises. Each side is generally knowledgeable of the people providing evidence and testimony for their opponents and the positions those people are taking. It is here, for the first time, that the statistician consultant is proposed to the court as an expert in a particular field of knowledge. For the statistician it may be statistics, statistics as applied to a particular field of law, probability, data processing, a specialty area such as sampling, or any combination of these and similar relevant areas.

The court is usually presented the statistician's résumé by retaining counsel and asked to qualify the individual as an expert witness in a specified area. Failure to qualify is considered a black mark, and so most consultants who testify regularly as expert witnesses do not allow themselves to be proposed as an expert in a field in which they do not feel qualified. Qualification itself, however, does not mean that the proposed individual must be an expert in the usual sense. It means only that the individual has specialized knowledge that would be of use to the court. I have seen graduate students and, on one occasion, an undergraduate sociology major qualify. Similarly, I have seen individuals with degrees in economics, engineering, psychology, and other fields in which statistics is applied qualified as "experts" in statistics. These can make particularly easy targets for opposing counsel, especially with the assistance of a statistician who can identify technical weaknesses.

One problem with frequently working as an expert witness is that over time one gives a large number of explanations of concepts, sometimes from the defendant's point of view and sometimes from that of the plaintiff. The expert must be willing to stand behind all previous testimony simultaneously—or have a good explanation for any apparent inconsistency. When one testifies in a particular case, one effectively provides testimony for all future cases as well.

In one instance when I was testifying, opposing counsel read to the court a paragraph concerning limitations of the use of statistics in legal matters. His question was whether I endorsed the points made. My response, that I not only agreed with them but thought they were well said, was greeted with what appeared to be a strange reaction. Only later in the day, when I was actually shown the book and asked to comment on another point from it, did I realize that I had authored the material first read to me. The point here is that opposing counsel had gone to the trouble of finding a minor publication at least partly in the hope that I would damage my position by commenting unfavorably. Sworn testimony is not an area in which one can allow professional judgments to differ based on the client or the case.

In fact, I have long been an advocate of the idea that two statisticians working on opposing sides of a case should be able to agree with respect to the statistical implications and conclusions subject to any specific set of assumptions. This would leave it to the attorneys and the statisticians to argue to the courts which assumptions should be considered appropriate and thus to know which agreed-upon statistical inferences are appropriate. The assumptions themselves often have a stronger legal component than a statistical one, which is another justification for the legal structure to take precedence over the statistical. As a corollary, I also believe that it is to the advantage of one's client that the opposing statistician be of high quality. Sometimes, the biggest problem in a courtroom presentation is providing proof of a relatively simple or obvious point.

Consider an example case in which the opposing statistician (actually an economist, chair of a department at a prestigious university) confused the tail probability of a nonstandard normal density function with its functional value. He presented page after page of absurdly small tabled numbers, claiming statistical significance at the levels identified.[5] It would have been no surprise to see a jury, presented with conflicting discussions of probability density functions and tail probabilities, to throw their hands up and dismiss all of statistics as incomprehensible and irrelevant. Had he been a reasonably good statistician the distraction

---

[5] As an illustrative example, consider the number of minorities hired to have a binomial distribution with $n = 100$ and $p = .1$ and assume that 2 minorities are selected. The standardized z value (not corrected for continuity) is -2.67 corresponding to a one-tail probability of .00383. The corresponding height of the density function at -2.67 is .000003.

would never have arisen. (Oddly enough the economist attempted to justify his conclusions by pointing out instances in which results were statistically significant regardless of which number was presented.)

A final and most interesting point on courtroom presentation is that it is presented under the familiar oath to tell "the truth, the whole truth, and nothing but the truth", but the meaning of this is not as obvious as it would seem. There actually should be a qualification to this of the form "in response to the question asked of you by counsel for either side or by the court." The expert witness is not generally given the opportunity to present all efforts and conclusions in full. Rather, he or she is required to respond to questions. Of course, the attorneys are free to ask broad questions permitting discursive answers, but they rarely do so. They prefer to maintain control over the details of the presentation. At first glance this might seem to put the statistician (or other expert) in an unprofessional position. It must be noted, however, that the rules governing this process have been worked out in detail, are familiar to all attorneys, and are under the control of the judge. Decisions such as what information is relevant (already possibly departing from the whole truth) are made by lawyers and judges, not by the statistician. The expert is only one of the tools relied upon by the legal system. Attorneys do sometimes ask for all conclusions reached, but as a practical matter, this is still generally done using a line of questions, each requiring a relatively short answer rather than as a request for the expert to provide a lengthy presentation. In most cases, when counsel hears that for which they have been waiting, the subject is changed.

Of course, opposing counsel can always reopen this subject on cross-examination, but one of the basic rules of examining a witness is that counsel should not ask a question without knowing what answer will be given. As much as this is an old saw, I have seen its violation work against the questioner often enough to understand why it is followed.

A related consequence of the adversarial system is that expert witnesses must watch out for their own interests. Except for the occasional long-term relationship, neither retaining counsel nor opposing counsel has much interest in the expert's future. Each has primary responsibility to their clients. The expert who, for example, wants to make a specific point cannot assume that counsel will offer an appropriate question. The point should be made at an appropriate moment or it may not be made at all.

It should also be remembered that one of the tools available to the opposing counsel is the deposition, in which he is able to learn the expert's opinions and reasoning prior to trial. This serves to avoid surprises for the questioner.

4 Testifying Expert v. Consulting Expert

Another aspect of the legal system as it relates to expert witnesses is that they can play two quite different roles. In recent years there has been an increased use of two experts by the same side, particularly for the defense. One is the "testifying expert" who plays the role we have been discussing. The testifying expert writes a report, is made available to the opposition to be deposed, and makes the courtroom presentations, the traditional role of the expert witness.

The other type of expert is the "consulting expert." This is a person who is not intended to make a courtroom presentation. Opposing counsel does not have the right to take their deposition or learn their opinions or results. Generally, the two experts are kept apart by counsel. Indeed, the testifying expert may never know whether a consulting expert has been retained. One of the common reasons for having two such experts is that the consulting expert may have a long-term relationship with the company and may be knowledgeable of activities not relevant to the case. They may have had conversations with senior executives or other workers who provided them with information that counsel does not consider proper or desirable to present in court. If he is not allowed on the witness stand, he will not be able to contradict counsel's position.

When statisticians first learn of this aspect of the legal process it may appear to be unfair, unprofessional, and unethical. Some statisticians have argued that statisticians should not participate in such a system. As indicated above, we may choose to participate or not, but it is unlikely that we are going to change it. Does that mean that we are forced to act in an unethical manner in order to participate in the legal system as described? I do not consider this to be the case.

In the first place, the concept of unethical suggests deceitful, dishonest, illegal or in some other way unfair behavior. Since all parties are aware of the rules and since opposing counsel has the right to make any inquiries whatever about the opinions and work of the testifying expert, it seems that no question exists concerning that individual's actions. Statisticians should not be faulted for following the rules of the legal system. The testifying experts are, of course, still responsible for their own ethical behavior and competence within that system as are the consulting statisticians in their relationships.

Consider a case in which testifying experts have been provided with issues or claims to investigate. They are not only free to request from retaining counsel any information they deem potentially relevant, they have an ethical obligation to make such a request. They should also ask whether there are consulting experts, and if so, what the consulting expert found. They should attempt to obtain the totality of relevant data with respect to the issue under consideration. In fact, I would argue that they are ethically responsible for inquiring about any information that might be relevant to the tasks with which they have been charged. Testifying experts are often asked by opposing counsel whether there is any information they would have liked to have had that was not provided to them. It is the responsibility of the testifying expert to ask the proper questions, request the appropriate information; be able to explain why use was not made of information that was provided, and to be able to explain why other information that might be considered relevant was not requested.

In other words, testifying statisticians must be prepared to take the stand and state that they would have liked to have analyzed specific data, but could not do so because counsel told them that it did not exist or because counsel said that they did not want such an analysis performed or because counsel simply refused to provide it without explanation. In any case, testifying experts must also be prepared to pass along whatever explanations have been provided to them and whatever limitations were put on their work. Of course, this should have been made clear to retaining counsel when the basic terms of their relationship were agreed upon.

The testifying expert who states that relevant information was not requested will look at least foolish, if not biased. Attorneys will have to take this into account in working with the testifying expert, but as officers of the court they are also under an obligation to follow the ethical positions of their own profession.

The give and take described above appears to allow the statistician greater control of the proceeding than it might have seemed at first. The reason for this is that the statistician is not an advocate for either side, but is, rather, an advocate of proper and ethical statistical analysis.

Other questions of ethical behavior will be discussed in what follows. It is important that the reader consider the distinction between failing to provide good quality statistical analysis and failing to provide ethical statistical analysis. Perhaps the most important aspect of the distinction is whether the audience is misled intentionally or by incompetence. One question that should arise in the mind of a statistician considering working in the legal field is what happens if their analysis does not produce the results that retaining counsel and client would like. Remembering the advocacy principle, the answer is that if timing permits, you will in all likelihood be replaced. To the extent that your analysis is proper and thorough, this should not be a professional concern. Regrettably, many attorneys act as if they believe that they will eventually find a statistician to defend whatever position they have taken. More regrettably, they may often be correct. A word of warning here: Attorneys may seek to use statisticians without litigation experience in the hope that they may be more likely to be intimidated and somewhat blindly responsive to counsel's requests than are statisticians with extensive courtroom experience.

5 A Real-Life Scenario Regarding Ethical Considerations

Assume that there is a quantitative procedure that has been developed by regulatory agencies and accepted by the courts. Further, assume that the procedure is not statistically sound and also that plaintiff's statistician applies the procedure incorrectly, concluding, as retaining counsel would like, that there is reason to believe at the .05 level of significance that the percentage of women in a particular portion of the defendant's workforce is below what it should be based on an estimated availability rate agreed upon by both sides. (A reminder: This is being presented to explore ethical considerations; modifications of the assumptions or alternative definitions of the issue are not of interest here.)

In this scenario, you have been requested to serve as the defendant's expert witness and you are asked to review the opposing statistician's report. You note the error made and indicate that, had the analysis been performed correctly, the results would have been favorable to the defense instead of to the plaintiff, as was the plaintiff's expert's position. You also note, however, that you do not consider the procedure he used appropriate for the issue at hand. In fact, you identify a standard statistical procedure that you do consider appropriate.

Consider first what you would do if you were told to perform no further analysis. Should you accept this instruction or not? Is it unethical to stop work? In accordance with the discussion above, I would answer "no." Moreover, why should the client pay for further analysis that counsel believes is not needed for presentation of the case? In fact, it may violate your agreement with your client for you to continue without permission. Is having such an agreement unethical? Again, I would say no because of opposing counsel's ability to inquire about your reasons and any restrictions placed on your work. The testifying expert is commonly required to provide a copy of the retention agreement to opposing counsel.

Alternatively, suppose you are allowed to analyze the data using the methodology you believe is correct and you obtain results that are in agreement with the opposing statistician's original, but in your mind inappropriately obtained, conclusions. You are then asked by retaining counsel to provide a report that will criticize your opponent's analysis, but not describe the additional work you performed. More specifically you are asked to demonstrate the impropriety of his analysis, but not permitted to discuss whether you ultimately agree with his conclusion or not. Would acceding to this request be unethical?

The product requested of you will be presented in a hearing being held to determine whether the case should be allowed to continue or be dismissed. The question is whether your acquiescence would be professionally unethical. On the one hand, it can be argued that you are failing to identify your true belief regarding the situation. You are criticizing a conclusion because of how it was determined, not because you consider it to be incorrect. On the other hand, you are not saying that the conclusion is false, only that it has not been properly justified by the opposing statistician (even though you believe that you have justified it properly).

I suggest that the resolution of the problem lies in the forum. Under the procedures followed, opposing counsel may ask you in deposition, prior to the hearing, what you object to in your opponent's analysis, what you believe should have been done differently, whether you actually did what you are proposing, what results you obtained, and what your conclusion is with respect to the actual issue as opposed to your opponent's methodologies. They may also, of course, benefit from the guidance of their experts and the response of their experts to your criticisms. Finally, you may warn your client and retaining counsel that you will reveal the additional information as to what you did and what conclusions you have formed given any opportunity to do so. They are then in a position to make an informed decision as to how to proceed.

I have discussed the above with a variety of statisticians and in my mind have found that those who are involved professionally in courtroom work generally find the resolution described satisfactory, and those who are not, disagree.

I suggest that the difference is that the former group has come to terms with the idea that the statistician is working in the legal arena, not in a statistical arena. As professionals, statisticians want to provide truth, but as a participants in legal proceedings the forensic statisticians recognize that determination of the methodology of how truth is to be shown is not up to them. It is in the purview of the court. In civil matters, it is the burden of the plaintiff to prove his case. It is not the obligation of the defense to prove the plaintiff's case. Thus, if plaintiff fails to properly demonstrate his conclusion, defendant does not have to concede the point. The concept again is that two skilled adversaries will, in fact, arrive at the truth, and in the example above all the means are there to do so. In a sense, the only question to be resolved is whose rules will be used for the purpose. Society has clearly chosen those of the law.

6   Positive Aspects of Working in the Legal Arena

At this point the reader may be thinking that with all the unpleasantries of the adversary system, with all the detail associated with justifying the analyses performed, and with all the complications associated in working in a field with its own rules and, in some sense, minimal respect for others, why would anyone choose to work as a statistician in the legal environment?

The answer, of course, is that there is a variety of positive factors that have not received proper emphasis. Different individuals will accord differing weights to these considerations. My own views will now be presented.

To begin with, I believe that among the most important reasons for working in legal statistics is that attorneys are bright! In particular, the attorneys involved in major complex litigation are bright in the sense of their logical analysis of the situations at hand. More specifically, they are bright in a way that statisticians, with strong mathematical backgrounds, respect. I have at various times consulted with professors, businessmen, and researchers in a large number of diverse fields. My opinion is that in the aggregate, no other group is as logical and thorough in their work as are attorneys. Making use of the statistician is just one of a host of complex tasks they must perform in litigation, and yet they quickly learn well the underlying philosophy and concepts of statistics.

We are all familiar with the common reaction we get when we tell a stranger that we are statisticians. Attorneys make the standard comments about never having been good in mathematics, or not being able to handle numbers, or saying that they never could understand, no less make use of, all those formulae. They then proceed to develop and demonstrate an understanding of statistical concepts that surpasses that which might be demonstrated by a student with years of formal academic study in the field. It is my belief that the reason for this is the common underpinning of logic. The attorney reasons through problems in the same way, using the same logical methodologies, as does the statistician in developing proofs. The main differences are simply subject matter and notation.

As a simple example, a trial results in a verdict of guilty or a verdict of not guilty, and a statistical test of hypothesis results in rejection of the null hypothesis or failure to reject the null hypothesis. It takes no effort to explain to attorneys that the statistician has not proved the null hypothesis just because it has not been rejected. They understand that failure to find guilt is not the same as finding innocence.

The attorney understands that there are differing levels of proof corresponding to the choice of a level of significance because in his own work the degree of proof is substantially different in a criminal proceeding (beyond a reasonable doubt) than in a civil case (preponderance of the evidence). In designing analyses and evaluating data, the attorneys often form insights before the statisticians. They will not know what formula to use, but they are capable of spotting erroneous conclusions.

In addition to being bright, attorneys at the level of working with statistical consultants are hard-working. Evening, weekend, and even late-night hours are common. This may sound like a detriment to working with them, but in practice it is an indicator of their intensity. It is rewarding to work in such an atmosphere.

Another positive point in working with attorneys is the opportunity to participate in strategic issues. Getting to devise and analyze strategic issues adds a level of gamesmanship that makes the required efforts enjoyable in the same sense as do ordinary puzzles and games. The difference between the strategic issues and the statistical issues is that the latter are those that are routinely performed by the statistician using his substantial specific education, whereas the former are generally broader in that they make use of more general aspects of intelligence and logic.

An advantage to the entrepreneurial statistician is the magnitude of the efforts that are requested. With relatively rare exceptions, the statistician is able to provide the necessary consulting efforts as an individual. Programming and clerical support may justify additional staff, but the statistical tasks to be performed are generally within the scope of an individual. The great majority of efforts last between a few weeks and a few years. Thus, statisticians can see their efforts through to their ultimate impact. Even in the rare instance when a case lingers for exceptionally long periods, even for decades, it is possible for the same statistician to be involved throughout.

In addition, other benefits of working on legal matters include the importance of the work, its impact on society, and the opportunity to see immediate implementation of our statistical results. Here, the statistician works on matters that will affect society in a real and observable way. Our efforts permit the courts to quantify issues such as the existence and amount of damage done to an individual or class of individuals. When the courts seek to meet their goal of making these individuals whole, we provide the means to determine what that will require.

Finally, it would be disingenuous not to mention that legal statistics is a relatively highly paid field. It must be remembered, however, that in addition to the stresses resulting from the adversarial system, the time demands are unique. The statistician is literally on call for the lawyers at all times. Because we are merely one among many tools being used simultaneously, we may not be kept informed of deadlines or of their revision. On many occasions I have worked through a night only to find that the court had granted a postponement of which we were not informed. One learns to try to anticipate and confirm such developments, but it is not always possible.

The issues involved in forensic statistics go beyond the mechanics. The underlying concepts of statistical matters are often brought to light in a new manner requiring more than mathematics to resolve. Examples may help to demonstrate the points made above.

7   Examples of the Application of Statistical Reasoning

Consider the following relatively simple and noncontentious finding. A court has determined that regression analyses based on the available data are sufficient to determine that African-Americans have been paid less than would have been expected given their characteristics and the salary structure of Caucasians. The statisticians have ultimately agreed on the data and have developed a salary model for Caucasians that is satisfactory to all concerned. Further, the court wishes to remedy the situation, at least in part, by compensating the individual African-Americans for what they should have received, but did not. It is agreed that the Caucasian model will be used to determine an expectation for each African-American and that the difference between that expectation and the actual salary will be the basis of the distribution.[6] Suppose that the total of all such differences is $4,000,000 because African-Americans who earned less than expected did so by a total of $5,000,000 and the total for those who earned more than expected was $1,000,000.

Ignoring all complications such as interest and compensatory damages, what amount should the class receive? Here, I would expect the court to offset the earnings that were higher than expected and distribute a total of $4,000,000. But, how should this be distributed to the members of the class? Should African-Americans earning more than their expected salaries receive any award? Should they receive a larger award because they are earning more than corresponding Caucasians even though they are functioning in an admittedly (by this point) discriminatory system? Should all African-Americans receive the same amount because all suffered the indignities associated with discrimination and it has not been shown that they have been disadvantaged differently? Should the amount of time they were employed (presumably, the amount of time they endured the negative atmosphere) be taken

---

[6]This may be identified as a Peters–Belson procedure such as discussed in Cochran and Rubin (1973), Peters (1941), Belson (1956), and Gastwirth (1989). A detailed example is presented in Gastwirth and Greenhouse (1995).

into account beyond its inclusion in the back-pay model? It is not the statistician's job to make this decision. Nevertheless, because of his quantitative orientation and skills it is commonly his job to devise such alternative procedures, to present their assumptions and justifications, and to implement the ultimate decision. In practice, a form of each of these and various permutations of them have all actually been implemented. See, for example, the settlement agreement filed in *Roberts v. Texaco* (1997).

8 Examples of Statistical Issues

At this point it appears worthwhile to provide examples of statistical methodology having a major impact on the conduct of litigation. In order to make insights available to a wide range of statisticians, these are based on relatively simple statistical issues. In actual practice, consideration is often given to the difficulty of explaining a concept to a jury. Counsel may choose to offer a simpler point that a court or a jury will grasp rather than a more sophisticated argument that they may ignore.

The first example involves a procedure known as the "eighty percent rule" or "$\frac{4}{5}$ rule." This term encompasses a variety of procedures based on similar, but differing, definitions. According to "legend," the rule was initially developed by a group of California industrial psychologists who were advising a federal agency as to when the results of a selection device should be looked into in detail to determine whether they were having an adverse impact on minority or female applicants. The original procedure actually included provision for traditional statistical analysis, but the procedures that have evolved in the courtroom tend to be simpler. For our purpose we will consider the rule to say that a selection device has adverse impact against, say, nonwhites, if the "pass rate" for nonwhites is less than 80% of the pass rate for whites.[7] The term "pass rate" here may mean either the rate at which the applicant has demonstrated sufficient knowledge to be able to perform in the position applied for as judged by the test developers, or the actual rate of selection for the job. (The reason for the ambiguity is that if there are a large number of test takers there may be too few positions to provide jobs to all that achieve the passing score. If selection is made in decreasing order of score, then there may be adverse impact with regard to who gets positions even if all applicants pass the test.) Remaining complications will not be discussed here in detail.

Supposedly, based on their knowledge of the number of test takers for whom data was available for the types of tests at issue, the psychologists decided on the 80% ratio as that which would be meaningful. It is crucial to note, however, that

---

[7]The original procedure also used the highest-scoring group as the basis for comparison. This appears to have been abandoned for two reasons: the statistical complications caused by failing to predetermine the comparison groups and the fact that the best-scoring group frequently consisted of a small number of Asian-Americans.

while such a standard is properly established by nonstatisticians, the methodology for determining whether the standard has been met should satisfy the standards of proper statistical analysis. Rather than utilize a statistical hypothesis test to test a null hypothesis that the pass ratio is at least .8 against the alternative hypothesis that it is less than .8, the procedure immediately became to make a decision based on the empirical results and not on the probability structure. Thus, even for a fixed sample size, levels of neither Type I nor Type II error were specified.[8] The four-fifths rule as written for employment selection may be found in *The Uniform Guidelines on Employee Selection Procedures* (1978).[9]

This has led to many decisions that appear absurd. Consider the simplest situation. One out of one hundred white test-takers passes. Neither of two non-white test takers passes. The adverse impact ratio is $0/.01 = 0$, which is less than .8. It took years for the federal agency to acknowledge that this was an inappropriate conclusion, and they still request that it be carried out as described. (They now commonly concede, when confronted, that if the shortfall is less than a whole person, it may be ignored.) On the other hand, however, when the number of test takers is large, they do not permit the use of the 80% rule. This is, of course, the circumstance under which the 80% rule would favor the employer because achieving the 80% figure is more likely than failing to obtain statistical significance when testing equality of the proportions. Differences of little practical significance might still correspond to statistical significance.

Note that given the numbers of test takers and fixing the pass rate of whites (usually the larger group) as equal to its empirical value (or as known from previous applications), the critical region is established, and the statistician can compute the power curve associated with the 80% rule. In particular, the size of the Type I error probability can be calculated. It is interesting to confront social scientists, who generally advocate use of the .05 level of statistical significance, with the dilemma posed by use of the 80% rule, which in real-world applications often corresponds to substantially higher Type I error levels for small sample sizes. (Where sample sizes are sufficiently large, Type I error levels may be substantially smaller than .05, but the enforcement agency, the Office of Federal Contract Compliance Programs (OFCCP), does not permit the 80% rule to be used in this situation without the additional requirement of a traditional test of significance.)

While some of the implications of use of the 80% rule as fully defined ease the concerns of the rule as it is practically applied, the current impact, decades after its development, still frequently leads to statistically unsubstantiated conclusions. Further, the reader may want to note that even given the great simplicity of the issue as stated here, courts still seem to give great deference to the 80% rule. See the discussion of *Boston Police Superior Officers Federation v. City of Boston* in

---

[8]One version of the origin of the original 80% rule says that the figure 80% was arrived at by attempting to obtain a "reasonable" Type I error probability for a "typical number of test takers."

[9]Federal Register, vol. 43, 38295-38309 (1978).

Seymour and Brown 1999. For early criticisms of the four-fifths rule see Greenberg 1979 and Boardman 1979.

A similar situation arises in connection with development of an estimated availability rate as discussed above. Department of Labor regulations[10] require the consideration of at least eight specific factors in estimating the availability rate of minorities and women for each job group.[11] In the early 1970s a federal monitoring agency developed a form to be used to estimate an availability rate using these factors. The eight factors as stated for minorities (numbered as in the regulation)[12] are (i) the minority population of the labor area surrounding the facility; (ii) the size of the minority unemployment force in the labor area surrounding the facility; (iii) the percentage of the minority work force as compared with the total work force in the immediate labor area; (iv) the general availability of minorities having requisite skills in the immediate labor area; (v) the availability of minorities having requisite skills in an area in which the contractor can reasonably recruit; (vi) the availability of promotable and transferable minorities within the contractor's organization; (vii) the existence of training institutions capable of training persons in the requisite skills; and (viii) the degree of training that the contractor is reasonably able to undertake as a means of making all job classes available to minorities.

In order to construct a weighted average, one must obtain or assign a weight and a rate to each of (at least) the eight factors. It has never been formally conceded that implementation of the regulations need not require such a weighted average, but that is a legal matter and not a statistical issue. Fortunately, it was conceded after years of discussion that it was not necessary for each factor to have a weight greater than zero. Thus, one could "consider" factor (i) by dismissing it as irrelevant for positions with specific requisite skills. Similarly, of what value is factor (ii) if taken literally? Even considering the more consistent measure, the proportion of minorities among the unemployed in the immediate labor area is of no relevance without considering at least the proportion of unemployed in the job group of interest and the appropriateness of the immediate labor area. What information is there in the overall unemployment data about the availability of minorities for, say, mechanical engineering positions? This seemingly simple regulation has been involved in disagreements between the regulated companies and the regulators for years. A major reason for this is that the government endorsed, and regulated companies (government contractors) tried to use, a rubric that, while it would have been appropriate for considering applicants from a true

---

[10]41 CFR 60-2.11

[11]Defined in 41 CFR 60-2.11 by "('job groups' herein meaning one or a group of jobs having similar content, wage rates and opportunities)."

[12]Minority and female factors are numbered differently, and the first factor for minorities is replaced by the fifth factor for women: the availability of women seeking employment in the labor or recruitment area of the contractor. This takes into account the reality that women are more likely than men to opt out of the labor force.

partition[13] (mutually exclusive, disjoint sets) of sources, was in effect based on the use of meaningless weighted averages of incommensurate numbers. Because of their quantitative abilities, statisticians are again often the most able to identify why there are conflicts.

Further, consider such a situation in which an estimated availability rate (EAR) for minorities has been agreed upon. The regulations then require the contractor to determine whether each of its job groups is underutilized where, " 'Underutilization' is defined as having fewer minorities or women in a particular job group than would reasonably be expected by their availability." Interestingly, and due in part to the specific use of the term "reasonably be expected," this has become an issue with which statisticians have been involved since the regulation went into effect. To demonstrate the most interesting aspect of what has become a conflict between statistics and bureaucracy, both agree that given the size of a job group, its number of minority (or female) incumbents, and a corresponding EAR, the appropriate statistical test to determine whether underutilization exists when the size of the group is sufficiently large is the normal approximation to the binomial distribution. (Even so, there is also a conflict with respect to whether that test should be of a one-tail or two-tail form.) And yet, when the size of the group is small (defined to be less than a calculated number[14] based on the EAR, which turns out to be at least 37), the OFCCP argues that the binomial distribution is inappropriate. What do they recommend in its place? Most often, the eighty percent rule discussed above! For further discussion see the author's "underutilization" entry in Kotz and Johnson (1988).

9 Summary

This article attempts to demonstrate that the legal arena is an unusually difficult forum in which to work. This is a consequence of the amount of control that statistics and scientific disciplines have to defer to the legal profession. Nevertheless, it is a rewarding area. The applications are real and immediate, and it provides opportunity to quantify complex issues. It also has raised methodological questions that have led to the development of new techniques and provided interesting data sets for the application of statistical methodology. It is an evolving field in which the statistician may still have a major and important role.

---

[13]Clearly neither set of 8 factors forms a partition since, for example, the "immediate labor area" is a subset of the "area in which the contractor can reasonably recruit"; the minority "unemployment force" is a subset of the minority "population"; and the female "unemployment force" is a subset of the females "seeking employment."

[14]The calculation procedure is known as "the rule of nines." It requires $n \times p \times (1 - p) > 9$, or a sample size greater than $9/(p \times (1 - p))$, where p is the EAR, for use of the normal approximation to the binomial distribution. Thus, the smallest acceptable sample size (corresponding to $p = .5$) is 37, and the minimum acceptable sample size for $p = .1$ is 101.

10 Cases Cited

Boston Police Superior Officers Federation v. City of Boston, 147 F.3d 13, 21 (1st Cir.1998).
Roberts v. Texaco, Inc. Case No. 94 Civ. 2015 (S.D.N.Y. 1997).

REFERENCES

[1] Belson, W.A. (1956), A technique for studying the effects of a television broadcast, *Applied Statistics*, 195–202.

[2] Boardman, A.E. (1979), Another analysis of the EEOC "four-fifths" rule, *Management Science*, 25, 770–776.

[3] Cochran, W.C. and Rubin, D.B. (1973), Controlling bias in observational studies: A Review, *Sankhya A*, 35(4), 417–446.

[4] Fienberg, S.E. (Ed.) (1989), *The Evolving Role of Statistical Assessments in the Courts*. New York: Springer.

[5] Finkelstein, M.O. and Levin, B. (1990), *Statistics for Lawyers*, New York: Springer.

[6] Gastwirth, J.L.(1988), *Statistical Reasoning in Law and Public Policy*. Orlando: Academic Press.

[7] Gastwirth, J.L. (1989), A clarification of some statistical issues in *Watson v. Fort Worth Bank and Trust, Jurimetrics*, 29, 267–284.

[8] Gastwirth, J.L. and Greenhouse, S.W. (1995), Biostatistical concepts and methods in the legal setting, *Statistics in Medicine*, 14, 1641–1653.

[9] Greenberg, I. (1979), An analysis of the EEOC "four-fifths rule", *Management Science* 25, 762–769.

[10] Kendall, M.G. and Stuart, A. (1961), *The Advanced Theory of Statistics*, Vol. 2, p. 279, London: Griffin.

[11] Kotz, S. and Johnson, N.L. (1988), *Encyclopedia of Statistical Sciences*, Vol. 9, New York: Wiley-Interscience.

[12] Meier, P. (1986), Damned Liars and Expert Witnesses, *Journal of the American Statistical Association*, 81, 269–276.

[13] Peters, C.C. (1941), A method of matching groups for experiment with no loss of population, *Journal of Educational Research*, 34, 606–61.

[14] Seymour, R.T. and Brown, B.B. (1999), *Equal Employment Law Update Fall 1998 Edition*, Washington, D.C.: BNA Books.

Epidemiological Causation in the Legal Context: Substance and Procedures

Sana Loue

Abstract

Reliance on epidemiological evidence has become increasingly common in a number of contexts. These include toxic torts, where injury is alleged to have resulted from exposure to a specific substance or product; personal injury, where one individual may seek to recover damages from another for infecting him or her with a disease; the regulation of medical products and devices; and the prosecution of an individual for conduct allegedly resulting in the transmission of a fatal disease to another. However, law and epidemiology differ significantly in their goals and in their investigative processes. This chapter discusses the use of epidemiological evidence in the context of toxic torts, focusing on epidemiological and legal principles of causation, legal procedures for establishing causation, and legal standards for the use of epidemiological evidence.

Key Words: causation, evidence, discovery, study design

1 Introduction

Reliance on epidemiological evidence has become increasingly common in various legal contexts. Toxic tort cases, in which injury is alleged to have resulted from exposure to a specific substance or product, such as Bendectin, Agent Orange, tobacco, tampons, and silicone breast implants, constitute one of the most common settings for the use of epidemiological evidence (*In re Agent Orange Products Liability Litigation*, 1984; *Kehm v. Procter and Gamble Manufacturing Company*, 1983; Fitzpatrick and Shainwald, 1996; Glantz, Slade, Bero, Hanauer, and Barnes, 1996; Sanders, 1992; Schuck, 1987).

Epidemiological evidence may also prove critical in the context of regulatory, criminal, and other civil matters. In a regulatory context, for instance, the Food and Drug Administration (FDA) relied on epidemiological studies indicating an association between aspirin use and Reye's syndrome as the basis for requiring a warning label on aspirin containers (Novick, 1987; Schwartz, 1988). Currently, the FDA is relying on epidemiological data as the basis for seeking stricter controls on the sale and distribution of tobacco products. In a criminal context, epidemiological evidence may be required in cases in which a defendant is accused of attempting to harm another individual by infecting him or her with a particular disease, such as human immunodeficiency virus (HIV). Civil lawsuits may focus on an individual's attempt to recover damages from another for infecting him or her with a disease, such as herpes; an action to involuntarily quarantine an individual who has active tuberculosis but is not following the prescribed regimen; or an action by a community to force a corporation to comply with air or water quality standards that have been established by regulation.

This chapter focuses on the use of epidemiological evidence in the context of toxic torts. The chapter discusses principles of causation in both a scientific and a legal context. Standards for the use of epidemiological evidence are reviewed, as well as the legal procedures available for establishing causation.

2   Epidemiology and Law: Divergent Purposes

An understanding of the use of epidemiology in the litigation context requires an understanding of the different processes and goals inherent in the legal and scientific spheres. As Justice Harry Blackmun observed:

> It is true that open debate is an essential part of both legal and scientific analyses. Yet there are important differences between the quest for truth in the courtroom and the quest for truth in the laboratory. Scientific conclusions are subject to perpetual revision. Law, on the other hand, must resolve disputes finally and quickly (*Daubert*, 1993: 113 S.Ct. at 2798).

Additionally, epidemiology is concerned with the quest for truth on a population level and seeks to explain disease occurrence and prevention on a population level. In the context of litigation, such as actions to recover damages for injuries alleged to have arisen due to exposure to specific products or substances, law is concerned with truth on an individual level, and seeks a determination as to whether the disease or condition at issue in a specific individual is attributable to a specific cause or factor. This dissonance in both purpose and perspective creates a tension between the two disciplines that is perhaps most apparent in their approach to an evaluation and a determination of causation.

3   Causation in Epidemiology

3.1   The Operationalization of Causation

Various models of causation have been used in the context of epidemiological research. Pure determinism has as its foundation the specificity of both cause and effect: A specific factor constitutes the one and only cause of a specific disease or condition, i.e., the factor is both necessary and sufficient to produce the disease or condition (Kleinbaum, Kupper, and Morgenstern, 1982). Koch's enunciation of the postulates underlying pure determinism hold, in essence, that the organism of interest (the exposure) must be found in all cases of disease; that the organism can be isolated from patients with the disease and cultivated outside of the organism; and that the cultivated organism must produce the disease when introduced into susceptible organisms (Carter, 1985).

A modified form of determinism is reflected in Rothman's description of causation:

> A cause is an act or event or a state of nature which initiates or permits, alone or in conjunction with other causes, a sequence of events resulting in an *effect*. A cause which inevitably produces the event is *sufficient*. A specific effect may result from a variety of different sufficient causes . . . . If there exists a component cause which is a member of every sufficient cause, such a component cause is a necessary cause (Rothman, 1976: 587–92).

Accordingly, the relative prevalence of a component cause necessarily determines, at least in part, the strength of a specific causal factor. For instance, a rare factor may be a strong cause if the complementary causes are common. Where the joint effect of two or more component causes exceeds the sums of their separate effects, they are said to be synergistic (Rothman, 1986).

Hill enunciated nine criteria to be considered in determining whether a causal association exists (Morabia, 1991). These criteria include strength, consistency, specificity, temporality, biological gradient, plausibility, coherence, experimental evidence, and analogy. The strength of a specific factor is directly related to the frequency with which it is found in cases of the disease under investigation and the frequency with which it occurs in the absence of the specific disease. Consistency refers to the repeated observation of an association between the factor under investigation and the putative effect across differing populations, times, and circumstances.

Specificity refers to the correspondence between a specific postulated causal factor and a specific effect. Temporality refers to the occurrence of the postulated cause prior to the effect. Biological gradient refers to a dose–response curve. The hypothesized relationship between the postulated causal factor and the resulting effect must be both biologically plausible (plausibility) and consistent with our knowledge of the natural history of the disease in question (coherence). Analogy to other known examples, such as an association between a specific outcome and a similar pharmaceutical product, may also support the existence of a causal relationship. It should be noted that experimental evidence is rarely available for human populations (Hill, 1965).

3.2 Methods for Determining Causation

Numerous elements must be considered in evaluating whether a causal association exists between a specific factor and a specific outcome. These include the study design; the measures used; the presence, absence, and extent of bias and confounding; the success of any strategies used to increase internal validity; and the ability to assess random error. Each of these elements is discussed below briefly.

3.2.1 Study Design

The study design provides a vehicle for the examination of the relationship between a specific exposure and an outcome in specific populations. There are three major types of epidemiologic study designs: experimental, quasi-experimental, and observational.

Experimental research involves the randomization of individuals into one or more comparison groups and one or more treatment groups, which are also known as study arms. The randomization serves to reduce the possibility of selection bias. Clinical trials are the most common type of experimental study, and are often referred to as the " 'gold standard' for causality inference" (Gray-Donald and Kramer, 1988). They are used to test the efficacy of a specific intervention, to test etiologic hypotheses, or to estimate long-term health effects. Clinical trials often utilize double blinding, so that neither the persons conducting the study nor the persons participating in the study know who is in the experimental arm(s) or the comparison arm(s).

Experimental studies can also be conducted on a community level to identify persons at high risk for a particular disease or to test the efficacy and effectiveness of a population intervention to prevent disease or promote health. For instance, one can compare the incidence of caries in communities in which fluoride is added to the water with the incidence of caries in communities with unfluoridated water.

Like experimental designs, quasi-experimental designs involve the comparison of one group either to itself or to others. Unlike experimental studies, however, quasi-experimental designs do not permit randomization. Consequently, the investigator does not have the same degree of control over the study factor of interest as he or she might have in an experimental study. Quasi- experimental designs are often used to test etiologic hypotheses, to evaluate the efficacy of an intervention, or to estimate the long-term effects of an intervention (Kleinbaum, Kupper, and Morgenstern, 1982). The following scenario provides an example of a quasi-experimental study. Assume, for instance, that a particular pesticide is hypothesized to be a risk factor for specific types of respiratory disorders. The use of that pesticide in a small area within a community is ubiquitous. Residents are offered the opportunity to leave the pesticide-exposed area and move elsewhere. Approximately one-half of the residents choose to leave, and the other half chooses to remain in the exposed area. The investigator can then follow both groups over time to determine whether there is a difference between the exposed and the unexposed groups with respect to the incidence of respiratory disorders. Unlike participants in an experiment, the participants here are not randomized, but make their own decision regarding exposure.

Epidemiological studies most frequently utilize an observational design. This is because reliance on an experimental design may not be logistically feasible or ethically permissible. For example, although one might wish to examine whether exposure to a particular substance is associated with the development of cancer, an experimental design might not be logistically feasible due to the length of follow-up time that would be required to observe the development of cancer. And, where there is prior knowledge to indicate that such an exposure could be associated with cancer, such as multiple animal studies and toxicological data, it would be unethical to subject research participants to the associated risk of harm.

Basic observational designs include the cohort study, the case-control study, and the cross- sectional study. Each of these study designs offers distinct advantages and disadvantages.

Cohort studies are conducted either prospectively or retrospectively. Individuals enrolled into cohort studies are identified on the basis of their exposure or nonexposure to a factor of interest and are followed over time to observe the number of new cases of the disease or condition of interest that develops in the exposed and the unexposed groups (Kelsey, Thompson, and Evans, 1986).

Prospective studies often require many participants and can be quite expensive to conduct (Kelsey, Thompson, and Evans, 1986). (What is considered a large sample size depends on the disease and the exposure under study.) Second, there may be errors in classifying individuals on the basis of their exposure. For instance, some individuals classified as unexposed may actually have been exposed. This may be a particular problem in situations in which the exposure under study is ubiquitous, such as pesticide use in an agricultural community. Third, although individuals enrolled in the study must be disease-free to participate, the disease process may have already commenced in some participants but may be undetectable with available technology. Classification of individuals as diseased and ineligible or nondiseased and eligible may also be problematic in studies involving diseases that occur along a spectrum, such as high blood pressure (Kelsey, Thompson, and Evans, 1986). Prospective cohort studies must follow individuals for a minimum period of time to permit a biologically appropriate induction period and an adequate latent period (the time after causation but prior to disease detection). Where we lack sufficient knowledge about the induction and latency periods, we must make various assumptions. Additionally, a portion of the individuals who must be followed in a prospective cohort study may drop out or be lost to follow-up during this long period of time. This attrition may result in bias. (See the discussion of internal validity, below.)

Retrospective cohort studies, although less costly than prospective cohort studies, share many of the same difficulties. Retrospective studies follow exposed and unexposed individuals forward in time from a specific point in the past to the present. For instance, a retrospective cohort study examining the relationship between exposure to asbestos and the development of lung cancer might follow a cohort of employees in a particular industry from a point in time twenty-five years ago to the present, to determine how many cases of lung cancer developed in those who were exposed and those who were unexposed to the asbestos. Records may be incomplete with respect to exposure data and may lack any information regarding extraneous variables. (See the discussion on confounding, below.)

Case-control studies require the identification of study participants on the basis of their current disease status. They are then examined to determine their past exposure to the factor of interest. Case-control studies are often utilized to evaluate risk factors for rare diseases and for diseases of rapid onset (Kelsey, Thompson, and Evans, 1986). The cases and controls for case-control studies must be selected from separate populations (Lasky and Stolley, 1994). In order to make causal inferences, the controls must be "representative of the same candidate population . . . from which the cases . . . developed" (Kelsey, Thompson, and Evans, 1986: 68).

As in cohort studies, the determination of who is and who is not diseased may be problematic. For instance, numerous case-control studies have been conducted to determine whether there exists an association between silicone breast implants and the development of an autoimmune disorder (Chang, 1993; Hirmand, Latenta, and Hoffman, 1993; Swan, 1994). The diagnosis of individuals with "human adjuvant disease," a term used to refer to the constellation of symptoms alleged to have arisen as the result of exposure to silicone, was difficult at best due to the imprecision of this term and the broad range of symptoms that it encompassed.

Although case-control studies require the identification of diseased and nondiseased individuals and an examination of their past exposure, temporality may still be at issue. As an example, Reye's syndrome is an acute encephalopathy that tends to occur among children ages 5 through 15 in the fall and winter. Most cases in the United States are preceded by a brief, acute viral infection, or prodromal viral illness. Although aspirin has been found to be a causative exposure for this syndrome (Public Health Service, 1985; Novick, 1987; Wallace, 1992), at least one research group has argued that it may be difficult to distinguish when the prodromal viral illness ended and when the symptoms of Reye's syndrome began (Horwitz, Feinstein, and Harvey, 1984).

Cross-sectional studies assess disease and exposure at the same point in time. Consequently, it may be difficult to determine whether the exposure preceded the disease or the disease preceded the factor hypothesized to be the cause. This temporal ambiguity precludes the use of cross- sectional studies as the basis for making causal inferences (Kelsey, Thompson, and Evans, 1986).

3.2.2 Measures

Clearly, an evaluation of causation in the context of epidemiology requires an evaluation of the study designs used, including the strengths and weaknesses of design. The evaluation must also consider the measures resulting from the studies. Epidemiology utilizes measures of disease frequency, which focus on the occurrence of disease; measures of association, which estimate the strength of the statistical association between a factor under study and the disease under study; and measures of impact, which help to explain the extent to which a particular factor has contributed to the cause or prevention of a specific outcome in a population. These measures have been discussed extensively elsewhere and will be reviewed here only briefly.

The incidence rate refers to the number of new cases of a disease in a specific population divided by the total of the time periods of observation of all the individuals in the same population. Incidence rates can be calculated from the data obtained from cohort studies. Unlike incidence, which refers to the number of new cases that develop during a specified time period, prevalence relates to the proportion of a specific population that has the disease at a specific point in time or during a specific period of time (Kleinbaum, Kupper, and Morgenstern, 1982).

The concept of risk refers to the probability of developing a disease during a specific time period (Kleinbaum, Kupper, and Morgenstern, 1982). Probability can be thought of as a continuum between one and zero, where a value close to zero indicates that an event is unlikely to occur and a value close to one indicates that the event is very likely to happen. Probabilities are often expressed as percentages. Risk is approximately equal to the incidence rate multiplied by time, over a short period of time (Rothman, 1986).

Measures of association are derived from a comparison of one or more study groups to another study group that has been designated as the reference group. The risk ratio, used with cohort studies, involves a comparison of the risk of disease in the group exposed to the factor of interest with the risk of disease in the group that has been unexposed to the factor of interest. The odds ratio, used with case-control studies, is derived from a comparison of the odds of having been exposed given the presence of the disease with the odds of not having been exposed given the presence of disease. This ratio is then compared to the odds resulting from a comparison of the odds of having been exposed given the absence of disease with the odds of not having been exposed given the absence of disease (Kelsey, Thompson, and Evans, 1986).

Cross-sectional studies often rely on the prevalence ratio, which results from a comparison of the prevalence of the disease in the exposed population and the prevalence of the disease in the unexposed population (Kelsey, Thompson, and Evans, 1986). It is unlikely that the prevalence ratio will be encountered very often in the context of litigation due to our inability to draw causal inferences from cross-sectional studies.

Measures of impact can be calculated from any ratio measure of association (Kleinbaum, Kupper, and Morgenstern, 1982). The attributable fraction, also called the attributable risk percent for the exposed, is calculated by subtracting the rate of disease among the unexposed from the rate of disease among the exposed and then dividing that difference by the rate among the exposed (Kelsey, Thompson, and Evans, 1986). The formula for this calculation is (rate for exposed)−(rate for unexposed)/rate for exposed. The attributable risk fraction, also known as the etiologic fraction, attributable risk, and population attributable risk (Kleinbaum, Kupper, and Morgenstern, 1982), is calculated by subtracting the rate of disease among the unexposed from the rate of disease among the entire population. This is written as (rate for the entire population)−(rate for unexposed)/rate for entire population. That difference is then divided by the rate for the entire population. The fraction that results depends on the prevalance of the exposure in the population and the magnitude of the rate ratio (Kelsey, Thompson, and Evans, 1986). Some writers have used the terms attributable fraction and attributable risk synonymously (Black, Jacobson, Madeira, and See, 1997).

Consider, as an example, the use of the risk ratio to calculate the attributable fraction. Suppose that a retrospective cohort study has indicated that exposure to a particular substance carries twice the risk of developing a specific form of cancer, compared to nonexposure, i.e., the relative risk is 2. The attributable fraction would be calculated by subtracting the risk of disease among the unexposed, which would be 1, thereby indicating no increased risk, from the risk of disease among the unexposed, 2. That difference is then divided by the risk among the exposed, 2. This yields an attributable fraction of .5.

3.2.3   Internal and External Validity

The scientific validity of a study, and hence its legal reliability (see below), depends on both the internal and external validity of the study. The internal validity refers to inferences that relate to the study participants, while the external validity refers to the ability to generalize the results of the study to populations or groups other than the study population.

The internal validity of the study can be impacted by selection bias, information bias, and/or confounding. Selection bias results from flaws in the procedures used to select participants for the study. This can occur, for instance, where the study utilizes volunteers, because individuals may refer themselves to the study for reasons related to the outcome under study (Kleinbaum, Kupper, and Morgenstern, 1982).

Information bias can lead to a distortion of the effect estimate as the result of misclassification of the research participants on one or more variables. For instance, participants' memories pertaining to a specific exposure may differ between the cases (diseased) and control (nondiseased) participating in a case-control study because particular exposures may have taken on greater significance for the cases because they are trying to understand why they have a specific disease (Kelsey, Thompson, and Evans, 1986; Rothman, 1986).

Confounding occurs where the exposure of interest is closely linked to another variable that is also linked to the disease of interest. To be a confounder, the factor must be associated with the exposure of interest and the disease of interest. Additionally, it must be associated with exposure among the cases and it cannot be a step in the causal process between the exposure and the disease (Greenland and Robins, 1985; Rothman, 1986).

The validity of an observational study can be increased through restriction and matching. Restriction refers to the practice of limiting enrollment of individuals to those who meet specified predetermined eligibility criteria, thereby reducing the possibility of bias resulting from the presence of extraneous factors (Gray-Donald and Kramer, 1988). Matching involves the selection of a comparison group that is comparable to the study group with respect to specified variables that would bias the results, such as sex or age. Matching results in a reduction of the potential variability between the study and comparison groups with respect to the matched variables (Kelsey, Thompson, and Evans, 1986). Stratification and modeling, discussed extensively in other sources, can also be used to increase the validity of the study (Breslow and Day, 1980, 1987).

Hill advised that:

> All scientific work is incomplete—whether it be observational or experimental. All scientific work is liable to be upset or modified by advancing knowledge. That does not confer upon us freedom to ignore the knowledge we already have, or to postpone action that it appears to demand at a given time (Hill, 1965).

This admonition is particularly relevant to the use of epidemiological data in the context of litigation, where, as demonstrated below, prompt action may be required even in the absence of perfect, or even extensive, knowledge.

4   Causation in Law

4.1   Methods for Determining Causation

Assessing the Reliability of the Scientific Evidence. Expert testimony in the area of epidemiology is permitted if the testimony is scientific or technical or involves other specialized knowledge and if the testimony will "assist the trier of fact to understand the evidence or to determine a fact in issue" (Federal Rule of Evidence 702). The epidemiologist can provide his or her testimony in the form of an opinion or an inference. In order to testify, however, the epidemiologist must be qualified as an expert "by knowledge, skill, experience, training, or education . . . " (Federal Rule of Evidence 702).

In order to be considered scientific knowledge for the purpose of testifying, the evidence to be proffered must be both relevant and reliable. Evidence is relevant if it has a "tendency to make the existence of any fact that is of consequence to the determination of the action more probable or less probable than it would be without the evidence" (Federal Rule of Evidence 401). Evidence that is not relevant will not be admitted. Additionally, evidence that is relevant will be excluded "if its probative value is substantially outweighed by the danger of unfair prejudice, confusion of the issues, or misleading the jury, or by considerations of undue delay, waste of time, or needless presentation of cumulative evidence" (Federal Rule of Evidence 403). For instance, in *In re Bendectin Litigation* (1988), in which damages were sought against the manufacturers of the drug Bendectin for injuries alleged to have been caused to the children of mothers who ingested Bendectin during their pregnancies, the court refused to admit evidence relating to the drug thalidomide, manufactured by the same company, because of the danger of unfair prejudice.

In order to be considered reliable, the scientific testimony "must be supported by appropriate validation" (*Daubert*, 1993: 113 S.Ct. at 2787). An assessment of the (legal) validity of the scientific testimony requires that the court (1) determine whether the theory or technique at issue could have been tested; (2) determine whether the methodology has been subjected to peer review; (3) consider the potential rate of error associated with a particular method or technique; and (4) assess the extent to which the proffered methodology has been accepted within the identified relevant scientific community (*Daubert*, 1993).

Various mechanisms can be utilized to determine whether the proffered epidemiological evidence is (legally) reliable. These include (1) a full pretrial hearing to assess the reliability of the evidence; (2) an examination of the pleadings, depositions, answers to interrogatories, admissions on file, and affidavits in the context of a motion for summary judgment; and (3) direct and cross-examination in the context of the trial itself. The court may also appoint its own expert to examine the evidence to be offered.

A full pretrial hearing on the admissibility of the scientific evidence is known as an in limine *Daubert*-type hearing. This type of hearing occurs before the actual trial and focuses on the qualifications of the experts who will testify, the nature of the areas of expertise, their examination of already existing studies, and the validity of current scientific studies. If the judge finds in the context of this in limine hearing that the scientific evidence is unreliable, and therefore inadmissible, neither the plaintiffs nor the defendants will be able to use that evidence at trial.

Under the Federal Rules of Civil Procedure, interrogatories may be directed only to a party to the action. Interrogatories are written questions addressed to the opposing party, to which they will respond in writing. Under the current Rules of Civil Procedure, the expert witness–epidemiologist who has been retained to provide expert testimony in a case must prepare and sign a written report, which must include a statement of the expert's opinions, including the basis for those opinions; any exhibits that the expert will be using; a statement of the expert's qualifications; and a list of any other cases during the previous four years in which the epidemiologist–expert testified as an expert either at trial or by deposition (Federal Rule of Civil Procedure 26). It is believed that the production of this report will reduce the need for interrogatories and the length of depositions.

A deposition is a record of testimony that is taken outside of the courtroom. Unlike interrogatories, a deposition can be directed to an expert witness, such as an epidemiologist. Questions during a deposition usually focus on four areas: the expert's qualifications as an expert, the procedures that the expert relied upon to form and render a professional opinion, the expert's opinion itself, and the process by which the expert arrived at his or her opinion (Matson, 1994).

Either the plaintiff or the defendant can bring a motion for summary judgment. This is a pretrial motion. The court can grant the motion only if "there is no genuine issue as to any material fact" (Federal Rule of Civil Procedure 56). If the party bringing the motion has the burden of proof on an issue raised by the motion, the court may grant the motion only if the evidence supporting the moving party's position is sufficient to permit a rational factfinder to find for the moving party under the appropriate standard. (The burden of proof refers to the facts that the plaintiff must prove in order to establish a *prima facie* case, such as duty, breach of duty, and harm, among others.) If the moving party does not have the burden of proof, the court may grant summary judgment only if the opposing party that does have the burden of proof does not produce evidence sufficient to permit a jury to find in its favor. Although the epidemiologist–expert witness is unlikely to testify in conjunction with a motion for summary judgment, he or she may be involved by helping a party to the action to identify relevant issues.

Direct examination of the epidemiologist–expert at trial is conducted by the attorney for the party for whom the epidemiologist is testifying. The direct examination generally addresses the following areas: the expert's credentials, the methodology that the expert used to evaluate the relevant epidemiological research, and the methods used to conduct the studies in which the expert was involved. Direct testimony of the epidemiologist–expert provides an opportunity to educate the jury regarding the subject matter at hand, the relevant methodology, and the peer review process (Karns, 1994).

Unlike direct examination, which is conducted by the attorney for the party for whom the expert is appearing, cross-examination is conducted by the attorney for the opposing party. While direct testimony seeks to establish the epidemiologist–expert as an expert and to underscore his or her competence and ability to evaluate the case at bar, cross-examination seeks to cast doubt on his or her ability or opinion. Cross-examination frequently focuses on the limitations of the expert's expertise, the methodology utilized by the expert, the nature of the epidemiological evidence, possible alternative causes of the plaintiff's disease or injury, and any differential diagnoses. Cross-examination may attempt to discredit the expert on the basis of poor memory, a conflict of interest, or lack of qualifications as an expert (Voke, 1994).

Assessing the Qualifications of the Epidemiologist as an Expert. Even though an epidemiologist may have used a methodology that the court finds is reliable, the individual may or may not qualify to testify as an expert witness. Various factors are considered in determining whether an individual should be deemed to be an expert in his or her field, including the individual's education in the specific area; whether he or she has performed or supervised any research in the specific area of inquiry; whether he or she has published any articles in the particular field; and the extent of the prospective witness's familiarity with the scientific literature that addresses the issue at hand, such as the relationship between a particular exposure and a specified disease outcome.

4.2 The Operationalization of Causation

In the context of toxic torts, the plaintiff must establish that the alleged injury arose from the conduct of the defendant. The plaintiff is required to demonstrate that but for the defendant's conduct, the injury would not have occurred. Alternatively, some jurisdictions permit the plaintiff to rely on the "substantial factor test," under which the plaintiff must demonstrate that the defendant's conduct was a substantial factor in bringing about the harm that the plaintiff suffered (Keeton et al., 1994). It is important to recognize that if there is no association between the putative exposure and the alleged disease or injury, there cannot be an inquiry into whether or not the injury to the plaintiff arose from the conduct of the defendant. If at an *in limine* hearing it is determined that the proffered evidence relating Substance A to Disease B is unreliable, that evidence is inadmissible at trial. If that was the only evidence available to the plaintiff to demonstrate the relationship between plaintiff's injury and defendant's conduct, then there is no basis left on which to proceed. For instance, suppose that a plaintiff claims that his stomach cancer resulted from extensive and prolonged exposure to aspirin. Unless he can establish that an association exists between aspirin usage and stomach cancer, his case cannot go forward to determine whether the injury arose from the conduct of the defendant aspirin manufacturer, such as the provision of an inadequate warning with respect to the dangers of extensive aspirin exposure.

In attempting to reconcile the operationalization of causation in an epidemiological context with that used in a legal context, some courts have held that evidence will not be admissible unless it is statistically significant at a 95 percent confidence level, and have equated the scientific standard with the legal standard (Poole, 1987). This interpretation ignores the fact that the significance level is chosen arbitrarily. Other courts have erroneously equated the magnitude of the relative risk with statistical significance. For instance, the court in *In re Joint Eastern and Southern Asbestos Litigation* (1993) held that "a [relative risk] of less than 1.50 is statistically insignificant." Several courts, however, have properly recognized that the absence of statistical significance does not foreclose the existence of a causal relationship between the exposure of interest and the alleged resulting injury (*Allen v. United States*, 1984; *In re TMI Litigation Cases Consolidated II*, 1996).

Some writers have argued that because the legal system requires that the probability of causation have exceeded 50 percent, a person's disease "more likely than not" would have been caused by the alleged exposure only if the relative risk is equal to or greater than 2 or the etiologic fraction is greater than 50 percent (Muscat and Huncharek, 1989). This view has been adopted by some courts. For instance, the court in *Marder v. G.D. Searle and Co.* (1986: 1092) found that:

> a two-fold increase is an important showing for plaintiffs to make because it is the equivalent of the required legal burden of proof—a showing of causation by the preponderance of the evidence or, in other words, a probability of greater than 50 percent. In epidemiological terms, a figure

of 1.0 indicates no change in the risk, and a figure of 2.0 indicates a two-fold risk.

Other writers have taken an even more restrictive approach, arguing that the courts should require a minimum relative risk of 3.0 to establish causation (Black, Jacobson, Madeira, and See, 1997). This restrictive approach is problematic for several reasons.

First, strict adherence to a risk ratio of 2.0 or more ignores many of the issues inherent in any epidemiological study that affect the magnitude of the resulting measure of association, including sample size and bias. Second, as a matter of policy, the adoption of such a threshold requirement is ill-advised because it would a priori preclude recovery by individuals actually harmed by a specific exposure where less than a relative risk of 2.0 is demonstrated.

This discussion of a threshold requirement based upon the magnitude of relative risk or attributable fraction can be analogized to the epidemiological concepts of sensitivity and specificity (Loue, 1999), used in conjunction with screening tests. Sensitivity refers to the proportion of individuals who truly have a specific characteristic that is correctly classified by the screening strategy as having that characteristic. Specificity refers to the proportion of individuals who do not have a specific characteristic, that is correctly classified by the screening strategy as not having that characteristic. Sensitivity and specificity are related in that attempts to reduce the proportion of individuals incorrectly classified as having a characteristic (false positives) may result in an increase in the proportion of individuals misclassified as not having the characteristic (false negatives) (Roht, Selwyn, Holguin, and Christensen, 1982).

Accordingly, in the context of litigation, a high threshold requirement, such as a relative risk of 3.0, would result in a lesser proportion of unharmed individuals being erroneously classified as harmed, but would also result in a larger proportion of truly harmed individuals being misclassified as unharmed, thereby precluding recovery for those injuries. Conversely, formal adoption of a lower relative risk as a threshold requirement would result in misclassification of a greater proportion of the unharmed as harmed.

The establishment of a threshold requirement can also be likened to the issue of Type I and Type II errors. Assume, for instance, that the null hypothesis (H_0) states that a risk ratio of less than or equal to 2.0 indicates no causal association in the legal and epidemiological contexts, while the alternative hypothesis (H_A) states that a risk ratio of greater than 2.0 indicates that a causal association exists. In any specific situation, one of the following must be true:

1. The null hypothesis is rejected when it is true, and as a result, a Type I error is committed. This means, for instance, that a jury may conclude that a causal association exists and damages should be awarded when, in fact, there is no such causal relationship.
2. The null hypothesis is rejected when the alternative hypothesis is true, i.e., a correct decision has been made.

3. The null hypothesis is not rejected when the alternative hypothesis is true. This constitutes a Type II error. Practically, this means that the jury may conclude that there is no causal association and no damages should be awarded when, in fact, such a relationship does exist.
4. The null hypothesis is not rejected when the null hypothesis is true.

Both Type I and Type II errors are serious. A Type I error would result in an award to an allegedly injured party when in actuality the putative exposure is not causally associated with the disease or injury. A Type II error would result in the denial of an award to an individual whose injury or disease may be associated with the exposure under examination. Whether a Type I or Type II error can be considered more serious in this context rests on a policy determination.

Third, it has been argued that the requirement of a relative risk of 2.0 to establish that an individual's injury was "more likely than not" brought about by the alleged exposure collapses the burden of proof with the burden of persuasion. As previously indicated, the burden of proof refers to the facts that the plaintiff must prove in order to establish a *prima facie* case, such as duty, breach of duty, and harm, among others. The burden of persuasion refers to the level of confidence that the jury must have in order to find a fact true for the party that has the burden of proof to prove that fact (Gold, 1986). There are three different burdens of persuasion. "By a preponderance of the evidence" is the standard that is applied in most civil cases, although the standard of "clear and convincing" is also applicable to civil cases. In criminal cases, the burden of persuasion is that of "beyond a reasonable doubt." By collapsing the burden of proof and the burden of persuasion, the standard of proof may be lowered from that of true versus false to that of a probability greater than 50 percent. The burden of persuasion, though, may be heightened (Gold, 1986).

Gold (1986: 382-383) uses the following example to illustrate this difference:

> A traffic light fails to turn red and a crash ensues. The city, sued for its defective light, argues that the car could not have stopped in time even had the light worked, so the light did not cause the accident.

Using a traditional analysis, under which the plaintiff bears both the burden of proof and the burden of persuasion, the plaintiff must prove first that the car could have stopped in time (burden of proof). After finding that the light truly caused the accident, the jury must then evaluate whether the plaintiff has met his burden of persuasion, i.e., that causation was more likely than not, meaning that the jury is more than 50% confident in this fact.

Gold's (1986: 382-383) alternative interpretation of the car accident illustrates the collapsing of the burden of proof and the burden of persuasion. In this scenario, we have no information available with respect to the individual car that was involved in the accident. The jury finds that:

> We accept the undisputed fact that 53% of cars could have stopped. With no reason to find your car atypical, we infer that your car more likely than not would have stopped, since most cars would have.

Gold (1986) has recommended that the "substantial factor" test be utilized as the burden of proof. This standard recognizes that there may be multiple factors involved in causation and meshes well with Rothman's conceptualization of multiple-factor disease causation. Exposures resulting in a substantially increased risk of disease would consequently result in liability, even if other factors were also implicated in producing the outcome. And rather than relying solely on a specific test statistic, such as a risk ratio of 2 or an attributable fraction of 50 percent, it is suggested that a determination of causality consider the totality of the circumstances.

The court in *Landrigan v. Celotex Corp.* (1992: 1087) arrived at a similar conclusion, finding that

a relative risk of 2.0 is not so much a password to a finding of causation as one piece of evidence, among others, for the court to consider in determining whether the expert has employed a sound methodology in reaching his or her conclusion.

Accordingly, the court granted recovery for injuries alleged to have arisen as the result of exposure to asbestos, although the demonstrated relative risk was 1.5.

Acknowledgments

The author thanks Joseph Gastwirth for both his invitation and editorial suggestions that improved this chapter. The author also acknowledges the helpful comments of an anonymous reviewer, whose suggestions were also helpful.

5 Cases Cited

Allen v. United States (1984), 588 F. Supp. 247 (D. Utah), *reversed on other grounds*, 816 F.2d 1417 (10th Cir. 1987), *cert. denied*, 484 U.S. 1004 (1988).

Daubert v. Merrell Dow Pharmaceuticals, Inc. (1993), 509 U.S. 579, 113 S.Ct. 2786, 125 L.Ed. 2d 469.

In re Agent Orange Products Liability Litigation (1984), 597 F. Supp. 740 (E.D.N.Y.), 603 F. Supp. 239 (E.D.N.Y. 1985); 611 F. Supp. 1223 (E.D.N.Y.), *affirmed* 818 F.2d 187 (2d Cir. 1987).

In re Bendectin Litigation (1988), 857 F.2d 290 (6th Cir.), *cert. denied*, 1989 US LEXIS 168.

In re Joint Eastern and Southern Asbestos Litigation (1993), 827 F. Supp. 1014 (S.D.N.Y.), *reversed*, 52 F.3d 1124 (2d Cir. 1995).

Kehm v. Procter and Gamble Manufacturing Company (1983), 724 F.2d 613 (8th Cir.).

Landrigan v. Celotex Corp. (1992), 605 A.2d 1079 (N.J.).

Marder v. G.D. Searle and Co. (1986), 630 F. Supp. 1087 (D. Md.), *affirmed* 814 F.2d 655 (4th Cir. 1987).

In re TMI Litigation Cases Consolidated II (1996), 922 F. Supp. 997 (M.D. Pa.).

REFERENCES

[1] Black, B., Jacobson, J.A., Madeira, E.W. Jr., and See, A. (1997), Guide to epidemiology. In B. Black and P.W. Lee (eds.), *Expert Evidence: A Practitioner's Guide to Law, Science, and the FJC Manual* (pp. 73–115). St. Paul, Minnesota: West Group.

[2] Breslow, N.E. and Day, N.E. (1980), *Statistical Methods in Cancer Research.* Volume I, *The Analysis of Case-Control Studies.* Lyon, France: International Agency for Research on Cancer.

[3] Breslow, N.E. and Day, N.E. (1987), Statistical Methods in Cancer Research. Volume II, *The Analysis of Cohort Studies.* Lyon, France: International Agency for Research on Cancer.

[4] Carter, K.C. (1985), Koch's postulates in relation to the work of Jacob Henle and Edwin Klebs. Medical History, **29**, 353–374.

[5] Chang, Y.H. (1993), Adjuvanticity and arthrogenicity of silicone. *Plastic and Reconstructive Surgery*, **92**, 469–473.

[6] Federal Rules of Civil Procedure 26, 56, 28 U.S.C.A.

[7] Federal Rules of Evidence 401, 403, 28 U.S.C.A.

[8] Fitzpatrick, J.M. and Shainwald, S. (1996), *Breast Implant Litigation.* New York: Law Journal Seminars-Press.

[9] Glantz, S.A., Slade, J., Bero, L.A., Hanauer, P., and Barnes, D.E. (1996), *The Cigarette Papers.* Berkeley, California: University of California Press.

[10] Gold, S. (1986), Causation in toxic torts: The burdens of proof, standards of persuasion, and statistical evidence. *Yale Law Journal*, **96**, 376–402.

[11] Gray-Donald, K. and Kramer, M.S. (1988), Causality inference on observational vs. experimental studies: An empirical comparison. *American Journal of Epidemiology*, **127**, 885–892.

[12] Greenland, S. and Robins, J.M. (1985), Confounding and misclassification. *American Journal of Epidemiology*, **122**, 495–506.

[13] Hill, A.B. (1965), The environment and disease: Association or causation? *Proceedings of the Royal Society of Medicine*, **58**, 295–300.

[14] Hirmand, H., Latenta, G.S., and Hoffman, L.A. (1993), Autoimmune disease and silicone breast implants. *Oncology*, **7**, 17–24.

[15] Horwitz, R.I., Feinstein, A.R., and Harvey, M.B. (1984), Case-control research: Temporal precedence and other problems of the exposure-disease relationship. *Archives of Internal Medicine*, **144**, 1257–1259.

[16] Karns, E. (1994), Understanding epidemiological evidence: What to ask the expert witness. *Trial*, 30, 48.

[17] Keeton, P. et al. (1984), *Prosser and Keeton on the Law of Torts*, 5th ed. St. Paul, Minnesota: West Publishing.

[18] Kelsey, J.L., Thompson, W.D., and Evans, A.S. (1986), *Methods in Observational Epidemiology*. New York: Oxford University Press.

[19] Kleinbaum, D.G., Kupper, L.L., and Morgenstern, H. (1982), *Epidemiologic Research: Principles and Quantitative Methods*. New York: Van Nostrand Reinhold.

[20] Lasky, T. and Stolley, P.D. (1994), Selections of cases and controls. *Epidemiologic Reviews*, **16**, 6–17.

[21] Loue, S. (1999), *Forensic Epidemiology: A Comprehensive Guide for Legal and Epidemiology Professionals*. Carbondale, Illinois: Southern Illinois University Press.

[22] MacHovec, F.J. (1987), *The Expert Witness Survival Manual*. Springfield, Illinois: Charles C. Thomas.

[23] Matson, J.V. (1994), *Effective Expert Witnessing*, 2d ed. Boca Raton, Florida: Lewis Publishers.

[24] Morabia, A. (1991), On the origin of Hill's causal criteria. *Epidemiology*, **2**, 367–369.

[25] Muscat, J.E. and Huncharek, M.S. (1989), Causation and disease: Biomedical science in toxic tort litigation. *Journal of Occupational Medicine*, **31**, 997–1002.

[26] Novick, J. (1987), Use of epidemiological studies to prove legal causation: Aspirin and Reye's syndrome, a case in point. *Tort and Insurance Law Journal*, **23**, 536–557.

[27] Poole, C. (1987), Beyond the confidence interval. *American Journal of Public Health*, **77**, 195–199.

[28] Public Health Service (1985), Public health service study on Reye's syndrome and medications. *New England Journal of Medicine*, **313**, 849–857.

[29] Roht, L.H., Selwyn, B.J., Holguin, A.H., and Christensen, B.L. (1982), *Principles of Epidemiology: A Self-Teaching Guide*. New York: Academic Press, Inc.

[30] Rothman, K.J. (1976), Causes. *American Journal of Epidemiology*, **104**, 587–592.

[31] Rothman, K.J. (1986). *Modern Epidemiology*. Boston: Little, Brown.

[32] Sanders, J. (1992), The Bendectin litigation: A case study in the life cycle of mass torts. *Hastings Law Journal*, **43**, 301–418.

[33] Schuck, P.H. (1987), *Agent Orange on Trial: Mass Toxic Disasters in the Courts*. Cambridge., Massachusetts: Belknap Press.

[34] Schwartz, T.M. (1988), The role of federal safety regulations in products liability actions. *Vanderbilt Law Review*, **41**, 1121–1169.

[35] Swan, S.S. (1994), Epidemiology of silicone-related disease. *Seminars in Arthritis and Rheumatism*, **24**, 38–43.

[36] Voke, B.P. (1994), Sources of proof of causation in toxic tort cases. *Defense Counsel Journal*, **61**, 45–50.

[37] Wallace, R.B. (1992), Reye's syndrome. In J.M. Last and R.B. Wallace (Eds.), *Public Health and Preventive Medicine*, 13th ed. (pp. 306–310). Norwalk, Connecticut: Appleton and Lange.

Judicial Review of Statistical Analyses in Environmental Rulemakings

Wendy E. Wagner

Abstract

In the review of environmental regulations, prominent appellate courts have demanded that agencies provide definitive-looking quantitative support for their rulemakings, but then defer to the agencies once this certain-looking information is provided. In this article the author argues that these demands by the courts are not only unrealistic, but they provide agencies like the Environmental Protection Agency (EPA) with perverse incentives to adopt poor statistical practices. Rather than admitting to errors and uncertainties, under the current approach to judicial review the EPA is rewarded for downplaying or even ignoring the variability and uncertainty in its data; is deterred from employing statistical techniques that provide richer information about the data set that might also tend to magnify uncertainty and variability, and is encouraged to describe its basic assumptions and policy choices in highly technical language that escapes lay understanding. Despite the flaws in the courts' current approach, a few relatively modest adjustments and clarifications to the standard for review may be capable of improving the courts' role in reviewing environmental regulations.

Keywords: Judicial review, environmental law, statistical practices, regulation, Environmental Protection Agency (EPA), courts.

1 Introduction

A good part of a statistician's business involves describing the sources and extent of error in scientific studies. Yet for judges and juries tasked with resolving a dispute (or reviewing an agency decision), information about the statistical noise surrounding a method or point estimate is often unwelcome: Understanding this noise requires time and patience, and often it only reveals more questions than answers (Fienberg 1989, pp. 139–40). Fact-finders are in the mood for answers, not statistics.

When the U.S. Court of Appeals is reviewing the agency's use of statistical analysis in environmental rulemakings, it is not unusual to find the judiciary intolerant of admissions of uncertainties and sources of errors in an agency's quantitative analysis. The U.S. Court of Appeals is the forum that reviews most challenges to agency rulemakings under the vague review standards set forth under the Administrative Procedure Act (5 U.S.C. §706(2)). In their review, the message appellate courts have sent to agencies over the past few decades is that they expect and will sometimes demand definitive quantitative analysis. In response to these impossible judicial demands, the Environmental Protection Agency (EPA) seems to have decided that the less it admits or explains about the statistical realities of its data sets and accompanying risk assessments, the safer its rulemakings are from being invalidated or remanded. The judiciary's affinity for definitive quantitative analysis may in fact be the primary cause of some poor statistical practices currently employed by the EPA in its standard-setting efforts.

In this article I present an overview of the current problematic state of the judicial review of agencies' quantitative analyses in environmental rulemakings. The first section surveys the general, ad hoc approach the appellate courts take when reviewing statistical analyses in environmental rulemakings and describes how these ad hoc standards tend to reward agencies for overstating the certainty of the quantitative analysis in their regulations. Three well-recognized weaknesses in EPA's statistical practices are then highlighted in the second section that are likely linked, at least in part, to the courts' unrealistic demands for certainty. The third and final section presents a proposal for a reformed standard of judicial review that, if implemented, would encourage the agencies to use better statistical practices in their regulatory analyses.

2   The Courts' Review of Statistical Analyses in Agency Rulemakings

The appellate courts are charged with the critical role of ensuring both the accountability and general accuracy of agency rulemakings. Yet ironically, in their review of technical rules, the courts may be exerting a net negative influence on these key features of administrative practice. Unrealistic judicial expectations of far greater certainty in agency risk assessments than the agency can provide, coupled with a few particularly bad opinions that take these demands to extremes, combine to reward some poor statistical practices in agency rulemakings.

Bad opinions or "wrong law" are commonplace in all areas of law. Yet because agencies are understandably risk averse in anticipating judicial review of their rules, opinions that place unrealistic demands on agency regulatory analysis tend to exert an important influence on how the agency believes it must prepare its rules in order to survive judicial review. Aberrational opinions, such as *Gulf South* and its progeny discussed below, in which the courts inexpertly critiqued highly technical aspects of the agency's decision and demanded an impossible level of certainty in the agency's quantitative analysis, often have a distorting influence on agency rulemakings. Thus efforts to average opinions in the search for a general standard for review is unlikely to replicate how agencies actually process and react to appellate review of their rules.

Yet, even if the agencies concern themselves only with what appear to be mainstream judicial requirements, existing ad hoc standards for review seem to provide few rewards and considerable penalties for honest and sophisticated statistical analysis. Although the guidelines governing judicial review of highly technical rules are far from consistent (Jasanoff 1990, p. 59), in the courts' collective utterance of various tests and approaches, three ad hoc standards for reviewing agency regulations emerge in the majority of opinions. Unfortunately, each of these ad hoc standards actually tends to lower, rather than improve, the quality of the agencies' statistical analyses. Each is discussed in turn.

2.1   Substantial Evidence or the Equivalent

The first ad hoc standard imposed by many courts in their review of agency technical regulations is that agency rules or quantitative standards be supported with "substantial evidence" or something essentially equivalent, a standard that comes directly from the Administrative Procedure Act (5 U.S.C. §706(2)(A)).[1] By requiring agencies to "justify the rule in detail and respond to all substantial objections raised by the public comments" (Scalia 1981, p. 26), quantitative analysis is encouraged, but good statistical practices may not be. Instead, frank and accessible disclosures by the agencies of uncertainties, sources of error, or even qualitative factors that necessarily influenced their final regulation may be met with a remand of the rule, since these disclosures reflect lapses in the certainty and definitiveness of the agency's analysis (Cross 1986, pp. 12–43; McGarity 1979, p. 750; Pierce 1979, p. 311). In environmental rulemakings where scientific uncertainties are particularly substantial, legal academics have observed that this requirement has, on occasion, prevented agencies from taking any action or has caused delays in the promulgation of regulations that can extend for decades (McGarity 1992, p. 1403; Mazurek et al. 1995, p. 87 n. 24; Pierce 1979, pp. 302–03).

   The most prominent example of the judicial requirement for certainty in agency quantitative analysis is the Supreme Court's 1980 pronouncement in the *Benzene* case, which involved a challenge to the Occupational Safety and Health Administration's (OSHA's) proposed occupational health standard for benzene (*Industrial Union Dep't v. American Petroleum Inst.* 1980). The Court struck down OSHA's standard in large part because, as OSHA itself had conceded, the quantitative standard was based on highly uncertain evidence. In the future in order to survive challenge, the Court warned, the agency must "show, on the basis of substantial evidence, that it is at least more likely than not that long-term exposure to ten parts per million of benzene presents a significant risk of material health impairment," a showing that would benefit from, if not require, sophisticated quantitative analyses (ibid. at 653, 655).[2] As a result of the *Benzene* case, careful observers

---

[1] Appellate courts have indicated that the "substantial evidence" standard used for the review of formal rules is essentially the same as the "arbitrary and capricious" standard used for the review of informal rules (*Association of Data Processing Service Orgs., Inc. v. Board of Governors* 1984; Pierce, et al. 1992, 341–42).

[2] In the D.C. Circuit's recent remand of EPA's national air quality standards for ozone and particulates, Judge Williams suggested that comprehensive scientific explanations might

of agency risk assessments have noted that "federal agencies ... conclude that they must provide quantitative risk estimates, even if they lack confidence in the resulting judgments" (Graham, et al. 1988, p. 151; Latin 1988, p. 132).

Subsequent appellate decisions, at least in the Fifth Circuit, take this requirement one step further by explicitly requiring from the agencies the equivalent of a definitive risk analysis in order to support a safety standard. In invalidating the Consumer Product Safety Commission ban of UFFI [urea-formaldehyde foam insulation], for example, the Fifth Circuit panel in *Gulf South Insulation v. CPSC* (1983, p. 1148), stated that "[t]he failure to quantify the risk at the exposure levels actually associated with UFFI is the finding's Achilles' heel." Although the court was correct in chastising the agency for uncritically relying on a study that used nonrandom data (two-thirds of the UFFI homes tested for formaldehyde in the study were "complaint-homes" where the occupants had previously complained about UFFI-related health problems: ibid. at 1144), the courts' invalidation of the CPSC rule was based predominantly on its impatience with unpreventable scientific gaps that the agency openly conceded were present, but that could not be resolved in the near future without postponing preventative regulation entirely (ibid. at 1142 n. 8). Most striking was the court's refusal to permit the Commission to rely on a large rodent study as the basis for extrapolating the effects of formaldehyde to man, even though the study was concededly valid and represented the only study available that informed the dose–response relationship between formaldehyde and adverse health effects. Instead, the court held that "[t]o make precise estimates, precise data are required" (ibid. at 1146).[3]

The more extreme *Gulf South* demand that a conclusive risk assessment support agency rulemakings is repeated in several subsequent cases. In *Asbestos Information Association v. OSHA* (1984, pp. 425–26), the Fifth Circuit suspended OSHA's emergency standard for asbestos in part because the court found that the significant uncertainties associated with the agencies' risk assessment contradicted the agency' claim that urgent action was necessary to regulate asbestos. Six years later, the court invalidated EPA's 1989 asbestos ban and phaseout rule on similar

---

also be essential in order for the agency to survive a nondelegation doctrine challenge. Specifically, Judge Williams opined that "an agency wielding the power over American life possessed by EPA should be capable of developing the rough equivalent of a generic unit of harm that takes into account population affected, severity and probability" in justifying why it selected one quantitative standard over alternatives (*American Trucking Associations, Inc., v. EPA* 1999, p. 7). The extent to which this call for more precise scientific criteria is what the D.C. Circuit actually *requires* from the agencies to survive nondelegation doctrine challenges will undoubtedly be clarified in future opinions.

[3] For a fuller critique of *Gulf South*, see Ashford 1983 and Fienberg 1989, pp. 46–60. The Panel on Statistical Assessments as Evidence in the Courts concluded that while the *Gulf South* court "correctly understood several technical issues" it "also revealed confusion with regard to complex scientific arguments" and exemplifies some of the dangers of lay judges "decid[ing] what scientific evidence is or is not adequate to support an agency conclusion."

grounds (*Corrosion-Proof Fittings v. EPA* 1991). The Fifth Circuit in *Corrosion-Proof* held that EPA had not presented sufficient evidence to justify the ban of all commercial uses of asbestos, but ignored EPA's arguments that evidence on such critical considerations as the number and value of lives saved by the ban past the year 2000 were unquantifiable, although qualitatively significant enough to justify a ban (ibid., pp. 1218–19).[4] In the court's own words: "Unquantified benefits can, at times, permissibly tip the balance in close cases. They cannot, however, be used to effect a wholesale shift on the balance beam" (ibid. p. 1219).

More recently, a district court in North Carolina took a similar approach in vacating EPA's "Environmental Tobacco Smoke" study (*Flue-Cured Tobacco Cooperative Stabilization Corp. v. EPA* 1998). While the court repeatedly and perhaps appropriately reprimanded EPA for failing to explain some of its technical decisions, its rejection of the EPA's study was based generally on the court's intolerance of the unresolvable uncertainties endemic to risk analysis. For example, EPA's use of a "total weight of the evidence" approach to conclude that environmental tobacco smoke is chemically similar to direct tobacco smoke was flatly rejected by the court as too incomplete. In doing so the court openly chastised the agency for conceding unpreventable uncertainties in its analysis in determining the chemical similarities (ibid. at 457 & n. 31), and took issue with inherent uncertainties in the underlying studies, such as the extent to which "air-diluted cigarette smoke (1:15) replicate[s] . . . [environmental tobacco smoke]" (ibid. at 456).[5] While *Gulf South*

---

[4]For a technical critique of the *Corrosion-Proof* decision, see Mark R. Powell (1997c). The Fifth Circuit appeared to echo this *Gulf South* theme in at least one other case, albeit less explicitly. In *Texas Independent Ginners Association v. Marshall* (1980, p. 409), the court cited *Benzene* as authority in concluding that OSHA had not provided "substantial evidence that byssinosis and other chronic disease arise from the exposure level to cotton dust in the ginning industry with its significantly different conditions and its significantly different exposure level," again discounting the agency's assumptions that were necessitated by inherently limited data.

[5]The court also rejected other key aspects of EPA's analysis that were based on assumptions due to limitations in the available scientific research. The courts' rejection of EPA's choice of epidemiological studies for its meta-analysis had some legitimacy because the agency had not explained its selection criteria clearly in advance of conducting the analysis. In its final analysis, EPA limited its meta-analysis to available epidemiological studies on nonsmoking females married to smoking spouses, and rejected childhood and workplace studies involving nonsmoker exposures to second-hand smoke. Unfortunately, however, the court did not stop at condemning the agency for these significant explanatory deficiencies. It then proceeded to substantively reject EPA's post hoc explanations that may in fact have guided its initial selection (a selection that its own science advisory board (the IAQC) endorsed). Specifically, the court rejected EPA's decision not to include workplace studies, a decision EPA justified because the workplace studies were very small in size, involved significant potential confounders outside the workplace, and had no available exposure data. The court also rejected EPA's decision not to use childhood studies, even though EPA justified this decision based on problems associated with these studies' necessary reliance on distant memories for exposure data, as well as the more limited lifetime exposures gen-

and its progeny appear extreme in demanding extensive scientific evidence from the agencies, such judicially imposed demands for definitive quantitative analysis are not likely to be dismissed lightly by an agency as it prepares its rules and preambulatory statements.

2.2 Extra Deference to Garbled Agency Technical Decisions

A second ad hoc tenet in the judicial review of agency rules counsels that extra deference be granted to agency fact-finding when the evidence appears highly technical in nature or is otherwise on "the frontiers of scientific inquiry." The U.S. Supreme Court stated this rule most succinctly: "When examining this kind of scientific determination [i.e., one at the 'frontiers of scientific knowledge'], as opposed to simple findings of fact, a reviewing court must generally be at its most deferential" (*Baltimore Gas & Elec. Co. v. NRDC* 1983, p. 103). Many courts are steadfast in following this extra-deference test, granting the agency wide latitude in technical areas as diverse as emission measurement technologies (*Pennsylvania v. EPA* 1991, p. 272), air pollution modeling (*Connecticut Fund for the Env't v. EPA 1982, p. 178*), and exposure modeling (*United Steelworkers v. Marshall* 1980, p. 1263). In regulatory decisions that involve statistics some courts are super-deferential. In responding to challenges to EPA's statistical methods for developing a technology-based standard for the organic chemical industry, the Fifth Circuit seemed almost to imply that agency statistical choices were immunized from judicial review and instead "committed to the sound discretion of the Administrator" (*Chemical Manufacturers Association v. EPA* 1989, p. 227). Other opinions from the First and Fourth Circuits similarly highlight statistical choices as an area where the court will grant the agency nearly complete decision-making authority (*BASF Wyandotte Corp. v. Costle* 1979, p. 655; *Reynolds Metals Co. v. EPA* 1985, p. 559).[6]

In applying this deference standard, however, these same courts generally pay little attention to whether the agency has actually explained its technical methods and studies in a way that assures that the court can adequately understand and follow its reasoning.[7] Indeed, in a few cases where the courts have rejected the

---

erally experienced by children growing up in smoking homes (*Flue-Cured Tobacco* 1998, pp. 458–60).

EPA also switched from using a standard 95% confidence to a 90% confidence interval in analyzing the meta-analysis. Again, the court rightly berated EPA for making this change without adequate explanation (ibid. at 462). But the court went further and essentially rejected the validity of ever using anything other than the "standard methodology" of a 95% confidence interval (ibid. at 461).

[6]For citations to still more cases that advocate great deference to agency statistical analyses, see Fienberg (1989, p. 120–22).

[7]The courts have paid at least lip service to the need for explanation (*Environmental Defense Fund v. Hardin* 1970, p. 1100), and have at times stated the requirement rather

extra-deference test and engaged in active review of an agency's scientific and technical decisions, such as *Gulf South* and *Corrosion-Proof Fittings* discussed above, it appears that the courts' concerns were aggravated by the agency's own frank concessions about the sources of error, variability, and incompleteness of the underlying data. Thus, a principle of judicial review that initially and quite admirably was intended to give agencies fact-finding and policy-making space has evolved into a standard that immunizes those technical rules that escape understanding as long as definitive-looking facts and figures support agency findings.

2.3 Scrutiny of Policy Judgments

Third and finally, if an agency does boldly admit to the policy judgments it has made when filling in gaps created by limited data, it will increase the vulnerability of the rule to invalidation or remand, particularly if the panel of judges collectively find the agency's rule to be politically unpalatable. In *American Trucking Associations, Inc. v. EPA* (1999, p. 5), for example, the D.C. Circuit remanded the EPA's ozone and particulate standards specifically because it found that the EPA's candid struggle to compare imprecise and uncertain health effects occurring at incremental pollution levels was neither "coherent" nor "principled." Several prominent legal scholars have specifically observed that agency rules are most at risk when the policy implications of the regulation are clear (Breyer 1986, p. 384; Mashaw & Harfst 1987, p. 273–74, 303; Melnick 1983, p. 371; Pierce 1988, p. 301–02). Empirical analyses of decisions by various D.C. Circuit panels confirm the tendency of judges to adopt different presumptions about the legality of agency rules depending on their political allegiance before taking the bench (Revesz 1997; Tiller 1998). If an agency is candid about its tendency to err on

---

boldly. The clearest statement comes from the First Circuit, which held that "[w]e will not remand so long as the Agency has explained the facts and policies on which it relied; the facts have some basis in the record; and a reasonable person could make the judgment the Agency made" (*BASF Wyandotte Corp. v. Costle* 1979, p. 652).

Yet despite these noble declarations, in most and perhaps all cases the "clear explanation" requirement appears to have been imposed only in the most egregious circumstances when the agency provided *no* explanation or one that was inconsistent with the agency's remaining analysis (*Natural Resources Defense Council, Inc. v. EPA* 1987, pp. 1287–89; *Dry Color Manufacturers' Association, Inc. v. Dept. of Labor* 1973, p. 106; *PPG Indus., Inc. v. Costle* 1980, p. 466; *Kennecott Copper Corp. v. EPA* 1972, p. 850). Indeed, one can read the opinions in this area to imply that if an agency provides a highly technical explanation that on its face purports to explain a judgment, the rule would be upheld and possibly even applauded (*National Nutritional Foods Association v. Weinberger* 1975, pp. 701–03). For example, the Tenth Circuit held in *Kennecott Copper Corp. v. EPA* (1979, pp. 1240–41), that EPA's explanations underlying its effluent limitation regulations were adequate because "[d]ata was set forth in detail, appropriate technology is noted, and conclusions are derived therefrom," although it is not clear from the opinion whether EPA also explained its policy choices or highlighted sources of error.

the side of human health by adopting quantitative models that are uniformly the most conservative, then that agency is increasing the risk that a panel will disagree with its judgment and find a way to reverse it. On the other hand, highly complicated and even unintelligible statistical explanations for agency standards provide shelter from such political winds and increase the chance that regulations will be upheld. Thus this ad hoc feature of judicial review also rewards the presentation of quantitative results that appear misleadingly precise or are presented in unintelligible ways that conceal from lay judges sources of error and underlying policy judgments.

3 Problems with EPA's Statistical Practices

The courts' uneven and often counterproductive approach to reviewing technical rules leaves the agencies with a clear, albeit unintended, message: the more unequivocal the agency's supporting quantitative analysis appears, the more likely the rule will survive judicial review. Indeed, a preambulatory discussion and accompanying rule that camouflages the numerous scientific uncertainties with technical-sounding, albeit not necessarily accessible or intelligible, explanations faces a greater chance of surviving judicial review than a more forthright discussion of the significant uncertainties associated with setting a standard that protects the public health.

Several recurring problems that surface in agency analyses can in fact be traced, either directly or indirectly, to these unrealistic judicial requirements. The influence of judicial review on agency analyses will obviously be most profound during the latter stages of an agency rulemaking. Yet even if agency scientists conducting initial studies and risk assessments remain relatively insulated from the courts' legal messages, they may still be affected indirectly to the extent that they are already predisposed to understate or obfuscate data gaps and uncertainties in their assessments (Wagner 1995, pp. 1632–40). Although in this instance the courts' approach to judicial review cannot be blamed for initiating the particular statistical errors, the courts' legal pronouncements do serve to discourage the agency from correcting the errors and ultimately may cultivate a bureaucratic climate that tolerates, if not rewards, certain poor statistical practices.

EPA's risk assessments and resulting protective standards have in fact been consistently criticized for the inadequate discussions (or even mention) of critical scientific uncertainties. Despite public acknowledgment of these problems, however, EPA has steered a rather steady course in tolerating certain poor statistical practices. Although the courts' demands for certainty may not be the only cause of the agency's lapses, the perverse impact of the courts' approach to reviewing technical regulations is likely a significant contributor to many of the statistical errors that continue to be tolerated by the EPA in developing regulatory standards. Three specific types of statistical weaknesses in the agency's rulemakings are discussed in the subsections that follow.

3.1   Significant Analytical Gaps Not Disclosed

EPA's reluctance to admit to large analytical gaps in its risk assessment or quantitative assessment constitutes the first and perhaps most important problem with EPA's statistical practices. Arriving at a plausible safety standard for fine particulates in the air, for example, requires a series of measurements (or in lieu of such scientific measurements, assumptions) that begin with ambient concentrations in the air and follow the particles to individual exposures and ultimately trace their effects in the lungs. Each step in the external and internal exposure chain is critical. Yet much of this information, such as the range of variability in the types and extent of personal outdoor exposures, may be poorly understood or even nonquantifiable based on the present state of scientific knowledge (NRC 1998, pp. 34–39, 44–97).

Perhaps due in part to the judiciary's intolerance of uncertainties and unquantified variables (and undoubtedly exacerbated by the fear of political reprisal for exposed policy judgments), the EPA has on numerous occasions addressed gaping voids in this analytical sequence by simply ignoring or otherwise camouflaging them. In developing a drinking water standard for lead, for example, EPA employed a biostatistician to do a study to determine children's drinking water patterns, but for reasons that are not clear, EPA did not use the study in conducting its analysis. Rather than admitting to this resulting, important informational gap in the final rule, however, EPA neither identified nor discussed the need for such a consumption study, nor did it "specify the presumed underlying drinking water consumption pattern" that ultimately formed the basis for its standard (Powell 1997a, p. 13). EPA's controversial fine particulate standard promulgated in 1997 as a national ambient air quality standard revealed similar sins of omission (EPA 1997). EPA, for example, fended off concerns by commenters that it needed to address the uncertainties associated with correlating outdoor ambient concentrations of fine particulates with personal exposures (both outdoor and total exposures) (ibid., pp. 38656, 38659, 38664). Yet by discounting this problem, EPA effectively obscures important gaps in its analysis and underutilizes key opportunities for encouraging further research on important unresolved problems arising in environmental and public health science (NRC 1998, pp. 32, 34–39, 40, 42–43).

3.2   Inadequate Characterization of Uncertainty and Variability

EPA's related tendency to summarize its analyses without providing basic accompanying parameters such as confidence intervals or discussions of uncertainty and variability provides a second illustration of EPA's reluctance to explain uncertainties. For over fifteen years the National Research Council of the National Academy of Sciences has criticized EPA's affinity for "a single point estimate" of risk, which "suppresses information about sources of error that result from choices of model, data sets, and techniques for estimating values of parameters from data" (NRC 1994, p. 184; NRC 1983, pp. 7–8).

Frank discussions about uncertainty, variability, and methodological choices—
the foundation of good statistical analysis—are also often wanting in many EPA
rulemakings. Somewhat predictably, EPA's failure to discuss uncertainties or explain why it selected some models or assumptions over other plausible options has
exposed the agency to sharp criticism (Graham et al. 1988, p. 158; Landy et al.
1990, p. 279; Latin 1988, pp. 100–105). In the National Research Council's most
recent report on this issue, the Academy Committee reiterated their uniform concern "that EPA often does not clearly articulate in its risk-assessment guidelines
that a specific assumption is a default option and that EPA does not fully explain in
its guidelines the basis for each default option" (NRC, p. 7, 1994). For example, in
setting air standards EPA has generally avoided preambulatory discussions of why
it selected one plausible model over others, referring to its final choices simply
as "agency judgments" or "health policies" (Wagner 1995, pp. 1630–31). Similar explanatory sleights of hand pervade EPA's study of environmental tobacco
smoke. Indeed, EPA appeared so intent upon making its risk assessment appear
scientifically complete that the agency lost valuable opportunities to improve the
quality of its analysis by openly explaining inherent uncertainties in the available
epidemiology studies, in determining the chemical composition of environmental
tobacco smoke, and in justifying the agency's selection of a ninety percent confidence interval for analyzing its meta-study (*Flue Cured Tobacco Cooperative
Stabilization Corp. v. EPA* 1998, pp. 455–62).[8]

EPA has also been criticized for avoiding statistical techniques that provide
richer characterization of the underlying variability in its data sets, information that
again tends only to underscore the numerous uncertainties in its risk assessment
(NRC 1994, p. 12; Thompson and Graham 1996).[9] For example, in calculating the
risk from exposure to multiple chemicals, EPA often relies on the simple addition of
point estimate risks for each chemical, rather than employing, when possible, more
illuminating statistical procedures to aggregate risks from exposure to multiple

---

[8]Even though its selection of a 90% confidence interval could have been justified in
part by the tendency of epidemiological studies to underestimate adverse effects when data
on individual exposures is not available (Gastwirth 1988, p. 896), as well as by the higher
costs of a Type I error relative to a Type II error in light of the scientific consensus that
smoking causes lung cancer and heart problems, EPA instead resorted to contorted, technical
justifications that were much less compelling (ibid., p. 461). Specifically, the EPA provided
the following explanation for its use of a 90 percent confidence interval:

Before this court, EPA explains the 'use of the 95 percent confidence interval with the
one-tailed test ... would have produced an apparent discrepancy: study results that
were statistically significant using the standard p-value of .05 might nevertheless have
a 95 percent confidence interval that included a relative risk of 1.' (citations omitted)
(ibid. p. 461).

[9]The USDA has also been criticized for failing to use more sophisticated techniques
in its risk assessment. Mark Powell, for example, argues that USDA's aggregation of bulk
pesticide loadings in risk assessments caused much information to be lost that could have
been preserved simply by weighting individual pesticides according to their toxicity (Powell
1997b, p. 24).

compounds (NRC 1994, p. 13). In the past several years and in response to this criticism, the EPA has produced several policy documents that encourage the use of more sophisticated statistical techniques when the data and other characteristics permit (EPA 1997; Hansen 1997; Poulter 1998, pp. 7–9). It remains to be seen, however, how much of this analysis will actually be conducted or discussed in agency regulatory preambles or how the courts will react to these discussions in their review of the regulations (Poulter 1998, pp. 22–23).[10]

3.3 Reliance on Incomplete or Questionable Studies

The third and final type of poor statistical practice tolerated by EPA likely stems from its often hurried and data-desperate administrative state of being. EPA's eagerness to support its time-sensitive regulatory standards occasionally leads it to rely on studies that are incomplete or of questionable quality. In such instances, the agency is not always candid about the potential problems in the studies.[11] In at least one case—EPA's heavy reliance on the Six Cities study in its formulation of the 1997 fine particulate standard—the agency's failure to ensure the quality of the results led to considerable regulatory backlash. In response to both public and congressional pressure regarding possible flaws in the Six Cities study, EPA has commissioned a statistical reanalysis of the study that includes a quality assurance audit on a sample of the original data and sensitivity analyses to test the robustness of the original findings and interpretations to alternative analytic approaches (BNA 1997). EPA's unquestioning reliance on the Six Cities study also led Congress to establish a National Academy of Sciences panel to review the agency's scientific needs in the regulation of fine particulates in order to ensure that the agency takes both a more critical and a more comprehensive review of existing studies and remaining data gaps (NRC 1998, pp. 19–21).

---

[10]The EPA policies do encourage more open discussions about the choice of statistical tools (EPA 1997, pp. 14–20). However, EPA also expressly states that compliance with its guidance documents advocating more comprehensive statistical analyses is neither legally binding nor necessarily appropriate for some rulemaking (Hansen 1997, p. 3).

[11]EPA, for example, relied on a study by Herbert Needleman that was important to developing a lead drinking water standard (Needleman et al. 1979). The study came under heated attack from other scientists alleging errors in Needleman's data collection methods as well as with other statistical practices. EPA provided Needleman with funding to reanalyze the data using the appropriate statistical tools, but again his study was attacked, and both his 1979 and 1990 studies were ultimately judged flawed because of "sloppy statistics," although there was determined to be no scientific misconduct. (Powell 1997a, p. 10) (citing ORI letter dated March 3, 1994). Despite the controversy, there is evidence that EPA officials relied on Needleman's work throughout the decision-making process, even at points when his statistical analyses had been called into question (ibid., p. 9). Since Needleman's conclusions were ultimately corroborated by independent studies before EPA released its final decision document (ibid.), however, EPA's alleged over-reliance on a study adjudged to have statistical flaws proved relatively harmless in the lead standard case.

4   Reform

While EPA's poor statistical practices may seem unforgivable when viewed in isolation, when set against the backdrop of judicial review they seem eminently rational. Omitting the often gaping sources of uncertainties and errors in their analysis, the EPA is able to massage risk assessments to appear more scientifically certain pursuant to the courts' general expectations and, in some cases, demands. Yet this science charade has significant detrimental impacts on the quality of statistical analyses. Once the uncertainties are uncovered in a risk assessment—usually as a result of political opposition to a particular standard or rulemaking—EPA's scientific credibility is undermined. What might have initially been a rational administrative reluctance to explain unpreventable uncertainties for fear of political controversy and judicial reprisal becomes an indication to congresspersons and the public at large that the agency is captured, politicized, or otherwise engaged in some clandestine, ends-oriented analysis. EPA's effort to make its rulemakings look as definitive as possible not only alienates policymakers and lay commentators, it may also complicate if not preclude the ability of scientists and statisticians to judge the reliability of its analysis and comment meaningfully on the agency's regulatory proposals (Preuss and White 1985, p. 335).

Despite periodic vows to change its ways, many of which are codified in the legally impotent form of policy guidances, it seems doubtful that EPA will have sufficient incentive to change its poor statistical habits as long as the courts effectively reward the agency for producing regulations that appear more certain than they actually are. But fortunately, the courts' counterproductive approach to judicial review is capable of reform. Since the appellate courts' current ad hoc rules for reviewing agency regulations seem the result of inattention, rather than a deliberated conception of what judicial review should be, clearer and more appropriate guidelines for the review of agency technical rules seem the perfect antidote. Such guidelines would set forth more appropriate rules for review, while simultaneously overruling past judicial decisions that tend to discourage agencies from conducting sophisticated and accessible quantitative analysis.

4.1   An Improved Standard for Judicial Review

A reformed standard of review for agency rules would require only minor clarifications to the existing approach, but could substantially improve the quality of agency quantitative analysis and fit comfortably within the vague guidelines currently set down in the Administrative Procedure Act (5 U.S.C. §706(2)).[12] Under a reformed standard for review, appellate courts would require only that the agency provide accessible explanations for the technical and policy analyses supporting their decisions. Once explained, the agency's actual substantive

---

[12]Additional legislative clarification of this refined standard would also be welcome reinforcement, although it is not essential.

decisions would be afforded great deference. This may in fact be the approach Skelly Wright took in authoring the opinion in *Ethyl*, although he was not explicit about the specific analytical steps used in his review (*Ethyl Corp. v. EPA* 1976; Wagner 1996). It is also the approach advocated by Judge Bazelon, if not in his judicial opinions, at least in his law review writings (Bazelon 1977, p. 823).[13]

Applying this revised and clarified standard would involve primarily procedural review, a type of review for which the courts are particularly well suited. In the review of an ambient air quality standard, for example, the court (assisted by those challenging the regulation) would review carefully whether the agency has stated all of the critical steps of its analysis, including assumptions where the current science is highly uncertain. The court would also scrutinize whether the agency has endeavored to highlight and characterize the uncertainties and variability in the data it does have available.[14] Finally, the court would ensure that the agency has provided accessible explanations for its selection of models and other statistical tools. Once these assumptions, technical choices, and other features of the rulemaking are identified and explained, however, the court's oversight role nears an end. The court would afford both the agency's technical and policy conclusions great deference. Technical judgments, such as the selection of statistical models, would be reviewed only under a highly deferential "arbitrary and capricious" standard: An agency's substantive technical decision, once explained, would be reversed *only* if it is clearly contrary to generally accepted statistical or scientific practices. Policy conclusions would similarly receive great deference and be invalidated only when they fall outside the permissible bounds of the agency's statutory mandate. This standard for review thus limits the courts to ensuring that the agency has stayed within the "policy space" left by Congress in the authorizing statute, and that even

---

[13]At least two opinions involving the review of agency rulemakings appear to illustrate this approach to judicial review of technical rulemakings. In *National Lime Association v. EPA* (1980), the D.C. Circuit remanded EPA's rule because the agency did not consider the representativeness of its data or explain why existing data was sufficient for setting a technology-based water pollution discharge standard promulgated for lime-manufacturing plants. The Sixth Circuit remanded an even more mysterious EPA regulation in *Cincinnati Gas & Electric Co. v. EPA* (1978) for "further study," because EPA did not explain why it ignored important, relevant studies or conclusions of an experts' conference that EPA itself had convened. Thus, in both cases, the EPA's divergence from what appeared to be good statistical practices, coupled with the absence of an explanation for the divergence, led the courts to remand the rules.

[14]The agency should also highlight additional research that, if undertaken, would likely assist it in understanding a particular environmental regulatory problem. Indeed, the general unavailability of many industry-sponsored, unpublished studies may need to be factored (or at least noted) in the agency's analysis of existing data (Gastwirth 1997, p. 298). The extent to which the agency should be required to locate unpublished studies and the more general problem of deficient incentives for industry to make internal studies publicly available are critical issues to improving the quality of agency regulatory analyses, but these issues deserve much more detailed attention than is possible in this article.

if within this "policy space," the resulting rulemaking is not arbitrary based on the facts available to the agency at the time of its decision (Percival 1996, p. 180).

The proposal alters the current set of ad hoc rules that govern judicial review by changing the "extra-deference" test to require deference *not* when the rule appears incomprehensibly complex and technical, but instead only after the agency has clearly explained how it got from the data to the ultimate standard or proposed regulation. This explanation would include "an explicit statement of the models used in the analysis, an assessment of the fit of the model . . . the reasons why some studies were selected as reliable and others were not . . . [and] the logical thought process of assessing the effect of the various assumptions on the resulting estimates of risk" (Gastwirth 1988, p. 900). Judicial demands for "substantial evidence" or the equivalent requirement of extensive technical support for a rule would similarly be replaced with extra deference, again provided that the agency clearly explains what it has done and explicitly identifies issues that escape quantitative analysis, that require policy judgments, or that may benefit from additional research.

Such an adjustment to the standard for judicial review thus corrects the major detrimental features of the courts' current ad hoc approach without requiring a complete overhaul of the state of judicial review. It also respects the separate roles the judiciary and the expert scientific community should play in improving the regulatory process. First, the proposed "explain and defer" approach to judicial review reinforces current judicial and academic consensus that the courts should *not* be in the business of scrutinizing the adequacy of agency technical and statistical decisions (*Craig v. Boren* 1976, p. 204; *Ethyl Corp. v. EPA* 1976, p. 67 (Bazelon, C.J., concurring); Abraham and Merrill 1986, p. 99; Fienberg 1989, pp. 15, 60; Finkelstein and Levin 1990, pp. 170–71; Kaye 1991, pp. 1543–44; Pierce 1990, p. 516). Yet it takes full advantage of the fact that "what courts and judges can do . . . and do well . . . is scrutinize and monitor the decisionmaking process to make sure that it is thorough, complete, and rational" (Bazelon 1977, p. 823). If the agency uses a Monte Carlo simulation in its analysis and its technical decision is challenged, for example, the court should give great deference to the agency's choice, provided that it has explained the advantages and disadvantages of the technique under the circumstances and followed generally established practices for disclosing assumptions and verifying the statistical methods (by, for example, conducting a sensitivity analysis) (Gastwirth 1989, p. 193).

Second, the reform reinforces the notion that better explanations of error and uncertainties will ultimately result in better science (Bazelon 1977, p. 823). Open communication is a fundamental tenet of good science, and one that can be impaired by litigation, including challenges to agency rules. If agencies concede their own misgivings about their data and methods of analysis and explain openly why they made the choices they did, both public policy-making and scientific and statistical research will be improved. But agency frankness about inherent weaknesses in quantitative analysis will surface only once the agencies are relatively confident that courts will provide them wide latitude in exercising their technical and policy-making discretion.

4.2   Response to Critics

The most obvious problem with a reform that reorients the courts toward policing the quality of the agencies' disclosures is that this type of test still requires the court to become expert in statistical and scientific analysis, albeit only with regard to detecting omitted discussions of sources of error, uncertainties, and variability encountered in data collection and analysis. To assist the courts in this endeavor, reference manuals or even abbreviated checklists of statistical and scientific considerations, such as those that are provided in recent handbooks on scientific evidence, might prove particularly valuable (Iancu and Steitz 1997; Kaye and Freedman 1994). Even the court appointment of statistician experts to assist in judging the adequacy of the agency's explanations may prove desirable in some cases.[15]

Another danger of the proposal is that some courts may be more inclined to find that the explanatory requirements have not been met when they are displeased with the agencies' policy choices. This is a current shortcoming of judicial review and one that likely would persist to some extent even if this reform were implemented. The danger may be minimized, however, if the guidelines and expectations for agency explanations are clear.[16] For example, explanations should be required for agency policy and technical choices, but if an agency openly concedes the uncertainties and establishes that the statute adopts the precautionary principle of regulation, the courts must defer. These guidelines would in theory thus preclude some of the dissatisfied nitpicking that can occur in cases like *Flue-Cured Tobacco Stabilization Cooperative Corp. v. EPA* (1998), where the district court demanded from the agency fuller explanations, but conveyed the impression that these explanations had to be backed up with additional data rather than detailed discussions of scientific uncertainty.

If the guidelines also could be paired with a viable threat of Supreme Court review of appellate remands based on inadequate explanations, this would further improve the constraints the test would impose on judicial decision-making (Revesz 1997, pp. 1731, 1767–68). Appellate courts will be wary of such remands and thus will exercise greater restraint in resisting politically motivated decisions. In any case, even if some biases in judicial review remain under the reformed standard,

---

[15]The use of experts by appellate courts in the review of agency rulemakings appears to have received no consideration, particularly with regard to their assistance in determining whether an agency's explanation is complete, transparent, and accessible (Cecil and Willging 1994, pp. 1009–12). Yet using court-appointed experts to provide assistance in judging the comprehensiveness of agencies' technical explanations seems a completely natural extension of the current use of these expert advisors.

[16]If guidelines were prepared for the courts, they could be legislatively directed (prepared by Congress directly or through the establishment of an expert panel like the National Academy of Sciences) or prepared by the Federal Judicial Center. In fact, the Federal Judicial Center has been quite effective in preparing these types of reference manuals for related technical issues; see, for example, Kaye and Freedman 1994 and accompanying manual.

the adverse ramifications may be less significant compared with the adverse consequences resulting from the courts' current ad hoc approach to review. A court that requires from an agency an inordinately detailed explanation might slow the rule making process down, but as a substantive matter the decision would not impair the agency's candidness in highlighting uncertainties, nor would it impact the integrity of the agency's scientific and policy analyses.

A final concern with the proposal could question whether it gives the agency too much discretion to continue poor statistical practices. This concern is mitigated to some extent by the fact that the courts still reserve legal authority to remand agency analyses that are clearly arbitrary or otherwise erroneous. It is further counterbalanced by virtue of the fact that in requiring the agency to explain its steps more clearly, its choice of statistical tools will be exposed and explained, leaving the agency more vulnerable to pressure from Congress and possibly the White House (generally via the Office of Management and the Budget). These extrajudicial pressures on agencies often can be formidable and serve as potent deterrents to poor agency statistical practices, irrespective of the role of the courts (Lazarus 1991).

In any case, the judiciary's demonstrated incapacity to review agency statistical practices in detail, discussed above, leaves no other choice. Between the costs of occasional judicial invalidation of an agency's good statistical practices and the costs of judicial affirmation of an agency's poor statistical practices, then, the costs of error are likely lower under the latter deference approach. Although affirming a rule based on poor (but not arbitrary) statistical practices will result in an unnecessarily imperfect regulatory program (to the extent that the errors are not ultimately corrected by political pressures), striking down good analyses is likely to have more serious adverse ramifications. If agencies risk having good statistical practices invalidated, their administrative concerns will likely be expressed in the form of extended regulatory delays and possibly in their avoidance of those specific good statistical practices that have been rejected by one or more courts. The occasional erroneous invalidation of agencies' good statistical practices will also likely lead agencies to continue to produce regulatory analyses and explanations that are often inaccessible and that fail to disclose critical uncertainties and assumptions. Finally, simply from the perspective of controlling burgeoning court dockets, occasionally deferring to poor statistical analyses as compared to occasionally invalidating good statistical practices will deter challenges to rulemakings and reduce the judicial resources expended in reviewing each challenge.

5 Conclusion

Several ad hoc rules and patterns have emerged in the appellate courts' review of technical agency rules. Taken together, these rules tend to impede the agency's adherence to good statistical practices. Patterns of weaknesses in the agency's use and disclosure of its statistical analysis further suggest that the agencies are either being rewarded for certain bad practices or are not sufficiently encouraged to use good statistical practices. But because the appellate courts' weaknesses appear to be the result of inattention, reform by clarifying and fine-tuning the standard for review of agency rules should go a long way toward correcting the problem.

Acknowledgments

I am grateful to Joseph Gastwirth, John Graham, and two anonymous reviewers for exceedingly helpful comments and editorial suggestions. Jonathan Entin and Steven Nutt also provided valuable assistance in refining many of the arguments advanced in this article, and Christina Tuggey provided excellent research assistance.

6 Cases and Statutes Cited

American Trucking Associations, Inc. v. EPA, 1999 WL 300618 (D.C. Cir. 1999).

Asbestos Information Association v. Occupational Safety and Health Administration, 727 F.2d 415 (5th Cir. 1984).

Association of Data Processing Service Organizations, Inc. v. Board of Governors, 745 F.2d 677 (D.C. Cir. 1984).

Baltimore Gas & Elec. Co. v. Natural Resources Defense Council, Inc., 462 U.S. 87 (1983).

BASF Wyandotte Corp. v. Costle, 598 F.2d 637 (1st Cir. 1979).

Chemical Manufacturers Association v. EPA, 870 F.2d 177 (5th Cir. 1989).

Cincinnati Gas & Electric Co. v. EPA, 578 F.2d 660 (6th Cir. 1978).

Connecticut Fund for the Env't v. EPA, 696 F.2d 169 (2d Cir. 1982).

Corrosion-Proof Fittings v. EPA, 947 F.2d 1201 (5th Cir. 1991).

Craig v. Boren, 429 U.S. 190 (1976).

Dry Color Manufacturers' Association, Inc. v. Dept. of Labor, 486 F.2d 98 (3d Cir. 1973).

Environmental Defense Fund v. Hardin, 428 F.2d 1093 (D.C. Cir. 1970).

Ethyl Corp. v. EPA, 541 F.2d 1 (D.C. Cir. 1976).

Flue-Cured Tobacco Cooperative Stabilization Corp. v. EPA, 4 F. Supp. 2d 435 (M.D.N.C. 1998).

Gulf South Insulation v. Consumer Product Safety Commission, 701 F.2d 1137 (5th Cir. 1983).

Industrial Union Dep't v. American Petroleum Inst., 448 U.S. 607 (1980).

Kennecott Copper Corp. v. EPA, 462 F.2d 846 (D.C. Cir. 1972).

Kennecott Copper Corp. v. EPA, 612 F.2d 1232 (10th Cir. 1979).

National Lime Association v. EPA, 627 F.2d 416 (D.C. Cir. 1980).

National Nutritional Foods Association v. Weinberger, 512 F.2d 688 (2d Cir.), *cert. denied*, 423 U.S. 827 (1975).

Natural Resources Defense Council, Inc. v. EPA, 824 F.2d 1258 (1st Cir. 1987).

Pennsylvania v. EPA, 932 F.2d 269 (3d Cir. 1991).
PPG Indus., Inc. v. Costle, 630 F.2d 462 (6th Cir. 1980).
Reynolds Metals Co. v. EPA, 760 F.2d 549 (4th Cir. 1985).
Texas Independent Ginners Association v. Marshall, 630 F.2d 398 (5th Cir. 1980).
United Steelworkers v. Marshall, 647 F.2d 1189 (D.C. Cir. 1980), *cert. denied*, 453 U.S. 913 (1981) 5 U.S.C. §706(2).

REFERENCES

[1] Abraham, K.S. and Merrill, R.A. (Winter 1986). Scientific Uncertainty in the Courts, *Issues in Science and Technology*, 2, 93–107.

[2] Ashford, N.A., et al., (1983). A Hard Look at Federal Regulation of Formaldehyde: A Departure from Reasoned Decisionmaking, *Harvard Environmental Law Review*, 7, 297–370.

[3] Bazelon, D.L. (1977). Coping with Technology through the Legal Process, *Cornell Law Review*, 62, 817–832.

[4] Bureau of National Affairs (BNA). (1997). Air Quality Standards: Research Panel to Take Another Look at Studies Used by EPA to Set PM Rule, *Environment Reporter*, 28, 712.

[5] Breyer, S.G. (1986). Judicial Review of Questions of Law and Policy, *Administrative Law Review*, 38, 363–98.

[6] Cecil, J.S. and Willging, T.E. (1994). Accepting Daubert's Invitation: Defining a Role for Court-Appointed Experts in Assessing Scientific Validity, *Emory Law Journal*, 43, 995–1070.

[7] Cross, F.B. (1986). Beyond Benzene: Establishing Principles for a Significance Threshold on Regulatable Risks of Cancer, *Emory Law Journal*, 35, 1–57.

[8] Environmental Protection Agency. (1997). National Ambient Air Quality Standards for Particulate Matter, Federal Register, 62, 38652–760.

[9] Fienberg, S.E. (1989). *The Evolving Role of Statistical Assessments as Evidence in the Courts*, New York: Springer-Verlag.

[10] Gastwirth, J.L. (1988). *Statistical Reasoning in Law and Public Policy, Vol. 2: Tort Law, Evidence, and Health*, Boston: Academic Press.

[11] Gastwirth, J.L. (1989). The Potential Effect of Unchecked Statistical Assumptions: A Fault in *San Luis Obispo Mothers for Peace v. United States Nuclear Regulatory Commission, Journal of Energy Law & Policy*, 9, 177–94.

[12] Gastwirth, J.L. (1998). Review of "Reference Manual on Scientific Evidence," *The American Statistician*, 51, 297–99.

[13] Graham, J.R., Green, L.C., and Roberts, M.J. (1988). *In Search of Safety: Chemicals and Cancer Risk*, Cambridge, MA: Harvard University Press.

[14] Hansen, F. (May 15, 1997). *Policy for Use of Probabilistic Analysis in Risk Assessment at the U.S. Environmental Protection Agency*, Washington, DC: U.S. EPA.

[15] Environmental Protection Agency. (1997). *Building Principles for Monte Carlo Analysis*, Washington, DC: U.S. EPA.

[16] Finkelstein, M.O. and Levin, B. (1990). *Statistics for Lawyers*, New York: Springer-Verlag.

[17] Iancu, C.A. and Steitz, P.W. (1997). Guide to Statistics, In *Expert Evidence: A Practitioner's Guide to Law, Science, and the FJC Manual* (eds. B. Black and P. W. Lee) St. Paul, MN: West Publishing Co., pp. 267–318.

[18] Jasanoff, S. (1990). *The Fifth Branch: Science Advisers as Policymakers*, Cambridge, MA: Harvard University Press.

[19] Kaye, D.H. (1991). Statistics for Lawyers and Law for Statistics (Book Review), *Michigan Law Review*, 89, 1520–44.

[20] Kaye, D.H. and Freedman, D.A. (1994). Reference Guide on Statistics, In *Federal Judicial Center, Reference Manual on Scientific Evidence*, Washington, DC: Federal Judicial Center., pp. 331–414.

[21] Landy, M.K., Roberts, M.J., and Thomas, S.R. (1990). *The Environmental Protection Agency: Asking the Wrong Questions*, New York: Oxford University Press.

[22] Latin, H. (1988). Good Science, Bad Regulation, and Toxic Risk Assessment, *Yale Journal on Regulation*, 5, 89–148.

[23] Lazarus, R.J., (Autumn 1991). The Neglected Question of Congressional Oversight of EPA: Quis Custodiet Ipsos Custodes (Who Shall Watch the Watchers Themselves?), *Law & Contemporary Problems* 54, 205–39.

[24] McGarity, T.O. (1979). Substantive and Procedural Discretion in Administrative Resolution of Science Policy Questions: Regulating Carcinogens in EPA and OSHA, *Georgetown Law Journal*, 67, 729–810.

[25] McGarity, T.O. (1992). Some Thoughts on "Deossifying" the Rulemaking Process, *Duke Law Journal*, 41, 1385–1462.

[26] Mashaw, J.L. and Harfst, D.L. (1987). Regulation and Legal Culture: The Case of Motor Vehicle Safety, *Yale Journal on Regulation*, 4, 257–316.

[27] Mazurek, J., et al. (1995). Shifting to Prevention: The Limits of Current Policy, In *Reducing Toxics: A New Approach to Policy and Industrial Decisionmaking* (ed. R. Gottlieb) Washington, DC: Island Press., pp. 58–94.

[28] Melnick, R.S. (1983). *Regulation and the Courts: The Case of the Clean Air Act*, Washington, DC: Brookings Institution.

[29] National Research Council, Committee on the Institutional Means for Assessment of Risks to Public Health. (1983). *Risk Assessment in the Federal Government: Managing the Process*, Washington, DC: National Academy Press.

[30] National Research Council, Committee on Risk Assessment of Hazardous Air Pollutants. (1994). *Science and Judgment in Risk Assessment*, Washington, DC: National Academy Press.

[31] National Research Council, Committee on Research Priorities for Airborne Particu-
late Matter. (1998). *Research Priorities for Airborne Particulate Matter: I. Immediate
Priorities and a Long-Range Research Portfolio*, Washington, DC: National Academy
Press.

[32] Needleman, H., et al. (1979). Deficits in psychological and classroom performance
in children with elevated dentine lead levels, *New England Journal of Medicine*, 300,
423–440.

[33] Needleman, H., et al. (1990). The Long-term Effects of Exposure to Low Doses of
lead in Childhood, *New England Journal of Medicine*, 322, 83–88.

[34] Percival, R., et al. (1996). *Environmental Regulation: Law, Science, and Policy*,
Boston, Mass: Little, Brown and Co.

[35] Pierce, R.J. (1979). Two Problems in Administrative Law: Political Polarity on the
District of Columbia Circuit and Judicial Deterrence of Agency Rulemaking, *Duke
Law Journal*, 1988, 300–28.

[36] Pierce, R.J. (1990). Political Control Versus Impermissible Bias in Agency Decision-
making: Lessons from *Chevron and Mistretta, University of Chicago Law Review*,
57, 481–519.

[37] Pierce, R.J., Shapiro, S.A., and Verkuil, P.R. (1992). *Administrative Law and Process*,
Westbury, NY: Foundation Press.

[38] Poulter, S.R. (Winter 1998). Monte Carlo Simulation in Environmental Risk
Assessment—Science, Policy And Legal Issues, *Risk: Health, Safety & Environment*
7–26.

[39] Powell, M. (1997a). The 1991 Lead/Copper Drinking Water Rule & the 1995 De-
cision Not to Revise the Arsenic Drinking Water Rule: Two Case Studies in EPA's
Use of Science, Resources for the Future Discussion Paper 97-05, Washington, DC:
Resources for the Future.

[40] Powell, M. (1997b). Science in Sanitary and Phytosanitary Dispute Resolution, Resources for the Future Discussion Paper 97-50, Washington, DC: Resources for the
Future.

[41] Powell, M. (1997c). The 1983–84 Suspensions of EDB under FIFRA and the 1989
Asbestos Ban and Phaseout Rule under TSCA: Two Case Studies in EPA's Use of Science, Resources for the Future Discussion Paper 97-06, Washington, DC: Resources
for the Future.

[42] Preuss, P.N. and White, P.D. (1985). The Changing Role of Risk Assessment in
Federal Regulation, In *Risk Quantitation and Regulatory Policy* (eds. D.G.Hoel, R.A.
Merrill, F.P. Perera) Cold Spring Harbor, NY: Cold Spring Harbor Laboratory, pp.
331–37.

[43] Revesz, R.L. (1997). Environmental Regulation, Ideology, and the D.C. Circuit,
Virginia Law Review, 83, 1717–72.

[44] Rodgers, W. (1981). Judicial Review of Risk Assessment: The Role of Decision
Theory in Unscrambling the *Benzene* Decision, *Environmental Law*, 11, 301–20.

[45] Scalia, A. (July-Aug. 1981). Back to Basics: Making Law Without Making Rules, *Regulation* 5, 25–28.

[46] Thompson, K.M. and Graham, J.D. (1996). Going Beyond the Single Number: Using Probabilistic Risk Assessment to Improve Risk Management, *Human & Ecological Risk Assessment*, 4, 1008–34.

[47] Tiller, E.H. (1998). Controlling Policy by Controlling Process: Judicial Influence on Regulatory Decision-making, *Journal of Law, Economics & Organization*, 14, 114–35.

[48] Wagner, W.E. (1995). The Science Charade in Toxic Risk Regulation, *Columbia Law Review*, 95, 1613–1723.

[49] Wagner, W.E. (1996). Ethyl: Bridging the Science-Law Divide, *Texas Law Review*, 74, 1291–95.

Statistical Testimony on Damages in

Minnesota v. Tobacco Industry

Scott L. Zeger, Timothy Wyant, Leonard S. Miller,
and Jonathan Samet

Abstract

In 1994, the state of Minnesota and Minnesota Blue Cross/Blue Shield filed suit in Minnesota District Court against Philip Morris, six other tobacco companies, and two tobacco trade groups ("Tobacco") alleging that the defendants had acted fraudulently, conspired to prevent development of a less hazardous cigarette, and violated a public trust to communicate accurately about the health effects of smoking. After a four-month trial, the judge instructed the jury in Minnesota law. But before a decision could be rendered, the two sides settled with Tobacco agreeing to pay $6.5 billion and to restrict advertising and trade of cigarettes in the state of Minnesota.

This paper gives an overview of the *Minnesota v. Philip Morris et al.* case and the role of statistical experts for the plaintiffs. We describe our approach to assessing damages in terms of the smoking-attributable expenditures. The data sets relied upon and the statistical methods used to estimate damages are summarized. We also discuss the "death benefit" and "indivisible damages," two legal concepts that had substantial impact upon the relevance of particular statistical arguments within the case.

Keywords: smoking-attributable expenditure; regression; death benefit; indivisible damages; smoking, statistical expert; National Medical Expenditure Survey; Medicaid; Blue Cross/Blue Shield; tobacco; Behavioral Risk Factor Surveillance System

1   Introduction

In August 1994, the Minneapolis law firm of Robins, Kaplan, Miller and Ciresi filed suit in Minnesota state court on behalf of the state of Minnesota ("State") and Minnesota Blue Cross/Blue Shield (BCBS) against Phillip Morris, RJ Reynolds, five other tobacco companies, and two tobacco trade organizations ("Tobacco"). The plaintiffs alleged that the tobacco companies had conspired with one another to commit a fraud on the citizens of Minnesota by withholding information about the deleterious health effects of cigarette smoking, failing to compete in the development of a safer cigarette, and misrepresenting themselves as committed to protecting the public's health in a series of advertisements across the country, now known as the "frank statement" letter.

As part of their case, the plaintiffs attempted to demonstrate first that the alleged fraud and antitrust behavior had taken place, and second that the plaintiffs were entitled to receive damages as the result of these illegal activities. To establish damages, Minnesota presented expert testimony by one of us (JS), that smoking causes disease resulting in smoking-attributable expenditures by the State and Blue Cross/Blue Shield. Two others (SLZ and TW) then testified about damages, that "smoking-attributable expenditures" (SAEs) by Minnesota totaled $1.77 billion. This finding was based upon detailed statistical and econometric analyses (led by LM) of more than 280 million medical bills as well as national and state survey data. After nearly three years of preparation, Minnesota and the tobacco industry presented their cases to the jury in early 1998. When the testimony was complete, the judge instructed the jury on Minnesota law. But prior to jury deliberation, Minnesota and Tobacco announced they had reached a settlement in which industry agreed to restrictions on the advertisement and sale of cigarettes and to pay a total of $6.5 billion to the State and BCBS over an extended period of time.

The purpose of this paper is to describe the role of a statistical team in a large civil action such as *Minnesota v. Philip Morris et al.* In particular, our goal is to describe the legal setting and illustrate the interplay of statistical science and legal questions being addressed by the court.

Section 2 gives some additional background on *Minnesota v. Phillip Morris et al.* Section 3 gives an overview of the statistical models used to calculate damages. Section 4 addresses two specific legal issues: the "death benefit" and "indivisible damages" and how statistical testimony and issues were interpreted by the court. Section 5 is a closing discussion of the role of statistical experts for the plaintiffs in this case. Elsewhere, one of us has provided a personal perspective on testifying in the case (Samet, 1999).

2   The Case

2.1   The Complaint

On August 17, 1994, Hubert H. Humphrey III, for the state of Minnesota, and Thomas F. Gilde, for Blue Cross/Blue Shield of Minnesota, represented by Michael Ciresi and Roberta Walburn of Robins, Kaplan, Miller, and Ciresi, filed suit in State of Minnesota District Court, 2nd Judicial District, against Philip Morris Incorporated, RJ Reynolds Tobacco Company, Brown and Williamson Tobacco Corporation, British American Tobacco Industries PLC, Lorillard Tobacco Company, The American Tobacco Company, Liggett Group Inc., and two industry organizations, The Council for Tobacco Research - USA, Inc., and The Tobacco Institute, Inc. This section briefly summarizes the causes of action comprising nine counts.

The first count alleged that the defendants had undertaken a special duty, "to render services for the protection of the public health...by their representation and undertaking to accept an interest in the public's health as a basic and paramount responsibility" (*State by Humphrey v. Philip Morris Inc.*, 1996). Plaintiffs alleged that this special duty was undertaken in part in a January 4, 1954, newspaper advertisement placed in Minneapolis, St. Paul, and Duluth entitled "A frank statement to cigarette smokers." There, the industry said, "we accept an interest in people's health as a basic responsibility paramount to every other consideration in our business." "We believe the products we make are not injurious to health." "We always have and always will cooperate closely with those whose task it is to safeguard the public health." The plaintiffs alleged that these statements and others like them constituted a special duty that the industry subsequently violated.

The second count related to Minnesota antitrust law and alleged that the defendants had conspired to unreasonably restrain trade and commerce. Plaintiffs alleged that defendants had suppressed research on the harmful effects of smoking and had conspired not to produce a safer cigarette, thereby restraining competition in the market for cigarettes. Count three was a related charge having to do with monopolization of the cigarette market, which similarly constrained competition and prevented the creation of a safer cigarette.

Count four alleged that the defendants had made fraudulent, misleading, and deceptive statements and practices about smoking and health and that they had falsely promised to conduct and disclose research on smoking. Counts five through seven related to specific Minnesota statutes regarding fair trade and advertising as it related to the dissemination of false information by the industry. Count eight alleged that "defendants assumed and owe a duty to pay for the harm caused by their wrongful conduct..." and that "plaintiffs have been and will be required by statutory and contractual obligations to expend large sums of money to pay for the harm caused by the wrongful conduct of the defendants." Finally, the complaint alleged "unjust enrichment." It states "defendants, through their wrongful conduct...have reaped substantial and unconscionable profits from the sale of cigarettes in Minnesota. These cigarette sales, in turn, have resulted in increased health costs directly attributable to cigarette smoking.... As a result, plaintiffs have been required to pay for the medical costs stemming from defendants' unlawful acts.... In equity and good conscience, it would be unjust for defendants to enrich themselves at the expense of plaintiffs."

2.2 The Trial

The trial began on January 20, 1998, in the state of Minnesota, county of Ramsey District Court, 2nd Judicial District, Chief Judge Kenneth Fitzpatrick presiding. Jury selection was completed on January 27, when opening statements were given.

Over the next ten weeks, the plaintiffs presented more than twenty witnesses, listed in Table 1. Plaintiff witnesses attempted to establish that tobacco is an addictive drug that causes lung cancer, chronic obstructive pulmonary disease, coronary heart disease, stroke, and other specific diseases, poor health, and death. This testimony by a number of physicians and scientists was interspersed with testimony from chief executive officers (CEOs), senior scientists, and other representatives of the tobacco industry for the purpose of establishing the alleged misconduct by the industry. The jury spent many days during the plaintiff's case in reviewing tobacco documents. More than 39 million documents were petitioned by Minnesota and ultimately turned over. Documents were becoming available while the trial was proceeding, so plaintiffs interwove the presentation of documents with scientific experts and tobacco industry personnel.

After testimony to establish that tobacco is addictive and causes disease, plaintiffs presented testimony by Drs. Zeger and Wyant about the damages attributable to smoking and the statistical models that were developed with Dr. Miller to calculate those damages. The plaintiff's case was completed with testimony on youth smoking and antitrust behavior by the tobacco industry.

On March 26, 1998, the tobacco industry began its defense. Ten witnesses were presented as listed in Table 1. A main thrust of the statistical experts of the defense (Donald Rubin, Harvard University; Brian McCall, University of Minnesota, and William Wecker, private consultant) was that damage estimates by the plaintiffs were not reliable. Their criticisms included the following: smoking-attributable expenditures as defined by the plaintiffs' experts was the wrong quantity to estimate; key confounders had not been controlled for, so that the estimates were biased; substantial missing data in national surveys rendered the estimates unreliable; and the confidence intervals on the SAEs were too wide.

2.3 Settlement

On Friday, May 8, 1998, after hearing three and a half months of testimony, the twelve jurors were not allowed to decide the Minnesota case. During the preceding evening, Minnesota and Tobacco came to an historic settlement. The main components of the settlement are as follows. The state of Minnesota is to receive $6.1 billion over twenty-five years; Blue Cross and Blue Shield will receive $469 million over five years. The law firm of Robins, Kaplan, Miller, and Ciresi, representing the state, will receive roughly $440 million over three years from the tobacco companies. In addition, Tobacco agreed to a permanent injunction against marketing cigarettes to children in Minnesota with a penalty of contempt of court citations for violations. Cigarette billboards and merchandise with cigarette company logos cannot be displayed or sold or given away within Minnesota. Tobacco industry documents will be maintained for public use for a period of ten years. Other provisions on payments to the entertainment industry to display cigarettes, false claims about health impacts of smoking, and lobbying in Minnesota are also included (Pioneer Press, May 9, 1998).

Table 1. List of Witnesses

Plaintiffs:

Person	Title	Expertise
Dr. Richard Hurt	Director of Nicotine Dependency Center, Mayo Clinic, Rochester, MN	Nicotine Addiction
Channing R. Robertson	Professor, Department of Chemical Engineering, Stanford University	Cigarette Design
Walker P. Merryman	Vice President and spokesman, The Tobacco Institute	
Bennett S. LeBow	Chairman of Brook Group, parent of Liggett Group	
Dr. Jonathan M. Samet	Professor and Chairman, Department of Epidemiology, Johns Hopkins University	Epidemiology of smoking related diseases
Thomas S. Osdene	Retired Philip Morris VP of science and technology and former Philip Morris Research Director	Industry consultant
Dr. Scott F. Davies	Director of Pulmonary and Critical Care Medicine, Hennepin County Medical Center	Lung cancer
Dr. Kevin J. Graham	Director, Preventive Cardiology, Minneapolis Heart Institute	Atherosclerosis and coronary heart disease
Helmut Wakem	Former researcher, Philip Morris	
James Charles	Former researcher, Philip Morris	
Robert Heiman	Former CEO for American Tobacco Company, now deceased; videotaped deposition used	
Dr. James F. Glenn	President, chairman and CEO, Council for Tobacco Research, 1993–Present	
Dr. Scott L. Zeger	Professor and Chair, Department of Biostatistics, Johns Hopkins University	Biostatistics
Dr. Timothy Wyant	President, DECIPHER; Former statistical consultant for Dalkon Shield Claimants Trust	Biostatistics

Table 1. (Continued).

Plaintiffs:

Person	Title	Expertise
James Morgan	Former Philip Morris CEO (videotaped deposition)	
Geoffrey Bible	Philip Morris, president and CEO	
Andrew J. Schindler	President and CEO, R.J. Reynolds Tobacco Co.	
Dr. Cheryl L. Perry	Professor, Division of Epidemiology, School of Public Health, University of MN	Youth smoking
Murray Senkus	Retired, former director of research, R.J. Reynolds (videotaped deposition)	
Robert Sanford	Retired, former director of research and development, Brown and Williamson (videotaped deposition)	
Byron Price	Current director of analytical research, Brown and Williamson, former director of research for American Tobacco (videotaped deposition)	
David Wilson	Corporate Secretary, B.A.T Industries, PLC	
Roger Black	Researcher, Brown and Williamson (videotaped deposition)	Tobacco growth/nicotine
Robert J. Dolan	Professor of Business Administration, Graduate School of Business, Harvard University	Advertising, marketing and promotion expert
Dr. Adam B. Jaffe	Associate Professor of Economics, Brandeis University	Antitrust economics
Paul J. Much	Senior managing director, Houlihand, Lokey, Howard & Zukin	Financial analysis of tobacco industry
Clifton Lilly	VP of Technology, Philip Morris	Nicotine research
James Morgan	Recent Philip Morris President and CEO	

Table 1. (Continued).

Defendants:

Person	Title	Expertise
Dr. David T. Scheffman	Professor, Owen Graduate School of Management, Vanderbilt University	Antitrust expert
Dr. William Wecker	Private consultant	Statistics
Dr. Donald R. Rubin	Professor, Department of Statistics, Harvard University	Statistics
Dr. Brian McCall	Professor, Department of Human Resources and Industrial Relations, Carlson School of Management, University of MN	Econometrics
Dr. Hyman Berman	Professor of History, University of MN	History of smoking and the media
B. Scott Appleton	Director of Scientific & Regulatory Affairs, Brown & Williamson Tobacco	Toxicology/cigarette design
Michael Dixon	Principal Research Scientist, B.A.T. Co	Physiology of smoking
David E. Townsend	VP of Product Development and Assessment, RJ Reynolds Tobacco Co.	Cigarette design

3 Smoking Attributable Expenditures

3.1 Overview

As described in Section 1, the objective of the statistical modeling in this case was to estimate the dollars actually expended by the state of Minnesota and Blue Cross/Blue Shield from 1978 to 1996 for medical services that were attributable to smoking. Medical and epidemiological testimony established that smoking causes disease and general medical morbidity. We built the damages model on this medical foundation, hence, our analysis started with identification of the total expenditures for medical services and nursing home maintenance. These total expenditures were classified into three broad categories: treatment of major smoking-attributable diseases (MSADs); other expenditures for medical services possibly related to poor health; and nursing home maintenance expenditures. Data files comprising more than 280 million billing records were built (by TW) to establish the total state and BCBS expenditures in these categories.

Given total expenditures, the next step was to estimate the fraction of expenditures that were reasonably attributable to smoking using statistical and econometric models whose development was led by Dr. Miller. In simplest terms, to obtain the smoking-attributable expenditures (SAEs), the total expenditures were reduced to account for the following three factors:

- only a fraction of Minnesotans with a given medical condition were smokers;
- even among smokers, only a fraction of their disease is caused by their smoking;
- even for smokers whose disease is caused by smoking, only a fraction of their medical expenditures is for the treatment of their smoking-attributable disease.

Our approach was to estimate the smoking-attributable fraction, or SAF, for medical services using data on smoking, disease, and expenditures from the National Medical Expenditure Survey, or NMES (1987). The smoking-attributable fraction was modeled as a function of several potential confounding variables identified by Dr. Jonathan Samet, the plaintiffs' medical and epidemiological expert. More details on the SAF estimation are provided below in Section 3.3.

Having developed a statistical model that estimates the fraction of expenditures attributable to smoking as a function of covariates, it was desirable to use an additional source of information to ensure that the SAFs applied to expenditures for Minnesotans reflected the covariate information typical of the Minnesota population. Toward this end, we also used 34,000 interviews from the Minnesota Behavioral Risk Factor Surveillance Survey (BRFSS), an annual survey of health risk behaviors conducted by the state's Department of Health and coordinated by the Centers for Disease Control (CDC) (1984–1994).

To summarize the approach, we estimated the smoking-attributable expenditures, dollars actually expended by the state that were attributable to smoking, in the following steps:

(1) enumerate the total expenditures for medical services from State and Blue Cross/Blue Shield billing records;
(2) build regression models of medical expenditures (or nursing home maintenance fees) as a function of smoking and other covariates from the National Medical Expenditure Survey (or the National Health and Nutrition Evaluation Survey for nursing home maintenance fees);
(3) use the regression results to calculate a smoking-attributable fraction (SAF) given covariate values;
(4) identify typical covariate values for Minnesotans in given demographic strata from the Minnesota Behavioral Risk Factor Surveillance Survey;
(5) calculate and total the smoking-attributable expenditures from each of the bills paid by the state or Blue Cross/Blue Shield over the period.

The steps described above were applied separately for expenditures in the following categories: major smoking-attributable diseases, other medical expenditures; and nursing home maintenance fees. In the remainder of this paper, we focus on the estimation of the smoking-attributable expenditures, for persons suffering from major smoking-attributable diseases. Variations of this approach were used for expenditures for other medical expenditures and nursing home maintenance.

3.2　Data Sources

We used federal and state health care studies, and state and Blue Cross billing information to determine SAEs, as briefly summarized in this section.

National Medical Expenditure Survey (NMES) Every ten years, the federal government conducts a major study of health care expenditures called the National Medical Expenditure Survey (NMES). The most recent completed survey for which data are available was conducted in 1987, the center of our nineteen-year analysis period (1978–1996).

The 1987 NMES collected information from a sample of about 35,000 persons in the civilian, noninstitutionalized population. Detailed information was collected on diseases requiring medical care; insurance coverage (in particular, whether coverage is through Medicaid, some other public program, or through an employer); behavioral habits with health implications such as smoking or seat belt use; region of residence; and personal characteristics including sex, age, race, income, household size, marital status, education level, height, and weight.

NMES is strong in areas where most other surveys about disease and expenditures are limited. The study continues throughout a full year with five interviews of each household. In NMES, many of the interviews are in person, thereby avoiding some of the limitations of telephone interviews. Interviewers are trained in disease coding, and maintain a detailed record throughout the year of chronic and acute diseases reported. Formalized steps are taken to check newly reported chronic conditions to be sure that they are not already being reported under another name and to keep coding consistent. Expenditures reported by participants are verified in the extensive survey of the medical care providers named by them.

Minnesota Behavioral Risk Factor Surveillance System (BRFSS) Since 1984 Minnesota has collected information on behavioral risk factors such as smoking through monthly telephone surveys of representative samples of about 3,400 Minnesota residents per year, as part of the Minnesota Behavioral Risk Factors Surveillance System (BRFSS), coordinated by the Centers for Disease Control and Prevention (CDC). Minnesota is one of a large number of participating states that ask the same core questions and use the same survey methods. During most years, Minnesota also asked whether persons obtained health insurance through their employer, and whether they were covered by Medicaid.

Billing and Medicaid enrollment data. The most important information for calculating SAEs was obtained from the State and Blue Cross/Blue Shield billing records including diagnoses, types of treatment, and costs for each medical encounter. We obtained this information from more than 280 million of the plaintiffs' billing records, which we retrieved and assembled into a longitudinal database.

From the billing records and enrollment files, we specifically obtained diagnoses, payments, date of treatment, type of service (e.g., ambulatory medical visit, prescription drugs), place of service (e.g., inpatient hospital, clinic, doctor's office), age, sex, marital status, residence zip code, dates of eligibility, and race and level of education for each patient.

One of the most important uses of these analysis files was to identify persons being treated for at least one of the major smoking-attributable diseases. Doctors and other medical care providers include their diagnoses, coded using the *International Classification of Diseases system* (ICD-9), on bills submitted to Medicaid or other health insurers. In keeping with the Surgeon General's reports on smoking and disease, our medical expert defined the major smoking-attributable diseases using ICD-9 codes as listed in Table 2.

To identify persons being treated for one of the major smoking-attributable diseases in any given year, we matched the billing records for each person against the ICD-9 codes in the master list in Table 2. If we found one or more of the codes for those diseases, the person was provisionally categorized as being treated for a smoking attributable disease during the year. To guard against overstating the prevalence of these diseases in the population covered by the state, we then applied several additional validity screens.

3.3 Regression Models

Regression analyses were conducted using the NMES data described in Section 3.2 to estimate the fraction of total expenditures that were attributable to smoking as a function of covariate information. In what we have termed the "refined analysis"

Table 2. International Classification of Diseases (IDC-9) diagnoses covered under major smoking-attributable diseases in the damages model

Atherosclerosis (440–441, 444)
Bladder cancer (188)
Cerebrovascular disease (342, 430–438)
Chronic obstructive pulmonary disease (COPD) (491–492, 496)
Coronary heart disease (410–414, 425, 427–428)
Esophageal cancer (150)
Kidney cancer (189)
Laryngeal cancer (161)
Oral cancer (140–141, 143–149)
Pancreatic cancer (157)
Peptic ulcer disease (531–533)

Table 3. Smoking-Attributable Expenditures (SAEs) and Smoking-Attributable Fractions (SAFs) for major smoking-attributable diseases by payer comparing core model that has only age, gender, payer, and disease as covariates with refined model that includes all covariates discussed in Section 3.3, 1978–1996.

Disease Category	Payer	Total Expenditures	Smoking-attributable			
			Core model		Refined model	
Lung cancer/ COPD			SAE	SAF	SAE	SAF
	Total	$427	$243	56.8%	$225	52.6%
	BCBSM[+]	85	52	61.2%	51	59.7%
	GAMC[*]	32	15	46.6%	18	57.0%
	Medicaid	311	176	56.6%	156	50.2%
CHD/Stroke/ Other						
	Total	$1,618	$383	23.7%	$411	25.4%
	BCBSM[+]	496	132	26.7%	170	34.3%
	GAMC[*]	143	65	45.7%	46	32.0%
	Medicaid	979	186	19.0%	195	20.0%

Note: All dollars in millions.

Numbers may not add to total due to rounding.

[+] BCBSM is Blue Cross/Blue Shield of Minnesota

[*] General Assistant Medical Care—last resort state program for indigent

(Table 3), four regression models were used to compute an SAF for the major smoking-attributable diseases. The first two models are probit regressions for indicator variables of whether a person was a smoker and whether the person was currently treated for a major smoking-attributable disease. They were fit simultaneously because these two outcomes were assumed to be correlated by an amount that could vary by gender, age, and disease strata. The third and fourth models also form a pair. The third regression was a probit model describing the probability of having any medical expenditures in a given year. The fourth regression described the size of the expenditures on a logarithmic scale given that expenditures had occurred. The predictor variables used for each of the four regressions were drawn from among the following: smoking (current, former, never), age, race, region of country, insurer (private, public), marital status, education attainment, relative income, overweight (binary BMI), and seat belt use as a surrogate for risk-taking behavior.

The analysis was conducted separately for several different strata defined by the following: age (19–34, 35–65, 65+); gender; and type of medical service (hospital, ambulatory, pharmacy, home health). We investigated the possibility that persons who failed to complete the NMES Survey questions on smoking (approximately 15%) might be different from the remainder of the population. The first two models were fit using Heckman–Lee (1976, 1979) adjustments for nonignorable missingness. These had little effect on the estimated SAEs. Because the fourth equation is a model of log expenditures among persons whose expenditures were positive, and because it is undesirable to rely upon the assumed normal distribution for the log expenditures, smearing coefficients (Duan, 1983) were estimated separately for smokers and nonsmokers within each of the strata. By using smearing coefficients, the model closely reproduced the total expenditures observed for smokers and nonsmokers within a stratum.

The four regression models allowed us to calculate the SAFs of expenditures as a ratio of two terms. The numerator is the difference in the expected expenditures for smokers with a given set of covariate values as might appear on a particular bill and otherwise similar nonsmokers. The denominator is the predicted total expenditures for the person, so that the ratio is the smoking-attributable fraction. Each is a fraction of the predicted values from the regression models. In the absence of covariates, this equation is well approximated by the product of the population attributable risk (Rothman, 1986) and the third reduction—the fraction of total expenditures for a person with disease caused by smoking that is for the treatment of their smoking condition. Hence, the SAF is a natural extension of the population attributable risk to the problem of attributing dollars rather than disease events. Several authors in previous research (Adams et al., 1997; Bartlett et al., 1994; and Miller et al., 1998) have used smoking-attributable fractions.

As a check on the results for the MSADs, a simpler "core model" was also estimated in which no covariates other than the defining strata age (19–34, 35–64, 65+), gender, payer (Medicaid, BC/BS), and type of medical service (hospital, ambulatory, pharmacy, home health) were included.

3.4 Application of SAFs to Minnesota Expenditures

The more than 280 million billing records included basic information about the type, date, and costs of service; diagnostic codes indicating the disease or condition being treated; and very basic demographic information such as age, gender, and marital status, and in some cases education, of the person being treated. They did not include smoking status. The regression models estimated from NMES predict a SAF while controlling for the demographic variables on the bills and other, possibly useful, covariates such as overweight, seat belt use as a proxy for risk-taking behavior, and socioeconomic status measures. The following approach was used to apply the most appropriate SAF to a given bill. First, bills were stratified into groups based upon the disease (lung cancer/chronic obstructive pulmonary disease; other MSADs), five-year age strata, gender, type of service provided, year of service, and payer (private, public). The more than 30,000 Behavioral Risk Factor Surveillance Survey (BRFSS) participants were similarly stratified. The smoking-attributable fraction for a given stratum of bills was the average SAF obtained by integrating over the empirical distribution of additional covariates as obtained from BRFSS. In this way, the SAF takes account of known differences between the Minnesota population to which SAFs are applied and the national population from which they were estimated.

3.5   Damage Estimates

Tables 3 and 4 present the estimates of total smoking-attributable expenditures by Blue Cross/Blue Shield and by the state of Minnesota over a 19-year period (Table 3) as well as the break-out of the three reductions comprising the SAF by age and gender (Table 4). Of the total $19 billion of medical expenditures for this period, roughly $2 billion was spent to provide health care services for MSADs. Of those, we estimate that $630 million was attributable to smoking. The results from the core model, which includes the covariates payer, age, gender, and disease category, were similar to those obtained with a refined regression model that includes all of the covariates discussed in Section 3.3. Hence, for major smoking-attributable diseases, the refined adjustment for several additional covariates such as SES did not substantially affect the results. Note that the smoking-attributable fraction was in the 50–60% range for lung cancer and COPD and only between 20–35% for CHD/stroke. This is because the attributable risk for the former diseases are much higher than for the latter. Note also the variations among payer groups in the SAFs. This reflects differences across these groups in age, gender, and other covariate values. Table 4 shows the SAEs by disease class, age, and gender as well as the three percentage reductions that make up the SAF as described in Section 3.1. These figures were from the original expert report and were revised slightly in subsequent analyses, which addressed questions raised by defense experts.

4   Biostatistics in the Courtroom

This section illustrates how the legal context shapes the questions that a biostatistician expert witness must address by reviewing two major issues that arose in the Minnesota case. It is intended to illustrate the interplay between science and the law.

4.1   The Death Benefit

Minnesota asked its statistical experts to determine the dollars actually spent by the state and Blue Cross/Blue Shield between 1978 and 1996 to cover expenditures for medical services (including nursing home maintenance) attributable to diseases and conditions caused by smoking. Another method one might consider using to assess damages would be to estimate the medical expenditures by Minnesota that would have occurred in the absence of smoking, or perhaps in the absence of the alleged misconduct by the defendants, and to assess damages as the difference between these estimated expenditures and those that actually occurred in the presence of smoking. This is the "causal inference" approach (Rubin, 1978; Holland

Table 4. Smoking-attributable expenditures in $ millions by disease class, age, and gender as well as three percentage reductions as described in Section 3.1

Disease	Sex	Age	Total Dollars	How many smokers	How much extra disease	How many more dollars	Smoking-attributable dollars	Percent of dollars attributable
Lung cancer/COPD	Female	35–64	$101.87	85.3%	83.5%	80.0%	$58.03	57.0%
		65+	78.70	93.8	96.3	71.8	51.06	64.9
	Male	35–64	76.35	87.5	68.3	76.5	34.90	45.7
		65+	54.27	97.1 92.4	65.9	32.05	59.0	
	Total		311.19	90.0	84.9	74.0	176.04	56.6
CHD/Stroke/Other	Female	35–64	252.36	77.0	49.0	77.6	73.80	29.2
		65+	366.49	42.6	9.7	53.3	8.08	2.2
	Male	35–64	216.99	95.7	60.8	76.2	96.33	44.4
		65+	143.28	78.8	11.6	55.9	7.34	5.1
	Total		979.12	68.6	37.2	74.3	185.55	19.0
Total	Female	35–64	354.23	79.4	59.6	78.6	131.83	37.2
		65+	445.20	51.7	37.5	68.5	59.15	13.3
	Male	35–64	293.34	93.6	62.6	76.3	131.23	44.7
		65+	197.55	83.8	37.3	63.7	39.38	19.9
	Total		1,290.31	73.7	51.3	74.1	361.60	28.0

Note: All dollars in millions

1986), advocated by tobacco's statistical experts (see Professor Rubin's article in this volume).

This approach had two limitations in the *Minnesota v. Tobacco case.* The first is that such a definition of damages requires substantially greater modeling assumptions and data relevant to what might have occurred absent smoking or the alleged misconduct by the defendants in Minnesota. Plaintiff's statistical experts were unwilling to speculate about how such modeling might be undertaken, nor was a specific proposal about how to estimate what might have occurred absent smoking presented by defense experts.

The second limitation of the causal approach was that the court ruled it out; specifically, the judge ruled that Tobacco could not challenge the damage estimates of the plaintiffs by invoking what became known as the "death benefit."

Consider the main difference between annual smoking-attributable expenditures as defined in Section 3 and the "causal measure" of damages defined to be the difference between the actual expenditures over the period in question and expenditures that would have occurred absent smoking. The "causal measure" includes the smoking-attributable expenditures as a major component. That is, dollars actually expended to treat diseases and conditions caused by smoking are included in it. But the "causal measure" also includes a rebate for any savings in health expenditures incurred by smoking having caused, in addition to lung cancer or other MSADs, premature death of a Minnesotan over this period. These savings became known as the "death benefit." On January 24, 1998, Judge Fitzpatrick ruled:

> Whereas, the Court finds it abhorrent and horrendously contrary to public policy that a party should, in whatever guise, claim that the killing of individuals should be used as a defense or as a factor in mitigating damages.... It is hereby ordered 1. Plaintiffs' Motion for Summary Judgment Dismissing Defenses based upon Alleged Benefits from the Premature Deaths of Smokers is DENIED because Defendants have not raised and shall not raise any defense so predicated (Fitzpatrick, C1-94-8565, 1998).

Hence, arguments in favor of the "causal measure" of damages were not allowed if they included the death benefit. Questioning of plaintiff's statistical experts about literature on costs of smoking that included the death benefit was also disallowed.

4.2 Indivisible Damages

In a Minnesota civil case, it is plaintiffs' responsibility to establish the damages that are specifically attributable to the alleged misconduct of the defendant. But in some situations, that misconduct has taken place over an extended period of time and comprises many smaller actions that in total are alleged to have produced the damages. This is an example of what is called "indivisible damages." In this case, under Minnesota law (Fitzpatrick, CLAD #2146, 1998), a plaintiff can indicate an inability to separate out the specific damages attributable to individual actions of the defendants, in which case the defendants become responsible for providing a methodology for identifying the specific damages. If they are unable to do so, then the plaintiffs may be entitled to the total damages, whether or not they can be allocated to specific defendant actions.

In the Minnesota tobacco case, the plaintiffs estimated the total medical expenditures attributable to smoking, not those attributable to specific actions of the defendants. Plaintiffs argued that the damages were indivisible. It therefore became defendant's responsibility to indicate a methodology for dividing the damages. Defendants did not present a specific proposal for doing so. Plaintiffs requested indivisible damages. The court therefore ruled:

> Whereas, Defendants have failed to sustain their burden under Minnesota's single individual injury rule, entitling a Plaintiff to recover its full damages unless the defendant can establish that it did not cause an identifiable portion of that injury ... Defendant's Motion for Summary Judgment is summarily Denied. . . .

The "death benefit" and "indivisible damages" examples illustrate how the legal context determines the utility and relevance of particular statistical arguments by expert witnesses. Because most statistical experts are not also legal experts, the utility of statistical testimony in a particular case is often compromised by legal decisions that are beyond the control of the statistical expert. To be maximally useful to the court, a statistical expert benefits from a general understanding of the theories of the case, as well as any major legal issues that would affect the ultimate use of his or her testimony, background which emerges from pretrial motions and hearings. With this basic understanding, it is possible for a statistical expert to address the questions that the court needs to resolve rather than others that ultimately do not bear on the legal issues as defined by the court in the particular case.

5 Summary

This paper has briefly summarized the role of statistical experts for the plaintiffs in the Minnesota vs. Tobacco case. We have described our approach to estimating "smoking-attributable expenditures," the dollars actually expended by Minnesota to cover health care services and nursing home maintenance that are attributable to smoking. Our analyses were based upon the medical model and testimony that smoking causes disease, which results in additional expenditures, and were therefore the first to disaggregate medical expenditures by disease and type of service in addition to key covariates including age, gender, and payer. The modeling described here focused on major smoking-attributable diseases. Extensions of these ideas were used to estimate SAFs for all other medical expenditures and for nursing home maintenance.

Our damage estimates were built upon enormous data systems, including 280 million medical bills, the National Medical Expenditure Survey, and the Behavioral Risk Factor Survey for Minnesota. The use of physicians' bills on millions of Minnesotans of which more than 100,000 had contracted a major smoking-attributable disease during the period of interest was, in plaintiffs' opinion, an essential strength of their case.

We have contrasted smoking-attributable expenditures with an estimate of damages derived from a "causal model" that includes the "death benefit." In the end, the death benefit was disallowed by the court. This is an excellent example of how court rulings can dramatically affect the utility of any particular statistical expert's testimony.

In many civil cases, both plaintiffs' and defendants' experts present damage estimates. In this case, only plaintiffs offered one. Defendants criticized the methodology and results of the plaintiffs' damage models, but did not have specific models of their own. It is interesting to speculate how the court proceedings might have differed had two statistical assessments of damages been presented.

REFERENCES

[1] Adams, E.K., Solanki, G., Miller, L.S., and Program Services and Development Branch, Division of Reproductive Health, National Center for Chronic Disease Prevention and Health Promotion, CDC (November, 1997). Medical Care expenditures Attributable to Cigarette Smoking during Pregnancy - United States, 1995. *Morbidity and Mortality Weekly Report (MMWR)* 45, 1048–1050.

[2] Bartlett, J.C., Miller, L.S., Rice, D.P., Max, W.B., and Office on Smoking and Health, National Center for Chronic Disease Prevention and Health Promotion, Public Health Practice Program Office, CDC (July 8, 1994). Medical Care Expenditures Attributable to Cigarette Smoking - United States, 1993. *Morbidity and Mortality Weekly Report (MMWR)* 43(26), 469–472.

[3] Behavioral Risk Factor Surveillance System (1984–1994) Division of Adult and Community Health, National Center for Chronic Disease Prevention and Health Promotion. Centers for Disease Control.

[4] Duan, M. (1983) Smearing estimate. *Journal of the American Statistical Association* 78, 605–610.

[5] Fitzpatrick, K. (1998a) Order Denying Plaintiffs Motion for Summary Judgment Dismissing Defenses Based Upon Alleged Benefits from the Premature Deaths of Smokers and Granting Plaintiffs' Motion in Limine for an Order Excluding all Evidence of Alleged Benefits from the Premature Deaths of Smokers. State of Minnesota, Second Judicial District Court, Ramsey County, Court File No. C1-94-8565, 1–3.

[6] Fitzpatrick, K. (1998b) Order Denying Defendants' Motion for Summary Judgment Dismissal of Plaintiffs' Antitrust Claims. State of Minnesota, Second Judicial District Court, Ramsey County, CLAD #2146, 7–8.

[7] Heckman, J. (1979) Sample Selection Bias as a Specification Error. *Econometrica* 47, 153–161.

[8] Holland, P.W. (1986). Statistics and Causal Inference. *Journal of the American Statistical Association* 81, 945–960.

[9] Lee, L. (1976) Estimation of Limited Dependent Variable Models by Two-Stage Methods. Ph.D. dissertation, University of Rochester.

[10] Miller, L.S., Zhang, X., Novotny, T., Rice, D., Max, W. (Mar/Apr 1998) State Estimates of Medicaid Expenditures Attributable to Cigarette Smoking, Fiscal Year 1993. *Public Health Reports*, 140–151.

[11] National Medical Expenditure Survey (1987) Agency for Health Care Policy and Research, U.S. Department of Health and Human Services.

[12] Rothman, K.J. (1986) *Modern Epidemiology*. Little, Brown and Company, Boston, MA.

[13] Rubin, D.B. (1978) Bayesian Inference for Causal Effects: The role of randomization. *The Annals of Statistics* 6, 34–58.

[14] Samet, J. (1999) Reflections: testifying in the Minnesota tobacco lawsuit. *Tobacco Control* 8, 101–105.

[15] *State by Humphrey v. Philip Morris Inc.*, (Minn. 1996) 551 N.W.2d 490, 495.

Statistical Issues in the Estimation of the Causal Effects of Smoking Due to the Conduct of the Tobacco Industry

Donald B. Rubin

1 Summary

A major legal issue for the past several years has been the tobacco industry's liability for health-care expenditures incurred because of its alleged misconduct beginning in the mid-1950s. Quantifying answers to such causal questions is a statistical enterprise, which has been especially active in the last quarter century.

This chapter summarizes my formulation of a statistically valid approach for estimating the potential damages in the tobacco litigation. Six distinct statistical tasks are outlined, although no specific estimates are produced. These six tasks are: formulation of mathematical statistical framework; assembly of data to estimate health-care-expenditure relative risks of smoking in the actual world; design of the statistical analyses to estimate these expenditure relative risks—a problem closely related to causal inference in observational studies; assembly and analysis of appropriate data to estimate the prevalence of different types of smoking behaviors and other health-expenditure-related factors in the relevant population—a problem of survey inference; assembly and analysis of appropriate data to estimate the dollar pots of health-care expenditures of various types in the relevant population—another problem of survey inference; assembly and analysis of information concerning the prevalence of smoking and other health-expenditure-related factors in a counterfactual world without the alleged misconduct of the tobacco industry—a problem involving explicit assumptions justified by actual-world experimental and observational data. This sixth task is the critical step where the alleged misconduct, and thus causal inferences, enter the equation; the second through fifth tasks involve the careful assembly and analysis of actual-world data. The outputs from the last five tasks (2 – 6) are input into an equation, which is derived in the first task, to give an estimate of the causal effect of the alleged misconduct on health-care expenditures.

The plausibility and validity of the results depend critically on the use of detailed information on health-care expenditures, smoking behavior, and covariates (i.e., background characteristics and nonsmoking health-care-expenditure-related factors). The reason is that this detail is used to justify the key assumption in the mathematical statistical formulation in the first task. The need for this level of detailed information places extra demands on the data-based efforts in the last five tasks.

The formulation presented here distinguishes issues of fact about the actual world, involving the health-care-expenditure relative risks of smoking and the prevalence of smoking behaviors and other health-care-expenditure-related factors, from issues using actual-world facts to conjecture about the counterfactual world. The results show that, under the key assumption, counterfactual-world estimation enters the equation only through the differences between actual- and counterfactual-world prevalences of smoking and other health-expenditure-related behaviors in subpopulations defined by background charactertics.

2   Statistical Tasks Needed to Estimate the Causal Effect of the Tobacco Industry's Alleged Misconduct on Health Expenditures

Six major statistical tasks can be delineated.

Task 1 is the formulation of the assumptions and the kinds of information needed to estimate the causal effects of smoking. This task also provides an explicit mathematical expression for this estimation under a key assumption. Task 1 is the most technically demanding, but has been done in a preliminary form in Rubin (1998) and in a comprehensive form in Rubin (2000). The major result will be summarized here in Section 3 because it forms the basis for the other tasks. That is, the mathematical expression for the potential excess health-care expenditures due to the alleged misconduct of the tobacco industry is a function of several quantities, each of which must be estimated in relevant subpopulations. Their estimation is the topic of Sections 5–8. The real-world implications of the key assumption is the topic of Section 4.

Task 2 involves the assembly of data that can be used to estimate relative risks of various smoking behaviors for various types of health-care expenditures in subpopulations of the relevant population during the relevant time period. Task 2, discussed in Section 5, requires the existence or creation of a large database with substantial information on smoking behavior, health-care expenditures, background demographic variables, and other health-care-expenditure-related factors. The 1987 NMES (National Medical Expenditure Survey; Agency for Health Care Policy and Research, 1992) is an important candidate database. There are other possible data sets as well, but they lack the extensive medical expenditure, smoking, and covariate information of NMES. All data sets have limitations and complications, and NMES is no exception. Dealing with one complication in NMES, missing data, is an important problem briefly addressed in the discussion of Section 5.

Task 3 involves the proper analysis of the data assembled in Task 2 to provide reliable estimates of the relative risks on health-care expenditures of smoking behaviors in subpopulations defined by covariates, i.e., background variables and nonsmoking health-care-expenditure-related factors. Task 3 entails a form of descriptive inference that is closely related to methods used for causal inference in observational studies because it requires adjustment for covariates. This task is not as easy as one might expect, because many generally invalid methods of statistical analysis for causal effects from observational studies abound. There has been substantial work on how to obtain valid inferences of this type with databases like NMES, and some initial progress with NMES is outlined in Section 6.

Task 4 is the assembly and analysis of appropriate survey data to allow the estimation of the prevalence of different smoking behaviors and other health-care-expenditure-related factors during the relevant time periods in subpopulations defined by background factors. Task 5 is the assembly and analysis of appropriate survey data to allow the estimation of the health-care expenditures of various types in subpopulations defined by covariates. Tasks 4 and 5 are essentially survey tasks, which are straightforward conceptually and briefly discussed in Section 7.

Task 6 is the assembly and analysis of experimental and observational data addressing the issue of how, in a counterfactual world without the alleged misconduct by the tobacco industry, the prevalences of smoking behaviors and other health-expenditure-related factors would have changed in subpopulations defined by background factors. One cannot logically assume the complete absence of cigarette smoking in a counterfactual world without the alleged misconduct of the tobacco industry, and so only a fraction of all expenditures that may be attributable to smoking are attributable to the alleged misconduct of the tobacco industry.

This point has been made repeatedly by both plaintiffs' experts and defendants' experts (including me) in both their reports and their testimony. For example, Fisher (1999, p. 2, item #6), in an expert witness report for the plaintiffs, wrote:

> It is necessary to generate a stream of damages taking account that not all smoking-related expenditures result from the alleged behavior of the defendants. Thus, the smoking-related expenditures estimated by Glenn Harrison and Wendy Max, and Henry Miller [experts for the plaintiffs] need to be adjusted by what Jeffrey Harris [expert for the plaintiffs, Harris, 1999] has calculated to be the proportion of total smoking-attributable expenditures caused by defendants' improper conduct. The monetary amount of damage resulting from the defendants' alleged behavior in each past and future year is thus calculated by multiplying the annual smoking related expenditures by the proportion caused by defendants' improper conduct.

Also, in the September 22, 1999 news conference held to announce the United States filing of its lawsuit against the tobacco industry, Assistant Attorney General Ogden (1999) stated:

> The number that's in the complaint is not a number that reflects a particular demand for payment. What we've alleged is that each year the federal government expends in excess of $20 billion on *tobacco* related medical costs. What we would actually recover would be our portion of that annual toll that is the result of the illegal conduct that we allege occurred, and it

simply will be a matter of proof for the court, which will be developed through the course of discovery, what that amount will be. So, we have not put out a specific figure and we'll simply have to develop that as the case goes forward.

These positions are supported by the Federal Judicial Center's "Reference Manual on Scientific Evidence" (1994, Chapter 3, p. 481):

> The first step in a damages study is the translation of the legal theory of the harmful event into an analysis of the economic impact of that event. In most cases, the analysis considers the difference between the plaintiff's economic position if the harmful event had not occurred and the plaintiff's actual economic position. The damages study restates the plaintiff's position "but for" the harmful event; this part is often called the *but-for analysis*. Damages are the difference between the but-for value and the actual value.

Task 6 is the most challenging statistically, because it is here that we need to consider what would have happened in terms of prevalence of smoking behaviors and other health-care-expenditure-related factors in the counterfactual world without the alleged misconduct. Therefore, this is the issue most open to the judgment of a jury. Nevertheless, many sorts of existing data sets are quite suggestive of answers to this question, and this is the topic of Section 8.

3 Task 1: Formulation of Needed Assumptions, Data, and Mathematical Expressions

In this section we summarize the technical material developed in Rubin (2000). Although the notation is fairly demanding, the resulting expression for calculating excess expenditures due to the tobacco industry's alleged misconduct, given by equations (1) and (2), drives all statistical issues of data assembly and analysis. The key assumption underlying the expression has as its basic component that, given enough covariate detail describing individuals, the relative risks of particular smoking behaviors for specific health-care expenditures in a specific year are the same in the counterfactual world without the alleged misconduct as in the actual world. This assumption, discussed in Section 4, is effectively made in one version or another in all analyses estimating damages in the tobacco litigation. The formulation in this chapter is a statistically correct formalization of the implicit assumptions underlying these analyses.

3.1 Conduct-Attributable Health-Care Expenditures

In the litigation for a particular population, the damages plaintiffs seek are the total "conduct-attributable expenditures" due to the tobacco industry's alleged misconduct in the actual world relative to a counterfactual world without this alleged misconduct. Suppose there are C categories of health-care expenditures under consideration (e.g., costs for treating lung cancer, lip cancer, types of cardiovascular disease, nursing home fees, etc.) over a period of T years. This total can be calculated from a two-dimensional array (matrix) of expenditures with C rows corresponding to the C categories of expenditures and T columns corresponding to the T years under consideration. The total conduct-attributable expenditures are obtained by summing the entries in this matrix across the C categories of expenditures and across the T years, discounting costs in time as appropriate.

Each entry in this C by T matrix of conduct attributable expenditures, say the cth category of expenditures and the tth year, can be written as the sum of expenditures in covariate subpopulations. Each covariate subpopulation is defined first by background demographic characteristics X (e.g., birth date, sex, race), which are by definition unaffected by the alleged misconduct of the tobacco industry, and second by nonsmoking health-care-expenditure-related factors D (e.g., diet, education, marital status), which are possibly affected by the alleged misconduct; D includes an indicator for alive/dead so that the population of individuals in the actual and counterfactual worlds are the same across all years. An example of a particular (X, D) subpopulation is all males born in 1943, living in a northeastern urban area in 1999, who graduated high school in 1961, college in 1965, who have been 10 pounds overweight since 1978, have private health insurance, are married with two sons, etc. Both X and D imply matrices, with columns corresponding to the T years and rows corresponding to characteristics (e.g., sex and year of birth for X, and pounds overweight and education for D). Some of the rows in X (e.g., birth year) will be the same across all T columns, and X by itself also defines subpopulations (e.g., all males born in 1943 in the Midwest).

Letting CAE be the conduct attributable expenditures of category c in year t, we can write:

$$\text{CAE} = \sum_{X} \sum_{D} [\text{POT}(X, D) \cdot \text{CAF}(X, D)], \qquad (1)$$

where

POT(X, D) is the total expenditures in category c in year t for individuals in the covariate subpopulation with background demographic characteristics X and nonsmoking health-care-expenditure-related factors D,

and

CAF(X, D) is the conduct-attributable fraction of these subpopulation expenditures (category c in year t) due to the alleged misconduct in the actual world relative to the counterfactual world without this misconduct, some number less than or equal to one;

$\sum_{X} \sum_{D}$ is the standard "sigma" notation indicating the summation over all covariate subpopulations defined by the combination of X and D.

3.2 Conduct-Attributable Fraction in Terms of Prevalences and Relative Risks

Let S indicate the different kinds of smoking behaviors that can lead to different health-care-expenditure outcomes (e.g., never-smoker; heavy smoker of unfiltered cigarettes for 10 years, of filter cigarettes for 3 years, quit for 5 years). As with the other quantities, S implies a matrix with columns for the T years under consideration and rows corresponding to the various smoking behaviors. The prevalence of smoking behavior S is the proportion of individuals with smoking behavior S. The joint prevalence of S and D is the proportion of individuals with smoking behavior S and nonsmoking health-care-expenditure-related factors equal to D.

Under a key assumption, discussed here in Section 4 and at length in Rubin (2000) as Assumption 1, the conduct-attributable fraction in the (X, D) subpopulation, for category of expenditure c in year t, can be written as

$$\text{CAF}(X, D) = \frac{\sum_S [\text{PR}(S, D|X) - \text{PR}^*(S, D|X)] \cdot \text{RR\$}(S|X, D)}{\sum_S \text{PR}(S, D|X) \cdot \text{RR\$}(S|X, D)}, \qquad (2)$$

where

$\text{PR}(S, D|X) =$ the joint prevalence in year t in subpopulation X of smoking

   behavior S and other health-care-expenditure-related factors D

   in the actual world (i.e., the fraction of individuals with

   smoking behavior S and health-care-expenditure-related factors

   D in year t in the X subpopulation);

$\text{PR}^*(S, D|X) =$ the prevalence in year t in subpopulation X of smoking

   behavior S and other health-care-expenditure-related factors D

   in the counterfactual world (i.e., just like $\text{PR}(S, D|X)$

   except for the counterfactual world instead of the actual world);

and

$\text{RR\$}(S|X,D) =$ the "relative risk" of expenditures of smoking behavior S for

   category c of expenditures in year t for the (X,D) subpopulation

   in the actual world—this quantity is defined in Section 3.3.

Thus, from equations (1) and (2), under the key assumption, in each year the quantities that must be estimated to calculate the total excess expenditures in the actual world relative to the counterfactual world without the alleged misconduct by the tobacco industry are the following: the actual world expenditure total dollars for each category of health-care expenditure and the relative risks of expenditures for different smoking behaviors within each (X, D) subpopulation, and the actual world and the counterfactual world prevalences of (S, D) within X subpopulations, where the counterfactual-world prevalences enter the equation only as differences from the actual-world values.

3.3 Acutal-World Relative Risks for Expenditures of Smoking Behaviors

For each covariate subpopulation defined by (X, D), there is a C by T matrix of actual-world relative risks of expenditures for each of the various smoking behaviors indicated by S. For the cth category of expenditures and tth year, RR$\$(S|X, D)$ gives the ratio, in the subpopulation defined by (X, D), of: the average expenditures for those individuals with smoking behavior S, AV$\$(S, X, D)$, to the average expenditures for those individuals who never smoked, AV$\$(S = 0, X, D)$, where $S = 0$ indicates never-smokers. This is a purely descriptive quantity comparing expenditures for different kinds of smokers to expenditures for never-smokers in the (X, D) subpopulation. The key assumption allows these actual-world relative risks to substitute for their counterfactual-world counterparts.

3.4 Remarks on the Application of the Formulation

A modification of the definition of dollar pots may be needed to address a legal issue. At the individual level, define ΔH to be the C by T matrix of "excess" health-care expenditures in the actual world minus those in the counterfactual world. Some entries of ΔH could be negative. For example, suppose an individual smoked and died of lung cancer in his 70th year, but in the counterfactual world, did not smoke and lived from age 70 to 90 in a nursing home. Or in the counterfactual world, he did not smoke but grossly overate and had a series of nonfatal heart attacks starting in his 60th year that continued through his 80th year, when he died. The issue concerns whether to account for health-care expenditures avoided due to earlier death in one world or the other. The traditional economic perspective would account for differences in total health-care expenditures due to changes in longevity, (e.g., Warner et al., 1995, p. 382). However, moral objections have been raised, and some courts, such as the trial court in Minnesota, explicitly disallowed any evidence on this issue. To exclude the effect on health-care expenditures of differences in longevity, we could define ΔH to reflect expenditures only up to some point in time at the individual level, such as death in either the actual world or the counterfactual world. Under such a definition, if an individual died in the fourth year (column), for example, in the counterfactual world, but later in the actual world, all entries in columns $5, \ldots, T$ of ΔH for that individual would be set to zero. Corresponding changes would have to be made to POT(X, D) and RR$\$(S|X, D)$.

A related issue arises in cases brought by the states or by the federal government, namely, whether differences in the tobacco excise taxes collected in the actual and counterfactual worlds should be taken into account. If so, this excess actual-world income could be used to offset excess actual-world expenditures. A parallel "actual world versus counterfactual world" analysis works to calculate this excess income but is presumably simpler, because smoking behavior directly drives tobacco excise taxes.

Another remark concerns the need, when calculating the conduct-attributable fractions in equation (2), to use estimates of relative risks, actual-world prevalences, and actual-world minus counterfactual-world differences of prevalences that pertain to all individuals in each (X, D) subpopulation in the litigation. An exception occurs when POT(X, D) is zero for some category of expenditure in some year, in which case the (X, D) subpopulation can be omitted when calculating conduct-attributable fractions for that category of expenditure in that year. An error committed by some plaintiffs' experts (e.g., Harrison, 1998; Rabinovitz, 1999) is to omit individuals with no relevant heath-care expenditures from some part of the calculation of relative risks or prevalences in an (X, D) subpopulation with positive expenditures for the year and category of expenditure being considered. Such errors tend to overestimate systematically the conduct-attributable fractions and thus overestimate the conduct-attributable expenditures; Rubin (2000) provides details.

A final remark on this formulation concerns the need for detailed (S, X, D) and health-care expenditure information when applying equations (1) and (2). Although some plaintiff's expert reports use little detail for some or all factors (e.g., Harris, 1997), the scientific interpretation of the key assumption suggests the need for such detailed information, as we now discuss.

4   The Key Assumption

The key assumption, which allows us to write the conduct-attributable fraction as in Section 3.2, is the following. Suppose we look at the collection of individuals who in the counterfactual world are in the (X, D) subpopulation and have smoking behavior S, and we calculate their average category c health-care expenditures in year t, AV\$*(S, X, D). The key assumption is that this average is the same as that for the individuals in the actual world who are in (X, D) subpopulation and have smoking behavior S, AV\$$(S, X, D)$. A critical consequence of this assumption is that the covariate subpopulation expenditure relative risks RR\$$(S|X, D)$ in the actual world are identical to those in the counterfactual world without the alleged misconduct, RR\$*$(S|X, D)$. Moreover, it implies that for never-smokers in the (X, D) subpopulation, the counterfactual world average category c health-care expenditure in year t is identical to that in the actual world, for $c = 1, \ldots, C$ and $t = 1, \ldots, T$: AV\$*$(S = 0, X, D) = $ AV\$$(S = 0, X, D)$.

4.1   Changes in the Counterfactual World

The key assumption explicitly allows that in the counterfactual world without the alleged misconduct, individuals' behaviors, as reflected by S and D, may be different than in the actual world. Thus, in the counterfactual world in year t, a specific (S, X, D) subpopulation may consist of different individuals, and different numbers of individuals, than in the actual world in year t—under the key assumption, these changed numbers are the reason health-care expenditures generally differ in the actual and counterfactual worlds. For example, someone who is in the "male, normal weight, light smoker" subpopulation in the actual world in 1970 could be in the "male, overweight, never-smoker" subpopulation in the counterfactual world in 1970, and then his counterfactual-world expected health-care expenditures in 1970 would equal the actual-world average health-care expenditures for the "male, overweight, never-smoker" subpopulation in 1970, which could differ from his actual-world expenditures in 1970.

A colloquial way to express the key assumption is the following: If the alleged misconduct would not have changed your smoking or other health-care-expenditure-related behaviors, it could not have affected your health-care expenditures; and if the alleged misconduct would have changed your behaviors so that you would have been in a different subpopulation in the counterfactual world than in the actual world, your expected health-care expenditures in the counterfactual world would equal the actual world average health-care expenditures of those in that different subpopulation.

4.2   The Need for Detail in (S, X, D)

If actual-world expenditure relative risks of specific smoking behaviors S vary across detailed (X, D) subpopulations, then that specificity and detail need to be included for the key assumption to be plausible, because such varying expenditure relative risks are the only links between changed prevalences in the counterfactual world and changed expenditures. Thus, if smoking filtered versus unfiltered cigarettes has different actual-world expenditure relative risks, then we should estimate each; or if being a five-year quitter has different expenditure relative risks than being a ten-year quitter, then we should estimate each. Similarly, if the expenditure relative risks of smoking change for different groups of individuals defined by background characteristics, such as age and sex, or by health-care-expenditure-related factors, such as diet or depression, then we should estimate separate expenditure relative risks for each such subpopulation. For example, X could be too coarse if it does not distinguish, in 1970, between someone who is 35 years old and someone who is 64 years old, or D could be too coarse if it does not distinguish between someone who is somewhat overweight and someone who is severely overweight. The way to address potential criticisms is to include finer detail of measurement into S, X, and D, and generally include more characteristics and more interaction terms, such as ones that allow different effects for male and female former smokers for length of time since quitting. Many plaintiffs' experts either use or express the desirability of using quite detailed information when estimating relative risks (e.g., Harrison, 1998; Lauer, 1998; Samet, 1998).

4.3   A Medical/Economic/Sociological/Psychological Law of Gravity

In order to believe the key assumption, we must essentially believe that the actual-world health-care expenditure relative risks, RR$(S|X, D)$ reflect a medical/economic/sociological/psychological "law of gravity" that would apply in any counterfactual world without the alleged misconduct. The assumption involves medical, economic, sociological, and psychological considerations because health-care expenditures are affected by, not only types of disease, but decisions to utilize health-care services, which are influenced by economic, sociological, and psychological factors. The law of gravity interpretation implies that given (S, X, D), we can pretty much explain average health-care expenditures: Knowledge of other background characteristics beyond X, or other health-care-expenditure-related factors beyond D, or more detailed smoking information beyond S, would not materially change the average expenditures in category c in year t. Having a component for each category of expenditure is important to the plausibility of the law of gravity interpretation because of actual-world data suggest that the expenditure relative risks for two kinds of lung cancer differ materially, then we should estimate each. Indeed, in Florida, a jury decided that smoking is capable of causing most lung cancers, but not bronchioloaveolar carcinoma (Engle, 1999). Thus, having detail in categories of health-care expenditures can also be important to satisfy legal considerations.

If the expenditure relative risks for a certain smoking behavior and a particular category of expenditure in a specific covariate subpopulation vary in time, then we should estimate different relative risks in time, which may be a daunting task. Because the expenditure relative risks are ratios of dollars in detailed categories, and assuming enough detail in the other factors so that they include temporal information, (e.g., S can represent "heavy smoker for five years, quit for six years," rather than just "former" versus "current" versus "never"), it may be plausible to assume that the C by T expenditure-relative-risk matrix RR\$($S|X, D$) has all of its T columns the same, so that in each (X, D) subpopulation and for each smoking behavior S, RR\$($S|X, D$) gives a vector of C relative risks, one for each category of expenditures. This assumption means that we do not need to find a longitudinal data set from which to calculate expenditure relative risks of smoking repeatedly for each year in the relevant period. Rather, we can let all relevant time trends be reflected in the changing prevalences of smoking and other health-care-expenditure-related factors, but not in the law of gravity model for expenditure relative risks. However, we still need to find or assemble a data set with substantial expenditure, S, X, D detail during the relevant period in a population (e.g., the nation), such that expenditure relative risks estimated in its (X, D) subpopulations apply in (X, D) subpopulations in the relevant population for the litigation (e.g., a particular health-care program).

4.4 For Total Expenditures, Do We Really Need All This Detail?

A reasonable question that naturally arises when this demand for extensive and detailed data is made is the following: If all we want are accumulated excess expenditures across all types of people in a population, do we really need to get all this information at such a detailed level? That is, for example, if the expenditure relative risks of smoking are 1.5 in the population, does that not imply that they average about 1.5 across covariate subpopulations? The answer is no because the relative risk in the full population can be different from the relative risks in *all* covariate subpopulations (say 1.5 in the full population versus 1.0 in each subpopulation). This point becomes most clear, not through mathematics, but through the consideration of a modest example of a general class of extreme examples known as Simpson's paradox (1951).

The four cells in Table 1 display, for male and female smokers and never-smokers, the numbers of each and their average expenditures; the last column gives the expenditure relative risks of smoking. Here, male smokers and male never-smokers have identical average expenditures, and female smokers and female never-smokers have identical average expenditures, so for neither males nor females is there any evidence that smoking is associated with increased expenditures: The expenditure relative risks for smoking are 1.0 for both males and females. Nevertheless, the average expenditures for smokers are 50% larger than those for never-smokers, with a relative risk of 1.5 for increased expenditures for smokers! In order to get the correct inference in this little example, we must control for sex of smoker because it is associated with both smoking (males tend to smoke more) and expenditures (males tend to have more expenditures), despite the fact that for males and for females, smokers have exactly the same average expenditures as never-smokers.

The topic of the need to control for possible confounding variables has an extensive literature in statistics and epidemiology, and is sometimes referred to as "collapsibility for causal effects" (e.g., in Table 1, problems associated with collapsing across males and females); see, for example, Rothman and Greenland (1998). Related to this, Rubin (2000) shows that background characteristics X that do not affect the difference in joint prevalence of (S, D) between the actual and counterfactual worlds can be omitted; this is not surprising given the form of the numerator in equation (2). However, since the determination of changes in prevalences in the counterfactual world is subject to jurors' assessment, it is clearly best to include as much detail as possible when estimating expenditure relative risks.

Table 1. Illustration of Simpson's Paradox

	Smokers	Never-smokers	Expenditure Relative Risks
Males	$n = 200$ ave = \$2000	$n = 50$ ave = \$2000	1.0
Females	$n = 50$ ave = \$1000	$n = 200$ ave = \$1000	1.0
All	$n = 250$ ave = \$1800	$n = 250$ ave = \$1200	1.5

5   Task 2: Assembly of Data to Estimate Expenditure Relative Risks

As discussed in Section 4, in order to make it plausible that the expenditure relative risks of smoking in the actual world apply in the counterfactual world without the tobacco companies' alleged misconduct, and that these are relatively constant in time, there needs to be substantial detail in health-care-expenditure information, smoking behaviors, X, S, and covariates, (X, D). This puts demands on data. Because of these demands, it is natural to turn to large existing databases that possibly contain relevant information, such as the American Cancer Society's "Cancer Prevention Survey" (CPS-II, a volunteer sample; e.g., Stellman and Garfinkel, 1986), the National Center for Health Statistics' "National Health Interview Survey" (e.g., Massey et al., 1989), or its "National Health and Nutrition Evaluation Survey" (e.g., Ezzati-Rice et al., 1995), or the Agency for Health Care Policy and Research's (1992) "National Medical Examination Survey, NMES".

5.1   The National Medical Expenditure Survey: NMES

Although there are many data sets that have been used to address the potential ill-health effects of smoking, and analyses of some of these have been introduced in the tobacco litigation, the current set of lawsuits focus on health-care expenditures, not health in general (morbidity or mortality). One existing data set has played a prominent role because of its medical expenditures information, the 1987 version of NMES, which is a nationally representative sample of roughly 35,000 individuals in the United States taken by the Agency for Health Care Policy and Research. Of critical importance, NMES attempts to obtain extensive information on medical expenditures broken down into quite fine categories, fine enough so that medical expenditures for individuals can be assembled at levels of detail corresponding to the Surgeon General's categories of disease (ICD-9 codes) for which the health relative risks of smoking are reported to differ. Also, NMES has relatively detailed smoking information beyond "former," "never," "current," and relatively extensive information on both background characteristics and other health-care-expenditure-related factors.

Because of these attributes, NMES seems to be the best suited of available data sets for estimating the relative risks of many categories of health-care expenditures due to smoking behaviors, RR$\$(S|X, D)$, in many subpopulations of the U.S. population, at least assuming, that they are essentially constant over the relevant time period. Of course, if we could design and conduct new surveys or supplement NMES, we could obtain even more detailed information regarding expenditure relative risks, but none of the parties in the smoking litigation has, to the best of my knowledge, attempted to collect new data for the estimation of expenditure relative risks, for example, for the particular population of a litigation. Instead, for example, the plaintiffs' experts have argued that the covariates being controlled when estimating relative risks are detailed enough to allow the application of NMES-estimated expenditure relative risks in their population (e.g., state). For convenience, let us suppose we accept the adequacy of NMES for estimating relative risks.

5.2   Missing Data in NMES

A complicating issue with NMES, however, is the nontrivial problem of missing data on expenditures, smoking behaviors, and some covariates. In some situations, indicator variables or simple recoding tricks (e.g., Harrison, 1998) can be useful in missing data problems (e.g., see Little and Rubin, 1987). Here, however, the meaning of the measurements themselves are what justify the key assumption, and so these techniques are not appropriate.

A fairly massive editing/imputation effort was undertaken by AHCPR to impute missing medical-expenditure information (Barwick and Katikineni, 1992). This effort in some instances was more like editing than imputation, in that individual's medical records were sought, found, and actual values were essentially imputed. Thus, some subset of the imputed expenditure values are essentially reported values. Other imputations, however, are far more uncertain. Some imputations were the result of relatively crude hot-deck matching methods with no attempt to reflect uncertainty of prediction or to relate missing expenditure information consistently to observed expenditure information or to smoking behavior or covariates. The problem of missing data is not easy, but substantial progress has been made in the last quarter of a century, partially due to theoretical advancements and partially due to computational progress (e.g., Little and Rubin, 1987; Rubin, 1987; Greenland and Finkle, 1995; Schafer, 1997). However, it appears that none of the plaintiff's experts attempted to deal with the missing data using modern techniques. Instead, they accepted AHCPR'S imputations and used outdated techniques such as complete-cases, or best-value or hot-deck single imputation, to deal with other missing data. These efforts were criticized, including in the Minnesota trail, where the criticisms seemed to resonate to the jury (Rybak and Phelps, 1998, pp. 394–395).

Although the effort needed to handle all the missing data well is substantial, the problem should be addressed this year (2000) by the creation of a multiply-imputed version of NMES, which can form a valid basis for the estimation of expenditure relative risks, at least up to the level of detailed information provided by NMES and suggested by the plaintiff's experts in the cases.

5.3   Overview of Multiple Imputation

Multiple imputation (Rubin, 1987, 1996; Schafer, 1997) is now a standard method to address missing data, particularly appropriate with public-use data sets, where it has been used with substantial success, e.g., NHANES produced by the National Center for Health Statistics (Ezzati-Rice et al., 1995), the Consumer Expenditure

Survey of the Federal Reserve Board (Kennickell, 1991), the Fatal Accident Reporting System of the Department of Transportation's National Highway Traffic Safety Administration (U.S. Department of Transportation, 1998), and the Census Bureau's Occupational and Industry Codes (Clogg et al., 1991). Currently, other federal agencies are considering the use of multiple imputation (e.g., the Bureau of Labor Statistics, Paulin and Raghunathan, 1998). Moreover, commercial software for creating multiply-imputed datasets now exists (e.g., Statistical Solutions, Ltd., 1999).

Multiple imputation replaces each missing value by two or more imputations, which together reflect the information, including the uncertainty, as to which values should be imputed. Each set of imputations is used to create one data set with no missing data. Each such data set is analyzed using standard complete-data methods. The results of these complete-data analyses are then combined using generic combining rules. The final result is one answer, which properly reflects uncertainty due to the missing values and produces a statistically valid inference. Given the complexity of the missing data in NMES and the intended analyses of NMES to estimate expenditure relative risks, multiple imputation seems to be the only inferentially valid path to take.

5.4   Overview of the Plan to Multiply-Impute NMES

There are three distinct phases used to multiply-impute NMES. The first uses the expenditure values imputed by AHCPR to create "donor pools" of possible expenditure amounts for the missing expenditures. The second phase uses Markov chain Monte Carlo techniques to take a random draw from the posterior predictive distribution of the missing values, both missing expenditure amounts and missing covariate and smoking behavior values. This phase is a demanding exercise, consisting of several major steps. The third phase involves the allocation of expenditure amounts associated with "unreported" (i.e., missing) ICD-9 codes to actual ICD-9 codes. The final result will be M (e.g., $M = 5$ was used for NHANES, Ezzati-Rice et al., 1995) NMES data sets, each with no missing values; all M data sets will be identical where NMES has observed data, but the M will generally differ where NMES has missing data.

6   Task 3: Inference for Expenditure Relative Risks of Smoking in the Actual World

The estimation of expenditure relative risks has to be done very carefully because the process of estimating RR\$$(S|X, D)$ essentially involves a series of "observational studies," each study comparing average expenditures for individuals with a specific type of smoking behavior $(S > 0)$ to never-smokers $(S = 0)$ with the same value of covariates (X, D). Disappointingly, a simple "linear regression" or two-part "logit then linear" or "logit then linear log" model cannot be relied on to obtain valid answers, because when the two groups being compared have different distributions of covariates, some degree of extrapolation is needed. If there were a huge data set in each covariate subpopulation, which included many individuals with each type of smoking behavior, the estimation of RR$(S|X, D)$ would be relatively easy: We would simply calculate the ratio of the average expenditures for type S smokers to never-smokers within each (X, D) covariate subpopulation. However, no available data set appears to be that rich, and so we have to use some sort of modeling to adjust for differences in covariate distributions between each type of smoker and never-smokers when estimating relative risks.

6.1 Some Principles for the Estimation of Relative Risks

For more than a third of the twentieth century, the statistical literature has warned that regression analysis cannot reliably adjust for differences in covariates when there are substantial differences in the distribution of these covariates in the two groups. For example, William G. Cochran, who served on the advisory committee that wrote the 1964 Surgeon General's Report, worked extensively on methods for the analysis of observational studies (Rubin, 1984). Cochran (1957) stated:

> ... when the x-variables [i.e., covariates] show real differences among groups—the case in which adjustment is needed most—covariance adjustments [i.e., regression adjustments] involve a greater or less degree of extrapolation.

And in Cochran (1965), he wrote:

> If the original x-distributions diverge widely, none of the methods [e.g. regression adjustment] can be trusted to remove all, or nearly all, the bias. This discussion brings out the importance of finding comparison groups in which the initial differences among the distributions of the disturbing variables are small.

And in the same article he wrote:

> With several x-variables, the common practice is to compare the marginal distributions in the two groups for each x-variable separately. The above argument makes it clear, however, that if the form of the regression of y on the x's is unknown, identity of the whole multi-variate distribution is required for freedom from bias.

In particular, there are three basic distributional conditions that in general practice must simultaneously obtain for regression adjustment (whether by ordinary linear regression, linear logistic regression, or linear-log regression) to be trustworthy. If any of these conditions is not satisfied, the differences between the distributions of covariates in the two groups must be regarded as substantial, and regression adjustment alone is unreliable and cannot be trusted. These conditions are stated below in terms of the propensity score (Rosenbaum and Rubin, 1983) and the residuals of the original variables given the propensity score (both defined in Section 6.2).

1. The difference in the means, B, of the standardized propensity scores in the two groups being compared must be small (e.g., the means must be less than half a standard deviation apart), unless the situation is benign in the sense that
   (a) the distributions of the covariates in both groups are nearly symmetric,
   (b) the distributions of the covariates in both groups have nearly the same variances, and
   (c) the sample sizes are approximately the same.
2. The ratio of the variances of the propensity score in the two groups, R, must be close to one (e.g., one half or two are far too extreme).
3. The ratio of the variances of the residuals of the covariates after adjusting for the propensity score must be close to one (e.g., one half or two are far too extreme).

Specific tabulations and calculations relevant to these points can be found in a variety of places (e.g., Rubin; 1973, 1979). In particular, Cochran and Rubin (1973, p. 426) state that "linear regression on random samples gives wildly erratic results . . . sometimes markedly overcorrecting or even (with $B = \frac{1}{4}$ for e^x) greatly increasing the original bias [when the ratio of the variances is one-half]." Table 3.2.2 in that article implies that when the ratio of the variance of any covariate is one-half, regression can grossly overcorrect for bias or grossly undercorrect for bias. These three guidelines also address regression adjustments on the logit or linear log scale because they, too, rely on linear additive effects in the covariates (Anderson et al., 1980).

After considering the use of propensity score analyses in Section 6.2 to address the validity of simple modeling adjustments, Section 6.3 offers specific suggestions on the construction of better analyses to estimate the expenditure relative risks RR$(S|X, D)$.

6.2 Propensity Score Analyses

The propensity score is the conditional probability of being in the treated versus control group (e.g., smoker versus nonsmoker) given a set of covariates. Linear propensity scores are a transformation of these probabilities that are linear in the covariates (or linear in their interactions, powers, and transformations). Linear propensity scores are closely related theoretically to discriminant scores (Rubin and Thomas, 1992). Rosenbaum and Rubin (1983) showed that the propensity score is the most critical single summary of the covariates for removing bias due to them, because all the mean bias in the covariates is reflected in the propensity score. Thus, the theoretical results reviewed in Section 6.1 can be applied directly to differences on the propensity score, where B is the bias of the propensity score and R the ratio of variances of the propensity score. Because the residuals after adjusting for the propensity score have the same mean in the treated and control groups, the same theoretical results with $B = 0$ can be applied to each of the residuals, where now R is the ratio of the variances of the residuals in the treated and control groups.

To see how well the conditions in Section 6.1 are satisfied in NMES, propensity score analyses were conducted comparing former and current smokers with never-smokers. In these analyses, the NMES sampling weights were used to represent the national population corresponding to the NMES design. Also, the 32 covariates selected were the ones used by plaintiff's expert's report, Harrison (1998). For this analysis, missing values were handled, not in an appropriate way as outlined in Section 5.4, but for simplicity and ease of comparison with other analyses, the same way that Harrison (1998) did. The differences between smokers and never-smokers nationally, displayed in the first two rows of Table 2, are substantial enough that regression models cannot reliably adjust for even the background characteristics and other confounding factors included in the regressions.

Also, such differences between smokers and never-smokers apparently persist in subpopulations, which is relevant because some plaintiffs represent such groups of people in litigation. Moreover, such subpopulations are relevant when assessing the possible impact of smoking reduction programs that target particular groups, such as teenagers or blue-collar workers. As an example, consider the group of individuals in NMES who reported that they had private insurance provided by a union in any of the four rounds of interviews. To compute the propensity scores, the 32 variables in Harrison (1998) were again used. These results, again using the NMES sampling weights, are presented in rows 3 and 4 of Table 2. The differences between smokers and never-smokers observed nationally appear to be even more substantial in the subpopulation of NMES corresponding approximately to union workers.

Table 2. Propensity Score Analyses For Smokers Versus Never-Smokers in NMES (1987) and Union Subset of NMES (1987)

Smoking Group	Propensity Score Bias	Variance Ratio	$\left(0, \frac{1}{2}\right)$	$\left(\frac{1}{2}, \frac{4}{5}\right)$	$\left(\frac{4}{5}, \frac{5}{4}\right)$	$\left(\frac{5}{4}, 2\right)$	$(2, \infty)$
All Current	.81	.97	0	6	22	3	1
All Former	.75	1.24	0	5	21	4	2
Union Current	.59	.11	4	5	16	5	2
Union Former	.69	.23	5	7	16	4	0

(Residuals Orthogonal to Propensity Score — Variance Ratios in Range)

6.3   More Reliable Adjustments Combine Regression Modeling and Propensity Score Methods

The statistical literature suggesting that regression modeling alone is unreliable in the situations presented in Table 2 also suggests that in such situations, combining regression modeling with matching and/or subclassification using the propensity score should produce substantially more reliable estimates (e.g., Rubin, 1973, 1979; Rubin and Thomas, 2000; Dehejia and Wahba, 1999). To provide the flavor of a statistically valid analysis for estimating the relative risks for categories of expenditures for various levels of S as a function of (X, D), suppose that the missing data in NMES have been handled by multiple imputation, as addressed briefly in Section 5.4. Then the following analyses would be conducted on each imputed data set.

Suppose that we define four "important" levels of coarse smoking behavior (e.g., current heavy, current light, former heavy, former light) in addition to never smoking, but retain the more detailed smoking information for regression adjustments. Consider each of these four smoking groups, in turn, as the treated group to be compared to the full group of never-smokers (the controls) by creating a propensity score matched sample, using Mahalanobis metric matching within propensity score calipers, as in a variety of places (e.g., Rosenbaum and Rubin, 1985; Reinisch et al., 1995; Rubin and Thomas, 2000; see also Dehehjia and Wahba, 1999). The propensity scores are estimated by a logistic regression of the treatment/control indicator on the covariates, and the Mahalanobis metric uses important continuous covariates. This process will generate four matched samples, each consisting of matched treated-control pairs whose covariate distributions should be similar. Now, for each of the four matched samples, build a standard (two-part) regression model using detailed (S, X, D) information to predict each detailed type of health-care expenditure, H. The relative risk at each (X, D) is then given by the ratio of the predicted H as a function of (S, X, D) to the predicted H at the same (X, D) but with $S = 0$ (where there is a different prediction equation for each coarse type of smoking behavior). Standard errors for the entire estimation scheme can be approximated by use of the bootstrap (Efron and Tibshirani, 1993).

7   Tasks 4 and 5: Survey Inferences for Actual Prevalences and Dollar Pots in Relevant Population During Relevant Periods

The estimation of actual-world prevalences of smoking behavior and other health-expenditure-related factors, $PR(S, D|X)$, and the amounts of money in dollar pots, $POT(X, D)$, require different and simpler statistical techniques than the estimation of the actual-world expenditure relative risks of smoking, which involved methods of adjustment used for causal inference from observational (nonrandomized) studies. For dollar pots, in principle, all we need to do is to conduct audit surveys of health-care records to estimate dollar amounts in each

(X, D) subpopulation. For (S, D) prevalences, in principle, all we need to do is conduct surveys in the relevant X subpopulations. There are two limiting factors: the required time and effort to conduct the relevant surveys, and the complications created by trying to get data on past prevalences and past expenditures, especially at the level of detail that is required for the validity of the key assumption.

7.1   Estimation of Actual-World Smoking Prevalences

Ideally, one would have a statistically valid survey of the correct population from which to estimate the smoking and other health-care-expenditure-related prevalences in X subpopulations for each of the T years under consideration. There appears to be a variety of sources of data that show changes in national smoking prevalences by some demographic characteristics as in plaintiff's expert reports (e.g., Harris, 1997). Without direct data in the correct population under study, it is still possible to estimate changing prevalences in time under some explicitly stated assumptions using combinations of national, state-level, and local data sets. These assumptions most likely would posit the absence of certain interactions, and apply statistical techniques that fit main effects and only some low-order interaction effects. Some such estimation seems necessary because we appear to know that smoking prevalences (and the prevalences of other health-care-expenditure-related factors such as diet and exercise) have changed over the years, and differently by some demographic characteristics (e.g., sex, education, occupation). For example, Nelson et al. (1994) state:

> Since 1978 to 1980, the differences in smoking prevalence by occupation have widened, providing further evidence that smoking has moved from a relatively common behavior practiced by most segments of society to one that has become more concentrated among selected subpopulations.

7.2   Estimation of Dollar Pots

Although the dollar pots may be known by row (health-care expenditure category) and column (year), they may not be known at the appropriately disaggregated level, that is, within (X, D) covariate subpopulations, but perhaps only within X subpopulations; assume that this is the case. Recall that we cannot ignore D because we made it inclusive in order to make the key assumption more plausible. It may be possible to do small surveys of past medical records to try to obtain D information in addition to X information on some individuals in each year. Or if it is possible to survey only current health-care records of individuals, we can still estimate aspects of the joint distribution of (H, S, X, D) at this time. If we assume that the implied conditional distribution of D given (H, X) (or D given (H, S, X) if smoking behavior is available on past health-care records) is constant in time, we can then multiply-impute the missing D values from past records, thereby estimating dollar pots within (X, D) subpopulations and representing uncertainty in these imputations. Without some statistical effort like this, the implicit assumption is that in the past, H and D are independent given X, which we may know from the expenditure relative risk analyses of NMES is not correct. In any case, although demanding, the goal is the standard one in any complex survey activity.

8 Task 6: Evidence for Prevalences of Smoking and Other-Health-Care-Expenditure-Related Factors in Counterfactual World

We now come to the most litigious aspect of the statistical analyses for the smoking cases: the estimation of prevalences of smoking and other health-care-expenditure-related behaviors in X subpopulations in a counterfactual world without the alleged misconduct by the tobacco industry. It is here that the opposing lawyers need to try to convince the court and jury not only of what actions by the industry constituted misconduct, a legal issue, but also what would have been the prevalences of smoking and other health-care-expenditure-related factors without this misconduct, a question addressed largely on statistical evidence. This is a statistical issue because, although we have no data in a counterfactual world, we do have many actual-world data sets concerning the effects of interventions on smoking and other health-related behaviors, particularly those interventions that arguably parallel actions that the tobacco industry allegedly would have taken in a counterfactual world without misconduct, and these actual-world data sets can be used as a basis for estimation. To focus on the statistical issues here means trying to find evidence on what happens to smoking initiation, smoking cessation, and other health-care-expenditure-related behaviors as the world around us changes.

8.1 Nonintervention Studies

Some relevant evidence comes from studies without active interventions. For example, there is some evidence that former smokers often gain substantial amounts of weight, which may have its own negative consequences for health-care expenditures (e.g., O'Hara et al., 1998). For another example, it appears that most people already substantially overestimate the absolute overall health risks of smoking (Viscusi, 1991), with the associated claim that if people were told the real risks, it would have no effect. Some support for this position appears in the 1979 Surgeon General's Report on Smoking; for example, p. 1-35:

> Most educational programs are based on what seems reasonable rather than on sound theoretical models. It is logical to assume, for example, that young people who know about the harmful effects of cigarette smoking on health will resist smoking. Thus, many programs are based on knowledge dissemination and a health threat. However, we know that 94 percent of

teenagers say that smoking is harmful to health and 90 percent of teenage smokers are aware of the health threat.

More statistically rigorous evidence comes from actual intervention studies, preferably randomized experiments, where the treated group is exposed to an intervention designed to inhibit the initiation of smoking or encourage the cessation of smoking, whereas the control group is not exposed to any intervention. There is now an enormous literature on programs designed to reduce cigarette consumption, and some themes emerge that are relevant to the prevalence of smoking and other health-care-expenditure-related factors in a counterfactual world.

8.2 Smoking Initiation Studies

Strategies for preventing smoking initiation have evolved over time. Initially, the strategy was based on a model of filling an "information deficit" about the long-term health risks of smoking. This model seems relatively parallel to some aspects of what would have happened in a counterfactual world without the alleged misconduct of the tobacco industry. This model, however, did not appear to work to reduce smoking in practice; Flay (1985, p. 450) wrote:

> Most past programs have been based on the premise that if children know why cigarette smoking is bad for them, they should choose to not start smoking. Of those conventional smoking education programs evaluated, many have succeeded in changing students' knowledge, some their beliefs, and some their attitudes, but very few have consistently reduced the onset of smoking behavior (Green, 1979; Thompson, 1978).
> The failure of informational or fear programs to change behavior comes as no surprise to psychologists (Leventhal & Cleary, 1980).

The second strategy to evolve was based on an "affective education" model, which involved programs that, as the Surgeon General (1994, p. 217) wrote:

> ... sought to increase adolescents' perceptions of self-worth and to establish or clarify a health-related value system that would support a young person's decision not to smoke ... Reviews based on more than a decade of research have concluded that interventions based on the affective education model were no more effective in reducing adolescent smoking than those based on the information deficit model. Some studies have even suggested (that is, without conclusive findings) that these programs may have had the untoward effect of eliciting interest in the behaviors they attempted to discourage (Kinder, Pape and Walfish, 1980; Schaps et al., 1981; Hansen et al., 1988). Nonetheless, affective education programs marked the beginning of an era during which enormous effort was expended to design smoking-prevention interventions that were more directly related to the factors believed to cause smoking among adolescents.

The third strategy to evolve was based on a "social influence" model, which appeared to be somewhat more successful according to the Surgeon General (1994, pp. 225):

> ... the positive shorter-term intervention effects reported in adolescent smoking-prevention studies tend to dissipate over time ... This general trend has been particularly evident among school-based intervention studies that included little or no emphasis on booster sessions ... Only the social influence approaches have been scientifically demonstrated (through replicated research studies) to reduce or delay adolescent smoking.

A fourth strategy to evolve concerned the desirability of focusing tailored programs to be appropriate to individuals. For example, Best et al. (1995, p. S-59) wrote:

> Individual differences are important determinants of smoking onset and the impact of social influences programs. Prevention programs should provide for targeting or tailoring treatment to subpopulations predisposed toward smoking .... In particular, individual differences—the person (Figure 1)—need to be taken into account .... The need now is to develop and test strategies for targeting or tailoring programs to these individual differences, using the full range of knowledge we have about the broader developmental context within which smoking takes place.

This conclusion about the need to consider subpopulations is highly relevant to the tobacco litigation. It suggests that when estimating smoking prevalence in a counterfactual world without the alleged misconduct, conditioning on covariate information is critical because the effects of interventions on smoking initiation vary by these characteristics, and moreover, that interventions that are not tailored may not be effective.

8.3 Smoking Cessation Studies

The literature on smoking cessation programs for adults also seems to suggest the relative ineffectiveness of untargeted and information-based programs; Klausner (1997, pp. S-1) wrote:

> Findings from over 100 intervention trials continue to provide much new and important information about how to reach smokers and potential smokers. However, one of the major conclusions that one can draw from these studies is that large-scale reductions in smoking prevalence are unlikely using interventions that are primarily directed toward the individual and delivered through traditional intervention channels.

The COMMIT randomized trials, which used a community-level four-year intervention designed to increase quit rates of heavy smokers, found essentially no effect on these smokers, but a small effect on light to moderate smokers; they found essentially no effect on overall smoking prevalences (COMMIT I & II, 1995a,b). Also see Winkleby et al. (1997). Ebrahim and Smith (1997, p. 1666) wrote:

> More recent trials examining changes in risk factors have cast considerable doubt on the effectiveness of these multiple risk factor interventions and even interventions against smoking, prompting a review of the reasons for the frequent failure of such community experiments.

Also, later (p. 1668), they suggest that the advice of a doctor can be helpful, which is consistent with the conclusion of the Surgeon General (1979, p. 1-34).

Recently, there appears to be strong interest in targeting or tailoring smoking cessation programs to the individual's characteristics, including using special techniques to help focus on the individual (Strecher, 1999; Velicer et al., 1993). Evidently, to be effective, smoking intervention programs need to target different subpopulations differently. Thus, the prevalences of different smoking cessation behaviors in a counterfactual world with special smoking reduction efforts apparently would depend on detailed (S, X, D) characteristics.

8.4   Conclusion on Task 6

The first major statistical effort in Task 6 is to summarize the existing actual-world data concerning what features of the environment lead to reduced smoking, and how these interact with characteristics of an individual. At that point, we are ready to assess how the prevalences of smoking and other health-care-expenditure-related factors would have changed without the alleged misconduct. The differences between the actual and counterfactual world prevalences are then used in the numerator of equation (2), along with actual-world estimates of prevalences and relative risks, to calculate the conduct attributable fractions from equation (2), and thus the conduct attributable expenditures from equation (1).

9   Extensions Requiring More Than One Counterfactual World

The formulation here has discussed only one counterfactual world, but more than one can be relevant. For example, there may be different acts of alleged misconduct, and each combination of the existence of and absence of these acts constitutes a different counterfactual world. Or tobacco industry and plaintiff positions may differ on their assessment of the prevalences of smoking behaviors and other health-care-expenditure-related factors in the counterfactual world. In other situations, it is necessary to consider more than one counterfactual world simply to define the consequences of the alleged misconduct.

9.1 Two Distinct Effects of the Alleged Misconduct

In some cases, such as Ohio Iron Workers (e.g., Lauer, 1998), the plaintiff was a third-party payer of health care, which alleged that the misconduct of the tobacco industry affected not only the smoking behaviors of its participants, but also its own actions, such as initiating smoking cessation programs. In some of these cases, a legal issue that has arisen is whether the plaintiff may recover only excess expenditures that would have been saved through its actions and not excess expenditures that would have been saved even without its actions. Statistically, the separate effects of the defendant's alleged misconduct can be estimated using more than one counterfactual world.

More precisely, let the C by T matrix CAE* represent the excess actual-world health-care expenditures relative to the counterfactual world without the alleged misconduct by the tobacco industry and allowing both plaintiff-initiated and individual-initiated changes in behavior from the actual world. Also, let the C by T matrix CAE^{*P} represent the excess actual-world expenditures relative to the counterfactual world without the alleged misconduct and without any "plaintiff-initiated" actions; CAE^{*P} is due to the effect of the alleged misconduct on "individual-initiated" behaviors (e.g., information about the health effects of smoking that influenced individuals to reduce their smoking). Thus the alleged misconduct caused the plaintiff to "not initiate" actions that resulted in the C by T matrix of excess expenditures equal to the difference CAE* − CAE^{*P}. From equation (1), these excess expenditures can be written as

$$\text{CAE}^* - \text{CAE}^{*P} = \sum_X \sum_D \text{POT}(X, D) \cdot [\text{CAF}^*(X, D) - \text{CAF}^{*P}(X, D)],$$

where under the key assumption, an entry in the C by T matrix of $[\text{CAF}^*(X, D) - \text{CAF}^{*P}(X, D)]$ equals, from equation (2),

$$\frac{\sum_S [\text{PR}^{*P}(S, D|X) - \text{PR}^*(S, D|X)] \cdot \text{RR\$}(S|X, D)}{\sum_S \text{PR}(S, D|X) \cdot \text{RR\$}(S|X, D)}.$$

Thus, the expression for these excess expenditures, which would have been saved by actions of the plaintiffs that would have occurred but for the alleged misconduct, involves actual-world prevalences and relative risks, and the difference between two sets of counterfactual world prevalences: the set without the plaintiff's actions and the set allowing them.

9.2 Two Distinct Sources of Alleged Misconduct—Joint Causation

Now consider the situation with two industries accused of misconduct, both of which are alleged to have caused an increase in health-care expenditures. For example, consider the alleged misconduct of the asbestos (e.g., Gastwirth, 1988) and tobacco industries causing damages from lung cancer and related diseases (e.g., Nicholson, 1999). In such situations, there may be the need to apportion any damages due to their combined alleged acts of misconduct between the two industries. To do this in a formal way requires the consideration of three counterfactual worlds: the one without misconduct by the tobacco industry, with excess actual world expenditures of CAE^{*T}; the one without misconduct by the asbestos industry, with excess expenditures of CAE^{*A}; and the one with misconduct by neither industry, with excess expenditures of CAE^{**}.

The C by T matrix CAE^{*T} is due solely to the tobacco industry's alleged misconduct, CAE^{*A} is due solely to the asbestos industry's alleged misconduct, and CAE^{**} is due to their alleged joint misconduct; C^{**} is the amount that together both industries owe if both acts of alleged misconduct are accepted. If within each (X, D) subpopulation the matrices CAE^{*T} and CAE^{*A} add to CAE^{**}, then there is no problem in allocating amounts to the two industries: tobacco owes the sum of the $C \cdot T$ entries in CAE^{*T} and asbestos owes the sum of the $C \cdot T$ entries in CAE^{*A}. But in general, subpopulation matrices do not add this way; for example, with tobacco and asbestos, current medical understanding suggests that for many categories of health-care expenditures and in many years, $CAE^{**} > CAE^{*T} + CAE^{*A}$, especially in some subpopulations.

One possible solution to allocating joint costs, which, in principle, is consistent with work by Chase et al. (1985) and plaintiff's expert for the asbestos industry (Nicholson, 1999), is to assign damages in proportion to their sole effects: Within each cell of CAE^{**} and each subpopulation, the tobacco industry owes $CAE^{**} \cdot CAE^{*T}/(CAE^{*T} + CAE^{*A})$, and the asbestos industry owes $CAE^{**} \cdot CAE^{*A}/(CAE^{*T} + CAE^{*A})$. One must do this partitioning separately within each (X, D) subpopulation and within each year t and each category c of expenditure and then aggregate; otherwise, a mistake, or even a Simpson's paradox, can result. For an artificial example, suppose for males excess expenditures are all allocable to tobacco, with $CAE^{*T} = \$1$, $CAE^{*A} = 0$, and $CAE^{**} = \$2$, whereas for females they are allocable to asbestos, with $CAE^{*T} = 0$, $CAE^{*A} = \$1$, and $CAE^{**} = \$10$. Tobacco should pay its share, \$2, and asbestos its share, \$10. But if expenditures are aggregated over both subpopulations before partitioning, we have $CAE^{*T} = CAE^{*A} = \$1$ and $CAE^{**} = \$12$, and then each would pay $12 \cdot 1/(1 + 1) = \$6$. Doing the calculation at disaggregated levels can be needed even when the expenditures are additive in the aggregate. See Rubin (2000) for more details.

10   Conclusions

Because Task 1 is simply a mathematical statistical formulation that is consistent with the thrust of all technical work in epidemiology estimating the risks of exposures, there should be little debate about it or the role of the key assumption. Also, because Tasks 2–5 are about how to estimate actual-world quantities, there should be fairly good agreement among statisticians about how this should be done, at least if underlying assumptions that are being made to cope with weaknesses in existing data sets are explicated. The most complicated issue here involves dealing with the level of detail in health-care expenditures, smoking behaviors, background characteristics, and other health-care-expenditure-related factors that need to be included if one is to believe in the medical/economic/sociological/psychological law of gravity implied by the key assumption. Attempting to include all detail considered relevant by any of the experts is clearly the best pathway to try to take.

Task 6, however, concerning the prevalence of smoking and other health-care-expenditure-related behaviors in the counterfactual world, is the most contentious. Here, the court and jury first must decide what would have taken place in a counterfactual world without the alleged misconduct. Then the court and jury must decide how that counterfactual world situation relates to evidence from actual-world interventions concerning their effect on the prevalence of smoking and other health-care-expenditure-related factors. Having assessed these prevalences, estimates of the conduct-attributable expenditures follow from equations (1) and (2), or extensions discussed in Section 9.

This formulation crisply delineates issues of fact about the actual world from issues using actual-world facts to conjecture about the counterfactual world, and shows that the counterfactual world estimation enters the equation only through the difference between actual- and counterfactual-world prevalences of smoking and other health-expenditure-related behaviors.

REFERENCES

[1] Agency for Health Care Policy and Research (1992), *National Medical Expenditure Survey, Calendar Year 1987*, Center for General Health Services Research, AHCPR, Rockville, MD: Public Health Service.

[2] Anderson, S., Auquier, A., Hauck, W.W., Oakes, D., Vandaele, W., and Weisberg, H.I. (1980), *Statistical Methods for Comparative Studies*, New York: John Wiley.

[3] Barwick, J. and Katikineni, D. (1992), *Task NMS.3180 Report HHS Events Editing, Volume I*, Division of Intramural Research, Agency for Health Care Policy and Research, Rockville, MD.

[4] Best, J.A., Brown, K.S., Cameron, R., Manske, S.M., and Santi, S. (1995), Gender and predisposing attributes as predictors of smoking onset: implications for theory and practice, *Journal of Health Education*, 26, 2, S-59 to S-60.

[5] Chase, G.R., Kotin, P., Crump, K., Mitchell, R.S. (1985), Evaluation for compensation of asbestos-exposed individuals. II. Apportionment of risk for lung cancer and mesothelioma, *Journal of Occupational Medicine*, 27, 189–255.

[6] Clogg, C.C., Rubin, D.B., Schenker, N., Schultz, B., and Weidman, L. (1991), Multiple imputation of industry and occupation codes in Census public-use samples using Bayesian Logistic Regression, *The Journal of the American Statistical Association*, 86, 413, 68–78.

[7] Cochran, W.G. (1957), Analysis of covariance: its nature and uses, *Biometrics*, 13, 261–281.

[8] Cochran, W.G. (1965), The planning of observational studies of human populations, *The Journal of the Royal Statistical Society A*, 128, 234–265.

[9] Cochran, W.G. and Rubin, D.B. (1973), Controlling bias in observational studies: a review, *Sankya - A*, 35, 4, 417–446.

[10] COMMIT Research Group (1995a), Community intervention trial for smoking cessation (COMMIT): I. Cohort results from a four-year community intervention, *American Journal of Public Health*, 85, 183–192.

[11] COMMIT Research Group (1995b), Community intervention trial for smoking cessation (COMMIT): II. Changes in adult cigarette smoking prevalence, *American Journal of Public Health*, 85, 193–200.

[12] Dehejia, R. and Wahba, S. (1999), Causal effects in non-experimental studies: re-evaluating the evaluation of training programs, *The Journal of the American Statistical Association 94*, 448, 1053–1062.

[13] Ebrahim, S. and Smith, G.D. (1997), Systematic review of randomised controlled trials of multiple risk factor interventions for preventing coronary heart disease, *British Medical Journal*, 314, 1666–1674.

[14] Efron, B. and Tibshirani, R.J. (1993), *An Introduction to the Bootstrap*, New York: Chapman and Hall.

[15] Engle, H.A. (1999), Verdict form for Phase I, *Howard A. Engle, M.D., et al., Plaintiffs, v. R.J. Reynolds Tobacco Company et al., Defendants*, General Jurisdiction Division Case No 94-08273/c/a-22, Circuit Court of the Eleventh Judicial Circuit in and for Dade County, Florida.

[16] Ezzati-Rice, T., Johnson, W., Khare, M., Little, R.J.A., Rubin, D.B., and Schafer, J. (1995), A simulation study to evaluate the performance of model-based multiple imputations in NCHS Health Examination Surveys, *Bureau of the Census Eleventh Annual Research Conference*, 257–266.

[17] Federal Judicial Center (1994), *Reference Manual on Scientific Evidence*.

[18] Fisher, F. (1999), Preliminary expert report of Franklin M. Fisher, July 1, 1999. *Blue Cross/Blue Shield of New Jersey et al., Plaintiffs, vs. Philip Morris, Inc., et al., Defendants*, No. 98 Civ. 3287 (JBW).

[19] Flay, B.R. (1985), Psychosocial approaches to smoking prevention: a review of findings, *Health Psychology*, 1985, 4, (5), 450.

[20] Gastwirth, J.L. (1988), *Statistical Reasoning in Law and Public Policy, Vol. 2*, New York: Academic Press, Inc., 807–810.

[21] Greenland, S. and Finkle, W.D. (1995), A critical look at methods for handling missing covariates in epidemiologic regression analyses, *American Journal of Epidemiology*, 1995, 142, 1255–1264.

[22] Harris, J.E. (1997), Expert report, November 3, 1997: Health-care spending attributable to cigarette smoking and to cigarette manufacturers' anti-competitive conduct: State of Washington Medicaid Program, 1970–2001, *State of Washington, Plaintiff, v. American Tobacco, et al., Defendants*, Superior Court of Washington in and for King County, Washington.

[23] Harris, J.E. (1999), Final expert report, November 29,1999: Defendant's anti-competitive anddeceptive onduct was a significant contributing factor in the development of smokin-related diseases among beneficiaries of Blue Cross/Blue Shield plans and increased health-care spending by those plans. *Blue Cross and Blue Shield of New Jersey, Plaintiff, v. Philip Morris Incorporated, et al., Defendants*, No. 98 Civ. 3287 (JBW).

[24] Harrison, G.W. (1998), Expert report, April 27, 1998: Health care expenditures attributable to smoking in Oklahoma, *The State of Oklahoma, ex rel., et al., Plaintiffs, vs. Reynolds Tobacco Co., et al., Defendants*, Case No. CJ-96-1499-L, District Court of Cleveland County, Oklahoma.

[25] Kennickell, A.B. (1991), Imputation of the 1989 Survey of Consumer Finances: stochastic relaxation and multiple imputation, *Proceedings of the Survey Research Methods Section of the American Statistical Association*, 1–10.

[26] Klausner, R. (1997), Evolution of tobacco control studies at the National Cancer Institute, *Tobacco Control*, 1997, 6 (Suppl 2), S-1 to S-2.

[27] Lauer, M.S. (1998), Expert report: Smoking and coronary heart disease, undated; and Supplemental report: Smoking and stroke, October 22, 1998; *Iron Workers Local Union No. 17 Insurance Fund and Its Trustees, et al., Plaintiffs, v. Philip Morris Incorporated, et al., Defendants*, Civil Action No. 1:97 CV1422, District Court, Northeastern District of Ohio.

[28] Little, R.J.A. and Rubin, D.B. (1987), *Statistical Analysis with Missing Data*, New York: John Wiley and Sons. Translated into Russian in 1991: Finansy and Statistika Publishers: Moscow, Andrei Nikiforev, translator.

[29] Massey, J.T., Moore, T.F., Parsons, V.L., and Tadros, W. (1989), Design and estimation for the National Health Interview Survey, 1985-94, *Vital Health Statistics*, 2, 110, National Center for Health Statistics, DHHS Publication No. (PHS) 89–1384.

[30] Nelson, D.E., Emont, S.L., Brackbill, R.M., Cameron, L.L., Peddicord, J., and Fiore, M.C. (1994), Cigarette smoking prevalence by occupation in the United States, *Journal of Occupational Medicine*, 36, 5, 516–525.

[31] Nicholson, W.J. (1999), Expert report, August 30, 1999: Evaluation of cigarette smoking interactions in the development of asbestos-related disease, *Falise et al., Plaintiffs v. The American Tobacco Company et al., Defendants*, United States District Court Eastern District of New York, (CV97-76640).

[32] O'Hara, P., Connet, J.E., Lee, W.W., Nides, M., Murray, R., and Wise, R. (1998), Early and late weight gain following smoking cessation in the Lung Health Study, *American Journal of Epidemiology*, 148, 821–832.

[33] Ogden, D.W. (1999), News conference, September 22, 1999, *FDCH transcripts*, http://onCongress1.cq.com/PSUser/psrecord...newsanalysis/transcripts&NS_initial_frm=

[34] Paulin, G. and Raghunathan, T.E. (1998), Evaluation of multiple imputation inferences, *Proceedings of the American Statistical Association 1998 Survey Methods Research Section*.

[35] Reinisch, J.M., Sanders, S.A., Mortensen, E.L., and Rubin, D.B. (1995), In utero exposure to phenobarbital and intelligence deficits in adult men, *The Journal of the American Medical Association*, 274, 19, 1518–1525.

[36] Rabinovitz, F.F. (1999), Expert Report, September 1, 1999: Estimation value of the tobacco industry's share of the indemnity and expenses of the Manville personal injury settlement trust, *Robert A. Falise, et al., Plaintiffs v. The American Tobacco Company, et al., Defendants*, United States District Court, Eastern District of New York, (CV97-76640).

[37] Rosenbaum, P.R. and Rubin, D.B. (1983), The central role of the propensity score in observational studies for causal effects, *Biometrika*, 70, 41–55.

[38] Rosenbaum, P.R. and Rubin, D.B. (1985), Constructing a control group using multivariate matched sampling incorporating the propensity score, *The American Statistician*, 39, 33–38.

[39] Rothman, K.J. and Greenland, S. (1998), *Modern epidemiology*, 2nd ed., Lippincott-Raven, Philadelphia.

[40] Rubin, D.B. (1973), The use of matched sampling and regression adjustment to remove bias in observational studies, *Biometrics*, 29, 1, 184–203.

[41] Rubin, D.B. (1979), Using multivariate matched sampling and regression adjustment to control bias in observational studies, *The Journal of the American Statistical Association*, 74, 366, 318–328.

[42] Rubin, D.B. (1984), William G. Cochran's contributions to the design, analysis, and evaluation of observational studies, *W.G. Cochran's Impact on Statistics*, P.S.R.S. Rao and J. Sedransk (eds.), New York: John Wiley, 37–69.

[43] Rubin, D.B. (1987), *Multiple Imputation for Nonresponse in Surveys*, New York: John Wiley.

[44] Rubin, D.B. (1996), Multiple imputation after 18+ years, *Journal of the American Statistical Association*, 91, 473–489 (with discussion, 507–515, and rejoinder, 515–517).

[45] Rubin, D.B. (1998), What does it mean to estimate the causal effects of "smoking"?, *Proceedings of the Section on Statistics in Epidemiology of the American Statistical Association*, 18–27.

[46] Rubin, D.B. (2000), Estimating the causal effects of smoking, to appear in *Statistics in Medicine*.

[47] Rubin, D.B. and Thomas, N. (2000), Characterizing the effect of matching using linear propensity score methods with normal covariates, *Biometrika*, 79, 4, 797–809.

[48] Rubin, D.B. and Thomas, N. (2000), Combining propensity score matching with additional adjustments for prognostic covariates, to appear in *The Journal of the American Statistical Association*, 95, 573–585.

[49] Rybak, D.C. and Phelps, D. (1998), *Smoked: The Inside Story of the Minnesota Tobacco Trial*, MSP Books: Minneapolis, MN, 394–395.

[50] Samet, J.M. (1998), Trial testimony at 3482 and Deposition testimony at 369–370, *State of Minnesota and Blue Cross and Blue Shield of Minnesota, Plaintiffs, v. Philip Morris, Inc. et al., Defendants*, Court File No. C1-94-8565, District Court of Ramsey County, Minnesota.

[51] Schafer, J. (1997), *Analysis of Incomplete Multivariate Data, London: Chapman and Hall*.

[52] Simpson, E.H. (1951), The interpretation of interaction in contingency tables, *The Journal of the Royal Statistical Society B*, 13, 238–241.

[53] Statistical Solutions, Ltd. (1999), *SOLAS 2.0 for Missing Data Analysis*, http://www.statsolusa.com.

[54] Stellman, S.D., and Garfinkel, L. (1986), Smoking habits and tar levels in a new American Cancer Society prospective study of 1.2 million men and women, *Journal of the National Cancer Institute*, 76, 1057–1063.

[55] Strecher, V.J. (1999), Computer-tailored smoking cessation materials: a review and discussion, *Patient Education and Counseling*, 36, 107–117.

[56] U.S. Department of Health and Human Services, Public Health Service, Office of the Surgeon General, Publication No. 1103. (1964), *Smoking and Health: Report of the Advisory Committee to the Surgeon General of the Public Health Service*, U.S. Government Printing Office, Washington, DC.

[57] U.S. Department of Health and Human Services, Public Health Service, Office of the Surgeon General, (1994), *Preventing Tobacco Use Among Young People: A Report of the Surgeon General*, Centers for Disease Control and Prevention, Government Printing Office, Washington, DC.

[58] U.S. Department of Health, Education, and Welfare, Public Health Service, Office of the Surgeon General, Publication No. 79-50066, (1979), *Smoking and Health: A Report of the Surgeon General*, U.S. Government Printing Office, Washington, DC.

[59] U.S. Department of Transportation, NHTSA (1998), Multiple imputation of missing blood alcohol content (BAC) in FARS, *Research Note: National Highway Traffic Safety Administration*, Washington, DC.

[60] Velicer, W.F., Prochaska, J.O., Bellis, J.M., DiClemente, C.C., Rossi, J.S., Fava, J.L., and Steiger, J.H. (1993), An expert system intervention for smoking cessation, *Addictive Behaviors*, 18, 269–290.

[61] Viscusi, W.K. (1991), Age variations in risk perceptions and smoking decisions, *The Review of Economics and Statistics*, 73, 4, 577–588.

[62] Warner, K.E., Chalouka, F.J., Cook, P.J., Manning, W.G., Newhouse, J.P., Novotny, T.E., Schelling, T.C., and Townsend, J. (1995), Criteria for determining an optimal cigarette tax: the economists's perspective, *Tobacco Control*, 4, 380–386.

[63] Winkleby, M.A., Feldman, H.A., and Murray, D.M. (1997), Joint analysis of three U.S. community intervention trials for reduction of cardiovascular disease risk, *Journal of Clinical Epidemiology*, 50, 6, 645–658.

Forensic Statistics and Multiparty Bayesianism

Joseph B. Kadane

Abstract

The invitation to write for this volume affords me an extraordinary opportunity to trace the development of some of my theoretical ideas about statistics back to their origin in some of my encounters with the legal system. While most of this story is in chronological order, it is useful to start with my general approach to applied and theoretical statistics, in Section 1. Section 2 records some experiences with working on the random selection of jury venires, and Section 3 discusses work on the optimal use of peremptory challenges. Sections 4 and 5 discuss Bayesian theory and applications, respectively. Section 6 mentions other work on juries that readers may find to be of interest. Finally, Section 7 raises a question about how the legal system responds to issues about the fairness of the jury system.

Keywords: jury venire selection, peremptory challenges, backward induction, multiparty Bayesian theory, experimental design.

1   Statistical Inference

I study statistical inference: how conclusions are drawn from data. There is a wide body of theoretical ideas about how to do this; later I explain some of the major divisions in the field, and where my own experiences have led me. Much of the action comes from doing statistical inference, starting by working with someone in a particular field who wants to find out about something. At the moment of this writing, my applied work is in archaeology, demography, genetics, law, medicine, social psychology, and solid-state physics, but this list changes over the years as old projects conclude and new ones begin. I find it useful to have a wide range of experience, so that my ideas about statistical inference are not narrowed by exposure to too narrow a sampling of fields.

When I do applied work, my commitment is to the application. I use my theoretical ideas to help me decide what to do in an applied problem, but if I find a conflict between my current theoretical ideas and being effective in contributing to the applied area, the latter takes priority. Such conflicts are often fruitful in developing my theoretical ideas, as afterwards I revisit the problem, to see whether a more thorough or satisfying job can be done on it. So for me, theory and application interact, each deepening the other.

2 Random Selection of Jury Venires

Many of my contacts with the legal system start with receiving a phone call. This time, it was from the county court system, asking whether I had an interest in looking into a problem of selecting a jury venire from several source lists in such a way that overlaps in the source lists were properly accounted for. In the space of a few days, they lost interest in having me work on the problem, but I became fascinated. The traditional way to think about a jury venire is that it is a random sample drawn from a master list, and used to supply potential jurors to courts. An actual master list with names amalgamated from several source lists requires checking a great many names for duplication, most of which would not be called to be a jury venire. I wanted to explore the idea of a virtual master list, an algorithm that would have the favorable properties of a master list without so much wasted checking. The result was a clientless foray into how to obtain a random sample (each person having the same probability of being selected) from a union of lists, with arbitrary overlaps.

Together with my colleague John Lehoczky, we discovered that there are a number of different methods to do this. Perhaps the simplest is to put the lists in an arbitrary order, list 1 first, then list 2, then list 3, etc. Choose a random name from this large, strung-together list. If the random name came from the first list, keep it as a good name. If it came from the second list, keep it as a good name only if it does not appear on the first list. A name from list 3 is good only if it does not appear on the first two lists, etc. In this way, a person is regarded as a good name only on the highest list the person appears on. Thus each person has the same chance of being included. Furthermore, this method does not require the lists to be amalgamated—a time-consuming proposition in which most of the duplicate-checking effort is spent on persons not selected as venire persons.

The next question we addressed is the effort-minimizing order of the lists. In practice, the lists used—the voters list, drivers list, utility customer lists, etc.—are organized differently, making checking a name against a list more or less expensive. For example, a voters list may be organized by ward and precinct, while the drivers list may be alphabetical for the county. In this case, it would be convenient to have the drivers' list first, and check names against it. Putting the voters' list last would ensure that names would never have to be checked against it. For more details, see Kadane and Lehoczky (1976).

As this work came to fruition, the next natural question was whether any-one would use it. Somehow, I came across a paper by a Philadelphia lawyer named David Kairys (1972), advocating the use of significance testing to de-termine whether a jury venire adequately represented the community. While my graduate education at Stanford had stressed significance testing and hypothesis testing, I had become skeptical of those methods for both practical and theoret-ical reasons. Essentially, the problem is that by testing at a fixed level, like .05, with a small sample size virtually no hypothesis is rejected; while with a large sample size, virtually every null hypothesis is rejected. Thus, far from measuring the verisimilitude of the hypothesis, the procedure is measuring sample size, for which there are simpler measures.

As luck would have it, I was traveling to Philadelphia soon anyway, so I called up David, introduced myself, said that I had read his article and disagreed with some of it, and asked to meet. This was the start of a long and fruitful collaboration, the first result of which was Kairys, Kadane, and Lehoczky (1977), hereinafter KKL, setting out the legal case for using multiple-list methods for jury venires, documenting what the experience had been nationwide, and discussing various measures that courts could use to determine the adequacy of a jury venire. The paper had to be finished in a hurry, because David was testifying on the subject to a Senate committee considering removing the federal mandate for multiple source lists (the move was defeated and the mandate remains, to this day).

Preparation of KKL was aided by data supplied by Tom Munsterman, then of Bird Engineering and in recent years of the National Center for State Courts. In work with Tom, it became evident that the major cost in doing multiple-list juror selection properly is the cost of checking a name against a list. Each prospective juror is sent a questionnaire to make sure of their eligibility for jury service. It is simple to add a few more questions to see whether the prospective juror is, or ought to be, on the source lists other than the one from which their name was selected. This reduces the cost of list-checking practically to zero. Tom has been working with court administrators to implement these ideas.

3 Peremptory Challenges

There are several legal steps that occur between the jury venire and people who actually serve on juries. The first concerns who returns jury questionnaires, and who is granted an excuse from serving. In some jurisdictions, the proportion of returned questionnaires is very low, stemming from (1) poor quality lists (2) a tradition of seeing jury service as a tax-in-kind, to be avoided if possible, rather than a privilege of citizenship and an honor, and (3) long required service, making it a burden. The move to one-day-or-one-trial service in many jurisdictions addresses (3) directly and (2) indirectly. Even careful work in getting the use of multiple source lists demographically right can be obviated if nonrespondents and the excuse process bias the resulting panels.

Challenges to the service of a particular juror also allow a departure from the desideratum that juries should be a random cross-section of the community. These come in two sorts: challenges for cause and peremptory challenges. Challenges for cause have to do with specific reasons why a particular juror could not be fair and impartial, such as prior acquaintanceship with the parties, etc. By contrast, an attorney exercising a peremptory challenge does not have to explain why; the juror is not permitted to serve. Each side gets a number of challenges provided in state or federal law, and can, in principle, exercise them at will. (This legal standard has been modified a bit in recent years: prosecutors cannot systematically remove black jurors from hearing cases against blacks (*Batson v. Kentucky* (1986)). However, the Supreme Court decision in *Purkett v. Elam* (1995) makes it very difficult to show prosecutorial discrimination. See Johnson (1998) and King (1998).

My long-time colleague and friend Morrie DeGroot and I started to wonder about optimal strategies for each side to employ in deciding which potential jurors to challenge. To make the problem even approachable, we had to make a number of (rather unrealistic) simplifications. We assumed that jurors vote independently of each other (thus no interaction in the jury room). In a criminal trial, the prosecution would want to maximize the probability of conviction, while the defense would want to minimize it. Each side could have its own probability that a juror would favor it, and (most unrealistically), each side would know the other side's probability. This is, however, slightly more realistic than supposing the sides to agree on a probability (which each would therefore know).

The procedures used to exercise peremptory challenges confronted us with another problem. Each judge can invent her own procedure for each trial, and these practices vary. We chose what we took to be a tractable case: each potential juror surviving challenge for cause is subject to peremptory challenge. First, one side decides whether to use one of its challenges on the potential juror; if not challenged by that side, the other side decides. If not challenged peremptorily by either side, the juror is seated and cannot later be challenged. Fortunately, the number of peremptory challenges available to each side is set by law (state or federal as the case may be), although the trial judge can apparently modify those numbers in various special circumstances.

Appendix E of VanDyke (1977) gives the numbers of peremptory challenges permitted by jurisdiction and type of case. For example, federal law allows each side 12 peremptory challenges in capital cases, 5 for other felonies, 2 for misdemeanors, and 3 for civil cases. In Pennsylvania, each side gets 20 for capital cases, 8 for felonies, 6 for misdemeanors, and 4 for civil cases. A few states give differing numbers of peremptory challenges to prosecution and defense in criminal cases.

Together with Arthur Roth, a visitor in our department, we developed a backwards induction approach to this problem (Roth, Kadane, and DeGroot (1977), hereinafter RKD). Among the questions of interest to us were whether there was an advantage to being first to decide whether a juror is to be challenged peremptorily. Intuitively, the idea is that if I get to decide first, I can calculate exactly what you (the other side) will do. Only in the case in which neither of us wants the potential juror to serve does order matter. But in that case, by accepting the juror, I can force you to use one of your challenges, which is to my benefit.

Or is it? Implicit here is the idea that I am better off if I have more challenges and you have fewer, with the same jurors already chosen. We discovered this assumption, which we called "regularity," only late in the preparation of the paper. We reported being unable to prove or disprove it, so we assumed that it was true.

In later conversations culminating in DeGroot and Kadane (1980), hereinafter DK, we generalized the model by allowing each side to have an arbitrary utility function in which jurors can be characterized more subtly than in RKD. The same argument applies, showing that regularity implies no disadvantage in choosing first. But in this context we also found a counterexample to regularity, and a related example in which it is advantageous to choose second, not first. However, the issue of whether regularity held in the simpler RKD model remained open. (See DeGroot (1987) for an excellent review of the theory of the optimal use of peremptory challenges as it had been developed to that point in time.)

There is a parallel approach to our sequential view of the process of exercising jury challenges. At about the same time as RKD was being published, we became aware of Brams and Davis's (1978) work using a simultaneous-move game-theoretic framework. They refer to irregularity in their model as "absurd."

Stepping out of chronological order at this point, much later, I had the good fortune to be teaching a "fast" undergraduate statistics course for mathematics and computer science majors. While most students in the course found it challenging, two indicated that they were bored. I gave them the problem of determining whether regularity holds in the RKD model. The resulting paper (Kadane, Stone, and Wallstrom 1999) gives examples of the failure of regularity in the RKD model, but also shows that regularity holds (in both the RKD model and the more general DK model) if there are only two kinds of jurors. DeGroot would have enjoyed that work, and I very much regret that he did not live to see it.

4 Multiparty Bayesian Theory

As I have gained more experience in doing statistics, my theoretical ideas have settled on the Bayesian paradigm. The important aspects of Bayesianism for this paper are on the decision-theoretic side: that I choose to make decisions to maximize my expected utility, where the expectations are taken with respect to my current beliefs about all uncertain quantities. Thus, the decision maker is permitted (encouraged, required) to make a statement of values, in the form of a utility function, and of belief, in the form of a probability distribution. Both of these are personal, or subjective, in that they can legitimately be different for different persons, without any of them making a provable error.

In the formulation of the peremptory challenge problem described above, each side is permitted to have its own view, quite possibly different from that of the other side, about whether this juror will vote for conviction. (The less reasonable part of the model is that each side is assumed to know the other side's probability).

What happens if that assumption is relaxed? It quickly becomes apparent that the model becomes much more complicated, because now each side, in making its decisions, has to think about what the other side may learn of its views by its decisions, which in turn depends on a theory of the other side's knowledge and uncertainty, etc.

To clarify our thinking on these issues, DeGroot and I (DeGroot and Kadane 1983) studied a much simpler situation. There is an object on a line. Player 1 has target x; Player 2 target y. Player 1 can move the object in stages 1 and 3, and

Player 2 in stage 2. Each player is penalized proportionally to the square of the distance that player chooses to move the object, plus the square of the distance of the final location of the object from that player's goal. Each player is assumed to know his or her own goal.

When each player knows the other's goal as well, the computation of optimal strategies is quite simple. In Player 1's last move, both the location of the object and Player 1's target are known to Player 1. Hence, computation of the optimal move is simple: Player 1 will move the object part of the way from its then current location in the direction of x; the fraction of the distance is determined by the constant of proportionality in Player 1's penalty. Now consider Player 2's move. Knowing x, Player 2 can predict Player 1's last move with certainty. Hence, by substitution, Player 2 can calculate the consequences to Player 2 of each possible move, and hence find the optimal move to make. Similarly, working backwards, Player 1's first move is simple, as again the results of each available action can be forecast with certainty.

Now consider the case in which neither player knows the other's goal, but instead has a probability distribution about it. Player 1's last move is unaffected, because Player 2's goal is irrelevant to Player 1's last move. However, Player 2's move is a bit more complicated. Player 2 does not know x, Player 1's goal, and hence cannot compute with certainty what Player 1 will do in response to each possible move of Player 2. However, the optimal move for Player 2 is tractable, since under the quadratic loss functions assumed, only the expectation of x given Player 1's first move is relevant. The full force of the complication becomes apparent in considering Player 1's first move. Now Player 1 has to think about not just his uncertainty about Player 2's goal, y, but also about his opinion about how Player 2's opinion about Player 1's goal will be influenced by Player 1's first move. Hence, this very simple example illustrates the difficulty in relaxing the assumption in the peremptory challenge model that each side knows the other's probabilities. (For further use of this example to explore themes in game theory, see Kadane and Seidenfeld 1992).

5   Applying Multiparty Bayesian Theory

One of the more difficult aspects of Bayesian ideas for non-Bayesians to embrace is its emphasis on subjectivity, that is, on the beliefs and values of the person making the decisions. In data analysis, these enter through the choice of a likelihood function (the probability of the data given certain parameters) and a prior distribution of the parameters. For historical reasons, likelihood functions are regarded by non-Bayesians as "less subjective" than priors. Standard Bayesian practice now includes a careful statement of the reasons for the prior chosen and exploration of the consequences of using other prior distributions.

Not all statistical problems come in the form of data analyses, however. Some of the most important problems are in the design of experiments. Here the first problem is to choose a design; then the data are collected, and then they are analyzed. Using the backwards induction principle described above, optimal decisions would be made in reverse chronological order. For each possible data set you might be confronted with, what data analysis would you use, and what would your expected utility be? Then, moving back in time, under each possible design, what is your probability of each resulting data set? Now you are in a position to choose a design to maximize your expected utility, where you are taking into account both that you know neither what data set will ensue nor the truth of the matters you are gathering data about. Bayesian experimental design has been developed to compute what to do, either analytically (Chaloner and Verdinelli 1995) or computationally (Muller 1998).

Thinking about the peremptory challenge situation might lead to the following question: Why does the person choosing the design of the experiment have to be the same as the person who analyzes the data? Put that way, of course, it is obviously not necessary, and one can think of many examples in which it is not the case. It is widely recognized that a policeman may use his beliefs in deciding how to conduct a criminal investigation. Yet the policeman will be unsuccessful in invoking criminal sanctions on someone based on his beliefs. A judge or jury would require evidence that she, as a neutral unbiased person, finds convincing. Thus the policeman is searching for evidence, conducting experiments, if you will, not to convince himself, but to convince someone else with a rather different starting perspective (i.e., prior probability). The same kind of difference of opinion is evident when a pharmaceutical company designs a study to convince the Food and Drug Administration of the safety and efficacy of a new drug. The company is convinced and enthusiastic, but the FDA is more skeptical. This led Ruth Etzioni and me (Etzioni and Kadane 1993) to explore the optimal design of experiments from this perspective.

Later, Scott Berry and I (Berry and Kadane 1997) used these ideas to find a Bayesian explanation for why randomization is so popular in applied design of experiments. The issue here is that a Bayesian making a decision in a single-person scenario never finds it advantageous to randomize. Yet randomization is a widely used technique in experimental design. Using a three-person scenario, Berry and I find an example in which a Bayesian experimental designer would wish to randomize. I am excited about this line of research, and am convinced that there is a lot more to be done to explore it further and make it useful.

6   Other Matters, Other Work

Of course, there is a great deal of other activity concerning jury composition, decision-making, etc., that I will mention here in the hope that an interested reader might want to pursue some of it. Classic first work on jury behavior: Kalven and Zeisel (1966). Research on jury size: Fabian (1977), Friedman (1972), and Gelfand and Solomon (1974, 1977). Fair numbers of peremptory challenges:

Franklin (1987) and Kadane and Kairys (1979). Jury decision-making: Hastie (1993), Hastie, Penrod, and Pennington (1983), and Kalven and Zeisel (1966). Organizing a complex mass of evidence coherently: Kadane and Schum (1996).

7 Conclusion

As this recounting of personal experiences shows, one idea or problem leads to another. From a telephone call about jury venire from several source lists we come, over a period of years, to questions of optimal experimental design.

One final matter: Part of the invitation to write this paper included a request to address my reaction to the legal process.

Typically, the question of the adequacy of the jury venire would be brought in a pretrial motion. It might take a few weeks or months for such a motion to be heard and acted upon. If the judge rules against the motion, and the defendant is convicted, an appeal on the issue can take a year or more to be resolved. During the time that motion has not been definitively resolved, it would virtually be malpractice for every defense attorney to fail to raise the same issue at every trial, thus preserving the defendant's right to benefit should the jury system be found wanting. In this way, months or years of jury trials can come to depend on the resolution of a motion questioning the legal status of the jury venire.

Very often, the jury system is set up by, and subject to the administrative control of, a chief judge or the administrative office of the state court. Who, then, can impartially decide whether the law requires that system to be improved, say by the use of multiple list methods, or better methods of checking for duplicates, etc.? Currently, such a case would be heard by the same chief judge, or by another judge who reports to that chief judge. It seems inevitable to me that the designer or approver of a system being questioned has a conflict of interest, and is likely to be defensive about such a challenge. How can the legal structure be modified to give these issues the fair hearing they deserve?

8 Cases Cited

Batson v. Kentucky 476 US 79 (1986).
Purkett v. Elam 514 US 765 (1995).

REFERENCES

[1] Berry, S. and Kadane, J.B. (1997), Optimal Bayesian Randomization, *Journal of the Royal Statistical Society*, Series B, 59, No. 4., pp. 813–819.

[2] Brams, S.J. and Davis, M.D. (1978), Optimal Jury Selection: A Game Theoretic Model for the Exercise of Peremptory Challenges, *Operations Research*, 26, pp. 966–991.

[3] Chaloner, K. and Verdinelli, I. (1995), Bayesian Experimental Design: A Review, *Statistical Science*, 10, 273–304.

[4] DeGroot, M.H. (1987). The Use of Peremptory Challenges in Jury Selection, *Contributions to the Theory and Applications of Statistics*, A. Gelfand, ed. Academic Press, pp. 243–271.

[5] DeGroot, M. and Kadane, J.B. (1980). Optimal Challenges for Selection, *Operations Research*, (July–August), 28: 952–968.

[6] DeGroot, M.H. and Kadane, J.B. (1983), Optimal Sequential Decisions in Problems Involving More than One Decision Maker, *Recent Advances in Statistics*-Papers Submitted in Honor of Herman Chernoff's Sixtieth Birthday, editors H. Rizvi, J.S. Rustagi and D.Siegmund, Academic Press, 197–210.

[7] Etzioni, R. and Kadane, J.B. (1993), Optimal Experimental Design for Another's Analysis, *Journal of the American Statistical Association*, 88, 1404–1411.

[8] Fabian, V. (1977), On the Effect of Jury Size, *Journal of the American Statistical Association*, 72, 535–537.

[9] Friedman, H. (1972), Trial by jury: Criteria for Convictions, Jury Size and Type I and Type II Errors, The American Statistician, 26, 21–23.

[10] Franklin, L.A. (1987), Bayes' Theorem, Binomial Probabilities, and Fair Numbers of Peremptory Challenges in Jury Trials, *The College Mathematics Journal*, 18, 291–299.

[11] Gelfand, A.E. and Solomon, H. (1974), Modeling Jury Verdicts in the American legal System, *Journal of the American Statistical Association*, 69, 32–37.

[12] Gelfand, A.E. and Solomon, H. (1977) Comments on "On the Effect of Jury Size," *Journal of the American Statistical Association*, 72, 536–537.

[13] Hastie, R., Penrod, S.D., and Pennington, N. (1983), *Inside the Jury*, Cambridge, MA: Harvard University Press.

[14] Hastie, R. (editor), *Inside the Juror: The Psychology of Juror Decision Making*, (1993). Cambridge University Press.

[15] Johnson, S.L. (1998), Batson Ethics for Prosecutors and Trial Court Judges, *Chicago-Kent Law Review*, 73, 475.

[16] Kadane, J.B. and Kairys, D. (1979), Fair numbers of Peremptory Challenges in Jury Trials, *Journal of the American Statistical Association*, 74, 747–753.

[17] Kadane, J.B. and Lehoczky, J. (1976), Random Juror Selection from Multiple Lists, Operations Research, (March–April), 24: 207–19.

[18] Kadane, J.B. and Schum, D.A. (1996), *A Probabilistic Analysis of the Sacco and Vanzetti Evidence*, J. Wiley & Sons.

[19] Kadane, J.B. and Seidenfeld, T. (1992), Equilibrium, Common Knowledge and Optimal Sequential Decisions, *Knowledge, Belief, and Strategic Interaction*, C. Bicchieri and M.L. Dalla Chiara, editors, pp. 27–45, Cambridge University Press.

[20] Kadane, J.B., Stone, C., and Wallstrom, G. (1999), The Donation Paradox for Peremptory Challenges, *Theory and Decision*, 47: 139–151.

[21] Kairys, D. (1972), Jury Selection: The Law, a Mathematical Method of Analysis, and a Case Study, *American Criminal Law Review*, 10, 771, 785–789.

[22] Kairys, D., Kadane, J.B., and Lehoczky, J. (1977), Jury Representativeness: A Mandate for Multiple Source Lists, California Law Review, 65: 776–827. Reprinted in the record of a hearing before the Subcommittee on Improvements in Judicial Machinery of the Committee on the Judiciary, U.S. Senate, September 28, 1977.

[23] Kalven, H.K., Jr. and Zeisel, H. (1966), *The American Jury*, Boston: Little, Brown.

[24] King, N.L. (1998), Batson for the Bench? Regulating the Peremptory Challenges of Judges, Chicago-Kent Law Review, 73, 509.

[25] Muller, P. (1998), Simulation Based Optimal Design, to appear in *Bayesian Statistics* 6, J.M. Bernardo, J.O. Berger, A.P. Dawid and A.F.M. Smith, eds., Oxford University Press, Oxford.

[26] Roth, A., Kadane, J.B., and DeGroot, M. (1977), Optimal Peremptory Challenges in Trial by Juries: A Bilateral Sequential Process, *Operations Research*, (November), 25: 901–19.

[27] VanDyke, J.M. (1977), *Jury Selection Procedures: Our Uncertain Commitment to Representative Juries*, Ballinger: Cambridge, MA.

Warranty Contracts and Equilibrium Probabilities

Nozer D. Singpurwalla

Abstract

This article pertains to warranty contracts associated with the exchange of items that are selected from a large collection of similar items. Warranty contracts for item reliability and quality are, by their very nature, adversarial. They are crafted by lawyers representing one adversary, generally a seller, and are ratified by lawyers representing the other adversary, generally a buyer. The contractual requirements are stated in lay terms and involve only observables. These requirements may or may not be based on a consideration of the underlying failure propensity.

The purpose of this article is to point out that inherent to any meaningful warranty contract there exist values of the propensity that make the contract "fair" to each adversary. We call these values "equilibrium probabilities"; they can be viewed as logical probabilities in the sense of Carnap. A warranty contract is said to be "in equilibrium" if the equilibrium probabilities coincide, and a contract that is in equilibrium is said to be "just" if the common equilibrium probabilities coincide with propensity. The ratification of any warranty contract is based on an adversary's personal probability of the propensity. Thus the scenario of warranty contracts brings into perspective the three predominant notions of probability: objective, logical, and subjective.

The thrust of our message is that the existence of equilibrium probabilities be recognized in warranty contracts. Current practice does not do so. This message should be of particular relevance to those involved in industrial and government contracting wherein the exchange of large monies is at stake.

Keywords: Adversaries, Game Theory, Logical Probability, Propensity, Purchasing, Reliability, Quality, Subjective Probability, Utility.

1 Introduction

The topic of warranties is quite fascinating. It is at the interface of engineering, law, and mathematics. Its origins are in the moral and the legal sciences; see Singpurwalla and Wilson 1993. Its impact is on the behavioral and the decision sciences. Its mathematical content lies in the philosophical underpinnings of probability.

In this article we focus attention on warranties associated with the exchange of items that are selected from a *large* collection of similar items, between a manufacturer (seller) and a consumer (buyer). This is a commonly occurring situation in industrial and government contracting; for example, the purchase of microchips by a computer manufacturer. The case of warranties associated with one-of-a-kind items is much simpler; it is not considered here.

Warranty contracts pertaining to item reliability (or quality) are generally written by lawyers representing the manufacturer. The specifications of the contract are often based on marketing considerations, and involve observable quantities such as the number of failures within a prescribed time. These specifications may or may not be based on the underlying propensity of failure. The warranty contracts are ratified (i.e., accepted) by lawyers representing the buyer or consumer. These lawyers may or may not seek advice from engineers; the latter tend to be cognizant of the underlying probabilities. If, after the contract is ratified, actual experience reveals an excessive number of failures, then the contract is likely to be canceled, and the lawyers proceed to litigate. During the course of litigation, one of the two adversaries may seek salvation from statisticians (to include applied probabilists). But statisticians evaluate warranty contracts in the light of probability, and so a statistician's testimony will invariably include the term "probability." Use of this term could raise several questions, such as what kind of probability and whose probability? More important, since the word probability is nowhere in the contract, opposing counsel may move to strike out the statistical testimony. The above sequence of events therefore poses a dilemma. On the one hand, probability is a necessary ingredient for analyzing the experiences of an adversary. On the other hand, warranty contracts can be interpreted by lay persons only in terms of observables, and so probability is not a part of the terminology of a contract.

The purpose of this article is twofold. The first is to describe an actual occurrence—suitably camouflaged—wherein the above conflict occurred. The second is to point out that underlying any meaningful warranty contract, no matter how specified, there exist probabilities that can be interpreted as being objective, subjective, or logical, and whose role is either explanatory or decision-theoretic. When explanatory, the role of probabilities is analogous to that of hidden parameters in physics. Of particular relevance are what we call "equilibrium probabilities"; these are like the logical probabilities of Carnap [cf. Weatherford 1982, p. 85]. Deviations of the propensity (i.e., the objective probability) of failure from the equilibrium probabilities makes a contract unfair. The ratification of the contract by a buyer is based on the buyer's personal probability of the propensity. Thus, as a corollary to the above, we suggest that an explicit acknowledgment of the existence of equilibrium probabilities be inherent to warranty contracts. This will provide a rational basis for a decision should litigation occur. Making the equilibrium probabilities explicit, however, is de facto requiring that the adversaries declare their utilities. This proposition may not be palatable to many firms.

2 A Real-Life Scenario

The following warranty contract is typical of many transactions. A buyer B is interested in purchasing n supposedly identical items. Each item is required to last for τ units of time; for convenience, we may let $\tau = 1$. Suppose that B is willing to pay $ x per item, and is prepared to tolerate at most z failures in the time interval $[0, \tau]$. For each failure in excess of z, $\mathcal{B}$ needs to be compensated at the rate of $ y per item. In effect, the quantity τ can be viewed as the duration of a warranty.

A seller $\mathcal{L}$ has an inventory of N such items, where N is very large. Upon advice from marketing and legal, $\mathcal{L}$ is agreeable to delivering the n items needed by $\mathcal{B}$. $\mathcal{L}$ is also prepared to abide by $\mathcal{B}$'s requirement of price and the terms of the warranty. The specific values for x, z, y, n, and τ are decided upon by $\mathcal{B}$, or by $\mathcal{B}$ and $\mathcal{L}$ together, and it is not our aim to discuss how these choices have been arrived at. The warranty contract as described above was ratified by both $\mathcal{B}$ and $\mathcal{L}$.

It now so happens that $\mathcal{B}$ experiences an excessive number of failures within the time period $[0, \tau]$. This development has caused a loss of goodwill and reputation from $\mathcal{B}$'s customers. Since $\mathcal{L}$ has not delivered all the n items stipulated in the contract, $\mathcal{B}$ seizes this opportunity to cancel the contract and to sue $\mathcal{L}$ for monies in excess of the terms of the contract.

$\mathcal{L}$ argues that $\mathcal{B}$ has reneged on the contract, and consults a statistician $\mathcal{R}$, specializing in reliability, to testify that the reliability of the units is indeed acceptable, comparable to industry standards. $\mathcal{L}$ is of course perfectly willing to reimburse $\mathcal{B}$ the sum of $ y for every failure in the interval $[0, \tau]$ that exceeds z. Since the word "reliability" was nowhere mentioned in the terms of the contract, $\mathcal{B}$'s lawyers move to strike out $\mathcal{R}$'s testimony. Incidentally, $\mathcal{R}$'s testimony and analysis did conclude that the reliability of the items was in keeping with industry standards. Based upon this, $\mathcal{L}$ claimed that $\mathcal{B}$ misused the items and therefore experienced an excessive number of failures; however, $\mathcal{L}$ could not substantiate this assertion.

The above conflict, which actually did occur, was eventually settled out of court by a mediator sympathetic to probabilistic thinking. Even though the bottom line was in favor of $\mathcal{L}$, $\mathcal{R}$ was left with the issue of how to connect what the legal profession and the general public are comfortable doing, with the technology that $\mathcal{R}$ is trained to use. Given below is $\mathcal{R}$'s synthesis of the probabilistic issues that underlie warranty contracts of the type described above. The gist of this synthesis is that there often exist unique and computable probabilities, called "equilibrium probabilities," that are specific to a warranty contract of the type described above, and that the existence of such probabilities should be acknowledged in all such contracts. Were this to be done, then the equilibrium probabilities could serve as a fulcrum point around which litigation may rationally proceed.

3   A Prescription for $\mathcal{L}$'s Normative Behavior

By normative behavior we mean actions that do not lead to a "dutch book"; see Lindley 1985, p. 50. The simplest way to convey the spirit of a dutch book is to imagine a coin-tossing gamble of the type, "heads I win, tails you lose," i.e., a no-win situation for one side. It has been shown [cf. Lindley 1985] that a strict adherence to the calculus of probability ensures the avoidance of a dutch book.

To prescribe $\mathcal{L}$'s normative behavior, let us suppose that it costs $\mathcal{L}$ \$ c to produce a single unit of the item sold. Then, if $\mathcal{B}$ experiences z or fewer failures in $[0, \tau]$, $\mathcal{L}$'s profit will be $n(x - c)$. However, if $\mathcal{B}$ experiences i failures in $[0, \tau]$, with $i > z$, then $\mathcal{L}$'s liability will be $(i - z)y$. When the contract is ratified by $\mathcal{L}$, i is of course unknown. Suppose then that $\mathcal{P}(i)$ is the propensity (or an objective probability) of i failures in $[0, \tau]$. Then, $\mathcal{L}$'s *expected liability* is

$$\sum_{i=z+1}^{n} (i - z) y \mathcal{P}(i).$$

Since $\mathcal{L}$ is selecting n items (at random) from an inventory of N items, where N is large, it makes sense to think in terms of the propensity of a single item failing in $[0, \tau]$; let p denote this propensity. Since the N items are judged to be similar, it follows that were we to know p, then

$$\mathcal{P}(i) = \binom{n}{i} p^i (1 - p)^{n-i}, \qquad\qquad i = 0, \ldots, n.$$

Thus conditional on p, $\mathcal{L}$'s expected liability reduces, after some algebra, to the form

$$y \left\{ np - \sum_{i=0}^{z} i \binom{n}{i} p^i (1 - p)^{n-i} - z \sum_{i=z+1}^{n} \binom{n}{i} p^i (1 - p)^{n-i} \right\}.$$

The warranty contract is said to be *fair* to $\mathcal{L}$ if, conditional on p, $\mathcal{L}$'s expected liability equals $\mathcal{L}$'s receipts, i.e., $\mathcal{L}$ expects to break even. Thus,

$$n(x - c) = y \left\{ np - \sum_{i=0}^{z} i \binom{n}{i} p^i (1 - p)^{n-i} - z \sum_{i=z+1}^{n} \binom{n}{i} p^i (1 - p)^{n-i} \right\}. \tag{1}$$

Since n, x, y, τ and z are either known or are specified by the contract, and c is known to $\mathcal{L}$, the above can be solved by $\mathcal{L}$ for p, to yield a value $p_{\mathcal{L}}$, should such a value exist. We call $p_{\mathcal{L}}$ an *equilibrium probability* for $\mathcal{L}$. If the true propensity of failure is greater than $p_{\mathcal{L}}$, $\mathcal{L}$ is liable to experience losses; otherwise, $\mathcal{L}$ is likely to profit. $\mathcal{L}$'s decision to ratify the contract, as stated, will depend on $\pi_{\mathcal{L}}(p)$, $\mathcal{L}$'s personal probability for the unknown p. This issue is treated later, in Section 6.

4   A Model for $\mathcal{B}$'s Normative Behavior

$\mathcal{B}$'s position could be quite complicated. $\mathcal{B}$ is prepared to pay nx to buy n items, which are supposed to last for τ units of time. $\mathcal{B}$ will incur an unknown loss due to the items failing prior to time τ, and is going to receive an unknown amount in reimbursements from $\mathcal{L}$.

Let w denote the worth (in dollars) to $\mathcal{B}$ if a unit functions for τ units of time. Then for the contract to be *fair* to $\mathcal{B}$, we must have

$$nx = nw - \mathbb{E}(\text{Loss}) + \mathbb{E}(\text{Reimbursement}),$$

where $\mathbb{E}$ denotes expectation. Thus $\mathbb{E}$ (Loss) denotes $\mathcal{B}$'s expected loss due to a premature failure of units; similarly for $\mathbb{E}$ (Reimbursement).

4.1 Reimbursements to $\mathcal{B}$

If at the end of τ units of time i units have failed, then $\mathcal{B}$ will receive as a reimbursement $\$(i - z)y$, if $i \geq z + 1$, and nothing otherwise. Using an argument similar to that of Section 3, we can see that

$$\mathbb{E}[\text{Reimbursement}] = \sum_{i=z+1}^{n} (i - z)y \binom{n}{i} p^i (1 - p)^{n-i},$$

which after some algebra results in the expression

$$\mathbb{E}[\text{Reimbursement}] = y \left\{ np - \sum_{i=0}^{z} i \binom{n}{i} p^i (1 - p)^{n-i} - z \sum_{i=z+1}^{n} \binom{n}{i} p^i (1 - p)^{n-i} \right\}.$$

Note that the above expression is conditional on p, the propensity of failure.

4.2 A Model for Loss Incurred by $\mathcal{B}$

$\mathcal{B}$ is willing to pay $\$ x$ for an item that can last for τ units of time. If the item fails at inception, then we assume that $\mathcal{B}$ suffers a loss of $\$ x$; if the item serves until τ, then $\mathcal{B}$ incurs no loss. Thus it is reasonable to suppose that the loss suffered by $\mathcal{B}$ is a decreasing function of time, taking the value x at time 0 and decreasing to 0 at time τ. Figure 1 shows some possibilities for this loss function, i.e., $\mathcal{B}$'s disutility.

For simplicity, suppose that $\mathcal{B}$'s loss is linear in the time to failure. Thus $\mathcal{B}$'s loss should the item fail at time t, is $x - \frac{x}{\tau}t$, for $t \leq \tau$. Suppose that the items in question do not age with time so that the propensity of the failure times of the N items in $\mathcal{L}$'s lot is assumed to have an exponential distribution with a parameter λ; λ is, of course, unknown to both $\mathcal{B}$ and $\mathcal{L}$. Thus, if $f(t)$ denotes the true (or

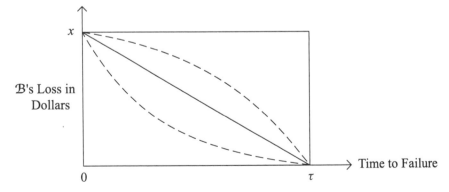

Figure 1. $\mathcal{B}$'s loss as a function of time to failure.

an objective) density function of the time to failure of an item at time t, then $f(t) = \lambda e^{-\lambda t}, t \geq 0, \lambda > 0$. Thus, conditional on $f(t)$ known, $\mathcal{B}$'s expected loss is

$$\mathbb{E}(\text{Loss}) = \sum_{i=1}^{n} \int_{\text{all } t} \left(x - \tfrac{x}{\tau} t \right) I(t \leq \tau) f(t) \, dt,$$

$$= nx \int_{0}^{\tau} f(t) \, dt - n \tfrac{x}{\tau} \int_{0}^{\tau} t f(t) \, dt.$$

Substituting $\lambda e^{-\lambda t}$ for $f(t)$, it is easy to see that

$$\mathbb{E}(\text{Loss}) = nx - \tfrac{nx}{\tau \lambda} \left(1 - e^{-\tau \lambda} \right).$$

For the contract to be fair to $\mathcal{B}$, the above expected loss, plus nx, the price paid by $\mathcal{B}$, should be equated to $\mathcal{B}$'s expected reimbursement, with p replaced by $1 - e^{-\tau \lambda}$, plus nw, the worth to $\mathcal{B}$ of the n items. That is,

$$nw + y \left\{ n(1 - e^{-\tau \lambda}) - \sum_{i=0}^{z} i \binom{n}{i} (1 - e^{-\tau \lambda})^i (e^{-\tau \lambda})^{n-i} \right.$$

$$\left. - z \sum_{i=z+1}^{n} \binom{n}{i} (1 - e^{-\tau \lambda})^i (e^{-\tau \lambda})^{n-i} \right\}$$

$$= 2nx - \tfrac{nx}{\tau \lambda}(1 - e^{-\tau \lambda}). \tag{2}$$

Since n, x, y, z, and τ are specified in the warranty contract, and since w is known to $\mathcal{B}$, the above can be solved by $\mathcal{B}$ for λ, and thence for p. We denote this value of p, should it exist, by p_B, and call it an *equilibrium probability* for $\mathcal{B}$. If the propensity of failure is different from p_B, $\mathcal{B}$ could incur a loss, depending on the values of the known constants. $\mathcal{B}$'s decision to ratify a contract (assuming that $\mathcal{B}$ did not craft it), will depend on $\pi_B(p)$, $\mathcal{B}$'s personal probability for the unknown p (or λ, in our case).

5 Contracts in Equilibrium—Just Warranties

In the previous two sections we have argued that given a warranty contract there may exist values of the propensity p that make the contract "fair" to each adversary. We say that a contract is fair to a particular party if that party neither suffers an expected loss nor enjoys an expected gain. That is, the party's expected profit is zero. We have termed these values of the propensity as "equilibrium probabilities," and have denoted them by p_B and p_L.

A warranty contract is said to be in *equilibrium* if p_B equals p_L, assuming, of course, that both p_B and p_L exist; see Section 5.1, which follows. Furthermore, a warranty contract that is in equilibrium is said to be *just* if the equilibrium probabilities coincide with the propensity of failure. The term "just" reflects the fact that if the propensity of failure is greater than the (identical) equilibrium probabilities, then both the adversaries will experience an expected loss;

vice versa otherwise. In the latter case, it is a *third* party, the party that is responsible for providing B with a worth w per unit, that is getting penalized. In actuality, it is unlikely that p_B equals p_L, unless the constants of the contract are so chosen. Thus contracts in equilibrium do not happen without forethought. Furthermore, when the contract is ratified, the propensity p is not known with certainty. Thus just warranties can only be retrospectively recognized, if they can be recognized at all. Finally, it is often the case that the third party referred to before is the public at large. Thus just contracts are beneficial to the general public.

5.1 The Existence of Equilibrium Probabilities

It is easy to verify [see equation (1)] that when $p_L = 0$, L's net gain (i.e., receipts−liability) is $n(x - c)$, which for $x > c$ is a positive quantity. Similarly, when $p_L = 1$, L's net gain is negative if $(x - c) < y$. Since L's net gain is a monotone function of p, there exists a value p_L, $0 < p_L < 1$, at which L's net gain is zero; see Figure 2. Figure 2 also shows that an equilibrium probability does not exist if $(x - c) > y$; this makes sense because now the penalty to L is always less than L's unit profit.

Analogous to Figure 2 is Figure 3; it is based on equation (2). It shows that when $p_B = 0$ (i.e., $\lambda = 0$), B's net gain is positive if $w > x$, and that when $p_B = 1$ (i.e., $\lambda \to \infty$), B's net gain is negative if $y < x$. Thus for $y < x < w$ there exists a value p_B, $0 < p_B < 1$, for which B's net gain is zero. Note that an equilibrium probability p_B does not exist if for $w > x$, it is so that $y > x$.

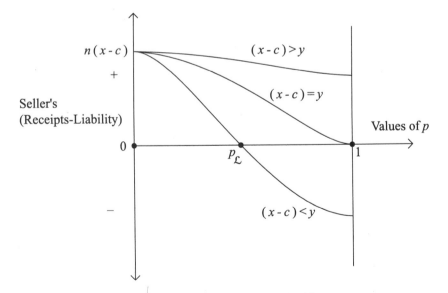

Figure 2. The seller's equilibrium probability, p_L.

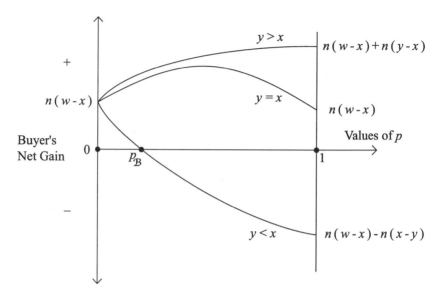

Figure 3. The buyer's equilibrium probability, p_B.

Figures 2 and 3 suggest that when the equilibrium probabilities do not take the extreme values 0 and 1, the constants of the warranty satisfy the following inequality: $x - c < y < x < w$. Assuming that $x > c$, and that $x, y > 0$, the values of x and y that correspond to having $p_B, p_L \in (0, 1)$ are shown by the hatched region of Figure 4.

5.2 Admissible Values of Equilibrium Probabilities

We have seen that when $p_B = p_L = 0$, $x = c = w$, and that when $p_B = p_L = 1$, $n = y = w$ and $c = 0$. It therefore follows that when $p_B = 0$ and $p_L = 1$, $x = y = w = 0$, which is meaningless. Thus we cannot have $p_B = 0$ and $p_L = 1$, nor can we have $p_B = 1$ and $p_L = 0$. This implies that equilibrium probabilities cannot take extreme values that are not identical. The case $p_B = p_L = 1$ is meaningful, but its consequence $c = 0$ is unrealistic. Thus for all intents and purposes, we shall regard the case $p_B = p_L = 1$ as being inadmissible. The consequence $x = c = w$ of the combination $p_B = p_L = 0$ may be viewed as idealistic.

Continuing along the above lines, note that when $p_L \in (0, 1)$, $x < y + c$, and when $p_B \in (0, 1)$, $y < x < w$. Thus it follows from these inequalities, plus those of the preceding paragraph, that the following combinations of equilibrium probabilities are *not* possible: $p_B \in (0, 1)$ and $p_L = 0$; $p_L \in (0, 1)$, and $p_B = 1$; $p_B \in (0, 1)$ and $p_L = 1$. The combination $p_B = 0$ and $p_L \in (0, 1)$ is feasible; it suggests that it is possible to have p_B smaller than p_L. However, we have not been able to show that for $p_B, p_L \in (0, 1)$, p_B is always less than p_L. Based on the

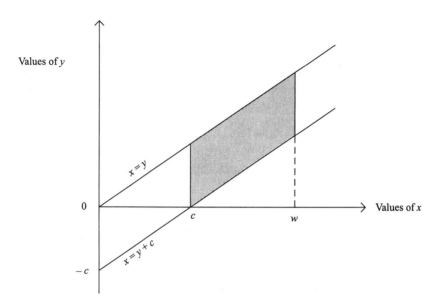

Figure 4. Values of x and y for nonextreme equilibrium probabilities.

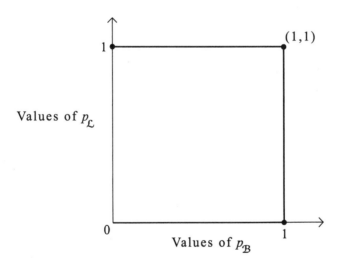

Figure 5. Inadmissible region for equilibrium probabilities (shown in boldface)

above, we show in Figure 5, the inadmissible values of p_B and p_L; they are shown by the boldface lines and dots. Thus for the model considered here, the search for equilibrium probabilities should be confined to the interior of the rectangular region of Figure 5, the vertical line on the left, and the point $(0, 0)$.

5.3   Existence of Equilibrium Warranty Contracts

We have stated that for a warranty contract to be in equilibrium, p_B and p_L must exist and be equal to each other. The case $p_B = p_L = 0$ of the previous section provides an example, albeit an idealistic one, of an equilibrium warranty contract. The case $p_B = p_L = 1$ is not admissible. Thus what remains to be explored are warranties in equilibrium, with p_B, $p_L \in (0, 1)$. To see whether such warranties can exist, and if so under what conditions, we recall, from Figure 4, that when p_B, $p_L \in (0, 1)$ the x and the y are constrained to lie in the hatched region of this figure. Thus requiring that $p_B = p_L$ would impose an additional constraint on x and y, assuming, of course that $x, y, c > 0$.

To investigate the above, we consider a special case of equation (1), namely, the case $z = 0$, that is, warranties that do not allow for any failures. For this case, it is easy to see that $p_s = (x - c)/y$. If this value is plugged in equation (2) with $z = 0$, and if $(1 - e^{-\lambda \tau})$, with $\tau = 1$, is replaced by p_B, then we can verify that for small values of p_B, x and y must satisfy the quadratic relationship

$$y = \frac{x}{2(w - c)}(x - w) + \tfrac{c}{2}$$

(see Appendix). Furthermore, to be assured that x and y lie in the hatched region of Figure 4, $c < x < w$ and $w < 3c/2$ (see Appendix). Figure 6 shows, via the boldface curve, the constrained values of x and y that yield an equilibrium warranty, with $p_B = p_L$, and $p_B \in (0, 1)$.

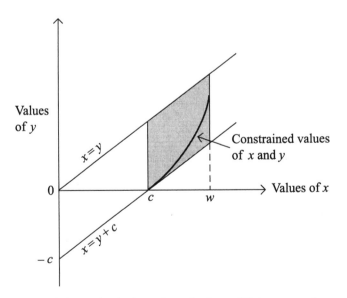

Figure 6. Constrained values of x and y for equilibrium warranties.

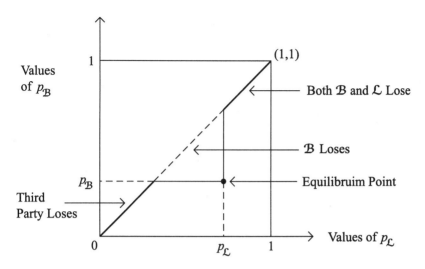

Figure 7. Regions in propensity that results in expected losses.

5.4   Warranties That Are Just

The equilibrium probabilities p_B and p_L have the defining feature that if the propensity of failure p deviates from them, then the contract becomes unfair; this is true even for contracts in equilibrium. Consequently, one or more of the two adversaries and the third party (mentioned before) will experience an expected loss. To be specific, suppose that $p_B < p_L$. Then, if $p > p_L$, both B and L will suffer an expected loss, whereas if $p_B < p < p_L$, it is B that will suffer a loss; L will enjoy an expected gain that is derived from either B's loss or the loss incurred by the third party. Finally, if $p < p_B$, then it is the third party that suffers a loss; both B and L will enjoy an expected gain. These contingencies are illustrated on the diagonal of Figure 7; it is on the diagonal that the propensity p should lie. The *equilibrium point* (p_B, p_L) is illustrated by the boldface dot of Figure 7.

In Figure 7 we have assumed that $p_B < p_L$. Should $p_L < p_B$, then features that mirror those of Figure 7 will be observed, in the sense that the equilibrium point will lie in the upper triangle and L instead of B will experience a loss.

When $p_B = p_L$, that is, when the warranty contract is in equilibrium, the middle portion of the diagonal of Figure 7 disappears. That is, the situation in which B experiences an expected loss but L enjoys an expected gain cannot exist. Rather, if $p < p_B = p_L$, then the third party experiences an expected loss, whereas if $p > p_B = p_L$, both B and L experience the loss. Thus the net effect of an equilibrium warranty is to eliminate the scenario in which one of the two adversaries experiences an expected loss and the other enjoys an expected gain. The diagonal of Figure 8, shown in boldface, shows the values of p_B and p_L that describe a warranty contract in equilibrium. Observe that the point $(1, 1)$, not being a feasible one, has been excluded; the point $(0, 0)$ is included.

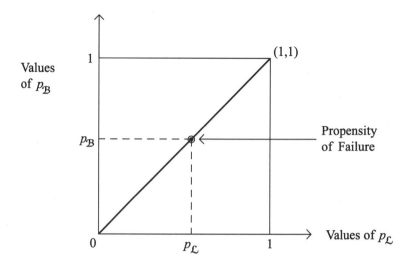

Figure 8. Admissible values of p_B and p_L for an equilibrium contract and an illustration of a just warranty.

An equilibrium warranty in which the propensity p equals $p_B (= p_L)$ results in the scenario wherein none of the players (the two adversaries and the third party) experience an expected loss. Thus such a warranty is termed a "just warranty." In essence, a just warranty is one that is fair to the buyer, the seller, and the public (i.e., the third party). The circled point on the diagonal of Figure 8 illustrates an example of a just warranty.

As stated before, a just warranty is an abstraction, because when the contract is negotiated, the propensity p is rarely, if ever, known. Indeed, it is the uncertainty about the propensity p that creates an adversarial situation involving the two risk takers, the buyer and the seller. The next section describes how these adversaries should act on a warranty contract in the presence of uncertainty about p.

6   The Ratification of a Warranty Contract

The material of Section 5 describes the structure of a warranty contract, in particular a contract that is in equilibrium and that strives to be just. The development there can be used for designing contracts that are equitable. However, in actuality, just contracts are an idealization for two reasons. The first is that the propensity p is unknown. The second is that the buyer and the seller tend to take actions that maximize their expected profits against each other, and also against the third party, which tends to be a passive player. It is often the case that B and L collaborate in their design of x and y in order to play "cooperative game" against a third party, so that w tends to be inflated. It is not our intention here to discuss this and related issues of warranty design. Rather, our aim is to describe how B

and $\mathcal{L}$ should act in the presence of a specified warranty, no matter how arrived upon, but under uncertainty about p.

The ratification of a warranty contract usually is preceded by negotiations between $\mathcal{B}$ and $\mathcal{L}$ about the constants of the contract. To see how these may proceed, recall, from Sections 3 and 4, that $\pi_{\mathcal{L}}(p)[\pi_{\mathcal{B}}(p)]$ were defined as the seller's (buyer's) subjective probabilities for the unknown p. Personal probabilities of the propensity are the appropriate probabilities to consider in making decisions. It is unlikely, though possible, that $\pi_{\mathcal{L}}(p)$ and $\pi_{\mathcal{B}}(p)$ will be identical. More important, since $\mathcal{B}$ and $\mathcal{L}$ tend to be adversaries, $\pi_{\mathcal{L}}(p)$ and $\pi_{\mathcal{B}}(p)$ will be known only to $\mathcal{L}$ and of $\mathcal{B}$, respectively. That is, $\mathcal{L}$ will not reveal $\pi_{\mathcal{L}}(p)$ to $\mathcal{B}$ and vice versa.

Clearly, if $\pi_{\mathcal{L}}(p)$ is degenerate, say at $p^* > 0$, and if $p^* = p_{\mathcal{L}}$, then $\mathcal{L}$ will ratify the contract. If $p^* > p_{\mathcal{L}}$, then $\mathcal{L}$ will not ratify the contract unless $\mathcal{B}$ is willing to lower y and/or to increase z. If $p^* < p_{\mathcal{L}}$, then $\mathcal{L}$ may either ratify the contract or may try to convince $\mathcal{B}$ that x needs to be increased and/or y needs to be lowered before the contract is ratified by $\mathcal{L}$. $\mathcal{B}$'s behavior will be analogous to $\mathcal{L}$'s if $\pi_{\mathcal{B}}(p)$ is degenerate, say at p_*. In particular, if $p_* > p_{\mathcal{B}}$, $\mathcal{B}$ will insist that x and z be lowered and/or y be increased in order for $\mathcal{B}$ to ratify the contract. If $p_* \leq p_{\mathcal{B}}$, then $\mathcal{B}$ will immediately ratify the contract as is. Under the latter circumstance, $\mathcal{B}$ may try to convince the third party that w be increased.

When $\pi_{\mathcal{L}}(p)$ is not degenerate, which is what we would expect, then $\mathcal{L}$ will ratify the contract if the $n(x - c)$ is greater than or equal to

$$\int_0^1 y \left\{ np - \sum_{i=0}^{z} i \binom{n}{i} p^i (1 - p)^{n-i} - z \sum_{i=z+1}^{n} \binom{n}{i} p^i (1 - p)^{n-i} \right\} \pi_{\mathcal{L}}(p) \, dp,$$

which is the expected value, with respect to $\pi_{\mathcal{L}}(p)$, of the right-hand side of equation (1). It is what $\mathcal{L}$ believes $\mathcal{L}$'s expected liability is. Prior to ratifying the contract $\mathcal{L}$ may still choose to negotiate with $\mathcal{B}$ along the lines discussed when $p^* < p_{\mathcal{L}}$.

When $\pi_{\mathcal{B}}(p)$ is not degenerate, then $\mathcal{B}$'s behavior will be similar to that of $\mathcal{L}$, mutatis mutandis.

7 Conclusion

In this article we have explored the structure of warranty contracts concerning product reliability. In particular, the concept of a just contract and its relationship to the respective parties' prior knowledge of the relevant costs and probability of failure are described. Other aspects of the problem deserve further study and analysis. Little attention has been paid to the game-theoretic aspects of this fundamentally adversarial problem. Cooperation between the adversaries to maximize their expected gains at a cost to a passive third party is an issue that needs to be pursued, because it seems to be the modus operandi of some organizations. Indeed antitrust laws are designed to prevent collusive behavior by firms. The scenario of warranties brings into focus the need to have several interpretations of probability. The objective view for its scientific base, the logical one for designing warranties that are fair to all players, and the subjective approach for decision-making. Irrespective of one's attitude to the three notions (concepts) of probability, the fact remains that probabilities are central to warranties and that an acknowledgment of their existence is essential for a warranty contract to have a scientific basis.

Acknowledgments

This paper is dedicated to the memory of the late Dr. W. Edwards Deming, who introduced the author to the role of a statistician in the courtroom by inviting him to serve as a collaborating expert witness on behalf of the Internal Revenue Service on two tax cases.

The author acknowledges the contribution of Chris Falkous in connection with the model of Section 4. Also acknowledged are the comments by Professors Joseph Gastwirth, Dennis Lindley, and Charles Mann. Professor Gastwirth's invitation to contribute an article to this book is deeply appreciated. Supported by Grant DAAG-55-97-1-0323, The U.S. Army Research Office, and subcontract Number 35352-6085 with Cornell University under WO8333-04 from the Electric Power Research Institute and the U.S. Army Research Office.

REFERENCES

[1] Lindley, D.V. (1985). *Making Decisions*. John Wiley and Sons, New York.

[2] Singpurwalla, N.D. and S. Wilson (1993). Warranties: Their Statistical and Game Theoretic Aspects. *SIAM Review*, 35 1: 17–42.

[3] Weatherford, Roy (1982). *Philosophical Foundations of Probability Theory*. Routledge and Kegan Paul, Ltd. London.

Appendix

Equation 2 states that for the contract to be fair to $\mathcal{B}$ we must have that

$$nw + y\left\{n(1 - e^{-\tau\lambda}) - \sum_{i=0}^{z} i\binom{n}{i}(1 - e^{-\tau\lambda})^i(e^{-\tau\lambda})^{n-i}\right.$$

$$\left. - z\sum_{i=z+1}^{n}\binom{n}{i}(1 - e^{-\tau\lambda})^i(e^{-\tau\lambda})^{n-i}\right\}$$

$$= 2nx - \frac{nx}{\tau\lambda}(1 - e^{-\tau\lambda}).$$

Now let $z = 0$ and $\tau = 1$ and replace $(1 - e^{-\tau\lambda})$ by p_B. Then the above reduces to

$$nw + ynp_B = 2nx + \frac{nx}{\ln(1 - p_B)}p_B$$

For small values of p_B we can approximate $\ln(1 - p_B)$ by $-p_B - p_B^2/2$, and hence the above becomes

$$w + yp_B = 2x - \frac{x}{1 + \frac{p_B}{2}} \Rightarrow w + yp_B + \tfrac{1}{2}wp_B + \tfrac{1}{2}yp_B^2 = 2x + xp_B - x.$$

Now, since $p_B = (x - c)/y$, we obtain

$$w + x - c + w\frac{x - c}{2y} + \frac{(x - c)^2}{2y} = x + x\frac{x - c}{y}$$

$$\Rightarrow 2wy + 2xy - 2cy + wx - wc + x^2 - 2xc + c^2 = 2xy + 2x^2 - 2xc$$

$$\Rightarrow y(2w - 2c) = x^2 - wx + wc - c^2$$

$$\Rightarrow y = \tfrac{1}{2}\frac{x}{w - c}(x - w) + \tfrac{c}{2}.$$

Now we have the inequalities $c < x < w$ and $x - c < y < x < w$. So

$$x - c < y = \tfrac{1}{2}\frac{x}{w - c}(x - w) + \tfrac{c}{2} = \tfrac{1}{2}(x - c)\frac{x - w + c}{w - c}$$

$$\Rightarrow 2(w - c) < x - w + c$$

$$\Rightarrow 3(w - c) < x < w$$

$$\Rightarrow 2w < 3c \Rightarrow +w < \tfrac{3}{2}c.$$

Death and Deterrence: Notes on a Still Inchoate Judicial Inquiry

Robert J. Cottrol

Abstract

This article examines the impact of the social science literature on the death penalty and deterrence on court decisions in capital punishment cases. The article examines two highly influential statistical studies, one done by sociologist Thorsten Sellin in 1959 and the other by economist Isaac Ehrlich in 1975 and uses both studies to illustrate the kinds of questions the courts can and should ask of quantitative studies in this area.

Keywords: Capital Punishment, Cruel and Unusual Punishment, Deterrence, Econometrics, Economics of Crime, Eighth Amendment, Judicial Review

1 Introduction

This article is about a line of inquiry that the courts by and large have avoided in recent years. Despite an extensive body of social science literature examining the issue of deterrence and the death penalty, state and federal courts have shown a marked unwillingness to grapple with that literature. Since the resumption of the death penalty after the Supreme Court's 1976 decision in *Gregg v. Georgia*, the judiciary has examined such issues as the constitutionality of the death penalty, fairness or proportionality in capital sentencing, the role of race in death sentences, and what constitutes proper argumentation in capital cases while paying only cursory attention to the social science literature on the deterrence issue. This has been true despite the briefing of the deterrence issue in death penalty cases.

The modern social science literature on the deterrence issue has been dominated by highly sophisticated quantitative examinations of the subject, most involving advanced regression and econometric analysis. This article is a guide by a decided nonstatistician on how the courts and others, especially nonspecialists, might ask intelligent questions of this body of literature and how that body of literature might be of value to courts and lawyers interested in the questions of death and deterrence. This article will focus on two landmark studies Thorsten Sellin's 1959 examination *The Death Penalty* (Sellin, 1959), and Isaac Ehrlich's 1975 article "The Deterrent Effects of Capital Punishment: A Question of Life and Death" (Ehrlich, 1975). Both studies set the agenda for the social science and policy debates on deterrence in their times. The Sellin study may have played a minor role in influencing the Supreme Court's 1972 decision in *Furman v. Georgia* to strike down then existing capital punishment statutes. Ehrlich's article may have had a similar influence on the Court in *Gregg*, which restored the death penalty. Both studies provide interesting methodological contrasts.

2   The Enduring Controversy

The controversy over the death penalty has been a long-standing one in the modern Western world (Sellin, 1959). In the United States, currently the only Western nation to apply the death penalty, the debate has been particularly strong since the end of the Second World War. The rationales advanced for and against capital punishment have echoed, in microcosm, larger and more fundamental questions concerning the purpose and function of the penal system. Thus, opponents and advocates of the death penalty have been part of a broader set of quarrels concerning the moral responsibility of offenders, the role of societal inequalities in producing criminal behavior, the proper role of retribution or desert in a system of punishment, the possibility of rehabilitating offenders, and the simple value of incapacitating criminals regardless of the ultimate causes or potential reformations of their antisocial behaviors.

One of the central issues in the debate over capital punishment has been the contention that the death penalty deters murder.[1] Certainly, there is a long-standing history of inflicting the death penalty because of its presumed deterrent powers. In Britain in the eighteenth century a host of relatively minor crimes were subject to the death penalty. Pickpockets and other petty thieves could and did end their lives on the gallows (Hay et al., 1975). By the nineteenth century sentiment in most Western countries had rebelled against such a brutal utilitarianism. Imprisonment would replace death as the punishment for most crimes not involving homicide. The movement against capital punishment also achieved some success in abolishing the

---

[1]Here we are principally concerned with social science literature and court opinions that have addressed or made reference to the issue of whether or not the death penalty deters murder. This is because the modern American death penalty (post *Gregg*) is largely reserved for crimes involving aggravated cases of first-degree murder. With the Supreme Court's decision in *Coker v. Georgia* (1977), invalidating the death penalty for the rape of an adult, the application of the death penalty for a crime not involving murder has become somewhat problematic. It should nonetheless be noted that the *Violent Crime Control and Law Enforcement Act of 1994* permits the death penalty for major drug traffickers even if no homicide is involved (*21 U.S.C.* 8489(e)-1994)). Also, some states have enacted statutes permitting the death penalty for aggravated rape of a minor under the age of 12 (La. Rev. Stat. Ann. 14:42 west, 1996). Another major exception or set of exceptions are federal death penalty statutes for wartime military offenses, most notably military espionage. The application of the death penalty in these contexts is rare enough, at this point, that we would probably find it difficult to draw any generalizable or scientific inferences concerning the death penalty and deterrence in cases not involving homicide. It should be noted that prior to the Supreme Court's decision in *Furman* a number of states made rape and kidnapping capital crimes [some states also made other crimes, like burglary, subject to potential death sentences.]

death penalty for murder. In the United States that effort would have some success in a number of states as early as the middle of the nineteenth century (Sellin, 1959). It would also become the subject of intense political and later judicial debate in the United States in the twentieth century.

The debate over the deterrent effect of the death penalty became a perennial criminological and political debate in twentieth-century America. At this point, I would like to try to offer a working definition of the term *deterrence* and see what forms of analysis and argumentation should reasonably be included in or excluded from any consideration of the issue. Probably the best way to think of the issue is to view it in economic terms, i.e., as aggregate, marginal deterrence. Assume two identical hypothetical populations. In the first those who commit murder are subject to the death penalty, while in the other those who commit that crime are subject to some other criminal sanction. Our question, assuming *ceteris paribus*, that is, all other things being equal, is, Are there fewer murders in the group with the death penalty than in the group without? In other words, can we say that the death penalty caused a decrease in the number of murders? Of course, the difficult problem in social science research is controlling for other conditions, determining wheter all other things really are equal—a condition often wished for, but rarely achieved.

It is important to frame the question in this manner for the following reasons. If we simply ask, Does the death penalty deter murder? the answer has to be yes. We can find individuals who will refrain from committing murder because of the existence of the death penalty. Of course, we can also find individuals who will not commit murder because of the possibility of long-term imprisonment. We can even, doubtless, find some individual whose homicidal impulses might be stemmed because of a $25.00 fine. To further complicate matters, it is entirely likely that there are some individuals who are enticed into committing murders precisely because of the possibility of the death penalty. In deciding between policy choices the question has to be, Does one alternative provide more of the desired good (in this case a reduction in murder) than its alternatives?

I am going into this somewhat labored analysis in part because the debate over death and deterrence has been peculiarly plagued by the problem of dueling anecdotes. Thus, opponents of capital punishment frequently present as evidence that the death penalty does not deter murder actual cases of people who have committed murder or other capital crimes despite the existence of the death penalty. The interview with the condemned inmate who did not think he would get caught, the historical example of the eighteenth-century English pickpocket who plied his trade during the public hanging of a pickpocket are frequent and familiar examples of this line of argumentation (Kaplan, 1983). Similarly, death penalty advocates readily bring up examples of robbers who carry unloaded weapons in order not to kill their victims and thus run the risk of execution.

These anecdotes, or perhaps more generously case studies, can have considerable value in giving us an insight into the psychology and perhaps microcultural backgrounds of individuals who are and who are not deterred. Nonetheless, these anecdotes cannot shed light on the larger question of whether or not the death penalty, in the aggregate, makes a difference. Clearly, there is a range of human responses to legal sanctions. Some will be deterred by a very minimal sanction; some will not, even with the harshest sanction. In order to answer the question of whether or not the death penalty makes a difference in the aggregate, statistical evaluation would seem to hold out more promise than the recitation of anecdotes and counteranecdotes often encountered in this area.

3   Thorsten Sellin and the Road to *Furman*

The modern social science inquiry into capital punishment and deterrence began with Thorsten Sellin's 1959 study *The Death Penalty*. Sellin, a University of Pennsylvania sociologist, conducted the study for the American Law Institute, which was in the process of drafting the Model Penal Code. He pioneered the systematic study of death penalty statistics including the contrasting of homicide rates in jurisdictions employing and those not employing capital punishment. His study also examined homicide rates in jurisdictions before and after the abolition of the death penalty. Concluding that the evidence did not support the conclusion that the death penalty deterred murder, the Sellin study would have considerable influence on the death penalty debate in the 1960s. It would also be noted in the landmark decision in *Furman*.[2]

Sellin's research sought to test four hypotheses or propositions regarding deterrence and the death penalty. According to Sellin, if the death penalty were a deterrent, the following should be true:

1. Murders should be less frequent in states that have the death penalty than in those that have abolished it, other factors being equal.
2. Murders should increase when the death penalty is abolished and should decline when it is restored.
3. The deterrent effect should be greatest and should affect murder rates most powerfully in those communities where the crime occurred and its consequences are most strongly brought home to the population.
4. Law enforcement officers would be safer from murderous attacks in states that have the death penalty than in those without it (Sellin, 1959).

Although Sellin framed the deterrence question in a way that seemingly invited empirical hypothesis testing, his study was limited by the quality of data available and by his own relative lack of statistical sophistication.[3] Available vital statistics records did not separate capital murder from other forms of homicide, so Sellin

---

[2]See especially Justice Marshall's concurring opinion in *Furman* at pp. 49–51, Lexis version.

[3]It should be noted that Sellin received his graduate training in sociology at the University of Pennsylvania in the 1920s. At the time and indeed until relatively recently such training was unlikely to entail the fairly sophisticated training in quantitative methodology common

was forced to use a state's homicide rate as a crude proxy for the capital murder rate. Sellin indicated that the homicide rate would still reveal the trend and its responsiveness or nonresponsiveness to the presence of the death penalty (Sellin, p. 22, 1959).

Sellin's statistical methodology was probably a more significant weakness of his study. Sellin's cross-sectional and longitudinal comparisons never employed more than basic descriptive statistics. Thus Sellin's report informs the reader that, among other things, between 1920 and 1955 homicide rates in Maine and Rhode Island, two New England states that had abolished the death penalty, were not higher than in those New England states—New Hampshire, Connecticut, and Rhode Island—that retained capital punishment. Similar analyses were performed for certain neighboring Midwestern and Western states. Although the Sellin report asserts that comparisons were made among states that were socially, culturally, and economically similar, the data did not indicate income, age, concentration of population, ethnicity, or other variables that are usually considered as potentially important in influencing the homicide rate. Sellin attempted no formal tests that might indicate whether the variations in the homicide rates between death penalty and non–death penalty states were significant. The report essentially let the descriptive statistics speak for themselves (Sellin, 1959).[4]

Two of Sellin's tables, 6 (p. 25) and 7 (p. 28), illustrate some of the methodological difficulties with his study. Table 6 examined homicide and the death penalty in the New England states between 1920 and 1955. At the time, Maine and Rhode Island had no death penalty. Capital punishment was legal and executions were performed in the other states. Table 6, as Sellin noted, showed similar rates of homicide in the New England states despite the differences in the law regarding capital punishment. Sellin assumed a basic cultural and socioeconomic similarity in the New England states that would make this a valid comparison. But

---

in graduate programs today. Training in the social sciences has in recent decades involved significantly more training in inferential statistics, in part because of the development of computers and statistical packages that make large-scale data analysis more accessible to researchers.

[4]While Sellin did not have access to modern computer packages, it is reasonable for us to analyze his data with them. As the homicide rates declined during the period, this variation between the years should be controlled for in order to obtain an accurate comparison of the differences in rates among the states. Thus we ran a two-way ANOVA. We focused on one contrast, the difference between the average homicide rates of the states without a death penalty and those having the death penalty. The overall model was statistically significant, and the R-square was .55. Both year and state factors were statistically significant ($p < .0001$). The contrast was only $-.063$, which was far from statistical significance (p-value$= .415$). This formal analysis is consistent with Sellin's conclusion that the data did not indicate that the death penalty had a major impact on homicide rates.

Calculations performed with SAS. Additional calculations supporting this note but not discussed here were performed with SPSS 9.0 and Minitab Release 11. I would like to thank especially Gang Zheng, Ph.D. candidate in statistics at George Washington University, for his assistance.

that similarity was assumed, not proved. If Maine, which had no death penalty during this period, and Massachusetts (which did have capital punishment at the same time) had roughly similar murder rates, can that be used as evidence of the lack of the deterrent power of the death penalty? At a minimum we would want to note that Massachusetts contains a large, diverse, multiethnic city, Boston, while Maine lacked a comparable city. Thus a major variable or set of variables likely to increase the homicide rate was not subject to any statistical controls in the Sellin study. Indeed, it was not even mentioned as a possible confounding factor.

Similarly, Table 7 examined capital punishment and the homicide rate in the Midwestern states of Michigan, Ohio, Indiana, Minnesota, Iowa, Wisconsin, North Dakota, and South Dakota. Here again, Sellin contrasted the rates in states he believed to be similar, finding no appreciable difference in the homicide rates attributable to capital punishment. For example, Sellin contrasted Michigan, a state that had abolished capital punishment in the nineteenth century, with Ohio and Indiana, which exercised the death penalty in the 1920–1955 period. Yet again the question of whether Sellin's numbers demonstrate the ineffectiveness of the death penalty as a deterrent is confounded by another potential variable. There is a considerable body of sociological literature debating the issue of whether or not a special southern subculture of violence exists (Cohen and Nisbett, 1994): Dixon and Lizotte, 1989: Ellison, 1991). We need not assess that body of literature or take part in the controversy to realize that it is relevant to this discussion. Southern Ohio and southern Indiana have, since before the Civil War, been in many ways culturally part of the American South. Michigan lacks the kind of distinctive "Southern" region that exists in both Ohio and Indiana. This again casts potential doubt on the Sellin study. An alternative way of interpreting his data might be that two states with a greater propensity for violence because of the presence of a strong "Southern" cultural element managed to achieve the same homicide rate as the more "Northern" Michigan because of the deterrent power of the death penalty. Again no statistical test attempting to filter out this factor or even a mention of this as a potential problem was present in the Sellin analysis.

If Sellin's statistical methodology might be considered too crude to be of value by the standards of present-day social science, its skepticism concerning the deterrent value of the death penalty fit into the larger spirit of postwar America's views on crime and punishment. The conventional wisdom among criminologists a half century ago was that the primary purpose of the penal system was to bring about rehabilitation. Retribution or revenge was seen as primitive and wrong-headed (Cottrol, 1997). The Warren Court was about the business of making the states respect the criminal procedure guarantees of the Bill of Rights.

And by the 1960s, the death penalty was meeting with increasing disfavor. During that decade appeals from death row inmates were getting increased attention in the federal courts. Fewer executions were performed each year. Public opinion was increasingly skeptical about the application of the ultimate penalty (Ellsworth and Gross, 1994). Sellin was frequently cited by opponents of capital punishment as evidence that the death penalty served no useful purpose.

This increased skepticism concerning capital punishment reached its highest point in *Furman*, the case that pronounced the death penalty, as it then existed, unconstitutional. While express consideration of the deterrence issue does not appear to have played a major part in any of the *Furman* opinions, Justice Marshall's opinion noted Sellin's study with approval. Although Marshall recognized evidentiary problems in the Sellin study, he accepted Sellin's basic conclusion that the death penalty appeared to have no influence on the homicide rate.[5] Marshall's concurring opinion was part of the majority striking down the existing death penalty statutes.

4   Ehrlich, *Gregg*, and the Modern Discussion

Furman, of course, would not be the last word on capital punishment. Although many at the time, including then Chief Justice Burger, believed that the decision would mean the effective end of the American death penalty, that would prove not to be the case. Many developments contributed to the return of capital punishment. A renewed emphasis on retribution regardless of deterrence or other utilitarian benefits helped bring about the return of the death penalty (Berns, 1979). Fear of rising crime and the emergence of crime as a national political issue also contributed to the resurrection of capital punishment.

The academic reconsideration of the deterrence issue also helped the case of death penalty advocates. The appearance in 1975 of Isaac Ehrlich's article "the Deterrent Effect of Capital Punishment: A Question of Life and Death" is rightly considered a watershed in the social science debate over deterrence (Ehrlich, 1975). The article represented something of a new strain in criminological discourse, the importation of explicit economic theory and methodology, particularly econometric methodology, into the study of criminal behavior. Gary Becker (1968) had been the chief pioneer in advocating the use of economic models to explain criminal behavior. In his view the economic assumptions of rationality and response to incentives could be imported from the study of consumer behavior into the discussion of the behavior of criminal actors. In the 1970s (and beyond) Ehrlich and other economists would take up Becker's challenge and invade a new world, criminology. That world, previously dominated by comparatively nonquantitative sociologists, would have to contend with the highly quantitative tools and indeed mathematical language of the sometimes strange imperial economic priesthood.

The Ehrlich study represented a direct challenge to the Sellin thesis in both methodology and conclusion. Where Sellin's was essentially a descriptive study with no explicit theoretical model, or at most one that was very loosely drawn, Ehrlich's examination explicitly assumed that offenders responded to incentives, that those responses could be measured, and that it was the job of the researcher to employ or design inferential tests that would allow an acceptance or rejection

---

[5]See note 3, supra.

of the null hypothesis concerning the relationship between the death penalty and deterrence.

Ehrlich's study also differed from Sellin's in that it did not attempt a contrast between abolitionist and retentionist jurisdictions. Instead, Ehrlich attempted to examine the deterrent effects of the death penalty through the use of regression analysis. Unlike Sellin, Ehrlich's technique involved explicit analysis of the effect of the number of executions on the homicide rate. Ehrlich's study, utilizing data for the years between 1933 and 1967, reported that for every execution performed in the indicated years eight lives were saved through deterrence.

An important aspect of Ehrlich's examination was his discussion of deterrence in terms of conditional probabilities. His study thus recognized that execution was conditional on conviction, which in turn was conditional on arrests or apprehension. More importantly, Ehrlich did not rest with an analysis of the deterrent effects of executions. He also calculated the deterrent effects of arrest and conviction. His calculations indicated that while the death penalty deterred murders, the increased probability of arrest or conviction provided even greater deterrence, i.e., higher partial elasticities were achieved with increases in arrest and conviction as opposed to increases in executions.[6]

It is at this point that Ehrlich's study and the response of many of his critics seem curiously lacking. Some of Ehrlich's critics have offered what are at least partially normative critiques of the study (Beyleveld, 1982). Others have criticized his data sources and his application of econometric method (Bowers and Pierce, 1975; Passell and Taylor, 1977). Yet one of the most glaring questions raised by Ehrlich's study, the issue of opportunity cost,[7] seems to be largely unaddressed in Ehrlich's original study, the response of his critics, and his responses to their criticisms.[8] Accepting the reliability of Ehrlich's data and the essential validity of his methodology, his conclusions concerning the deterrent effect of the death penalty are nonetheless rendered problematic by what he acknowledges to be the greater return on the investment that the criminal justice system gets from increased probability of arrest and conviction. Given the increased cost of the death penalty, any empirical claim that capital punishment is a superior deterrent should ask the question whether or not the resources put into the death penalty would achieve even greater preventive effect if they were shifted to increase po-

---

[6]Ehrlich (1975 pp. 411–414) indicates elasticities between -1.0 and -1.5 associated with probability of arrest, elasticities between -0.4 and -0.5 associated with probability of conviction, and elasticities of -0.06 and -0.065 associated with probability of execution.

[7]The idea of opportunity cost is one of the more important contributions that economists have made to social discourse. Simply put, economists have made us aware that the cost of a commodity is not simply the price we pay for the commodity, but opportunities that we for go. As Paul Samuelson reminds us, a university student paying $10,000 a year in tuition has an educational cost equal to that $10,000 plus the $16,000 a year job that he is not pursuing while he is at the university (Samuelson and Nordhaus, 1992).

[8]One partial exception to this is a study (Andreoni, 1995) discussing the question of whether or not capital punishment reduces the probability of conviction.

lice and prosecutorial resources that would enhance the likelihood of arrest and conviction.

Another question potentially raised by the Ehrlich study is whether or not the death penalty might create the illusion of deterrence not through an actual reduction of capital murders but instead by a distortion of the data. We know historically, particularly before *Furman*, where a number of jurisdictions imposed mandatory death penalties for first-degree murder, judges and juries often simply refused to convict defendants of that crime. Some defendants were acquitted. Others were convicted of lesser included offenses. Both were done to avoid death sentences in difficult cases. We also know that both before and after *Furman* prosecutors have used the possibility of death sentences to pressure defendants to plead guilty to lesser offenses. All of this has the potential to lead to a misclassification of data. In a hypothetical case where a murderer is convicted of manslaughter as a result of either jury sympathy or his own plea bargain, the criminal justice statistics are misreported. One murder fewer than actually occurred shows up on the record. Without some corrective mechanism to estimate how many such cases occur, the measurement of the influence of the death penalty on the murder rate becomes problematic. The Ehrlich study indicated no corrective mechanism for that potential problem.

In any event Ehrlich's study was greeted with enthusiasm by supporters of capital punishment (McGahey, 1980). At last, a rigorous social science study was available affirming what had long seemed to be simple common sense to advocates of capital punishment, that the death penalty indeed deters murder. If the Ehrlich thesis would remain controversial among the author's peers, it was assured of a warm reception on the part of many policy advocates. Solicitor General Robert Bork cited Ehrlich's study in briefs for the United States government in support of capital punishment.[9]

Ehrlich's analysis seems to have played relatively little role in the *Gregg* Court's decision permitting the states to employ the death penalty using statutes that had been drafted in the wake of the Court's earlier decision in *Furman*.[10] While

---

[9]Brief for the United States as Amicus Curiae at 35–38, *Fowler v. North Carolina*, 428 U.S. 904 (1976). Brief for the United States as Amicus Curiae at 34–45, 9a–16a, *Gregg v. Georgia*, (1976).

[10]In *Furman* there was a five to four vote to strike down existing death penalty statutes. Two of the Justices who voted to strike down the death penalty, Brennan and Marshall, held that capital punishment was per se cruel and unusual punishment. Three of the justices, Douglas, Stewart, and White, held that the death penalty was violative of the eighth amendment's cruel and unusual punishment clause because of the arbitrary manner in which the determination was made who would receive death sentences. After the decision a number of states redrafted their capital sentencing statutes. Post *Furman* statutes defined capital murder as a relatively narrow subset of the broader category of first-degree murder. Those statutes also mandated bifurcated trials in which there were really two trials, one to determine guilt or innocence and the other to determine sentence. During the sentencing phase death penalty statutes list statutorily defined aggravating and mitigating factors to guide the jury in determining sentencing.

Justice Potter Stewart's opinion for the Court acknowledged Ehrlich's study and the deterrence rationale, the opinion also noted that the evidence was not conclusive. Instead, the Stewart opinion argued that the issue of deterrence was the kind of complex, fact-based issue traditionally and best left to legislatures. The opinion also noted that retribution and other non-deterrence-based rationales could also serve as a legitimate basis for death penalty legislation.

Gregg represented a major shift by the Court. Where the *Furman* Court was willing to give a close scrutiny to the death penalty, attempting to balance its harshness against its potential benefits, the *Gregg* Court was more willing to defer to legislative determinations, real or assumed, when examining capital punishment. In such a judicial atmosphere consideration of the social science debate on deterrence was improbable. To a great extent American courts have largely followed the Supreme Court's lead, viewing the issue as complex, difficult, and altogether a matter for the legislatures and not the courts.[11] As one state court indicated:

> The legislature could reasonably find that the death penalty deters murder, just as it could find that it does not. Given that the evidence is conflicting and inconclusive, the court could not say that a legislative conclusion that the death penalty acts as a deterrent is so clearly arbitrary and irrational as to constitute an illegitimate exercise of power.[12]

At least one state court, the Supreme Court of Georgia, has gone so far as to exclude social science evidence for or against the general deterrent effect of capital punishment from the penalty phase of capital cases. Although prosecutor and defense attorneys are permitted to argue the cases for or against deterrence, several members of the Georgia high court reasoned that the social science evidence would tend to confuse juries, increase trial expense, and usurp an issue properly left to the legislature.[13]

All this would seem to leave little room for judicial scrutiny of Sellin, Ehrlich, and the others who have ventured into the murky waters of statistics, the death penalty, and deterrence. The immediate future seems to promise the kind of continued judicial conservatism that will be characterized by a pronounced reluctance to invade what appears to be purely a policy and hence legislative realm.

Yet I am not sure that the courts will be able to forever put aside the cross-sectional analysis of Sellin and the time series and logarithmic regressions of Ehrlich and their critics, supporters, and successors. At the beginning of the twenty-first century, the American death penalty has severe problems, problems

---

[11] In a recent case, *Harris v. Alabama*, 513 U.S. 504 (1995), Justice Sandra Day O'Connor delivered a majority opinion indicating that the Court had no jurisdiction over policy issues such as what purpose is served by capital punishment. Justice Stevens dissented, indicating, among other things, that the greater deterrent power of the death penalty was unsupported by persuasive evidence.

[12] *State v. Ramseur*, 106 N.J. 123, 524 A. 2d 188 (1987).

[13] *Fleming v. State*, 265 Ga. 541(1995).

that arguably trigger constitutional concerns. Critics of capital punishment have noted how economic discrimination, particularly in the form of ineffective assistance of counsel, plays a significant role in determining who receives death sentences. Some critics have indicated that race still plays an important role in selecting death row inmates. Embarrassingly large numbers of innocent persons have been found sentenced to death since capital punishment's return post *Gregg*.[14] All of this has the potential to cause future courts to revisit the equal protection and possibly the eighth amendment issues.

It is in that possible future revisitation where the deterrence issue would likely reemerge. If the harms and inequalities of the death penalty trigger judicial reconsideration, part of that reconsideration would doubtless involve a balancing of the harms of capital punishment with its asserted benefits—deterrence presumably being high on the list of such. One jurist, Justice Berdon of the Connecticut Supreme Court, in a dissenting opinion in a recent case briefly examined the issue of deterrence as a potential justification for capital punishment. Justice Berdon°s view was that the death penalty constituted cruel and unusual punishment under the Connecticut Constitution and that the death penalty's cruelty would have to be balanced by compelling justification. The opinion found no justification on deterrence grounds.[15]

The judicial examination of the deterrence literature has, at best, been cursory. Jurists have cited but have not given close scrutiny to the highly quantitative body of empirical literature on the subject. And yet just such an inquiry would be warranted if the courts decide that the deterrence issue is a proper area for judicial concern, given the difficulties existing with and perhaps inherent in capital punishment. How might the courts go about such a task? The judicial approach to date, even where individual jurists have clearly found certain studies and conclusions persuasive, has been to frankly admit the inconclusive nature of the literature and the disagreement among the experts. Can more be expected of jurists and lawyers, most of whom can be expected to have reasonably minimal statistical training and skills?

It would, of course, be unrealistic to expect significant percentages of the bench and bar to have quantitative skills equal to those who have gone through professional training in statistics, economics, or even some of the more quantitative programs in sociology. Courts in this area as in others can appoint and rely on outside experts. Judges are also, of course, accustomed to weighing any expert opinion against the prevailing consensus in the field. And of course, some jurists might simply throw up their hands and decline to get into the battle of the dueling statisticians, perhaps mumbling a few words such as "inconclusive," "you can

---

[14]The Death Penalty Information Center, an admittedly partisan source, lists 67 individuals released from death row since 1978 on the grounds of probable actual innocence. See "Innocence: Freed From Death Row," *Death Penalty Information Center* http://www.essential.org/dpic/Innocentlist.html.

[15]*State v. Ross*, 230 Conn. 183, 205–208 (1994), (Berdon, J. dissenting).

prove anything with statistics," and "I've always hated math, that's why I went to law school."

Yet, as I hope this discussion of Sellin and Ehrlich demonstrates, important, fundamental questions concerning an inherently quantitative subject can be asked by those with a fairly scant quantitative background. At bottom, the statistical examinations of the issue of death and deterrence raise questions concerning human behavior and human relationships. If lawyers and jurists will need help performing the proper statistical tests and analyzing the quality of data collection and sampling techniques, their training and experience in dealing with the complexities and varieties of human experience should help them to ask the right questions and to approach all proffered assertions with appropriate caution. That caution can provide a beginning for an inquiry that will be with us for some time to come.

5 Acknowledgments

I would like to acknowledge the careful reading and helpful suggestions of my colleagues, including Joseph Gastwirth, Sonia Suter, Steve Schooner. I would also like to thank Marc Rosenblum and Gang Zheng and also acknowledge the research assistance of Kamala Miller, second-year student, George Washington University Law School.

6 Cases

Coker v. Georgia, 433 U.S. 584 (1977).
Fleming v. State, 265 Georgia 541 (1995).
Furman v. Georgia, 408 U.S. 238 (1972).
Gregg v. Georgia, 428 U.S. 153 (1976).
Harris v. Alabama, 513 U.S. 504 (1995).
State v. Ross, 230 Conn 183 (1994).
Woodson v. North Carolina, 428 U.S. 280 (1976).

7 Statutes

21 U.S.C. 848(e) (1994).
La. Rev. Stat. Ann. 14:42 (West 1996).

REFERENCES

[1] James Andreoni (1995), "Criminal Deterrence in the Reduced Form: A New Perspective on Ehrlich's Seminal Study," *Economic Inquiry*, 476–483.

[2] Gary S. Becker (1968), "Crime and Punishment: An Economic Approach," *Journal of Political Economy*, 169–217.

[3] Deryck Beyleveld (1982), "Ehrlich's Analysis of Deterrence: Methodological Strategy and Ethics in Isaac Ehrlich's Research and Writing on the Death Penalty as a Deterrent," *British Journal of Criminology*, 101–123.

[4] Walter Berns (1979), *For Capital Punishment: Crime and the Morality of the Death Penalty*.

[5] William J. Bowers and Glenn L. Pierce (1975), "The Illusion of Deterrence in Isaac Ehrlich's Resarch on Capital Punishment," *Yale Law Journal*, 187–208.

[6] D. Cohen and Richard E. Nisbett (1994), "Self-Protection and the Culture of Honor-Explaining Southern Violence," *Personality and Social Psychology Bulletin*, 551–567.

[7] Robert J. Cottrol (1997), "Hard Choices and Shifted Burdens: American Crime and American Justice at the End of the Century" (Reviewing Michael Tonry, *Malign Neglect: Race, Crime and Punishment in America* (1995) in *George Washington University Law Review*, 506–529.

[8] Jo Dixon and Alan J. Lizotte (1989), "The Burden of Proof—Southern Subculture of Violence: Explanations of Gun Ownership and Homicide," *American Journal of Sociology*, 182–187.

[9] Isaac Ehrlich (1975), "The Deterrent Effect of Capital Punishment: A Question of Life and Death," *American Economic Review*, 397–417.

[10] C. G. Ellison (1991), "An Eye for an Eye—A Note on the Southern Subculture of Violence Thesis," *Social Forces* 1223–1239.

[11] Phoebe C. Ellsworth and Samuel R. Gross (1994), "Hardening of the Attitudes: Americans Views on the Death Penalty," *Journal of Social Issues*, 19–52.

[12] Douglas Hay, et al. (1975), *Albion's Fatal Tree: Crime and Society in Eighteenth Century England*.

[13] John Kaplan (1983), "The Problem of Capital Punishment," *University of Illinois Law Review*, 555–577.

[14] Richard M. McGahey (1980), "Dr. Ehrlich's Magic Bullet: Economic Theory, Econometrics and the Death Penalty," *Crime and Delinquency*, 485–502.

[15] Peter Passell and John B. Taylor (1977), "The Deterrent Effect of Capital Punishment: Another View," *American Economic Review*, 445–451.

[16] Paul A. Samuelson and William D. Nordhaus (1992), *Economics: Fourteenth Edition*.

[17] Thorsten Sellin (1959), *The Death Penalty*.

Introduction to Two Views on the *Shonubi* Case

Alan Julian Izenman

I

Both lawyers and statisticians have found much to criticise in the Second Circuit opinion *United States v. Shonubi*. At issue in this drug smuggling case was the estimation of an unknown total amount of heroin that was imported illegally in the digestive tract of the defendant during several trips from Nigeria into the United States. The only quantitative piece of information available was the amount of heroin found in the defendant's possession on his last such trip. Determining this unknown total was crucial in sentencing the defendant. In the two articles that follow, the authors, Professor Joseph L. Gastwirth, Dr. Boris Freidlin, and Dr. Weiwen Miao, and Professor Alan J. Izenman, consider various facets of the *Shonubi* case from legal and statistical perspectives. The general consensus among these authors is that the appellate court neither appreciated nor understood the complex role that statistics played in this case.

II

It must have seemed like a straightforward case at first. Charles O. Shonubi was convicted in October 1992 by the United States District Court (E.D. New York) of importation and possession of heroin with intent to distribute. Shonubi had been detained at John F. Kennedy International Airport on 10 December 1991 under suspicion of being a "balloon swallower," that is, a person who swallows a number of balloons filled with illicit drugs (usually cocaine or heroin) and enters the United States through a regularly-scheduled airline flight. Shonubi had apparently boarded a flight from Lagos, Nigeria, changed planes at Amsterdam, Holland, and continued on to New York. During the flight, the balloons had resided in his digestive tract. Upon clearing the airport, laxatives would relieve him of his precious cargo, which he would then pass on to others for distribution. Shonubi was found to have swallowed 103 balloons filled with an aggregate of 427.4 grams of heroin.

There was no problem convicting Shonubi. He had been caught red-handed with the drugs, and passport information and employment records strongly indicated that this was not his only foray into the world of drug smuggling. Shonubi had been employed during 1990–1991 as a toll collector at the George Washington Bridge, but had been fired for unexcused absences caused by his frequent traveling, which he could not possibly have afforded on his annual salary. There was also evidence that Shonubi had been using multiple passports to conceal his traveling schedule to and from Nigeria, a known "source" country for illicit drugs.

The prosecution presented evidence that Shonubi had made eight such smuggling trips, including the last one in which he was arrested.

Sentencing in the federal court system is separate from the trial itself and constitutes a second phase of the proceedings. The sentence for drug smuggling depends primarily upon the total quantity of drugs involved. The federal probation service interpreted that directive in this case more broadly than previously by incorporating estimates of past smuggling activity into the calculation of the total amount of drugs imported by Shonubi. Probation estimated that Shonubi had carried a grand total of $427.4 \times 8 = 3,419.2$ grams of heroin during his eight smuggling trips. The Federal Sentencing Guidelines state explicitly that 3,000–10,000 grams of heroin corresponds to a base offense level (BOL) of 34. Although the probation service further recommended that this BOL should be increased by two further levels (to 36) due to Shonubi's lies at trial and his general obstruction of justice, the sentencing judge (Jack B. Weinstein) declined to do so. With no criminal history, the defendant was sentenced to 151 months of imprisonment (*Shonubi I*). So much for Shonubi.

Well, not quite. Shonubi appealed his sentence, arguing that the total quantity of drugs on which his sentence was based was arrived at "by speculation." The government cross-appealed for the obstruction increase. The Second Circuit Court of Appeals arrived at two decisions in this case, both reflecting error on the part of the sentencing judge (*Shonubi II*). First, it vacated the sentence because it felt that the reasoning used by the government to arrive at 3,419.2 grams of heroin carried by Shonubi over eight smuggling trips had not been proven by a preponderance of the evidence. Second, it agreed with the government that a two-level increase for perjury and obstruction of justice was indeed justified.

The appellate court agreed with the district court's finding that Shonubi's previous seven trips constituted the same course of conduct as the last trip, namely, drug smuggling. However, the court insisted that "specific evidence" such as drug records, admissions, or live testimony must be presented to justify estimates of the total drug quantity imported by Shonubi over all eight trips. It noted that "[t]his careful practice is essential where a defendant's sentence depends in such large measure on the amount of drugs attributable to his conduct." The court agreed with Shonubi that "only speculation links appellant to any importation of drugs beyond 427.4 grams." The case was sent back to the district court for resentencing.

Which brings us to the third and most important act in the sentencing of Shonubi. Judge Weinstein wrote an extremely lengthy (71 pages) opinion regarding his decision (*Shonubi III*). This opinion is quite unusual in federal case law because of its lengthy descriptions of various statistical arguments. Weinstein described his opinion as "a memorandum ... largely devoted to explaining how a sentencing judge—and a trier of fact generally—reaches a decision." Prior to resentencing, he circulated draft versions of his opinion to legal scholars for comments, posed questions to his colleagues on the court, heard testimony regarding the economics of heroin smuggling, and, using Federal Rule of Evidence (FRE) 706, appointed a panel of two experts (Professors Peter Tillers and David Schum) to assist him with statistical arguments. The government relied upon the statistical expertise of

Dr. David Boyum, while the defendant retained Professor Michael Finkelstein for statistical assistance.

Boyum produced two data sets to aid the government in estimating the amount of heroin smuggled into the United States by Shonubi on his seven previous trips. The first data set was obtained from the Drug Enforcement Administration (DEA) and the second from the United States Customs Service. The DEA data consisted of information on 124 Nigerian balloon swallowers who had been arrested during the same period of time as Shonubi's eight trips. The original data records consisted of 142 pages, one for each smuggler; however, 17 of those pages displayed inconsistent data (gross weight being less than or equal to the corresponding net weight, which is impossible), one page that was missing, and one page that was a duplicate of another page. The DEA information on each smuggler included date of data collection, the number of balloons swallowed, the gross and net weights of the amount of heroin swallowed, and purity of the heroin. The Customs Service data consisted of arrest date, date of birth, gender, and gross weight of the heroin seized from 117 Nigerian balloon swallowers who were arrested at JFK Airport during the same period of time as the DEA data. Both sets of data are given in the Appendix to this Introduction.

Boyum first calculated the relationship between net and gross weight from the DEA data, and then used that relationship to convert the gross weights in the Customs Service data into net weights. Of the two data sets, Boyum seems to have concluded that the Customs Service data were of greater interest and use in this case. Once net weights were available for the Customs Service data, Boyum simulated 100,000 possible series of seven previous trips by Shonubi using repeated sampling with replacement of the 117 net weights. The simulations produced a Gaussian-looking histogram of seven-trip totals. Boyum concluded from these simulations that "there is a 99% chance that Shonubi carried at least 2,090.2 grams of heroin on the seven trips combined." Together with the 427.4 grams carried in his last trip, the government advanced the view that Shonubi smuggled approximately 2,500 grams of heroin in his eight trips.

The defense expert, Professor Finkelstein, challenged this determination in two ways. First, he introduced the idea of a "trip effect," in which smugglers would be expected to swallow a greater amount on each subsequent trip than was swallowed in the previous trip—sort of an experience factor. Because Boyum's simulation did not take such a trip effect into account, Finkelstein argued that it overestimated the total net weight for Shonubi. Second, the objection was made that the data that Boyum used in his estimation procedure consisted of data on other smugglers, not Shonubi, and hence did not constitute "specific evidence" as the appellate court had defined it.

The FRE 706 Panel agreed that Boyum's inferences derived from the DEA and Customs Service data did not constitute specific evidence about Shonubi, and agreed with the defense expert that the notion of a "trip effect" could well be important in this case. But the panel also found that Boyum's data did "provide evidence about a reference class of individuals to which Shonubi can reasonably be said to belong." The panel also carried out informal experiments that showed that a trip effect may be relevant. Using the Customs Service data, the panel then provided several scenarios that might lead to estimates of the total amount smuggled by Shonubi. The panel's estimates ranged from 1,479 grams to 2,527.4 grams based upon different assumptions of the nature of the "learning curve." Their overall conclusion was that, based upon all the available evidence, Shonubi had smuggled in excess of 1,000 grams of heroin.

The sentencing judge concluded that Shonubi smuggled between 1,000 and 3,000 grams of heroin in his eight trips. The corresponding BOL was 32, which, after adding the two-level enhancement, yielded a sentence of 151 months imprisonment, the same sentence originally imposed.

Again, Shonubi appealed. At this point, the appellate court decided (*Shonubi IV*) that the general use of the preponderance of the evidence standard for resolving all disputed aspects of relevant conduct at sentencing was too lenient a standard for situations "where such conduct, if proven, will significantly enhance a sentence." In the court's opinion, a "more rigorous" standard of proof should be applied. Although a higher standard of proof was never explicitly stated in their opinion, the court reiterated the requirement for "specific evidence" regarding Shonubi's past trips that presumably would satisfy a standard such as clear and convincing evidence. As a means of providing specific evidence about Shonubi's own prior smuggling activities, they could not accept the government's use of data on other drug smugglers. The court then noted that the government had had two opportunities to present the required specific evidence to the sentencing court, and therefore no further opportunity was warranted. So again, the appellate court vacated the sentence and remanded the case to the district court for resentencing. The sentence, they concluded, would have to be based only upon the amount of heroin found on Shonubi at the time of his arrest, plus the two-level increase in his BOL.

In *Shonubi V*, Judge Weinstein sentenced Shonubi to 97 months imprisonment as mandated by the Second Circuit.

III

What is *Shonubi*'s legacy? The Second Circuit's use of a "more rigorous" standard of proof than preponderance of the evidence for resolving certain disputed aspects of relevant conduct at sentencing is the main feature of the *Shonubi* case that is cited by other courts. Such a higher standard is to be employed only for those situations where a significant enhancement of a defendant's sentence is proposed. The Second Circuit had previously defined a *significant* enhancement of a relevant conduct increase as "a tail which wags the dog of the substantive offense" (*United States v. Ruggiero*, 1996).

In the few cases where the Second Circuit has considered a heavier standard of proof, such as the "clear and convincing evidence" standard, the results have been contradictory. On the one hand, an 8-level enhancement to the BOL in *Ruggiero* and an 18-level enhancement in *United States v. Gigante* (1996) were both regarded as not significant enough to trigger a higher standard of proof for relevant conduct. Yet, in *Shonubi IV* (p. 1089), the Second Circuit cited *Gigante* (thereby implicitly invoking the clear and convincing standard of proof) as precedent in order to deny a 6-level increase to the BOL.

At the district court level within the Second Circuit, contradictory decisions have also been made. Specifically, two district court judges in the Northern District of New York reached conflicting results, and both cited *Shonubi IV*'s use of the clear and convincing evidence standard as precedent. In *United States v. Murgas* (1998, pp. 253–254), the clear and convincing evidence standard was applied to deny a 9-level increase to the BOL. In *United States v. Howard* (1999), also a 9-level increase to the BOL, the district court rejected the need for the higher standard of proof.

In other federal circuits, the clear and convincing evidence standard of proof has also been applied in cases where the extent of relevant conduct increases were at issue. We refer the reader to *Howard* for a survey of those cases. In those cases, 4-level and 6-level increases did not trigger the higher standard of proof, whereas 18-level and 22-level increases did.

IV

The following two articles each focus attention on the opinion in *Shonubi III* and the response by the appellate court in *Shonubi IV*. In the first article, Gastwirth, Freidlin, and Miao discuss only the 117 net weights derived from the Customs Service data. They point out that (1) outliers in the data tend to distort implicit distributional assumptions and hence any resulting inferences; (2) the 427.4 grams Shonubi carried on his last trip was suspiciously smaller than would be expected based upon the data; (3) if a learning curve were used to impute missing data, the sensitivity of the resulting estimate of the total amount of heroin carried by Shonubi in his eight trips would depend upon the manner in which the learning curve is defined; (4) regardless of how the learning curve is defined, it would still be very difficult to obtain an estimate of that total that would be less than 1,000 grams; (5) as for the notion of "specific evidence," it would not be unreasonable to use data derived from other drug smugglers in the sentencing phase of this case; (6) the lack of pertinent data on Shonubi's drug smuggling activities can be contrasted with other cases that involve sample evidence but where the entire population of items, such as records in fraud cases, could be examined if deemed necessary; and (7) the appellate court's failure in this case to appreciate data analysis and statistical inference presented seems to reflect similar recent trends encountered in discrimination cases.

V

The second article is by Izenman, who is critical of the sentencing process on a number of different levels. He argues that (1) the DEA and Customs Service data were not the precise measurements they appeared to be, but that in fact, both data sets were contaminated by measurement error; (2) there is statistical evidence that the DEA forensic laboratory may have underestimated the amount of heroin carried by Shonubi in his last trip, a point also made by Gastwirth *et al.*; (3) there are statistical reasons for preferring the DEA data, rather than the 117 net weights derived from the Customs Service data, for estimating the unknown total drug quantity imported by Shonubi; (4) specific evidence, as introduced into this case by the appellate court, is a useful concept for convicting and sentencing inner-city drug traffickers, but it is impossible to obtain in drug smuggling cases; (5) even though there has been no published evidence for or against a learning curve or trip effect for balloon swallowers, a theory put forward by the defense and supported by the FRE 706 Panel, there is anecdotal evidence that smugglers learn to swallow up to their maximum capacity prior even to their first trip; and (6) simulations similar to those carried out by Boyum could perhaps have been more readily justified had attention also been paid to other related factors, such as the number of balloons swallowed.

Cases Cited

United States v. Gigante (1996), 94 F.3d 53 (2d Cir.).
United States v. Howard (1999), 37 F.Supp.2d 174 (N.D.N.Y.).
United States v. Murgas (1998), 31 F.Supp.2d 245 (N.D.N.Y.).
United States v. Ruggiero (1996), 100 F.3d 184 (2d Cir.).
United States v. Shonubi: *Shonubi V*: 962 F.Supp. 370 (E.D.N.Y. 1997); *Shonubi IV*: 103 F.3d 1085 (2d Cir. 1997); *Shonubi III*: 895 F.Supp. 460 (E.D.N.Y. 1995); *Shonubi II*: 998 F.2d 84 (2d Cir. 1993); *Shonubi I*: 802 F.Supp. 859 (E.D.N.Y. 1992).

Appendix

Combined DEA and Customs Service data sets

obs#	dataset	# balloons	gross wt	net wt	purity	age-yrs	gender
1	1	79	742.4	503.2	0.510	*	*
2	1	90	901.7	576.9	0.320	*	*
3	12	90	800.2	573.3	0.850	38	1
4	12	1	706.2	439.8	0.750	41	1
5	1	5	72.2	23.1	0.620	*	*
6	12	44	531.7	296.3	0.560	30	1
7	1	17	240.4	119.2	0.560	*	*
8	12	106	954.9	626.1	0.660	31	1
9	12	107	877.0	442.9	0.500	27	1
10	12	76	708.1	365.1	0.620	21	1
11	12	70	620.0	367.0	0.500	28	1
12	12	65	594.4	311.2	0.590	25	1
13	1	90	868.0	549.0	0.920	*	*
14	1	81	826.5	406.1	0.550	*	*
15	1	69	703.7	457.5	0.410	*	*
16	12	90	801.3	547.8	0.560	31	1
17	12	60	548.4	445.0	0.230	29	1
18	12	40	510.5	286.4	0.370	32	1
19	12	90	884.4	587.8	0.690	24	1
20	1	33	355.0	223.7	0.630	*	*
21	12	94	1001.2	692.7	0.860	34	1
22	12	67	482.4	286.0	0.460	34	1
23	12	61	580.7	392.2	0.350	29	1
24	12	60	513.1	295.8	0.960	37	1
25	12	69	557.1	303.6	0.470	32	1
26	1	85	585.6	408.0	0.970	*	*
27	1	80	573.3	376.0	0.990	*	*
28	12	50	489.3	266.6	0.740	24	1
29	12	58	690.2	328.9	0.810	35	1
30	1	104	951.6	640.6	0.880	*	*
31	1	29	146.8	100.3	0.620	*	*
32	1	117	642.9	339.3	0.660	*	*
33	1	22	367.0	195.8	0.900	*	*
34	1	8	185.9	63.8	0.940	*	*
35	12	39	459.4	272.9	0.490	36	1
36	1	69	845.7	552.1	0.660	*	*
37	12	25	484.6	160.6	0.920	26	1
38	12	85	835.7	540.8	0.460	31	1
39	12	45	635.1	313.0	0.400	32	1
40	1	128	1157.4	614.9	0.680	*	*
41	1	45	2577.6	2455.0	0.780	*	*
42	12	75	761.1	510.0	0.110	29	1
43	12	56	668.2	405.0	0.550	32	1
44	1	60	460.6	236.4	0.660	*	*

Combined DEA and Customs Service data sets (Continued).

obs#	dataset	# balloons	gross wt	net wt	purity	age-yrs	gender
45	1	30	340.6	185.0	0.520	*	*
46	1	28	312.4	182.1	0.520	*	*
47	12	79	648.5	421.3	0.800	31	1
48	1	62	*	436.6	0.034	*	*
49	12	49	578.9	247.2	0.660	29	1
50	1	130	1247.8	823.3	0.770	*	*
51	12	135	1312.0	895.1	0.500	32	1
52	12	39	399.2	132.3	0.620	34	1
53	12	62	655.1	380.6	0.760	25	0
54	1	55	380.9	328.2	0.740	*	*
55	1	3	50.1	20.0	0.670	*	*
56	1	110	*	619.7	0.660	*	*
57	1	70	865.6	480.2	0.820	*	*
58	1	83	827.1	551.1	0.610	*	*
59	1	93	778.4	512.8	0.820	*	*
60	1	39	*	219.3	0.990	*	*
61	1	95	1345.2	1020.0	0.550	*	*
62	1	80	613.6	364.0	0.800	*	*
63	1	72	747.2	461.6	0.640	*	*
64	1	15	*	500.8	0.830	*	*
65	1	152	1142.6	596.6	0.180	*	*
66	1	92	869.1	458.1	0.670	*	*
67	1	50	*	294.5	0.510	*	*
68	1	121	1208.7	434.2	0.310	*	*
69	1	48	539.1	311.7	0.680	*	*
70	1	70	1160.8	593.1	0.620	*	*
71	1	72	*	480.5	0.930	*	*
72	1	50	560.3	419.1	0.840	*	*
73	1	30	331.7	183.6	0.810	*	*
74	1	15	*	105.1	0.770	*	*
75	1	2	550.0	471.9	0.850	*	*
76	1	2	551.0	470.7	0.840	*	*
77	1	113	960.6	594.4	0.660	*	*
78	1	72	811.8	521.5	0.950	*	*
79	1	40	272.2	196.0	0.050	*	*
80	12	40	621.3	314.0	0.340	54	1
81	1	49	646.2	357.7	0.940	*	*
82	1	4	*	193.8	0.640	*	*
83	1	100	1275.0	906.0	0.990	*	*
84	1	73	782.4	476.7	0.690	*	*
85	1	91	1103.6	443.4	0.770	*	*
86	1	103	1849.6	652.3	0.940	*	*
87	1	45	774.7	445.5	0.660	*	*
88	12	71	522.6	293.2	0.880	45	1
89	1	124	1113.6	591.0	0.970	*	*
90	12	90	914.8	582.3	0.930	31	1

Combined DEA and Customs Service data sets (Continued).

obs#	dataset	# balloons	gross wt	net wt	purity	age-yrs	gender
91	1	67	955.6	512.0	0.350	*	*
92	12	84	826.5	494.3	0.790	39	1
93	12	35	321.2	205.1	0.700	34	1
94	1	61	679.4	342.2	0.840	*	*
95	1	8	97.7	45.3	0.830	*	*
96	1	71	856.7	413.9	0.960	*	*
97	1	42	452.1	240.2	0.620	*	*
98	1	81	683.0	472.5	0.860	*	*
99	1	71	735.5	355.0	0.820	*	*
100	12	49	740.0	491.8	0.750	23	1
101	12	80	875.6	510.6	0.470	37	1
102	1	79	509.6	373.4	0.310	*	*
103	1	4	122.7	22.6	0.940	*	*
104	1	1	139.1	106.5	0.960	*	*
105	1	27	223.3	145.8	0.950	*	*
106	12	84	617.7	504.0	0.850	44	1
107	12	68	781.6	471.2	0.890	33	1
108	1	96	1064.8	839.3	0.950	*	*
109	1	171	*	840.0	0.650	*	*
110	1	76	889.2	387.6	0.450	*	*
111	1	100	740.9	410.5	0.760	*	*
112	1	97	978.9	491.8	0.440	*	*
113	1	109	1313.4	763.0	0.970	*	*
114	1	99	1277.5	495.0	0.300	*	*
115	1	66	726.8	460.0	1.000	*	*
116	1	98	804.5	483.1	0.650	*	*
117	1	82	1015.9	562.5	0.280	*	*
118	1	66	770.7	426.4	0.650	*	*
119	12	71	610.5	356.7	0.810	46	1
120	1	101	857.5	531.3	0.740	*	*
121	1	68	856.2	320.4	0.460	*	*
122	1	94	968.4	545.2	0.620	*	*
123	1	35	519.3	373.2	0.910	*	*
124	1	105	859.8	469.1	0.660	*	*
125	1	54	393.1	249.4	0.540	*	*
126	1	80	742.1	412.0	0.790	*	*
127	1	69	682.8	426.3	0.660	*	*
128	1	75	916.5	475.0	0.580	*	*
129	1	67	906.4	462.3	0.980	*	*
130	1	110	1222.0	836.7	0.770	*	*
131	1	97	1108.9	582.0	0.710	*	*
132	1	75	886.3	467.3	0.640	*	*
133	1	239	*	2250.0	0.800	*	*
134	1	116	*	2250.0	0.680	*	*
135	1	55	*	286.6	0.530	*	*
136	1	2	*	101.1	0.300	*	*

Combined DEA and Customs Service data sets (Continued).

obs#	dataset	# balloons	gross wt	net wt	purity	age-yrs	gender
137	1	1	*	66.7	0.930	*	*
138	1	97	1033.9	455.9	0.780	*	*
139	1	18	*	143.5	0.760	*	*
140	1	116	*	345.5	0.810	*	*
141	1	2	*	312.4	0.710	*	*
142	2	*	331.0	*	*	38	0
143	2	*	572.0	*	*	26	0
144	2	*	698.0	*	*	41	1
145	2	*	594.0	*	*	29	1
146	2	*	204.0	*	*	29	1
147	2	*	687.0	*	*	34	1
148	2	*	788.0	*	*	25	1
149	2	*	808.0	*	*	31	1
150	2	*	1090.0	*	*	35	1
151	2	*	403.0	*	*	26	1
152	2	*	383.0	*	*	36	1
153	2	*	748.0	*	*	28	1
154	2	*	869.0	*	*	34	1
155	2	*	827.0	*	*	29	1
156	2	*	352.0	*	*	25	0
157	2	*	903.0	*	*	31	1
158	2	*	609.0	*	*	30	1
159	2	*	849.0	*	*	38	1
160	2	*	736.0	*	*	32	1
161	2	*	865.0	*	*	30	1
162	2	*	814.0	*	*	41	1
163	2	*	608.0	*	*	31	1
164	2	*	1130.0	*	*	37	1
165	2	*	690.0	*	*	30	1
166	2	*	298.0	*	*	30	1
167	2	*	817.0	*	*	34	1
168	2	*	1064.0	*	*	36	1
169	2	*	790.0	*	*	52	0
170	2	*	564.0	*	*	37	1
171	2	*	829.0	*	*	30	1
172	2	*	565.0	*	*	26	0
173	2	*	921.0	*	*	37	1
174	2	*	958.0	*	*	39	1
175	2	*	2093.0	*	*	40	1
176	2	*	600.0	*	*	32	1
177	2	*	594.0	*	*	47	0
178	2	*	895.0	*	*	38	1
179	2	*	1087.0	*	*	29	1
180	2	*	631.0	*	*	33	1
181	2	*	779.0	*	*	35	1
182	2	*	653.0	*	*	26	0

Combined DEA and Customs Service data sets (Continued).

obs#	dataset	# balloons	gross wt	net wt	purity	age-yrs	gender
183	2	*	677.0	*	*	35	1
184	2	*	993.0	*	*	38	1
185	2	*	652.0	*	*	30	0
186	2	*	511.0	*	*	42	1
187	2	*	899.0	*	*	31	1
188	2	*	835.0	*	*	35	0
189	2	*	734.0	*	*	44	0
190	2	*	400.0	*	*	35	1
191	2	*	1575.0	*	*	51	1
192	2	*	477.0	*	*	27	1
193	2	*	648.0	*	*	36	0
194	2	*	869.0	*	*	28	1
195	2	*	1472.0	*	*	44	1
196	2	*	746.0	*	*	34	1
197	2	*	870.0	*	*	28	1
198	2	*	966.0	*	*	31	1
199	2	*	628.0	*	*	37	1
200	2	*	397.0	*	*	33	1
201	2	*	916.0	*	*	33	1
202	2	*	513.0	*	*	51	1
203	2	*	613.0	*	*	37	1
204	2	*	631.0	*	*	35	1
205	2	*	1421.0	*	*	45	1
206	2	*	1658.0	*	*	44	1
207	2	*	1179.0	*	*	39	1
208	2	*	1138.0	*	*	41	1
209	2	*	792.0	*	*	43	1
210	2	*	193.0	*	*	35	1
211	2	*	323.0	*	*	24	1
212	2	*	974.0	*	*	42	1
213	2	*	715.0	*	*	28	1
214	2	*	876.0	*	*	39	1
215	2	*	855.0	*	*	24	0
216	2	*	795.0	*	*	38	1
217	2	*	323.0	*	*	30	1
218	2	*	762.0	*	*	31	0

Note 1: There are two data sets recorded here. The DEA data are coded as 1 and the U.S. Customs Service data are recorded as 2. There are 40 observations common to both data sets, and they are coded as 12. The DEA data consist of 141 observations and the U.S. Customs Service data consist of 117 observations.

Note 2: In general, an asterisk (*) denotes that the observation was not recorded. In the case of 17 of the gross weight values, an asterisk shows that each of those recorded values was less than or equal to the corresponding recorded net weight value, which is impossible.

Note 3: For the gender variable, a female is coded as 0 and a male is coded as 1.

Note 4: The age variable is given in years. It was calculated by subtracting date of birth from date of arrest.

The *Shonubi* Case as an Example of the Legal System's Failure to Appreciate Statistical Evidence

Joseph L. Gastwirth, Boris Freidlin, and Weiwen Miao

Abstract

This article illustrates shortcomings in the legal system's weighting of statistical evidence by examining one of the data sets submitted into evidence in the *U.S. v. Shonubi*. Using outlier methods to remove several unusually large observations and developing several models for the learning curve of drug runners, one can determine whether violations in reasonable assumptions can have a critical impact on sentencing. Courts should not insist on a "perfect" statistical study but need to assess the potential effect of missing data, omitted variables, etc. on the ultimate inference. Two other areas of law, sampling in false claims cases and possible discrimination in layoffs where strong statistical evidence may not be fully appreciated, are discussed. In the second type of case, courts have used an ad hoc measure of the impact of a layoff on protected group rather than proper measures such as odds ratios.

Key Words: sentencing, sampling, outlier detection, measures of effect, statistical evidence.

1 Introduction

The *Shonubi* case illustrates the legal system's failure to fully appreciate statistical evidence, perhaps because some of the judges are uncomfortable with its inherent uncertainty. The appellate court rejected virtually any estimate of the amount of heroin Shonubi carried on the seven earlier trips because it had to be based on what other drug runners had carried. The court required "specific evidence," i.e., evidence pertaining to the defendant. Furthermore, the court cited defendant's expert observation that the estimated amount *might* be biased due to omitted factors.[1] We believe that critics of a statistical analysis should be required to demonstrate that the "possible flaws" are sufficient to change the ultimate inference rather than simply suggest possible deficiencies. This view is similar to that expressed by Judge Posner in *Allen v. Seidman* (1988, p. 380):

> In a case like this, where the pool taking the challenged test is reasonably homogeneous in terms of qualifications and the racial disparity is very

---

[1] See footnote 4 and accompanying text, 1013 F.3d 1085 at 1092.

large, a simple statistical comparison will support a finding that the test had a disparate impart. See *Aguilera v. Cook County Police and Correction Merit Board*, supra 760 F.2d at 846 and cases cited there.

This is especially true in the present case since the defendant, while taking pot shots—none fatal—at the plaintiffs' statistical comparison, did not bother to conduct its own regression analysis, which for all we know would have confirmed and strengthened the plaintiffs' simple study.

We also note that statistical evidence in other types of cases recently has not been given its full evidentiary due, and we suggest that courts should use statistically valid measures that are consistent with the underlying model instead of creating their own.

2 Statistical Issues Deserving More Attention

The appellate decision was correct in noting that the estimate of 427.4 grams of heroin carried by the defendant was based on a sample of only four balloons out of 103. Apparently, the standard deviation of the amount of heroin in these balloons was not reported. In other forensic applications, e.g., DNA tests for paternity (Dodd, 1986; Gastwirth, 1988), it has been recommended that whenever possible two independent labs should perform the analysis. The variability in the measurements due to differences between laboratories and the possible variation in the purity of the drug in the balloons samples could then be incorporated into the analysis, thereby providing a more appropriate confidence interval for the estimated total amount of heroin.

The report of Professors Schum and Tillers, the court-appointed experts, noted the importance of assessing whether the data follow a normal distribution. Dr. Boyum, the government's expert, decided to use a resampling approach because the data did not appear to be normal. In Figure 1, we present a quantile–plot of the original 117 observations. The data do not fall on a straight line, as would be the case if the data were normal. However, the deviation from a normal curve occurs because of the largest few observations. Deleting the largest five observations yields data that is quite consistent with the normal curve. Indeed, the p-value of the Wilk–Shapiro test is .96. These 112 observations had a mean of 408.4 grams, a median of 406.3, and a standard deviation of 130.5. The lower end of a 95% confidence interval for the mean is 384.3. Using this value as an estimate of the average amount Shonubi carried on the seven previous trips yields 2690.1 grams. When the amount, 427.4 grams, carried on the eighth trip is added, the total is 3117.7, just over the critical value of 3000. Recall that individuals carrying 3000 or more grams of heroin receive larger sentences than those bringing in 1000–3000 grams. This does suggest that modest violations of the assumptions underlying the calculation could effect the ultimate inference as to whether the total carried exceeded 3000 grams.

Figure 1. Q-Q plot for the 117 observations

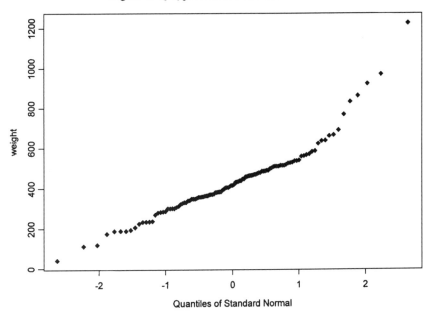

Quantiles of Standard Normal

Judge Weinstein's second opinion[2] noted that the smallest observation, 42.16, appeared to be an outlier and should be deleted. As the reduced data set, including that observation, did fit a normal curve, we decided to keep it in our analysis, which would favor the defendant. Moreover, using Grubb's Studentized extreme deviate test for an outlier (Barnett and Lewis, 1994; Sprent, 1998), from a normal sample we calculated a value of 2.80 for the reduced data set and 2.26 for all 117 observations. In neither case is the test statistically significant (at the .05 level). This indicates the need for judges to apply proper statistical procedures instead of just looking at the data.

It is also important to check the distributional assumptions like normality before relying on tests for outliers. This difference in the values of the outlier tests on the two data sets reflects the procedure's dependence on the assumed distribution. We note that the critical value of Grubbs's test for samples of 112 to 117 is about 3.24, so the smallest observation is noticeably closer to being declared an outlier in the reduced data set, which appears to be normally distributed.

Professor Finkelstein noted that the data on the 117 other Nigerian drug runners was not a random sample but should be considered an observational study subject to potential biases. He suggested that the probability of being caught would increase over time and also there would be a learning curve. Thus, runners who

---

were caught would have in their possession a greater than average amount of heroin. Neither he nor the appellate court quantified the potential impact of these possible flaws. Furthermore, he stated that the trip numbers for other drug runners were not available, so that a regression model relating the probability of being caught to the trip number could not be developed.[3] In his second district court opinion,[4] Judge Weinstein cites reports that smugglers practice swallowing oversized grapes *before* carrying heroin. This suggests that the learning curve should not be steep. A survey of his colleagues[5] indicated that most thought that first-time smugglers would be more likely to be caught and that they start close to the maximum amount they can carry. If one considers the five large values we deleted as "outliers," the remaining normal distribution of amounts carried is consistent with the judges' beliefs.

As the government's own expert testified that there was a modest learning curve that would level off at the third trip and that the probability of being caught was .25 for each trip, we will explore the sensitivity of the estimate to modest violations of these assumptions. If the ordered 112 observations are considered to follow a strong learning curve and the probability of being caught is .25, then the number of trips a smuggler makes until caught follows a geometric law. This implies that the first quarter of the ordered observations were from people caught on the first trip, the next 18.75% (.25 × (1 − .25)) were from runners caught on the second trip, and the remaining 56.25% were caught on or after their third trip. These last observations are assumed to be at the plateau. The average values of the data in each of these groups of order statistics are 241.8, 359.1, and 498.9. For example, the average of the lowest 25% of the observations equals 241.8, while that of the largest 56.25% is 498.9. It is surprising that none of the experts involved in the case noted that on his eighth trip, Shonubi carried only 427.4 grams, quite a bit less than the "plateau" average of 498.9. If we had not deleted the five largest values in order to ensure that the data appeared normally distributed, this difference would have been greater.

While it would be useful to know the trip numbers, the ratio of the amount Shonubi carried at his plateau relative to the smugglers in the data is 427.4/498.9=.856. It is sensible therefore to estimate the amounts he took at the earlier trips by multiplying those estimates (241.8 and 359.1) by .856. Using the resulting smaller values for the amounts carried on the first two trips and 427.4 for the remaining ones yields an estimate of 3076.4 grams for all eight trips. As the value .25 was given without any standard errors, we performed a sensitivity analysis assuming that the probability of being caught was .2 or .3. Those results were 3064.5 and 3092.9, respectively. This indicates that the result is not very

---

[3] 895 F.Supp. at 504
[4] 895 F.Supp. at 491
[5] 895 F.Supp. at 511 and 103 F.3d at 1088

sensitive to the presumed probability of being caught, assuming that the geometric model holds. It could be argued that Shonubi might also have had a more gradual learning curve. To explore the potential effect of the assumption that the plateau is reached on the third trip we assumed that the plateau was reached at the fourth trip. Now the average of those at the plateau (the last 42.19%) was 528.6, so Shonubi's ratio is just .808. A similar calculation, multiplying the averages of the groups of ordered data by this ratio, yields an estimate of 2953.3. This estimate is below the critical value of 3000 and indicates that the assumed learning curve is quite important.

Judge Weinstein's second opinion presents a variety of alternative estimates from the expert panel. All of these were above 1000 grams. In addition to the sensitivity analysis reported above, we also considered the potential effect of the claimed increase in probability of being caught as the amount carried increases. Assuming that the probability a smuggler carrying an amount at the lowest tenth percentile had of being caught is .1 while the probability for a smuggler with an amount at the ninetieth percentile is .2 had an effect of about 40 grams on the estimated average amount on each trip. This might affect a sentence at the 3000 level, but it is *not* plausible that this could reduce the estimate of the total amount carried to below 1000. Even a stronger relationship between the amount carried and the probability of being caught did not bring the overall estimate close to 1000 grams. Again, no evidence was offered indicating that the amount carried increases one's probability of being caught, and the survey of the trial judges did not support a strong relationship.

Another consideration is the degree of proof required at the sentencing phase. There are three distinct levels used in the legal setting: beyond a reasonable doubt, clear and convincing, and the preponderance of the evidence. In *U.S. v. Fatico* (1978) Judge Weinstein asked his fellow judges to assign probabilities to the different criteria. The results are also discussed in Gastwirth (1988, pp. 700–702) and used to define posterior probabilities in a Bayesian analysis of the data by Aitken, Bring, Leonard, and Papasoulitis (1997). The latter authors note that while the original conviction for drug-related crimes requires evidence satisfying the beyond a reasonable doubt standard, at sentencing the preponderance of the evidence standard is typically used. Indeed, judges are allowed to consider related criminal activity for which the criminal has *not* been found guilty in determining the sentence for a crime for which the defendant has been found guilty.

The preponderance of the evidence criterion would correspond to using the median or mean (for a symmetric distribution such as the normal curve) as the basis for an estimate. Of course, sampling error and measurement variability should be incorporated in a confidence interval. Even if one interpreted the beyond a reasonable doubt standard as a probability of .95 as used for illustration in Aitken et al. (1997), the estimated amount of heroin Shonubi smuggles in all eight trips easily exceeds 1000 grams. A conservative estimate is obtained by replacing the group averages 241.8, 359.1, and 498.9 by the fifth percentile of each group. These values are 113, 339, and 396.4, respectively, and the resulting estimate is 2861.4. Even accounting for sampling error would not reduce this value to less than 1000 grams. Our conclusion is similar to the models developed by Aitken et al. (1997).

A nonstatistical aspect of the *Shonubi* case concerned the definition of specific evidence. While we are statisticians, not lawyers, we should mention that requiring one party in a case to produce evidence about which the other party has more knowledge presents almost impossible task to the party with the burden of proof. This is why in illegal wagering cases, e.g., *Hamilton v. U.S.* (1969) and *Pinder v. U.S.* (1964), courts have accepted projections based on fragmentary data to estimate the total amount of bets and resulting tax due. Thus, it seems reasonable for the government to rely on the statistical evidence derived from other drug smugglers at the sentencing stage, as the defendant has the opportunity to rebut it.

Although estimates based on random sampling have been accepted by courts in a wide variety of cases (Diamond, 1994; Gastwirth, 1988; Izenman, 2000), a recent article, Behre and Ifrah 1999, argues that in False Claims Act cases estimates based on sampling are not sufficiently reliable as evidence of liability. In these cases the government needs to demonstrate that the claims were fraudulent and that the defendant knew they were. They contrast this type of case with recoupment claims under other laws pertaining to health care because the Social Security Act gives such power to the Department of Health and Human Services.

Before becoming involved as an expert in a sampling case, a statistician should find out which laws are applicable so that the sample estimate is sufficiently accurate or is based on data from a sufficiently large fraction of the population to meet the relevant requirements. Indeed, Behre and Ifrah (1999) point out that damage estimates may be based on statistical techniques but not liability. They note that while in *U.S. v. Krizek* (1994) a court did determine liability on estimates, in most fraud cases, courts are requiring that each claim be shown to be false. Thus, projections of the percentage of claims that were false based on statistical sampling were deemed insufficient, e.g., *U.S. ex. rel. Thompson* (1997).

Of greater interest is the list of challenges to random samples that Behre and Ifrah (1999) suggest. They discuss the *Protestant Memorial* (1998) case, where the defendant provided an expert who stated that simple random sampling is appropriate only when the units of analysis are homogeneous. Apparently, the expert stated that if the units are not homogeneous, a simple random sample would lead to an estimator with large variation and consequently a biased result. The expert said that only stratified sampling should be used. While stratified samples usually lead to estimates with lower standard errors, a properly conducted simple random sample still yields an unbiased estimate. In that opinion, the sampling error was not discussed at length. Rather than using the sample mean itself as an estimate of the amount owed, using the lower end of a 95% confidence interval for the average amount owed would protect the defendant from overpaying. It also provides an incentive for the government to use better sampling protocols, since confidence intervals from properly stratified samples are narrower than those from simple random samples.

It is important to distinguish cases under the False Claims Act from *Shonubi*. In those cases, assuming that the business records are preserved, it is possible to examine virtually all of the questionable claims. In drug runner cases, information on the amount of drugs smuggled on previous occasions is unavailable because the defendants do not keep records. Even in fraud cases, statistical sampling may prove useful at the first stage of an investigation. A modest sample should enable the government to ascertain which types of procedures or medications have the highest incidence of inaccurate billing. The second stage can examine the bills for those types of services.

Unfortunately, the failure of the Second Circuit to carefully consider the data appears to be part of a recent trend. In discrimination cases concerning layoffs (RIFs), the proper statistical analysis should compare the fractions of employees laid off in the protected and majority groups. Several cases, e.g., *Rose v. Wells Fargo & Co.* (1990), *Holley v. Sanyo Mfg., Inc.* (1985), *EEOC v. McDonnell Douglas*(1998), and *Council 31 v. Doherty* (1999), simply compared the fractions of employees in the protected class before and after the layoff or the average age of employees. If these representation rates differed by one percent or so, the courts deemed the effect minimal.

As the data from *Rose v. Wells Fargo* was discussed in Gastwirth (1992), we examine the data from *McDonnell Douglas*. Of the 3,389 employees aged 55 and over, 464, or 13.7% of them, were laid off. In contrast, of the 19,662 employees younger than 55, 1069, or 5.4% of them, lost their jobs. This means that older employees were two and one-half (13.7/5.4) times more likely to be laid off than younger employees. Applying Fisher's exact test yields a *p*-value less than one in ten million. StatXact4 yields a 95% confidence interval for the risk older employees had of being laid off relative to younger ones as (2.27, 2.79). The plaintiffs presented a logistic regression that incorporated performance evaluations and still yielded a statistically significant effect of age. One reason we believe that the *McDonnell Douglas* court might not have fully appreciated the statistical evidence is that the case was dismissed after a motion for summary judgment rather than after a trial on the merits. At a trial the statistical evidence and the explanation offered by the defendant might have been presented and evaluated by the jury.

The opinion noted that employees over 55 comprised 14.7% of all employees before the RIF and 13.6% afterwards and deemed the difference of 1.1% not meaningful. This way of looking at the data ignores the underlying statistical model and does not use appropriate statistical testing, unlike the Supreme Court's analysis in *Castenada v. Partida* (1977). Moreover, the appropriate statistical measure for termination data is the odds ratio (Gastwirth and Greenhouse, 1995), although the relative risk and the odds ratio are quite close when a small proportion of all employees are laid off. The fallacy of the court's approach of deeming a one-percent difference in the representation rates of a minority group before and after a layoff as legally insignificant can be illustrated as follows. An employer with 2000 employees half of whom were in a protected group lays off 39 of the 1000 employees in the protected group and *none* of the workers in the majority group.

Thus the protected groups' share of employees declines from fifty percent to forty-nine percent as a consequence of the lay off. The p-value of Fisher's exact test is zero to eight decimal places. StatXact4 calculates the 95% confidence interval for the odds-ratio as $(10.4, \infty)$ and Koopman's 95% confidence interval for the relative risk as $(10.19, \infty)$. Thus, members of the protected group would have been at least ten times more likely to have been laid off; a court granting judgment on the basis of a small difference in the representation rates would not even require the employer to provide a business-related justification for its policy.

It should be emphasized that some courts have shown increased sophistication in dealing with statistical evidence. In *Victory v. Hewlett Packard* (1999) the defendant moved for summary judgment. The plaintiff submitted data showing that 12 males sales representatives out of a total of 95 were promoted while none of the 25 female sales representatives were. Using Fisher's exact test, plaintiff's expert indicated that the data were significant at the .05 level. The defendant's expert argued that the data was not significant because the precise p-value was .052, rather then .05. Moreover, the employer noted that all of the men promoted had received the highest job evaluation. Judge Seybert's opinion notes that four women also had received top evaluation sometime in their career. Thus, that factor did not appear to fully explain the data. The opinion also noted that the defendant was reluctant to provide personnel records during discovery and this might have unduly limited the sample size available to the plaintiff. The judge's discussion of the role of statistical evidence at the summary judgment stage is well worth quoting:

> At summary judgment, a court does not meticulously weigh the evidence; rather, it considers whether admissible evidence raises a genuine issue of material fact. Statisticians may wish to quibble over two-tenths of one percent, and the meaning lying therein, which at this juncture this court views as a distinction without a difference. Resolution of the battle of experts is a matter best suited for the trier of fact.

Acknowledgments

The authors wish to thank Professors P. Tillers and D. Schum for providing them with the data and related expert reports and Professor A. Izenman for helpful suggestions. This research was supported in part by a grant from the National Science Foundation.

3   Cases Cited

Allen v. Seidman, 881 F.2d 375 (7th Cir. 1989).
Castenada v. Partida, 430 U.S. 482 (1977).
Council 31 v. Doherty, 79 FEP Cases 411 (7th Cir. 1999).
Hamilton v. U.S., 309 F.Supp. 468 (S.D.N.Y. 1969).

EEOC v. Mcdonnell-Douglas, 19 F.Supp 2d (E.D. Mo. 1998), *affirmed* 80 FEP Cases 13B (8th Cir. 1999).

Pinder v. U.S., 330 F.2d 119 (5th Cir. 1964).

Protestant Memorial Medical Center Inc. v. Department of Public Aid, 692 N.E. 2d 861 (Ill. App. 1998).

Rose v. Wells Fargo, 902 F.2d (9th Cir. 1990).

U.S. ex. Rel. Thompson v. Columbia/HCA Healthcare Corp., 125 F.3d 899 (5th Cir. 1997).

U.S. v. Fatico, 458 F.Supp. 338 (E.D.N.Y. 1978).

U.S. v. Krizek, 859 F.Supp. 5 (D.D.C. 1994).

U.S. v. Shonubi, 802 F.Supp. 859 (E.D.N.Y. 1992), *sentence vacated* 998 F.2d 84 (2d Cir. 1993).

U.S. v. Shonubi, 895 F.Supp. 460 (E.D.N.Y. 1995), *sentence vacated* 103 F.2d 1085 (2d Cir. 1997).

Victory v. Hewlett-Packard, 78 FEP Cases 1718 (E.D.N.Y. 1999).

REFERENCES

[1] Aitken, C.G.G., Bring, J., Leonard, T., and Papasouliotis, O. (1997). Estimation of quantities of drugs handled and the burden of proof. *Journal of the Royal Statistical Society* (A), 160, 333–350.

[2] Barnett, V. and Lewis, T. (1994). *Outliers in Statistical Data* (3rd edn. Chichester:John Wiley).

[3] Behre, K.D. and Ifrah, A.J. (1999). Statisticians at DOJ may overstate case. *National Law Journal*, March 29, B6–B11.

[4] Diamond, S.S. (1994). Reference guide on survey research, in *Reference Manual on Scientific Evidence*, Federal Judicial Center, Washington, D.C.: U.S. Government Printing Office, pp. 221–271.

[5] Dodd, B.E. (1986). DNA Fingerprinting in matters of family and crime. *Medicine, Science and Law*, 26, 5-7.

[6] Gastwirth, J.L. (1988). *Statistical Reasoning in Law and Public Policy: (Vol. 2) Tort Law, Evidence and Health*. San Diego, CA: Academic Press.

[7] Gastwirth, J.L. and Greenhouse, S.W. (1995). Biostatistical concepts and methods in the legal setting. *Statistics in Medicine*, 14, 1641–1653.

[8] Izenman, A.J. (2000). Statistical issues in the application of the federal sentencing guidelines in drug, pornography, and fraud cases. (this volume).

[9] Sprent, P. (1998). *Data Driven Statistical Methods*. London: Chapman & Hall.

[10] StatXact4 (1998). *User Manual*, Cytel Software Corporation, Cambridge, Massachusetts.

Assessing the Statistical Evidence in
the *Shonubi* Case

Alan Julian Izenman

Abstract

A number of interesting statistical issues arose in determining the total amount of heroin smuggled into the United States by Charles O. Shonubi in his eight trips to and from Nigeria. Smuggling on each trip was accomplished by swallowing heroin-filled balloons. The only evidence of actual narcotics smuggled in those eight trips, however, was the 427.4 grams smuggled on the last trip. The case, *United States v. Shonubi*, consists of a series of five opinions, three by the sentencing judge of the federal district (E.D.N.Y.) and two by the Court of Appeals for the Second Circuit. The primary issue in contention was the length of Shonubi's sentence. The federal sentencing guidelines required that his sentence be based not just on the total quantity of drugs he carried internally at the time he was arrested, but also on "all such acts and omissions that were part of the same course of conduct or common scheme or plan as the offense of conviction." The prosecution, therefore, argued that the total amount of drugs carried by Shonubi should include an estimate of the amount he carried on his seven previous trips. This latter estimate proved to be the most contentious part of the case. In this article we examine some of the statistical issues raised in the sentencing phase. These include whether the quantity of drugs carried by Shonubi on his last trip was correctly determined; the effects of using estimates of balloon weights of other smugglers in determining the amount of heroin carried by Shonubi on his seven previous trips; whether the modeling process should include a recognition of the existence of a learning curve for swallowing large numbers of heroin-filled balloons; the influence of covariates, such as age and gender, on the smuggling process; and the use of the bootstrap as a method of estimating drug amounts carried on prior trips. Three data sets on Nigerian heroin smugglers are used to provide information on constructing drug quantity estimates.

Key words and phrases: Balloon swallowing, bootstrap, covariates, errors in variables, heroin, illicit drug trafficking, learning curve, measurement error, ratio estimation, sample size determination, smuggling, specific evidence, statistics and the law, weighted least squares.

1 Introduction

Illicit drugs are often smuggled into the United States through couriers or "mules" who are found to have large numbers of balloons (a generic term, which may also refer to condoms, prophylactics, capsules, or pellets) filled with heroin or cocaine residing internally in their alimentary canal. Customs officials at U.S. international airports may suspect travelers whose journeys originated from a "source" country such as Colombia or Nigeria of being "balloon swallowers." Kadish (1997) gives a detailed discussion of "drug courier profiles"—identifying characteristics and behaviors—that have been used by customs officials or DEA agents to justify stopping and questioning suspicious-looking airport travelers about possible drug smuggling. Such travelers can be detained until it becomes clear that they are (or are not) indeed drug smugglers. One such detention (*United States v. Odofin* 1991) lasted twenty-four days before the defendant finally passed heroin-filled balloons. Whilst in detention, evidence of balloon swallowing may be obtained through personal admission, x-rays, body-cavity searches, monitored bowel movements, or involuntary surgery. The constitutional standard for non-routine detentions was delivered by the Supreme Court in *United States v. Montoya de Hernandez* (1985), which held that it was sufficient that there exist reasonable suspicion of internal smuggling. Because of the incriminating evidence discovered in their possession, very few of these balloon swallower cases ever proceed to trial, the defendant instead choosing to plead guilty in return for a reduced sentence.

Charles O. Shonubi was caught at New York's John F. Kennedy International Airport on 10 December 1991 smuggling heroin in his digestive tract. He was one of many Nigerian balloon swallowers arrested at JFK Airport during the early 1990s, and one of the few who elected to go to trial. For example, during the two years 1990 and 1991, there were 184 and 249 Nigerian passengers, respectively, who were arrested at JFK Airport for smuggling heroin (Vielmetti and Bennett 1990; Treaster 1992). Yet at the time, the Customs Service was convinced that "no more than five percent" of all Nigerian passengers who smuggled heroin through JFK Airport were being caught (Treaster 1992). Specifically, the Customs Service believed that an estimated two hundred Nigerian heroin smugglers arrived each day at U.S. airports (Barrett 1990) and that there could be as many as thirty to forty on some flights from Nigeria, and that "the Nigerian traffickers are using dozens of flights" (Treaster 1992). In fact, so many Nigerian balloon swallowers were being arrested at U.S. airports in those days that nearly all passengers from Nigeria became suspected drug smugglers (Vielmetti and Bennett 1990). The situation got so bad that JFK Airport had to be closed for two years (1993 and 1994) to flights from Lagos, Nigeria (Gregory 1994).

Successful balloon swallowers make repeated trips, usually of short duration, into the United States until either they are caught or they retire. In Wren (1999), a Colombian woman stated that "swallowers usually make ten trips before the organization lets them quit." Many smugglers carry new or replacement passports, possibly counterfeit, which show no prior travel history; others carry two or more passports to hide repeated journeys to "source" countries. In Shonubi's case, there was overwhelming evidence that he had used more than one passport to make a total of eight trips to and from Nigeria. In cases (involving smugglers other than Shonubi) when evidence of previous possible smuggling trips was found in a defendant's passport by U.S. customs officials, no use was made of those facts for sentencing purposes. See, for example, *United States v. Yakubu* (1989) (three trips to Nigeria during the six months prior to being arrested), *United States v. Onyema* (1991) (repeated journeys between Nigeria and the United States), and *Nwankwo v. United States* (1992) (three trips from Nigeria to the United States in the previous five months). In these and similar cases, the multiple trips served only to justify reasonable suspicion of drug smuggling and subsequent detention by U.S. customs officials.

This is not to say that a passport record of multiple trips between the United States and Nigeria always identifies a drug smuggler. Indeed, there have been many instances in which legitimate travelers from Nigeria were erroneously detained by U.S. customs officials on suspicion of drug smuggling based upon the fact that they had made multiple trips to Nigeria over a short time period. See, for example, *Adedeji v. United States* (1992). However, Shonubi appears to have been the first (and, so far, only) balloon swallower in which prior trips were used at a sentencing hearing for the express purpose of enhancing the defendant's sentence.

In this article we examine the case of *United States v. Shonubi*, and particularly the evidence with statistical content that was used to determine the defendant's sentence. The written evidence consists of a series of five opinions, which, for brevity, we shall refer to as *Shonubi I, II, III, IV*, and *V*. There are three District Court opinions (*I, III*, and *V*) written by the sentencing judge, Jack B. Weinstein, and two opinions of the Court of Appeals for the Second Circuit (*II*, written by Circuit Judge Cardamone, and *IV*, written by Chief Judge Newman). For specific citations of these cases and others mentioned in this article, see References.

This article is arranged as follows. In Section 2 we discuss at length the statistical issues of estimating the amount of heroin that Shonubi was caught with at JFK Airport. In Section 3 we discuss the difficulties that the appellate court had in dealing with the prosecution's estimates of the total amount of heroin imported by Shonubi in his seven previous trips. We focus our attention on the core argument of "specific evidence" that was used by the appellate court to judge the statistical estimates, and on the notion of a smuggler's "learning curve" that was put forth by the defense as a way of throwing doubt upon the prosecution's estimates. In Section 4 we describe the two interconnected data sets that were obtained by the prosecution from the Drug Enforcement Administration (DEA) and the United States Customs Service for the purpose of estimating the amounts of heroin that Shonubi carried in his seven previous trips. We also discuss a third data set extracted from published federal court opinions. In Section 5 we use the data sets from Section 4 to study the relationship between gross weight and net weight of the amounts smuggled into the United States by other Nigerian balloon swallowers. This relationship was used as an intermediate step by the prosecution to provide an estimate of Shonubi's past smuggling activities. Although we show that it was not necessary for the prosecution to incorporate any estimate of this relationship into their quantity determination, we feel that comments regarding this relationship are of general statistical interest. In Section 6, again using the data sets from Section 4, we provide a bootstrap estimate of the total amount of heroin that Shonubi carried in his seven previous trips. Our estimate supports the conclusion reached by the sentencing judge in *Shonubi III* that a total of between 1,000 and 3,000 grams of heroin was smuggled into the United States in Shonubi's eight trips.

2 Estimating Drug Quantity: The Last Trip

Shonubi was found to be carrying internally 103 multicolored balloons each filled with a white powdery substance. Four of those balloons were randomly chosen by a forensic chemist for testing and inference. Despite little information being available regarding the actual procedures followed by the chemist (a common occurrence in such court opinions), it is not difficult to reconstruct the sequence of events leading up to the stated quantities.

First, the four balloons were weighed together in their original state yielding a sample total gross weight of 27.44 grams and a sample average gross weight of 6.86 grams. The total gross weight of all 103 balloons was then *estimated* at 103×6.86 grams $= 706.6$ grams. Second, the substances were removed from each of the four balloons and combined into a composite mixture, which tested positive for heroin with purity 53%. The inference was then made that all 103 balloons contained heroin of 53% purity. Third, the heroin mixture was weighed, yielding a sample total net weight of 16.6 grams. The average net weight of the heroin in a sample balloon was therefore determined to be 4.15 grams. The total net weight of the heroin in all 103 balloons was estimated by the chemist using the following procedure:

> [By m]ultiplying the average [net] weight of the heroin mixture in the four
> tested balloons by 103, the chemist arrived at an aggregate [net] weight
> of 427.4 grams [*Shonubi III*, p. 465].

The defense and both trial and appellate courts accepted this net weight estimate of the heroin carried by Shonubi without objection.

There are several reasons for concern here. First, a sample of four out of 103 balloons is too few for accurate inference. This point was implied by a member of the Federal Rule of Evidence (FRE) 706 Panel (Tillers 1997, p. 1880, footnote 7), although not in the panel's report (Schum and Tillers 1995) to the sentencing judge. (The panel consisted of two expert witnesses appointed by the judge to help evaluate the statistical evidence put forward by the parties' experts.) Indeed, in comparison, the two most popular sample size rules (the 10% rule and the square-root rule, which operate as very crude guidelines with no theoretical justifications and which are used by many forensic laboratories for sampling from illicit drug seizures, see Izenman 1999) would both require a sample size of at least *eleven* in this case.

What size sample would have been more appropriate in Shonubi's case? Suppose we wish to sample a continuous random variable with known standard deviation S and finite population size N. What should be the sample size, n, if we specify a significance level α and an acceptable margin of error d? This is an elementary calculation, which can be found, for example, in Cochran (1977, Chapter 4). The required sample size is obtained from a confidence interval for the finite population mean $\bar{Y}$. Let $\bar{y}$ be the mean calculated from a simple random sample (SRS) of size n and suppose that $\bar{y}$ is normally distributed. Then, a $100(1 - \alpha)\%$ confidence interval for $\bar{Y}$ is given by $\bar{y} \pm d$, where the margin of error is

$$d = z_{\alpha/2} \left(1 - \frac{n}{N}\right)^{1/2} \frac{S}{\sqrt{n}}, \tag{1}$$

and where $z_{\alpha/2}$ is the upper $100\alpha/2\%$ point of the standard normal distribution. Solving (1) for n yields

$$n = \frac{n_0}{1 + \frac{n_0}{N}}, \quad \text{where } n_0 = \frac{z_{\alpha/2}^2 S^2}{d^2}. \tag{2}$$

Now, let $N = 103$ and $\alpha = 0.05$. If $S^2 = d^2$, which is highly unlikely, then (2) gives us $n = 4$, as was actually used. We expect, however, that S^2 would be much larger than d^2, in which case $n > 4$. For example, the various data sets of Section 3 suggest that S would be 150–250 grams. If $d = 100$ grams, then n would fall between 9 and 25. For smaller values of d, the sample size, n, would increase. (If $d = 50$ grams, then n would be 27–50.) Such choices of d therefore produce sample sizes well in excess of the $n = 4$ used by the chemist in this case. Such a small choice of n surely contributed to the poor precision of the resulting estimator and a low degree of confidence in that estimator.

We note in passing that other methods for sample size determination in illicit drug cases have been proposed. For example, Aitken (1998) suggested a Bayesian approach for estimating the proportion of the seized containers (which may take the form of plastic bags, ziplock "baggies," paper packets or envelopes, vials, or even bottles) whose contents contain an illicit drug. See also Aitken (2000). In cases involving smuggling, however, such a statistical problem would not really be of interest because there is no reason to suspect that any of the swallowed balloons contains a substance other than illicit drugs. This point was made by the court in *Shonubi III*, which noted that "no one carries sugar in balloons from Nigeria to New York."

An alternative sampling strategy suggests itself here. One of the things that was missing in this case (and, most likely, in all similar cases) is a consistency check on the sampling and subsequent inferences. Analyzing only four balloons cannot provide sufficient flexibility for consistency checks. If we take an SRS from the available N balloons using (2) to determine the sample size n, we can split that sample randomly into two subsamples, one of size n_1 and the other of size n_2 ($n = n_1 + n_2$), for comparative testing purposes, including tests for heroin and a purity measurement. For example, n_1 can be chosen to be roughly $n/2$. The two sets of balloons would each be weighed for average gross weight and their respective contents weighed for average net weight and then compared. Assuming that a high degree of consistency is achieved from the results of these two samples (keeping in mind, of course, that the balloons are all filled from the same source), then they can then be recombined back into the original SRS of size n for inferential purposes. This procedure would allow internal comparisons of the sampling procedure based upon interim estimates (from each sample) of gross weight, net weight, and purity of the heroin in all 103 balloons. Furthermore, the combined sample of size n would be large enough to provide acceptable official estimates of gross weight, net weight, and purity of the heroin.

In the event that the interim estimates are not sufficiently indicative of an overall consistency among all balloons seized, a third SRS could be taken from the remaining balloons and further consistency checks as necessary could be carried out on the contraband. In general, the more homogeneous the balloons and their contents, the smaller the combined sample needs to be, while the more heterogeneous the balloons and their contents, the more checking and double-checking need to be done to establish acceptable official estimates for the case in question.

Second, we are also sceptical about the stated amount of heroin found in Shonubi's possession. Figure 1 shows the net weight of heroin carried internally by 17 Nigerian smugglers (including Shonubi) plotted against the number of balloons they swallowed (see Section 4.1 for details). This scatterplot shows that the point corresponding to Shonubi has a relatively low net weight component given the number of balloons Shonubi actually carried. We would expect, based upon the evidence given in Figure 1, that Shonubi should have been carrying at least 600 grams (net weight) of heroin on his last trip. We can see this from the following computation. There were seven cases in the federal and DEA data sets (see Sections 4.1 and 4.2) where the individual carried between 100 and 105 balloons. We computed the average net weight of heroin for each of these seven smugglers and then multiplied those averages by 103. This was done to obtain reasonable comparisons with the 427.4 grams of heroin ostensibly carried in 103 balloons by Shonubi. The seven projected net weights had an average and standard deviation of 630.5 grams and 178.3 grams, respectively.

How can we explain the discrepancy between these numbers and the amount of heroin carried by Shonubi on his last trip? One way would have been to compare the average weight of the four sample balloons with the average weight of the remaining 99 balloons to check on sampling bias. Alas, the gross weight of the balloons was also an estimate from the same four balloons that provided the net weight estimate (an important point that everyone connected with the case seems to have missed), so that it would have been impossible to carry out such a comparison. We conjecture that either Shonubi was carrying a *smaller* amount of heroin than would have been expected of a person carrying 103 balloons or, more likely, given his demeanor and smuggling experience, that 427.4 grams was an *underestimate* of the net amount of heroin that Shonubi actually carried internally on his last smuggling trip. This latter possibility may explain why Shonubi never challenged the validity of the government's estimate.

3   The Seven Previous Trips, Specific Evidence, and the Learning Curve

Both the trial court and the Court of Appeals agreed that Shonubi had made eight smuggling trips between 1990 and 1991. They also agreed that for sentencing purposes, the eight trips should be considered as "a single course of conduct." What the court of appeals did not accept were the estimates by the sentencing judge of the amount of heroin that Shonubi had imported in the seven trips prior to the trip in which he was apprehended.

The first estimate, made by the U.S. Probation Department and accepted by the sentencing judge, was a simple guess that the total amount carried was eight times the amount carried on the last trip, that is, 8×427.4 grams $= 3419.2$ grams, which resulted in a sentence of 151 months. This estimate proved to be too simple for the Court of Appeals. The resulting sentence was remanded back to the sentencing judge for an estimate that incorporated specific knowledge of Shonubi's previous smuggling trips. The second estimate was based upon a lengthy investigation of the statistical and nonstatistical aspects of the case. These included extensive simulation studies involving the Customs Service data (see Section 4.3). These simulation studies (and other information) yielded an estimate of between 1,000 grams and 3,000 grams of heroin for Shonubi's eight trips, and, again, a sentence of 151 months. The Court of Appeals again threw out that sentence, but this time required the sentencing judge to incarcerate Shonubi to a sentence corresponding only to the amount he carried on his last trip. Shonubi was sentenced to 97 months in prison.

The core argument made by the court of appeals was that "specific evidence" was necessary (in this case) to prove relevant-conduct drug quantity. In other words, the prosecution was required to provide evidence specific to Shonubi of the amounts he had smuggled on prior trips. The court listed *records of defendant's drug transactions, defendant's own admissions, or live testimony about defendant's drug transactions* as examples of such specific evidence. Because the court felt that the prosecution in the *Shonubi* case had not produced such evidence, it vacated the same sentence twice, even though it clearly recognized that the prior trips were also smuggling trips and that Shonubi was more than a minor or minimal participant in the heroin smuggling trade.

The appellate court's notion of specific evidence (as set out in *Shonubi*) invites the following questions to be asked. What kind of specific evidence could be produced at a balloon swallower's sentencing hearing to show the amount of drugs that the defendant smuggled into the United States on prior trips? Is it likely that balloon swallowers would carry drug records from prior trips on their person during later trips? Hardly. Would they be expected to provide detailed information about their previous smuggling trips together with amounts smuggled? Unlikely. Although balloon swallowers do not act alone, they are often caught at international airports without accomplices, family members, or others who could or would testify in court about their previous drug smuggling activities. The prosecution could try to get such witnesses to testify in court, but for one reason or another, this typically does not happen. So, we have to expect that specific evidence of quantities smuggled on prior trips is unlikely to be presented at trial or at a sentencing hearing. Consequently, the Second Circuit Court of Appeals must have realized that requiring the prosecution to come up with specific evidence (as they defined it) of Shonubi's prior smuggling trips would be an impossible task.

International drug smuggling produces inherently different circumstances than those surrounding drug trafficking in the inner city. For prosecuting the latter, the notion of specific evidence certainly makes sense, and obtaining such evidence would not be an impossible, nor even a particularly onerous, task, especially in cases involving drug conspiracies. In fact, the Supreme Court has already recognized that a difference exists between the two types of situations. In *Montoya de Hernandez*, the Supreme Court held that:

> Since the founding of our Republic, Congress has granted the Executive plenary authority to conduct routine searches and seizures at the border, without probable cause or a warrant, in order to regulate the collection of duties and to prevent the introduction of contraband into this country. This Court has long recognized Congress'[s] power to police entrants at the border . . . Consistently, therefore, with Congress'[s] power to protect the Nation by stopping and examining persons entering this country, *the Fourth Amendment's balance of reasonableness is qualitatively different at the international border than in the interior.* . . . [This reflects a] long-standing concern for the protection of the integrity of the border. This concern is, if anything, heightened by the veritable national crisis in law enforcement caused by smuggling of illicit narcotics, and in particular by the increasing utilization of alimentary canal smuggling [Emphasis added].

The Supreme Court recognized that international drug smuggling presents such unique and distinguishable circumstances that a relaxation of the standard guidelines is necessary for a non-routine stop and search at airports. Similarly, the right to legal due process has often been suspended at airports for smuggling situations when a health hazard is suspected; if the government believes that drugs may be blocking a balloon swallower's digestive system, then surgical procedures may be performed without requesting or obtaining the suspect's consent (Gregory 1994). Such considerations play an important role in the conviction phase of a federal trial (such as *Shonubi's*), where the standard of proof required to convict (proof beyond a reasonable doubt) is higher than at the sentencing phase (proof by a preponderance of the evidence). See Izenman (1999) for a discussion of standards of proof used in illicit drug cases.

By insisting on the almost impossible notion of "specific evidence" (as enunciated in *Shonubi II* and *IV*), the Court of Appeals for the Second Circuit rejected the statistical evidence as to the extent of Shonubi's drug smuggling. As the FRE 706 Panel pointed out, all that had to be believed was that Shonubi carried at least

573 grams of heroin on his seven previous trips, an average of at least 82 grams per trip. The statistical arguments of Judge Weinstein and the panel should have been sufficient to convince the Court of Appeals that Shonubi carried in excess of 1,000 net grams of heroin.

The defense tried to provide doubt regarding the prosecution's estimate of the aggregate amount of heroin smuggled by Shonubi in his eight trips. They did this primarily through an interesting theory of a "learning curve" that was suggested by a defense expert. The basic idea is that smugglers begin carrying small amounts of drugs, and then increase their carrying load on each successive trip until their maximum internal capacity is reached. On the surface, this would appear to be a reasonable hypothesis of a drug smuggler's behavior. Unfortunately, there exists no published evidence that this hypothesis is true (or false). The sentencing judge and his district court bench colleagues also dismissed the learning curve as a viable model for explaining a typical smuggler's behavior. See, for example, the survey results of federal judges of the Eastern District of New York in *Shonubi III*, p. 511.

We believe instead, and the published evidence (such as Wren, 1999) also strongly suggests, that the most likely scenario is that internal smugglers start out as close to maximum capacity as possible and essentially stay at that limit for successive trips until they are caught or retire.

Balloon swallowing is a very difficult and unnatural task and has to be learned. One of the Panel members, Dr. Schum, tried to visualize what it would be like to swallow 103 balloons (filled with powdered sugar!). See *Shonubi III*, pp. 506–507. Schum examined the sugar-filled balloons and thought about the task of swallowing such a large number. His reaction was that swallowing would have to require "a certain amount of courage," and that there had to be a learning curve (Schum and Tillers 1992, p. 54). However, this argument did not reflect the cold business realities of drug-smuggling organizations, which send many balloon swallowers into the United States with the expectation that a certain percentage of them will get caught. A common concern of these organizations (Morton 1998) is to forestall any possible refusal by the smuggler to swallow the required amount. To help accomplish this, the organization apparently does not allow the smuggler to see beforehand the entire collection of balloons they are required to swallow; instead, the smugglers are handed the balloons one at a time. Thus, Schum's experiment gave little insight into the mechanics of balloon swallowing.

The learning curve hypothesis implicity assumes that balloon swallowing is learned on the job, one trip at a time. However, published accounts have been quite detailed in their descriptions of the type of intense preparation that potential smugglers have to go through before they even take their first smuggling trip. A compilation of accounts of balloon swallowing mechanics was given in *Shonubi III*, pp. 490–491, much of it culled from investigative newspaper reports. Smugglers are expected to carry as much as the "organization" that recruits them wants them to carry, every time, and the "organization" teaches them to do that from the beginning. More recently, in a *New York Times* article on heroin balloon swallowers

(Wren 1999), a Columbian woman described the preparation that she went through to become a "swallower":

> She [said she] underwent a 15-day procedure to prepare her body for ingesting the heroin, including prepping her throat by swallowing grapes and then carrots shaped like pellets. The day before the trip, she said, the courier is taken to a pharmacy and injected with a relaxant to facilitate swallowing. "They don't tell you the size of the pellets," she said in a recent interview. "They say it's very easy." Before the flight, she said, a swallower is given a pill to control the bowels, and a tranquilizer and a liquid anesthetic to numb the pain. "The pellets usually scratch your throat and it starts to bleed."

In her first trip, this woman nearly died because of poorly-wrapped pellets. Yet, she still made two more trips before she was arrested at Newark Airport. When asked why she continued to smuggle drugs, she replied,

> "Because when you get involved, they always need you," she said. "They look for you. And when you say no, they say they know where your family is and where your kids are, and please do them this favor."

By the time a smuggler is ready to take his or her first trip, they are already trained to swallow heroin-filled balloons near to or at full internal capacity. They do not need to "learn on the job." They have already learned everything about swallowing before undertaking the job. Even though balloon swallowers may be arrested after several smuggling trips between the "source" country and the United States, we have no reason to believe that there exists a so-called "trip effect."

4   Three Data Sets

In order to comment on the statistical issues involved in estimating the amount of heroin carried by Shonubi during his seven previous smuggling trips, it is worthwhile describing (in Sections 4.2 and 4.3) the two data sets that Boyum obtained in his attempt at that estimation problem. In Section 4.1, for comparison purposes, we also consider additional data we extracted from federal cases that had gone to trial.

Questions of interest include the following: What is the relationship between the number of balloons carried internally and the amount of heroin in those balloons? What is the relationship between the (gross) weight of balloons + tape + heroin and the (net) weight of the heroin only? And does age or gender appear to play any role in explaining the amount of heroin carried internally?

4.1   Data from Federal Court Cases

First, we carried out a LEXIS search of federal cases using the two key words "Nigeria" and "heroin." This search yielded 106 Federal District Court cases and

130 appellate cases. From those 236 cases, we found 30 cases that involved 32 different Nigerian balloon swallowers (including *Shonubi*). Information regarding both the number of balloons and the estimated total net weight of heroin found in those balloons was given for only 17 swallowers. (The remaining published opinions, unfortunately, gave at most one of the two numbers, and so could not be used here as bivariate pairs. It would have been very useful for the present work if the opinions of these cases had included the age and gender of the defendant, the number of balloons extracted, and the gross weight, net weight, and purity of the heroin seized.)

The average number of balloons carried internally by 26 individuals was 70.81 (median 80.5) with a standard deviation of 33.17, and the average net weight of heroin carried in balloons by 19 individuals was 414.4 grams (median 427.4 grams) with a standard deviation of 199.0 grams. It appears to be an interesting coincidence that the median amount is identical to the amount carried by Shonubi when caught at JFK Airport. The 17 individuals with both numbers given are plotted in Figure 1. The plot shows increasing variability in the amount of heroin as more balloons are swallowed. One can possibly visualize two groups of points in the scatterplot, a small, "lower" grouping of five points containing Shonubi and the only two female balloon swallowers in the data set, and a larger, "upper" grouping consisting only of male balloon swallowers. A comparison with the DEA data (see Section 4.2) shows that a gender grouping would appear to be an artifact of a small data set.

If additional information on the physical characteristics (height, weight) of each smuggler were available, one could try to make a case for the presence

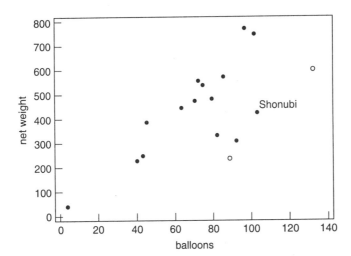

Figure 1. Net weight of heroin carried internally by 17 Nigerian smugglers (including Shonubi) plotted against the number of balloons they swallowed. Data are from federal court cases. Open circles show female smugglers and filled circles show male smugglers.

of *several* coincident regression lines (non-parallel lines, like rays, emanating from the origin) that might reflect the different capacity levels of balloon swallowers.

4.2 The DEA Data

The Drug Enforcement Administration (DEA) provided Boyum with data on the chemical analyses of heroin seized from 142 Nigerian balloon swallowers who had been arrested at JFK Airport during the period 1 September 1990 through 10 December 1991. The DEA records on eighteen of the swallowers showed incorrect gross weights, so that the working data set had $m = 124$ cases. The only statistical use that Boyum had for the DEA data was to help him derive a formula for converting gross weights into net weights. This was necessary because the Customs Service data (see Section 4.3) gave only gross weights of heroin seizures. It is not clear why Boyum preferred the Customs Service data to the DEA data for estimating the aggregate net weight that Shonubi smuggled in his past trips. The only information given in the Customs Service data that was not given in the DEA data was details on gender and age of the smugglers, information that neither Boyum nor the prosecution ever used!

In our study of each arrest record in the DEA data, we were interested primarily in the date on which the data were collected, and the number of balloons, gross weight, net weight, and purity of the heroin seized. In Figure 2 we plotted net weight against the number of balloons for the 17 Federal court cases (see Figure 1) and for 122 of the 124 DEA data cases. We deleted two DEA cases from the scatterplot, one with an abnormally high amount of heroin relative to the amounts carried by the other smugglers, and another whose net weight amount (652.3 grams) did not seem to be consistent with his gross weight amount (1849.6 grams).

We computed the averages and standard deviations of the four variables for the full data set of 124 smugglers (and for comparison, in parentheses, the same statistics for the reduced data set of 122 smugglers). The average number of balloons carried was 68.7 (68.6) with a standard deviation of 31.4 (31.5); the average gross weight of heroin carried was 736.5 grams (712.3 grams) with a standard deviation of 346.4 grams (288.8 grams); the average net weight of heroin carried was 437.1 grams (418.8 grams) with a standard deviation of 258.9 grams (184.5 grams); and the average purity was 67.8% (67.5%) with a standard deviation of 21% (21%). A matrix plot of the four variables for the reduced data set is shown in Figure 3. Further graphical analysis (not shown here) of the data showed that although there was no reason to doubt that gross weight was normally distributed, net weight had a lighter right-hand tail than a normal variable. Furthermore, customs agents apparently catch more smugglers who have swallowed high-purity heroin (purity greater than 90%) than would be expected if purity were a normally distributed variable.

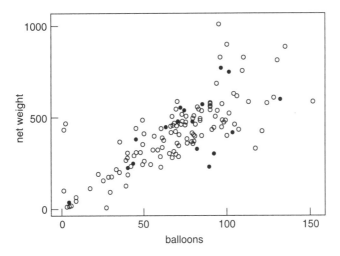

Figure 2. Net weight of heroin carried internally by Nigerian smugglers plotted against the number of balloons they swallowed. For comparison purposes, open circles show data from 122 DEA cases and filled circles show data from the 17 federal court cases.

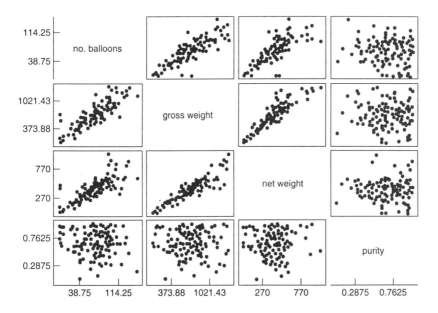

Figure 3. A scatterplot matrix for the four recorded variables, number of balloons swallowed, gross weight of heroin, net weight of heroin, and purity of heroin, from the DEA data.

4.3 The U.S. Customs Service Data

Boyum was also provided with United States Customs Service data on each individual arrested at JFK International Airport between 1 September 1990 and 10 December 1991 for importing heroin from Nigeria by balloon swallowing. The variables recorded were arrest date, name, date of birth (and hence, age), and gender of each of the 117 individuals arrested and the gross weight of the heroin seized in each case. The period of time of data collection for both the DEA and Customs Service was deliberately chosen to be the same as Shonubi's travel records, from first trip to eighth trip.

We therefore expected that the entire Customs Service data could be matched on a one-to-one basis to 117 of the 124 arrest records in the above DEA data. But this did not happen. Only 40 cases from each of the two data sets matched exactly the gross weight of heroin seized and the compatibility of the dates of arrest (Customs data) and data collection (DEA data). It is not clear why the remaining data do not match. Boyum's affidavit never recognized any connection, partial or complete, between the two data sets. Similarly, neither the government nor the defense mentioned in their memoranda any possible relationships between the two data sets.

The average gross amount smuggled in this data set was 742.2 grams with a standard deviation of 288.7 grams. Of the 117 internal drug smugglers in this data set, there were 107 men and 10 women and a wide range of ages (21–54 years old). In general, one would expect the majority of balloon swallowers to be men because their size would enable greater amounts of drugs to be swallowed. However, evidence (Wren 1999, Gregory 1994) suggests that more women are now being used to throw off suspicion at customs checks. Scatterplots of the Customs Service data (Figure 4) reveal no noticeable relationship between gender or age of the smuggler and the gross weight of heroin smuggled. As regards an age factor, Wren (1999) noted that drugs have been found on 13-year-olds and 84-year-olds.

5   The Relationship Between Gross Weight and Net Weight

The absence of net weights of heroin in the Customs Service data motivated Boyum to use the DEA data to derive a formula for converting gross weights into net weights. Although we find no reason why Boyum should have needed to convert gross weights into net weights, this statistical problem is of general interest.

Let X_i and Y_i represent gross weight and net weight, respectively, of the heroin swallowed by the ith smuggler in the DEA data set, $i = 1, 2, \ldots, m$. We shall generally take $m = 122$, unless stated otherwise. Figure 2 indicates that a straight line passing through the origin may summarize the scatter of points. We note, however, that the variability of net weights increases with increasing gross weight values. A scatterplot (Figure 5) of the individual ratios Y_i / X_i against X_i,

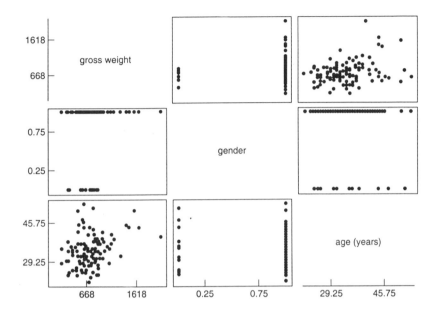

Figure 4. A scatterplot matrix of the three recorded variables, gross weight of heroin, gender of smuggler, and age (in years) of smuggler, from the U.S. Customs Service data.

$i = 1, 2, \ldots, m$, shows that (except for two points with very small ratios) the ratios appear to scatter randomly around a horizontal straight line.

In this section we model the relationship between gross weight and net weight using several methods. To adapt to the variance heterogeneity in the net weight variable, we compare differently weighted least-squares analyses, then develop a multiplicative model by transforming the variables. A more appropriate formulation, however, combines the multiplicative model with measurement errors in both variables.

5.1   Weighted Least-Squares

One way of dealing with such nonconstant variance is by using weighted least-squares (Sarndal, Swensson, and Wretman 1992, Chapter 7). From the discussion in Section 1, the 122 smugglers can be viewed as a random sample from the population of all Nigerian heroin balloon swallowers who pass through JFK Airport during the period in question. So, assume that the $\{(X_i, Y_i)\}$ are a random sample from a population in which

$$Y_i = \beta X_i + e_i, \tag{3}$$

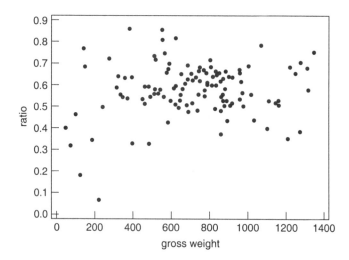

Figure 5. Scatterplot of the ratio Y/X against X, where X is the gross weight of heroin and Y is the net weight of heroin, from the DEA data.

where the e_i are independent of the X_i with

$$\mathcal{E}(e_i) = 0, \quad \mathrm{var}(e_i) = \sigma^2 X_i^\gamma, \tag{4}$$

γ is a known constant, and β and $\sigma > 0$ are unknown parameters. Because $Y < X$ for all data points, we expect $\beta < 1$.

The weighted least-squares regression estimator of β uses weights proportional to the $\{X_i^{-\gamma}\}$. Ordinary least-squares (OLS) corresponds to taking $\gamma = 0$. The OLS estimator of β is given by $\hat{\beta}_{OLS} = T_{xy}/T_{xx}$, where $T_{xx} = \sum_{i=1}^{m} X_i^2$ and $T_{xy} = \sum_{i=1}^{m} X_i Y_i$. When $\gamma = 1$, the regression estimator is the ratio-of-averages estimator

$$\hat{\beta}_{\mathrm{ratav}} = \frac{\bar{Y}}{\bar{X}}, \tag{5}$$

where $\bar{X} = m^{-1} \sum_{i=1}^{m} X_i$ and $\bar{Y} = m^{-1} \sum_{i=1}^{m} Y_i$. The corresponding estimate of σ is denoted by $\hat{\sigma}_{\mathrm{ratav}}$. When $\gamma = 2$, the weighted least-squares regression estimator of β reduces to the average-of-ratios estimator

$$\hat{\beta}_{\mathrm{avrat}} = \frac{1}{m} \sum_{i=1}^{m} \frac{Y_i}{X_i}. \tag{6}$$

The corresponding estimate of σ is denoted by $\hat{\sigma}_{\mathrm{avrat}}$. The weighted least-squares estimates for $\gamma = 0, 1, 2$ are given in Table 1 for both the complete data ($m = 124$) and the reduced data ($m = 122$).

The estimator (6) is the one that Boyum used to convert gross weights in the Customs Service data into net weights. Boyum's conversion formula was

$$\hat{Y}_i^B = 0.5855X_i, \quad i = 1, 2, \ldots, 117. \tag{7}$$

Because Figures 2 and 5 show greater variability of the points around the fitted line with $\gamma = 2$ than would be expected with $\gamma = 1$, Boyum's estimator (6) appears to be more appropriate than (5) for estimating β. See Sarndal et al. (1992, Section 7.3.4) for related comments.

5.2 Data Transformations

An alternative way of dealing with nonconstant error variance is to make a variance-stabilizing transformation of Y and/or a transformation of X. In this situation, where the range of both variables is very large, the most appropriate transformation is to take logarithms of both Y and X. Which logarithms are used is not important. Here, we used base-10 logarithms. See, for example, Weisberg (1985, Section 6.2). The pairs of transformed variables, $(\log(X_i), \log(Y_i)), i = 1, 2, \ldots, m$, are plotted in Figure 6, which shows that the transformations led to a close scatter of points along a straight line.

In terms of the original variables, a multiplicative model,

$$Y_i = (\alpha X_i^{\beta})(e_i), \quad i = 1, 2, \ldots, m, \tag{8}$$

would be appropriate, where e_i is the multiplicative error component having a continuous distribution with mean 1 and a finite variance. Under logarithmic

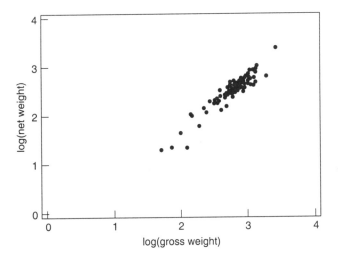

Figure 6. Scatterplot of transformed variables, $(\log(X), \log(Y))$, where X is the gross weight of heroin and Y is the net weight of heroin, for the DEA data.

transformations of X and Y, this nonlinear model is converted into the linear model

$$\log(Y_i) = \log(\alpha) + \beta\log(X_i) + \log(e_i), \tag{9}$$

where we assume that

$$\mathcal{E}(\log(e_i)) = 0, \quad \text{var}(\log(e_i)) = \sigma^2. \tag{10}$$

The values of α, β, and σ are unknown.

Let

$$\overline{\log(X)} = m^{-1}\sum_{i=1}^{m}\log(X_i), \quad \overline{\log(Y)} = m^{-1}\sum_{i=1}^{m}\log(Y_i),$$

$$S_{xx} = \sum_{i=1}^{m}(\log(X_i) - \overline{\log(X)})^2,$$

$$S_{yy} = \sum_{i=1}^{m}(\log(Y_i) - \overline{\log(Y)})^2,$$

$$S_{xy} = \sum_{i=1}^{m}(\log(X_i) - \overline{\log(X)})(\log(Y_i) - \overline{\log(Y)}).$$

Then, ordinary least-squares applied to the transformed data yields

$$\hat{\beta}_{\text{OLS}} = \frac{S_{xy}}{S_{xx}}, \quad \log(\hat{\alpha}_{\text{OLS}}) = \overline{\log(Y)} - \hat{\beta}_{\text{OLS}}\overline{\log(X)},$$

from which $\hat{\alpha}_{\text{OLS}}$ can be obtained. The corresponding estimate of σ is denoted by $\hat{\sigma}_{\text{OLS}}$. The fitted values are calculated from the expression

$$\hat{Y} = \hat{\alpha}_{\text{OLS}}X^{\hat{\beta}_{\text{OLS}}}. \tag{11}$$

Table 1 lists the estimates $\hat{\alpha}_{\text{OLS}}$, $\hat{\beta}_{\text{OLS}}$, and $\hat{\sigma}_{\text{OLS}}$ for both the complete data ($m = 124$) and the reduced data ($m = 122$).

Residual analysis for the ordinary least-squares fit (11) using the reduced data is given in Figure 7, with a plot of the residuals versus gross weights (Figure 7(a)) and a normal probability plot (Figure 7(b)). The residuals are reasonably normally distributed, but have some outlying points.

5.3 Measurement Error Model

We showed (in Section 3) that the net weight and gross weight of the 103 balloons in Shonubi's case were both estimated from the same four sample balloons. Furthermore, the DEA laboratory that analyzed the substances seized and calculated the net and gross weights of the evidence for each smuggling case at JFK Airport also did so for the *Shonubi* case. There is sufficient reason to believe, therefore,

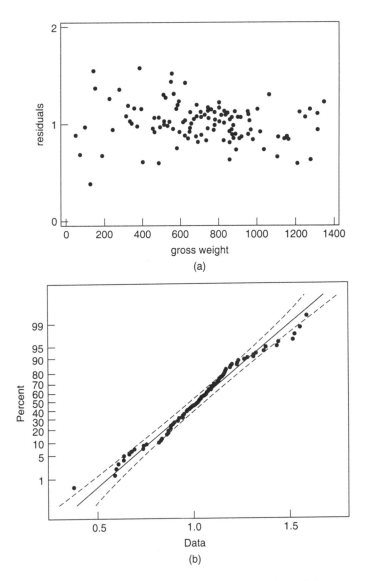

Figure 7. Residual analysis for ordinary least-squares fit of DEA data. (*a*) shows a scatterplot of residuals against gross weight of heroin; (*b*) shows a normal probability plot of residuals.

that an estimation procedure similar to that used in Shonubi's case was also routinely used in every one of the cases in this DEA data set, but where the number of sample balloons most likely varied from case to case.

Thus, the totality of the DEA data consists of pairs (X_i, Y_i) of *estimated values*, where X_i (gross weight) and Y_i (net weight) were both measured with error. Yet, the statistical methods given earlier in this section (weighted least-squares fit of the original data or ordinary least-squares fit of the transformed data) did not take into account the presence of measurement error. It is well known that ignoring measurement error in estimating the regression slope parameter using ordinary least squares will result in a biased (with magnitude of the bias in the direction of zero) and inconsistent estimate. A more appropriate model for relating estimated net and gross weights is a measurement error (or errors-in-variables) model. See, for example, Kendall and Stuart (1979, Chapter 29), Fuller (1987), and Casella and Berger (1990, Section 12.3).

The model can be expressed as follows. The "true" gross weight ξ and the "true" net weight η of the heroin balloons carried by a Nigerian heroin smuggler are unobservable quantities because they are not measured directly by the forensic chemist. Based upon our previous analyses, we assume that given ξ, a multiplicative model

$$\eta = (\alpha \xi^\beta)(\nu) \tag{12}$$

expresses the relationship between η and ξ, where ν is the multiplicative "equation error" having continuous distribution with mean unity and finite variance. See Fuller (1987, Section 2.2). A logarithmic transformation of (12) gives

$$\log(\eta) = \log(\alpha) + \beta \log(\xi) + u, \tag{13}$$

where we assume that $u = \log(\nu) \sim \mathcal{N}(0, \sigma_u^2)$. Instead of observing the true random variables $(\log(\xi_i), \log(\eta_i))$ for the ith smuggler, we actually observe $(\log(X_i), \log(Y_i))$, where

$$\log(X_i) = \log(\xi_i) + \delta_i, \quad \log(Y_i) = \log(\eta_i) + \epsilon_i, \quad i = 1, 2, \ldots, m, \tag{14}$$

are the true values plus independent additive measurement error. The measurement errors δ_i and ϵ_i are assumed to be independently normally distributed with $\delta_i \sim \mathcal{N}(0, \sigma_\delta^2)$ and $\epsilon_i \sim \mathcal{N}(0, \sigma_\epsilon^2)$.

We thus assume that, conditionally on $\xi_1, \xi_2, \ldots, \xi_m$, a linear relationship of the form

$$\log(\eta_i) = \log(\alpha) + \beta \log(\xi_i) + u_i, \quad i = 1, 2, \ldots, m, \tag{15}$$

exists between the transformed values. Furthermore, our discussion in Section 1 above suggests that it would not be unreasonable to assume that the $\{\xi_i\}$ constitute a random sample from a common population; that is, we assume that $\log(\xi_i) \sim \mathcal{N}(\mu_\xi, \sigma_\xi^2)$.

We can now put together the components of the linear structural model. We assume, conditionally on $\{\xi_i\}$, that the $\{X_i\}$ and $\{Y_i\}$ are independently distributed with

$$\log(X_i)|\xi_i \sim \mathcal{N}(\log(\xi_i), \sigma_\delta^2),$$
$$\log(Y_i)|\xi_i \sim \mathcal{N}(\log(\alpha) + \beta \log(\xi_i), \sigma_\epsilon^2 + \sigma_u^2),$$

and that the $\{\xi_i\}$ are assumed to be independently and identically distributed with

$$\log(\xi_i) \sim \mathcal{N}(\mu_\xi, \sigma_\xi^2).$$

The maximum likelihood estimator (MLE) of β in (15) can be obtained using the marginal distribution of $(\log(X_i), \log(Y_i))$ after integrating out $\xi_i, i = 1, 2, \ldots, m$.

If we integrate out ξ_i, the marginal distribution of $(\log(X_i), \log(Y_i))$ is bivariate normal,

$$\begin{bmatrix} \log(X_i) \\ \log(Y_i) \end{bmatrix} \sim \mathcal{N}_2 \left(\begin{bmatrix} \mu_\xi \\ \log(\alpha) + \beta \mu_\xi \end{bmatrix}, \begin{bmatrix} \sigma_\xi^2 + \sigma_\delta^2 & \beta \sigma_\xi^2 \\ \beta \sigma_\xi^2 & \beta^2 \sigma_\xi^2 + \sigma_\epsilon^2 + \sigma_u^2 \end{bmatrix} \right). \tag{16}$$

It follows that given the observations $\{(\log(X_i), \log(Y_i))\}$, the likelihood function of μ_ξ, $\log(\alpha)$, β, σ_δ^2, σ_ϵ^2, and σ_ξ^2 is bivariate normal. The MLEs of these seven parameters are the same as their "method of moments" (MOM) estimators, which can be found by equating sample quantities to the corresponding parameters. We now solve the following five MOM equations:

$$\overline{\log(X)} = \hat{\mu}_\xi,$$

$$\overline{\log(Y)} = \log(\hat{\alpha}) + \hat{\beta}\hat{\mu}_\xi,$$

$$\frac{1}{m} S_{xx} = \hat{\sigma}_\xi^2 + \hat{\sigma}_\delta^2,$$

$$\frac{1}{m} S_{yy} = \hat{\beta}^2 \hat{\sigma}_\xi^2 + \hat{\sigma}_\epsilon^2 + \sigma_u^2,$$

$$\frac{1}{m} S_{xy} = \hat{\beta}\hat{\sigma}_\xi^2.$$

There is an identifiability problem here, with five equations and seven unknown parameters. Without independent measurements (such as are described by Carroll and Ruppert 1996) on the measurement error variances, it is impossible to estimate σ_ϵ^2 and σ_u^2 separately. The best we can do is to estimate their sum $\sigma_\epsilon^2 + \sigma_u^2$, in which case the response measurement error σ_ϵ^2 is said to be "confounded" with the equation error σ_u^2 (Carroll 1998, p. 2513). Of course, if we assume that the model (12) does not include the multiplicative equation error v, then $\sigma_u^2 = 0$, and σ_ϵ^2 can be suitably estimated by ML. In the present case, this difficulty could have been resolved had the DEA routinely reported standard deviations of the sample measurements of gross and net weights for each smuggler.

From the first two MOM equations, we have that

$$\log(\hat{\alpha}_{\text{MLE}}) = \overline{\log(Y)} - \hat{\beta}_{\text{MLE}} \overline{\log(X)}, \tag{17}$$

from which the MLE of α can be obtained. An estimate of β is obtained from the latter three MOM equations, where we have five unknowns. We can partially resolve this identifiability problem by assuming that

$$\lambda = \frac{\sigma_\delta^2}{\sigma_\epsilon^2 + \sigma_u^2} \tag{18}$$

is known. It can then be shown that the MLE $\hat{\beta}$ of β satisfies the following quadratic equation:

$$(\lambda S_{xy})\hat{\beta}^2 + (S_{xx} - \lambda S_{yy})\hat{\beta} - S_{xy} = 0. \tag{19}$$

Solving (19) for $\hat{\beta}$ yields

$$\hat{\beta}_{\mathrm{MLE}}(\lambda) = \frac{-(S_{xx} - \lambda S_{yy}) + \sqrt{(S_{xx} - \lambda S_{yy})^2 + 4\lambda S_{xy}^2}}{2\lambda S_{xy}}. \tag{20}$$

ML estimates of σ_δ^2, $\sigma_\epsilon^2 + \sigma_u^2$, and σ_ξ^2 are given by

$$\hat{\sigma}_\delta^2 = \frac{1}{m}\left(S_{xx} - \frac{S_{xy}}{\hat{\beta}}\right),$$

$$\hat{\sigma}_\epsilon^2 + \hat{\sigma}_u^2 = \frac{1}{m}\left(S_{yy} - \hat{\beta}S_{xy}\right),$$

$$\hat{\sigma}_\xi^2 = \frac{1}{m}\frac{S_{xy}}{\hat{\beta}},$$

respectively. See, for example, Fuller (1987, Section 1.3) and Casella and Berger (1990, pp. 589, 591–2).

For the reduced ($m = 122$) set of transformed data, $S_{xx} = 7.6932$, $S_{yy} = 10.306$, and $S_{xy} = 8.4354$. We calculated $\hat{\beta}_{\mathrm{MLE}}(\lambda)$ for $0.001 \leq \lambda \leq 5.00$. The estimate (18) is monotonically increasing in λ, varying between 1.09663 and 1.20529 over the range of λ given. Recall that the OLS estimator of β in the multiplicative model (8) without measurement error being taken into consideration was $\hat{\beta}_{\mathrm{OLS}} = 1.09421$. Thus, for $\lambda > 0.001$, $\hat{\beta}_{\mathrm{MLE}}(\lambda) > \hat{\beta}_{\mathrm{OLS}}$, which supports our earlier assertion that the OLS estimator is attenuated toward zero whenever measurement error is not taken into account. Because we believe that λ is dominated by the equation error variance σ_u^2 and that σ_δ^2 is larger than σ_ϵ^2, we estimate that λ is approximately 0.4. Our measurement error model estimate of β is taken to be $\hat{\beta}_{\mathrm{MLE}}(0.4) = 1.1382$. The MLE of $\log(\alpha)$ is therefore $\log(\hat{\alpha}_{\mathrm{MLE}}) = 2.5562 - (1.1382)(2.7992) = -0.6298$, whence $\hat{\alpha}_{\mathrm{MLE}} = 0.2345$. The fitted regression function is therefore given by

$$\hat{Y} = (0.2345)X^{1.1382}. \tag{21}$$

A normal probability plot of the residuals is slightly better than that in Figure 7(b). The ML estimates of the variances are graphed against λ in Figure 8. At $\lambda = 0.4$, $\hat{\sigma}_\delta^2 = 0.0023$, $\hat{\sigma}_\epsilon^2 + \sigma_u^2 = 0.0058$ and $\hat{\sigma}_\xi^2 = 0.0607$. Table 1 lists the values of the parameter estimates $\hat{\alpha}_{\mathrm{MLE}}$ and $\hat{\beta}_{\mathrm{MLE}}$ and the estimated variances $\hat{\sigma}_\delta^2\hat{\sigma}_\epsilon^2 + \hat{\sigma}_u^2$ and $\hat{\sigma}_\xi^2$ for both the complete and reduced data.

We mention in passing an alternative method recently proposed by Cook and Stefanski (1994) for estimating β in the EIV model. Their idea, called SIMEX, is a two-stage computationally-intensive procedure involving simulation and extrapolation. Its theoretical properties have been studied by Stefanski and Cook (1995)

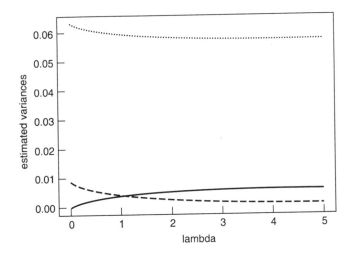

Figure 8. Maximum-likelihood estimates of variances in the measurement error model plotted against λ. Estimates were obtained from the reduced set of 122 DEA observations. The dotted line is $\hat{\sigma}_{\xi}^2$, the dashed line is $\hat{\sigma}_{\epsilon}^2 + \hat{\sigma}_{u}^2$, and the solid line is $\hat{\sigma}_{\delta}^2$.

Table 1. Parameter Estimates From DEA Data.

Estimator	Complete-Data Estimate (s.e.)	Reduced-Data Estimate (s.e.)
	Weighted Least-Squares	
$\hat{\beta}_{\text{OLS}}$	0.6062 (0.0134)	0.5863 (0.0094)
$\hat{\beta}_{\text{ratav}}$	0.5935 (0.0111)	0.5880 (0.0095)
$\hat{\beta}_{\text{avrat}}$	0.5855 (0.0109)	0.5844 (0.0104)
$\hat{\sigma}_{\text{OLS}}$	121.626	80.012
$\hat{\sigma}_{\text{ratav}}$	3.3590	2.796
$\hat{\sigma}_{\text{avrat}}$	0.1209	0.115
	Multiplicative Model	
$\hat{\alpha}_{\text{OLS}}$	0.3109 (0.0951*)	0.3069 (0.0951*)
$\hat{\beta}_{\text{OLS}}$	1.0942 (0.0337*)	1.0965 (0.0338*)
$\hat{\sigma}_{\text{OLS}}$	0.0970*	0.0938*
	Measurement Error Model ($\lambda = 0.4$)	
$\hat{\alpha}_{\text{MLE}}$	0.2368	0.2345
$\hat{\beta}_{\text{MLE}}$	1.1363	1.1382
$\hat{\sigma}_{\delta}^2$	0.0025	0.0023
$\hat{\sigma}_{\epsilon}^2 + \hat{\sigma}_{u}^2$	0.0057	0.0058
$\hat{\sigma}_{\xi}^2$	0.0639	0.0607

* indicates that estimated s.e. is given in log-scale

and Carroll, Kuchenhoff, Lombard, and Stefanski (1996). General treatments of SIMEX have been described in Carroll, Ruppert, and Stefanski (1995) and Carroll (1998).

6 Estimating Drug Quantity: The Bootstrap Estimate

In order to estimate the amount of heroin that Shonubi carried in his seven previous trips, Boyum had an ingenious idea. He obtained data from the DEA and Customs Service and used the bootstrap methodology (without explaining explicitly that that was what he was doing) to estimate that quantity. As expected, his idea was not appreciated sufficiently by the defense team. More importantly, it was not even appreciated by the FRE 706 Panel (who seemed to misunderstand the methodology) or by the Court of Appeals (who essentially ignored any value it might have had). Boyum's methodology was not flawless. But the basic idea was worth taking seriously. Without the data provided by the DEA and the Customs Service, it would have been impossible to justify *any* estimate of the missing data, as evidenced by the reaction of the Court of Appeals in *Shonubi II*.

The essence of the bootstrap is that one randomly selects a sample with replacement from the given data (resulting in a "bootstrap sample"), computes the appropriate statistic using the bootstrap sample, repeats the procedure B times, where B is a large number, and then draws inferences based upon the B values of the bootstrapped statistic (that is, from the "bootstrap distribution"). For details, see Efron and Tibshirani (1993) and Hall (1992). This popular statistics tool is a computationally-intensive, nonparametric procedure that has been used to provide reliable estimates of standard errors and percentiles of statistics that would otherwise be quite difficult to derive theoretically.

Boyum implicitly assumed that the 117 net weights were a random sample from some larger homogeneous population of Nigerian heroin balloon swallowers. Unlike the defense in this case (and also the FRE 706 Panel), we have no trouble with this assumption. From our discussion in Section 1, we believe that the smugglers who were caught at JFK Airport during the period of time covered by the DEA and Customs Service data can be regarded as a random sample of the total number of all smugglers who passed through that airport during that time period, some of whom got caught while the rest did not. Also, some legitimate travelers thought to be drug smugglers were stopped by customs officials and then released following detention. Furthermore, the homogeneity of the population of smugglers is dealt with by our rejection in Section 4.2 of the concept of a "learning curve."

We recall (from Section 4) that the 117 net weights were actually estimated from the gross weights of the Customs Service data, where the gross weights were themselves estimates based upon small random samples of balloons in each case. This *double* estimation procedure leads to higher measurement error in the 117 net weights, which, in turn, would have a greater effect on any subsequent statistical inferences. It can be argued, therefore, that the 117 net weights from the

Customs Service data that were used to produce inferences regarding Shonubi's past trips were certainly a much less precise set of measurements than Boyum and the prosecution would have us believe.

Boyum's strategy was to randomly draw seven observations from the 117 net weights and then compute the total of those seven observations. Although not stated explicitly in his affidavit, we see from Boyum's computer program that he sampled with replacement. This total acted as a single estimate of the aggregate net amount of heroin smuggled by Shonubi in his seven prior trips. Boyum took $B = 100,000$ replications in his "Monte Carlo" simulations and thereby obtained the bootstrap distribution of the total net weight. Boyum then concluded that on Shonubi's seven previous trips there was an estimated 99% chance that Shonubi carried more than 2,090.2 grams of heroin. (He also estimated that there was a 95% chance that Shonubi carried more than 2,341.4 grams in the first seven trips.) The prosecution then added the 427.4 grams to the 2,090.2 grams to render Shonubi accountable for a grand total of approximately 2,517.6 grams of heroin.

We take a different view of this methodology. As we see it, one of the problems with Boyum's bootstrap procedure is that it implicitly assumed that Shonubi's drug smuggling pattern could include every one of the 117 estimated net weights, including the very low and very high quantities. These extreme amounts would probably be out of character for Shonubi regardless of the trip number. (The smallest and largest estimated net weights included in the simulation were 42 grams and 1,225 grams, respectively.) What is really needed for a more realistic simulation is a set of net weights that are commensurate with the amount of heroin carried by Shonubi on his last trip.

A more appropriate starting point, therefore, is to restrict attention to those Nigerian heroin smugglers who swallowed roughly the same number of balloons as Shonubi. *We believe that the number of balloons, rather than the total amount of heroin in those balloons, controls.* In other words, instead of the "organization" trying to get a smuggler to swallow a given amount of heroin, it is more likely that the smuggler will be told to swallow a specific number of heroin-filled balloons, subject to an upper limit on the swallower's capacity, probably documented during the preparation phase. Accordingly, we selected those smugglers from the DEA data (rather than from the Customs Service data) who were found to have carried internally 50–100 balloons when arrested. To avoid unlikely amounts of heroin to be included in the simulation as Boyum did, we restricted the net amounts to less than 500 grams. For a person such as Shonubi, we feel that this combined range of possible smuggling items and amounts should not be unreasonable for previous trips. The DEA data already includes estimated net weights, unlike the Customs Service data, in which the estimated gross weights had to be converted into estimated net weights as Boyum had to do.

There were fifty such smugglers in the DEA data, and the corresponding net weights of those smugglers varied from 236.4 grams to 495.0 grams. See Figure 9. We carried out a bootstrap computation using S-Plus (Statistical Sciences 1995) by sampling seven times with replacement from the fifty net weights, and then

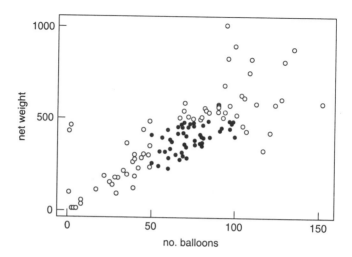

Figure 9. Scatterplot of net weight of heroin against number of balloons swallowed based upon the DEA data (see Figure 2). Filled circles show those smugglers who swallowed between 50 and 100 balloons containing between 236.4 grams and 495.0 grams of heroin.

computed the sum of those seven numbers. Following Boyum, we replicated this procedure 100,000 times. The results were as follows.

The mean of the bootstrapped totals was 2,782 grams and the median was 2,567 grams. The standard error of the mean was 195.4 grams. The bootstrap distribution, which is slightly skewed to the left, is shown in Figure 10. The bootstrap (BC_a) percentiles show that there is an estimated probability of 97.5% that the total net weight was greater than 2,003.0 grams. (Similarly, there was an estimated 95% probability that the total net weight was greater than 2,025.5 grams.) Adding 2,003.0 grams to the 427.4 grams actually found on Shonubi on his last trip yields an estimated probability of 97.5% that the grand total exceeded 2,430.4 grams. Our results, therefore, support the prosecution's claim that Shonubi carried between 1,000 and 3,000 grams of heroin in his eight trips.

Acknowledgments

The author thanks Joseph Gastwirth for the invitation to contribute to the literature on the *Shonubi* case, Peter Tillers for kindly sending copies of appropriate court documents (affidavits, government and defense memoranda, FRE 706 Panel Report, and data sets), Betty-Ann Soiefer Izenman for advice and guidance on legal issues that arose during the writing of this article, and Raymond Carroll, Leonard Stefanski, Sanat Sarkar, and D. Raghavarao for useful discussions that helped clarify ideas.

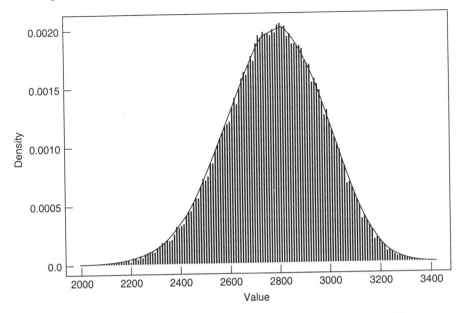

Figure 10. The bootstrap distribution of estimated total net weight of heroin carried internally by Shonubi during his previous seven smuggling trips. The data used in the bootstrap simulations were the filled circles from Figure 9.

7   Cases Cited

Adedeji v. United States (1992), 782 F.Supp. 688 (Mass.).
Nwankwo v. United States (1992), 92 CV 1695 (E.D.N.Y.), 1992 U.S. Dist. LEXIS 13472.
United States v. Montoya de Hernandez (1985), 473 U.S. 531, 105 S.Ct. 3304, 87 L.Ed.2d 381.
United States v. Odofin (1991), 929 F.2d 56 (2d Cir.).
United States v. Onyema (1991), 766 F.Supp. 76 (E.D.N.Y.).
United States v. Shonubi: *Shonubi V*: 962 F.Supp. 370 (E.D.N.Y. 1997); *Shonubi IV*: 103 F.3d 1085 (2d Cir. 1997); *Shonubi III*: 895 F.Supp. 460 (E.D.N.Y. 1995); *Shonubi II*: 998 F.2d 84 (2d Cir. 1993); *Shonubi I*: 802 F.Supp. 859 (E.D.N.Y. 1992).
United States v. Yakubu (1989), 1989 U.S. Dist. LEXIS 12386 (E.D.Ill).

REFERENCES

[1] Aitken, C.G.G. (1998), Sampling—how big a sample? *Journal of Forensic Sciences*, 44, 750–760.

[2] Aitken, C.G.G. (2000), Sample size determination and evidence interpretation. This volume.

[3] Barrett, P.M. (1990), Nigerians smuggling heroin in their stomachs pose fast-growing problem for federal agents. *Wall Street Journal*, November 16, 1990, Section A, page 16.

[4] Carroll, R.J. (1998), Measurement error in epidemiologic studies, *Encyclopedia of Biostatistics, Volume 3*, (eds. P. Armitage ad T. Colton). Chichester, U.K.: J. Wiley & Sons.

[5] Carroll, R.J. and Ruppert, D. (1996), The use and misuse of orthogonal regression in linear errors-in-variables models. *The American Statistician*, 50, 1–6.

[6] Carroll, R.J., Kuchenhoff, H., Lombard, F., and Stefanski, L.A. (1996), Asymptotics for the SIMEX estimator in nonlinear measurement error models. *Journal of the American Statistical Association*, 91, 242–250.

[7] Carroll, R.J., Ruppert, D., and Stefanski, L.A. (1995), *Measurement Error in Nonlinear Models*. London: Chapman & Hall.

[8] Casella, G. and Berger, R.L. (1990), *Statistical Inference*. Pacific Grove, CA: Wadsworth & Brooks/Cole.

[9] Cass, C. (1998), Customs Service drug searches prompt horror tales, lawsuits. Associated Press report, December 2, 1998.
http://www.foxnews.com/news/national/1202/d_ap_1202_149.sml.

[10] Cochran, W.G. (1977), *Sampling Techniques*, third edition, New York: J. Wiley & Sons.

[11] Cook, J.R. and Stefanski, L.A. (1994), Simulation-extrapolation estimation in parametric measurement error models. *Journal of the American Statistical Association*, 89, 1314–1328.

[12] Efron, B. and Tibshirani, R.J. (1993), *An Introduction to the Bootstrap*. New York: Chapman and Hall.

[13] Fuller, W.A. (1987), *Measurement Error Models*. New York: J. Wiley & Sons.

[14] Gregory, A.M. (1994), Smugglers who swallow: The constitutional issues posed by drug swallowers and their treatment. *University of Pittsburgh Law Review*, 56, 323–365.

[15] Hall, P. (1992), *The Bootstrap and Edgeworth Expansion*. New York: Springer-Verlag.

[16] Izenman, A.J. (1999), Legal and statistical aspects of the forensic study of illicit drugs. Submitted for publication.

[17] Kadish, M.J. (1997), The drug courier profile: in planes, trains, and automobiles; and now in the jury box. *American University Law Review*, 46, 747–791.

[18] Kendall, Sir M. and Stuart, A. (1979), *The Advanced Theory of Statistics, Volume 2. Inference and Relationship*. Fourth edition. Chapter 29. London: Griffin.

[19] Morton, W. (1998), In the bellies of "mules," a killer drug is smuggled. *Daily Record: Morris County's Online Newspaper*,
http://www.dailyrecord.com/heroin/heroin9805.htm

[20] Sarndal, C.-E., Swensson, B., and Wretman, J. (1992), *Model Assisted Survey Sampling*. New York: Springer-Verlag.

[21] Schum, D. and Tillers, P. (1995), Joint Report, Amended Appendix (Exhibit) B, 67 pages, United States District Court for the Eastern District of New York, 92 CR 0007 (JBW), *United States v. Shonubi*.

[22] Statistical Sciences (1995), *S-Plus Guide to Statistical and Mathematical Analysis, Version 3.3*. Seattle: StatSci, a division of MathSoft, Inc.

[23] Stefanski, L.A. and Cook, J.R. (1995), Simulation-extrapolation: The measurement error jackknife. *Journal of the American Statistical Association*, 90, 1247–1256.

[24] Tillers, P. (1997), Introduction: Three contributions to three important problems in evidence scholarship. *Cardozo Law Review*, 18, 1875–1889.

[25] Treaster, J.B. (1992), Nigerian connection floods U.S. airport with Asian heroin. *New York Times*, February 15, 1992, Section 1, Page 1.

[26] Vielmetti, B. and Bennett, K. (1990), Nigeria source of much heroin. *St. Petersburg Times*, November 2, 1990, page 1A.

[27] Weisberg, S. (1985), *Applied Linear Regression*. New York: J. Wiley & Sons.

[28] Wren, C.S. (1999), A pipeline of the poor feeds the flow of heroin. *New York Times*, February 21, 1999, Metro Section, page 37.